THE
UNITED STATES
IN
WORLD AFFAIRS
1948-1949

PUBLICATIONS OF THE

COUNCIL ON FOREIGN RELATIONS

FOREIGN AFFAIRS (quarterly), edited by Hamilton Fish Armstrong.
THE UNITED STATES IN WORLD AFFAIRS (annual). Volumes for 1931, 1932 and
  1933 by Walter Lippmann and William O. Scroggs; for 1934–1935, 1936,
  1937, 1938, 1939 and 1940 by Whitney H. Shepardson and William O.
  Scroggs; for 1945–1947, 1947–1948 and 1948–1949 by John C. Campbell.
POLITICAL HANDBOOK OF THE WORLD (annual), edited by Walter H. Mallory.
PUBLIC OPINION AND FOREIGN POLICY, by Lester Markel and Others.
THE PRICE OF POWER, by Hanson W. Baldwin.
OUR FARM PROGRAM AND FOREIGN TRADE, by C. Addison Hickman.
THE FOREIGN AFFAIRS READER, edited by Hamilton Fish Armstrong.
THE STUDY OF INTERNATIONAL RELATIONS IN AMERICAN COLLEGES AND UNI-
  VERSITIES, by Grayson Kirk.
FOREIGN AFFAIRS BIBLIOGRAPHY, 1932–1942, by Robert Gale Woolbert.
THE PROBLEM OF GERMANY, by Hoyt Price and Carl E. Schorske.
THE UNITED STATES IN A MULTI-NATIONAL ECONOMY, by Jacob Viner and
  Others.
THE STRUGGLE FOR AIRWAYS IN LATIN AMERICA, by William A. M. Burden.
THE FAR EASTERN CRISIS, by Henry L. Stimson.
LIMITS OF LAND SETTLEMENT, prepared under the direction of Isaiah Bowman.
WORLD ECONOMY IN TRANSITION, by Eugene Staley.
MOBILIZING CIVILIAN AMERICA, by Harold J. Tobin and Percy W. Bidwell.
THE INVISIBLE TARIFF, by Percy W. Bidwell.
RAW MATERIALS IN PEACE AND WAR, by Eugene Staley.
OUR TRADE WITH BRITAIN, by Percy W. Bidwell.
PEACEFUL CHANGE, by Frederick Sherwood Dunn.
CAN WE BE NEUTRAL?, by Allen W. Dulles and Hamilton Fish Armstrong.
ORES AND INDUSTRY IN THE FAR EAST, by H. Foster Bain.
INTERNATIONAL SECURITY, by Philip C. Jessup.
SURVEY OF AMERICAN FOREIGN RELATIONS (in four volumes, 1928–1931), pre-
  pared under the direction of Charles P. Howland.
DOLLARS IN LATIN AMERICA, by Willy Feuerlein and Elizabeth Hannan.
NEW DIRECTIONS IN OUR TRADE POLICY, by William Diebold, Jr.
INTERNATIONAL AIR TRANSPORT AND NATIONAL POLICY, by Oliver J. Lissitzyn.
AMERICAN AGENCIES INTERESTED IN INTERNATIONAL AFFAIRS, compiled by
  Ruth Savord.

THE
UNITED STATES
IN
WORLD AFFAIRS
1948-1949

By John C. Campbell
and the Research Staff of the
Council on Foreign Relations
with an introduction by
General George C. Marshall

Published for the
COUNCIL ON FOREIGN RELATIONS
by
HARPER & BROTHERS
NEW YORK
1949

The Council on Foreign Relations is a non-profit institution devoted to study of the international aspects of American political, economic and strategic problems. It takes no stand, expressed or implied, on American policy.

The authors of books published under the auspices of the Council are responsible for their statements of fact and expressions of opinion. The Council is responsible only for determining that they should be presented to the public.

COUNCIL ON FOREIGN RELATIONS

56618

ACKNOWLEDGMENTS

IN preparing this volume the author has received assistance from many quarters. He is particularly indebted to Percy W. Bidwell, Director of Studies at the Council on Foreign Relations, to Walter H. Mallory, Executive Director of the Council, and to Hamilton Fish Armstrong, Editor of *Foreign Affairs,* for their continuing advice and encouragement. Richard P. Stebbins and William Diebold, Jr., of the Council's research staff, have contributed substantial parts of the manuscript. Miss Ellen Hammer, Miss Joan Beaury, Miss Inez Viterbo, Alexander Park and Richard K. Carlton have given valuable aid in the preparation of material. Miss Ruth Savord, Librarian of the Council, Donald Wasson, and the entire library staff have been most helpful.

The author is under obligation to a number of officers of the Department of State and the Foreign Service whose cooperation, of course, entails no responsibility for anything appearing in these pages. Finally, thanks are extended to Dr. Henry M. Wriston, Chairman of the Council's Committee on Studies, and to the members of that Committee for their interest and constructive criticism. Other members of the Council have also been kind enough to read certain chapters in manuscript. Expressions of opinion, whenever they appear, are the author's own. The Council on Foreign Relations, its Directors, and its Committee on Studies have no responsibility in the matter beyond that of making it possible for a book such as this to appear.

INTRODUCTION

BY GENERAL GEORGE C. MARSHALL

THIS volume reviews the record of the United States in international affairs during 1948 and the early months of 1949. Never before have the broad objectives and even the day-to-day operations of our foreign policy been more widely and fully discussed than during this period. The account of these events set forth in the following chapters should, therefore, have a familiar ring to most of our reading public.

In this brief introduction I cannot attempt to discuss the problems in every region of the world which call for consideration. At most, emphasis can only be given issues which seemed at the time—and seem now—to be of decisive importance. In providing the introduction—which I am pleased to do—I do not necessarily endorse any particular statements or interpretation made in this volume.

The postwar effort of American diplomacy—which was actually initiated during the course of the war itself—has been directed both toward the restoration of stability in the world and toward the achievement of an international order that should make world peace more secure than it has been in the past. Those broad purposes have been sought in many ways through action in United Nations organs and otherwise. Secretary Byrnes necessarily devoted himself during most of his period in office to efforts to secure agreement on peace treaties that would provide a stable basis for reconstruction. But shortly after five peace treaties were signed in 1947, it became unmistakably evident that organized recovery efforts of great magnitude were necessary to obtain world stability and security.

The exhaustion, destruction and dislocations resulting from

the war left many countries unable either to meet their economic needs or to halt a most serious political and social deterioration. Moreover, the Soviet Union did not continue the cooperation with the Allies which it had carried on during the war and gave no support to their efforts to bring about general recovery. Quite the contrary was the case. The Soviet Government opposed and obstructed efforts to bring about general recovery. To take measures sufficiently effective to arrest this alarming decline in every country where it existed was obviously not practicable. In this situation the United States Government projected in 1947 a long-range program for providing assistance to states which were themselves putting forth efforts to restore their economies and to maintain their political independence.

The critical problem of 1948, therefore, was that of transforming these plans into action and of doing what was possible to provide additional safeguards for states against open or concealed aggression. To accomplish this task it was necessary that the Congress make appropriations for a program of large-scale economic assistance abroad. This was done through the Foreign Assistance Act of April 3, 1948, and the consequent appropriation measures. The progressive implementation of this vast program brought about a steady increase of strength and confidence to the peoples who were aided, especially to those in western European countries.

However, this was not enough. Since the problem throughout the world was moral and political as well as economic, it was necessary to supplement the effort to achieve recovery by other measures to assist free nations in maintaining their independence and stability.

With encouragement from the United States the Brussels Treaty was signed on March 17, 1948, providing for mutual defense and economic and cultural collaboration between Great Britain, France, the Netherlands, Belgium and Luxembourg. On the same day, the President, in addressing both houses of Congress, called the treaty a notable step toward peace and expressed confidence that the determination of the free countries of Europe to protect themselves would be matched by equal determination on our part to help them to do so. There then followed the Vandenberg Resolution in the Senate, calling for vigorous efforts to strengthen the United Nations; increased appropriations for the Voice of America; the revival of Selective Service, and an increased armament program.

The United States then participated in a further step of even greater significance. This was the negotiation of a North Atlantic pact which would lay the basis for effective individual and collective self-defense in conformity with Article 51 of the United Nations Charter. The pact or treaty was signed by the representatives of 12 states on April 4, 1949. This step, involving the assumption on our part of far-reaching obligations, is a positive recognition of the now generally accepted fact that the security and welfare of this country are intimately bound up with that of the other North Atlantic countries.

Another phase of this question as to whether the present unsettled conditions were to be exploited to extend and strengthen the Soviet system in Europe was presented by the Berlin problem. The failure of the U.S.S.R. to respect the provision of the Potsdam agreement that Germany should be treated as an economic unit led the western occupying powers, early in the year, to hold discussions in London concerning the establishment of a government in western Germany. The Soviet authorities thereupon initiated restrictions on transport and communications which became, in effect, a full blockade of the western sectors of Berlin. The western powers opposed this illegal attempt to force them out of Berlin, and after laborious and fruitless negotiations referred the matter to the Security Council of the United Nations, where a proposed solution was vetoed by the Soviet representative. While thus seeking a settlement through every peaceful means, the western powers succeeded in maintaining the economic life of their sectors through the airlift between Berlin and the western zones of Germany. This massive operation of carrying supplies into Berlin to surmount the blockade represented a most notable achievement and, incidentally, it developed the technique and skill of our Air Force to a remarkable extent.

On the other side of the globe, it was hoped that as China emerged victorious from its long war with Japan it would move rapidly to solve the problems of internal unity and reconstruction. As a stable, independent nation it could make a tremendously important contribution to the stability of Asia and to world peace and order. The people of the United States have watched with intense concern the efforts of the Chinese Government to solve those problems and, where possible, have sought through their government to lend a helping hand. During the past year, the China Aid Act of 1948 offered evidence of this concern. But it has become increasingly clear that the basic problems confronting the Chinese people cannot be resolved through external aid.

The final outcome of these particularly critical postwar policies is not yet apparent. Concrete advances have been achieved, however, which offer ground for optimism. The restoration of stability, confidence, and strength throughout the international community will create opportunities to reach equitable agreements with other states which will relax tension and promote peaceful relations. Such opportunities will not be overlooked, and proposals from other governments that such agreements be negotiated will not be disregarded provided the proposals are genuine. It is hardly useful at this point, however, to attempt to envisage the circumstances in which such occasions might arise. Our primary concern is—and probably must remain for some time—that of continuing to foster conditions which will enable states to achieve economic recovery and to maintain their independence. Under such conditions there should be a powerful development of the spiritual and moral forces which are essential to the life of free people.

It should always be kept in mind that it is the American people's support of the principles and purposes of the United Nations which guides the conduct of our foreign policy. The American people understand these principles to require that the precepts of democracy be carried out in international affairs, that important matters of international policy be decided through consultation with the countries affected by them, and that full consideration be given to the interests of all members of the international community.

The American public evidently approves a course which subordinates the affairs of the moment to larger and longer-range considerations. The prosecution of this affirmative policy is a notable achievement for this government. That such decisions could be taken by a Democratic President and Republican Congress in the year of a hard-fought presidential election is a brilliant demonstration of the ability of the American people to meet the great responsibilities of their new world position of leadership.

The most important function of such a history as this is to place these complex events, however recent they may be, in proper relation to one another and to the development of our policy and postwar international position. In doing this the present volume makes a very useful contribution to the understanding of current international affairs.

PREFACE

THIS third postwar volume of the Council on Foreign Relations' annual survey of American foreign policy covers roughly the period from the spring of 1948 to the spring of 1949. It is not, and cannot be, a final or complete history of diplomacy or of international relations in this period. It merely attempts, within the limited perspective of one year or less, to recount the most significant developments in world affairs as they affected the United States.

The historian a generation hence, with all the documentary sources at his disposal, may write a definitive account of our foreign relations in this momentous period, enabling us to judge with some degree of assurance our successes and our failures. But the present generation must make its decisions without waiting for the guidance of definitive histories. The public now plays a direct part in international affairs. In a democracy such as ours the great decisions must have the backing of the people. Such modest currently written "histories" as this serve a useful purpose if they contribute in any way to public knowledge and understanding of the great issues before the world today.

The dilemma of choosing between the topical and the chronological approach to such a book as this is a real one. While attempting to compromise, I have leaned toward the former as necessary to an intelligible presentation of the problems at hand. The early chapters deal with our world position and policies, particularly with respect to Europe, in the spring of 1948. There follows a series of chapters on special topics and areas—international trade and shipping, events in the Far East, inter-American affairs, relations with Canada, Palestine, and issues before the United Nations. Finally the narrative turns to the major developments of the latter part of 1948 and the first months of

1949: the new phase of the problem of Germany and the conclusion of the Atlantic pact. If Europe appears to have special prominence in comparison to other parts of the world, that is because American policy was directed first and foremost toward the recovery of Europe and the balancing of Soviet power in the old world.

Some subjects, passed over in earlier volumes of the survey, are treated here more extensively than is indicated by the dates on the title page. A case in point is shipping. Another is relations with Canada, barely mentioned in the last two volumes. The purpose is to maintain a certain elasticity in this series of volumes, giving special attention to certain subjects when it seems desirable to do so, and not being bound by a rigid system of starting and stopping dates.

This book is intended to be a straightforward, factual account of American foreign relations. It does not defend any particular policies nor does it attempt to weave the story round any theme or interpretation. It offers no solutions for the pressing problems we face in the international field. Its sole purpose is to contribute to a better understanding of the facts and issues involved.

J. C. C.

New York, 1949

CONTENTS

INTRODUCTION, by General George C. Marshall . . .   vii

PREFACE   xiii

  I.   OUTLINES OF AN AMERICAN POLICY   1
       1. U.S.A. and U.S.S.R.   3
       2. American Rearmament   7
       3. The Vandenberg Resolution   9
       4. Foreign Aid Program   15
       5. Diplomacy and Propaganda   21

 II.   THIRD FORCE AND WESTERN UNION   30
       1. Soviet Aims in Europe   34
       2. The Italian Election   41
       3. Unstable France   49
       4. Progress Toward Western Union   53

III.   DIVIDED GERMANY IN DIVIDED EUROPE   65
       1. Changes in Western Germany   67
       2. The Soviet Zone   79
       3. Eastern Europe and the German Question   88
       4. Political Forces in Germany   93

 IV.   BELGRADE AND BERLIN   102
       1. Communist Rule in Eastern Europe   103
       2. The Tito Heresy   116
       3. The Danube Conference   127
       4. The Battle of Berlin   133
       5. The Moscow Negotiations   139

  V.   PROGRESS OF EUROPEAN RECOVERY   150
       1. Administering Marshall Plan Aid   152
       2. Self-Help and Mutual Cooperation   165
       3. Western Germany in the Marshall Plan   182
       4. The Marshall Plan Splits World Labor   189
       5. East-West Trade   197

VI. SPECIAL ECONOMIC PROBLEMS   208
1. Trade Agreements and the ITO   210
2. International Agreement on Wheat   220
3. Shipping Policy   228
4. Paying for United States Exports   249

VII. AMERICAN POLICIES IN THE FAR EAST (I)   259
1. Nationalism, Communism, and Soviet Strategy   262
2. The Plight of Nationalist China   270
3. Red Star in the Ascendant   278

VIII. AMERICAN POLICIES IN THE FAR EAST (II)   288
1. Changes in Occupied Japan   288
2. Two States in Korea   306
3. The Indonesian Conflict   312
4. Ferment and Communism in Southeast Asia   322

IX. RELATIONS WITH NEW WORLD NEIGHBORS   330
1. Canada's Trade and Dollar Problem   333
2. The Defense of North America   340
3. Pan America or Atlantic Community?   351
4. The Bogotá Conference   355
5. Economic Aid and Good Neighbor Policy   367

X. WAR AND PEACE IN PALESTINE   375
1. Partition Plan Abandoned   378
2. The New State of Israel   383
3. Truce and Mediation Efforts   387
4. Solution by *Fait Accompli*   392
5. United Nations Mediation   400

XI. ISSUES BEFORE THE UNITED NATIONS   408
1. Continued Failure on Disarmament   410
2. The Balkans Again   419
3. Accomplishments of the General Assembly   430
4. The Record of the Security Council   437

XII. THE WEST AGREES ON GERMANY   450
1. Berlin Before the Security Council   452
2. Agreement on the Ruhr   464
3. Reparation and Security   475
4. The West German Constitution   482

XIII. DEFENSE OF THE WEST   497
     1. The Presidential Election   499
     2. ERP Enters the Second Year   509
     3. Development of the Brussels Union   512
     4. The Council of Europe   517
     5. North Atlantic Pact   527

SELECTED BIBLIOGRAPHY   543

CHRONOLOGY OF WORLD EVENTS   565

APPENDIX: TEXT OF THE NORTH ATLANTIC TREATY . .   587

INDEX   592

MAPS

Zones of Occupation in Germany   68

Indonesia   314

Palestine   380

THE
UNITED STATES
IN
WORLD AFFAIRS
1948-1949

CHAPTER ONE

OUTLINES OF AN AMERICAN POLICY

REPRESENTATIVES of 12 nations, on April 4, 1949, placed their signatures on a North Atlantic Security Pact. This was the west's answer to the dynamic and expansionist policies of the Soviet Union. Together with the European Recovery Program, it formalized the division of Europe and the division of the world. The United Nations organization, founded at San Francisco in the hour of victory, still stood as the symbol of the "one world" of the common war effort against the Axis powers, and as a promise of world order under law sometime in the future. The realities of international politics, however, were to be found less in the Charter and the proceedings of the United Nations than in the conflicts and tensions between two hostile blocs. Scientific advance and the rapidity of communications made the world one; politically there was not one world but two.

The United States, as the strongest and wealthiest power in one of those blocs, found itself with new and heavy responsibilities which required revolutionary changes in the American attitude toward world affairs. In the four years since V-E Day the American Government and people had been growing up to those responsibilities, although not without doubts and uncertainty as to their nature and extent, and as to what course they dictated. By response to events rather than by design, the United States developed policies to meet the challenges of Soviet power and of international communism. At the same time it had to chart a new course in relations with nations outside the Soviet bloc, especially the nations of western Europe, and to reassess, in the light of new conditions, its traditional policies in Latin America and the Far East. America's prosperity, in comparison to the economic troubles of other countries, posed the question of what sacrifices it would make, in loans and grants aimed at reviving international trade and developing backward areas, in order to promote world conditions on which its own future prosperity depended.

For several years, each spring had witnessed a new crisis in international relations and new, dramatic steps in the development of American policy. In March 1946, in the midst of deadlock on the peace treaties and tension over Iran, Secretary Byrnes had announced his policy of "firmness and patience." One year later came the crisis in Greece and the "Truman doctrine." In March 1948, after the Communist seizure of Czechoslovakia and renewed talk of the danger of war, President Truman called for peacetime conscription, increased armament, and the speedy passage of the European Recovery Program. In the year which followed, American policy moved forward with greater assurance. None of the fundamental problems were "solved." In the Far East the American position grew much more difficult as a result of the military victories of the Chinese Communists. No progress was made toward peace settlements. In Europe, however, where east and west were in direct contact and direct competition, the United States and other western nations had blocked the advance of Soviet power; they had set their own objectives and were making progress toward achieving them. It was a struggle in which considerations of power were all-important.

By the spring of 1949 the United States had come a long way from the days when Cordell Hull used to describe American foreign policy in terms of a set of moral and legal principles. It had come a long way also from the days at the close of the war when Hull's successors expected early agreement with our major Allies on a peace settlement and counted on the new United Nations organization to take the responsibility for maintaining world peace and security thereafter. American policy took shape in a postwar world in which there were but two powers capable of waging full-scale modern war and of conducting positive world policies, the United States and the Soviet Union. These two centers of power exercised an undeniable force of attraction on smaller nations—and on groups within those nations—which tended to gravitate, voluntarily or involuntarily, into the sphere of one or the other. This tendency was magnified by the fact that the U.S.S.R. was not only a state but also the headquarters of a world revolutionary movement. The events of the years 1945–1949 demanded a policy in which idealism was coupled with firmness, for if the United States did not maintain a substantial military establishment, make intelligent use of its great economic power, and assert itself boldly and adroitly in the field of diplomacy, it was apparent that large portions of the world would follow eastern Europe in falling under Soviet control.

1. U.S.A. and U.S.S.R.

These circumstances inevitably gave the "Russian problem" a special prominence in American thinking on foreign affairs. Secretary Byrnes, and Secretary Marshall after him, were compelled to devote a great part of their time and energies to sterile negotiation with Soviet diplomats, and simultaneously to develop ways and means of checking dynamic Soviet policies at various danger points around the globe: Germany, Austria, Trieste, the Balkans, Greece, Turkey, Iran, Manchuria, and even Latin America.

By overshadowing and coloring all others, the Soviet issue tended to be used as a measuring rod for American decisions on foreign policy, just as in wartime all questions were judged in the light of their relation to the main objective of military victory. "There is, in fact," writes a keen foreign observer, "a concentration upon the Russians and an exclusion of other international developments that is almost unhealthy in its intensity." [1] American disillusionment over the state of the world was expressed almost entirely in terms of blame for the Russians and resentment that they were so "difficult to get along with." President Truman, in his message to Congress of March 17, 1948, said that the critical world situation resulted from

[1] Max Beloff, "No Peace, No War," *Foreign Affairs*, XXVII, January 1949, 219.

the fact that one nation alone, the U.S.S.R., "not only refused to cooperate in the establishment of a just and honorable peace but—even worse—has actively sought to prevent it." That same nation and its agents, he went on, had destroyed the independence of a whole series of nations in eastern Europe; it had persistently obstructed the work of the United Nations by constant abuse of the veto. Because of obstruction and defiance on the part of one nation, the "great dream" of the Charter had not yet become a reality.

While the President's oversimplification of the international picture, in ascribing all ills to the perfidy and aggressiveness of the Russians, was typical of the tendency to overlook the complexity of world problems and the inadequacy of many aspects of U.S. policy, his interpretation was none the less largely valid. Concentration on the Soviet issue reflected a new realism in American foreign policy, a realism based on the thesis that first things, in this case a question on which peace and the fate of the western world depended, must come first. To deal effectively with that question required of the men responsible for American policy a knowledge of the Soviet system sufficient to understand Soviet statements and actions, a comprehension of American interests and of the temper of American public opinion, and continuing attention to the needs and aspirations of the millions of human beings inhabiting the large and important parts of the world which lay outside of the American and Soviet "empires." It was a large order. But the responsibilities, and the potential consequences of failure, were correspondingly large.

In 1947, the Byrnes policy of firmness and patience hardened into the policy of containment. Byrnes' thought had been that by patient negotiation, yielding on no essential American principle or interest, the United States could reach a general peace settlement with the U.S.S.R. which would bring about the withdrawal of occupation troops and a return to normal international relations.[2] After the Moscow conference on Germany, however, there seemed to be little hope of a negotiated general settlement within the next few years. Thenceforward, the main

[2] James F. Byrnes, *Speaking Frankly* (New York, Harper, 1947), 316.

emphasis of U.S. policy was on the so-called Truman doctrine and on strengthening the non-Soviet world. Within the framework of this global policy, the United States concentrated its attention and the major part of the resources available to support its foreign program on the rebuilding of western Europe, considered essential to world stability. At the same time a definite change took place in the American attitude toward the ex-enemy states, Germany and Japan. The emphasis shifted from ensuring their impotence as potential aggressors to ensuring their essential contribution to economic recovery in Europe and Asia and their attachment to the American sphere lest they fall into that of the Soviet Union.

With no apparent hope of a settlement, the lines were drawn for a long-term struggle for position and influence. The American purpose was to build up and consolidate, on the basis of free institutions wherever possible, the nations of the "in-between world"; to fill the vacuums the mere existence of which served to encourage Soviet expansion; to bring about a balance of world power which would force the Soviets to give up their attempts to subvert the independence of other nations. General Marshall frankly explained the American position with respect to Europe after his return from the London conference on Germany in December 1947. So long as the vacuum in Europe was not filled by the restoration of a healthy European community, he said, and so long as the struggle with the U.S.S.R. on this issue continued, there would be no realistic basis for a peace settlement.[3] In May 1948 he mentioned three fundamental tasks of U.S. foreign policy: to dispel the "serious misconceptions" in the minds of the Soviet leaders, to restore the balance of power relationships required for international security, and to assist in developing conditions of political and economic security so that democratic peoples would be able to preserve their freedom and independence in the face of totalitarian threats.[4]

[3] Department of State, *Bulletin,* XVII, December 28, 1947, 1244-1247.
[4] Statement to the House Committee on Foreign Affairs, May 5, 1948 (*ibid.,* XVIII, May 16, 1948, 623-625).

The Soviet leaders, far from abandoning their "misconceptions," regarded these moves as an American attempt to build up a capitalist-imperialist bloc encircling the Soviet Union. They redoubled their efforts to strengthen their own bloc, to wreck the Marshall plan, to create difficulties for the western powers in Asia, and to thwart American policies in Germany and Japan. Thus there arose, in the spring of 1948, a situation bearing a real danger of war. Congressional and military opinion tended to magnify rather than to underestimate that danger. The House Armed Services Committee, for example, reported its conviction that recent Soviet actions "raise the new and ominous possibility that the Soviet Union may now be willing to risk a showdown on the assumption that the future can bring only worsening of the Soviet position." [5] "We are not sure," declared General Bradley, Chief of Staff, "that there is no war right away." [6]

The question before the American policy-makers, for the immediate future, was whether the Soviet Union, preferring not to stand by while America rearmed and a strong western bloc took shape, would provoke war by moving into western Europe or by precipitate action at some point such as Berlin. Over the longer term, the question was whether the Soviet leaders would bide their time until they possessed the atomic bomb and then place the west before the alternative of atomic war or a peace settlement on Soviet terms.

To meet either contingency and to carry on its pursuit of a new world equilibrium promising peace and stability, the United States developed a four-point program which amplified and gave substance to the policy of containment worked out during the preceding year. It involved expansion of American military strength, extension of military support to western Europe and to other countries threatened by the Soviets, sustained economic assistance to such countries, and increased diplomatic and propaganda activity aimed at strengthening democratic, pro-American

[5] House Report No. 1881, 80th Congress, 2nd Session, May 7, 1948.
[6] Statement to the Senate Armed Forces Committee, April 25, quoted in *New York Times*, April 26, 1948.

elements and countering Communist influence throughout the world.

2. American Rearmament

President Truman, in his special message to Congress of March 17, 1948 on the "critical" situation in Europe, recommended as immediate measures to build up the country's military power the adoption of universal military training and temporary reenactment of selective service. Owing to the lag in recruiting, the Army had only about 541,000 officers and men, some 128,000 below the authorized and budgeted strength, and possessed no adequate strategic reserve of combat forces; the Navy (including the Marine Corps) and Air Force, at 473,000 and 336,000 respectively, were approximately at the level permitted by existing budget figures.[7] The intention of the Administration was not only to fill the existing gap in the Army but to increase the armed forces all along the line. To carry out this expansion the armed services needed a peacetime draft law and more money; they declared, furthermore, that it could not be fully effective without the adoption of universal military training. Air Force spokesmen, moreover, went over the head of the Secretary of Defense to maintain that the existing plans for a 55-group force were inadequate and that the 70 groups recommended by the President's Air Policy Commission were essential to provide the striking power necessary for national security.

The President proposed adding slightly over $3 billion to the $11 billion already requested for the military budget of the fiscal year beginning on July 1, 1948. A supposedly parsimonious Congress, taking its cue from military leaders and from the atmosphere of crisis created by the Administration itself, decided that these estimates, where they pertained to the Air Force, were too conservative. The arguments for a larger Air Force found immediate and wide support among Congressmen, partly because they leaned to the theory that air power would

[7] First Report of the Secretary of Defense (Washington, 1948), 2.

be decisive in any future war, partly because an expanded Air Force seemed to be a convenient substitute for the universal military training bill, which not many were anxious to see brought to a vote in an election year. After considerable discussion and debate the new military program took shape as follows: a limited selective service law, signed by the President on June 24, 1948; authorization of a military establishment, in terms of officers and men, well above the level which Secretary of Defense Forrestal had set as a minimum; a military budget of approximately $14 billion; and authorization by an overwhelming vote of both houses of Congress of funds to begin building the 70-group Air Force, a decision which would bring much higher military budgets in the next few years. Subject to the availability of funds, Forrestal and his colleagues laid plans for an Army of 25 fully equipped divisions, a Navy consisting of two major fleets with some 562,000 officers and men, and a 70-group Air Force.[8]

There could be no certainty as to precisely what size and type of military establishment the nation required for maximum security, since no one knew whether or when war might occur or the conditions under which it would be fought. Many non-military factors entered the picture, such as the danger of inflation and the necessity of drastic adjustments in the civilian economy if the outlay for armaments should be especially large. The planning of the top military and civilian officials was directed toward flexibility. They were trying to create a force which could meet an immediate emergency and which also would be a sound foundation for the military establishment of the future. The Joint Chiefs of Staff were working out both short-range and long-range strategic plans; conferences were held at Key West in March 1948 and Newport in August to settle interservice differences and to assign roles and missions to each service, so that such plans could be carried out with maximum effectiveness. The Air Force would not have its 70 groups for three or four years, but the decision to increase air power to that point did not lack meaning for the immediate

[8] *Ibid.*, 60-68.

future. The whole rearmament program was a measure of political warfare as well as of military preparedness. It was intended to deter the Russians from reckless action and to encourage nations living in the shadow of Soviet power. It was intended also to convince the American people that this was no time for complacency, that possession of the atomic bomb neither gave them immunity from attack nor guaranteed victory if war should come.

3. The Vandenberg Resolution

The second pillar of American policy, one which still had to be erected, was military support of western Europe. Two separate questions were involved: first, the provision of arms to the western nations, and second, an American guarantee to come to their aid in case of attack. On the former, the State and Defense departments in Washington agreed with the five nations of the Brussels pact [9] that only with military supplies from America, possibly through some form of lend-lease, would those nations be able to defend themselves. On March 17, 1948, the day the Brussels treaty was signed, the President expressed his confidence that the United States would extend support "by appropriate means." However, the European Recovery Program was still to be adopted. Even had the Administration worked out a companion program of additional billions to arm western Europe, it could hardly have expected its passage at that session of Congress.

The fundamental question remained: Was ERP enough? Did it make sense to pour out great sums for the economic recovery of the nations of western Europe when those nations remained so weak that they could be overrun almost without opposition? According to existing plans, all their productive energies would go into the recovery effort. They could not build up and supply large armies without diverting manpower and resources from civilian production and giving up all hope of reaching the ERP

[9] The United Kingdom, France, Netherlands, Belgium and Luxembourg. See *The United States in World Affairs, 1947-1948,* 496-500, and below, pp. 59-63.

targets. Yet an atmosphere of security was also necessary to recovery. The Brussels pact gave evidence of willingness to combine forces for security. Defense chiefs of the five nations were already meeting to plan joint strategy. But they needed the assurance of military supplies, which they did not have the dollars to pay for. No American military representatives attended these first five-power talks in May and June of 1948. They could hardly do so until the Administration and Congress took some definite stand and until arrangements were made on the diplomatic level. On the technical side, the machinery for American military aid and advice probably would be in readiness as soon as the political decision to make it available should be taken.

In addition to an assured supply of armaments, the western European nations wanted a specific guarantee that the United States would come to their aid in the event of war. This was a new chapter of an old story. President Wilson had promised France such a guarantee in 1919 but his Congress had repudiated him. A generation later, after involvement in another world war, the American people had again debated the question of alliances and security arrangements; they chose to accept the general obligations of the United Nations Charter and to avoid specific military commitments to individual nations. But the three years following the San Francisco conference brought changed conditions and a need to reassess the American position. The Charter was not the bulwark of peace that Americans had hoped it would become. It could not give Europe security when one great power, vested by the Charter with a veto power over action by the United Nations, threatened the independence of other states.

In 1946 Secretary Byrnes, with bipartisan support, had proposed a four-power treaty to guarantee the demilitarization and disarmament of Germany. Soviet opposition killed it. Now France and other western European nations wished to know whether the United States would commit itself to support them militarily against a revived Germany and against Russia as well. America had encouraged them to form an economic and military bloc, a policy which the Soviet Government regarded as provocative; therefore, they reasoned, America should back them in facing the consequences of that policy.

The U.S. Congress, regardless of changed conditions, remained reluctant to accept a military alliance involving the automatic obligation to fight in support of any European nation. That was regarded as too great a departure from tradition and as placing in the hands of foreign nations the power to take this country into war, a power vested in the Congress by the Constitution of the United States. Senator Vandenberg was not anxious to take the lead in urging such a momentous decision on the 80th Congress. Administration leaders decided not to press the issue. Nevertheless, both the State Department and Vandenberg felt that some declaration of policy was called for in order to reassure western Europe and to warn the leaders of the Soviet Union. At this time Congress had before it a number of resolutions proposing the reorganization of the United Nations through elimination of the veto and other drastic changes. The State Department and the Senate Foreign Relations Committee decided to deal with both questions simultaneously by preparing a draft resolution for the consideration of the Senate. This was the genesis of the so-called Vandenberg Resolution.

Both Secretary Marshall and Senator Vandenberg believed it inadvisable to insist on revision of the Charter, which would surely break up the United Nations as presently constituted. They took the position that the United States could best achieve the purpose of promoting security by encouraging regional defense arrangements within the framework of the Charter, while maintaining U.N. machinery and procedures intact as a necessary avenue of negotiation and as the foundation on which a functioning world order might later be built.

The resolution presented to the Senate with the approval of the Committee on Foreign Relations on May 19, 1948, reaffirmed that it was the policy of the United States to achieve international peace and security through the United Nations. It then recommended voluntary agreement to exclude the veto in questions involving pacific settlement of international disputes and the admission of new members; maximum efforts to obtain agreement on providing the United Nations with armed forces and on the regulation of armaments under dependable guarantee against violations; and if necessary, after adequate efforts toward strengthening the United Nations, review of the Charter "at an appropriate time." These points set forth the position with respect to the United Nations which the United States had already taken in U.N. deliberations.

The remainder of the resolution, dealing with regional agreements, laid down in general terms the American approach to the problem of security in Europe. The United States Government should further "the progressive development of regional and other collective arrangements for individual and collective self-defense in accordance with the purposes, principles, and provisions of the Charter." It should make clear its own determination to exercise the right of individual or collective self-defense under Article 51 should any armed attack occur affecting its national security. Finally, it should promote "association of the United States, by constitutional process, with such regional and other collective arrangements as are based on continuous and effective self-help and mutual aid, and as affect its national security." [10]

This country was already a party to one such regional agreement, the Inter-American Treaty of Reciprocal Assistance signed at Rio de Janeiro on September 2, 1947. Under that treaty it was obligated to assist any American state subjected to armed attack, but retained the right to decide whether or not to employ its armed forces. Under this Senate resolution, the United States would be prepared to "associate" with a regional defensive alliance of European states. Whether that association would go as far as, or further than, the inter-American commitment was left for future decision.

The committee's report stated that the defense arrangements mentioned were "not to be confused with military alliances."

[10] S. Res. 239 (*Reaffirming the Policy of the United States to Achieve International Peace and Security Through the United Nations and Indicating Certain Objectives to Be Pursued*). See Senate Report No. 1361, 80th Congress, 2nd Session, May 19, 1948.

American commitments could not be "open-ended or unlimited" and must require reciprocity of aid. Our national security would have to be involved. Any treaty obligations would require Senate ratification. Any program of material assistance would require legislative authorization. As in ERP, the European nations would be expected to give maximum support to each other before they could expect help from the United States. These conditions were intended to protect American interests. They illustrated the reluctance of the U.S. Congress to give as automatic and binding a guarantee as the western European nations seemed to want.

On June 11, 1948, the Senate passed the Vandenberg Resolution by a vote of 64 to 4 without extended debate.[11] Although the western European nations were left in some uncertainty as to how far the United States would go in their support, this formal decision of the Senate was sufficient encouragement to the Brussels pact signatories to continue their planning for joint defense and to count on eventual American assistance. They could also count, for some time to come, on the presence of American troops in Germany, Austria, and Trieste. These forces acted as a shield for western Europe, though not for Sweden and Norway. Although they could hardly put up effective opposition to a strong Soviet attack, it seemed unlikely that the Soviets would launch such an attack at the risk of almost certain war with the United States. Aggression anywhere in western Europe carried that risk, although the United States was not formally committed to resist it.

What the western European governments wanted was time to build up their defenses with the moral and material support of the United States. The Vandenberg Resolution and the concurrent strong line of Washington's policy toward the U.S.S.R. made it possible for them to go ahead with the political, economic and military arrangements that went under the name of Western Union, and to open negotiations with the United States and Canada on how the military arrangements might be ex-

---

[11] A similar declaration approved by the House Committee on Foreign Affairs was not acted upon by the House during the 80th Congress.

panded to cover not only western Europe but the entire North Atlantic region.

A policy of military assistance to countries threatened by international communism was already in effect in other parts of the world: Greece, Turkey, and China. In these areas there was no question of regional arrangements nor of formal American guarantees. Military aid, in varying forms and degrees, was being supplied under bilateral agreements with the purpose of meeting particular situations. The U.S. Congress, in April 1948, authorized $275 million for military aid to Greece and Turkey, carrying on the original program adopted the year before. At the same time the Government of China was granted $125 million which it was permitted to use for the purchase of American military supplies.[12] The policy had met with success in Greece and Turkey in that those two countries had been kept out of the Soviet orbit, but the expectations that American assistance could be limited to one year had proved too optimistic. In the case of China the Administration had been skeptical that American military supplies would be used effectively by Chiang Kai-shek's government or that they would assure his success against the Communists unless provided on a massive scale constituting a burden that the American people would not accept. The decision to make $125 million available was due largely to pressure in Congress, particularly from the Republican side. As yet no firm military policy with respect to the Asiatic mainland had been adopted. While controversy continued between those who urged more support for Chiang Kai-shek and those who believed it useless, both sides tended to look more toward Japan as a bastion of America's military position in the Far East.

Both Greece and China illustrated the difficulties involved in military aid to countries where the political and economic basis for its effective use was, to say the least, shaky. One such difficulty was the hazard that our allies in these areas, who were expected to "contain" Soviet-Communist expansion with the

[12] The sums for these countries were authorized by the omnibus Foreign Assistance Act of 1948, which included ERP as well. Only $225 million was actually appropriated for Greece and Turkey (Public Law 793, approved June 28, 1948).

help of U.S. supplies and advice, were likely to be weak and disorganized peoples with undemocratic governments; Walter Lippmann rather contemptuously described them as "a heterogeneous array of satellites, clients, dependents and puppets, . . . a coalition of disorganized, disunited, feeble or disorderly nations around the perimeter of the Soviet Union." [13] In contrast to the positive American policy in Europe, expressed through ERP and the Vandenberg Resolution, the military side of the Truman doctrine in the Near East and of the program of aid to China was more in the nature of a holding action, and in the latter case the dike against the Communist flood was not holding.

Despite disappointing results, these programs could not be abandoned without the risk of damaging losses in prestige and strategic positions. On the other hand, they could not be expanded indefinitely without depleting American supplies needed elsewhere and leading to open military intervention, a course likely to be rejected by the people both in America and in the countries being helped. But the problem remained and would have to be met, by military or other means, if the United States was to succeed in holding the existing balance of power and in retaining its influence in the Near East and in Asia.

4. Foreign Aid Program

The third pillar of American policy consisted of ERP and the more limited programs of economic aid in other parts of the world. It rested on the assumption that, in general, economic health was necessary to world security, and, in particular, the economic health of certain regions was necessary to the security of the United States. General Marshall, in explaining the State Department's approach to the problem of maintaining peace, spoke of the necessity of restoring equilibrium to international society before the United Nations could function as contemplated at San Francisco. "The underlying problem in the immediate future is to bring about the restoration of economic,

[13] Walter Lippmann, *The Cold War* (New York, Harper, 1947), 21.

social, and political health in the world and to give to the peoples of the world a sense of security . . . What is needed for the achievement of a world order based on law and dedicated to peace and progress is a widespread improvement in the material and social well-being of the peoples of the world." [14]

The American contribution to the material well-being of the peoples of the world was being channeled to those areas, notably western Europe, where it served the double purpose of alleviating distress and promoting recovery on the one hand, and of supporting American strategic and political aims on the other. The purpose of combating "hunger, poverty, desperation and chaos," as General Marshall put it in his Harvard speech of June 1947, was a real and sincere one, held by a great body of American opinion. The "equilibrium" at which U.S. policy was aiming, however, was not just a matter of greater stability and order in individual countries; it was, necessarily, an equilibrium of power which would prevent Soviet expansion and possible domination of the Eurasian land mass. In this sense, American economic policy could rightly be called "dollar diplomacy." American dollars were intended to strengthen those countries, our potential allies, which were struggling with economic troubles beyond their power to meet unaided. Indubitably the flow of dollars increased American influence in the receiving countries and strengthened those elements opposed to the Soviet Union and the local Communist parties. But dollar diplomacy in the sense of "domination of other countries by Wall Street trusts through their lackeys in the U.S. Government and abroad" remained a figment of the imagination of Communist propagandists.

The European Recovery Program, adopted by substantial majorities in Congress, promised to be for the next four or five years the main effort of U.S. foreign economic policy. The estimated four-year total for ERP, in the neighborhood of $17 billion, represented an unprecedented peacetime undertaking. Although the United States was not committed to the program

[14] Statement to the House Committee on Foreign Affairs, May 5, 1948 (Department of State, *Bulletin*, XVIII, May 16, 1948, 623-625).

beyond the first year, it had a certain moral obligation to see it through, having encouraged the European nations to make their plans on a four-year basis. Congress authorized, in April 1948, the expenditure of $5.3 billion in the first year. In June, however, the economy-minded House of Representatives voted to appropriate only $4 billion for the program (one billion had already been appropriated) and proposed that it be spent over a 15-month period instead of over 12 months as contemplated. This was a cut of over 20 percent. The reaction to this "meat-axe technique," as Senator Vandenberg called it, was immediate. There was disillusionment in western Europe, jubilation in Communist quarters. Marshall protested that such a reduction would change the program from one of recovery to one of mere relief. Vandenberg, appearing at his own request as a witness before the Senate Committee on Appropriations, termed it a cynical reversal of a major policy decision. Both insisted that the United States had made a commitment and must keep it. The Senate responded by restoring all the cuts made by the House, and eventually the two houses agreed on $4 billion to be spent in 12 months if the Administration should decide to do so. The program could thus go ahead as planned, but the affair had proved most damaging to American prestige as evidence that a large group in Congress misread the purpose of the program, the nature of the commitment already made, and the political effect of such "economies" on the situation in Europe.

ERP had both a negative and a positive aspect. Although theoretically open to adherence by the nations of eastern Europe, that adherence naturally would have to be on terms acceptable to the United States, terms which the Soviet Government felt that it could not accept and could not allow its satellites to accept. The Soviet decision to fight the Marshall plan, and to line up the satellite states and the European Communist parties to fight it also, inevitably made it a first-class political issue in every country of Europe. Its negative, anti-Communist aspect was magnified. Marshall's original statement at Harvard—"any government that is willing to assist in the task of recovery will find full cooperation, I am sure, on the part of the United States

Government"—can be compared with the outspoken anti-Soviet mood of Congress when it finally approved ERP in April 1948. The House Committee on Foreign Affairs, reporting the bill favorably, concluded that "the program is necessary to prevent the United States from being confronted with a world so unbalanced and hostile as to present almost insuperable burdens to the people of the United States . . ." [15]

It was certainly a major purpose of ERP to bolster western Europe so that it would be able to withstand encroachment on the part of Russia. It had also a more positive and constructive purpose: to bring about economic recovery in western Europe, in order that this area might end its special dependence on American aid, regain its share of world production, resume its active role in world trade, and establish a solid underpinning for democratic institutions. The general objective of American foreign economic policy remained that of the early postwar period: greater world prosperity through increased international trade, investment, and financial stability, aided by such agencies as the new International Trade Organization, the International Bank for Reconstruction and Development, and the International Monetary Fund. It was a goal which could not even be approached until western Europe stood on its own feet. That was why the success of ERP was regarded as essential to our future economic position in the world, just as it was essential to our political and strategic position.

Other areas, notably Greece and China, came within the scope of the American program of emergency economic assistance. At first Greece was granted such assistance under the special act of Congress, passed in May 1947, for aid to Greece and Turkey (assistance to Turkey was purely military). This was supposed to be a one-year program under which, it was hoped, Greece would attain sufficient economic recovery and stability to be able to support itself thereafter with the help of a loan from the International Bank.[16] At the end of that

[15] House Report No. 1585, 80th Congress, 2nd Session, March 20, 1948, 12.
[16] Statements of Under-Secretaries of State Acheson and Clayton, March 24, 25, 1947 (*Hearings* before the Senate Committee on Foreign Relations, 80th Congress, 1st Session, on S.938, Washington, 1947, 20, 68-69).

year, however, the Greek economy had not recovered, and the situation which had motivated the original grant of aid remained. Communist-led guerrillas, supported by the states of the Soviet bloc on Greece's northern frontier and indirectly by the U.S.S.R., were still active. They thrived not only on aid from across the borders but also on the parlous state of the Greek economy. Assistance had to be continued unless the United States wished to face the consequences of the probable exhaustion of the country's resources and the resulting anarchy which might bring the Communists to power and swing Greece into the Soviet orbit.

After the expiration of the Greek aid program adopted in 1947, further civilian (as distinguished from military) aid was to be extended through ERP, in which both Greece and Turkey participated. Set apart by geography, these two countries presented special problems different from those of the other participants; there was, indeed, some feeling in the west that they did not belong in the program at all and should be dealt with by the United States on a separate basis. Aside from questions of administration, American economic aid to Greece differed in being a front-line operation in a bankrupt country torn by civil war. Its purpose was more closely related to the immediate problem of containing Soviet expansion, and for Greece there was certainly less hope of solvency after four years of the Marshall plan than there was for the stronger and less demoralized nations of the west.

Nationalist China was the other major recipient of American economic support. There no clear-cut economic policy was developed by the United States, largely because of a chaotic situation which made it virtually impossible to devise an aid program giving some promise of creating stability. President Truman had stated American readiness to give loans and other support to the Chinese Government, "as China moves toward peace and unity," [17] but China moved in the opposite direction. The Export-Import Bank, in 1946, had earmarked $500 million

[17] Statement of December 16, 1945 (Department of State, *Bulletin*, XIII, December 16, 1945, 946).

for loans to China, yet no loans were approved since the Bank
saw no chance of repayment. As civil war continued and the
situation of the Chinese Government became more desperate,
American opinion became increasingly concerned over the prospects of a complete victory for the Communists.

The Administration proposed, early in 1948, a program of
limited economic aid intended to give the Chinese Government
"a respite from rapid economic deterioration." In June the
Congress appropriated $275 million for this purpose in the fol-
lowing fiscal year, in addition to the $125 million available for
military aid. As a means of containing the Communists, this
measure gave but slight promise of bringing results, for the
sum was small in relation to China's needs and the armies and
administration of Chiang Kai-shek's regime were showing grave
weaknesses approaching disintegration. China and the Far East
were not suited to a closely integrated and planned economic
program such as ERP. On the other hand, political and strategic
considerations demanded that something be done to counter
Communist advances. What to do in China and the Far East
was an aspect of U.S. foreign policy which clearly required
reassessment and review in the light of our world position in
the spring and summer of 1948 as the Chinese Communists
rapidly extended their sphere of control.

In other parts of the world farther removed from the Soviet
Union, U.S. economic policy did not have the same emergency
character as in western Europe, the eastern Mediterranean, and
China. Mutually beneficial trade, not grants for recovery, was
the main consideration in our economic relations with the
British dominions, Latin America, the Middle East, and South-
east Asia. These areas, however, might in the future come to
the forefront of the conflict between the United States and the
U.S.S.R. Furthermore, they consisted largely of "underdevel-
oped" countries bent on industrialization and looking to the
United States to provide them with capital. The dollar crisis
was not limited to Europe. The whole future of the inter-
American system might well depend on whether the United
States could satisfy the Latin American demand for U.S. loans

and goods. In working out its economic policies in these areas the United States would have to relate them both to its immediate aim of restoring world equilibrium and to the long-term economic objectives of increased trade and prosperity throughout the globe.

5. Diplomacy and Propaganda

The aims which the United States Government had set for itself required sustained and concentrated activity along many lines, not the least important of which were the political and ideological. Since it was waging with the Soviet Government a limited kind of war, a war for the allegiance and support of men and nations, the old norms of international conduct gave way to the use of economic, political and propaganda weapons which both governments had learned to use so well in the recent war against Germany. The United States, with its stronger responsiveness to public opinion and its traditional attachment to ethical standards in international relations, often found itself at a disadvantage in competing with the U.S.S.R. on this terrain. Even in Washington, however, the old distinctions between "legitimate" and "illegitimate" methods of conducting foreign relations tended to lose their meaning as both powers became more and more openly engaged in what might be described as political warfare.

The rulers of the Soviet Union, because of their connections with Communist parties all over the world, possessed a particularly effective instrument for influencing the political affairs of other nations. The United States did not find it easy to combat that influence. Diplomacy, even with its new array of public affairs officers, cultural attachés and labor attachés, was of limited use in that it was largely restricted to contacts between governments. To put its side of the story before the political parties, the labor unions, the business groups and the universities, to explain its policies and to dispel suspicion of its motives, the United States had to widen the base of its conduct of foreign relations. It had to engage in publicity and propaganda on a large scale, in other words to attempt to reach the peoples of the world in addition to, and sometimes over the heads of, their governments.

Since the abolition of the Office of War Information at the close of the war, foreign propaganda operations on a smaller scale had been conducted by the State Department. As differences with Russia developed, the Administration thought it necessary to continue and expand these activities in order to correct the distortions of Soviet propaganda. In such regions as eastern Europe, where freedom of the press was curtailed, the people were being given a picture of America as ruled by Wall Street capitalists bent on exploiting their own and other peoples and driving the world toward war in order to avert economic collapse at home. Radio broadcasts constituted one of the few weapons which the western powers could use in trying to oppose Soviet policies in eastern Europe. In other areas, where the scales were more evenly balanced, publicity became an adjunct of our political and economic policies.

One reason why American propaganda abroad had great difficulty in competing with that of the Soviets was lack of support on the part of Congress, which controlled the allocation of funds for that purpose. It took some time before Congress became convinced of the need for a program of even moderate scope. In July 1947 it adjourned without specifically authorizing any program and cut down the State Department appropriation for informational and cultural activities to a bare $12.4 million. Evidence of waste and amateurishness in the conduct of these activities was seized upon by many Congressmen as a good reason for not supporting them at all. Others believed that propaganda was not a proper function of government, that the dissemination of news was the business of America's publishers, press agencies, and radio networks. That same summer of 1947, however, witnessed a widening of the split with Russia and an intensification of the Soviet propaganda barrage against the Marshall plan and against American policy in general. Many Congressmen, including members of a joint Senate-House committee which made investigations in 22 countries, returned from visits to Europe convinced that the U.S. information program should be improved and expanded. That committee pointed out that the British were maintaining a program three times the size of ours and the Soviet Union one "so colossal that there is no practical means of estimating its exact cost." [18] The Senate Foreign Relations Committee, in endorsing a bill to expand existing services, pointed to "the urgent need for an adequate information program to interpret the spirit of America to the world." "The character of modern international relations and communications," it stated, "as well as the place held by the United States in world civilization, demand and warrant increased activities abroad in the field of public relations." Furthermore, "the present hostile propaganda campaigns directed against democracy, human welfare, freedom, truth, and the United States, spearheaded by the Government of the Soviet Union and the Communist Parties throughout the world, call for urgent, forthright, and dynamic measures to disseminate the truth." [19]

On January 27, 1948, President Truman signed the Smith-Mundt Act, passed unanimously by both houses, giving permanent legislative authorization for operations in the fields of dissemination of information and educational exchange. The former included the putting out of news and comment through radio, the press, motion pictures, and special information centers; the latter included exchange of professors and students, maintenance of libraries abroad, and provision for sending technical specialists to foreign countries. The official Voice of America radio broadcasts in 22 languages were regarded as the principal means by which the world was to be blanketed with a "barrage of truth." How effective this barrage would be in supporting American foreign policy objectives was difficult to measure. Henceforward, at any rate, it was accepted as one of the necessary instruments for the attainment of those objectives. Planning went forward to reorganize the Voice of America,

[18] *The United States Information Service in Europe,* Senate Report No. 855, Part I, January 30, 1948, 80th Congress, 2nd Session, 17.
[19] Senate Report No. 811, 80th Congress, 2nd Session, January 7, 1948, 3-4.

turning from its rather cautious, factual presentations of the American side of the story, which were ineffective in many countries, to harder-hitting but still factual propaganda, openly critical of the Soviet policies and directed at certain "target areas," most of them in Europe. The "line," judging from an exposition of the program given by the Assistant Secretary of State in charge of it, was to present the conflict with the U.S.S.R. as "not a struggle between two powerful nations [but] a struggle between two concepts or ideas, . . . between good and evil, the good represented by human liberty and the evil by the totalitarian police state." [20]

At the same time that the United States was pursuing its worldwide propaganda offensive, its program of aid to countries threatened by Russia, and its policy of containment, the men responsible for the conduct of American foreign relations had constantly to take stock of our long-range objectives. While preparing for a war that might come at any time, the United States remained willing to engage in negotiations with the Soviet Union, through appropriate channels, on the outstanding problems which barred the way to a general settlement in Europe and elsewhere. But American officials held little hope that any general settlement could be reached at this stage, since they felt unable to make any major concessions and saw no indications of a softer policy on the part of the Soviet Union. Limited settlements on particular problems or areas might be possible, but hardly a general settlement which would mean the end of the "cold war." Each power, rather than make damaging concessions in early negotiations, preferred to devote its efforts to shifting the world balance of power to the point where the other would be "reasonable." This was the logical conclusion to be drawn from the diplomatic exchange which took place between the two governments in May, 1948.

On May 4 Ambassador Walter Bedell Smith made a formal

[20] Address of George V. Allen at the Mount Holyoke College Institute on the United Nations, June 29, 1948 (Department of State, *Bulletin*, XVIII, July 18, 1948, 90). Many of the problems facing the U.S. in this field are surveyed in Lester Markel and others, *Public Opinion and Foreign Policy* (New York, Harper, for the Council on Foreign Relations, 1949).

statement to Foreign Minister Molotov dealing with the situation "of great seriousness" which had developed in American-Soviet relations in the past two years. He spoke of the progressive extension of the Soviet power, the establishment in eastern Europe of Communist regimes subservient to the U.S.S.R., and the "inexplicable" Soviet hostility to the Marshall plan, all of which had led the non-Soviet world to draw together for the purpose of recovery and self-defense. The United States, as the strongest nation in that community, had been forced to take a leading part in the movement and to increase its military establishment to meet the threatening world situation. Smith then emphasized that this foreign policy had the support of the overwhelming majority of the American people, and that it would be a grave error to assume that domestic considerations, political or economic, would produce any radical change in it. In closing he assured Molotov that the United States had no aggressive designs whatever and that it hoped to find the road to a decent and reasonable relationship between the two countries. "As far as the United States is concerned, the door is always open for full discussion and the composing of our differences."

Molotov's reply, delivered on May 9, agreed that it was desirable to improve relations, then stated that the Soviet Government accepted the proposal to begin "a discussion and settlement of the differences existing between us." The remainder of the note was devoted to denials of the allegations made by Smith with respect to Soviet policy in eastern Europe, interference in the affairs of other nations, and opposition to European recovery. It charged that the present unsatisfactory state of Soviet-American relations was due not to the U.S.S.R., which consistently followed a policy of peace, but to the United States, which was developing military bases all over the globe and forming military alliances against the U.S.S.R.

On the following day, without notice to the United States, the Moscow radio broadcast the texts of the American proposal, with significant omissions, and of the Soviet reply, implying that bilateral negotiations for a general settlement of differences were about to begin. The result was a flurry of speculation all over the world on the prospects of an early Soviet-American settlement, confusion in Washington, where there was no belief in the possibility of reaching a settlement on satisfactory terms, and astonishment and some indignation in capitals such as London and Paris, which had had no previous notice of a new American approach to problems which concerned third powers as intimately as they concerned the United States and Soviet Russia. The State Department came under fire at home and abroad, both from those who feared that the approach heralded some new "appeasement" of the U.S.S.R. and from those who felt that it confirmed the Department's unwillingness to arrive at a genuine understanding with the Russians.

If there had been any serious intention on the part of either government to begin at this time a high-level negotiation of major differences, the Soviet decision to make the whole thing public, an obvious propaganda manoeuvre, would have reduced the chances of successful negotiation virtually to zero. In actual fact, that was not the intention of the United States, if later official explanations are to be taken at face value. The thinking which lay behind the American statement of May 4 was the following: that the Soviet leaders seemed to have certain misconceptions concerning American policy; that they might overestimate the importance of Henry Wallace and others who opposed that policy; that they might be counting on the presidential campaign and an economic crisis to weaken American firmness against Soviet expansion; that they might take adventurous decisions leading to war as a consequence of such miscalculations; and that it was desirable to convince them not only of the firmness and consistency of U.S. policy but also of the fact that it was defensive, with no thought of aggression against the U.S.S.R. or any other state. The main purpose of the statement was to explain the position the United States had taken and to warn that an accommodation could not be expected unless the Soviet Government changed its own policies. The remark about the door being open for discussion and negotiation was more or less perfunctory; it was a point which had been made several times before in official American statements. Careless drafting was responsible for its being put in a context which could be taken as a proposal to begin bilateral negotiations, thus giving the Russians the opportunity to seize on it for propaganda purposes. Truman immediately made a statement to the effect that Smith's *démarche* represented no new departure in the policy of the American Government.

Examination of the texts of the two communications indicated no intention on the part of either government to make concessions to the other's point of view. Each said that the other could contribute to peace by changing its present policies. If the Soviet Government had wished to negotiate, perhaps to prepare the ground for a "Big Two" deal on a world scale, it could have pursued the matter through diplomatic channels. Instead, it told the world that it was ready to confer in an effort to reach agreement, leaving to the State Department the awkward task of explaining that it had not really proposed bilateral discussions and had not intended to negotiate on world problems directly with Russia in the absence of other interested states.

After the publication of the documents the whole affair degenerated into public recriminations. Soviet statements continued to contrast the peace policy of the U.S.S.R. with the war policy of the United States. Stalin declared that the proposals which were now put forward in an open letter by Henry Wallace could serve as "a good and fruitful basis" for agreement, but hardly with the expectation that Washington would regard them in the same light. Most of Wallace's points either followed the Soviet line, such as substituting a new UNRRA for the Marshall plan, or were vague generalities. American spokesmen cited Soviet violations of treaties and blocking of action on a host of outstanding issues; they said that if the Soviets wished to negotiate, let them make new proposals on Germany, Greece, Korea or any other outstanding problem in the proper place for such negotiations, the Council of Foreign Ministers or the United Nations. In so far as any negotiated settlement was concerned, matters returned to where they were before the exchange took place.

Winston Churchill, a few months before, had declared that the best chance of avoiding war was "to bring matters to a head with the Soviet Government, and, by formal diplomatic processes, with all their privacy and gravity, to arrive at a lasting settlement." [21] The American initiative of May 4 was not based on this approach to the problem. The main effort of American policy was directed not toward negotiation but toward strengthening the non-Soviet world, on the theory that success in this endeavor was the best means of guarding American security, deterring the Soviet leaders from war, and bringing about a situation where an enduring world settlement might be reached. A growing body of American opinion, including many Congressmen, even believed that no lasting settlement could be achieved by agreement with the Soviet Union. A House committee's report on world communism concluded that "the Communists do not believe in the things we believe in and cannot collaborate with us in the work of peace." [22] It did not, however, regard a third world war as inevitable, believing that a strong America, exercising vigilance and pursuing a constructive policy of its own, could show the way to peace, presumably through making the non-Soviet part of the world a going concern which the Communists would be powerless to disturb.

Simultaneously, official American statements spoke of continued support of the United Nations, without trying to force Russia's withdrawal or to convert the world organization into an anti-Russian bloc. The purpose was to maintain the United Nations as a point of contact and place of negotiations which could eventually become, when the world situation permitted, the mainstay of international peace and security. These were the main lines of an American foreign policy to which the Russian threat had given a consistency heretofore lacking. It

[21] *Parliamentary Debates, Weekly Hansard,* House of Commons, January 23, 1948, 563.
[22] *The Strategy and Tactics of World Communism,* House Document No. 619, 80th Congress, 2nd Session, Subcommittee No. 5 of the Committee on Foreign Affairs (Washington, 1948), 61.

had bipartisan support in the Congress and broad popular backing. No one could be sure that it was the soundest and best conceived policy possible. But its existence, and the clarity with which official Washington explained and defended it, provided an answer to the many people who had so often asked since the war whether the United States had a foreign policy.

CHAPTER TWO

THIRD FORCE AND WESTERN UNION

No FEATURE of the postwar world was more ominous than the
uncertainty which hung over the fate of Europe, for centuries
the center of the world's power, the hub of a world-wide economic system, and the source of political institutions and cultural
values which had spread to all other continents. As a result of
the war and of trends which began long before the war, Europe
had lost its power and its leadership. Liberation from Nazi domination revealed a continent economically prostrate, spiritually
divided, uncertain of the future, and completely dependent on
the victorious great powers for finding the way to a new equilibrium. There could be no quick recovery. "What is Europe now?"
asked Winston Churchill two years after V-E Day. "It is a
rubble-heap, a charnel house, a breeding-ground of pestilence
and hate." [1]

Destruction or exhaustion of productive facilities and the
disappearance of old trade patterns were obvious causes of
Europe's sickness. The failure of the major Allies to agree on a
peace settlement was both a cause and a symptom. There were
no unifying ideas, such as those of President Wilson a generation before, holding out the prospect of a just and stable peace.
Europe, as a geographic entity and as a society, was pulled apart
by political and ideological conflicts. The eastern half of the
continent, exchanging Nazi for Soviet domination, was unable
to renew its historic cultural and commercial ties with the west.
The Germans, as the price of defeat, lived under military occupation in a ruined country, their political and social institutions
in a state of disintegration and flux. But it was the nations of

[1] Speech at the Royal Albert Hall, May 14, 1947 (*United Europe*, London,
1947, 6).

the west, the nations most closely associated with the origins and development of western civilization and the age of European leadership, which were experiencing the real "crisis of Europe."

The economic difficulties were thought at first to be temporary, capable of solution as soon as the European countries, with emergency aid from outside, could get back into production. However, the best efforts of the European governments and workers, with the help of UNRRA and direct American loans, proved insufficient to surmount the recurring food crises or to solve the problem of the dollar shortage. Despite the recovery of production in 1946 nearly to the prewar level, many aspects of the world picture had changed so radically from those of 1938 that western Europe still required large-scale loans or grants from America in order to ward off collapse.

There had been a considerable over-all growth in population, at the same time that so many of the able-bodied had been lost in the war. Trade between eastern and western Europe had virtually ceased. The western nations could no longer count on their colonial possessions in Asia as a major source of raw materials, investment income, and foreign exchange derived from colonial exports to other parts of the world. They were no longer receiving a substantial income from shipping and insurance services. Over and beyond these recent changes was a long-term trend toward increasing disequilibrium between European and American production resulting from America's technological advantages and mass production methods. Western Europe was dependent on the American continent for food and raw materials, and could export to America only a fraction of what was needed to meet the cost of importing them. This was the fundamental cause of the chronic dollar shortage, to which loans and grants had provided but a temporary answer.

Western Europe's economic troubles were a reflection and a cause of a drastic change in the world balance of power. The destruction of the power of Germany left a vacuum in the heart of Europe. France and Italy, reckoned as great powers before the war, both emerged from it as second-class military nations, their weakness magnified by political and social strife. England, still the center of a world empire, remained a great power, but its financial assets and its industrial machine were near the point of exhaustion; with the changes in India, Ceylon and Burma the Empire itself had begun to shrink, although without great damage to England's position since for the most part the Empire's loss was the Commonwealth's gain. These "tired" nations stood facing, over the ruins of Germany, a dynamic nation whose empire stretched from the Pacific to the Elbe and the Adriatic and whose armed strength far outweighed any that could be mustered by western Europe. In the absence of a peace settlement based on common respect for a European order, this disproportion in military strength was a constant threat to tranquility. Indeed it was itself a major reason why no general peace settlement had been made.

The revolutionary shift in the balance of power was the essence of the problem of Europe. At the same time it was the factor which made it inevitably a world problem. Put bluntly, without slighting either the interests and importance of the Europeans themselves or the frequently idealistic motivation of American policy, the continent had become the stakes of the world-wide rivalry of the two greatest world powers, both of which were, by strict definition, non-European. While these two powers, with Britain and France, were going through the motions of negotiating a European settlement, they were in fact working at cross purposes everywhere on the continent. The Soviet Union seemed determined to exclude the United States from all influnce in that part of Europe which lay behind the line reached by the Red Army in 1945, and to encourage such instability in the rest of Europe that the United States would withdraw, as it had after the First World War. American policy, however, despite a rapid reduction of military forces immediately after the surrender of Germany, became firmer as time went on. The absence of a peace settlement for Europe as a whole made the United States all the more determined to hold firm in western Europe. The Marshall plan gave formal sanction to that policy, for it was intended not only to restore western Europe's financial solvency but also to give it the strength to serve as a barrier against Soviet power. Western Europe was a vacuum in the sense that, if American power did not remain there until those nations had the strength and stability to defend themselves, Soviet power would inevitably flow westward to the Atlantic.

From the military standpoint the United States could not afford to see Scandinavia, the British Isles, the ports of France and Spain or the coast of West Africa in the hands of a potentially hostile rival power. As in 1940, America could not allow the manpower, the resources and the technical skills of Europe to be brought under the domination of a single totalitarian state. Economic considerations led to the same conclusion. The United States saw no real prospect for its own continued prosperity if it should be unable to trade with free nations in western Europe. On the Marshall plan the issue between the United States and the U.S.S.R. was truly joined. The former was committed to its success, the latter to its defeat. As Andrei Zhdanov announced when the Communist Information Bureau (Cominform) was established in 1947, the Soviet Union would "bend every effort in order that this plan be doomed to failure."

There was a mixture of the offensive and the defensive in the policies of both powers. Each was, undoubtedly, concerned over the "imperialism" of the other. Under those circumstances it was scarcely possible to reach agreement on a European peace settlement. Even if it could be assumed that the policy of each of the two rival powers was directed not toward dominating western Europe but merely toward assuring that the other should not dominate it, the effect was the same since neither would risk the possibly irreparable consequences of not suspecting the worst of the other. In the absence of any firm basis for mutual confidence, any agreement on "neutralizing" western Europe, or any higher enforceable law or world organization, the result could hardly have been otherwise. There was no such higher law, for at the time of the formation of the United Nations neither of the two had been willing to give up its sovereignty to the new world organization.

1. Soviet Aims in Europe

Any attempt to describe the aims of the Soviet Union in Europe is hazardous in view of the secrecy of the process by which Soviet decisions on foreign policy are reached. The members of the Politburo allow their people no free and open debate, nor are they required by their political system or by a demanding public opinion to give any explanation of their policies beyond what seems to them desirable. Nevertheless, there is a certain body of evidence on which one can draw: the writings of Lenin and Stalin, public statements of Soviet leaders, articles in the Soviet press, and above all the actual record of Soviet diplomacy and action.

The difficulty comes in interpreting the writings, in judging the significance of the often contradictory public statements and the motives behind them, and in drawing definite conclusions from the recent record of Soviet behavior. Even that record, clear as it is in showing the dynamic and aggressive character of Soviet policies, provides no conclusive answers to questions of life-and-death importance to America and to the world: whether Soviet moves in Europe have been primarily defensive, aimed at preventing diplomatic and military encirclement and neutralizing potentially hostile forces, or offensive, aimed at domination of Europe and eventually of the world; whether such a distinction exists at all in the Soviet mind or has any practical relevance; whether Soviet policies are based on the assumption of inevitable war between the U.S.S.R. and the west; whether the Soviet leaders would risk such a war in the near future, or would merely bluff, avoiding a showdown until such time as they would have at hand more effective weapons including the atomic bomb. These points were of utmost importance to responsible officials who had the task of working out a European policy for the United States. For, whether the two powers might be moving toward a conflict or toward a settlement in Europe, the realism and effectiveness of American policies would be measured by their success in meeting the policies and the actions of the Soviet Union and its "apparatus" of international communism.

By 1948 there were many indications of an increasing rigidity in the Soviet attitude, an insistence on the fundamental hostility between the capitalist world and the U.S.S.R. That concept had always been present in Soviet thinking. Stalin's own writings over a period of 30 years indicate no deviation, except for temporary tactical reasons, from Lenin's dictum that "the existence of the Soviet Republic side by side with the imperialist states for a long time is unthinkable. In the end either one or the other will conquer. And until that end comes, a series of the most terrible collisions between the Soviet Republic and the bourgeois states is inevitable." Stalin's occasional published statements to foreigners, as to Harold Stassen in 1947, in which he spoke of the possible peaceful coexistence of the two systems, appear to have been tactical and intended for foreign consumption. [2]

If Stalin and his colleagues envisaged war or a series of wars with the capitalist world, they did not necessarily expect it in the near future. According to their doctrine, it would come when the structure of world capitalism, of which the United States was the citadel, should break down in crisis, driving the capitalist-imperialist powers into war with each other or with the stronghold of socialism, the Soviet Union. The task of the latter was to prepare for that struggle, strengthening the socialist sector of the world and exploiting the weaknesses shown by the capitalist states both internally and on the international front. This strategy did not exclude temporary periods of peaceful coexistence or even limited collaboration with capitalist states, should capitalism become stabilized, a development which Soviet leaders appeared not to expect. The U.S.S.R. had accepted such collaboration in the 1930's, in order to counter the menace of Hitler, and had finally come to terms with Hitler himself in order to buy time to prepare for war and to establish its own power at strategic points in eastern Europe. In the

[2] Historicus, "Stalin on Revolution," *Foreign Affairs*, XXVII, January 1949, 174-214.

"Second Imperialist War" it had allied itself with the western democracies as a means of saving its own existence and smashing the power of Germany and Japan. The Soviet leaders were willing to continue that collaboration after the war, but only on terms which the western powers were unwilling to accept. While Soviet spokesmen pleaded for the unity of the great powers, they denounced American and British policies which did not conform to theirs as disruptive of unity and as sowing the seeds of a new war. Meanwhile, they did not hesitate to take full advantage of the chaotic conditions left by the war to expand the "socialist sector" of the world and to promote revolutionary activity elsewhere.

The record of Soviet policy in Europe, from 1944 to 1948, showed Stalin as the legitimate heir to the Tsars in pushing Russia's frontiers westward, in attempting to dominate the Balkans, and in seeking security against the power of Germany. There could be no doubt that here he was defending Russian national interests and that a primary motive was security. However, the establishment of absolute control over eastern Europe through the installation of "friendly," later purely Communist, governments seemed to western opinion to go much further than was justified by the legitimate requirements of security. Combined with the direction of Communist movements far from Russia's frontiers, it seemed to project Soviet ambitions well beyond those of the Tsars. The western powers made great concessions to satisfy Soviet demands for security. The Soviets took these and much more. They established their power in a zone which extended as far west as Norway, the Elbe, Bohemia, Vienna, and the Adriatic. The combined mass of the U.S.S.R. and its bloc of satellites cast a long shadow over western Europe and maintained a constant pressure on such critical points as Austria, Trieste and northern Greece.

There is little doubt that the Soviet leaders hoped, at the end of the war, that the United States would withdraw its armies and influence from Europe and that Communists might come into power in western and in eastern Europe. As Dean Acheson pointed out in the introduction to the preceding volume of this survey, the situation seemed to offer them the chance "to win the greatest prize of history without military effort on their part —a power system extending from the Atlantic to the Pacific including the Mediterranean and North Africa and most of the population and resources of the world." [3] Their technique was not open revolution, which had failed signally after the First World War, but infiltration at key points of the political and social structure. The core of each national Communist party was a small group of intelligent and capable leaders devoted to Moscow; for them there was no conflict between Marxist doctrine and the policies of the state where Marxism had triumphed, no conflict between the interests of their own nations and those of the Soviet Union. They had followed the twists and turns of the party line for years, since before the wartime dissolution of the Comintern which they had served. After the war they campaigned avidly, appealing to nationalism, local interests, and the wants of diverse sectors of the population, for popular support which might help them win political power. Through propaganda and diligent recruiting the Communist parties of Europe sought to expand their membership. Through "front" organizations they sought to win the support of non-Communists. But the essential element in the whole equation in each country was the concentration of authority in a small group of men who, in turn, were agents of another small group of men in the Kremlin.

Because of their role in the anti-Nazi resistance movements and the strength of their popular following, the Communist parties won representation in the postwar governments of France, Italy, and other western nations. Had they succeeded in obtaining key ministries as they did in eastern Europe, they might have been able to match the success which they had there. They failed, however, owing to the vigilance of the non-Communist parties and the absence of the Red Army. In their controversy with the Yugoslav Communists in 1948 the Soviet leaders themselves touched on this latter point, using an argument that would have been even more apposite if applied to

[3] *The United States in World Affairs, 1947–1948*, x.

Poland, Rumania, Bulgaria or Hungary. "In that the French and Italian Communist parties had for the time being less success than the Yugoslav Communist party, that cannot be explained by some extraordinary qualities in the Yugoslav Communist party, but mainly by the fact that . . . the Soviet Armies rushed along to the assistance of the Yugoslav people, broke down the resistance of the German occupying army, freed Belgrade, and thus . . . created the preconditions needed in order to open the way for the Communist party to power. It is a matter for regret that the Soviet Army did not and could not give this same help to the French and Italian Communist parties." [4]

By 1947 the dynamic policies of the Soviet Union, accompanied as they were by threats against other nations, violent propaganda attacks, and the obstruction of efforts at international collaboration, were bringing into being a consolidation of counterforces under the leadership of the only power which could match Soviet strength, the United States. It found expression in the so-called Truman doctrine, aimed at halting Soviet expansion into Greece, Turkey and the Near East, and in the Marshall plan, with its purpose of stabilizing the economies and the free institutions of western Europe. The offer of aid to Europe made by General Marshall in his Harvard speech was addressed to all European states, but from the outset there was slight chance that the Soviet Government would accept it on the terms set by the United States, or that its satellites would be permitted by Moscow to accept on any terms. The Marshall plan put the Soviets on the defensive in Europe, since it rallied the west behind a constructive idea and program and served as a temptation to nations of the east which were sorely in need of American credits and supplies. In Czechoslovakia, Hungary and Poland even the Communists had wished to accept American aid, until the Kremlin laid down the law.

The result of the American initiative was not to soften but to toughen the Soviet attitude. In October 1947, Communist

[4] *The Correspondence Between the Central Committee of the Communist Party of Yugoslavia and the Central Committee of the All-Union Communist Party (Bolsheviks)* (Belgrade, 1948), 63.

representatives from eight European states met the leaders of
the Soviet Communist party in Poland to be told how to deal
with the "new historical situation." [5] It was at this meeting that
the establishment of the Cominform, in some respects a successor
to the old Comintern, was announced. In the east the Communist parties were speedily to complete the liquidation of the
remnants of bourgeois power and influence and to purge their
own ranks of doubtful elements. In the west the main object was
to wreck the Marshall plan.

This latter task fell principally to the French and Italian
parties, the only two western parties in the Cominform, which
were publicly criticized for their "errors" by Zhdanov. They
obediently launched a program of strikes and violence. Despite
their control of the principal trade unions, the campaign of
direct action in the west met with only limited success. Although recovery in France and Italy was delayed, the general
strikes in the closing months of 1947 ended in failure, the
Communists were defeated in the Italian election of April 1948,
and the Communist-led French coal strike later in the same year
was finally broken. The mass parties built up by the Communists
since the war were not well suited to direct revolutionary action.
Nowhere were they able to unseat existing regimes. Nevertheless,
although the United States and its western allies had seized
the initiative by embarking on an ambitious plan, the Soviets
still had manifold opportunities to exercise initiative of their
own. It is much easier and less costly to promote disorder and
encourage economic chaos than to carry through a complex and
long-term program for the economic rehabilitation, closer union,
and defense of 16 or more separate nations. There was every
indication, during the year 1948, that this would continue to
be the policy of the Soviet Union.

Probably the crucial area in the unfolding of Soviet policy
was Germany. Ever since the Communists came to power in
Russia in 1917 their leaders had devoted special thought and
consideration to the role of Germany. In the view of Lenin,

[5] The nine Communist parties were those of the U.S.S.R., Poland, Czechoslovakia, Hungary, Rumania, Yugoslavia, Bulgaria, France and Italy.

success of the revolution in Europe depended on its success in Germany, which had the industrial power and the numerous, advanced proletariat which Russia lacked. In the unsettled years which followed the First World War the Soviet leaders did what they could to bring about a revolution in Germany which would establish Communist power in the heart of Europe. The failure of the Communist revolts in Germany in 1923 put an end to these hopes, but the idea of a great Eurasian bloc, with Germany's industries and skills joined to Russia's manpower and resources, found expression in other ways: in secret contacts between the Red Army and the Reichswehr, in trade relations maintained despite the suppression of the German Communist party by the Nazis and a continuous propaganda war, and ultimately in the Nazi-Soviet pact of 1939.

Such a bloc could dominate Europe and defy the western democratic powers; it could prevent the latter's using Germany as a spearhead of attack—or a bastion of defense—against the Soviet Union. However, although the pact of 1939 meant the extinction of Anglo-French influence in eastern Europe and the end of independence for the unfortunate nations situated between the two giants, Europe was not big enough for both Nazi Germany and Soviet Russia. Hitler made the attempt to win the great Eurasian empire for Germany. His final and complete defeat, accomplished by the joint efforts of Russia and the western powers, opened the possibility that the same empire might be won by Stalin.

While the war was still in progress, there were some signs indicating Soviet policy for postwar Germany. The Soviet Government established a Free Germany Committee in Moscow in 1943. Propaganda was its main purpose, but the combination of captured German officers and old German Communists was significant. When German military power was smashed, the Soviet Union joined the western Allies in establishing four-power occupation and in agreement on a set of principles, those of Potsdam, for the treatment of Germany. At the same time the Soviet rulers, interpreting those principles to suit themselves, pursued their own political program: in the Soviet zone, a directed social revolution and what amounted to a one-party system of government; throughout the country, propaganda and other activities which, if successful, might bring all Germany eventually into the orbit of the Soviet Union.

As the years passed, with no prospect of an agreed peace settlement, four-power control and the Potsdam decisions became more and more of a formality, while the reality lay in the conflicting purposes of the occupying powers. American policy aimed at promoting Germany's economic revival while guarding against military revival. The main purpose was essentially negative: to prevent the creation of a Soviet Germany under the control of Soviet Russia. That was the esssence of the problem of Germany and, indirectly, of the problem of Europe.

2. The Italian Election

In May 1947 the Communist ministers were dropped from the governing coalitions in both France and Italy. Premiers Paul Ramadier and Alcide De Gasperi, who remained in office with reduced parliamentary support, took the risk of facing Communist opposition not only in the parliaments but in the factories and on the streets. This momentous decision coincided roughly with a hardening of American policy against Russia and the adoption of measures of aid to Greece and Turkey widely referred to as the Truman doctrine, a doctrine of support for anti-Communist regimes against Soviet pressure and against their local Communist enemies. The charge that the United States demanded the exit of the Communist ministers in France and Italy was unfounded. But it can hardly be doubted that De Gasperi and Ramadier and their colleagues acted in the hope of American support and in the knowledge that the United States would welcome their decision. In any case, May 1947 marked a turning point. Thereafter the governments of France and Italy were unreservedly in the western camp. France no longer seriously tried to play the role of mediator between east and west. In June came the Marshall proposal of American aid for a long-term program of European recovery, which both France and Italy, along with Britain, supported wholeheartedly despite Soviet denunciation of the plan as American imperialism.

The big question in French and Italian politics was whether orderly government could be maintained and plans for recovery carried out in the face of the open hostility of the Soviet Government and of the French and Italian Communist parties. Political stability and economic recovery were absolutely essential to the success of the Marshall plan. Conversely, American aid was necessary if the French and Italian governments were to succeed in their efforts to maintain representative institutions and to stave off economic collapse. Success depended largely on the capacity for cooperation of the moderate political groups: the Catholic parties, the Socialists and, of lesser importance, the bourgeois liberals. Deep differences existed between them. The Socialists, whatever their attitude toward the Communists might be, considered themselves a Marxist and working-class group, while the Catholic parties, although advocating social reform, remained essentially clerical in outlook and seemed to be veering to the right in 1947 and 1948. Within the Catholic ranks were many who had supported authoritarian Catholic groups before and during the war and who followed the lead of the Vatican rather than any definite political program. The issues of nationalization and of clerical versus lay education sharply divided Socialists and Catholics, as they always had. Successful cooperation depended on the degree to which doctrinaire considerations would be outweighed by common devotion to constitutional representative government.

In Holland and Belgium the Christian and Socialist parties, representing the great majority of the people, consistently supported the democratic process; the frequent ministerial crises in Belgium resulted from party manoeuvres rather than from any threat to the system itself. The governmental crises in Italy and France, on the other hand, reflected the pressure of large, organized groups which did not accept the existing order, as well as the divisions between the parties which did accept it. On the left were the Communists, and on the right the unreconstructed fascists plus new groups which decried the weakness

of the governments in combating the Communists and in dealing with pressing political and economic problems. The Soviet
threat to western Europe led to a corresponding growth of
parties of the right, which, after being in discredit immediately after the war, were beginning to make a comeback.
Between the extreme right and extreme left the middle-of-the-
road parties had to construct a "third force." If they should
collapse as a result of their own divisions or be swept aside by
the militant forces of right or left, it was hard to see how the
cooperative effort to rebuild western Europe could succeed or
how American policy could find any firm support on the continent.

In Italy the decision of the Socialist party, under the leadership of Pietro Nenni, to continue working with the Communists
added immeasurably to the difficulty of forming a strong democratic regime. The Socialist wing of the "third force" was composed only of those fractions of the party which broke away
from the party on the Communist issue. Giuseppe Saragat, one
of the right-wing leaders, joined the De Gasperi government in
December 1947, and later another group led by Ivan Matteo
Lombardo formed an alliance with the Saragat faction to run
a "united Socialist" list in the election of 1948.

The men responsible for American policy knew that a Communist victory in that election would install Italy behind the
"iron curtain" and put the Soviet Union in a position to dominate the central Mediterranean. It would outflank the American position in Austria and Greece and bring Soviet Europe to
the borders of France. The Italian voter had it in his power
to deal a crushing blow to American policy in Europe. He also
had the opportunity, if he chose to use it, to deliver a decisive
rebuke to the Communist cause. As a consistent advocate of free
elections, the United States could not object to the Italians'
exercising their right to choose freely between communism and
democracy, between east and west. On the other hand it could,
and did, make preparations to counter any move by the Communists to seize power illegally either before or after the elections. It could, and did, make determined efforts to strengthen

the Italian Government's hand during the campaign and to persuade the voters to vote against the Communists.

Backing the other side was the Soviet Union, working in its time-tested manner through the Italian Communist party. For the Soviets, however, the matter was less critical. From the strategic standpoint they had nothing to lose and much to gain, since Italy was already in the orbit of the western powers. They could afford to gamble, as long as their gamble did not draw the Soviet Union into a war for which it was not prepared. But they could ill afford the loss of prestige which they would suffer should the Communists be badly defeated at the polls.

Thus the stage was set for an electoral campaign which went far beyond domestic Italian issues. Its international significance was fully recognized on both sides. Premier De Gasperi, head of the Christian Democratic party, frankly defended his policy of reliance on the United States, "the only country from which our salvation can come." It was a policy, he said, of "solid European collaboration made possible by American economic aid." Palmiro Togliatti, the Communist leader, publicly agreed with the thesis, which he noted in the American press, that the election was a great event in international affairs, of decisive significance "not merely for us Italians but for the whole world." [6] De Gasperi charged that the campaign of the Italian Communists was being waged in accordance with the strategy laid down by the Cominform. Thus far that strategy had been thwarted, he maintained, by the failure of the Communist-led general strikes, by the salutary action taken by the government to maintain order, and by the "interest" which the United States had shown in western Europe. The anti-Communist parties must win, De Gasperi exhorted the voters, or there would be no more free elections in Italy. The choice, in his view, was whether Italy should remain a part of western civilization or become an enslaved, pauperized, Balkan state. The Communists replied that, on the contrary, it was the United States, the Vatican, and their puppet Italian politicians who wished to enslave Italy,

[6] De Gasperi's speech at Turin, March 7, 1948 (*Popolo,* March 9, 1948); Togliatti's speech at Genoa, March 6, 1948 (*Unità,* March 7, 1948).

to keep the people in bondage to the landlords and to American capital.

The United States and the Soviet Union were not willing to leave all the campaigning to the Italians. Both powers engaged in a search for ways and means of influencing the Italian voters. The Soviets made full use of radio and press propaganda. They argued that the United States and the Christian Democrats stood for reaction and war, the U.S.S.R. and the Italian Communists for democracy and peace. They advertised widely minor diplomatic concessions made to Italy by Yugoslavia and Albania. A more effective stroke was a Soviet statement of February 16 in favor of Italian trusteeship over Italy's former colonies in Africa, although on other international issues of equal or greater importance to Italians—Trieste, reparations, and Italy's admission to the United Nations—the Soviet Government did not find it possible to offer concessions. Finally, behind the propaganda front lay the threat that the Italian Communists might use force. They had a private army, based on their wartime partisan formations. They were known to be receiving shipments of small arms from Yugoslavia. Knowledge that the Communists possessed military force and probable outside support might cause some Italians to feel that they were certain to come to power anyhow, regardless of the volume of opinion or the number of votes against them.

In comparison to the Soviet Union, the United States had many advantages in the battle to influence Italians and used them to good effect. On the material side was the constant flow of American goods into Italy under legislation for interim aid, with the promise of much more to come under the Marshall plan. Ambassador James Clement Dunn, by making telling speeches as American ships arrived laden with food, reminded Italians where their interests lay. U.S. naval vessels made a good-will visit to Italian ports, and additional Marines were sent to the Mediterranean, as a sign of American support. In addition the United States was able to make a number of gestures which could not fail to create an impression: conclu-

sion of a treaty of friendship, commerce and navigation; [7] renunciation of the share of the Italian fleet allotted to the United
States under the peace treaty (Britain took the same step);
transfer of 14 Italian merchantmen captured in the war and 15
Liberty ships; support of Italy's claim to readmission to the
international government of Tangier.

In some measures the three western powers acted together.
The most important campaign manifesto was an announcement
by French Foreign Minister Bidault on March 20 at Turin,
where he shared the speakers' platform with De Gasperi. The
author of the "French line," which when embodied in the peace
treaty had cut Trieste off from Italy, publicly proclaimed the
desire of the three western powers to see that city and the surrounding area returned to Italian sovereignty. The apparent
failure of the "free territory" experiment and the deterioration
of relations with Russia provided sufficient motivation for this
proposal. But its timing was a master stroke of election strategy.
Its effect in Italy was enormous. Italians could put full blame on
Russia for their failure to recover Trieste, and the Russians
were unable to do anything about it since the other party involved was their ally, Yugoslavia.

As April 18, election day, approached, American efforts to
ensure the Communists' defeat were intensified. Particularly
effective use was made of motion pictures, radio broadcasts, information bulletins and other means of propaganda.[8] The question of Italy's membership in the United Nations was again
brought up in the Security Council, and the resulting Soviet
veto well publicized. The Congress, with the Italian situation
very much in mind, passed the European Recovery Program by
a large majority. The State Department warned that a Communist victory would disqualify Italy for further American aid;
Italian leftists, while denouncing the aid as a manifestation of
imperialism and saying that Italy's needs would be met by the

[7] This treaty was signed at Rome on February 2, presented to the U.S. Senate
for ratification on April 14, and ratified on June 2, 1948.
[8] See "Report from Italy" written by Arnaldo Cortesi in Lester Markel and
others, Public Opinion and Foreign Policy (New York, Harper, for the Council
on Foreign Relations, 1949), 198-204.

U.S.S.R., had felt obliged to tell the voters that supplies from America would continue to arrive no matter who won the election.

Private American citizens and organizations also joined in the campaign. The American Federation of Labor sent help to the right-wing Socialists. With the blessings of the State Department and of influential Congressmen, Italian-Americans wrote letters to their relatives and friends in the old country, pointing out the evils of communism and warning that a Communist victory would mean no more food parcels. Well-known Americans ranging from former Secretary Stimson and Mrs. Roosevelt to Rocky Graziano, the disbarred middleweight boxer, appealed to Italians to vote for liberty. Acting Mayor Vincent Impelliteri of New York, in a broadcast of April 7, pleaded with the Italian voter not to cast a ballot that "would permit your beautiful country to become enslaved under the crushing heel of Communism."

The cumulative effect of all these favors, promises, pleas and warnings on the Italian people cannot be measured but it must have been considerable. Combined with the influence of the Vatican, which called the issue one of Christianity against atheistic communism and instructed the clergy to campaign openly for the Christian Democrats, it lengthened greatly the odds against the Communists. By the day of election, there seemed to be little doubt that the Popular Democratic Front of Communists and their left-wing Socialist allies would fall short of winning a majority. The possibility remained that they might win 40 percent or more of the votes and thus make it impossible for De Gasperi to form a stable coalition without including them. But the results of the election settled that question. The Christian Democrats won an impressive victory.

Over 90 percent of the eligible voters went to the polls. In the vote for the Chamber of Deputies the Christian Democrats won 48.7 percent of the popular vote and an outright majority of the seats. Their allies, the right-wing Socialists and Republicans, won nearly 10 percent of the vote. The leftist bloc won only 30.7 percent. The most significant conclusion to be drawn from the election returns was that over two-thirds of the Italian people were determined to reject Communist rule and not to forfeit American aid. Normal party preferences and widely felt dissatisfaction with the De Gasperi government's record were subordinated to the larger consideration that this was a plebiscite on communism. Analysis of the election results shows that the Christian Democratic party was the beneficiary of many votes which in previous elections had gone to the Socialists, Republicans, and parties of the extreme right.

No one could deny that this was a victory for American policy and a great encouragement to those in Europe who had chosen the path of rebuilding, uniting and defending the west within the framework of the Marshall plan. It was a round won by the west in the struggle for Europe. Yet it was only a round. The Soviet Union retained its hold on one-half of the continent, and the other half still had many weak spots. The Marshall plan was only getting started; it had not yet proved that it could save Europe. In Italy itself there would be other rounds to come. Over eight million people had voted for the Communist-led bloc. The Socialist party and the bulk of the trade unions remained under Communist control. De Gasperi's new government had before it many problems which would be most difficult to solve, even with American aid.

The election having resulted disastrously for the Nenni Socialists,[9] new opposition arose within the party to the tie with the Communists, but the leaders were able to prevent further large-scale defections. On the other side of the ledger, the remarkable showing of the Christian Democrats in the election put De Gasperi in a position to constitute a government not dependent on Socialist support. A real danger, as the situation developed after the election, resulted, paradoxically, from the very magnitude of the Christian Democratic victory. De Gasperi

[9] Since they ran on a common list with the Communists, there is no way of telling how many of the 8 million votes for the People's Democratic Front were Socialist rather than Communist. But the failure of the bloc to win as much as one-third of the votes, added to the self-evident fact that the Socialist leaders subordinated their party completely to the Communists, severely damaged the Socialist party's prestige throughout Italy.

himself held to the idea of the "third force" by keeping the right-wing Socialists and the Republicans within the government. The heavy rightist vote which the Christian Democrats received, however, while removing the threat from neo-fascist groups, strengthened the conservative elements in the party; it lessened the likelihood that the new government would undertake the drastic reforms necessary to win the urban workers away from the Communists and to prevent the latter from making further inroads among the poverty-stricken peasants of southern Italy. By stern police measures the government was able to make its authority felt and to break Communist-inspired strikes. After the election it could act more surely and effectively than in the strikes of November and December 1947. Yet, as many of its own supporters conceded, it could not feel itself firmly based on popular support until it took the economic and social measures necessary to break the hold of Communist organization and Communist propaganda on the underprivileged classes.

3. Unstable France

France, because of its size, population, resources and geographical position, was in many respects the center of the entire effort to rebuild a stable and prosperous western Europe. Owing to its cultural tradition and its historical role of leadership, France had an influence extending far beyond its borders. Developments in France, almost inevitably, would make or break American policy in Europe and the plans for western recovery. That was why the obvious weakness of France was viewed with concern not only on the continent but also in London and Washington. The experience of France provided the real test of whether the "third force" was a fiction or a reality.

The French Government was operating under the constitution of the Fourth Republic, which had come into force in December 1946. This constitution, in the drafting of which the Communists had had an important part, did not make for strong and effective government. As under the Third Republic, the weakness of the executive in combination with the multi-party system produced a series of unstable coalition cabinets whose terms of office depended on uncertain majorities in the National Assembly. While France was governed by a coalition of Communists, Socialists and the Catholic *Mouvement Républicain Populaire* (MRP), the cabinet usually had behind it an overwhelming majority in the Assembly. After the Communist ministers resigned, the Ramadier and Schuman cabinets commanded only a bare majority in the Assembly, and probably less than a majority in the country. The Communists still claimed to be "the first party of France" in popular following, and the new movement led by General de Gaulle, the *Rassemblement du Peuple Français* (RPF), was rapidly gaining adherents, if the municipal elections of October 1947 were any criterion. De Gaulle demanded new national elections, but the government avoided that issue; it could still muster a majority in the Assembly, and only the Assembly could make the decision for a new election.

Growth of Gaullist sentiment was a natural reaction to the new militancy of the Communists and the ineffectiveness of the government. De Gaulle wished to restore French prestige and glory both at home and abroad. He felt that France must be strong in order to meet the Russian menace, and the German menace, and in order not to become a client of the United States. He condemned the present constitution and the system of government by parties as productive only of weakness. His program called for a more disciplined regime in France, with a strong executive not dependent on the shifting sands of party politics. His opponents said that he wanted a dictatorship, which he denied. Yet his was plainly a movement with authoritarian tendencies. Few Frenchmen had any clear idea what de Gaulle would do if he got into power. But a great many, in the government camp and to the left of it, felt that his ideals of extreme nationalism and strong executive power were not easily distinguishable from fascism. This was the main reason why the Schuman government held on to power so grimly, hoping that both Gaullist and Communist strength would recede if only

France could enjoy a period of economic stability and consolidation of democratic institutions. It counted heavily on American economic aid to make that possible.

When Robert Schuman took the post of premier in the midst of the crisis over Communist-led strikes in November 1947, the general expectation was that his tenure of office would be brief and would pave the way for de Gaulle. By its action in dealing with the strikes, however, through a combination of conciliation and firmness, the Schuman government won considerable prestige. At the same time the Socialists gained new strength through the withdrawal of Socialist-led unions from the Communist-controlled General Confederation of Labor to form a rival organization called *Force Ouvrière.* The Communists lost ground both with the general public and with the workers when it became obvious that their strikes had been called to serve the political interests of a foreign power and to disrupt the national recovery effort. Nevertheless, the government could not expect to hold its gains unless it could check inflation and increase the real wages of the workers. Schuman came forward with a bold program, which called for governmental economies, increased tax receipts, strict controls, and stabilized wages, with the purpose of stopping the disastrous rise in prices. But there were formidable obstacles to the success of this program. One was the inability of the government to collect taxes and to enforce controls. Another was the political difficulty in refusing further wage increases to the workers. The Socialists were especially sensitive on this issue since it enabled the Communists, who championed higher wages, to win over their working-class supporters.

Both Communists and Gaullists continued to make propaganda against the government. The former, by their conduct in the Assembly, did much to obstruct the ordinary processes of legislation. They did not slacken their assault on the moderate parties even though they knew that the result of success would probably be not a Communist but a Gaullist regime. The combination of internal weakness and virulent attack from both sides made the position of the "third force" extremely shaky.

A polarization of political forces both inside and outside the country drove many Frenchmen, to whom the struggle against the Communist menace seemed the main issue, into de Gaulle's camp. Schuman, however, was able to keep his parliamentary majority together and to keep his government in office during the first half of 1948.

The need for a strong stand against the Communists, the fear of desertions to the RPF, and the difficult economic situation were factors pushing the government toward the right. Schuman and his Minister of Finance, René Mayer, turned away from the "directed economy" approach toward greater economic liberalism. Their program was intended to combat inflation, stimulate production, and put government finance on a sound basis. Devaluation of the franc and a freer money market was one side of it; a determination to hold firmly against demands for big wage increases was another. The Radical Socialists, the great bourgeois party of the Third Republic, took an increasingly prominent place in the government. The Socialists, on the other hand, who did not like the new economic policies, felt that their views were being slighted; and they were in a position to destroy the government by deserting it. Léon Blum and other Socialist leaders feared that such a move might bring to an end the entire "third force" experiment, a grave responsibility for a democratic party to take, but pressure from the party's left wing was particularly strong.

To arrest the drift to the right which was making their position even more difficult, the Socialists finally took the step of breaking with the government. Having lost their support, the Schuman cabinet was forced to resign in July 1948. But with de Gaulle waiting in the wings, the parties of the "third force" could not afford to let their own disputes reach the breaking point. The Socialists gave reluctant and temporary support to a new government headed by André Marie, a Radical Socialist, although they found his economic program, under the guidance of Paul Reynaud, most distasteful. In the end they could not stomach Reynaud's wage policy, which they thought would undermine their labor support. Marie felt unable to carry on with a divided cabinet. His resignation at the end of August provoked a new ministerial crisis in which the very existence of the Fourth Republic hung in the balance. The Socialist Paul Ramadier was unable to form a government. Schuman, at the urging of President Auriol, who used every recourse to bring Socialists, MRP and Radicals together again, tried twice but could not line up a stable majority in the Assembly. Only on September 10, after a period of nearly two weeks without a government, was the crisis ended when the Assembly approved a cabinet headed by Henri Queuille, a veteran Radical parliamentarian.

The Queuille cabinet, opposed by the Communists and a few rightists, represented a political truce. The Socialists were given the important ministries of interior, national defense, and labor. Schuman kept the portfolio of foreign affairs, which he had held under Marie. But the economic difficulties, which underlay the disputes on inflation, wage raises, taxation and retrenchment, were not yet overcome. The situation of the workers, caught in the inflationary squeeze, remained desperate, a standing invitation to further gains by the Communists. To maintain the "third force" coalition and improve its own precarious situation the new government looked not only to necessary measures of government finance but also to general economic progress with the assistance of ERP supplies and of ERP "counterpart funds," which could be made available only with the consent of the United States. The State Department and the Economic Cooperation Administration, for their part, were ready to give such assistance as they could to strengthen the French Government's position and preserve the "third force" as a political reality in France and in western Europe.

4. Progress Toward Western Union

On the broader international front the concept of the "third force" meant not only the defense of representative democratic institutions but closer association among the nations of western Europe. Such association, "western union" as Secretary Bevin called it in his speech to the House of Commons on January 22, 1948, presumably would enable western Europe more easily to recover economically and to defend itself against an attack from the east. Some who supported the idea envisaged western Europe in the role of a "third force" in world politics, a great power independent of both Russian and American leading strings. It was at one time the thought of a number of Europeans that a socialist Europe, pursuing a middle course between American capitalism and Soviet communism, could bring about a compromise between them. Later this approach began to seem unrealistic and the main contest to be one of power and survival rather than a conflict of economic systems. But Europeans still thought of the third force as a possible balancing factor in world politics. In England both Conservative and Laborite opinion tended to envisage a western Europe-British Commonwealth combination, with Great Britain as the pivot, as a third great power in the world.[10] Official American statements mentioned this goal of a strong Europe standing on its own feet as the hoped-for end result of the process of filling the existing "power vacuum."

For the immediate future, however, western union could only be thought of in terms of far-reaching collaboration with the United States. It was a postulate of the original Marshall proposal that European recovery was possible only on the basis of greater unity in western Europe, and a postulate of the recovery program worked out by the western European nations themselves that they could not avoid economic disaster, much less regain economic stability, without large-scale American support over a number of years. Similarly, a pooling of western Europe's resources for defense obviously would not balance Russia's forces at this stage unless it were buttressed by American military strength, a fact that was recognized on both sides of the

[10] See Churchill's address at the opening of the unofficial Congress of Europe at The Hague, May 7, 1948 (*The Grand Design*, London, United Europe Movement, 1948, 7), Bevin's speech in the House of Commons (*Parliamentary Debates, Weekly Hansard*, House of Commons, September 15, 1948, 106-107), and the Labor party pamphlet stating that "the final aim of Western Union must be to produce a third center of power independent alike of America and Russia" (*Feet on the Ground*, London, 1948, 5).

Atlantic. Even the advocates of a socialist western union as a third force in world politics conceded that there were now but two choices in foreign policy, the Soviet alignment and the American alignment, and they chose the latter. Nevertheless, the unity of western Europe was not something which could be imposed or engineered by America. The initiative and the drive had to come from the Europeans themselves.

There was ample evidence, in the first months of 1948, that this "one hopeful new political idea which has emerged in Europe since the war" [11] had strong popular support in victor and vanquished nations alike. Unofficial movements working for European federation, some of them since before the war, suddenly came into the limelight as events seemed to bring closer to reality what had been but a vague ideal held by a few enthusiasts. Following Bevin's speech of January 22, and the alarm caused by events in Czechoslovakia and Soviet demands on Finland, concrete proposals for action made their appearance in the British Parliament and in the French Assembly. In March a motion was presented to the House of Commons by over 70 back-bench members (later subscribed to by nearly 200), of all three major parties, the avowed purpose of which was "to create in Western Europe a political union strong enough to save European democracy and the values of Western civilization, and a trading area large enough, with the Colonial Territories, to enable its component parts to achieve economic recovery and stability." The declaration urged first, as an emergency policy, the creation of a Council of Western Europe, consisting of representatives of the 16 "Marshall plan countries" and western Germany, with power to set up permanent international staffs to coordinate military, economic and social policies. Second, in pursuance of the long-term goal of a real federation, with common citizenship and a single direction of foreign affairs, defense, currency and major economic policies, the governments concerned should take steps to convene as soon as practicable a constituent assembly of representatives chosen by

[11] Robert Strausz-Hupé, "France and the Future German State," *Yale Review,* XXXVIII, Winter 1949, 313.

the parliaments of the participating states.[12] A few days later a group of French Deputies presented a parallel resolution to the National Assembly in Paris; similar action was taken in the Netherlands.

At the same time preparations were going forward for an unofficial "Congress of Europe" at The Hague, where delegates from six different European organizations would attempt to agree on a common program.[13] Among them was a galaxy of former premiers, foreign ministers, cabinet members and diplomats including Winston Churchill, Paul Ramadier, Paul Reynaud, Salvador de Madariaga, and Paul van Zeeland; some delegates, still holding political office, attended in their capacity as individuals. The balance was tipped somewhat on the conservative side. It was for this reason and because of Churchill's prominent part in it that the British Government was cool toward the Hague Congress. A congress of 14 European Socialist parties held in Paris shortly before the Hague meeting, although declaring its support of the idea of a European federation "open to countries whose policies are other than Socialist," decided at British insistence not to participate in the Congress of Europe. Nevertheless, 23 British M.P.'s and a number of continental Socialists and trade union representatives attended as individuals; they pressed the point that a union would be meaningless without the collaboration of the working class, but did not insist that western union must be a union of socialist states.

Churchill, who had taken the lead in this movement since his "United States of Europe" speech at Zurich in September 1946, served as honorary chairman of the congress, which met early in May. Its resolutions called for the creation of a political and economic union of European nations, free from outside control and not directed against any other nations. To this end, "as a matter of real urgency," a European assembly chosen by

[12] *Parliamentary Debates, Weekly Hansard,* House of Commons, May 5, 1948, 1280-1281.
[13] United Europe Movement, Conseil Français pour l'Europe Unie, Ligue Indépendente de Co-opération Européenne, Nouvelles Equipes Internationales, Union Européenne des Fédéralistes, Union Parlementaire Européenne.

the parliaments of the participating nations was to be convened to advise the governments on practical measures to be taken and to work out the necessary plans. This was something less than the elected constituent assembly which the "federalists" had urged. As to economic matters, the congress recommended steps to abolish obstacles to trade and pave the way for free convertibility of currencies, to work out a common plan for the development of resources, and to raise the standard of living, with a view to achieving the free circulation of capital, unification of currencies, coordination of budgetary policy, and a full customs union. Furthermore, the political and economic union would have to be based on a genuine and living unity, the common heritage of Christian and other cultural values and common loyalty to the fundamental rights of man.

Perhaps more significant than resolutions and proposals, since the main purpose of the congress was to rouse the peoples of Europe, was the "Message to Europeans": "Europe is threatened, Europe is divided, and the greatest danger comes from her divisions . . . Alone, no one of our countries can hope seriously to defend its independence. Alone, no one of our countries can solve the economic problems of today. Without a freely agreed union our present anarchy will expose us tomorrow to forcible unification whether by the intervention of a foreign empire or usurpation by a political party . . . We can tomorrow build the greatest political formation and the greatest economic unit our age has seen . . . Between this great peril and this great hope, Europe's mission is clear . . . The union of our continent is now needed not only for the salvation of the liberties we have won, but also for the extension of their benefits to all mankind. Upon this union depends Europe's destiny and the world's peace." [14]

As they were dealing in generalities, the delegates at The Hague did not have to find solutions to such problems as Germany's place in a united Europe, relations with the British Commonwealth, and the future of the nations in the Soviet

[14] International Committee of the Movements for European Unity, *Congress of Europe, The Hague, May 1948, Resolutions* (London, 1948).

half of Europe. Their resolutions spoke of Europe, not of
western Europe alone. German representatives were present,
and the congress declared that Germany's inclusion in a united
Europe provided the solution of the German problem. However, the existing partition of Germany and the absence of a
peace settlement were facts which governments would have to
deal with before they could go very far toward European union.
That union could hardly be built except on a solid basis of
Franco-German understanding, as Churchill himself had pointed
out at Zurich, but such an understanding did not exist. As for
eastern Europe, exiled opponents of the existing regimes took
part in the Hague congress as a reminder that the Soviet-
dominated countries belonged to the European community, but
there was no question of inviting the satellite governments to
take part in the movement for union. That union was to be
"open to all European nations democratically governed," and
no state was entitled to be called a democracy unless it guaranteed to its citizens, in fact as well as in law, liberty of thought,
expression and assembly, as well as the right to form a political
opposition.

In comparison with the plans and aspirations of the Congress
of Europe, which seemed to outrun the immediate political
realities, the western European governments were making slow
progress toward union. There were two avenues of approach:
closer economic ties among the 16 "Marshall plan countries,"
as a foundation on which political union might later be built,
and the bolder path of political decisions in favor of regional
alliance or federation. Steps toward economic integration, envisaged as an essential part of the Marshall plan, were cautious
and restricted in scope. Of the measures cited when the 16
nations met again in Paris in March 1948, the majority had
resulted from the work of the U.N. Economic Commission for
Europe. The western nations had held a conference on manpower problems, achieved a limited multilateral clearing arrangement, and begun discussion on a western European customs union. France and Italy were studying the possibility of a
Franco-Italian customs union. France, Britain and the Benelux

nations, in the Brussels pact of March 17, pledged the gradual elimination of all divergences in their economic policies by harmonizing production and developing trade. Depending on what followed, this might be a pious wish or it might be the foundation of a real economic union.

That nothing more positive was done was due partly to advice from the American State Department to go slow so long as the European Recovery Program was still a bill before the U.S. Congress and not yet an actuality. Another and more fundamental reason was the difficulty in breaking down the traditional national economic patterns and in producing immediate results on such inherently long-range projects as a customs union. At their Paris meeting the 16 nations rededicated themselves to cooperation and set up a continuing Organization for European Economic Cooperation (OEEC). Study of the concrete measures of cooperation went forward, but the pace was slow even in terms of the goals set by the European Recovery Program.[15] Toward the broader objective of a European union this was hardly even a timid first step.

The political events which followed Bevin's speech were more spectacular. The British Government proposed to France, Holland, Belgium and Luxembourg that they form an alliance, taking as a model the Anglo-French treaty of Dunkirk of March 1947, which was directed against Germany. In subsequent negotiations the scope of the proposed five-power pact was broadened. In its final form, the Treaty of Brussels of March 17, 1948 was a 50-year defensive agreement within the framework of the United Nations Charter, modeled on the inter-American defense treaty recently concluded at Rio de Janeiro as well as on the Treaty of Dunkirk. Its provisions covered economic and cultural cooperation as well as defense, but the latter was the heart of the treaty. It was, indeed, a hard-and-fast defensive military alliance, binding each member to come immediately to the aid of any member that should be attacked in its European territory by any power; in this automatic obligation of mutual assistance the Brussels pact went beyond that of Rio,

15 See below, pp. 165-182.

which left to each member state the decision whether it would go to war.

The Treaty of Brussels bound its members more closely together than before the war, when Britain and France had had no formal alliance and the smaller states had clung to their neutrality until the moment that Germany attacked them. Still, it was an old-fashioned military alliance. It did not represent any pooling of sovereignty. Only in a very limited way, both juridically and geographically, was it a western union in the sense that Secretary Bevin's phrase had been generally understood. Yet it was a foundation on which political union might gradually be built. At the moment, although the pact provided that they might be invited to join, other western European states were unwilling or unable to do so. Italy would gladly have joined but could not easily assume such obligations with its armed forces restricted by the peace treaty and its admission to the United Nations still pending. Austria was still occupied and awaiting a treaty. Switzerland was wedded to its traditional neutrality. Portugal, Iceland and Eire, all three key points in Atlantic strategy and participants in the Marshall plan, were too far afield for consideration at this point in what was thought of as a nuclear western European bloc. Scandinavia, by contrast, was in the direct line of any attack on western Europe from the east. The decision of the Scandinavian nations not to join a western alliance therefore seemed to call for some explanation.

The strongest voice in Scandinavia, since it spoke for the largest population and had behind it the strongest army, was that of Sweden. Although Sweden, unlike Switzerland, had joined the United Nations and accepted the obligations of the Charter, the developing great-power conflict led the Swedish Government to reaffirm its prewar attitude of neutrality. The purpose was to remain on good terms with both east and west, to avoid joining any political or military bloc, other than a defensive Scandinavian bloc, and to take refuge in neutrality if war should break out elsewhere. Swedish opinion, while recognizing that the country might not again be able to escape involvement in a major war, supported this position. The same view also had its advocates in Denmark and in Norway, but in both those countries there was less disposition to place reliance on neutrality and a greater willingness to turn to the west. This had been the lesson of their experience in the recent war. They were, more than Sweden, Atlantic nations in their location, outlook and economic relations. Nevertheless, the idea of Scandinavian solidarity was real. The ties binding the three nations together seemed stronger than those which pulled any of them toward other partners, and for the moment the balance of Scandinavian policy and sentiment swung toward neutrality.

Soon after Bevin proposed the idea of western union, the three Scandinavian governments stressed their desire to keep clear of alliances and blocs. They were, however, already cooperating with other nations in the economic sphere and were willing to continue participation in what was in effect a western bloc, the European Recovery Program. Regardless of the distinction which Scandinavian officials drew between economic and political cooperation, Scandinavia's participation in the former was not accepted by the Soviet Government as nonpolitical and as consistent with the proclaimed desire to avoid taking sides in the quarrels of the big powers. It was, indeed, an indication that the interests and feeling of the Scandinavian countries lay with western Europe. Their cultural traditions and devotion to parliamentary democracy, in which the Social Democrats played a leading role in all three states, left little doubt of their stand on the issue of Communist and Soviet expansion.

A sector of public opinion in Scandinavia held the view that all three countries must turn without equivocation to the west and join a political and military bloc backed by the United States. According to this reasoning, the risk of war involved in such a course was less than that of remaining alone and unprotected in an illusory neutrality. The governments felt, however, that it would be foolish to declare in favor of a policy certain to offend Russia when there was as yet no certainty that western Europe and the United States could defend Scandinavia or would commit themselves to do so. Therefore they must remain free to claim the right of neutrality in case of war.

It was certainly true that the five nations which signed the Brussels pact were in no position to give Scandinavia adequate assistance in case of war. With the exception of Great Britain, they lacked even the means to defend themselves, so great were the efforts required of them to rebuild their economies. Organization for defense, however, was the core of the treaty, for the western nations could not overlook the possibility of war within the next few years. Economic and political union remained as goals for the future, but the immediate task was to create a common high command and to build up and equip the necessary armed forces. The foreign ministers of the five signatory powers, meeting in Paris on April 17, 1948, as the Consultative Council provided for in the treaty, decided to set up a permanent organization in London, including a military committee. This was followed by discussions among the five ministers of defense and by staff talks intended to lay the basis for joint command, joint planning, and a coordinated system of supply.

As these talks progressed, it was quite apparent that concrete plans could hardly be made without knowledge of the extent of support to be expected from the United States. As the London *Observer* remarked in a lead editorial: ". . . for the next few years no effective defense of western Europe is possible without the full participation of America, both in the actual fighting force and in the supply of that force. This absolute condition of successful Western European defense must be fully understood on both sides of the Atlantic." [16]

Although the United States Government apparently expected the five nations, on the analogy of the Marshall plan procedure, to work out a fairly complete plan of armament and operations before deciding what the United States could do to help, the overriding importance of the American contribution was not minimized in Washington. Premier Paul-Henri Spaak of Belgium, on a special mission to the United States in April, warned that the Brussels alliance could not succeed without American support and urged immediate practical cooperation. There were

16 *The Observer*, April 25, 1948.

no early public pronouncements of policy other than the State Department's "hearty welcome" to the Brussels pact and the President's remark in his March 17 address to Congress that the United States would, "by appropriate means, extend to the free nations the support which the situation requires . . . I am sure," the President continued, "that the determination of the free countries of Europe to protect themselves will be matched by an equal determination on our part to help them to do so." The main question was how far Congress, in an election year, would be willing to go in committing the United States to give arms and a military guarantee to the nations of western Europe.

Steps toward greater political unity in Europe did not depend so much on what America might do. Yet there were many other obstacles more complex than those involved in building a combined military force. Political union or federation required giving up national control over certain phases of policy. Even the looser concept of "western association" [17] entailed similar sacrifices. Bevin, in proposing western union, had purposely used vague terminology. He spoke of it as "more of a brotherhood and less of a rigid system." When the five foreign ministers met in July 1948, the French Government felt that the time had come for more definite proposals. Foreign Minister Bidault, taking his cue from the resolutions of the Congress of Europe at The Hague, proposed the creation of a European parliament of representatives named by the legislatures of the western nations. A second French proposal called for the rapid realization of an economic and customs union of the five powers, later to include others. When Bevin and Spaak, while offering no objection in principle, received these plans coldly, no action was taken on them.

Great Britain, whose participation was essential, had not yet arrived at any definite policy on political union. Bevin, in a review of foreign affairs before the House of Commons on May 4, praised the "consolidation of the western democracies"

[17] This is the term used by Barbara Ward in *The West at Bay* (London and New York, Norton, 1948).

that had taken place but warned that it was necessary to proceed realistically step by step. A dramatic move toward union in the sense of federation or a pooling of sovereignty might appeal to idealists, he said, but could only set back the whole movement so well begun. Understandably, there was considerable reluctance to take bold steps toward union with France at a time when the latter was demonstrating the instability of its governmental system. Furthermore, the question of how Britain's position in a western union would dovetail with its membership in the British Commonwealth was not resolved. There was much argument on this point in the British press, and the dominions had still to be consulted on the highest level. Meanwhile the Labor Government, desirous of not appearing to follow in the wake of Churchill's initiative, was proceeding slowly and cautiously. Western European union, if it was to be established at all, would not be established in a hurry.

CHAPTER THREE

DIVIDED GERMANY IN DIVIDED EUROPE

AFTER the fruitless London session of the Council of Foreign Ministers in December 1947, no further attempt was made to reach four-power agreement on a peace settlement for Germany. It was futile to keep on repeating the same old arguments with no prospect that either the U.S.S.R. or the western powers would yield on the key issues of economic unity, reparation, frontiers and the formation of a German government. It was futile also to continue a procedure based on the assumption that the victorious Allies had sufficient community of interest to fix the general lines of occupation policy in defeated Germany and to agree on peace terms. American policy-makers became convinced that the Soviet Union was striving not for a stable settlement in Europe but to exploit existing instability in order to get control of Germany and of all Europe.

Devoting its major energies to combating Soviet pressures, the United States saw the German problem in a different light than in 1945. Unilateral Soviet action in eastern Germany had made it impossible to deal with the country as an economic unit. The answer of the United States and Great Britain was economic merger of their zones and an attempt to make western Germany self-sustaining, without waiting indefinitely to reach four-power decisions. Their double motive was to lighten their own financial burden and to speed European recovery. To the western powers the possible future menace of a revived Germany seemed less alarming than the more immediate Soviet threat to the west. These trends, together with the adoption of the Marshall plan, brought the United States to a more clearly defined German policy based on recognition of the essential role of industrial western Germany in the recovery of western Europe.

The concrete application of that policy led logically from the merger of the U.S. and U.K. zones toward closer association of "Bizonia" with the French zone and toward creation of a west German government. The prospect of this last step—outlined in the decisions taken by the three western powers, together with the Benelux nations, at London in June 1948—pushed the German question to a state of crisis, for the Soviet reaction was sharp. It took the form of increased pressure to drive the western powers from Berlin. Whether the latter could have avoided this crisis by less hasty action in western Germany is doubtful. The Soviet squeeze on Berlin started as early as January 1948. While Moscow later justified its action as provoked by the "partition policy" of the western powers, and while the latter did anticipate the Soviets in announcing their intention to set up a German government, it need not be assumed that it was solely the moves of the western powers that set the pattern and timetable of Soviet action in Germany. The Soviet leaders, who always sought to appear as champions of German unity, took advantage of the opportunity to accuse the western powers of dividing Germany, ignoring the four-power machinery, and violating the Potsdam agreements. They were sponsoring a German People's Congress and a People's Political Council around which they hoped to crystallize German sentiment for national unity. That they had not yet set up a German government in their own zone was a matter of tactics rather than of loyalty to the Potsdam agreements.

Western Germany remained a congested slum in the heart of Europe. Shortages, low productivity, and a population swollen by refugees made their zones a burden on Britain and America, which had to supply food at great expense to keep the people from starvation. Furthermore, these conditions jeopardized the success of the Marshall plan, on which the United States had staked the success of its European policy. Not only Germany but Europe needed German resources, skills and goods. For the economic revival of western Germany, the United States and Britain, with the reluctant consent of France, found it necessary to put increasing responsibility in German hands. Since the halting operation of the first bizonal institutions, limited to economic functions, could be ascribed in large part to the absence of political responsibility, the decision was taken to create a German political regime for the western zones.

In taking this decision the western powers were not trying, as Moscow charged, to torpedo further negotiations in the Council of Foreign Ministers, yet they recognized that four-power negotiations were not getting anywhere. While they explicitly stated that they were still prepared to negotiate with the U.S.S.R. on a peace settlement for all Germany, the effect was to put an end, for the time being, to any possibility of four-power negotiations and to hasten the disintegration of what remained of the four-power administration for governing Germany. By the summer of 1948 the Allied Control Council and the Allied Kommandatura, supreme authorities over Germany and Berlin respectively, had ceased to function, Soviet representatives having refused to attend. Also by virtue of Soviet action, the German problem then took on a new and more acute form, with the spotlight on Berlin. Germany was now partitioned and Europe divided by the line of the "iron curtain." The presence of the western Allies in the German capital was the one glaring rent in the curtain.

1. Changes in Western Germany

Plans for reorganizing Bizonia, held in abeyance while the Big Four were meeting in London, marched rapidly ahead after the London conference adjourned in failure. Early in January 1948 the American and British military governors produced the blueprint of a German Bizonal Economic Administration at Frankfort to replace the more limited organs which they had established the previous May. It provided for the expansion of the already existing Economic Council (*Wirtschaftsrat*) in size and in legislative powers, for the establishment of a second chamber known as the *Länderrat,* composed of two appointees of each *Land* (state) government, and for a new Executive Committee, a High Court for Economic Affairs, and a central

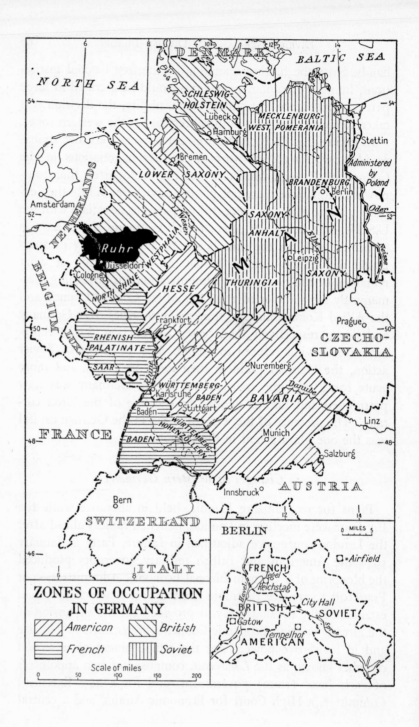

ZONES OF OCCUPATION
IN GERMANY

American   British

French   Soviet

Scale of miles
0   50   100   150   200

bank. These proposals, after being placed before the minister-presidents of the various *Länder* of the two zones and altered in some details as a result of their criticisms, were put into effect on February 9, 1948.[1]

Bizonia thereby acquired something much nearer to a German government that it had had before. It was, by definition, only an economic administration and was of course subordinated to the over-all authority of the American and British military governors. Definitions, however, could not keep German politics out of the new administration, especially since the members of the Economic Council were chosen by the *Land* parliaments on the basis of the strength of the various political parties in those parliaments. Moreover, the retention of ultimate authority in Anglo-American hands did not disguise the fact that a large measure of responsibility had been turned over to the Germans.

At the same time the British and American authorities agreed on a reorganization of military government through the establishment of joint agencies for commerce and industry, food and agriculture, civil service, transport, communications, and finance. The first three, along with the Joint Export-Import Agency, were to be headed by Americans, each with a British deputy, and the latter three by Britons, each with an American deputy; at the top were the two military governors as joint chairmen of the Bipartite Control Office. The new organization was reminiscent of the combined Anglo-American wartime arrangements for civil affairs in the Mediterranean and European theaters. "Economic fusion" of the two zones had been decided upon as long ago as the summer of 1946. Now for the first time the necessary changes in military government were made whereby economic affairs in the combined zones could actually be run on a uniform basis and German agencies could be given unified direction.

The Soviet Government registered strong protests against these steps as violating the agreements on four-power government of Germany. The United States and Britain expected these protests and more or less discounted them in advance. But they

[1] The Bank of German States was established on March 1, 1948.

felt obliged to pay more attention to the objections which came from France. Technically, Britain and the United States did not have to consult France on decisions affecting only their own zones. However, the three western powers had stood together on the major issues at the London conference of 1947. Having abandoned its middle position between Russia and the Anglo-American combination, France could legitimately claim the right to be heard. The intensity of French interest and feeling concerning the future of Germany was well known to the British and Americans. They could hardly have been surprised at French displeasure over the announcement of measures for the reorganization of Bizonia without any prior consultation with Paris.

France had given up hope of attaining its original aims, which included the separation of the Rhineland and the Ruhr from Germany. This retreat had made the French Government all the more anxious to win satisfaction on those points for which it was still pressing: the incorporation of the Saar territory into the French economy, international control of the Ruhr, and guarantees against centralization in Germany. The United States and Britain, already committed to the French position on the Saar, agreed with France in February on measures which would complete the incorporation of that territory into the French economy. On the other two issues the French made little headway. Britain and the United States remained unenthusiastic over French proposals for international ownership and management of the mines and industries of the Ruhr; meanwhile they were making plans to revive Ruhr industries as an indispensable aid to German and European recovery. On the matter of the form of government in Germany they stood for a federal rather than a centralized regime, but the new German institutions they were setting up in Bizonia impressed the French as constituting far too big a step in the direction of centralized government.

The immediate purpose behind the revamping of administration in Bizonia was to meet more effectively the urgent problems of food, fuel, transport, and the black market. The French were less concerned with such matters than with the long-term aspects, with what these decisions would mean for the future of Germany, and of France. In its detailed criticism of the Anglo-American measures the French Government objected that the trend toward centralized government would be difficult to reverse later. The Economic Council, it held, was the forerunner of a future German Reichstag. Instead of emanating from the *Land* governments in a truly federal system, the central organs established in Bizonia would be in a position to dominate those governments.

The questions raised by France required more than a perfunctory reply. Both Britain and the United States realized the need of French support in organizing western Germany in defiance of Soviet protests. A conference of the three powers was convened in London, to which Holland, Belgium and Luxembourg, as interested parties, were also invited. All six western nations whose representatives met at London in February 1948 felt that the time had come to settle at least the urgent problems of western Germany, without ruling out a later settlement for all Germany in which the U.S.S.R. and other eastern European nations would participate. Economic conditions demanded immediate constructive action if Germany was to make its indispensable contribution to western Europe's recovery. Furthermore, the Soviet Union was bidding for the political support of all Germans, not just those in the Soviet zone. Chaos and divided councils in the three western zones would play directly into Soviet hands.

The absence of the Russians from the London talks did not guarantee their success. When they were recessed early in March there was still no firm agreement between French views and those of the United States and Great Britain. The official communiqué announced that economic policies in Bizonia and the French zone would be coordinated and that the three western zones would be associated in the European Recovery Program. Agreement was reached in principle that "a federal form of government is best adapted for the eventual reestablishment of German unity, at present disrupted." As for the Ruhr, recommendations for the establishment of a system of international control, the nature of which was not divulged, were to be submitted to the six governments.

These had been preliminary talks. Until they were resumed in April, again at London, it was not clear whether common ground between the Anglo-American and French views had been or could be found. By that time the European Recovery Program, counted on to compensate France for concessions on the German question, had become law. By that time also the four-power Allied Control Council in Berlin was no longer meeting. The session of March 20 was abruptly terminated by the Soviet Chairman, Marshal Sokolovsky, after the western representatives had refused to give the Council an account of the six-power London talks, against which Moscow had already protested as a flagrant violation of the four-power agreements on control of Germany. A few days later the State Department delivered its reply to the Soviet protest, repeating the point made in an earlier note that no provision of the Potsdam agreement prevented any of the occupying powers from discussing outside the Control Council matters of concern to themselves. The reason why the three western powers felt obliged to consult together, said the note, was precisely that the Soviet Government itself had proved unwilling to implement the principles of the Potsdam agreement, notably the principle of German economic unity. The United States rejected the assertion that its actions were a threat to the authority of the Allied Control Council, throwing the blame on "the consistent pursuit by the Soviet Government in the eastern zone of Germany of a systematic unilateral policy of its own." [2] Britain and France replied in the same vein.

The only point on which there was four-power agreement was that the machinery for governing Germany (the Allied Control Council and its many subordinate committees, subcommittees and "working parties") had broken down. The Soviet action in walking out of the Council on March 20 and the fail-

<hr />

[2] Note of March 25, 1948 (Department of State, *Bulletin*, XVIII, April 4, 1948, 457-459).

ure of General Clay, as next chairman, to call a meeting in April registered recognition, on both sides, of that fact. In this situation the United States and Great Britain indicated their readiness to see established a German government with jurisdiction over all three western zones. General Sir Brian Robertson revealed British and American intentions in a speech made in Düsseldorf on April 7. He announced that ". . . we must accept as a fact that an iron curtain splits Germany. For the time being we must be content with unity so far as it can be achieved, and do not forget that this means the unity of two-thirds of Germany." [3] Premier Schuman of France, speaking a few days later to the congress of the MRP, his political party, stated that "if a four-power accord becomes impossible, we shall make a three-power agreement." [4] A four-power accord had already become impossible, at least for the foreseeable future. The issue at London, then, was not whether but how the three powers would reorganize western Germany politically.

France made real concessions in the London negotiations. At the root of the French attitude was the fear of the resurgence of German military power. The French hoped to ensure Germany's permanent inferiority to France industrially for reasons of security and also in order to eliminate German competition. Britain and America, in the French view, had consistently shown disregard for the interests of France in rejecting the series of French proposals on the Rhineland, the Ruhr, and the future organization of Germany. Foreign Minister Bidault was in a difficult position. He had cast France's lot with the west and sincerely desired a three-power agreement on western Germany. But he had to take account of the depth of French feeling on the subject and of the weakness of the Schuman cabinet. Its opponents on both left and right were waiting for a good opportunity to attack a German policy which could be labeled a betrayal of vital French interests.

Early in June 1948 the delegates meeting in London an-

[3] *Monthly Report of the Control Commission for Germany (British Element).* III, April 1948, 14.
[4] *New York Times,* April 12, 1948.

nounced their agreement on a number of recommendations to their respective governments.[5] The long-predicted merger of the French zone with Bizonia was not one of them. The decisions to coordinate economic policies and to establish a west German government, however, made formal merger an academic question. The Germans were to be allowed to establish political institutions and assume those governmental responsibilities which were compatible with the minimum requirements of occupation and control. The minister-presidents of the *Länder* were to be authorized to convene a constituent assembly, each *Land* choosing its delegates in its own way. The constitution to be drawn up, according to the London agreement, should be such as to enable the Germans to play their part in bringing to an end the present division of Germany, not by reconstitution of a centralized Reich but by means of a federal form of government. The French delegation did not wish to see a constituent assembly called at this early stage but took consolation in the abandonment of an American proposal that it be chosen by universal suffrage and in the knowledge that the Americans and British would not, as they had hitherto feared, establish a full-fledged government based on the institutions already set up at Frankfort.

Bidault could not accept the prospective formation of a German government without getting in return certain guarantees on security matters and on the Ruhr. To guard against the immediate danger that Russia might resort to force against western Europe and the more distant threat of a strong Germany, possibly acting in partnership with Russia, Bidault obtained American and British agreement on the following points: (1) the three powers would not withdraw their troops from Germany until the peace of Europe was "secured" nor without prior consultation; (2) they would consult together if any one of them considered that there was a danger of resur-

5 The London conference was a meeting of ambassadors and experts, not of foreign ministers. The chief delegates were Sir William Strang (U.K.), Lewis W. Douglas (U.S.), René Massigli (France), Michiels van Verduynen (Netherlands), Vicomte Obert de Thiesieus (Belgium), M. Claessen (Luxembourg). Their agreements were in the form of recommendations, not of treaty obligations.

gence of German military power or of the adoption by Germany of a policy of aggression; (3) during the period of occupation the existing prohibitions on German armed forces and controls with respect to disarmament and the level of industry would be maintained; (4) prior to giving up supreme authority, the occupying powers would agree on such permanent measures of disarmament, control of industry, and occupation of key areas as were judged necessary.

The decision on international control of the Ruhr was the other major concession to the French viewpoint. Its terms bore many marks of the long process of give-and-take which finally produced a compromise between the French insistence on security and the Anglo-American desire to revive the Ruhr production in the interest of Europe's recovery. The three Benelux countries were somewhere in the middle of the argument. Invaded by Germany in the past, they shared the French concern with security. But their own prosperity was dependent on German economic recovery. The ports of Holland and Belgium could not thrive without the revival of Germany's trade. They did not support the French proposal for international management of Ruhr industries, and were ready to accept any system of control on which the three great powers could agree. The important thing, they felt, was to put an end to the uncertainty which was bringing neither security nor prosperity.

According to the London agreement, international security and general economic recovery required that the resources of the Ruhr should be used in the interests of peace, not for purposes of aggression, and that access to its coal, coke and steel should be guaranteed without discrimination to "the countries of Europe cooperating in the common economic good." To this end international control was to be exercised through an International Authority composed of representatives of the six contracting nations and Germany. The United States, Britain and France each would have three votes on the Authority, Germany would have three, and the Benelux nations one apiece. For the time being Germany's votes were to be exercised by the powers responsible for economic administration of that part of Germany which includes the Ruhr.[6] Among the Authority's main functions would be the allocation of coal, coke and steel as between German consumption and export, these decisions to be implemented by the Allied military governors so long as they held supreme authority in Germany, after that by the German government.

French opinion seemed dissatisfied with the bargain which Bidault had made. De Gaulle assailed it as a betrayal of French interests. The rightist *Aurore* stated that "France has just sustained in London the greatest diplomatic defeat she has known for a long time—a defeat that not only lowers her prestige but threatens to place her sooner or later in serious danger." On the left, *Franc-Tireur* asserted that the result of the London conference confirmed the breakdown of the foreign policy of the Quai d'Orsay, while *l'Humanité*, organ of the Communist party, wrote that it had been useless to speak of security or of an independent French policy ever since Bidault had begun tripartite conversations behind the back of the U.S.S.R. and meekly followed Washington's lead. Some journals maintained that France had done as well as could be expected and that the accords should be upheld, but the critics were more numerous and surer of their backing than the defenders. The prominent journalist Pertinax wrote in *France-Soir:* "Now we have nothing left but our illusions. Germany will not have a federal structure . . . there is nothing left of our plans for control based on Allied management of the German mines and iron and steel production." [7]

Bidault faced a cold and hostile Assembly when he presented the agreement for approval on June 11. Strictly speaking, the London decisions were recommendations to the participating governments. They were accepted without controversy in London and Washington.[8] In Paris it was a different story. Bidault

[6] Great Britain and the United States. France would be added at such time as a full merger of the three zones should take place.

[7] French Embassy, Information Division, *News from France*, III, June 24, 1948, 9-10.

[8] Not being a treaty, the agreements were not submitted to the U.S. Congress. In general, the Congressional and public reaction in the United States was

defended himself by explaining the difficulties of his position. There was nothing to be gained, he said, merely by repeating proposals that France's allies rejected. France had to make concessions, or else be content to see the future of western Germany determined by the United States and Great Britain without regard to French interests. It was a choice between isolation and cooperation, and France could not afford to be isolated. Bidault naturally stressed what France had gained: Anglo-American acceptance of an international regime for the Ruhr during the occupation period, postponement of the formation of a centralized German government and acceptance of the federal principle, and American assurances of security. He made much of the "not negligible" guarantees given by the United States on keeping troops in Germany and agreeing to designate key regions for permanent occupation. He mentioned America's closer association with western Europe through Truman's speech of March 17, promising support of the five-power Brussels pact, and through the Vandenberg resolution then before the Senate. Bidault was on the defensive, but he was not apologetic. He felt that he had obtained the maximum possible in the circumstances. France, he said, had to take the world as it was. It could not separate itself from those nations which had the same goal as France, that of constructing a viable Europe.[9]

The Foreign Minister's policies were then subjected to bitter attack from both right and left and were criticized also by some Socialists. He was charged with cruel deception of the French

---

favorable. One current of opinion, however, opposed the London accords on the ground that they represented a "Germany first" policy and opened the way for the renascence of German industrial and military power. Others who favored partition of Germany into smaller states deplored the plan to set up a central government for western Germany in an attempt to outbid the U.S.S.R. for German support. Such an approach, they felt, must encourage rabid German nationalism and probably would fail (see Sumner Welles in the *New York Herald Tribune*, June 15, 1948; Eugene V. Rostow, "Germany: a Warning," *New York Times Magazine*, June 6, 1948, 9 ff.). Henry Wallace and his supporters attacked U.S. policy on the two counts that it forsook agreement with Russia and was rebuilding "the old Prussian-Nazi, cartel-ridden Germany of Hitler's munition magnates."

[9] *Journal Officiel, Débats Parlementaires, Assemblée Nationale*, June 12, 1948, 3454-3461.

people and blindness to the German danger. These speakers were not impressed by the so-called guarantees obtained from the United States. Communist spokesmen denounced him for slavishly following the anti-Soviet policy of Washington. Pierre Cot, whose point of view was near that of the Communists, delivered the most forceful and stirring speech of the debate, a frank appeal to nationalism. Speaking "not as a party man but as a Frenchman to other Frenchmen," he stated that the "great French idea," that of making the French-Belgian-Dutch steel industry the largest in Europe, was being abandoned in favor of the reconstruction of Germany. "France cannot accept!" he concluded, asking every deputy to search in his heart and listen to "the voice of natural instinct, the voice of France." [10]

After four days of debate the Assembly passed a resolution giving qualified approval to the London accords by a margin of 8 votes, with 26 abstentions. In accepting a German policy on which it had serious doubts the Assembly majority enjoined the government (1) to reaffirm the French position on the necessity for internationalization of the mines and basic industries of the Ruhr, obtaining the extension of the Ruhr Authority's control to include actual management of those mines and industries; (2) to safeguard the security of France by the occupation of Germany for a long period, the withdrawal of Allied troops to be conditional upon a definite agreement on security guarantees and occupation of key areas; (3) to eliminate all risks of the reconstitution of a centralized authoritarian Reich; (4) to continue to seek a final four-power agreement on Germany. It solemnly reminded the government of its promise to oppose any decisions running counter to those aims. Even on the government side there was little enthusiasm for the London recommendations. More emphasis was placed on the reservations than on the acceptance, although to the British and Americans it was the acceptance which counted. The decisive factor, however, as American representatives in Paris may have helped to point out, was that this vote did not concern German policy

10 *Ibid.*, June 13, 1948, 3484-3488.

alone. It involved Europe, and the common effort to rebuild Europe. It involved the Marshall plan and the Brussels pact and the project of western union. Association with the western powers was more important to France than sterile insistence on a German policy which could never be put into practice.

2. The Soviet Zone

There was no mistaking Soviet displeasure over the decision of the western powers to set up a government in western Germany. In diplomatic notes and in its press and radio propaganda Moscow made loud and repeated protests against this action as a violation of the Potsdam agreements. The Soviet leaders knew, however, that the future of Germany was being determined by what was going on in Germany, not by protests and diplomatic exchanges. The new and more positive policy of the western powers, aimed at making the greater part of Germany a going concern under western direction, represented a real threat to Russia's long-range objectives. The Kremlin found several ways to reply: by putting pressure on the western powers in Berlin, by launching a propaganda campaign for German unity, and by taking new measures of its own in eastern Germany.

The position of the western powers in Berlin was vulnerable to interference with the lines of communication and supply between their occupation zones and the capital, for these lines ran through the Soviet zone. As early as January 1948, the Soviet authorities were putting obstacles in the way of traffic. At the end of March they began to discover "technical" difficulties making it necessary to impose restrictions on passenger and freight traffic between the western zones and Berlin. It was not clear whether these were conceived as measures of reprisal for the constitutional changes being made in Bizonia and for the six-power London decisions, or were the initial steps of a concerted plan to drive the western powers out of Berlin.[11] In any event, coupled with the intensified Soviet

[11] See below, pp. 133-137.

propaganda for a united, "democratic" Germany, they heralded determined Soviet efforts to achieve a double objective: to ensure that Anglo-American policies in western Germany should fail and that any united Germany emerging from the current wrangling should be tied to the Soviet bloc and not to the west.

Such was the purpose of the German People's Congress organized under Soviet auspices in December 1947. This body, completely dominated by the Soviet-sponsored Socialist Unity party (SED), put forward a claim to present Germany's views at the London meeting of the Council of Foreign Ministers and later set about organizing a plebiscite on German unity. Where it could operate, in the Soviet zone of Germany and the Soviet sector of Berlin, the People's Congress enjoyed wide publicity and collected thousands of "yes" votes. In its attempts to influence the course of events in the remainder of Berlin and in the western zones it was less successful. It was repudiated by all the political parties except the Communists and on that ground was denied permission to carry on its activities in the bizonal area. While it was probably true, as the U.S. State Department charged in a public statement, that the People's Congress was a Communist-dominated organization representing but a small minority of the German population, it had significant potentialities which the Soviets obviously intended to exploit. Recent western actions put them in a position to accuse the western powers of splitting Germany and to pose as the champions of German unity. They could use the Congress as a propaganda weapon and rallying point of German nationalism in support of their aims, and, if things developed favorably, could build on it a government claiming jurisdiction over all Germany.

Meanwhile the outlines of the "new democratic Germany" so frequently mentioned in Soviet propaganda were apparent from what was going on in the one part of Germany where its sponsors had a free hand, the Soviet zone of occupation. Since the start of the occupation the line between eastern and western Germany had been a formidable barrier. The areas placed under Polish "administration" by the decision of the Big Three at

Potsdam (southern East Prussia, Silesia, and parts of Pomerania and Brandenburg) were being governed as an integral part of Poland. The U.S.S.R. and Poland regarded that decision as a final territorial settlement, and none of the objections registered by Byrnes at Stuttgart or by Marshall and Bevin at Moscow and London could alter the fact that the Poles were in possession. To the west of these territories lay the Soviet zone, difficult of access from the west and in many ways tied more closely to the Soviet-dominated states of eastern Europe than to the rest of Germany. There the new rulers implanted a political and economic system of significance not only to the Germans living under it but to all Germans and to the future of Europe.

When the Russians came into eastern Germany in 1945 they wasted no time in clearing the ground for a new political regime in which Germans should play a role from the first. The leading part was reserved for those German Communists like Wilhelm Pieck and Walter Ulbricht who had spent many years in Moscow preparing for this very opportunity. Four parties were permitted to carry on political activities: the Communists, Social Democrats, Christian Democrats and Liberals. Within less than a year it became clear to the Soviet authorities that the Communist party did not have sufficient popular support to carry the Soviet program through. In 1946 they engineered its merger with the Social Democratic party to form the Socialist Unity party (SED), which became the chosen instrument for carrying the Soviet program into effect. The new party, in which Communist leaders held the reins, was given a privileged position with respect to jobs, propaganda facilities, and all the other factors which are important in maintaining political power. It had the active support of the Soviet Military Administration.

The two bourgeois parties, the Christian Democratic Union (CDU) and the Liberal Democrats, were allowed to continue in existence. In elections they did fairly well. They were represented in the *Land* and local governments. Their influence on policy, however, was unimportant. In government blocs they were invariably outnumbered by representatives of the SED and of other Communist-sponsored organizations such as the labor unions and the youth movement. Wilhelm Külz, the Liberal leader, was known for his complaisance to the Russians and to the SED. Jakob Kaiser, leader of the CDU in the Soviet zone and a man who sincerely desired cooperation with the Russians, was permitted to follow a more independent line until December 1947 but was then removed from his position by the direct intervention of the Soviet authorities after refusing to take part in the People's Congress. His supporters were gradually eliminated from the administration, and the party leadership was placed in "safe" hands. By 1948 the Soviet zone had acquired a political structure very much like those of the states of eastern Europe in which the Communists had eliminated or reduced to docility the historic bourgeois and agrarian parties and swallowed up the Socialists.

Early in the occupation the Soviet authorities established central economic agencies, staffed by Germans, in their zone. In July 1947, shortly after German economic institutions were created in Bizonia, they expanded the powers of these agencies and created a German Economic Commission. In February 1948 this commission was given further powers at the expense of the *Land* governments. Composed of representatives of the central agencies, of the *Land* governments, and of the trade union movement and the peasants' organization, and having power to enforce its decrees, it could have served as the nucleus of a government for the zone. The People's Congress could have become a parliament. In the summer of 1948 the Soviet-licensed press in eastern Germany published a draft constitution for a "democratic and indivisible German republic" bearing a superficial resemblance to the Weimar constitution of 1919. The Soviet authorities, however, did not choose to establish a German government at this time. They were making capital of the western powers' moves toward a separate government for western Germany, hoping to throw on them the onus of "partition."

In their economic program the Soviets pursued two main objectives: to obtain from Germany material benefits which would compensate at least partially for Russia's great war losses, and to create in eastern Germany an economic system working in favor of Communist control and the orientation of Germany to the east. The two could not be reconciled. The Soviet authorities found difficulty in winning friends and influencing people while stripping the zone of many of its industrial resources.

Soviet reparation claims on Germany, stated in money terms, amounted to $10 billion. This was the figure first put forward by Stalin at Yalta and demanded by Molotov in the Council of Foreign Ministers in 1946 and 1947. The western powers had not agreed to that sum, or any specific sum, but only to the arrangement made at Potsdam whereby Germany would hand over as reparation industrial plant and equipment over and above a level fixed by the four occupying powers as necessary for the German peacetime economy. Under the Potsdam agreement the U.S.S.R. was to get all such equipment in the Soviet zone plus 25 percent of that in the western zones, in addition to a share of Germany's external assets.[12] This arrangement had not satisfied the Soviet Government. Their continued insistence on the $10 billion total and on getting reparation from current German production contributed more than any other single issue to the failure to reach four-power agreement on a German settlement. The western powers, who were pouring in goods to keep western Germany afloat, could not agree to allow Russia to drain them off in reparation payments. In its own zone, however, the Soviet Union was able to do as it liked, and to exact reparation without regard to the wishes of the other occupying powers or the precise stipulations of applicable agreements.

The Soviet zone possessed important industries, although it had no heavy industrial concentration comparable to the Ruhr area; Upper Silesia, with its mines and steel mills, had been turned over to Poland. Aircraft, machinery and precision instruments were among the major items produced in the Soviet zone. The Soviet authorities began to dismantle factories and ship them back to Russia as soon as their armies came in. Among them were the great printing establishments of Leipzig, the

---

[12] A part of the reparation removals from the western zones was to be compensated by food and raw materials provided by the Soviet Union, which also undertook to satisfy Poland's reparation claims from its own share.

aviation factories at Dessau, much of the Zeiss optical works at Jena, a number of steel mills, and a great quantity of mining equipment. After the process had gone on for more than a year it became apparent to the Soviet Government that the value of such transplanted factories in the U.S.S.R. was very limited. Removals were slowed down, although not entirely discontinued. In order to obtain a greater return, and at the same time to still criticism from the Germans, the Soviets shifted to a policy of leaving factories in Germany, where they could produce more efficiently the goods which the Soviet Union needed. Some were left in German hands, all or part of their production being taken on reparation account for use in Russia or for sale abroad. Others, chiefly capital goods industries, were actually taken over by the Soviet Government and operated as "Soviet companies," coordinated by a huge trust with headquarters in Berlin and actually controlled from Moscow. The ownership and direction of these industries (of which there were at first about 200, later reduced to 126 when some were transferred to the respective *Land* governments) were entirely in Soviet hands; they were effectively tied into the economy of the U.S.S.R. The industries controlled by these companies had a total producing capacity of about 30 percent of all industry in the zone. They included coal, oil, iron and steel, machinery, chemicals, electrical goods and synthetic rubber.[13]

No official figures of the total "takings" from the Soviet zone were given out. American and British estimates ran quite high. Marshall at the London conference of November 1947 stated that Russian acquisitions in one form or another came to over $500 million a year. Bevin named a total of $7 billion since the end of the war, the greater part of the total that the Soviet Government was demanding from all Germany. These figures in-

---

[13] The Soviet companies' share of production in various industries ranged from 77 percent in potash and petroleum, 69 percent in rubber and 56 percent in electrical goods, down to 4 percent in textiles; they employed some 300,000 workers not counting those working in the uranium mines, or about one-fifth of the industrial workers in the zone. See Deutsches Institut für Wirtschafts-forschung, *Wirtschaftsprobleme der Besatzungszonen* (Berlin, 1948), 230; "Die Wirtschaftliche Entwicklung in der sowjetische Zone Deutschlands seit Potsdam," *Europa Archiv*, II, December 1947, 1027-1040.

cluded, in addition to reparations, huge quantities of goods
delivered to the Soviet occupation forces for use in Germany.

Of the industrial enterprises not under Soviet ownership,
many became public property through socialization laws. These
volkseigene Betriebe or "People's Industries" were administered by the *Land* governments and coordinated in a common
plan for the zone by the German Economic Commission. The remainder, chiefly small establishments, were owned by cooperatives or were left in private hands. Planning for all these enterprises, public and private, was centered in the Soviet Military
Administration. How the latter used its complete control over
industry depended on the weight given, at any particular time,
to different and sometimes conflicting aims. Alongside the aim
of gaining direct material advantages for the economy of the
U.S.S.R. was that of breaking the power of the old industrialists
and building a new system based on a Communist-led proletariat. That meant that some attention had to be paid to public
opinion and to living standards. Some consideration had to be
given to what plant and resources were necessary to keep the
economy of the zone from collapse.

In agricultural policy the Soviet authorities could follow a
more consistent line. There the principal objective was to end
forever the great estates of the Junkers and to create an agricultural class loyal to the new regime. By a thoroughgoing land
reform the large landowners were expropriated without compensation; their estates and former government holdings, about
three million hectares according to Soviet sources, were divided
among landless and poor peasants and German refugees from
territories taken over by Poland. About ten percent of the land
was given over to experimental state farms, perhaps to pave
the way for collectivization on a larger scale at some later date.

The Soviet authorities, having organized the peasants first
into revolutionary committees and then into mutual aid societies,
set up a system of planning quotas fixed for each *Land* and each
village. Through the mutual aid societies, the agrarian counterpart of the Communist-led trade unions, the Soviets apparently
hoped to build an organization of assured loyalty to the regime

as well as to encourage maximum food production. But many difficulties beset both the peasants and the agricultural planners. The war and Germany's collapse had disorganized the entire agricultural system. The creation of thousands of small holdings did not make for efficiency and high levels of production. Many of the former inhabitants had fled westward. Livestock was gravely depleted, and there was not enough farm machinery. Deliveries to the cities were cut down.

In working out an economic plan for their zone the Soviet authorities kept one eye on the rest of Germany and the other on the other countries of eastern Europe. The Soviet zone was a part of Germany. What was done with its economic resources was of immense importance for the future of Germany. In any choice to be made between east and west the Germans would inevitably measure the prosperity, or poverty, of the Soviet zone against the productivity and living standards in the western zones. Economic chaos or stagnation would hardly win converts to communism in an area where Communists exercised full power. On the other hand, pending some kind of settlement of the German problem, the Soviet zone remained a part of the Soviet "empire" in eastern Europe. Its foreign trade was managed to suit the interests of the U.S.S.R. It had resources, products and skills needed by the states of eastern Europe, including the U.S.S.R., all of which had embarked on ambitious two-, three-, or five-year plans. In mid-1948 the Soviet administration worked out with its German economic experts an economic program for the latter half of the year, to be followed by a two-year plan for 1949 and 1950, calling for increased production and closer trade relations with eastern European states. The Soviets apparently hoped also to maintain their zone's trade relations with western Europe (especially Scandinavia, Benelux and Switzerland) and with western Germany. In November 1947 an agreement was signed with U.S. and U.K. military authorities for trade with Bizonia in 1948 approximately 50 percent higher than in 1947. This trade did not develop, however, since the Soviet zone did not have the goods to deliver; moreover, the Soviet blockade of Berlin was followed by a halt, by order of the U.S.-

U.K. authorities, in the shipment of goods from Bizonia into the Soviet zone. For that zone, both by design and by circumstance, the emphasis for the future was on ties with the U.S.S.R. and the states of the Soviet bloc.

However skillfully the two-year plan might be advertised to the Germans of the Soviet zone, there was no escaping the fact that conditions were deteriorating. The drain of goods to the east, the lack of raw materials and of new machinery needed by key industries, and the drop in output flowing from changes in ownership, management and personnel all contributed to a decline in living standards noted by Germans and foreign observers able to get into the Soviet zone from the west. The 1947 drought hit crops badly. Russia's demands for agricultural produce remained heavy. Eastern Germany, in 1948, no longer had the surplus of food which in earlier years would have been available to the western zones if the Potsdam decision to treat Germany as an economic unit had been observed by the Russians. Now, as western Germany moved toward recovery while eastern Germany stagnated, economic unity no longer looked so attractive to the western powers.

The Soviet Government, for its part, was not likely to propose, or to accept, any plan for the organization of a united Germany which did not make allowance for the political and economic structure developed in the Soviet zone. The political organization—including government, administration, courts, trade unions, peasant cooperatives, the educational system, and use of the secret police and the concentration camp—made the German regime an instrument of Soviet policy. The economic organization included socialization of industry and planned economy on the one hand, and on the other direct Soviet participation and vested interest in the most important sector of German industry. Exploitation had been the principal motive. Should it be replaced by reconstruction, it would be a reconstruction geared to Soviet interests. The western powers could not accept German unity on such terms. And the longer the Russians stayed in eastern Germany, tying it more and more closely to their own system, the greater would be the difficulties in putting Germany

back together again even if at some future date the four powers
might agree that it should be done.

3. Eastern Europe and the German Question

In the struggle of the great powers over Germany the interests of the smaller nations which were Germany's immediate
neighbors were often overlooked. For the people of Belgium and
Holland, Denmark and Norway, Poland and Czechoslovakia,
solution of the German problem was a question of national survival. They had experienced German aggression and ruthlessness, and they had to live as neighbors to the Germans, come
what may. They had little to gain from any competition between
the great powers for the support of a united Germany, and
might be the first to pay for any mistakes made by those powers
in dealing with Germany.

Representatives of the smaller nations were permitted to
state their views on a German settlement to the Deputies of the
Council of Foreign Ministers early in 1947 before the Council
met at Moscow in March. When the Council itself was in session, in Moscow and later in London, only occasionally was a
small nation invited to state its case on a particular subject. The
United States consistently argued in favor of having the small
powers share in drafting the German peace treaty, but so long
as the Big Four could not agree on how to go ahead with the
treaty, the only German "settlement" consisted in the decisions
which they took as occupying powers, in concert or separately.
Accordingly, the smaller powers had little or no influence on
decisions of the greatest significance for their own future. The
indefinite postponement of peace treaty negotiations and the
virtual end of four-power administration in Germany in 1948
meant that the U.S.S.R. and the western bloc each would make
its own *de facto* peace settlement in its own part of Germany.
Each would choose to what extent it wished to associate the
small powers in its partial peace settlement. The western powers
brought the three Benelux nations into the London negotiations
which resulted in the six-power agreement of June 1948 on

western Germany. The U.S.S.R. countered with a meeting of eastern European Foreign Ministers held in Warsaw later in June.

Past experience and fear for the future were the prime reasons why the people of Poland, Czechoslovakia, and to a lesser extent Yugoslavia supported the idea of alliance with the U.S.S.R. against German resurgence. In Hungary and Rumania, which had been Germany's allies in the war, anti-German feeling had never been so strong; there the Russian menace, in the popular mind, was a graver danger than the German menace. More distant Bulgaria had managed to be on good terms with both Germany and Russia, each at the proper time, and to profit from both connections.

Poland, ravaged and plundered during the war, had taken over extensive German territories and driven out millions of Germans. Once Germany recovered its strength its first move, almost inevitably, would be to try to recover those lost territories. Against that threat Poland had no choice but to rely on Russia. Before the Poles was the picture of what had happened to them when they had attempted to maintain a policy independent of, and antagonistic to, both Germany and Russia. No matter what the complexion of its government, Poland was impelled toward a policy of keeping Germany impotent. Soviet measures directed to that end were sure of Polish support. Polish views on the German settlement, presented to the Council of Foreign Ministers in 1947, stressed demilitarization, denazification, and reparation. On the other hand, despite their official stand against decentralization, Poles could hardly fail to be alarmed over Soviet policies aimed at reconstituting a centralized Germany as a Soviet ally. Poland's "regained territories" in the west might be used as bait for Germany to accept a Soviet alignment, and the two could at any time strike a bargain, as they had in 1939, to effect a fifth partition of Poland.

The Czech people had the same deep-seated fear of Germany, without the Poles' tradition of hatred and distrust of Russia. Czechoslovakia demanded small territorial cessions from Germany, heavy reparations, free zones in German ports, and treaty guarantees against German aggression. But the Czechs also wanted the assurance that outside help would be forthcoming. After the soul-searing experience of Munich they were no longer willing to rely for security on possible help from the west. German lands, which might some day be reconstituted as "greater Germany," still surrounded Czechoslovakia on three sides. It became an axiom of Czechoslovak thinking that an alliance with the U.S.S.R. must be the anchor of the country's foreign policy. Geography determined Prague's position and severely limited the possibilities of an independent policy. In practice, Czechoslovakia had to take its place as a member of the Soviet bloc, even before the Communists took power in February 1948, this subservience being accepted by Czech opinion as a necessary price to pay for security against the hereditary enemy. After that date the government in Prague, like that in Warsaw, was completely under the Kremlin's control.

For these reasons Polish and Czech opinion could always be rallied in support of Soviet protests against Anglo-American attempts to revive industrial production in the Ruhr. The very fact of revival was disturbing, whether the purpose were the recovery of the European economy, as the western powers alleged, or the rebuilding of war industries and the return to power of the German steel barons, as Soviet propaganda so positively claimed. By the same token, Soviet policies which tended to strengthen Germany and to promote German nationalism may well have been equally disturbing, although the Polish and Czechoslovak governments did not say so openly.

The Soviet Government was plainly annoyed at the decision to hold the six-power meetings in London, and even more at the results. Its annoyance was shared by the governments of Poland, Czechoslovakia and Yugoslavia. But their protests against the "violation of Yalta and Potsdam" were curtly rejected.

The next move of the Soviet bloc was a conference of eight Foreign Ministers in Warsaw on June 23, 1948. Including three ex-enemy states and another, Albania, which was neither Allied nor enemy, this conference had no legal standing with respect to the formal peacemaking with Germany. It was a demonstration of the solidarity of the Soviet bloc in opposition to western policies in Europe. The eastern European countries were mobilized to speak with one voice on the German problem. The voice was that of Molotov. The final document, adopted after three brief meetings, declared that the London conference had been called in violation of Potsdam and with the purpose of liquidating the Council of Foreign Ministers and the Allied Control Council; that the western powers had abandoned the agreements on German disarmament, demilitarization, and reparation; that the London decisions were directed toward rebuilding German industries and the war potential of the Ruhr in the service of monopoly capitalists and of the military and strategic aims of the United States; that the western powers were dividing and dismembering Germany in opposition to the legitimate wishes of the German people; that the federal structure for Germany proposed at London was antidemocratic; and that all these gross violations of the Yalta and Potsdam accords would facilitate a new German aggression and hinder Europe's economic recovery. The declaration then recommended that the occupying powers work together to assure Germany's demilitarization, establish four-power control over the Ruhr, form a democratic central government in Germany composed of democratic parties and organizations, make Germany pay its reparation obligations, and proceed to the conclusion of a treaty of peace; all occupation forces should be withdrawn one year after the conclusion of the treaty.

This declaration, except for the item on withdrawal, amounted to a repetition of proposals already made many times by the U.S.S.R. within the past year in the Council of Foreign Ministers and elsewhere. Although it made no mention of the establishment of a German government for the Soviet zone or for all Germany, it was aimed principally at winning support among the German people.[14] The Soviet program won unani-

[14] According to one newspaper report, Molotov proposed establishment of a German government but dropped it when the Poles and Czechs registered violent objections (Joseph and Stewart Alsop in the *New York Herald Tribune*, August 25, 1948).

mous approval at Warsaw because six of the Communist governments represented there had no policy independent of the U.S.S.R., and the seventh was Yugoslavia, whose regime had taken the decision to maintain 100 percent solidarity with Soviet foreign policy while fighting for its life against the expected attack of the Communist Information Bureau. All these countries, however, regardless of regime, had certain interests in the future of Germany which were not those of the Soviet Union. Even though the Oder-Neisse frontier was declared "indestructible," Poland and Czechoslovakia could not look ahead with equanimity to the revival of even a "democratic" centralized Germany. For the U.S.S.R., Germany was the great prize. To win Germany was to win Europe. In comparison the Poles, Czechs and Hungarians were unimportant, and they knew it. But no conflicting views were voiced at Warsaw. The Soviet grip on eastern Europe was too strong.

Foreign Secretary Bevin expressed the western powers' reaction to what he called the Warsaw "statement of Soviet policy" when he referred to it as invoking the need for four-power agreement while continuing to insist on Soviet predominance in Germany. The fundamental difficulty, he said, was the insistence on a "so-called democratic, that is to say Communist-controlled, central German Government." No progress could be made toward four-power agreement so long as that was the Soviet program.[15]

There was every indication that this was, and would continue to be, the Soviet program. The greatest obstacle to its success, in the eyes of the Soviet leaders, was the independent action of the other powers in western Germany, embodied in their London decisions. Against the dangers of this action no available form of retaliation could be neglected. Thus, at the same time that they were making verbal assaults on it such as the Warsaw declaration, they were also going methodically ahead with more effective countermeasures at a point where the western powers were particularly vulnerable, Berlin.[16]

[15] *Parliamentary Debates, Weekly Hansard,* House of Commons, June 30, 1948, 2339.
[16] See below, pp. 133-139.

4. Political Forces in Germany

In all consideration of the future of Germany the thoughts and aspirations of the Germans themselves had to be taken increasingly into account. Russia and the west were competing not only for strategic positions in Germany but also for the support of the German people. The common Allied policy of "democratizing" the Germans, as laid down by the Potsdam agreements, had proved to be no common policy at all. Each occupying power set out to inculcate democracy in its own way. The absence of a common approach gave the Germans more room for manoeuvre, more room to make their own views felt in the Germany which was emerging from the collapse of Hitler's Third Reich. They saw that their country was a coveted prize for which the victors seemed willing to risk a new war.

Under the occupation, of course, supreme authority rested with the Allied military governments. German political parties were handicapped in seeking popular support for the obvious reason that they were engaged in "shadow politics." The occupying powers, while placing more and more of the business of government in German hands, tended to give them responsibility without authority. Their leaders were, for the most part, survivors from the pre-Hitler era. Only a few had wide prestige. It was difficult to persuade the first-rate leaders to serve under a foreign occupation. Those who accepted office could not be sure that they would not be swept aside after the occupation was over, tarred with the brush of collaboration with those who had defeated and humiliated Germany. Nevertheless, Germany had to be governed, and Germans had to take part in it. As the war faded into the past, the objectives of the occupying powers demanded increasing attention to trends in Germany, both those of a more formal political nature and the less easily discernible trends in public opinion, religion and cultural life.

With the destruction of the Nazi state, the class antagonisms which had been repressed by the totalitarian system again appeared. The middle class, which had been rather closely identified with National Socialism, strove to save what it could from the wreck of German society and to face the challenge of well-organized working-class parties. In the western zones the middle-class groups, so far as they were able to survive loss of material possessions and denazification proceedings, managed to maintain a semblance of their position in industry, the professions, the bureaucracy and the universities. In the Soviet zone their economic power was largely destroyed through the Soviet program of reparation removals, nationalization, and sponsorship of working-class leadership in both political and economic life. Throughout Germany the middle class tended to support the Christian Democratic Union (CDU), which included both Protestants and Catholics, and the less important Liberal Democratic and allied parties. The program of the CDU varied from one part of Germany to another. In Bavaria, where it was known as the Christian Social Union (CSU), it was quite conservative; in the Soviet zone CDU leaders accepted nationalization and attempted to cooperate with the Communists. Nor was it an exclusively middle-class party. Like the old Center party, it had some working-class following.

The working-class parties were the Social Democrats (SPD) and Communists (KPD), bitter opponents except in the Soviet zone, where the Communists had swallowed their rivals thanks to Soviet pressure in forcing their merger into the new Socialist Unity party (SED) in 1946. In the western zones, where they resisted such a merger, the Social Democrats consistently came out far ahead of the Communists in free elections. Strongest in the U.K. zone, which included the Ruhr industrial area, the SPD was a factor to be reckoned with by the western powers, both because of its influence in the trade unions and because of its tendency to preach German nationalism as well as social democracy. The Communist party, numerically weak, had little more than nuisance value in the western zones. Even in Berlin, surrounded by Soviet-occupied territory, the SPD could easily outbid the SED for popular support. It was because of their failure at the polls that the Soviet authorities and the German Communists had to adopt more direct and forceful methods in their attempt to get control of the machinery of government in Berlin.

German politics in the western zones at first centered in the separate *Länder,* by decision of the occupying powers. In the U.S. zone the conservative CSU stood forth as the leading party in Bavaria, the CDU in Württemberg-Baden, the SPD in more industrial Hesse and in the city of Bremen. In the British zone the SPD had the lead in Schleswig-Holstein, Lower Saxony and Hamburg, while the CDU held a slight edge in North Rhine-Westphalia. The latter state included the Ruhr, where Communist strength in the western zones was concentrated. The CDU was the leading party in all three states of the largely agricultural French zone. In general terms the SPD and CDU were at odds on the two major problems of policy: centralism versus federalism, and socialism versus private enterprise. Yet these issues were never sharply defined, chiefly because their solution, in the short run, lay not with Germans but with foreign powers. Moreover, within the parties there were splits over doctrine, methods, and the personal ambitions of individual leaders. The leaders within each *Land* and each zone kept an eye on their prospects in an eventually unified Germany. On the ability of the two main parties to cooperate, as in Austria, might depend the chances for a relatively stable government in the future, for in combination they would constitute a "third force" much stronger than any existing parties of extreme right or left.

The establishment of bizonal agencies in 1947 gave the parties of the American and British zones the opportunity to operate on a wider stage than before. In the first Economic Council there was an even balance between the SPD and the CDU, with 20 members each, but the minor party representation (except for three Communist members) was on the conservative side, thus giving a stronger voice to the CDU. This it maintained after the reorganization of the bizonal institutions at Frankfort early in 1948. The CDU swept the board in the nomination of members of the Executive Committee, which controlled the various administrative departments. The Social

Democrats, who chose to abstain from voting when the Executive Committee was elected, became a sort of unofficial opposition in the bizonal administration, a rather unfortunate situation since their cooperation was necessary in making the administration's decisions effective in industrial areas like the Ruhr. The position of the six Communist members of the Economic Council, as a British report pointed out, was somewhat peculiar.[17] They held their seats despite the fact that their party condemned the entire bizonal administration as an illegal instrument of the western powers designed to bring about the final division of Germany.

The big question for the German parties in 1948 was not socialism versus private enterprise but the future structure of Germany. The London decisions of the western powers, providing for the formation of a west German government, forced the leadership of each German party to take a stand for or against. "The German people," read the London agreement, ". . . should now be free to establish for themselves the political organization and institutions which will enable them to assume those governmental responsibilities which are compatible with the minimum requirements of occupation and control and which ultimately will enable them to assume full governmental responsibility." The minister-presidents of the Länder of the three western zones were therefore authorized to convene an assembly to draft a constitution which would "enable the Germans to play their part in bringing to an end the present division of Germany not by the reconstitution of a centralized Reich but by means of a federal form of government which adequately protects the rights of the respective states, and at the same time provides for adequate central authority and which guarantees the rights and freedoms of the individual."

The questions before the Germans in the western zones were, first, did they want to establish a separate government, and second, if so, what degree of centralism did they prefer. In general, the working-class parties were hostile to the idea of setting

17 *Monthly Report of the Control Commission for Germany (British Element)*, III, May 1948, 10.

up a government for western Germany alone, the Communists because they followed the line of Soviet policy, the Social Democrats because they wished to avoid responsibility for acts which seemed to recognize the permanent division of Germany. The first SPD reaction was to condemn the London agreement as "a unilateral foreign decision which entails no German responsibility." The CDU also had objections but was more inclined to go along, accepting as a fact, unpleasant though it was, the temporary absence of eastern Germany from a venture which had nevertheless to be undertaken. It seemed the only alternative to the present uncertainty and drifting; and it did offer the possibility that, with economic improvement, a stable and self-governing western Germany would serve as a magnet for the east rather than vice versa. The apparent determination of the western powers to remain in Berlin was another factor which finally brought western German leaders of both major parties to qualified acceptance of the London decisions. Ernst Reuter, SPD leader in Berlin, who would have been mayor but for the Soviet refusal to recognize his election, encouraged them to do so, saying that the consolidation of western Germany was an essential preliminary to an improvement in Berlin's situation and to the return of eastern Germany to the common motherland.

The CDU, and especially the CSU in Bavaria, favored a government structure under which the central organs would exercise only the minimum esssential powers and the *Länder* would retain wide autonomy. Here they were at odds, however, with the SPD leaders, who thought in national rather than in provincial terms, and also with the parties of the right, which held to the strong nationalism with which the German middle class had long been associated. The SPD tradition and organization had always been centralist. Socialists felt that the historic movement toward German unity could not be reversed, and that provincial autonomy, especially in south Germany, would play into the hands of reactionaries.

On July 1, 1948, the three Allied military governors presented to the minister-presidents of the 11 western *Länder* three documents covering the conditions for convening a constituent assembly by September 1, modification of certain *Land* boundaries, and proposals for an occupation statute. The Germans raised some objections. They did not wish to have the new regime called a government, nor to designate the assembly as constituent and the basic law as a constitution. They maintained that the regime must be clearly provisional, owing its existence solely to the temporary state of affairs caused by the occupation of Germany. Their view was that there could be no German constitution until the whole German people could have a voice in framing it. The risk of appearing to be advocates of partition was one which German politicians did not care to assume, even those who were quite ready to go ahead on the basis of the London decisions. Their hesitation was due even more to the terms proposed for an occupation statute. This statute, a sort of preliminary peace treaty, would define the powers handed over to the new German government and those retained by the Allied authorities. In the view of the Germans, the Allies wanted to keep too much authority. They did not want a constitution at all if wide powers of supervision and intervention at all levels were to be reserved by the military governors.

Toward the end of July these difficulties were resolved by compromise. The 11 minister-presidents formally accepted the responsibility for selecting representatives to a "parliamentary council" which would draft a "provisional fundamental law," to be ratified not by the people, as the London agreement provided, but by the separate states. This solution met some of the German, and also French, objections to the London decisions but meant no essential change in them.

As delegates from the 11 *Länder* convened at the Chiemsee in Bavaria to prepare drafts to be submitted to the assembly, lively discussion on the subject took place throughout western Germany. Despite the tendency to keep attention riveted on eastern Germany and Berlin, many German leaders were prepared to think in terms of Germany's political association with western Europe; economic association already existed as a result

of the admission of western Germany (represented by the occupation authorities) into the Organization for European Economic Cooperation. Some Germans, mostly those of CDU
persuasion, believed western Germany could exert a considerable degree of initiative toward formation of a European union.
The draft constitution prepared at the Chiemsee envisaged the
eventual transfer of a measure of sovereignty to an international
authority, with the express purpose of facilitating adherence
to a European federation. This was an approach designed to
restore Germany to equal status, and to provide a simultaneous
solution for the German and for the European problem, although there was no certainty that other nations of western
Europe would feel comfortable in a federation which Germany,
even western Germany, might tend to dominate because of its
greater population and resources.

Party programs and tentative plans for a German constitution
necessarily gave an inadequate and possibly misleading picture
of political forces in Germany. Germany's future was bound up
in the outcome of the struggle between east and west. While
the occupation continued, politics in the eastern zone conformed
to a pattern set by the Soviet Union, and in the western zones
to a pattern set by the western powers. As occupation controls
relaxed, as troops were withdrawn, the Germans themselves
would have a greater influence both on their own affairs and on
the east-west conflict.

It was still too early to say whether Germany would lean
toward democracy and the western system, would turn to communism and Russia, or would again take the road to authoritarian nationalism. The overriding fact in the picture was that
the line of partition cut through the German nation. No German politician or party could ignore it. Furthermore, beneath
the surface were many disquieting factors. In western Germany
were two large groups which had found no place in the body
politic: the former Nazis and the refugees from Czechoslovakia,
Poland and the eastern areas taken over by Poland. Neither
"denazification" nor "reeducation" had accomplished what
Allied planners had hoped they would accomplish. Denazifica-

tion in the American and British zones, although successful in removing Nazi elements from the top positions in public and private life, had bogged down in a maze of detailed procedures and delays and had become discredited in the eyes of many Germans who had no sympathy with the Nazis. The French had never undertaken it systematically, and the Russians used it flexibly as a means of furthering their own political purposes. Reeducation, in the brief time available, could be effective only in opening ways for the Germans to reeducate themselves. Foreign tutelage of an advanced people could not easily overcome habits of mind and action which were a product of generations of historical evolution. Education in the principles of democracy, in French culture, or in the dogmas of Marxism-Leninism counted less with the Germans than the hard facts of their everyday life and of the existing international situation.

Among those facts were the improving economic conditions in the western zones and the contrasting state of affairs in the Soviet zone, where the SED was purging its leadership of all but those of tried and true loyalty to the Soviets and where living standards were sinking. Western Germans who were able to visit the Soviet zone came back with appalling stories of tyranny and misery. There could be little doubt that the great mass of Germans was strongly anti-Russian and anti-Communist. But so long as the Russians and their Communist followers had a free hand to organize eastern Germany as they wished, they as well as the western powers could seek German nationalism as an ally; and they alone could, without a war, play the card of the return of the lost eastern provinces. This was an issue with a special appeal to the two disinherited groups, the ex-Nazis and the eastern refugees.

In the opinion of a wide variety of German leaders and foreign observers, the great majority of the German people, and especially the German youth, was anything but responsive to the activities and programs of the various political parties. It was impossible to tell what direction the mass of the people would take. Subjected to Nazi rule and propaganda for over a decade, they had no loyalty to the old Weimar form of democracy or to the old Weimar politicians who were again on the political scene. The churches, despite a marked religious revival following the collapse of the Nazi state, did not offer leadership rising above social and political divisions and prejudices. Nor did the universities. Nationalism, growing daily according to every indication, seemed stronger in appeal than anything offered either by party leaders, churches, or intellectuals. Under conditions of hardship and despair, social antagonisms, and the threat of civil war between two mutually hostile Germanies, the potential for democratic development in Germany could not be rated very high.

CHAPTER FOUR

BELGRADE AND BERLIN

THE TREND in eastern Europe was toward consolidation of
Soviet power. Ever since the Red Army swept into Poland, the
Danube valley and the Balkans in 1944, political developments
in those states had followed a regular pattern of which the
end result was the assumption of full power by Communists
with the direct and indirect support of the Soviet Union. Here
the record of east-west conflict was one of unbroken Soviet and
Communist success, punctuated by ineffective protests from
Washington and London. Yet there were, in the summer of
1948, two weak spots in the Soviet empire east of the Lübeck-
Trieste line. One, unexpectedly, was Yugoslavia, the southern
and western anchor of the Soviet position in Europe. The other
was eastern Germany, where the western powers still retained
their garrisons, their military government personnel, and their
influence in the former capital of the Reich, located in the heart
of the Soviet zone. The world's attention was focused on two
cities, Belgrade and Berlin.

Yugoslavia, ruled by its Communist party since 1945, had
been considered Moscow's most loyal ally. Belgrade, as the seat
of the Cominform, was a junior capital of international communism. When the story of Tito's heresy broke in June 1948,
the world was astonished and incredulous. Was this a hoax or
a real declaration of independence of Moscow? Was Tito attempting to found a new national communism? Was this a
dispute over doctrine or over power? Would the rift prove of
benefit to the west? To these questions the western powers
found no certain answers. At the Danube conference held in
Belgrade, and in the United Nations, there was no sign of
deviation by Yugoslavia from the Soviet line on foreign policy.

Against the "western imperialists" the Soviet bloc still presented a united front. Yet the leaders of the Soviet Union and of the other satellites did not cease to proclaim the need for the overthrow of the Communist leaders of Yugoslavia.

Belgrade was a symbol of defiance in the area already engulfed by the westward push of Soviet power. Berlin was the symbol of western, and German, resistance in a struggle not yet decided, the struggle for Germany. The historic capital of Germany was occupied by the four powers. So long as the western powers remained in their sectors of the city, the Russians were denied the opportunity to exploit its potentialities as capital of a future Soviet Germany or even to combat effectively the moves of the western powers in setting up a west German government. Hence the application of pressure to get them out. At Berlin, for the first time, the conflict over Germany passed from a contest of words to a naked test of fortitude, tenacity, and ingenuity, a test on which both sides staked their prestige and which involved the danger of war.

1. Communist Rule in Eastern Europe

Since the end of the war the Soviet Union had wielded predominant influence in eight states of eastern Europe: Finland, Poland, Czechoslovakia, Hungary, Yugoslavia, Rumania, Bulgaria and Albania. The United States never explicitly recognized this region as a Soviet sphere of influence and in fact rejected that concept.[1] Nevertheless, as a result of certain wartime military and political decisions (including two specific Anglo-Soviet arrangements on the Balkans in 1944), the armistice terms with the defeated Axis satellites, and the physical presence of Soviet armed forces, the Soviet Union gained a position of primacy which it soon converted into one of dominance.

The western powers had hoped to save something of their influence, and some measure of independence for the peoples of eastern Europe, through the Yalta Declaration on Liberated

[1] *The Memoirs of Cordell Hull* (New York, Macmillan, 1948), II, 1451-1459.

Europe and the Yalta agreements on Poland and Yugoslavia. The Soviet Government, however, interpreted in its own way these pledges of tripartite action and free elections. After the decisive Communist defeat in the Hungarian elections of 1945, it soon became apparent that Moscow had no intention of allowing further free elections in eastern Europe which would bring to power elements it considered hostile. As the western powers were not prepared to challenge the Soviet position in this region with force, their opposition was confined to a series of protests, for the record, over violations of Yalta, of the armistice agreements, and of the peace treaties. France, not a signatory to these agreements, did not participate in the battle of words until the Communist seizure of power in Czechoslovakia in February 1948. On that occasion all three western powers joined in a public statement voicing the indignation and alarm of the western world "over developments which place in jeopardy the very existence of the principles of liberty to which all democratic nations are attached." The events in Czechoslovakia, though following the pattern made familiar elsewhere in eastern Europe, made a much deeper impression on western opinion because of Czechoslovakia's tradition of political democracy and strong economic and cultural ties with the west. But the western powers were not prepared to take any action, although they supported the move to bring before the Security Council the charge of Soviet intervention. Moscow knew that it had a free hand in eastern Europe.

The speed with which consolidation of Communist power was carried through reflected and contributed to the growing danger of war in Europe. According to Stanislaw Mikolajczyk, in 1947 Communist party workers in Poland had been given instructions as follows: "There will be a war with the west. It will be won by the U.S.S.R. First we must indoctrinate the people of Poland for that war . . . We must quickly prepare for that war by liquidating the Peasant Party and the remnants of independent thought in the Socialist Party." [2] Mikolajczyk charges Russia

[2] Stanislaw Mikolajczyk, The Rape of Poland (New York, McGraw-Hill, 1948), 224-225.

with preparing to wage a world war against civilization. Whether the preparations were viewed as offensive or defensive, the possibility of war was certainly a major consideration behind the Soviet leaders' decision to waste no time in eliminating all possible opposition to their rule in eastern Europe.

By the spring of 1948 all the states of the Soviet sphere, with the one exception of Finland, had passed from the stage of coalition and compromise with "bourgeois" groups and institutions to the new stage of "people's democracy." The old ruling groups, including the remaining kings, had been swept away. Men and institutions associated with western influence and with prewar nationalism were marked for liquidation. The pro-western middle-class parties, except in Czechoslovakia, did not have the popular strength to resist the forces which the war and the Soviet victory had let loose, and the February *coup* broke their power in Czechoslovakia. The most formidable obstacle to full Communist political control in these predominantly peasant countries had been the peasant parties. Among their leaders were men not lacking in ability, courage and devotion to principle: Mikolajczyk in Poland, Nagy in Hungary, Maniu in Rumania, Petkov in Bulgaria, Dragoljub Jovanović in Yugoslavia. Yet by 1948 the first two were in exile, Maniu and Jovanović were in prison, and Petkov had been hanged. The Peasant party in Poland, taken over by its pro-Communist wing after Mikolajczyk's flight in 1947, had become a minor and powerless partner of the Communists. The Smallholders' party of Hungary, which had won an absolute majority in the national election of 1945, had broken up into a number of parties; those which did not accept Communist guidance were in turn harried, persecuted and rendered impotent. Maniu's National Peasant party and Petkov's Agrarian Union were declared subversive and officially dissolved.

The peasant parties, whose popular following far outnumbered that of the Communists, lost out because they could not compete with the latter's disciplined organization and ruthless methods backed by Soviet power. It was true that they were not always truly representative of the peasantry either in organization or in leadership, and that some of their leaders were compromised by association with reactionary elements which flocked to their banner in order to combat communism. Yet they were the nearest to representative national parties that existed in these countries. The decisive reason for their failure to stand their ground was the outside aid which the Communists had at their disposal. Their destruction was encompassed with the active help of the Soviet Union. From the western powers they had only moral support, which encouraged but did not save them.

The Social Democratic parties in some of the eastern European countries might have been in a position to offer effective opposition to the Communists as they did in the west, but they faced heavy psychological as well as material handicaps. Socialists had to make a choice between working-class solidarity with the Communists and democratic solidarity with other parties which were associated in their minds with the old order. The weakness of democratic traditions and the strength of the Communists' position turned many Socialist leaders toward collaboration with them. With their help the Communists were able to split the Social Democratic party where they could not capture it intact. Those who chose to fight for democracy and political liberties met the same fate as the peasant party leaders: trials for treason, death, imprisonment, or exile. Those who collaborated were often rewarded with high office. Arpád Szakasits became President of Hungary, Józef Cyrankiewicz was made Premier of Poland; Zdeněk Fierlinger became Vice Premier of Czechoslovakia. But these men lost their identity as Social Democrats.

Throughout eastern Europe Communists proceeded to push toward formal merger of the two parties. Rumania was the first country where such a "United Workers' party" was formed in February 1948. Hungary and Czechoslovakia followed in June, Bulgaria in August, and Poland in December. Thus ended any hope that eastern Europe's Socialists, who had had historic ties with the Socialist parties of western Europe, might survive as a nucleus of the non-Communist left.

In Finland alone the Social Democratic party continued to

lead an independent existence. There the Soviet Union did not choose to insist on Communist rule, probably because it saw no need to provoke civil disturbances in a country which was "correct" in its foreign policy and was meeting its reparation obligations; probably also because it did not wish to cause alarm throughout Scandinavia and push Sweden into a western bloc. For the time being the Soviet Government seemed satisfied with the mutual assistance treaty which the Finns accepted in April 1948. A democratic Finland was allowed to continue in existence and to show a surprising degree of independence. In May the Communists were actually forced to give up the ministry of the interior, with its control of the police. In July Finland held a free election in which the Communists suffered severe losses. The new Social Democratic government of Karl August Fagerholm was anti-Communist but was careful not to be anti-Soviet. This was the line which Mikolajczyk and Maniu had publicly preached but had not been permitted to practice. In a sense this was the "third force" flourishing on Russia's doorstep, but flourishing only so long as Russia should choose to tolerate it.

Two other countries of eastern Europe also held elections in 1948. Their outcome was never in doubt. No real opposition parties were allowed to put up candidates or to conduct electoral campaigns. A Rumanian election held in March gave 405 out of 414 seats to the Communist-dominated National Democratic Front, with the remainder going to the subservient splinter groups of the old historic parties. In the Czechoslovak election of May 30 only the list of the National Front (the Communists and their allies) was on the ballot; even so, approximately one million persons cast blank and "invalid" votes according to official tally, in addition to those who abstained or were excluded from voting. Hungary, which had held an election following the Communist *coup* in 1947, retained a nominal coalition government with a non-Communist premier; but the last of the opposition parties were eliminated by February 1949. Of all the satellites, Hungary was the slowest in reaching the stage of open Communist rule. Yet there was no question about where real power lay. Hungary's policies were determined by Mátyás Rákosi and his Communist colleagues. The Bulgarian Government, having expelled all the opposition deputies from the national assembly, chosen in 1946, held no new election. The Fatherland Front coalition was brought under even tighter Communist control by a reorganization of the Front into what Georgi Dimitrov called "a united people's social-political organization with a common new program."[3]

Having disposed of the "bourgeois" parties, the Communist-led regimes turned to the churches as the last stronghold of opposition, with the purpose of curbing their influence and bringing them under the full control of the state. Especially marked for attack were those churches and religious organizations—Catholic, Protestant or Jewish—having ties with religious bodies in the west. The trial of 15 Protestant pastors in Bulgaria in March 1949, with its series of remarkable confessions obtained from the accused by the security police and its fabrications concerning espionage by American and British officials, was clearly intended to discredit western influence in Bulgaria. The Orthodox churches, by tradition and organization linked to the state authorities, were brought under control without great difficulty in Rumania and Bulgaria through the appointment of subservient church officials. Laws regulating the practice of religion brought the churches under the unchallenged domination of the state authorities. In Rumania the Greek Catholic (Uniate) Church was forced into joining the Rumanian Orthodox Church and dissolved by government decree in December 1948.

The strongest opposition came from the Roman Catholic Church, as might have been expected in view of its organization, discipline, and outspoken enmity toward communism. The issue was most clearly joined in Hungary, where the government undertook to dissolve Catholic organizations, nationalize denominational schools, and destroy the influence of the Primate of Hungary, Jozsef Cardinal Mindszenty. There was no doubt

[3] Report to the 2nd Fatherland Front Congress (*Free Bulgaria*, III, February 18, 1948, 31).

of the cardinal's deep hostility to a regime which was trampling upon right and justice and the moral law as he saw it. Because of that hostility he became a symbol for all who opposed the Communists, even though his own views on political and social problems tended to be reactionary rather than liberal. In December 1948, Mindszenty was arrested, charged with plotting to overthrow the republic and with black market operations. His arrest and his trial, held the following February, called forth a wave of indignation and protest from individuals, organizations and governments all over the world. The American press was virtually unanimous in condemning the Hungarian Government. The House of Representatives passed a resolution expressing its indignation. Secretary of State Acheson denounced the treatment of Mindszenty as a "conscienceless attack upon religious and personal freedom" and a further development in the process of totalitarian police control which had divested the Hungarian people of any real independence. Hungarian-American relations neared the breaking point when the Budapest government requested the recall of the American Minister, Selden Chapin, on February 12, 1949. The United States Government refused the demand but called him home "for consultation."

The violation of human rights in Hungary, Rumania and Bulgaria had shocked the conscience of the world, as the United States and Britain pointed out in sharply worded notes, on April 2, 1949, formally charging those three governments with disregarding their peace treaty obligations to protect human rights and fundamental freedoms. Hungary had also challenged the power of the Roman Catholic Church, which history has shown to be a formidable foe. Similar struggles seemed to be in store between church and state in Czechoslovakia and also in Poland, the most strongly Catholic of all the satellite states. So divergent were the doctrines of Communists and Catholics, and so firmly held on each side, that such struggles could hardly be avoided. The odds, at least in the short run, favored the Communists, who had in their hands the force and the governmental authority to impose their will on religious leaders, church bodies, and the mass of the people.

Once the Communist leaders had made sure of the elimination of their opponents they undertook some housecleaning of their own. The elimination of the "remnants of the bourgeoisie," by methods which included terror and deportation, was followed by a purge in the party ranks. Since the war the Communist parties, under guidance from Moscow, had sought to gain mass support. In seeking members and votes they had opened their doors to hundreds of thousands of recruits. They had soft-pedaled the class struggle in making appeals and promises to all sections of the population. They had exerted pressures which in practice compelled many to join. Consequently, it was not surprising that opportunists, ex-fascists, and many others who could show no record of loyalty to Marxism flocked to their banner. Then the merger with the Social Democrats brought in many more whose traditions and training had been Marxist but certainly not Stalinist.

By broadening the base of their parties, the Communist leaders in the satellite states had eased their path to power. At the same time they had made their parties less dependable from the Kremlin's point of view. Consequently, a campaign to purge "nationalists" and doubtful elements was undertaken throughout Europe and pursued with added zeal after Moscow's condemnation of the Communist rulers of Yugoslavia. The leaders of the Czech Communist party, which had let in hordes of new members after the February revolution, confessed a few months later that they had made a serious mistake since the party could carry out its mission of leadership "only when it is really a party of the most conscientious and advanced fighters for socialism." [4] A system of "verification" was instituted in order to purge the party of "alien elements." The new law for the defense of the republic, which came into force in October 1948, meant persecution and imprisonment for many Communists as well as non-Communists. In Rumania the former cabinet member and party leader, Lucretiu Patrascanu, was expelled early in 1948 as a bearer of bourgeois ideology within the ranks of the

[4] *For a Lasting Peace, For a People's Democracy! Organ of the Information Bureau of the Communist and Workers' Parties,* Bucharest, July 15, 1948.

party. The Hungarian Communists were told by their chief, Rákosi, that the party's rapid growth had endangered order and discipline. In Poland, where a large Communist party could scarcely avoid infection with the widespread anti-Russian feeling, the crisis which arose over the "nationalist deviation" of party secretary Wladyslaw Gomulka, following the Cominform action against Tito, was the signal for a purge in the leadership and in the ranks. Everywhere but in Yugoslavia the apt graduates of the Comintern (Berman and Bierut, Gottwald, Rákosi, Ana Pauker, Dimitrov and Kolarov) tightened their party organizations in accordance with the line currently put forth by Moscow. In Yugoslavia the same process went on, but with opposite aims.

As the Communists turned from the task of winning power to that of consolidating and organizing their victory, the shape of the "people's democracies" could be more clearly observed. New constitutions provided the institutional framework for Communist rule. Czechoslovakia and Rumania adopted constitutions in 1948. Bulgaria and Poland had done likewise the year before, Hungary, Yugoslavia and Albania in 1946.[5] In many articles these documents were similar to the Soviet constitution of 1936. The political structure, based ostensibly on the principle of popular sovereignty, was roughly the same, with a single-chamber legislature elected by the people and a council of ministers responsible to it. Suffrage was universal, but under the electoral laws certain categories of persons, including those "guilty of an antidemocratic attitude," were barred from voting or engaging in political campaigns. Freedom of the press, of assembly and of religious worship were guaranteed, but in practice denied. Organizations with a "fascist" or "antidemocratic" character or which "facilitate imperialist aggression" were prohibited. Although the façade of collaboration with non-Communist groups and splinter parties was generally retained, as in the

---

[5] Poland's "little constitution" of February 19, 1947, was intended to be temporary. It was a combination of the old constitution of 1921 and of new principles introduced since 1944. Hungary adopted not a complete new constitution but an Act on the State Form of Hungary (January 31, 1946) and supplementary fundamental legislation.

U.S.S.R. the entire political structure was adapted to the exercise of real power by the political bureau of the Communist party, whose instructions were translated into law by the council of ministers and the elected assembly, or acted upon directly by "people's committees" or "action committees" throughout the country. President Beneš of Czechoslovakia regarded the single-list elections and the introduction of the new constitution as the formalization of the extinction of political liberty in his country. Convinced that he could do nothing to check the Communists, he resigned on June 7, without having signed the constitution.[6]

The people's republics did not, however, have the same economic and social system as the U.S.S.R. Although they were said to be "born of the struggle led by the people with the working class at its head," [7] they did guarantee the rights of private property and of private initiative, although it was a declared function of the state to plan and direct the national economy. The land was declared to belong to those who till it, ostensibly a confirmation of the principle of peasant ownership and of the land reforms which the Communists had carried through in Hungary, Poland and Rumania.

The people's democracies, according to the official theory, were no longer capitalist states, but neither were they socialist states. Communist leaders, not wanting to antagonize too many groups during their struggle for political power, had given assurances that this would be their status for the indefinite future. But they would not have been Communists had they regarded it as anything more than a way station on the road to socialism as practiced in the great socialist fatherland, the U.S.S.R. In 1948, when the dispute with Tito developed and a purge of Communist ranks was found necessary, the word went out to speed the process of "socialization." This was both an

---

[6] Although Beneš's health was bad and he died a few months later, a record of conversation between him and his successor, Gottwald, indicates that his refusal to accept the constitution and the single-list election were behind his resignation (article in the *Manchester Guardian*, October 12, 1948, by the former editor of *Národní Osvobození*). The crucial decisions, of course, had been made the previous February, when Beneš agreed to accept a Communist-dominated government.

[7] Article 2 of the Rumanian constitution.

ideological and a tactical move. It coincided with the current turn in Moscow toward Marxist orthodoxy; at the same time it was aimed at making absolutely sure that power would remain in the hands of Communists loyal to Moscow and at eliminating groups, such as an independent peasantry, which might in the future be a center of opposition to Soviet power.

Soviet pronouncements left no doubt that the stage of people's democracy was a temporary one. The "right-wing deviationists" in the Polish Socialist and Communist parties, for example, were denounced for trying "to represent the people's democracy as a sort of complete and self-sufficient system, . . . a golden mean reconciling capitalism and Socialism . . . This group failed to realize that the experience of building Socialism in the Soviet Union is international in its significance . . . The people's democracies are advancing to Socialism by concrete ways of their own, . . . but these concrete forms are only variations on the main path blazed by the epoch-making experience of the first Land of Socialism—the Soviet Union . . . The main and basic features of the successful construction of Socialism in the Soviet Union are valid for all countries advancing to Socialism." [8] Premier Georgi Dimitrov, speaking at the congress of the Bulgarian Communist party in December 1948, spoke of the need of introducing full clarity into the question of the character of the people's democracy. The Soviet regime and the people's democratic regime, he said, were two forms of the same system of government. Both were based on the dictatorship of the proletariat.

Expropriation of private industrial and commercial enterprises, already well advanced, was carried further through the enactment of increasingly drastic nationalization laws in Czechoslovakia, Hungary, Rumania and Bulgaria. These measures, though they posed some thorny economic problems owing to the lack of capital, urgently needed goods and management skills, caused the regimes no great political difficulties either internally or in foreign relations. There was no strong industrial

[8] I. Kovalsky, "The People's Poland on the Upgrade," *New Times,* No. 46, November 10, 1948, 7.

middle class in eastern Europe; business and banking had always tended to be dependent on the state, and now the state was in Communist hands. The former owners were generally either foreigners or individuals already dispossessed or open to attack as supporters of earlier political regimes. The U.S. Government, which had hoped that American-owned firms in eastern Europe would find it possible to continue in business, did not contest the governments' right to nationalize them, as this was deemed a domestic matter in each country; American diplomatic efforts were devoted to seeking prompt and adequate compensation for American citizens whose property was taken over.

The "socialist offensive" in agriculture, on the other hand, raised formidable political as well as economic difficulties. Land reform and the destruction of the old peasant parties had not turned the peasants into Communists nor provided a solution for their fundamental problems of overcrowding on the land, low productivity, insufficient credit and lack of modern farm equipment. The Communist answer, in the spring and summer of 1948, was to prepare the way for collectivization.

Hungarian, Rumanian and Bulgarian Communists wrote in the Cominform journal of the need for "socialist construction" of agriculture. The Communist press spoke of the need of intensifying the class struggle in the rural areas, of liquidating the kulaks. In July the Polish Communist party adopted "a program for the socialist reorganization of the countryside through the all-round development of cooperatives, socialization of the principal means of production and the elimination of capitalist elements." In August, Hungary established new regulations governing cooperatives as a first step toward the mechanized state agriculture set by Rákosi as the goal. Hilary Minc, a leading member of the Polish cabinet and of the political bureau of the Workers' (Communist) party, pointed to the agricultural cooperatives as the simplest and most acceptable way for the peasants to make the transition "to new farming methods—to large-scale collective farming." [9] The Bulgarian five-year plan proposed to extend collective farms to cover 60 percent of

[9] *For a Lasting Peace, For a People's Democracy!*, August 1 and October 1, 1948.

agricultural production by 1953. The satellite governments were not, however, rushing into large-scale programs for the collectivization of agriculture. In order not to alarm the peasants, officials felt compelled to deny that collectivization was imminent. Minc, in introducing his new program, stressed its voluntary and gradual character. Premier Zápotocký of Czechoslovakia even declared that there would be no collectivization of the land, which belonged to the peasants "for all time." In these countries the tradition of individual peasant proprietorship was far stronger than in the Russia of 1917. It was difficult enough to get the peasants to deliver their quotas of grain to government collectors. Tito had discovered in Yugoslavia that he could not afford to alienate the peasants without shaking the foundations of his regime, since the industrial working class was still too small to support it. The Soviet Union and the Communist parties might have the power to impose "socialist construction" on the peasants of eastern Europe, but in doing so they were certain to stir up against them the strong currents of nationalism and devotion to individual peasant property.

The rapid pace of sovietization in each country was matched by feverish diplomatic activity in building an eastern bloc. With the Soviet-Finnish treaty of April 6, 1948, the U.S.S.R. completed a series of pacts covering all of its European satellites except Albania. These were mutual assistance treaties directed against Germany or any state associated with Germany. Finland was given special consideration in that the treaty would apply only in case of an attack on Finland or on the Soviet Union across Finnish territory, Finland would fight only within its own boundaries, and Soviet military aid on Finnish territory would be a matter for mutual agreement. Among themselves the satellite states created a network of bilateral alliances to complete the structure, some of them directed against Germany, others against any state attacking one of the parties to the treaty.[10] As

10 In addition to those concluded before May 1, 1948 (listed in footnote 4, page 449 of *The United States in World Affairs, 1947–1948*) were the following: Bulgaria-Poland, May 29, 1948; Hungary-Poland, June 18, 1948; Hungary-Bulgaria, July 16, 1948; Czechoslovakia-Rumania, July 21, 1948; Rumania-Poland, January 26, 1949; Czechoslovakia-Hungary, April 16, 1949.

the Soviet denunciation of those who were trying to form a western bloc reached new heights, the eastern bloc became an established fact.

2. The Tito Heresy

Just as Moscow appeared to be nearing successful completion of its campaign to consolidate Soviet power in eastern Europe through the elimination of the last vestiges of "bourgeois" influence, it was faced with the new and more difficult problem of disaffection within the Communist camp itself. Marshal Tito of Yugoslavia, at the head of the most conspicuously successful of the Communist regimes in southeastern Europe, presumed to follow policies of which Moscow did not approve.

Appreciation of some basic facts about Yugoslavia and about Tito's position helps to explain how such an unexpected breach in the solid Communist front was possible. Yugoslavia had been the most loyal, the most active of all the Soviet satellites in the war of nerves against the west. Yugoslavia had led the campaign to push the frontiers of the Soviet world to the head of the Adriatic Sea at Trieste and to the eastern Mediterranean. Tito and his colleagues led one of the strongest and best organized Communist parties in Europe outside the U.S.S.R. In recognition of Yugoslavia's special favored position, Belgrade was chosen in October 1947 as the seat of the Cominform. Yet this very strength of Tito and of Communist Yugoslavia made possible the independence of action which developed into an open public dispute between Belgrade and Moscow.

In contrast to the Communist leaders of other eastern countries, who had sat out the war in Moscow and returned home in the baggage of the Red Army, Tito had come to power in Yugoslavia the hard way. He had organized guerrilla forces which fought continuously, under the most difficult conditions, against the Germans and their puppets and against his rival for future power in Yugoslavia, General Mihailović. As early as 1942 the Yugoslav Partisans had established governmental institutions in territory which they held. Without ceasing to be good Communists, they had built their institutions and doctrine on their experience within Yugoslavia as well as on Marx and Lenin. When they took over the entire country at the end of the war, they felt that they, not outside armies, had accomplished Yugoslavia's liberation. Furthermore, despite popular resentment against the dictatorial rule of Tito and his party, the Communist-led Partisan movement had had a mass basis, especially in areas where the ideas of national liberation and social change were linked in the popular mind. Tito took seriously the concept of the mass organization, which the Soviets by 1948 were abandoning in favor of the older revolutionary concept of a small, highly organized and disciplined elite recruited primarily from the working class.

In a real sense, Tito was a Yugoslav nationalist as well as a Communist, and this nationalism was greatly encouraged during the war by Soviet propaganda itself as a weapon against the Germans. The Yugoslavs, in particular the Serbs, have throughout history shown a remarkable spirit of independence, as the Turks, the Austrians, and the Germans in turn discovered. Yugoslavia's foolhardy but magnificent defiance of Germany in March 1941 was characteristic. Even Communist leaders, trained to take orders from Moscow, have now proved capable of asserting the national interest, as they see it, against Soviet interference. Yugoslavia's geographical location was another factor which made possible an independence not open to Rumania, for example, or to Hungary; Yugoslavia did not border on the U.S.S.R., had open lines of communication to the outside world, and was not dependent in the same degree as Poland and Czechoslovakia on Russian protection against the menace of a revived Germany. In addition, Yugoslavia had been moderately successful in restoring its economy, although it was having difficulty in meeting the goals of its ambitious five-year plan; assistance from the Soviet Union to overcome those difficulties was notable by its absence. This Soviet failure to supply Yugoslavia with even a minimum of capital goods in return for Yugoslav ore and other materials going to the U.S.S.R. made a real contribution to the rift.

On March 27, 1948, the Central Committee of the Communist

Party of the U.S.S.R., without first informing the Yugoslav party, circulated to the members of the Cominform [11] a letter containing a number of accusations against the leaders of the Communist Party of Yugoslavia. Among the "errors" cited were the following: slander against the Soviet Union, the Soviet Communist party, and the Red Army; shadowing of Soviet citizens in Yugoslavia by the secret police; absence of democracy in the Yugoslav Communist party; dissolution of the party in a people's front; abandonment of the Marxist-Leninist path with regard to the leading role of the proletariat; acceptance of "reformist" theories of peaceful growth from capitalism to socialism; attempts to win the favor of imperialist states and place Yugoslavia under their control; treating the Soviet Union and its representatives on the same plane as the imperialist states. The letter claimed also that the Yugoslav Communists had never ceased to boast of their successes in the war, although they could not claim greater merits than those of Poland, Czechoslovakia, Rumania and other countries, and had in fact been able to come to power only because the Soviet army liberated Yugoslavia.

The decision to circulate these charges obviously meant that the Soviet leaders regarded the situation in Yugoslavia as beyond control merely by admonition or by direct, unpublicized pressure on Tito. By placing the case before the other satellites, they gave a timely warning to those in Poland, Czechoslovakia and elsewhere who may have been tempted to stray from the path of orthodoxy, but they also staked Soviet prestige on the expectation that the Yugoslav leaders would recant or could be overthrown. What was Tito's great crime? It did not appear clearly from the list of charges, some of which were true, others plainly false. Undoubtedly Soviet agents in Yugoslavia had been shadowed. Undoubtedly the Yugoslav Communist party used undemocratic methods. In these matters the Yugoslavs were only showing that they could copy the Soviet model and knew how to set up an effective dictatorship. The charges of

[11] The Communist parties of Poland, Czechoslovakia, Hungary, Rumania, Bulgaria, Yugoslavia, France and Italy.

"bourgeois deviation" were scarcely justified. Of all the satellites, Yugoslavia had proceeded farthest and most rapidly on the road to a collective system. Mindful of their peasant problem and concentrating on industrialization, the Yugoslav Communists felt that they alone must be the judges of the pace of agricultural collectivization. The "popular front" was a device which the Soviet leaders themselves had supported time and again; it happened to be out of favor in Moscow at the moment. As for favoring the "imperialist" powers, there was nothing in the Yugoslav record to support that accusation. Tito's real crime was insubordination.

For some months there had been indications that Yugoslavia was outgrowing the role of satellite. The Yugoslav Government took an interest in world affairs beyond the confines of eastern Europe. It sent trade delegations, apparently without Soviet consent, as far afield as the Near East and India. There seem to have been differences between the Yugoslav and Soviet ideas on how to handle the issues of Greece, Trieste and Austrian Carinthia. As early as 1945 the Soviet Government had protested formally in Belgrade against a speech of Tito on Trieste which it called "an inimical attack on the Soviet Union." [12] Several observers have reported that the U.S.S.R., in 1948, wanted Tito to drop his claims on Trieste and Gorizia, which interfered with Soviet attempts to influence Italian opinion before the April election. It is worth noting that, after the Cominform resolution against Tito, Communist organizations outside Yugoslavia, including those in Trieste,[13] gave no further support to Yugoslavia on territorial issues. On the question of Balkan federation the Soviets, through *Pravda,* had delivered a

[12] In its letter of May 4, 1948 the Soviet Communist party argued that Tito in 1945 and 1946 had criticized the Soviet Government for not getting Trieste for Yugoslavia, although the only way to get it would have been to wage war against the Anglo-Americans, which the U.S.S.R. was not prepared to do (*Correspondence between the Central Committee of the Communist Party of Yugoslavia and the Central Committee of the All-Union Party (Bolsheviks)*, Belgrade, 1948, 45-50).

[13] There was a struggle for power between pro-Cominform and pro-Tito factions of the Communist party of the Free Territory of Trieste, with the result that the former came out on top in the U.S.-U.K. zone while the latter held control in the Yugoslav zone.

blast against Premier Dimitrov of Bulgaria when he suggested it in January 1948. Dimitrov recanted publicly, but Tito, who was known to have similar ideas, did not.

Probably the most important single reason for the clash concerned the control of the Yugoslav army. Tito had a big army and a well-organized secret police, loyal to Yugoslav rather than Soviet leadership, and refused to let Soviet "advisers" take over control as they had in other satellite states. The advisers were withdrawn in March 1948 because the Soviet Government did not want them to remain "in hostile surroundings." Tito, in defending his course, complained of Soviet interference in Yugoslav affairs. He insisted that it was "incorrect" for Soviet agents in Yugoslavia to recruit Yugoslav citizens for the Soviet intelligence service.

The exercise of power had an exhilarating effect on the Yugoslav leaders. It bred a spirit of independence. In answering Soviet charges, Tito said: "However much affection any of us may cherish toward the country of Socialism, the U.S.S.R., in no way should he have less affection for his own country in which Socialism is being built as well." [14] As early as 1945, according to the documents which the Soviets finally published to support their case, the Yugoslav Communist leaders were "slandering" the Soviet Union. The whole system in eastern Europe, and Communist discipline throughout the world, would suffer if they remained unchecked. These considerations apparently convinced Moscow that Tito and his principal aides (Edvard Kardelj, Aleksandar Ranković, and Milovan Djilas) had grown too big for their boots and would have to be ousted. The vital question of unreserved obedience had been posed and had to be answered.

If the Soviet leaders expected a confession of error or quick overturn in Yugoslavia, they were mistaken. On April 13 the Yugoslav Communists sent back a reply which was a denial of the "unjust fabrications" and a spirited defense of their policies as being fully in line with the holy writ of Marx and Lenin.

[14] Letter of Tito and Kardelj to Stalin and Molotov, April 13, 1948 (*Correspondence* . . . , 29-30).

They then proceeded to expel and arrest two high-ranking Communists, Sreten Zujović and Andrija Hebrang, for "anti-party activity." These two were Moscow's men. The Yugoslav leaders then refused to attend the Cominform meeting called to pass judgment on them, knowing that all the other Communist parties had already lined up with Moscow. The meeting was held in Rumania in June. It produced a lengthy resolution which, when made public on June 28, placed before the world for the first time the sensational news of discord within the Communist family. The quarrel had gone so far that it was probably impossible to keep it secret any longer. Having brought it out in the open, the Soviets had to carry through to a successful conclusion or suffer unprecedented loss of face.

The resolution of the Cominform, whose headquarters were moved from Belgrade to Bucharest,[15] repeated the accusations of the earlier letters. It compared the Yugoslav Communists' ideas and policies to those of Trotsky, of Bukharin, of the Mensheviks, of capitalist kulaks and petty-bourgeois nationalists. Tito and his colleagues were accused of having set up a "purely Turkish terrorist regime" in the Communist party, and of having disgracefully expelled and arrested Zujović and Hebrang for daring to criticize their anti-Soviet attitude. Such a regime, said the Cominform, could not be tolerated. The resolution was full of criticisms of Yugoslav domestic policies, particularly the coddling of the peasants, but the real gravamen was that Tito had broken with the international tradition and "taken the road of nationalism." "Considerably overestimating the internal, national forces of Yugoslavia and their influence, the Yugoslav leaders think that they can maintain Yugoslavia's independence and build socialism without the support of the Communist Parties of other countries, . . . of the people's democracies, . . . of the Soviet Union . . . The Information Bureau does not doubt that inside the Communist Party of Yugoslavia there are sufficient healthy elements, loyal to Marxism-Leninism . . . Their

[15] The July 1 issue of the Cominform journal was put in type in Belgrade with the front page left open for the text of the resolution. The editors, although they had the text in Belgrade, took everything to Bucharest and brought out the issue there.

task is to compel their present leaders to recognize their mistakes openly and honestly and to rectify them . . . Should the present leaders prove to be incapable of doing this, their job is to replace them and to advance a new internationalist leadership of the Party." [16]

This was an invitation to revolution. Apparently the Soviet leaders, on the basis of reports from their diplomats and other agents in Yugoslavia, expected that a movement strong enough to overthrow Tito and his group could be developed within the ranks of the Yugoslav Communist party. Yet no such movement appeared. Tito and Kardelj kept their control of the party. Ranković could count on his secret police. The army was loyal. There was some disaffection in Montenegro and Bosnia, but anti-Tito elements among officials there were quickly replaced. A prominent general, prospective leader of a revolt, was shot while trying to get across the border into Rumania. Meanwhile Tito and his friends did all they could to rally Yugoslav opinion behind them, not without some success. Even though disclaiming the nationalist label, they were defending Yugoslavia against outside interference.

The Yugoslav Communist leaders repeated their defiance at the fifth congress of their party, held in Belgrade at the end of July. The Cominform parties were invited to send representatives but refused to do so. The Moscow *Pravda* carried an article which proclaimed that the congress was being held "under conditions of terror." The break appeared complete when Tito, Kardelj, and the others made long and fiery speeches, with no admission of error. They showed no hesitancy and no doubt of their ability to stay in power. The congress, efficiently managed by the Tito group, which entirely controlled all committees and allowed no floor debate, endorsed the policies condemned by the Cominform and voted a new program pledging the party to continue along its own road to socialism.

Up to this time the dispute had been between Communist parties, not between governments,[17] and the Yugoslav leaders

16 For a Lasting Peace, For a People's Democracy!, Bucharest, July 1, 1948.
17 The sole exception was the case of Albania (see below).

were trying to keep it that way. They stressed their loyalty to the foreign policy of the U.S.S.R. and to Stalin personally. They appealed to him to disavow the Cominform. Stalin's picture, despite Soviet protests, appeared everywhere in Belgrade alongside that of Tito during the party congress. Yet the differences could hardly be kept on the party level, since party chiefs were also leaders of governments. Despite all the diatribes and the controversy over Marxist-Leninist dogma, the real issue was whether the Yugoslavs would be permitted to run their own affairs. As Djilas explained it, Yugoslavia's relationship with the U.S.S.R. and the people's democracies must be "on the basis of mutual cooperation, taking into account historical differences and degrees of development, on the basis of voluntary agreement and mutal confidence." [18] Moscow could not tolerate this threat to the principle of absolute obedience on the part of satellites, especially after the public excommunication of the heretics. Significantly, the first Soviet letter of March 27 had accused the Tito group not only of deviations from Marxism but of a hateful attitude toward the Soviet Union and its foreign policy.

The quarrel with the other satellites was patently concerned with power, influence and even territory rather than doctrine. Many Communists were shaken by the news of the alleged treason of one of international communism's great heroes. To the rank and file it brought perplexity, to the leaders a warning of a possible wider purge of "nationalists" throughout eastern Europe. The official reaction everywhere was solidarity with the Soviet Union. Yugoslavia was isolated. Old Balkan disputes and jealousies, kept under the surface when all the talk was of brotherly relations among people's republics, flared up anew. Yugoslavia's neighbors did not lose the opportunity to seek Moscow's favor and to settle some old scores. Yugoslavia had been promoting a Yugoslav-Bulgarian-Albanian federation. Now Albania denounced the economic treaty and customs union between the two countries and began to expel its Yugoslav advisers and experts. Bulgaria was more circumspect but fully

18 *Borba*, Belgrade, July 5, 1948.

supported the Cominform resolution and was soon engaged in a bitter controversy with the Yugoslavs over the age-old problem of Macedonia, which supposedly had been settled on a basis of brotherly understanding in a secret protocol to the Bled agreements of July 1947.[19] The Communist party of Yugoslav Macedonia publicly accused Albania and Bulgaria of seeking to annex Yugoslav territory, and the Yugoslav Communist party congress took cognizance of the fact that federation or even normal relations with the two neighbor countries were out of the question under existing circumstances.

Yugoslavia's relations with Czechoslovakia, Rumania and Hungary also were embittered by press attacks, mistreatment and expulsion of Yugoslav diplomats and students, dissolution of Yugoslav minority organizations, and calls for revolt in Yugoslavia. In formal diplomatic notes Belgrade accused the Rumanian and Hungarian governments of "hostile outrages" and a "monstrous anti-Yugoslav campaign" in which high officials, including Rákosi and Ana Pauker, were openly calling on Yugoslav citizens to overthrow their legal government. The Yugoslavs had also to contend with limited economic sanctions, the most telling of which were interruptions and delays in deliveries of Albanian and Rumanian oil, Polish coal, and machinery from Czechoslovakia.

The pressure on Tito and his group was great, but it was not sufficient to shake their hold on Yugoslavia. The break seemed irreparable when a series of articles in the official newspaper of

[19] The Bulgarian Communist party revealed this secret agreement in a resolution published on July 15, 1948, condemning Tito for failing to live up to it. It provided for the joining of Bulgarian with Yugoslav Macedonia and the return to Bulgaria of certain districts on the Yugoslav frontier, all within the framework of a South Slav federation. Stoyan Pribichevich, a journalist who knows Tito personally, states that he "has been constantly against a union with Bulgaria on the ground that three times in our generation the Bulgars have stabbed the Serbs in the back" (*New Republic,* CXIX, July 12, 1948, 6). Even after the *Pravda* reproof to Dimitrov on the question of a Balkan federation (see above, pp. 119-120), the latter made several public statements favoring the more limited idea of a South Slav union of Bulgaria and Yugoslavia; after the Cominform resolution, he stated that Bulgarian Communists still adhered to this ideal, but that the chauvinist policies of the present Yugoslav Communist leaders made it unattainable for the moment.

the Yugoslav Communist party, which surely were approved by Tito himself, concluded with this judgment: "Stalin is the greatest living authority in the democratic world today. But in the argument between the Yugoslav Communist party and the Soviet Communist party right is not on his side." [20] The Soviet leaders chose to avoid direct military intervention. Consequently, the deadlock was not broken. Every day that passed, with Tito still in power, added to his prestige and damaged that of the Soviets. Yet the odds were against him. Yugoslavia could not count on solving its economic problems in isolation. The Soviets could use force in the end if they found it necessary. They might attempt to use the time-honored Balkan weapon of assassination. Meanwhile they kept up their war of nerves. In the early months of 1949 a rising tide of accusations and frontier incidents involving Yugoslavia and its neighbors indicated that Moscow was doing its best to infiltrate its agents into Yugoslavia. The raising of the Macedonian question by Greek and Bulgarian Communists appeared to be aimed at Yugoslavia even more than at Greece.

How did this struggle affect the world picture? Superficially, it did not change it at all, as Yugoslavia made no move to desert the Soviet bloc. The Yugoslav leaders were still Communists. They continued to follow domestic policies which they considered to be Marxist and Leninist, and a foreign policy of solidarity with the "great country of socialism," the U.S.S.R. They made no conciliatory gestures toward non-Communists in Yugoslavia or toward the western "imperialists."

Nevertheless the Tito schism had enormous implications. Basically, it was an attempt to maintain independence of policy. If successful, it would mean that Moscow was denied control of the Yugoslav Government and the Yugoslav army. Tito's Yugoslavia would stand as an example of "independent" communism, a living refutation of the theory of monolithic uniformity of the Communist world. It might be the nucleus of a new "power center" in southeastern Europe, small but nevertheless standing on its own feet. The Soviet leaders were well

[20] *Borba.* October 4, 1948.

aware of the dangers of such a development. Nationalism, which had been lauded when eastern European Communist leaders were leading the fight against the Germans, was now a deadly sin.

The arguments on both sides in this whole controversy did much to puncture some of the myths of Soviet propaganda. Henceforth there could be no further question that the Cominform was anything but an instrument of Soviet policy. It was openly admitted that Communist alliances with non-Communist parties in popular fronts were but a tactical manoeuvre bearing no relationship to the national interests of the countries in question. Moscow now stated frankly that they should be discarded in favor of direct control by Communist parties when they held power, direct revolutionary action when they were still in opposition. Nationalism was for Communists a mortal sin. Their first loyalty must be to "international" communism, that is, to the policies of the Soviet Union.

The internecine quarrels of Communists and the frank exposition of Communist aims and methods provided unexpected propaganda opportunities for the western powers. The appearance of nationalism as a potent force within the Soviet bloc was naturally welcome to the United States and to the other western powers without, of course, altering their distaste for the type of totalitarian police regime which Tito headed. Although Yugoslavia redoubled its denunciations of the west and declared that it must follow a socialist, i.e. pro-Soviet, foreign policy, there was no denying that the rift with Russia weakened the Soviet bloc. The western powers would have liked to exploit that weakness. At some future time, in order to stay in power, Tito might move toward closer relations with them. Yet overt moves or expressions of support, unpalatable in themselves, would only hinder him in his fight for survival. And it was in their interest that he should survive, if he continued to oppose Soviet domination and if the only alternative was a completely Moscow-directed Communist regime. For the time being they could do little except take some minor steps such as completing the settlement, long under negotiation, of all outstanding claims between Yugoslavia and the United States,[21] continuing negotiations for a long-term Anglo-Yugoslav trade agreement, seeing that Yugoslavia got supplies of oil and other goods to replace what did not come in from other eastern countries, and encouraging Yugoslav trade with western Europe.

The American attitude was one of watchful waiting. The Yugoslav situation called for artful diplomacy and for going full speed ahead with the Marshall plan, to which some observers gave much of the credit for the cracks appearing in the Soviet bloc. In any case ERP had an undeniable power of attraction on eastern Europe and could be used to exploit fissiparous tendencies. It was true that popular liberties were scorned and trampled upon by the rulers of Yugoslavia, and that "national communism" could be as great a threat to democratic institutions in Europe as Russian communism. But the detachment of Yugoslavia from the Soviet bloc, or the breakup of the Communist world into separate states able to act independently of the U.S.S.R., would weaken the Soviet menace to Europe and to the world. It was a development which the western powers could not fail to hope for and encourage.

3. The Danube Conference

In the summer of 1948 Belgrade played host to an international conference to establish a new regime for the Danube. The subject matter of the conference was not of momentous importance in the existing state of world affairs. The eyes of the world were on Belgrade for other reasons, for this was the first formal conference since the Smith-Molotov exchange of the previous May [22] and since the rift between Yugoslavia and the Cominform had come out into the open. Would the U.S.S.R. and the western powers make a start, at Belgrade, toward a negotiated settlement of their differences? And would the crack

---

[21] The agreements, signed on July 19, 1948, covered compensation to the United States for nationalized U.S. property in Yugoslavia and for lend-lease and pre-UNRRA civilian relief. At the same time the U.S. Treasury unblocked Yugoslav gold and other assets in the United States.

[22] See above, pp. 24-28.

in the solidarity of the Soviet bloc have any effect on Yugoslavia's foreign policy and relations with the west?

The conference was held pursuant to a decision of the Council of Foreign Ministers in December 1946. When the western powers finally persuaded Molotov to insert in the Balkan peace treaties a uniform clause guaranteeing freedom of navigation on the Danube, they agreed also to hold a conference within six months of the entry into force of the treaties to work out a convention for a new Danube regime. The conference was to be composed of the Big Four plus the following riparian states: Czechoslovakia, Hungary, Yugoslavia, Bulgaria, Rumania and the Ukrainian S.S.R. Austria would be admitted to such a conference "after the question of a Treaty with Austria has been settled." It was apparent from this list that, unless there should be a surprising shift in the orientation of the Danube states, the U.S.S.R. would control a clear majority of the votes.

The peace treaties came into force on September 15, 1947. Relations between Russia and the west had deteriorated sadly since December 1946. The U.S.S.R. controlled the Danube from the Black Sea up to Linz in Austria and could impose a new convention on the satellite states whenever it chose. The western powers saw little chance of getting agreement on a new regime which would really guarantee freedom of navigation and equality of treatment. However, the United States, which had led the fight on this issue in the peace treaty negotiations, did not wish to let the March 15, 1948 deadline pass by in silence. Late in February Washington proposed that the conference be convoked and that Austria be invited to participate. After the other three powers agreed that it should meet, several months were consumed in deciding on the time and place of meeting and on the status of Austria. Moscow objected strongly to accepting Austria as a full-fledged member, since this was the one riparian state whose delegate could not be counted on to parrot the Soviet arguments and vote according to Soviet dictates. The December 1946 decision of the Council of Foreign Ministers supported the Soviet position—it was not easy to argue that "the question of a treaty with Austria" had been "settled"—and the United States ultimately agreed that Austria should be invited to Belgrade only "in a consultative capacity."

The conference finally opened on July 30, 1948. The Soviet Government sent Vyshinsky and most of the satellite governments sent their foreign ministers, indicating an intention to exploit to the full this first postwar conference at which the eastern bloc would have a voting majority, and perhaps also to impress the rulers of Yugoslavia. From the start it was plain that it was a political and not a technical conference. The Soviets intended to use it to demonstrate both to the satellite nations and to the west who was the master in eastern Europe. Vyshinsky made no conciliatory gestures. At the opening session he gratuitously insulted the English-speaking delegations by insisting on the exclusion of English as an official language. He showed no disposition to negotiate. He came with a ready-made Danube convention and with a ready-made majority of seven votes to three. The satellite delegations endorsed the Soviet draft convention *in toto* before it was even discussed.

After the very first meetings it was apparent that, if Moscow was seeking an accommodation with the west, it had not chosen the Danube conference as the place to begin. It was evident also that Yugoslavia was not straying from the Soviet reservation, at least in so far as speaking and voting at the conference table was concerned. On the contrary the Yugoslav delegate, Aleš Bebler, went out of his way to emphasize his government's solidarity with the Soviet Union and opposition to the "imperialistic designs" of the western powers. Their very presence at the conference, he said, was "not in accord with democratic principles."

From the record of Soviet policy in the Danube basin since 1944, indeed from the whole history of Tsarist and Soviet Russian policy on the Danube since the end of the eighteenth century, it was obvious that Moscow would not accept anything like the prewar international regime for the regulation of shipping on the river. The draft convention which Vyshinsky presented at Belgrade was a blueprint for Soviet domination of the entire Danube. The new convention could not be effective above Linz without the agreement of Austria and the western powers, but the latter could not prevent its application to the greater part of the river. Control of the Danube was directly related to control of the Danubian countries. Restoration of the prewar regime of freedom of navigation and equality of treatment, with nonriparian representation on the Danube commissions,[23] might give the western powers a means of loosening the Soviet grip on eastern Europe. The Soviet leaders would not accept it any more than they would accept western "interference" in Balkan elections. They would agree to an innocuous statement of the principle of freedom of navigation. They would not agree to a detailed convention and an administration of the river which would really put that principle into practice.

Since Vyshinsky's overbearing tactics doomed the Danube conference to failure before discussion began on the merits of the question, the western delegates had to decide whether to walk out or to continue to sit there and talk back, knowing that the assorted Communist speakers around the table would talk at greater length and more insultingly and would vote down every western proposal whether of procedure or of substance. Whatever they did, the western powers wished to act together, especially in order not to weaken their solidarity in the concurrent and more important Moscow negotiations on Berlin. The United States wished to sit through to the end, placing its case on the record and showing that it could take part with dignity in an international conference where it was consistently outvoted by a "mechanical majority" far more consistent and more obviously managed than any of which the Soviet Union had so loudly complained in the United Nations. This was the strategy ultimately adopted by all three western delegations.

[23] Before the war there were two commissions, the European Commission of the Danube (established in 1856) for the maritime Danube (Braila to the Black Sea), and the International Commission of the Danube (established in 1919) for the fluvial Danube (Ulm to Braila). After 1919, Great Britain, France, Italy and Rumania were members of the first; these same states and the remaining riparians were members of the second.

The American delegation argued that the pressing need for the immediate future was to get ships and trade moving again, trade which was important to both eastern and western Europe. An increase in east-west trade was one of the basic assumptions of the Marshall plan. Under the American proposals for freedom of navigation and nondiscrimination, British, French, Italian and Greek ships would again appear on the lower Danube; Austrian and German craft would again bring goods to Bratislava, Budapest and Belgrade; English, American and Austrian firms would be able to do business in Danube ports. This was precisely what the Soviet Union did not want. Having already acquired control of the bulk of Rumanian and Hungarian shipping and port facilities, it had no desire to open the field to competitors. With full control of Danube navigation in its own hands, the U.S.S.R. and its obedient satellites denounced efforts to break down the monopoly as "western imperialism" and as attempts to destroy the sovereignty of the Danubian nations.

When the proposed new Danubian commission was discussed, the Soviet bloc insisted on limiting membership to riparian states; thus the U.S.S.R., which by virtue of its annexation of Bessarabia bordered on the lower Danube, would be the only great power on the commission. The satellite spokesmen made much of the "Danube for the Danubian peoples" theme. Ana Pauker of Rumania inveighed against the French and British insistence on "acquired rights," which she called rights to oppress and to exploit. Bebler said that the presence of nonriparians on previous international regimes was based on their "political predominance and dictatorial treaties of peace [1856, 1919] by which they succeeded in imposing their will on the Danubian states." [24] The western powers held to the principle that nonriparian interests must be represented. Britain and France both wished to be members of the commission, as they had been before the war. The United States also claimed the right to be represented, both because of its temporary responsi-

[24] Danube Conference, 5th plenary meeting, August 4, 1948, Document Plen. 29, 18-19.

bilities as occupying power in that part of Germany through which the Danube flowed and because of its role as a great power participating in the European peace settlement and making an enormous material contribution to Europe's reconstruction. The United States also championed Austria's right to membership immediately instead of after the conclusion of the Austrian treaty, just as it had backed Austria for full participation in the Belgrade conference. On all these points the western proposals were voted down 7 to 3, and the Soviet proposals accepted.

Once the decision was made to restrict membership on the commission to the riparian states, there was little point in talking at length on its powers and functions. Speaking for the record, the western delegates made known their view that under the provisions of the Soviet draft convention the commission would not be able to do the job of regulating navigation and keeping the river open. For one thing, the Soviet draft placed the two most important sectors, the Iron Gates and the mouths of the river, under the special administrations of the two riparian states; thus the mouths would be under Soviet-Rumanian administration, which in practice would mean Soviet control. Riparians and nonriparians alike would suffer from this type of exclusive arrangement.

Attached to the Soviet draft convention was a supplementary protocol which declared previous Danube conventions null and void and abolished the former commissions; assets of the latter were to be taken over by the new commission, and their debts, held chiefly in England and France, were to be canceled. The French and British delegations registered strong objections. Throughout the conference, they insisted on their rights under the Convention of 1921, the continued validity of which the U.S.S.R. denied and refused to refer to the International Court for an advisory opinion. The United States, like the U.S.S.R. not a party to that convention, had favored placing major emphasis on working out a new regime based on the principle of freedom of navigation and on consideration for the interests of all nations concerned, instead of insisting on the sanctity of the earlier treaty provisions. Ultimately, however, owing to the need for maximum western solidarity and the extreme position taken by the Soviet Union, the U.S. delegation supported the view that the Convention of 1921 remained valid and that its signatories could not be deprived of their rights under it without their consent.

Every one of the American, British and French amendments was rejected by seven votes to three. On the final day of the conference the three western delegates declared their unwillingness to accept the convention endorsed by the majority. When the final vote was taken in plenary session, the well-disciplined majority dutifully recorded seven votes for each of 47 articles, two annexes, and one supplementary protocol. The U.S. delegate, Cavendish Cannon, recorded an abstention on each article, then voted against the convention as a whole. The British and French ignored the final voting, on the theory that the whole procedure was illegal.

The new convention was signed on August 18 by the seven nations of the Soviet bloc. The Danube, or that part of it which was under Soviet control, was given a new "international" status. But that status was not recognized by nations outside the Soviet sphere as supplanting the international regime of 1921. The deadlock remained, and the Danube was likely to remain a dead waterway.

Belgrade had taken on importance as a focal point in Europe. Should Tito maintain his independence of Moscow, pressures from east and west might well converge there. At the Danube Conference, however, Yugoslavia was still 100 percent on the Soviet side in opposition to the west. Belgrade was a point of potential rather than actual conflict in the east-west struggle. The real center of crisis, in the summer of 1948, was Berlin.

4. The Battle of Berlin

Soon after the Council of Foreign Ministers adjourned in December 1947, with no progress registered toward a German settlement, there were rumblings of future trouble over Berlin.

The determination of the United States and Britain to go ahead with the organization of Bizonia, bringing in the French zone if possible, was matched by Soviet pressure on the western Allies in Berlin. Communist propaganda took the line that the western powers had nullified four-power administration, split Germany in two, and therefore had no business remaining in the German capital. A series of minor annoyances and pinpricks, including interference with passenger traffic on western trains to and from Berlin, accompanied these statements, which apparently were intended to convince both the Berliners and the western representatives that the latter soon would have to withdraw. After the Communist victory in Prague at the end of February 1948, Berlin seemed to be marked as the next item on the Soviet program.

On March 30 the Soviet authorities in Berlin announced a number of regulations, effective April 1, affecting transport and communications between Berlin and the western zones. For the most part these restrictions provided for Soviet checking and inspection of passengers and freight shipments. Despite immediate protests on the part of western military representatives in Berlin, they were put into effect and were followed shortly by more drastic measures which interfered with rail, barge and automobile traffic. "Technical difficulties" were put forward as the reason for the restrictions, but the controversy which ensued between the Soviet and the western military authorities in Berlin went into the question of the western powers' right to "free and unmolested use of the established corridors" and, inferentially, their right to be in Berlin at all.

The basic agreements establishing the rights of the four powers in Germany and in Berlin were concluded in the European Advisory Commission prior to the surrender of Germany. These agreements defined the sectors of Berlin to be occupied by the four powers and affirmed the right of all four to participate in the joint control of the city. A later agreement in the Allied Control Council affirmed the joint responsibility of all four occupying powers for feeding and supplying the population of Berlin.

Since Berlin was an island in the Soviet zone, the western powers had also to arrange for access to it across Soviet-held territory. Here the rights and obligations were not so clearly and irrefutably established. Truman and Churchill, in June 1945, affirmed the right of "free access by air, road and rail" to the U.S. and U.K. forces in Berlin, in letters to Stalin which dealt also with the entry of the western garrisons into the capital and the withdrawal of American troops from certain areas in the Soviet zone which they had occupied in pursuing the Germans.[25] Stalin's replies indicated tacit acceptance of the western proposals. Thereafter Marshal Zhukov confirmed orally that the western powers would have free access to Berlin subject only to normal regulation of movements, and separate agreements were reached laying out "corridors" for rail, road, water and air traffic which they could use. Unfortunately for the western powers, the right of unrestricted access to Berlin by surface routes, a logical corollary of the agreements on four-power occupation and administration, was not nailed down beyond contention in written agreements. When they asserted such a right in protesting the Soviet restrictions of April 1, 1948, the Soviet commander replied that there was no agreement guaranteeing unrestricted traffic of persons and goods through the Soviet zone and that control of such traffic was an internal matter of zonal administration which concerned only the Soviet authorities.

Whatever the merits of this controversy, the compelling arguments were not legal but physical and political. The Russians were in a position to hinder or to cut traffic between the western zones and Berlin. They could find reasons for doing so no matter what the legal situation might be. Facing the pros-

[25] The United States argued later that it had agreed to withdraw American troops from Saxony and Thuringia in consideration for Soviet agreement to free access to Berlin (note of July 6, 1948, to the Soviet Government, Department of State, *Bulletin*, XIX, July 18, 1948, 85). The Soviets replied that the U.S. Government was well aware that in bringing its forces back to the boundaries of the U.S. zone it was only carrying out obligations which it had already assumed when the zonal boundaries were agreed upon (note of July 14, 1948, Ministry of Foreign Affairs of the U.S.S.R., *The Soviet Union and the Berlin Question, Documents*, Moscow, 1948, 44-45).

pect of more restrictions, the western powers had to make a crucial political decision. They had assumed military and governmental responsibilities in Berlin and had undertaken to supply food to the more than two million inhabitants of their sectors. Should the Russians bar access to the city by land, Allied personnel and the German population could be supplied only by air, a seemingly impossible task which carried with it the risk of Soviet interference and inflammatory incidents. The collision of a British transport and a Soviet fighter plane over Berlin on April 5, with loss of life, was a warning that the situation might well get out of hand. In making their calculations and decisions, both sides had to take account of the real possibility of war.

For the west, Berlin was an exposed position; in the military sense it was at the mercy of the Soviets. Surrounding it on all sides, the latter had every advantage. By measures which required no effort on their part they could force the western powers into great expenditures and great risks to maintain themselves without knowing whether they might not have to withdraw in the end. Even should the Soviets agree to lift their restrictions on traffic, for a price, they could always reimpose them. The western nations would be subject to recurring blackmail. These were considerations which might have induced them to withdraw, especially if they could get a suitable *quid pro quo* in return. Such an agreement might have been made at this stage, in the spring of 1948, before each side became too deeply committed to an unyielding stand.

The Soviet moves seemed directed toward persuading the western powers to take such a decision. They were supported in Soviet propaganda with the argument that the western "partition policy" had nullified the entire four-power system of government; that, having made Frankfort the capital of a future west German state, they had no right to remain in Berlin as capital of all Germany. In other words, ran the Soviet argument, they had to give up their partition policy or give up Berlin; they could not have it both ways.

The western powers accepted neither the Soviet reasoning

nor any other arguments in favor of withdrawal from Berlin. They found weightier considerations on the other side. They had legal rights in Berlin which, they maintained, could be modified only by agreement. The political consequences of giving up those rights as a result of Soviet pressure would be extremely unfavorable, possibly disastrous, to the western cause in Germany and in Europe. The Germans had their eyes fixed on Berlin as a test of the western powers' intention to stay in Germany. If they should leave to the mercies of the Russians the German inhabitants of the western sectors of the capital, whom they had encouraged to speak out freely against Communist totalitarianism, then Germans would have little confidence that they would not abandon western Germany as well when sufficient pressure was applied.

All Europe was nervously eyeing Berlin in the spring of 1948. Signs of weakness on the part of the west would have had repercussions in Italy, approaching its crucial election, and in many other countries where the balance of internal forces was closely related to the balance of power on the continent. The United States, which took the leadership of the three western powers on this issue, felt that the pressure on Berlin must be regarded not as an isolated phenomenon but as a move in the Soviet offensive aimed at control of Germany and Europe. General Clay, with the support of Washington, took the decision to sit tight. The British reaction was the same. The French were more inclined to seek a settlement and to contemplate the possibility of withdrawal, but they too stood on their rights and followed their western partners in refusing to yield to pressure.

Thus far Soviet interference had been confined principally to the movement of passengers and of supplies for the western missions and garrisons in Berlin. The trains carrying food for the population of the western sectors of the city were still going through. Until they should be stopped, the Soviet restrictions put into effect in April would be troublesome but not decisive. They were followed in May and June, however, by further regulations, by disputes over operation of the railroad yards in

Berlin, and by continued friction over the administration of governmental and trade union affairs in the capital.

The strain was too great for the four-power Allied Kommandatura, under whose supervision the city government was carried on. While the representatives of the four powers engaged in endless wrangles and gave the German administration no unified direction, the administration itself began to break down. Although the city council supposedly exercised jurisdiction over all four sectors, the decisive influence in each sector, as in Germany as a whole, rested with the occupying power. The municipal government, elected in 1946 by a city-wide election which gave the majority to non-Communist parties, tended to look to the western powers to maintain its authority, while the Communists did what they could to discredit it. In the Soviet sector the occupation authorities often interfered arbitrarily in the city administration. On June 16 the Kommandatura held a long and stormy meeting, from which the Soviet delegation, on the excuse of American "rudeness," walked out before it was over. On July 1 the Soviet authorities announced that the Kommandatura no longer existed. Henceforward German city officials took orders from no common Allied authority.

The announcement of the currency reform in the western zones on June 18 [26] was the signal for new Soviet measures which cut most of the remaining surface traffic between the western zones and Berlin. The new western Deutsche Mark was not at first introduced into Berlin, as the western powers still hoped to arrange four-power control of currency there. The Soviets, however, did not agree to this and issued orders for their own currency reform in the Soviet zone and all of Berlin. The western powers then announced on June 23 that, in view of "the attempt of the Soviet Military Administration to dominate the economic affairs of Berlin and issue its own currency for the quadripartite city," they found it necessary to introduce the western mark into their sectors of Berlin. At the same time the Russians halted all traffic between the capital and the western zones. The American and British authorities, as a counter-

[26] See below, pp. 186-187.

measure, then halted the movement of freight from Bizonia into the Soviet zone.

The new situation forced the western powers to take to the air not only to supply their own forces in Berlin but to bring in the food and other materials needed by the people of the western sectors of the city. With stocks on hand and with what could be flown in, the western position could be maintained for some weeks. How long the period of grace would last depended on the success of the airlift and on the morale of the western garrisons and the Berliners in their sectors. The western powers decided against adventurous tactics such as trying to force armed supply trains through to Berlin in defiance of Soviet orders, a course which could hardly fail to result in open acts of war. On the other hand, they stated their firm intention to stay and to maintain the air supply route; if the Russians chose to interfere with it the blame for any provocative acts would fall on them. Both Democratic and Republican leaders in the United States were united in support of this stand. In London Foreign Secretary Bevin, backed by both major parties, told the House of Commons that the British people must face the risk of war, for the alternative course of action, appeasement, would make war almost certain.

Exchanges of protests and explanations among the military commanders in Berlin brought no results. Generals Clay and Robertson asked for an end to the blockade. Marshal Sokolovsky replied that traffic might be resumed when technical difficulties were overcome and the currency problem settled. The western powers concluded that they could get no further by pursuing the argument in Berlin. Not wishing to abandon hope that the Soviet Union could be persuaded to lift the blockade, especially since the pressure was on the west, they decided on a direct approach to the Soviet Government in Moscow.

5. The Moscow Negotiations

The governments of the United States, Great Britain and France had some differences of view on how to deal with the

Berlin crisis. France, in a more exposed position and with a weak government, was less partial to a firm stand, more anxious to seek an agreement with Russia not merely on the blockade but on the entire German problem. The French had expected just such a strong Soviet reaction to the London decisions on western Germany. The French Assembly had insisted, in reluctantly accepting those decisions, that a new effort be made to reopen four-power talks on a German settlement. Nevertheless, the blockade was a clear-cut challenge to the rights of all three western powers in Berlin and to their influence on the future course of events in Europe. They decided that they must present a united front, consulting together and harmonizing their respective views before presenting them to Moscow.

On July 6, 1948, the three powers sent similar notes to the Soviet Government protesting against the blockade and insisting that it be lifted. Their tone and language were firm and unequivocal. The American note cited the relevant agreements establishing the right of the United States to its position in Berlin, a right stemming from the same source as that of the Soviet Union. It declared that for any of the occupying powers to attempt to impose a blockade on the people of Berlin was "intolerable"; there could be no delay in restoring essential transportation on which their well-being depended. The western powers declared their willingness to discuss, in Berlin, any dispute over the city administration but not to negotiate under duress; that is, the lifting of the blockade must precede any negotiation and not form a part of it.

The Soviet reply to these notes was the most complete and authoritative statement of the Soviet position yet made. The blockade was admitted to be not a consequence of technical difficulties but retaliation for what was going on in western Germany. The situation in Berlin was ascribed to the western powers' systematic violations of four-power agreements, in particular to the separate currency reform in the western zones, the introduction of a special currency in the western sectors of Berlin, and "the policy of the dismemberment of Germany." The Soviet note alleged that by destroying the system of four-power administration in Germany and in Berlin the western powers "thereby undermined as well the legal basis which assured their right to participate in the administration of Berlin" and were reducing to naught their right to occupy it. Berlin, said the note, lay in the center of the Soviet zone and was a part of that zone; the Soviet Union had been forced to take urgent measures (the blockade) to protect the people of Berlin and the economy of the Soviet zone from the disruptive effects of the introduction of the western mark in Berlin.

At the end of the Soviet note came the reply to the western refusal to negotiate under duress. The Soviet Government would not link the beginning of negotiations with the fulfillment of "any preliminary conditions whatsoever." And it saw no point in negotiations on Berlin alone, since that question could not be severed from the general question of Germany. This last statement gave some indication of Soviet intentions. Apparently the Soviet leaders were concerned over the progress made by the western powers in organizing western Germany and linking its economy with western Europe. The Ruhr, instead of being placed under four-power control as they had urged, was being used exclusively to further the aims of the western powers. The strategy of the Soviets was directed toward pressing their advantage in the battle for Berlin, where the west was vulnerable, in order to reverse the trend of the battle for Germany. The Soviet Union appeared to wish to force its adversaries not into war but into a new round of negotiation in the Council of Foreign Ministers.

Although they considered the Soviet reply completely unsatisfactory, the western governments decided to try once more. They proposed that their envoys in Moscow [27] have a personal talk with Stalin and Molotov. A meeting with Stalin took place on August 2. Ambassador Smith presented the case for the three powers in clear and blunt terms. He called their right to be in Berlin "unquestionable and absolute." He asked Stalin what were the motives behind the imposition of the blockade.

[27] Ambassador Walter Bedell Smith (U.S.), Special Envoy Frank Roberts (U.K.) and Ambassador Yves Chataigneau (France).

If there were technical difficulties, the western powers would cooperate in overcoming them. If it was the currency question, the restrictions were uncalled-for, since this question could be settled by four-power negotiations in Berlin. If the Soviet aim was to bring about new discussions on German problems, the western powers were always willing to discuss any and all such problems, but not under duress. If, on the other hand, the purpose of the blockade was to compel the western governments to abandon their rights as occupying powers in Berlin, "such an attempt could not be allowed to succeed."

Stalin, according to the American account of the meeting, repeated the contention that the western powers no longer had a juridical right to occupy Berlin, although he disclaimed any intention to push them out.[28] He then developed the argument that the blockade measures had been made necessary by the London decisions on western Germany and the introduction of the western mark into Berlin. At the end of a long discussion he linked the blockade and currency questions in a compromise proposal: the Soviet zone mark to be introduced as the sole currency for all sectors of Berlin, and simultaneously all restrictions on transport to be removed. He did not make deferment of the London program for western Germany a necessary condition of the agreement, although he wished this to be recorded as the "insistent wish" of the Soviet Government.

Since Stalin appeared willing to lift the blockade, the western powers were prepared to continue discussions on the plan to introduce the Soviet mark into Berlin, although in a sense this was negotiation under duress as the blockade remained in effect. In a series of meetings with Molotov during August the three western envoys tried to work out a specific agreement based on what seemed to be a general understanding reached in the conversation with Stalin. These talks revealed that fundamental differences persisted. Molotov's proposals included provisions that the Berlin currency should be under exclusive Soviet control and that only the transport restrictions imposed

[28] U.S. Department of State, *The Berlin Crisis, a Report on the Moscow Discussions* (Washington, 1948), 19.

since the currency reform (June 18) should be removed. He also brought up again the question of deferring implementation of the London decisions. The western powers remained firm on all these points. They insisted that the issue and circulation of the Soviet mark in Berlin must be under quadripartite control, that all transport restrictions must be lifted, and that the London program for western Germany was not under discussion. The difference on the currency question was a real one, for if the Soviets were to have exclusive control over the Berlin currency they would be in a position to control the economic and political life of the city. The western powers also objected to what seemed to be the fundamental Soviet thesis that they had no rights in Berlin other than those which they might acquire by the agreement then under negotiation.

The lack of progress with Molotov caused the western envoys to go back for another try with Stalin on August 23. Judging from the American account of the conversation, he proved willing to meet the western representatives more than half way on all the major points of difference. He agreed to lift all traffic restrictions including those imposed before June 18; he agreed that a four-power financial commission would control the operations of the German Bank of Issue of the Soviet zone in regard to the provision of currency in Berlin; he still wanted the western powers to reverse their decision to set up a government in western Germany but did not insist on it as a part of the proposed agreement on Berlin. Stalin's statement of the Soviet position seemed to meet the following four "basic requirements" of the western powers: (1) recognition of their right to be in Berlin; (2) no abandonment of their decisions on western Germany; (3) unconditional lifting of the blockade; (4) adequate quadripartite control of the issue and continued use of the Soviet mark in Berlin. If these were met, they were willing to renew four-power talks on Berlin and on Germany as a whole.

On the basis of this apparent agreement the three envoys attempted to work out with Molotov and Vyshinsky a joint communiqué and directive to the four military governors in

Berlin. The directive, agreed upon and sent to the military governors on August 30, called upon them to work out the practical details of the simultaneous lifting of the blockade and introduction of the Soviet mark as the sole currency for Berlin, naming a date on which this could be done. The arrangements for the currency changeover and for the continued provision and use of the Soviet zone mark in Berlin were to ensure, *inter alia,* no discrimination against holders of western marks, adequate safeguards against disruption of the stability of currency in the Soviet zone, and a "satisfactory" basis for Berlin's trade with the western zones and with other countries. A four-power financial commission was to "control the practical implementation of the financial arrangements indicated above, involved in the introduction and continued circulation of a single currency in Berlin." [29] The proposed communiqué, however, which mentioned these matters and also the agreement to hold four-power talks on general German problems, was never issued since Molotov insisted on inclusion of a final paragraph dealing with the London decisions.

While the diplomats consumed days and weeks in trying to reconcile views that were probably irreconcilable under existing circumstances, in Berlin itself the siege continued. The western sectors of the city were now completely dependent on supplies brought in by air. This meant, of course, shorter supplies of coal and other materials, although food rations were maintained and even increased. Unless there should be a break in the blockade, the prospect was that they would become even shorter, that homes would have little or no heat in the coming winter, that industries, crippled by lack of raw materials and by being cut off from power stations in the Soviet sector, would have to close down. But those who counted on an early crisis of supply did not foresee the great effort of which the U.S. Air Force and the RAF were capable. The airlift exceeded expectations. At the end of June American and British planes were flying a daily average of slightly over 1,000 tons of supplies, mostly food, into Berlin. At the beginning of September the

[29] Department of State, *The Berlin Crisis,* 40-41.

daily average was approaching 4,000 tons, with coal the major item in total tonnage.[30] The quantity of supplies was still only about one-half that which had come in by surface transport before the blockade was imposed, but it was sufficient to postpone indefinitely any prospect of the forced withdrawal of the western garrisons. Moreover, the success of the airlift was having a psychological effect in Berlin and in Germany. Transport planes were landing at Tempelhof in the U.S. sector at the rate of one every three minutes. At Gatow in the British sector, used by both U.S. and RAF planes, the rate in September was one every two minutes. Landing and unloading facilities were being expanded at both airports, and a new field at Tegel in the French sector was being prepared to take part of the load. The western powers were showing their determination to hold on, and they were showing it by a spectacular demonstration of air power which could not fail to impress the Germans and the Russians as well.

Political developments within the city reflected the mounting tension and the clash of world policies and ideas now concentrated at this one point on the map, the ruined capital of the nation which lost the war. Soviet policies seemed to be directed at nullifying the city government's authority in the Soviet sector, and at building up Communist-dominated organizations which could eventually take over the government of the whole city. There were already two sets of departments for labor, finance, and food supply. The western powers attempted to uphold the authority of the city government, which had a Social Democrat as mayor and a non-Communist majority in the assembly and the city council. The Soviet-licensed press stirred up feeling with strident attacks on the government. Publications in other sectors replied in kind, but were repeatedly confiscated in the Soviet sector. Communists were placed in control of the police in that sector, while the remainder of the police force remained loyal to the city government.

[30] For exact weekly totals, see Office of Military Government for Germany (U.S.), *Report of the Military Governor*, No. 39, September 1948, *Statistical Annex,* Issue No. XIX, 69.

All the elements for trouble were present if any of the occupying authorities should choose to encourage it. Disorders broke out at the end of August and in the first week of September when a Communist-led mob prevented the city assembly from carrying on its sessions at the city hall, which was in the Soviet sector. Amid riotous scenes the assembly was in effect driven out of the hall; police from the western sectors guarding the building were arrested. These events drew from the United States the charge that the Soviet authorities had "condoned and encouraged public disorders in the Soviet sector." [31] The assembly took refuge in the British sector, where it prepared to carry on. Meanwhile, SED leaders in the Soviet sector, declaring that the assembly and city council had been repudiated by the people, prepared to substitute hand-picked bodies of their own. A few days later a huge anti-Communist and anti-Soviet demonstration in the British sector near the Brandenburg Gate, on the boundary of the Soviet sector, erupted in violence when German police from that sector were provoked into firing on the demonstrators.

Under these circumstances, dangerous to peace in Berlin and in the world, the four military governors were meeting to discuss means of carrying out the directive sent by the four governments on August 30. The western representatives concluded from Marshal Sokolovsky's attitude that he was not ready to honor the understandings reached at Moscow. Although agreeable to the removal of surface transport restrictions imposed since March 30, he proposed new restrictions on air traffic. On the currency question he took the position that the proposed four-power commission should not have authority to control all operations of the German Bank of Issue with respect to Berlin. He also asserted for the Soviet authorities the exclusive right to control Berlin's trade with the western zones and other countries.

The western powers considered Sokolovsky's position contrary to the explicit assurances given by Stalin in Moscow. The

[31] Statement of Philip C. Jessup to the Security Council, October 6, 1948 (U.N. Security Council, *Official Records: Third Year*, No. 115, October 6, 1948, 18).

Soviet Government, on the other hand, backed up Sokolovsky completely, declaring that it was the western representatives who had departed from the agreed directive. Answering the specific points raised, it claimed that the proposed restrictions on air traffic were based on a decision of the Allied Control Council in 1945;[32] that the four-power financial commission was not intended to control all operations of the German Bank of Issue with respect to Berlin but only those involved in the introduction and circulation, not issuance, of the Soviet currency; that, on the trade question, the directive merely said that the military governors should work out a "satisfactory basis," that Sokolovsky had proposed nothing in contravention of that directive, and that in any case the Soviet Government now agreed that this trade should be placed under the control of the four-power financial commission.

Whether the Soviet commander had dishonored or had loyally carried out the pledge given by Stalin was not of great importance. The directive of August 30 was not as precise as it might have been. The significant fact was that each side was accusing the other of a unilateral and wrong interpretation of the directive. Like Yalta and Potsdam, this agreement turned out in practice to be no agreement at all. If Stalin had really agreed to what the western envoys thought he agreed to on August 23, by September he had lost interest, having seen that he could neither get the western powers out of Berlin nor persuade them to postpone their plans for western Germany. The differences on the currency question were certainly not insuperable, but weeks of negotiation had left each side convinced of the bad faith of the other. In an exchange of blunt notes, the Soviet Union accused the western powers of trying to disrupt the economy of the Soviet zone "and ultimately to force the U.S.S.R. to withdraw therefrom,"[33] and was in turn charged

[32] This alleged decision of November 30, 1945, according to the State Department, was in fact only a Soviet proposal that air traffic be restricted to the needs of the military forces; it was not accepted by the other powers (*The Berlin Crisis*, 48).
[33] Note of September 25, 1948 (*The Soviet Union and the Berlin Question, Documents*, 55-56).

with the intention "to impose conditions nullifying the authority of the western occupying powers and to acquire complete control over the city of Berlin." [34] Convinced that the Russians were merely playing for time and that further negotiation through diplomatic channels would be futile, the three western powers decided to appeal to the Security Council of the United Nations.

The intricacies of the currency problem meant little to the people of Europe and of America, who did not form a clear opinion as to the merits of the specific points on which discussions in Moscow and Berlin broke down. The main point at issue, however, was clear. It was whether the Soviet Union would succeed in forcing the western powers out of Berlin. By September the latter had committed themselves so firmly on this issue that it was no longer possible to withdraw without suffering untold damage to their prestige and position in Europe. The firmness of both sides was what made the situation so dangerous to the peace, although there was no evidence that either wished to push it to the point of war. The western powers refrained from trying to break the land blockade by force. And the Soviets stopped short of shooting down the planes which were circumventing that blockade.

On the larger question of the future of Germany, the Soviet Union wished to bring about a renewal of four-power negotiations in the hope that it might reverse the trend which had begun when the western powers decided to revive production in the Ruhr, include western Germany in the Marshall plan, set up a German government for the three western zones, and conclude a western military alliance. The United States and Britain were not anxious to renew four-power negotiations, seeing no basis for an acceptable settlement with Russia until western Europe had built up greater economic and military strength. They did not flatly refuse to negotiate, but insisted that they could not do so "under duress." With some reluctance France took the same line. Neither side wished to give up its present advantages: the west would not go back on the London

[34] U.S. note of September 26, 1948 (*The Berlin Crisis,* 59).

decisions; the Russians would not relax their grip on the Soviet zone nor ease the pressure on Berlin. For each side felt that it must retain those advantages or else risk losing out ultimately in Germany and in Europe.

CHAPTER FIVE

PROGRESS OF EUROPEAN RECOVERY

THE EFFORTS of the Soviet Government to strengthen its influence in Europe during the early months of 1948 were probably stimulated in no small degree by the successful launching of the program for western European recovery which had been worked out pursuant to Secretary Marshall's Harvard speech of June 1947. The Soviet leaders were conscious that this program was directed against precisely those conditions of economic prostration and chaos which had hitherto favored the advance of communism in Europe. In the spring of 1948 the Marshall plan was rapidly being transformed into a reality, and seemed to promise a progressive strengthening in western Europe's economic and social fabric which would make further Communist and Soviet gains in that area increasingly difficult. For the Soviets the year 1948 might very well be the last good opportunity to extend their influence on the European continent without an open resort to arms.

To judge by its immediate political effects in Europe the Marshall plan was already holding out great hope of success. The mere prospect of continued American aid was having a heartening effect on the peoples of the more seriously threatened countries, as was strikingly evidenced by the outcome of the Italian elections in April. As a long-term proposition, however, the European Recovery Program had still to prove itself. It was, after all, much more than a scheme for stopping European communism with American dollars. It was an enormously complex undertaking which aimed at nothing less than a radical renovation of the entire economy of western Europe.

The basic objective of the program, as presented to Congress in the first months of 1948, was to enable the participating countries to achieve equilibrium in their balance of international payments by the year 1952, a date whose finality was stressed time and again by Administration and Congressional spokesmen. This goal, decidedly ambitious in view of western Europe's wartime losses of productive capacity and of income from overseas investments and other sources of invisible earnings, was to be achieved primarily by a vast increase in the rate of capital investment leading to an equally great expansion of industrial production and of exports. The need for external assistance was to be held down by a vigorous application of the principles of "self-help and mutual cooperation" among the participating countries with the object of ensuring a maximum utilization of available resources, a lowering of trade barriers within Europe, and a progressive integration of the various national economies which might ultimately lead to full customs or economic union.

The practicality of some of these aims would become apparent only as the four-year program progressed toward completion. It was clear from the beginning, however, that they would require a sustained cooperative effort of unprecedented dimensions by all the countries involved; and a few months' experience made it plain that the program would be subject to innumerable contradictory pressures which threatened to modify its scope and character in many critical respects.

Among the unpredictable influences that would have a crucial bearing on the operation would be the behavior of the United States itself as the sponsor of the entire program. In providing and administering the billions which were intended ultimately to close Europe's "dollar gap," the United States would necessarily exert tremendous direct influence over the whole future of the European economy. Americans responsible for discharging this responsibility would be guided not only by the stated objectives of the program but by legitimate concern over its domestic impact, two separate considerations that might not always prove easy to reconcile. For four successive years, furthermore, ERP would have to run the gauntlet of a skeptical Congress which would be especially sensitive to its domestic fiscal implications and solicitous for the welfare of a host of specialized economic interests in the United States.

The course of European recovery would also be vitally affected by the strained political conditions in Europe which it was hoped ERP would play some part in alleviating. The Soviet Union, sworn enemy of the Marshall plan, retained sufficient influence in the western European labor movements to hamper the recovery process by sporadic strikes and disturbances as well as by tireless propaganda. Soviet economic imperialism in eastern Europe, in conjunction with the American policy of denying exports of strategic commodities to the U.S.S.R. and its satellites, would impede the revival of intra-European trade on which all recovery calculations were based. The fear of Soviet aggression which was impelling the western nations to undertake measures for their collective self-defense would tend to limit the revival of popular morale and would probably call for expanded military establishments and armaments which, for the most part, could be had only at the expense of the program's strictly economic objectives.

These and many other factors made it questionable how closely Europe's recovery would follow the course originally charted in Paris and Washington. They did not, however, affect the validity of the basic concept that underlay the entire program. The Marshall plan, or some approximation of it, still seemed the only practicable way of restoring Europe as a force for peace and world stability. However much they might quarrel with specific features of the unfolding recovery program as directed by the Economic Cooperation Administration (ECA), neither the American people nor the mass of Europeans seemed disposed to challenge its underlying principles.

1. Administering Marshall Plan Aid

"America's answer to the challenge facing the free world today," President Truman called the ECA when he signed the Foreign Assistance Act of 1948 on April 3.[1] Three days later

[1] Title I, the Economic Cooperation Act of 1948, was ECA's basic law. The other three titles concerned aid to China, Greece and Turkey, and the U.S. contribution to the International Children's Emergency Fund.

he sent to the Senate the appointment of Paul G. Hoffman, president of the Studebaker Corporation, as Administrator. A Republican, Hoffman had gained a reputation as a progressive and broad-gauged businessman, largely through his service as head of the Committee for Economic Development, a business group formed in 1942 that sponsored serious research into public problems and encouraged businessmen to take an active and responsible part in helping to maintain a high and stable level of employment and economic activity, not leaving it all to the government. Hoffman was acceptable to both liberal and conservative groups interested in the Marshall plan. His appointment was welcomed by Vandenberg and after a short hearing was unanimously confirmed by the Senate on April 7.

The day he took office Hoffman authorized procurement of $21 million worth of goods to meet emergency needs in Austria, France, Greece, the Netherlands and Italy. Six days later the S.S. *John H. Quick* cleared Galveston for France, carrying the first ECA cargo, and Austria signed the first "letter of intent" indicating that it would negotiate a bilateral aid agreement with the United States. Such quick action was largely the result of the tentative aid plans the State Department had prepared during the winter to save valuable time for the new agency.

Staffing ECA was another matter, and a slower one. Deluged with applications, Hoffman announced that he would have "a comparatively small staff consisting largely of technicians and experts." [2] The top posts in Washington and abroad went mainly to businessmen and lawyers. Recognizing that the support of European labor was crucial to the political and economic success of the program, Hoffman appointed labor advisers to serve both in Washington and in the missions abroad. W. Averell Harriman resigned as Secretary of Commerce to take a key position as the Special Representative of ECA in Paris. As "ambassador at large" Harriman's job was to deal at first hand with the Europeans, especially the newly created Organization for European Economic Cooperation (OEEC) in Paris, super-

[2] Form letter to applicants, Press Release ECA-6, April 19, 1948.

vise the ECA country missions, and represent the United States
on the U.N. Economic Commission for Europe.[3]

During the first three months of its existence ECA paid its
bills out of a billion-dollar loan from the Reconstruction Finance Corporation, authorized by the Economic Cooperation
Act. Though aid to Europe was established as public policy, it
faced another set of hurdles in the appropriation process. The
April 3 Act authorized appropriation of $4.3 billion to be ex-
pended over a 12-month period; in addition the Administration could borrow $1 billion from the Treasury for loans to
Europe. Stop-gap aid to France, Austria and Italy totaling $55
million was separately appropriated, so the Administration
was asking Congress for $4.245 billion. Led by their chairman,
Taber of New York, the Republican majority on the House
Appropriations Committee cut the amount to $4 billion, which
it said was to last 15 months and provide aid to Trieste, Japan,
Korea and the Ryukyus as well as the OEEC countries. "The
architects of this world-wide relief program have no definite
plan and no definite program," Taber told the House on June
4. He considered the budget estimates "the result of a series of
after-dinner conversations" and referred to "the complete lack
of substantiating evidence on the proposed needs and requirements of the participating countries . . ." The mass of statistics
submitted by the executive branch seemed to him full of discrepancies. "I am satisfied that with proper housekeeping ECA
can get along for 15 months on the $4,000,000,000 which have
been recommended and with that sum provide necessary relief
and proper rehabilitation."[4] With the aid of the Republican
leaders in the House, the Committee's version of the bill was
speedily passed at one sitting by a voice vote.

In the Senate Vandenberg, supported by statements from
Republican presidential aspirants Dewey and Stassen, strongly
challenged the House action. After hearing his testimony as

[3] Most of the missions remained quite small. The largest by the end of the year
were Athens (a special case) with 129 people, Paris with 87, London with 62,
and Rome with 45. By then Harriman's office had over 400 American employees
plus foreign help. ECA's Washington staff numbered 842 on December 31.
[4] *Congressional Record* (Daily edition), June 4, 1948, 7341-7342.

well as that of Marshall and Hoffman, the Senate Appropriations Committee approved a compromise formula, leaving the appropriation at $4 billion (plus the billion-dollar loan authorized in the recovery act) but restoring the 12-month period and removing Japan, Korea and the Ryukyus from the list of recipients. Taber fought hard for his original position during the three days the bill was in conference. At one point it looked as if the fight would have to be carried to the floor of the Republican convention before the conferees would agree. But on June 19 Taber's colleagues began leaving him one by one. Taber himself remained adamant till the last. The conferees accepted the Senate bill with one concession of form to the House: the appropriation would run for 15 months but the President, on the advice of the Administrator, could use it up in 12. Vandenberg had won. The conference report was accepted by both Houses on June 20 (in the House by 318 to 62 and in the Senate without dissent); the President signed the bill on June 28.

ECA's first big diplomatic job was to negotiate aid agreements with the Marshall plan countries. Some Americans had argued that since the United States was urging close cooperation on the western European countries, its dealings should be solely with the OEEC, their common organ. Government officials felt differently and preferred, partly for legal reasons, to make the basic commitments bilateral. Their view was adopted by Congress, and the Economic Cooperation Act specified that each country receiving aid would have to sign an agreement with the United States including a number of commitments set out in the Act. Since ECA's staff was not yet assembled most of the negotiation fell to the State Department, which began talks in Washington in early June with representatives of Britain, France, Sweden and Denmark, figuring that an agreement worked out with these countries could serve as a pattern for all the rest. There were difficulties at first, arising largely from the fears of some Europeans that the language of the draft agreement proposed by the American negotiators would give the United States virtual control—or at least veto power—over the policies of European governments in important spheres. This was not the American intention, and after some clarification negotiations proceeded more smoothly.

Most of the agreements were signed in late June and early July.[5] Negotiations with the American and British authorities in the Bizone proved as hard as or harder than those with the independent countries. Military government officials saw no need for another American mission in Germany and felt it would be quite satisfactory to have ECA turn over to them the funds allocated for western Germany to use as part of their import program. ECA and the State Department disagreed, arguing that much the same conditions had to apply to Germany as to the other participating countries. The final agreement was that Harriman would head the German mission, in addition to his regular job as Special Representative, being represented in Frankfort by a deputy. A bilateral aid agreement similar to the others was signed July 14.

Only Switzerland refused to sign an agreement. Since they were not applying for aid, the Swiss saw no need to make commitments to the United States about their future policy. Signature of the convention creating OEEC seemed to them sufficient guarantee of their wish to cooperate in European recovery. American negotiators argued that as a participant in ERP Switzerland would be able to buy some relatively scarce American products for which export licenses might otherwise be denied. The Swiss were not impressed; countries in Latin America and elsewhere were getting some of these goods without signing special agreements; Switzerland itself had scarce goods for export and did not require its customers to promise that they would follow Swiss ideas of sound economic policy. In fact, suggested one Swiss newspaper, Swiss credits to other European countries were themselves a kind of little Marshall plan and perhaps everything would be clearer if the Swiss Government set up an ECA to make sure everyone understood that

[5] June 28, France, Ireland, Italy; June 29, Denmark; July 2, Austria, Belgium, Greece, Netherlands; July 3, Iceland, Luxembourg, Norway, Sweden; July 4, Turkey; July 6, United Kingdom; July 9, French zone of Germany; July 14, Bizone; September 28, Portugal; October 15, Trieste.

it was in a different category from other ERP countries.[6] Since the negotiations were fruitless, the United States dropped the matter in November 1948. Portugal, which also did not receive aid from ECA during the first year of the recovery program, accepted a bilateral agreement.

The 18 bilateral aid agreements were similar in most respects, with occasional variations in the text or differences in the interpretative notes, according to the special problems of each recipient country. Broadly speaking, the United States undertook to render aid and the recipient country to pursue recovery policies, independently and in cooperation with other OEEC nations. In addition to trying to meet production targets, encouraging trade, and ensuring that American aid was effectively used, the recipient's obligations covered measures to balance its governmental budget and establish "a valid rate of exchange," provisions which had worried some of the European governments during the negotiations. Other sections of the agreements dealt with investment guarantees, the handling of local currency counterpart funds arising out of American grants, the purchase of strategic materials by the United States, voluntary relief supplies, the promotion of travel, and foreign publicity about American aid.

All this was framework. ECA's main job, of course, was to get supplies to Europe—the right goods, to the right places in the right amounts. ECA did not actually go out and buy goods to ship to Europe. Instead it operated as a financing agency, providing funds for the purchase of approved quantities of goods needed for recovery, most of which moved through private trade channels in the United States. At first ECA's operation was largely a continuation of the Interim Aid program; food, feed, fertilizer and fuel, all for current consumption, comprised 75 percent of the first quarter's shipments. Later emphasis shifted toward the purchase of raw materials and machinery for reconstruction as well as immediate consumption needs. By the end of March, 1949, ECA procurement authorizations were divided in the following proportions:

[6] *Neue Zürcher Zeitung,* August 27, 1948.

	Millions of dollars	Approximate percent of total
Food, feed and fertilizer	$1,649	35
Fuel	693	14
Raw materials and semifinished goods	1,269	27
Machinery and vehicles	578	12
Tobacco	125	3
Ocean freight	406	8
Miscellaneous	50	1
Total	$4,770	100

ECA financing was not simply a matter of filling the justified needs of the OEEC countries. The Economic Cooperation Act instructed the Administrator to conduct procurement in such a way as to "minimize the drain upon the resources of the United States and the impact . . . upon the domestic economy"; he was to "avoid impairing the fulfillment of vital needs of the people of the United States." Apart from the impact of foreign aid as a whole on the economy, this was largely a matter of limiting shipments of scarce goods such as meat, nonferrous metals, and farm machinery.

In addition to its control over procurement for ERP countries, ECA had a voice in the export control system. But it also had a more supple instrument to help cushion the impact of European aid on United States supplies. Offshore purchasing—the use of ECA funds to buy goods in Canada, Latin America or elsewhere for shipment to western Europe—made it possible to get some of the goods Europe needed without taking them out of the domestic supply. Moreover, this device gave flexibility to the program, made it possible to supply some goods to Europe more advantageously than if they had had to be bought in the United States, and helped lay the groundwork for trade patterns more likely to reflect Europe's needs after the Marshall plan than 100 percent dependence on the United States would have done. By the end of 1948, 38 percent of all ECA procurement authorizations were for offshore purchases. Of the $1.4 billion allocated in this way, about $593 million was for purchases in Canada and $353 million for Latin America;

$245 million was spent by the participating countries in buying from each other, and the remaining $217 million in purchases elsewhere, $31.6 million of it in eastern Europe. Among commodities the amount purchased offshore varied greatly, of course, from 100 percent of the sugar to .1 percent of the cotton. The Economic Cooperation Act directed the Administrator to procure as much of Europe's oil abroad as he could; he managed to get approximately 80 percent of it, by volume, from other areas.[7] Canada supplied about 35 percent of the wheat ECA financed.

Congress had been concerned with "protecting" the domestic economy from plenty as well as from scarcity. The law encouraged the Administrator to use domestic agricultural surpluses as much as possible and forbade him to buy these goods offshore (except within the participating countries themselves when he and the Secretary of Agriculture agreed that this was desirable). ECA's procedure was to inform recipient countries what products were in surplus and encourage them to use these goods wherever possible in meeting their consumption goals. The Department of Agriculture, authorized to pay subsidies up to 50 percent of the sales price of surplus farm products, helped to purchase frozen eggs, fruit, flaxseed, and tobacco. Other products shipped from government surplus stocks were tung oil, turpentine, linseed oil, and hemp fiber. However, as farm prices fell in the United States many producer groups called on ECA to ship more of their products abroad. Mr. Hoffman resisted the pressure, pointing out that the purpose of the program was European recovery, not farm relief. After a two-hour conference with southern Congressmen and tobacco-growers, he said, "I don't believe that American industry and agriculture are entitled to a subsidy under this program. If that was the intent of the law then I don't belong down here." [8]

Not all the $5 billion worth of goods ECA planned to ship to Europe during its first year would be given away; one-fifth of the aid had to be in the form of loans. The European coun-

---

[7] The value distribution was 66 percent offshore, 34 percent domestic, because the higher-priced petroleum products came from this country.
[8] *New York Times,* September 29, 1948.

tries were not altogether prepared for this and some of them disliked the idea of adding to their already heavy debt burdens. The National Advisory Council recommended that ECA offer liberal terms: up to 35 years at 2.5 percent interest starting in 1952; amortization starting sometime between 1952 and 1956; provision for postponement of principal or interest if the United States agreed. Having trouble finding willing borrowers, ECA in October 1948 announced temporary suspension of procurement authorizations to nine countries until they concluded loan agreements. Austria, western Germany, Trieste and Greece were exempted; fully solvent countries, like Belgium, Sweden, Turkey, Ireland and Iceland, got more aid in loans than in grants; [9] but for the most part, the loans bore a more or less proportional relation to total aid. The Congressional "watchdog committee" criticized this arrangement and remarked that ECA placed emphasis "on lending the full amount of money authorized by the act, even though repayment may be uncertain, rather than treating the $1,000,000,000 authorized for loans as a sum available to be used to the extent that borrowers can be found who qualify." [10]

The criticism accurately describes the position in which ECA found itself; any other course would have cut the amount of aid it could give. For the second year of the program ECA recommended to Congress that loans cover a smaller proportion of aid. One-eighth the dollar earnings of ERP countries in 1948–1949 went for amortization and interest on dollar obligations; ". . . a further large charge upon their future dollar receipts would in all likelihood be a deterrent to the achievement of the objectives of the recovery program." [11] It would

[9] These countries got no direct grants at all up to March 1949 except for Belgium, which got $3 million. However, all but Ireland got "conditional grants" connected with the European payments scheme (see below) which in some cases exceeded the amount of their loans.
[10] *Report on Progress of the Economic Cooperation Administration*, of the Joint Committee on Foreign Economic Cooperation, 81st Congress, 1st Session (Washington, 1949), 98.
[11] Economic Cooperation Administration, *A Report on Recovery Progress and United States Aid* (Washington, 1949), 113.

certainly give pause to private investors and international lending agencies.

Out of the billion dollars authorized for lending, ECA was also to provide funds to guarantee the convertibility of private American investments in the participating countries. This activity got a slow start and by the end of March, 1949, ECA industrial guarantees totaled only $2.6 million, all for investments in the United Kingdom. Another $892,414 was used in accordance with special provisions in the Economic Cooperation Act to encourage wider distribution of American films and publications in Europe by ensuring the convertibility of their earnings in European currencies. Part of the difficulty of expanding the investment guarantee program lay in the hesitancy of American investors about putting new capital into unsettled Europe, and in the inevitable slowness of surveys, negotiations, etc. Another handicap was the fact that European governments— which had to approve the investments—generally preferred to take as a loan the money that would otherwise go into the guarantee. On the recommendation of ECA, Congress tried to meet this problem when it extended the Act for a second year by permitting the Administrator to borrow $150 million (minus the amount already committed in guarantees) for guarantee purposes over and above the $1 billion he could borrow for loans to governments.

ECA's financial responsibilities did not end with providing goods, loans and guarantees. As prescribed by the Economic Cooperation Act, the bilateral agreements required the countries receiving aid to set up "counterpart funds" into which they paid in their own currencies the cost to the U.S. Government of the goods they received as grants from ECA.[12] Five percent of this fund could be drawn on by ECA to meet administrative expenses of the U.S. Government and to help pay

[12] Since Portugal, Sweden and Turkey were not to receive any grants, the provision was omitted from these bilateral agreements. "Conditional" aid in connection with the European payments plan is in a special category since the dollars received are matched by local currency grants to other participating countries. However, the country which receives the indirect aid (i.e., goods from another participating country) must add its value to the counterpart fund.

for strategic materials. The rest (minus internal transportation costs of private relief parcels) was to be used by agreement between ECA and the recipient government in ways that would promote recovery and improve the financial position of the latter. This meant different things in different places. In Britain, all the releases from the counterpart funds went into cancellation of the government's internal debt, to help check inflationary pressures. In Italy, where there was unemployment and money was tight, all the releases went into investment to stimulate reconstruction; a public works program financed partly from the counterpart fund was launched to provide jobs. France was an especially difficult case, with heavy inflation, a large investment program, and a volatile political situation. Of the 140 billion francs released from the counterpart fund during 1948, 105 billion went into investments and 25 billion into debt retirement. (The remaining 10 billion went into development of French colonial resources in which the United States is deficient.) Releases for investment were paid into the special government budget for this purpose, thus helping indirectly to balance the budget for current expenses. The timing and use of these releases was of great political importance in France and played an important part in keeping the Queuille government in power. At the same time, David Bruce, head of the ECA mission to France, pressed hard for strong French measures to check inflation before releasing any of the funds.

When giving an account of their doings to members of the public, ECA officials frequently called attention to the numerous and varied duties the law imposed on the Administrator. Some of these duties, such as the acquisition of strategic materials for the United States, seemed a bit off the main line of his job of promoting European recovery. The Economic Cooperation Act specified that the bilateral agreements should commit the European countries to "facilitate the transfer" of materials of which the United States was short; to negotiate "a future schedule of minimum availabilities to the United States of America for future purchase and delivery of a fair share" of such materials; to promote the production of such materials;

to negotiate for "suitable protection" of the rights of Americans to share in the development of that production "on terms of treatment equivalent to those afforded to the nationals of the country concerned"; and to negotiate a schedule of increased production of strategic materials, and transfer to the United States of an agreed share of the increase, "on a long-term basis in consideration of assistance furnished" by the United States.

Always an attractive idea to Congress, obtaining strategic materials in return for foreign aid proved a headache to ECA. From the point of view of foreign countries, exportable strategic materials were potential dollar-earners, not things to be "given away" if they could help it. Foreign participation in the development of national resources of strategic materials raised many touchy questions. Producers were traditionally wary of governmental stockpiles that might depress prices by overhanging the market. At the end of 1948 ECA reported that "in spite of its utmost efforts to accomplish these objectives, the ECA is not satisfied with the progress made . . ." [13] ERP countries and their dependencies had known surpluses of only ten or a dozen strategic minerals. To require these countries to deliver materials not in surplus would only force them to look elsewhere for additional supplies, and would probably run contrary to the main purposes of ECA. By the end of the year ECA had bought only $22 million worth of rubber, sisal, and industrial diamonds from the United Kingdom, although negotiations for further supplies were in progress.

Part of the slowness was due to the time it took to locate new resources and work out development projects. Missions explored possible fields of development and made surveys. ECA offered various sorts of financial assistance both to foreign governments and to private American interests, but takers were few. The use of counterpart funds was limited by the fact that these were available in sizable amounts only for three areas important as possible suppliers of strategic materials: the colonial possessions of Britain, France, and the Netherlands. There

[13] *A Report on Recovery Progress and United States Aid,* 229.

were few funds in Belgium, none at all in Turkey or Portugal. All these factors contributed to ECA's inability to negotiate any "future schedules of minimum availabilities" by the end of 1948. But the difficulty ECA put first on the list was "the lack of adequate and long-term purchasing power in any United States Government agency." [14] To do a proper job of securing strategic materials, it felt, there ought to be an agency able to place long-term contracts for the purchase of foreign strategic materials so as to assure a market for expanded production and to permit amortization of investment costs. The implication was that ECA would prefer to get out of this line of business.

The Joint Congressional Committee on Foreign Economic Cooperation was not very sympathetic with the ECA view. "The lack of speed with which ECA has operated with respect to obtaining some repayment in strategic materials against either loans or grants is in sharp contrast with its activity as a disbursing agency . . . ECA, having more bargaining power than any other executive agency with the possible exception of the Department of State, has failed to stand up to the diplomacy of the European nations, and has assumed that dollars alone will buy access and deliveries against a historical repugnance on the part of the foreign governments and private producers to the idea of an American stock pile." [15] Without altogether turning down the idea that a separate agency with long-term contracting authority should be set up to procure strategic materials, the committee disapproved ECA's wish to get rid of the job. "If Congress places a sufficiently high priority on stock piling, the ECA might well be given increasing responsibility in this field rather than be relieved of its obligations." [16]

A defense-minded Congress took some of the Committee's advice. In renewing the Act in the spring of 1949 it strengthened the language of the mandate to the Administrator to get strategic materials and increase their production and gave him

[14] *Ibid.*
[15] *Report on Progress of the Economic Cooperation Administration*, 123-124.
[16] *Ibid.*, 6.

the authority, in agreement with the Director of the Bureau of Federal Supply (the procurement agency for stockpiling), to enter into contracts lasting up to 20 years for their purchase. Payment might precede delivery, but the purchases were to be for the account of the Bureau and subject to the limits of its appropriations and contract authority. The idea seemed to be to marry ECA's bargaining power with the long-term functions of the stockpiling agency. Another source of possible help lay in ECA's colonial development work, which, though not confined to strategic materials, promised to be much more active in 1949 than in 1948. As work began on implementation of the President's program for technical assistance to underdeveloped areas, enunciated as Point Four in his inaugural address of January 20, 1949, the strategic materials program took on new overtones and the chances of increased imports improved.

2. Self-Help and Mutual Cooperation

"Mindful of the advantages which the United States has enjoyed through the existence of a large domestic market with no internal trade barriers, and believing that similar advantages can accrue to the countries of Europe, it is declared to be the policy of the people of the United States to encourage these countries through a joint organization to exert sustained common efforts as set forth in the report of the Commmittee of European Economic Cooperation signed at Paris on September 22, 1947, which will speedily achieve that economic cooperation in Europe which is essential for lasting peace and prosperity." Thus Congress, in the Economic Cooperation Act, gave legislative form to the American desire to see the Europeans extend their "mutual cooperation," which Secretary Marshall had bracketed with "self-help" as necessary conditions for new American aid.

To many Americans the idea of a "United States of Europe" was a natural, desirable concept; by achieving unity the Europeans would automatically dispose of a lot of their difficulties. From this point of view, Marshall plan aid should be both a carrot and a stick moving Europe on the path toward some kind of unification. When the Economic Cooperation Act was being discussed in Congress, Senator Fulbright led a group that proposed stronger language on the subject of cooperation and unification, but Vandenberg, Lodge, and Connally, backed by the Administration, argued that it would be unwise for the United States to prescribe too concretely the ways and means of carrying out a difficult process, the burden of which would inevitably rest mostly on the Europeans themselves.

In Europe views were mixed. There were those who felt that western Europe could once more play a decisive role in the world only if it became, in some sense, an integrated unit. Others were more inclined to see the difficulties of overcoming centuries of separation, of reconciling real differences in national interests, and of putting together contradictory systems of economic organization. Almost everyone was for "cooperation," which could mean many different kinds of things, but there was a good bit of evidence to support the view of a well-placed British observer that "none of the governments or peoples of Western Europe is prepared to face the economic, financial, and social consequences of any real measure of integration." [17] Anything as ambitious as "integration" lay in the future; the first question was: In what way would the cooperation on the recovery program begun at Paris be continued?

The Paris report said that if the United States provided the financial help that was expected, "a joint organisation to review progress achieved in the execution of the programme will be necessary." The participating countries said they would be ready to set up such a body to "ensure, to the fullest extent possible by joint action, the realisation of the economic conditions necessary to enable the general objectives to which each country has pledged itself to be effectively achieved." The organization would report to the participating governments on the progress of recovery and they would give it whatever information it needed. "The organisation will be of a temporary

[17] A. D. Marris, *Prospects for Closer European Economic Integration* (London, Royal Institute of International Affairs, 1948), 17.

character and will cease to exist when the special assistance necessary for the recovery of Europe comes to an end." [18] "Even the anodyne wording" of this paragraph "took days of negotiation," according to the deputy leader of the British delegation to the Paris conference.[19]

After the Paris report was delivered to Washington there was a lull in matters of European cooperation. A committee continued to work on intra-European payments problems, a study group began work on customs unions matters, and in January a manpower conference was held in Rome. But nothing overt was done about bringing together the 16 countries to make more detailed recovery plans.

During the Senate hearings on the ERP bill that began in January, questions were raised about the willingness of the Europeans to cooperate. By the middle of the month Britain and France were reported ready to call another meeting of the sixteen, but the State Department opposed the idea. Supposedly it was worried about the effect on Congress of having the Europeans working on plans to divide up funds which the United States had not yet provided, and, also, about the possibility that the Europeans would announce their opposition to some of the possible conditions to the aid that Congress was debating. After he and the British Ambassador had spent 40 minutes with Under-Secretary Lovett, Henri Bonnet, the French Ambassador, said, "It would be premature to have a full and formal meeting of the sixteen countries as long as there are no concrete developments here in Washington." [20]

The Communist *coup* in Czechoslovakia increased the pressure. On March 15, after the Senate had passed the European aid bill but before the House had begun to debate, the Committee of European Economic Cooperation met again in Paris and created a working party to draft a multilateral recovery agreement setting up a continuing organization. Thanks to the preliminary work already done, the working party had a draft

[18] Committee of European Economic Cooperation, *Report* (Washington, 1947), I, 39-40.
[19] Marris, *op. cit.,* 13.
[20] *New York Times,* January 16, 1948.

ready to submit to the governments by March 26. Truman signed the Economic Cooperation Act on April 3. Two days later the conferees met again in Paris, and by April 15 a final draft of a Convention for European Economic Cooperation was ready, which was signed the next day by ministers of the 16 participating countries and the Commanders in Chief of the western zones of Germany.[21]

Like the preamble, Article I of the convention emphasized cooperation as a means of recovery: "As their immediate task" the signatory nations agreed to "undertake the elaboration and execution of a joint recovery program." There followed commitments to develop production, draw up programs of production and trade, stimulate trade among themselves, "strengthen their economic links by all methods which they may determine will further the objectives" of the agreement, reduce trade barriers, maintain financial stability and "sound rates of exchange," and make full use of their manpower. At the heart of the new agreement lay the provisions concerning the Organization for European Economic Cooperation. Each country would have one representative (and one vote) on the Council, the OEEC's governing body. A seven-member Executive Committee was to carry on work between Council sessions with the aid of a Secretariat headed by a Secretary-General, who would have the right to submit proposals to the Council as well as to carry on the affairs of the staff. The OEEC's decisions were to be "by mutual agreement of all the Members," but a country might declare itself not interested in a particular subject and its abstention would be no veto.[22]

Behind the negotiations about the text of the convention lay a difference in view as to how strong the OEEC should be. Not that any government proposed to go very far in subordinating

[21] The Anglo-American zone of Trieste acceded to the agreement on October 14, 1948.

[22] This proviso was of particular interest to the Swiss, who were anxious not to be caught in a position where their reluctance to go along with a degree of planning they disapproved of, or to jeopardize their traditional neutrality in some indirect fashion, would stand in the way of cooperation by other members of the Organization.

itself to the new body, but the French were generally credited with wanting the OEEC to have strong powers to initiate action and make plans for recovery that applied to all the participating countries. The British, on the other hand, seemed inclined to emphasize "self-help," giving national governments the main job of working out recovery, leaving to the OEEC the role of reconciling national plans and providing for the necessary international action. Naturally, the convention did not provide a clear-cut decision. Perhaps partly as a result of United States pressure, the language of the agreement sounded more like the French view, but what was really done would plainly depend more on the future actions of governments and on the competence and initiative of the OEEC Secretariat than on the terms of the agreement.

On their face, the OEEC's powers were broad. It was "to prepare and implement within the sphere of the collective action of the Members concerned the measures necessary to achieve . . . a sound European economy . . . and to facilitate, promote and coordinate the individual action of Members." On the basis of study and review of what was being done it was "to take such action as may be found appropriate in order to ensure [the] execution" of the convention. It was to provide information to the United States Government and make recommendations to it, help in negotiations, make agreements with government and international organizations and "take decisions for implementation by Members." Nothing was said about the obligations of members with regard to the OEEC's recommendations or decisions, but the plain implication of each country's general obligations to promote recovery was that once it had agreed to a particular action by OEEC it was bound to do its best to carry out that decision.

The OEEC began work shortly after it was created. Robert Marjolin, a French civil servant who had been active in the preparatory work, became first Secretary-General. Sir Edmund Hall-Patch became chairman of the Executive Committee, while Premier Spaak of Belgium served as chairman of the Council, with Baron Jean Charles Snoy et d'Oppuers as his alternate.

Technical committees were established on which members of the national delegations worked closely with the Secretariat.[23]

Since a large part of its work involved cooperating with the Americans, the OEEC was handicapped during the first weeks of its existence by the fact that Harriman's office was not yet set up and working. Meanwhile the OEEC had been pushed into rapid activity by the ECA's announcement that the program for dividing up United States aid during the third quarter of the year (July–September) should be done in the first instance by OEEC. The previous quarter's aid—the first that had been given—had been divided by ECA and it was difficult for OEEC to move into action so quickly. However, a program was submitted to ECA by June 5.[24] On the same day Harriman officially told the OEEC Council that in the American view they ought not only to work out a program of aid for the first fiscal year (ending June 30, 1949) but to make it a coherent program by reconciling national requests. In other words, it would be OEEC's job to decide how much of the expected American aid was to go to each participating country; that meant cutting down national requests, which in turn involved analysis of each national plan to see where savings might be made. That would be a tough job, thrusting the international body right into the middle of each member's national affairs. There was opposition to the American suggestion, particularly from the British, who feared the task might wreck the new organization, but the United States pressed its point and the job was accepted. This did not mean, of course, that the United States would automatically accept all OEEC recommendations;

[23] Member countries could send representatives to any committee, but in practice only those countries particularly interested in the problems under discussion attended. At the end of the year there were five "horizontal" committees dealing with programs, balance of payments, trade, intra-European payments, and manpower. Fourteen "vertical" committees dealt with food and agriculture, agricultural machinery, coal, electricity, oil, iron and steel, raw materials, machinery, nonferrous metals, chemicals, timber, pulp and paper, textiles, inland transport, and maritime transport.

[24] Subsequently OEEC was relieved of the job of making quarterly allocations because it was fully occupied with the first two annual programs and the long-range plans. ECA worked out the quarterly shipments in direct negotiations with the countries involved.

ECA was accountable to Congress for its funds and would have to be satisfied that the proposed division and use of the money was sound, but the initial burden would be on the Europeans (in constant touch with Harriman's group) to produce a reasonable proposal.

To make an annual program, OEEC had to know more than just how much American aid each country wanted; total import plans were needed, which greatly increased the burden of a job that had to be done under high pressure. Adding to the complications was the fact that no one knew how much aid would actually be available until the end of June, so original estimates had to be revised and assumptions changed. When it got the answers to the questionnaires it had sent to each government the OEEC found, naturally enough, that requests for aid considerably exceeded what would be available. A Committee of Four was appointed to scale down the programs until they fitted into the possibilities. These "four wise men" had to analyze national programs to find where cuts could be made, negotiate with national delegations, and try to switch prospective purchases from dollar countries to the sterling area or European sources. But for the latter method to work there had to be a more effective system of financing intra-European trade than had heretofore existed. A Committee of Five was set up to develop such a system.

When the work of the two committees was finally presented to the Council, many matters had to be referred back to the member governments. Throughout the process bargaining was hard; dollars and plans were at stake; there was some acrimony; doubt was cast on the soundness of other nations' plans and statistics; the fact that the German representatives at the Council "spoke with an American accent" made matters worse; there was talk of excluding Greece and Turkey as special cases and not western European countries. But the need to reach agreement was compelling and by October 16 the Council was ready to approve a plan which was sent to Washington.

The Agreement for Intra-European Payments and Compensations which was concluded as part of the first year's allocations was regarded by many people as a major achievement of the OEEC. It was certainly the most ambitious attempt to date to deal with a central problem in European recovery. Before the war about half of Europe's trade was among the countries of the continent. After the war intra-European trade revived much more slowly than European production or trade with the rest of the world. The virtual elimination of Germany was the major cause of this decline, but the fact that almost no European currencies could be used outside of a single country was also an important hindrance. At Paris the OEEC set up a Committee of Financial Experts which considered remedial proposals and eventually succeeded in working out a payments agreement. On November 18, 1947, France, Italy and the Benelux countries signed the first Agreement on Multilateral Monetary Compensation; later the Bizone joined and eight other countries became "occasional members." Clearings through the Bank for International Settlements in Basel were on a very modest scale, partly for technical reasons and because of the agreement's limited scope, but mostly because the disparity in trade among European countries arose from more fundamental causes than the lack of effective monetary exchange machinery. Different rates of recovery and production, differing needs and availabilities led some countries to become chronic debtors and others chronic creditors; the willingness of the creditors to lend additional sums was limited. The scope of this agreement was not great enough to overcome the difficulties hampering expansion of intra-European trade.

ECA alleviated the situation by allocating dollars for offshore purchases by one European country from another, but it was not willing to continue this practice indefinitely since it was cumbersome and showed no prospects of creating a system of intra-European trade that could survive the end of American aid. Alternative arrangements were rejected for one reason or another, or proved impracticable. The agreement finally worked out by OEEC enlarged the scope of the existing arrangement and used American aid to force additional goods into European trade channels.

All of the ERP countries signed the new agreement.[25] Just as before there were to be automatic monthly clearings that involved no increase in one country's holdings of another's currency. The main new feature was the creation of "drawing rights" by one country on another. As a result of the many sets of bilateral negotiations supervised by the Committee of Five, an annual balance of payments was estimated between each set of countries. Then the debtor of the pair was given drawing rights on the creditor sufficient to fill the gap.[26] For instance, Britain got drawing rights of $30 million on Belgium, while France got $200 million worth of drawing rights against Britain. The net contribution of each country to the others in the group under this scheme was matched by "conditional aid" from the United States; should the contributing country not fulfill its pledge, it might lose a share of the dollar aid. Arrangements were also made for transferring drawing rights from one country to another with the idea of making the system more flexible and encouraging multilateral trade. However, since such shifts would involve a transfer of dollars from one country to another, they would plainly be met with considerable resistance.

The following table shows the effect of the payments agreement in redistributing dollar aid among the European countries. France was the greatest gainer by the scheme, getting two-fifths of the drawing rights. Britain and Belgium were by far the largest creditors, providing two-thirds of all contributions.[27] Most of Britain's credits went to France; those of Belgium were more widely spread, with the Netherlands, France and Britain leading the list of countries that received aid in the form of drawing rights.

[25] Portugal and Switzerland were not to be included in clearings unless they specifically assented to each transaction.

[26] This was the theory; actually the size of the gap was not a scientific estimate but the product of negotiations since it amounted to a gift from one country to the other. In the case of Belgium the sum of the estimated export balances was much larger than the total contribution Belgium was willing to make.

[27] This and the next sentence refer to total (not net) drawing rights and contributions, which do not appear in the table.

AMERICAN AID AND EUROPEAN DRAWING RIGHTS
FISCAL YEAR 1949 [28]
(in millions of dollars)

	Gross ECA aid (1)	Net drawing rights received (+) or extended (−) (2)	Net ERP aid (col. 1 plus col. 2) (3)
Austria	215.2	+ 63.5	278.7
Belgium-Luxembourg and Belgian dependent overseas territories	247.9	− 207.5	40.4
Denmark	109.1	+ 6.8	115.9
Free Territory of Trieste	17.8	. . . .	17.8
France and dependent overseas territories	980.9	+ 323.3	1,304.2
Germany: Bizone	410.6	− 6.7	403.9
French zone	99.2	+ 0.8	100.0
Greece	144.8	+ 66.8	211.6
Iceland	5.2	− 3.5	1.7
Ireland	78.3	. . . .	78.3
Italy	555.5	− 20.3	535.2
Netherlands and dependent overseas territories	469.6	+ 71.7	541.3
Norway	83.3	+ 31.8	115.1
Sweden	46.6	− 25.0	21.6
Turkey	39.7	− 11.7	28.0
United Kingdom	1,239.0	− 290.0	949.0
Commodity reserve	13.5	. . . .	13.5
Total	4,756.2	0.0	4,756.2

The first clearing took place early in November, 1948. As time passed the balances showed that some countries were using up their drawing rights more quickly than others. More serious was the growing criticism that the agreement put the incentives in the wrong places. Specifically, it encouraged France not to press exports to countries on which she had large drawing rights, since she could count on free imports from them; it permitted exporters in some countries to charge high prices, since their customers were not really paying for the goods they were buying, thus distorting trade. The OEEC Council had adopted a set of commercial policy principles to

[28] Economic Cooperation Administration, *A Report on Recovery Progress and United States Aid*, Table 1, p. 10.

prevent misuse of the system, but these were adjurations without sanctions to enforce them. The payments agreement had been presented as an interim step to be reexamined and revised in time for the second year's allocation of aid. As that time approached various proposals were made for returning to offshore purchasing or for the introduction of dollars into the clearing fund. But by late spring 1949 there were no definite indications of how OEEC or ECA would try to solve the problem.

Before it was finished with the first annual program, OEEC had started on an even larger task: a long-term program for European recovery, extending through the presumed end of the Marshall plan in 1952. When Hoffman told OEEC in July that he wanted to see a long-term plan, some eyebrows were raised about free-enterprise America pressing planning on Europe. But Hoffman had said: "I want to make clear as crystal the fact that what I have in mind is a programme of action, not a rigid and ponderous five year plan which tries to compress the life processes of a nation into a set of formulae and a sheaf of statistical tables." [29] The practical difficulties were immense. Nevertheless, there were sensible reasons for Hoffman's view; Congress wanted to know what Europe proposed to do with the American taxpayers' money and where the Europeans were headed; without a program aimed at ending the European dollar deficit by 1952, the United States might find itself in the difficult position of risking the loss of benefits from the aid already given unless it was ready to extend the Marshall plan; knowledge that aid would definitely come to an end (and be smaller each year before then) would in itself be a stimulus to European activity. So questionnaires and instructions went out from OEEC to each participating country.

The job was not simply a statistical one. Indeed, the value of statistical estimates of what would happen four years hence in unsettled Europe was strictly limited; the basic data differed in accuracy from one country to another, and were often not comparable as between them. Each national program actually had to include a pattern of policy, tentative decisions on major

[29] *The Economist*, CLV, July 31, 1948, 175.

issues, and an estimate of what could be achieved in the years
to come. Even the Socialist planners of Great Britain cautioned
that "a long-term plan can be no more and no less than a statement of economic strategy. It will not attempt to be a complete
and rigid set of instructions for several years ahead." [30]

When it received the national plans, the OEEC studied them,
analyzed questions, and discussed issues at length with the national delegations. Naturally enough, the OEEC reported that
"comparison of the several national programmes has shown
that, taken together, they do not solve the problems of Western
Europe." [31] To fit the divergent plans together would be a long
and complicated job. As a start, OEEC published an *Interim
Report* which totaled the national estimates of production and
trade, questioned some of them, pointed out discrepancies, and
outlined some of the problems which OEEC would have to
tackle in the future if European recovery was to be cooperative,
harmonious and effective. "It should be stressed that this report
is not a joint European recovery programme," said the OEEC;
it was, however, the biggest step the European countries had
taken in concert to determine the real nature of their problems
and to suggest how they could find a cooperative solution—or
the impossibility of one.

The main assumptions of the *Interim Report*, as of the national plans, were: peace, a high level of employment throughout the world and especially in the United States, a high level
of world trade, control of inflation, continued cooperation,
planned governmental attacks on major economic problems and
continued aid from the United States. On this basis, the participating countries looked for an increase of about 25 percent
in their industrial production by 1952,[32] which would place
them about 30 percent above the prewar level. Especially large
advances were expected in the refining of crude oil, electricity

[30] Long-term Programme of the United Kingdom, OEEC, *Interim Report on the
European Recovery Programme* (Paris, 1949), II, 890.
[31] *Ibid.*, I, 12.
[32] Most of these figures exclude Switzerland, which reported that it "cannot
draw up a Long Term Programme properly so called because the motive force
of its economy lies in private enterprise" (*Ibid.*, I, 172).

production, and the output of aluminum, nitrogenous fertilizers, potash, phosphates and commercial motor cars. By the end of the program, coal output was to be 11 percent higher than in 1935–38, and finished steel 40 percent (or, if western Germany is omitted, 71 percent). Agricultural production by 1952 was to be about 15 percent above prewar, which would require increases of from 25 to 40 percent over the good harvests of 1948–49. An important part of this program rested on France's expectation of increasing its farm output to 25 percent above the prewar level, which would permit substantial exports of wheat and meat to other European countries.

To achieve these high levels of production, the OEEC estimated that the productivity of European labor would have to rise more than 15 percent during the four years of the program. "This is a bold assumption. Yet no other assumption is more important . . . Whether it can be fully effected . . . is, however, doubtful, and therefore no effort should be spared to secure as great an increase as possible." [33] Also necessary would be substantial investment to increase the capacity to produce. The national plans called for a high level of investment but the OEEC felt that "the total claims of investment on national resources greatly exceed, in most countries, the resources which are at all likely to be available." [34] Hence it was important that the best possible use be made of whatever investment could be achieved, and the OEEC set as a major task reconsideration of the investment programs and examination of the possibilities of coordinating them with each other to prevent redundancy. The uncertainties in the program made it hard to judge what levels of consumption Europe was likely to attain by 1952. Full achievement of the national programs would bring consumption per head up to the 1938 level, but the OEEC thought it would be more realistic to expect a level 10 to 15 percent lower than that. There would be considerable variations from one country to another, of course, and in the amounts of different products to be consumed compared with prewar.

[33] *Ibid.*, I, 45.
[34] *Ibid.*, I, 96.

When added together the national programs of imports and exports showed that western Europe in 1952 would still have a deficit of $800 million in its balance of payments with the rest of the world. The OEEC thought these calculations a good bit too optimistic and judged it more likely that the deficit would run to $3 billion. Even this would require a very large expansion of exports, including such feats as taking away from the United States half of its current Latin American market. Some students found even OEEC's calculations overoptimistic, pointing, for example, to the very large exports of machinery and metal products for which western Europe would have to find customers. Like OEEC, they were pessimistic about expanding European sales to the United States. Others felt that OEEC had perhaps made things look worse than they were by instructing the participating countries to make their calculations on the basis of prices and exchange rates prevailing in mid-1948; these people thought it likely that the prices Europe paid for its imports might well fall faster than the prices it got for its exports, and they put considerable reliance on what exchange devaluation would do to help sell Europe's goods. According to OEEC calculations, even "drastic changes in present policies" aimed at making European exports more competitive in world markets—a diplomatic way of talking about devaluation of currencies—would not fill the gap. Still, there was growing pressure to tackle this problem and the indications were that OEEC would try it in 1949.

The *Interim Report* covered many other matters, including the possibility of expanding intra-European trade and possible measures of cooperation to speed recovery. Whether the OEEC was going to be able to turn the separate national programs into a coherent long-term plan for the group as a whole seemed problematical. It was faced with many difficulties. For instance, British recovery—which progressed very well during the year—was premised on a continued austerity program that would virtually wipe out the United Kingdom's import surplus from the continent. The French and Belgians objected strongly, pointing out that their export programs assumed the sale of at least some luxury goods to England and that in prewar days Britain's excess of imports in trade with the continent was an important source of exchange for that area. Whether there was to be a long-term plan or not, without doubt the *Interim Report* played an important role in stimulating more careful and realistic study of the problems of recovery. It dispelled some illusions, and began to make many Americans wonder whether 1952 would really see the end of emergency aid. As one eminent economist said, the report's conclusion on the probable deficit in the European balance of payments "will come as a shock to the American people, who have been assured that the Marshall Plan is a program of aid to end aid. It should also shake whatever complacency there may have been in Europe." [35]

While it was preparing the long-term program, OEEC also had to work on the plan for the second year of its activities, 1949–50. Heavily burdened as they were with other OEEC work, most governments submitted their programs late. Not knowing how much American aid would be available and hesitating to make precise forecasts for a year that would not begin for another six months, OEEC did not try to put these all together into a coherent whole. Instead it passed along the national programs to the ECA in December 1948 with a number of comments on them, pointing to the areas in which more work would have to be done. When asking for their national plans OEEC called the attention of the participating governments to the fact that since less American aid would probably be available, most countries would have to get along with fewer ECA dollars in 1948–49. Similarly there would be less indirect aid available under an intra-European payments agreement. Ten countries and the French zone of Germany, however, asked for more aid than they had received in 1948–49. The national requests added up to $4,690.1 million, just $66.1 million less than the previous year. In an "illustrative program" prepared for Con-

[35] John H. Williams, "Europe After 1952," *Foreign Affairs*, XXVII, April 1949, 428.

gress, ECA reduced this total to $4,202 million. It cut every national request except the British.[36]

Outside the OEEC, governments were cooperating in a variety of ways to achieve immediate or long-run recovery goals, but there, too, they ran into difficulties. The Benelux customs union, which had been launched by the Belgian and Dutch governments in exile in wartime London, came into effect on January 1, 1948. Elimination of tariffs between the partners was not followed by great material changes, since quotas and exchange controls continued to regulate trade. Plans called for a fuller economic union, but there were fundamental difficulties in bringing the two economies into harmony. Belgium had rapidly removed most wartime controls; its prices and wages were high, and large quantities of consumers' goods were available. Holland had continued rationing, price controls and food subsidies, and held down imports. In each country some agricultural or industrial producers worried about the effect on their business of free competition from their rivals in the other country. Conversations continued and plans were made to approach amalgamation gradually.

At the original CEEC conference in Paris, France and Italy announced their intention of forming a customs union. At the end of 1947 a joint commission issued a report examining the relations of the two economies in all major fields. Though there were many sectors in which Italian and French production was competitive, the commission stressed the advantages of a customs union in providing for combined action in exporting and importing. Industrial agreements could prevent undesirable competition between the partners. The commission emphasized that a customs union alone would not yield the hoped-for benefits; it would have to be the first step toward a full economic union. In March 1948, Bidault and Sforza signed a protocol at Turin in which both countries expressed their desire to

---

[36] The cuts ranged from 90 percent in the case of Portugal to less than 1 percent for Denmark. Greece, Iceland, Norway, Portugal, Sweden and the French zone of Germany were left with larger allocations than the year before. Italy and Denmark were to get within a few hundred thousand dollars of their previous allocations.

form such a union and set up another commission to draft a plan of action. On March 26, 1949, a customs union agreement was signed in Paris. If both legislatures approved it, a joint council would be set up to bring about removal of customs duties between the two countries and adoption of a common tariff by the end of one year. In the second year the council was to elaborate a program for a full economic union to be achieved, it was hoped, over a period of six years.

The Scandinavian countries held a number of conferences at which various measures of economic cooperation were discussed. Their committee on a customs union—like the all-European committee set up at Paris—moved slowly, preparing technical groundwork. Countries interested in manpower problems continued discussions through the organization set up in Rome and through the International Labor Organization. While technical work progressed, obstacles grew to the use of immigrant Italian labor as France greatly reduced the number it planned to take and as unemployment emerged in Belgium. Meanwhile the work of the Economic Commission for Europe in Geneva helped improve Europe's production and use of timber, coke, steel and silica bricks. The Commission continued to bring together countries in and out of the OEEC to deal with problems of mutual concern, and moved ahead with its interesting research work that had already greatly influenced thinking about recovery problems.

There were no readily acceptable yardsticks for measuring the pace of European cooperation. Progress was certainly slow compared with the high expectations of many people—especially Americans—formed in the months after Secretary Marshall's Harvard speech. But that was only to be expected once the difficulties were looked at clearly and objectively. Compared with the experience of prewar days, the work being done by the OEEC was a substantial advance in cooperation. The question was whether the new organization could gather momentum once the initial push had worn itself out. In the spring of 1949, OEEC, largely in response to American pressure, set up a steering committee of cabinet ministers from eight countries [37] with the aim of strengthening the organization's position. (It had been said that the national delegations at Paris were not on a high enough political level to carry adequate weight at home.) At its first session the committee worked out a program of action for 1949 which was subsequently adopted by the full Council of the OEEC. It centered on stabilization of currencies and the coordination of some aspects of the national plans—which was enough to show that the most difficult jobs were still ahead.

3. Western Germany in the Marshall Plan

Motives of self-interest dictated the decision to include western Germany in the European Recovery Program. The 16 countries represented in the OEEC included nine which had suffered Nazi occupation. Various others had incurred heavy losses in the war which the Germans had forced upon them or had preserved a precarious neutrality. All had reason to fear the rebuilding of German industrial power, yet all recognized that their own economic recovery was dependent on Germany's recovery. Faced with universal shortages, Europe's factories needed Germany's coal, steel and iron, chemicals and heavy equipment; storekeepers wanted to fill empty shelves with German cameras, chinaware and leather goods; workmen and their wives and children needed German shoes and textiles.

From motives of self-interest, the United States also was not averse to seeing western Germany included among the participants in the Marshall plan. We were about to invest billions in a plan for European recovery; the inclusion of Germany increased the chances of success of that plan, in fact seemed vital to its success. This interest in German recovery was supplementary to the more direct interest in reducing the burden of spending hundreds of millions each year in keeping our former enemies alive. So long as the occupation of Germany lasted, the only way to remove this millstone from the necks of American taxpayers was to revive bizonal industrial produc-

[37] Britain, France, Belgium, the Netherlands, Italy, Switzerland, Sweden and Turkey.

tion so that exports of manufactures could pay for essential imports of food and raw materials. Such a revival of German production could be made to serve not only Germany itself but other European countries as well, for Germany remained, despite the destruction of the war, the industrial heart of Europe.

Acceptance of western Germany as a participant in the Marshall plan proved an easier decision than the determination of that area's share in the $5 billion which Congress appropriated for European aid for 1948–49. The bizonal military authorities, represented principally by General Clay, had set their sights on making the area for which they were responsible self-sustaining. They wanted as large a share as they could get. OEEC officials, on the other hand, had their attention fixed primarily on European recovery, to which they regarded German recovery as only subsidiary. They regarded Germany as a necessary, but in no sense as a privileged, partner. In this conflict of views Hoffman and ECA took on the role of mediator.

In the estimates submitted to Congress by the Department of State as the basis of its appropriation for the 1948–49 recovery program, a figure of $437 million was included to cover the needs of the bizonal area.[38] Congress, however, appropriated a global sum; it did not attempt to allocate the shares of western Germany or of the other recipient countries. That difficult task was eventually assigned by ECA to the Council of OEEC.

Responding to the Council's request to each of the participating countries for detailed information concerning their probable dollar requirements and resources, Generals Clay and Robertson, representing Bizonia, asked for $450 million of direct aid, plus $102 million of net drawing rights in European currencies.[39] Taken together, this meant that Bizonia's claim on the total $5 billion of dollar aid would amount to about

[38] This sum was in addition to the sum of approximately $700 million requested by the U.S. Military Government for the relief of the German civilian population. In addition, $100 million was suggested as necessary to cover the dollar deficit of the French zone. This figure seems not to have been seriously questioned in the ensuing discussion.

[39] Bizonal officials estimated that in trade with OEEC countries the Bizone's exports would be $263 million and imports $365 million.

$550 million, or more than 10 percent of the total. The claim was buttressed by statistical analyses prepared by German experts attached to the Bizonal Economic Council.

When the experts of OEEC added up the requests of all of the claimants for dollar aid, they found that the total was greatly in excess of the amount appropriated by Congress. Obviously, an all-round paring down of estimates was necessary. In this process the bizonal allotment was reduced to $367 million of direct dollar aid. Furthermore, instead of acquiring drawing rights of $102 million (net) on other participating countries, Bizonia was to be required to put $90 million (net) of its goods at the disposal of the other countries. In other words, OEEC's allotment practically cut in half the sum requested by the American and British Military Governments. This action was so strongly protested, particularly by the representatives of the American Military Government, that a deadlock ensued which for a fortnight during the late summer of 1948 brought the operations of OEEC to a standstill. Since the global amount was fixed, no increase could be made in the bizonal allotment without decreasing those of other claimants. And none of them was willing to forego dollars on which it was counting in order to aid German recovery.

The stubborn refusal of General Clay to accept the OEEC allotment put Hoffman in an embarrassing position. He had told the Europeans that they should decide how the cake should be cut, and western Germany was not excepted from this rule. But now another American official was defying an OEEC decision. The dispute highlighted the anomalous position of western Germany. Although technically it was a participant in the European Recovery Program on the same basis as Britain, France, Italy and the other countries, actually it was a special case. The three zones did not constitute a "country," their claims for dollar aid were presented not by defeated Germans but by their military governors. Since the dominant power in the trizonal economy was the American Military Government, the United States was involved in a dual capacity, as donor of dollar aid and as one of the recipients.

General Clay took the position that no foreign organization could assume the right to apportion American dollars to an agency of the U.S. Government. On the other hand, the OEEC assumed that the $5 billion granted by Congress was already its property, over which its control was final. The outcome, as might have been expected, was a compromise. OEEC raised its allocation of direct aid by $47 million (from $367 to $414 million) and in addition cut down the requirement of net German credits to be granted to other countries from $90 to $10.2 million. This action, of course, required downward adjustment in other allotments, particularly those of France, Italy and the Netherlands. Commenting on this situation, the London *Economist* charged that the ECA administrator in Europe, W. Averell Harriman, had intervened on the side of the American Military Government, compelling OEEC to raise the allotment to Germany, and implied that this action weakened the organization by depriving it of responsibility.[40] Robert Marjolin, the Secretary-General of OEEC, denied this charge with the statement that "at no time did the Americans try to exert pressure on us." [41]

The incident brought into bold relief the fear, expressed both in the United States and in Europe, that American Military Government was concerned primarily with bringing about a maximum recovery in western German in a minimum of time and was only incidentally concerned with Germany's contribution to European recovery. Clay had already aroused considerable resentment among western European nations by his insistence that Bizonia's foreign trade be on a dollar basis and that oversea shipments be routed through Hamburg and Bremen instead of through such ports as Rotterdam and Antwerp, whose prosperity depended on transit trade.

While the debate over funds was proceeding in Paris, the economic situation in western Germany had undergone a spectacular transformation. After two years of stagnation, production of coal, steel and other basic commodites showed rapid

[40] *The Economist,* CLV, September 11, 1948, 407.
[41] *New York Times,* September 12, 1948.

increases, and business of all kinds suddenly revived. Literally overnight, supplies of consumers' goods which had not been seen for years, furniture, household articles, electric appliances, bicycles, radios, reappeared in show windows. In restaurants the bills of fare featured eggs, real coffee, fruits and vegetables. Many factors contributed to what seemed a miracle. A gradual improvement had been under way for several months. The knowledge that Marshall plan aid would soon be available revived business confidence. The American military authorities had taken the risk of spending a large sum to bring in crucial raw materials in the spring of 1948. The immediate and most important factor, however, was the long-awaited currency reform.

An overhauling of the German currency and financial structure, which in the western zones had been left virtually intact under the original military government directives and the Potsdam agreement, had been under consideration in the Allied Control Council for over a year, during which the Soviet representatives had raised numerous objections to American proposals for replacing the existing Reichsmark with a new currency, enacting a capital levy and scaling down the German national debt. Inflationary conditions in the west had meanwhile reached a point where they were a major obstacle to economic recovery. Shortages of essential goods, uneven price controls and the freezing of wages at prewar levels had given the abundant Reichsmark currency a purely fictitious value, encouraged black-market and barter trading at the expense of normal trade, and promoted the diversion of resources into nonessential production, thus frustrating efforts to create a sound economy in the western zones.

In the absence of four-power agreement, a currency reform for the three western zones was officially promulgated by the western military governors on June 18, 1948. The conversion operation was regulated by three laws issued during the following week. The first provided for the surrender of the old Reichsmark currency and a preliminary issue of 60 new "Deutsche Marks" to each member of the population on a one-for-one

basis. The second defined the conditions for issuance of up to
10 billion Deutsche Marks by the Bank of German States, which
was given authority to fix the minimum reserves of financial
institutions. The third law established a general conversion
rate of 1 Deutsche Mark for 10 Reichsmarks, applicable both
to currency holdings and to most debts and contractual obligations, and at the same time temporarily blocked one-half of the
new Deutsche Mark accounts. Debts of financial institutions in
the western zones were dissolved; debts of the Reich and Reich
agencies were left to be settled under an equalization of burdens
law to be drafted by German authorities.[42]

Results of the currency reform exceeded the most optimistic
expectations. The drastic conversion restored normal economic
incentives for the first time since the occupation and greatly
stimulated activity in all fields. Supplementary measures which
tended to reinforce the economic revival were substantial tax
reductions and the lifting of the majority of price controls.
Assuming that increased production plus the arrival of Marshall
plan goods would soon do away with shortages, the military
governments moved rapidly toward reestablishing something
like a free economy. A general revival of the morale of the
German population accompanied the economic revival. One
correspondent wrote: "For the first time since the end of the
war the Western Germans view approaching winter without
dread and despair." [43]

So rapid was the pace of recovery that at the end of September 1948 production in the bizonal area had already reached
some of the goals set in the European Recovery Program for
June 1949. The general index of industrial production in
November reached 75 percent of the 1936 level; the December
figure was 78, three points above the June 1949 target. For
production of hard coal, a key commodity in the German econ-

[42] The currency reform was not originally applied in the western sectors of
Berlin, which were still considered to be under four-power rule. The sharp
reaction of the Soviets in immediately proclaiming their own currency conversion
for the eastern zone and all of Berlin led the western powers to introduce the
Deutsche Mark in their sectors of the former capital on June 23 (see above,
p. 138).

[43] Edwin Hartrich, in the *New York Herald Tribune*, September 6, 1948.

omy, the target goal for 1948–49 was set at 83 million tons, equivalent to a monthly average of somewhat less than 7 million tons. Actual production in the six months from April to September 1948 averaged 7.2 million tons. The export goal for the bizonal area for 1948–49 was set at $666 million, or a monthly average of $55 million. During the first six months of the program, April to September 1948, exports reached $397 million, or a rate of $66 million per month.

How long revived activity could be maintained at the new level was a matter of some doubt. The economic outlook in the early months of 1949 was not altogether favorable. The rising curve seemed to be leveling off. The failure of wages to keep pace with the rising cost of living caused labor and consumer unrest, and fears were expressed for the stability of the new currency. The additional capital sorely needed for both short-term and long-term investment was not available from foreign sources, and private savings were entirely inadequate. The new Deutsche Mark was quoted in foreign markets, particularly in Switzerland, at a heavy discount. Moreover, with the rapid expansion of certain lines of production, bottlenecks appeared. With the demand for electric power at the capacity of existing equipment, for example, many months were required for the installation of new boilers, engines and generators.

The success of the Marshall plan for western Germany was predicated on a vast expansion of exports. Yet the ability of German manufacturers to keep their costs low enough to compete in foreign markets was open to question. The official 30-cent foreign exchange value of the new Deutsche Mark [44] appeared to be an overvaluation which would handicap sales abroad. Export industries had to reckon also with the inefficiency of labor resulting from undernourishment, bad housing and the decline of morale. In coal mining the daily output per worker at the end of 1948 was 39 percent less than in 1936. In

[44] At the time of the currency reform the military governments decided to establish a uniform conversion for imports and exports from the bizonal area at the rate of 30 cents to one mark, with certain temporary exceptions. This restored to some extent a relationship between internal German prices and world prices.

general, according to an official estimate in the summer of 1948, 15 or 20 workers were required to produce what 10 had turned out in prewar years.

German businessmen found it difficult to raise funds for working capital and for equipment. They were troubled by continued uncertainty regarding the denazification, decartelization and dismantling programs. Optimism generated by the success of the currency reform was tempered by these factors and many others, not the least of which was the question of the future of Germany and of the political status of the western zones.

4. The Marshall Plan Splits World Labor

Increased production is the heart of the European Recovery Program. It was recognized from the start that the participating countries would have to attain levels of production well above those prevailing before the war or give up all hope of achieving a balance of payments with America. The ambitious plans made by governments, however, could not be realized without great efforts and full cooperation on the part of organized labor. Two questions were of special importance in assessing the role of labor in the recovery program. One was that of Communist influence in the labor movements of various countries as a factor which could slow down and possibly defeat the recovery effort; France and Italy had become a testing ground even before the Marshall plan became a reality. The second question concerned the role of international labor organizations and their support of, or opposition to, the recovery program.

The largest such organization was the World Federation of Trade Unions (WFTU), founded in 1945 on the initiative of the Soviet All-Union Congress of Trade Unions, the British Trades Union Congress (TUC), and the American Congress of Industrial Organizations (CIO). It grew out of the wartime spirit of the unity of workers in all three countries in the common struggle against the Axis powers. More specifically, it grew out of the desire of the Soviet Government to play a leading role, through its unions, in world labor, and the desire of the leaders of the TUC and CIO to take part in a new and more active world organization than the prewar International Federation of Trade Unions (IFTU), to which neither the Soviet unions nor the CIO belonged. All were willing, for the moment, to overlook the fundamental differences between the government-controlled unions of the U.S.S.R., the free, non-revolutionary unions of Britain and the United States, and the essentially revolutionary Communist-led unions in various countries outside the U.S.S.R.

The new organization proposed to speak out on behalf of labor on world affairs and to exercise a much greater influence than the old IFTU. Nominally representing some 70 million workers, it sought recognition as the authoritative voice of world labor. American labor was not unanimous in according it such a voice. Although the CIO joined, the American Federation of Labor (AFL) and the Railway Brotherhoods remained aloof. The AFL undertook an active opposition to the WFTU on the grounds that the Soviet trade unions were not free unions at all but instruments of the Soviet Government and that the latter was in a position to dominate any world labor organization in which the Soviet and other Communist unions were represented.

The most important factor in determining the course taken by the WFTU was, indeed, the attitude of the Soviet Government. The Soviet unions, representing some 30 million workers, with the support of the recently inflated unions of the satellite states and some colonial countries and the Communist-led federations in France, Italy and Latin America, were in a position to dominate the WFTU. Should they attempt to do so, the chances were that the British, American and other unions from western democratic states would abandon it, a result which the Soviets did not wish to see since then the WFTU could no longer serve them as a channel of influence into the labor movements of those states. At the beginning they took a moderate attitude. In the procedural arrangements they did not claim votes in proportion to their membership. The presidency of the WFTU was given to a British labor leader, Arthur Deakin, while a Frenchman, Louis Saillant, became secretary-general.

During the immediate postwar years, while a semblance of unity was maintained among the great powers on the governmental level, there was no real threat to the unity of labor as expressed in the WFTU, although the AFL remained hostile to it. The British and American unions, however, did not like the WFTU's emphasis on political matters. They believed that more attention should be given to practical union problems than to such things as pronouncements against "fascist" practices in Argentina and Greece. The real test came with the Marshall plan in 1947. The Soviet leadership wished to use the WFTU in its concerted campaign to sabotage and defeat recovery in western Europe. This was an out-and-out challenge to the British and American unions, for the TUC was at one with the Labor government in regarding the Marshall plan as Britain's salvation, and the CIO had endorsed it without qualification.

In November 1947 the Soviet trade union leadership declared its support of the decision of Europe's chief Communist parties, organized in the Cominform, to fight against "imperialist aggression." Labor federations in the satellite states passed resolutions denouncing the United States for intimidating and trying to enslave other peoples, abetting reaction, waging war on the working class, and striving for world hegemony. Louis Saillant, the pro-Communist secretary-general of the WFTU, used his official position and the organization's publications as means of spreading the same propaganda. He also refused to call a meeting of the WFTU to discuss labor's role in the Marshall plan, as the British and American unions had requested. The Soviet leadership, foreseeing the breakup of the organization if such a meeting were held, naturally wished to avoid it. Arthur Deakin, British labor leader who was president of the WFTU, denounced Saillant in strong terms for yielding to Soviet pressure. "If," he said, "the position now is that the

WFTU is to be merely a political body dealing with those questions acceptable to the U.S.S.R., we know where we stand." [45]

The TUC then came forward with plans for a separate conference of the labor unions of Marshall plan countries, to which the CIO and AFL would also be invited. At this juncture, in February 1948, James Carey of the CIO undertook a trip to Moscow to explain his organization's attitude and to ask the Russians to lay their cards on the table. The CIO leadership did not favor withdrawal from the WFTU. Its idea was that the organization served as an avenue by which the views of American labor could be carried to workingmen all over the world, to people who would never be reached by government agencies or by official propaganda. Yet this approach could hardly make headway where unions were dominated by Communists, whose conception of the interests of world labor was always that of the party line laid down by Moscow. Carey talked plainly with V. V. Kuznetsov, chief of the Soviet trade unions. Saying that the original community of spirit that had brought the WFTU affiliates together had been dissipated, he made it clear that American labor did not regard the Marshall plan as an attempt of American capitalists to enslave Europe. While the CIO hoped that the WFTU would hold together, it believed that the issue of the Marshall plan must be faced. If compelled to choose between its support of ERP and its ties to the WFTU, the CIO would choose the former. In dealing with the Russians the CIO had considerable bargaining power since its withdrawal would puncture the claim that Soviet policy and the WFTU had the support of the toiling masses everywhere.

The British unions, determined to have a conference to discuss the Marshall plan inside or outside the WFTU, went ahead with a meeting in London on March 9. In its makeup this conference was representative of non-Communist labor in western Europe and the United States. Unions of the Benelux countries shared in sponsoring it. The powerful Communist-led general confederations of labor in France and Italy remained aloof, but Léon Jouhaux' Force Ouvrière, the French anti-Communist trade union federation, and independent Italian unions sent representatives. The main labor organizations of Scandinavia, Switzerland, Eire, Austria, and western Germany took part. From America came delegates from both the CIO and the AFL. The conference had no real disagreements. It welcomed American aid to Europe, confirmed that no unacceptable conditions were attached to such aid and called on the workers of all participating countries to cooperate in support of ERP. Without engaging in anti-Communist polemics, by setting up a permanent advisory committee it laid the basis for what might become a new international organization of non-Communist unions. These unions, as it appeared even more clearly after their second meeting in July, were prepared to work with their governments to make the Marshall plan a success, while the Soviet and other Communist-dominated unions were doing what they could to ensure its failure. In that situation the WFTU was in fact split even though the non-Communist unions did not withdraw and were not ready, at this stage, to form the new international favored by the AFL. The latter already had a permanent mission in Europe and was giving advice and financial support to non-Communist labor organizations, especially to *Force Ouvrière.*

When the WFTU executive bureau finally met in Rome at the end of April, Carey indicated that the CIO would withdraw unless it were given assurance that the organization would no longer be used as an instrument and mouthpiece of Communist policy. He was no longer insisting that the WFTU discuss the European Recovery Program. "The Marshall plan is a fact and will go ahead despite all opposition," Carey told the press. "Organized labor has already created machinery to give it its full support." [46] The removal of this issue made a compromise possible. The Russians and their supporters accepted a number of demands put forward by Carey, with the support of the British and other delegates, aimed at curbing the political activities and pronouncements of WFTU officials like Saillant and ensuring consultation on policy matters with the

[46] *New York Times,* May 5, 1948.

various affiliated national organizations. Communist delegates succeeded, on the other hand, in postponing a decision on the admission of *Force Ouvrière.*

These uneasy compromises made it possible for the WFTU to continue in existence without defections. They left unresolved the deep-seated differences between Communist and non-Communist unions which made the unity of world labor a fiction. The question before western labor leaders was whether there was anything to be gained by maintaining that fiction. Philip Murray and the CIO leadership still felt that there was, that free unions could by active participation strengthen democratic tendencies within the world organization. The AFL maintained that in taking this course the CIO was doing a disservice to the cause of democracy and free trade unionism the world over. Carey had boasted that he would teach the Communists a lesson, wrote Matthew Woll, AFL vice-president, but at Rome he had surrendered completely and ignominiously. Carey replied that the CIO had chosen to carry on the fight with reactionary totalitarianism in the arena, not from an ivory tower; it would "continue to run interference for the free trade unionists of Europe . . . against Communists and all other forces of reaction," including, presumably, the AFL leadership.[47]

Subsequent developments seemed to bear out the AFL's view that the WFTU was dominated by Moscow and that democratic unions could accomplish nothing by remaining in it. In September the WFTU was scathingly indicted by its own president, Arthur Deakin, who told the British Trades Union Congress that the Communists had captured the organization and were using it as an agency to carry out Cominform policies and a platform for advancing Soviet propaganda. The congress then overwhelmingly defeated a resolution expressing support of the WFTU. So far as its influence outside the Soviet sphere and outside Communist-dominated unions was concerned, the WFTU was already dead.

[47] "The CIO Role in the WFTU," *The New Leader,* July 3, 24, 1948, an article by Matthew Woll and reply by James Carey.

Regardless of the CIO-AFL disputes on domestic labor issues and on the WFTU issue, the two organizations were united in support of the Marshall plan. Their attitude was of the greatest value to the Administration, as there could be no better advertisement to European workers that the recovery program was no capitalist plot. The success of the program depended, in the final analysis, on the support of those workers and on their rejection of Communist attempts to defeat it. Both ECA and OEEC took this factor into account in associating labor representatives with their work.

As the program developed, labor's role was likely to become greater. In an address which Philip Murray said would ring around the world, Supreme Court Justice William O. Douglas told a CIO convention in November 1948 that the new times had brought challenges which should make labor an active participant in international affairs. It could help Europe to understand that the real struggle for peace and prosperity was not class warfare but the struggle to make the modern industrial plant operate productively for the benefit of all; and it could help America to understand that Europe under the political management of Socialist and labor parties "is not a continent turning communist but a people struggling for things that are precious to men everywhere . . . the rights of man, his liberty, his dignity, his security . . ." [48] Unless the competition of the Communists could be successfully met on the labor front, Douglas concluded, it was difficult to see how the United States and the governments associated together in the European Recovery Program would be able to "contain" communism on the diplomatic or any other front.

The disruption of the WFTU, which finally occurred at the Paris meeting of its executive bureau in January 1949, indicated a clear perception of the Communist issue by the TUC and CIO leadership. Nevertheless, it did not come in a manner which allowed the pro-Marshall plan groups to claim all the advantages. In a prearranged move to force the issue to a head, the British demanded that the WFTU suspend its activities for

[48] *New York Times,* November 25, 1948.

one year in view of the absence of any basis for agreement on a majority of the questions before the organization. This motion was supported by Carey of the CIO and Evert Kupers, chairman of the Dutch Federation of Labor. The Soviet, French, Italian and Chinese delegates refused on constitutional grounds to entertain either this motion or a subsequent Anglo-American proposal that the WFTU be dissolved outright. Deakin, Carey and Kupers thereupon formally withdrew.

The Executive Committee of the WFTU General Council convened in Paris at the end of January to condemn the secessionists. It proclaimed that the WFTU was still in business, accepted the membership of labor federations in seven additional non-European countries, scheduled a new World Trade Union Congress for the summer of 1949, and confirmed the selection of Giuseppe di Vittorio, Communist secretary-general of the Italian General Confederation of Labor, as acting WFTU president to replace Deakin. Soviet and Communist spokesmen denounced the "splitters" as conscienceless puppets of Anglo-American capitalism, and admitted that their treacherous action would temporarily lessen the WFTU's effectiveness. But they loudly insisted that there would be no relaxation of the effort to strengthen a movement on which the hopes of the world's laboring masses were focused.[49]

As against the three national labor organizations that had withdrawn—including, to be sure, the TUC and the CIO, the two most powerful bodies outside the Soviet trade unions, accounting for nearly one-fourth of the affiliated WFTU membership—over 60 remained within the WFTU, whose left-wing leaders now made effective propaganda use of the role of injured innocents. The main French and Italian labor confederations (excluding the *Force Ouvrière* and a new anti-Communist Italian federation headed by Giulio Pastore) remained inside the WFTU. So, for the time being at least, did those of the Scandinavian and most of the other OEEC countries. Even

[49] See especially *New Times*, No. 5, January 26, 1949, 3-5 and supplement; February 23, 1949, 3-7.

within the TUC and the CIO some left-wing voices were raised in criticism of the disruptive action of the parent bodies.

The TUC-CIO plan of withdrawal from the WFTU had envisaged the possibility of setting up a new non-Communist world labor federation, urged by the AFL for at least a year. It speedily appeared, however, that those who had split the WFTU had nothing ready to replace it. A meeting at Bern of the ERP Trade Union Advisory Committee served to throw into relief rivalries and jealousies between AFL and CIO, and between AFL and TUC, which appeared likely to delay action along this line for months. Meanwhile there was no body which could compete with the WFTU for the allegiance of the important western European unions remaining within that now frankly Communist-dominated organization. Unless the Anglo-American groups could speedily compose their differences and initiate a concrete and well-conceived program, the battle for labor's allegiance to the European Recovery Program was still far from won.

5. East-West Trade

While the nations of western Europe were slowly mastering the techniques of economic cooperation under the guidance of the OEEC and the ECA, a parallel movement, inspired by different principles but similar in many of its effects, was taking place in the belt of Communist-dominated eastern European states whose dependence on the U.S.S.R. had barred them from participation in the European Recovery Program. The political homogeneity of these new "countries of people's democracy," their governments' adherence to a common ideology and unwavering loyalty to the Kremlin—with the exception of Finland and, in 1948, Yugoslavia—favored a uniformity of economic plans and policies which increasingly took on the appearance of a coordinated movement toward goals already fixed in Moscow.

Postwar economic planning in eastern Europe rested on the assumption of maximum cooperation of each satellite country with the U.S.S.R. and with its sister satellites. Only such cooperation, Communist writers insisted, could guarantee to each of these "complementary" economies the necessary raw materials and machinery and assure "a steady tempo of socialist production." In contrast, the Marshall plan was pictured as impoverishing the nations of western Europe and enslaving them to American capital.[50] Up to the beginning of 1949 intra-Orbit economic cooperation was carried on principally through the medium of bilateral treaties and agreements between the U.S.S.R. and the individual satellites and between different pairs of satellite governments. Such agreements occasionally contemplated a measure of joint economic planning, as with the Polish-Czechoslovak plans for development of the Katowice-Moravska Ostrava industrial area, but were normally concerned mainly with commercial and financial matters. Ordinarily they set the total value of projected trade exchanges between the signatories over a definite period, in most cases specifying fixed quotas of commodities to be supplied by each party.

The prime requirement of all of the satellites was for the capital goods, particularly such items as machinery and electrical equipment, called for by their economic development plans. These neither the Soviet Union nor the satellites themselves could supply in anything like the desired quantities, while the prospect of obtaining them from other sources was increasingly limited by the discontinuance of American credits, the tightening of American export controls, and the increasingly rigid east-west alignment in Europe. Eastern European economic planners thus found the realization of their projects chronically threatened and their ingenuity perpetually challenged by the lack of essential items which were virtually impossible to procure under prevailing political conditions.

An obvious solution lay in intensifying the trading relationships between eastern and western Europe. From an economic standpoint, a revival of such trade was in the interest of both east and west. To a large degree the achievement of the goals

[50] J. Goldman, "Problems of Planning in New Democracies," *For a Lasting Peace, For a People's Democracy!*, February 1, 1949.

set by both sides depended on it. The machinery, steel and other industrial products required to industrialize and mechanize the eastern economies could be obtained more readily in western Europe than anywhere else outside the United States itself. The west, in turn, was badly in need of certain critical items—especially coal, timber and timber products, grains, and potash (from eastern Germany)—which eastern Europe could supply and which otherwise would have to be obtained, if at all, largely from the dollar area. Importation of such materials from eastern Europe was, indeed, one of the basic assumptions of ERP.

Although east-west trade during 1947 and 1948 showed a tendency toward steady recovery from the stagnation into which it had fallen at the end of the war, it remained well below prewar levels. During 1948 both eastern and western European countries continued with some success their efforts to negotiate advantageous bilateral trade agreements, linked in some instances with settlements of western claims to compensation for properties nationalized in the east and other finanical questions. Conspicuous in this regard were two agreements concluded by the United Kingdom: a one-year trade agreement with Yugoslavia, signed December 23, 1948, and providing for an exchange of commodities in the amount of £30 million, and a long-term trade and financial agreement with Poland, signed on January 14, 1949 and providing for a total trade of £260 million over a five-year period. A further stimulus to east-west trade was provided in ECA's authorization for purchase in dollars, where other means of payment were lacking, of Polish coal, Yugoslav nonferrous metals, and eastern German potash for use by western countries.[51] Favorable results were also expected from a "timber program" developed by the Economic Commission for Europe (ECE) under which the western countries and the International Bank would extend loans to Czechoslovakia, Finland and Yugoslavia for the procurement of timber equipment to increase the latter countries' productivity.

[51] Economic Cooperation Administration, *A Report on Recovery Progress and United States Aid*, 220.

Despite these favorable auguries the status of east-west commercial relations remained unsatisfactory to both sides. Gunnar Myrdal, executive secretary of the ECE, stated on February 7, 1949 that intra-European trade in 1948 had reached only two-thirds of its 1938 volume and called this deficiency, due in large measure to trade restrictions arising from currency difficulties and to the greatly diminished role of Germany, the principal obstacle to economic recovery in Europe.[52] Much of the most fruitful work of ECE, the one technical economic body in which east and west continued to cooperate, was concerned with efforts to discover and circumvent obstacles to expanded east-west exchanges. Agreement to establish a committee for this purpose was reached in October 1948, and an international conference was held at Geneva in February 1949 to explore the possibilities of increasing multilateral trade within Europe. It commissioned ECE to prepare a list of commodities in short supply in Europe for presentation to a second east-west conference in May; at this second conference the eastern countries were to be asked specifically what western credits and other assistance would be required to increase their production of food and raw materials to meet western needs.

A restraining factor in the expansion of east-west trade was the American policy designed to prevent export of strategic commodities to members of the Soviet bloc. American sponsorship of ERP was influenced by two distinct and not entirely compatible objectives. On the one hand the United States desired to stimulate increased commercial exchanges among all countries, including those of the Soviet bloc, in line with its basic concern for expanding world trade as the best answer to communism and with its recognition of the concrete need of the ERP countries for commodities which could be obtained from eastern Europe more readily than elsewhere and without spending dollars. On the other hand, the United States was unwilling to sponsor a policy which would result in unduly strengthening a group of countries with which it might conceivably find itself at war at some not distant date. In particu-

[52] *Relazioni Internazionali,* XIII, February 19, 1949, 114.

lar, it was wholly unwilling to see the Soviet bloc countries gain possession of items of even indirect military use, whether of American or western European manufacture.

The U.S. Government had possessed since 1940 statutory authority to control American exports in the interests of the national policy. The Second Decontrol Act of 1947 extended these powers by authorizing the maintenance of emergency wartime controls where necessary to protect the domestic economy or "to aid in carrying out the foreign policy of the United States." Although export controls had been largely discontinued by the middle of 1947, the Department of Commerce began to reimpose them shortly thereafter. Control over all important exports to European and certain neighboring destinations was instituted on March 1, 1948, with the twofold aim of furthering the objectives of ERP and "safeguarding the national interest" with regard to shipments to the U.S.S.R. and other eastern European nations. Apart from certain goods in plentiful supply which had "no relation to the building up of war potential or to the strengthening of industry in eastern Europe," [53] all applications for export licenses to eastern Europe were carefully screened by an interdepartmental committee of the interested civilian and military agencies preliminary to final action by the Secretary of Commerce.

This screening operation was largely responsible for the drastic reduction of American exports to eastern Europe from an annual rate of $400 million in the second quarter of 1947 to an annual rate of $125 million in the third quarter of 1948.[54] Meanwhile shipment of many kinds of manufactured goods—including oil-drilling machinery, glazing equipment, truck tires, and steel mill equipment—which had been manufactured expressly for eastern European customers, and in some instances already paid for, was held up for want of export licenses.

In addition, the United States sought to induce the other

[53] *Twenty-Sixth Annual Report of the Secretary of Commerce, 1948* (Washington, 1948), 177-178.
[54] *Export Control and Allocation Powers: Fifth Quarterly Report by the Secretary of Commerce* (Washington, 1948), 2.

countries participating in ERP to adopt a similar policy. Under the Economic Cooperation Act the Administrator was obligated to deny participating countries any items which would go into production of commodities for eastern Europe for which the United States itself would have refused an export license. ECA's endeavors to promote a revival of east-west trade were thus confined "within the limits of national security," and numerous commodities of presumed military utility were withheld from intra-European trade. The system was by no means foolproof, however. There were numerous leaks and evasions, and Switzerland, a major supplier of capital goods, stood virtually outside it.

This situation gave rise to criticism in the United States as well as in both eastern and western Europe. American business interests, irked by the hazards and delays of the licensing procedure, claimed that its main result was to hand over traditional American markets to Great Britain and other western European countries.[55] Western Europeans complained at the restriction of their opportunities to reopen trade with the east even in tractors and other seemingly pacific items. The scope of the restricted lists served to exclude from east-west trade many products of direct economic importance which they were as eager to export as the east was to receive. Eastern European spokesmen, led by the Poles, exhausted every rhetorical resource in denouncing, at meetings of United Nations bodies and elsewhere, the conspiracy organized by the United States to hamper the development of the "new democracies" by denying them essential products. The U.S.S.R. and Czechoslovakia also claimed that the United States was violating the most-favored-nation provisions of existing commercial treaties. The limited availability to the east of loans from the International Bank, allegedly controlled by the United States, was cited by eastern spokesmen as a further manifestation of America's discriminatory policy.

Despite their manifest annoyance and distress, the eastern

[55] "Red Tape vs. U.S. Exports," U.S. News and World Report, XXVI, No. 3, January 21, 1949, 40-42.

European countries gave no indication that they would retaliate. Without overlooking the bargaining power accruing to them through western dependence on such items as Polish coal, they undoubtedly realized that they would stand to lose more than they gained by an economic rupture with the west. The Kremlin, for its part, while unable to offer its satellites advantages equivalent to those obtainable from the west, was not remiss in making gestures designed to alleviate their difficulties while strengthening its own dominant position. In the summer of 1948 it reduced by one-half the remaining reparation and related obligations of Finland, Hungary, and Rumania, although these concessions were less than appeared on the surface, as the cuts were in agricultural rather than in industrial goods.

With Poland and Czechoslovakia, whose highly developed economies felt most keenly the absence of a well-balanced foreign trade, the U.S.S.R. signed special agreements of far-reaching importance. The Soviet-Polish five-year trade agreement of January 26, 1948 provided for an exchange of commodities to a value of $1 billion in the five-year period 1948–52, and for Soviet deliveries of industrial equipment to an aggregate value of $450 million repayable over a five-year period. Among other items it promised to supply the equipment for a huge iron and steel works at Gliwice whose projected annual capacity of 1.5 million tons was to account for much of the doubled steel output (as compared with prewar) envisaged in Poland's six-year plan. In December 1948, a Czechoslovak delegation headed by Prime Minister Zápotocký went to Moscow to plead Czechoslovakia's cause and received assurances of a greatly increased exchange of goods, Soviet industrial equipment and technical cooperation, and Soviet loans of undisclosed amounts in both gold and free currency.

Whatever the net worth of such bilateral deals, from the standpoint of the Soviet bloc as a whole they could not compensate or mask the disadvantages of eastern Europe's self-imposed exclusion from the European Recovery Program. The eastern bloc opened the year 1949 with its own venture into the field of regional economic coordination. Representatives of Poland, Czechoslovakia, Hungary, Rumania, Bulgaria and the U.S.S.R., meeting in Moscow, set up a "Council for Mutual Economic Assistance" for the purpose of "rendering each other technical assistance, [and] rendering mutual aid in supplies of raw materials, food, machinery, equipment, etc." Established on a basis of equal representation and ostensible respect for the independence of the participating countries, the Council was declared open to other European states which agreed with its principles and wished to participate in "broad economic co-operation" with the original members [56]—an invitation of which no states outside the Soviet bloc could be expected to take advantage.

Through its influence on the economic planning and trade of the individual countries of eastern Europe, the U.S.S.R. was already in a position to exercise centralized direction over the economic development of the region. Establishment of a regular organization, meeting in rotation in the capitals of the participating countries, might be no more than a publicity device to counter the attractions of ERP and dramatize the superiority of the eastern approach to economic problems. It might be merely an instrument for facilitating Soviet exploitation of the satellite economies. On the other hand, it could provide a mechanism for both resisting and exerting economic pressure outside of the Soviet economic bloc, promoting multilateral trade exchanges within it, and conducting economic planning on a regional scale.

Yugoslavia, alone among the major states of the Soviet bloc, was absent from the conference which set up the Council for Mutual Economic Assistance. A Yugoslav protest elicited the tart Soviet rejoinder that Yugoslavia's participation was possible only if its government renounced its "hostile policy toward the U.S.S.R. and the countries of people's democracy." For the Yugoslav Communist leaders the rebuff was rather more ominous than their exclusion from meetings of the Comin-

[56] USSR Information Bulletin, IX, February 11, 1949, 66. Albania's admission to the Council was announced February 22, 1949.

form. The Council for Mutual Economic Assistance was not a party but a governmental body; its ostracism of Yugoslavia was characteristic of the hardening policy of the other eastern governments toward their recalcitrant sister regime. Tito and his supporters had every reason to fear that the new Council might become a potent instrument for reinforcing the economic pressure which had already imperiled their ambitious plans and might eventually threaten their very survival.

In the months that followed the original Cominform resolution the other Soviet bloc states, while penalizing Yugoslavia by slowing down or cutting off deliveries of eastern goods, had been slow to invoke drastic sanctions that might hurt Belgrade but would also invite retaliation. The full measure of Yugoslavia's fall from grace became apparent only at the very end of 1948 with a Soviet announcement that the new Yugoslav-Soviet trade protocol, signed in Moscow on December 27 after weeks of negotiation, provided for no less than a seven-eighths reduction in commercial exchanges for 1949 as compared with 1948, "in view of the unfriendly policy of the Yugoslav Government toward the Soviet Union." Poland, Czechoslovakia and Hungary, already in default on deliveries scheduled for 1948, followed with major reductions in the volume of their projected 1949 trade with Yugoslavia. Cuts of this magnitude could not fail to inflict heavy damage on a country whose economy was none too strong at best, which had been directing 55 percent of its trade to countries of the eastern bloc, and whose five-year plan presupposed heavy imports of industrial equipment from those countries.

In a series of speeches in the last days of December 1948, Tito and his lieutenants breathed defiance of the Cominform, castigated the other people's democracies for nonfulfillment of commitments, reaffirmed their own determination to persevere with the five-year plan—which, however, would be stripped to its bare essentials—and declared that Yugoslavia would not hesitate to ship its raw materials elsewhere, even to capitalist countries, in order to secure the necessary industrial equipment. These declarations were accompanied by other indications that Yugoslavia was seriously looking for wider trade outlets outside the Soviet bloc. Efforts were made to negotiate long-term commercial treaties with Italy and with the United Kingdom. Yugoslavia turned also to the United States, in the hope that a relaxation of export controls would permit the purchase of American machinery to build up heavy industry.

For the United States the problem of future economic relations with Yugoslavia presented itself mainly in political terms. The possible economic advantages of reopening Yugoslavia's commercial bridges to the west were clearly subordinate to the major question of that country's future relation to the east-west political alignment. Tito's five-year plan, and his entire regime, might fall without imports of machinery from the west. Limited economic aid would help to keep Tito afloat for some time, although it was always possible that the Cominform would find means to liquidate him and reintegrate a penitent Yugoslavia into the Soviet bloc. The continuing existence of Tito's regime was important to the United States, since the only apparent alternative was a Yugoslav government controlled entirely by Moscow. The advantages of keeping the Cominform rift open, as a standing refutation of Communist dogma and an incitement to "national" Communists elsewhere, were not inconsiderable. Tito's defiance of Moscow gravely weakened the Soviet bloc, even if it did not directly add an ally to the camp of the west.

Any judgment on the past and prospective success of the Soviet-Communist economic plans for eastern Europe depends on the motives behind those plans. To the extent that they were aimed at long-term solutions of the basic economic problems of the area—overpopulation on the land, low productivity, undeveloped industry, technical backwardness—they registered some indisputable gains (often at a high cost in human rights and welfare), though these were difficult to measure in view of the policy of secrecy in regard to statistics. They still faced formidable obstacles in attempting to reach the ambitious goals of vastly increased production and higher living standards set in the various national plans. Shortages of skilled manpower and of capital goods could hardly be met without an influx of goods, technical assistance and credits from the west, of which there was no immediate prospect except in the case of Yugoslavia, which was no longer a part of the Soviet economic sphere.

If the guiding principles of the new planned order in that sphere were to be found in the military rather than in the economic realm, then the main problem was not the long-range economic viability of the new eastern Europe but the contribution which the satellites could make to the military potential of the great Soviet empire stretching from Bohemia to the Pacific. The expansion of heavy industry, especially in Poland and Czechoslovakia, added to that military potential, although it was at least questionable whether the Kremlin would choose precisely this most vulnerable portion of its domain for the creation of a sizable military industry. In any event, whatever the various motives behind Soviet economic policy in eastern Europe might be and whatever the difficulties caused by the comparative isolation from the west, it seemed likely that the area would be drawn ever more closely into alignment with the Soviet Union's own economic planning, for war or for peace.

CHAPTER SIX

SPECIAL ECONOMIC PROBLEMS

THE MARSHALL plan dominated the foreign economic relations of the United States in 1948. Its size and portent not only distracted attention from less dramatic sectors of economic policy, but also set them in a new perspective and influenced the scope, methods, and pace of some of these efforts. Still, the conditions peculiar to each problem, the policy line established in previous years, and the forces shaping action did not wholly change. Multiplicity of aims continued to mark the foreign economic policy of the United States. Some, like the aims of the reciprocal trade agreements policy and the plans for an International Trade Organization, principally concerned the future, when the world might be more nearly "normal" once again; they bore a direct relation to the Marshall plan's possibilities of success. Other aims were more immediate, like those sought in the proposed International Wheat Agreement; their bearing on the Marshall plan was more limited. Still other policies involved both long-run and immediate aims; shipping was one of them, and American policy in this field seemed to clash at several points with the aims of the European Recovery Program.

At the beginning of 1949 President Truman said something which increased the complexity of American foreign economic relations for the time being but might later provide another unifying theme. In his inaugural address Truman said: "We must embark on a bold new program for making the benefits of our scientific advances and industrial progress available for the improvement and growth of underdeveloped areas . . . And, in cooperation with other nations, we should foster capital investment in areas needing development . . . The old imperialism—exploitation for foreign profit—has no place in our plans. What we envisage is . . . democratic fair-dealing."

The thought was not new. Most economic postwar planning had stressed the importance of developing the backward areas of the world if there was to be prosperity, stability and peace. The U.S. Government had repeatedly professed its support for just such ideas. But the President's endorsement of this concept as Point Four of his high policy program was timely. People were beginning to wonder what came after the Marshall plan; the OEEC's *Interim Report* had strengthened fears that even with much success in carrying out the recovery program Europe would still have difficulty after 1952 in finding foreign markets for its manufactured goods and non-dollar sources of raw materials; there was concern that the American focus on Europe, while necessary and valid in the immediate postwar years, would blind us to our interests in other parts of the world; Communist victory in China and our slippery footing in Greece suggested that emergency aid was of questionable value in backward areas—preventive treatment might be better; existing means of financing development of backward areas—the World Bank, the Export-Import Bank, private investment— were yielding very limited results.

The President's proposal was well received, at home and abroad. Of course, the Russians called it imperialism and some domestic critics saw in it a new form of "globaloney." But on the whole Americans welcomed the initiative; business groups and others began work on their own proposals for carrying it out. In Washington an interdepartmental committee started to put together the pieces out of which a program could be constructed. At Lake Success the idea was discussed in the Economic and Social Council, and U.N. officials began looking for ways in which their organization could take part and compensate somewhat for its exclusion from the Marshall plan. Throughout the country Cabinet members made speeches about the kind of activity they envisaged under Point Four. Three months after Truman's speech there was still no clear, official program, but there were many ideas and much work was being done, the outcome of which was likely to shape American policy in the years to come.

1. Trade Agreements and the ITO

American commercial policy in 1948–49 was largely concerned with the implementation of two basic agreements to which the United States had become a party, the General Agreement on Tariffs and Trade (GATT) signed at Geneva by 23 countries on October 30, 1947 and the Charter for an International Trade Organization (ITO) signed at Havana by 53 nations on March 24, 1948. Both documents laid down rules for a multilateral system of trade relations based on nondiscrimination, selective reduction of tariffs, and elimination of other restrictions detrimental to international trade.

Although the United States had taken the lead in promoting these agreements, the compromises necessary to gain international acceptance left them in a form which in many respects fell short of the State Department's ideals. American protectionist interests attacked them for going too far; other groups complained that they did not do enough to liberalize trade. Attention now shifted to Congress, which would have to accept or reject the Havana Charter and also to pass judgment indirectly upon GATT by passing on the renewal of the Reciprocal Trade Agreements Act, under which the tariff concessions embodied in the Geneva agreement had been negotiated.

The existing Reciprocal Trade Agreements Act was due to expire on June 12, 1948. When President Truman on March 1, 1948 asked Congress to extend it without change for another three years, he knew the chances of a favorable answer were poor. The program initiated by Cordell Hull was before a Republican Congress for the first time in its 14 years on the statute books. Though there had always been some Republican support for the program, the party's Congressional representatives had usually voted quite heavily against it. The new chairman of the House Ways and Means Committee was Harold Knutson of Minnesota, who for years had been a leading opponent of the Hull program; its Tariff Subcommittee was headed by Bertram Gearhart of California, another archenemy of the trade agreements.

Contrary to the usual practice, the House hearings on renewal were held in closed session. The bill that emerged provided for a restriction on the President's power to reduce tariff rates. The Tariff Commission was to be divorced from the interdepartmental machinery that advised the President what changes in duty might usefully be made in negotiations with foreign governments. Instead, the Commission was to hold separate hearings and decide limits below which duties could not be reduced without danger to domestic industry or agriculture. If the President exceeded these limits the agreement would be subject to Congressional veto. The Act was to be renewed for one year only.

The Administration assailed the bill, saying it would wreck the program. "Only a shadow of the original act is preserved while its substance is destroyed," Secretary Marshall wrote to Representative Doughton.[1] He said he would prefer to see the Act expire rather than have the new bill go through. But the Republicans had control and used it effectively. The House Steering Committee under Speaker Martin agreed on strategy and got the bill onto the floor under a rule that limited debate and forbade amendments. A closed meeting of all the Republican Representatives rallied support for the revised measure. Representative Eaton, chairman of the Foreign Affairs Committee, who had said he would oppose the measure, changed his mind on the ground that the Republicans could write a new law next year. After rejecting a Democratic move to renew the Act unchanged, the House passed the bill 234 to 149 on May 26. Five Republicans voted with the minority, and 16 Democrats with the majority.

In the Senate the bill fell athwart the provinces of both Vandenberg, who led the Republicans on foreign affairs, and Taft, who guided policy on domestic issues. Millikin of Colorado was a key figure as chairman of the Finance Committee and the

[1] *Congressional Record* (Daily edition), May 26, 1948, 6669.

man who had conducted the hearings on the International Trade Organization the year before. Vandenberg opposed the idea of a Congressional veto on the pacts and said it was "indispensable" to preserve the reciprocal trade agreements principle "unweakened." He argued that it would be sufficient check on the President if he had to explain to Congress why he had put a tariff rate below the "peril point" set by the Tariff Commission. Taft seemed inclined to hold out for the veto, but then agreed to dropping it from the bill.

The Administration continued to fight hard against the proposed changes, attacking the cumbersomeness of the new procedure, which would involve two sets of hearings and deprive the interdepartmental trade agreements organization of the direct participation of the Tariff Commission. Even more serious, to the minds of Administration spokesmen, was the fact that the sole criterion for the Tariff Commission to apply was the possible danger to domestic interests. This seemed to be a throwback to the "cost-of-production formula" for tariff-making. It spotlighted too narrow a segment of the national interests, ignoring the benefits of a reciprocal trade bargain to the economy as a whole. William L. Clayton, testifying for the State Department, told the Senate Finance Committee that while the greatest care was taken to assess the probable effects of each tariff cut, any change might involve some risks; the escape clause of the trade agreements would protect domestic interests against any real dangers.

Behind these arguments lay the view, probably shared by the Administration and the bill's supporters, that the Tariff Commission, standing alone, would be more influenced by Congressional pressure than were the interdepartmental committees under the existing arrangements. Oscar Ryder, Democratic chairman of the Tariff Commission, expressed the view that it would be better if the Commission were not given the new powers provided in the bill. On the other hand, Commissioner Gregg, a Republican, welcomed them.

Having dropped the veto provisions of the House bill, the Senate Republican leaders presented the measure as a compromise which made only "procedural changes" and did not reduce the President's real powers. Vandenberg said that it did not offend against the canons of our foreign policy. But the only compromise the Democrats could see was one among the Republicans themselves, and they were skeptical of a bill that was fully accepted by men who had always opposed the whole reciprocal trade agreements program. When the time came to vote, Barkley's proposals for straight extensions for three years, two years, and finally one year were defeated 48-41, 47-42, and 46-43.[2] Then the Republican bill passed 70 to 18, with a number of Democrats obviously supporting it as the only alternative to letting the Trade Agreements Act expire. Next day the House concurred and the bill went to the President.

Truman had either to sign the bill or let the Act lapse. The latter course would have blocked U.S. participation in the second round of tariff negotiations scheduled under the Geneva Agreement. So, despite the "new, complicated, time-consuming and unnecessary procedure," he signed the bill with "regret." Next year, he hoped, the bill would be restored "as a fully effective instrument of permanent United States policy." He was concerned at the prospect that the one-year limitation would "cast some doubt upon our intentions for the future," and in this he was echoed by some parts of the foreign press, which saw the bill as an indicator of what the Republicans might do if they came into power. The *Neue Zürcher Zeitung,* for instance, said of the House bill that "one would not go wrong to call it a victory for the protectionists."[3]

The trade agreements and related aspects of U.S. commercial policy played almost no part in the Presidential election campaign. The Democratic platform called for a return to the original form of the Hull Act. The language of the Republican plank reflected the compromise which lay behind the party's virtual unanimity in the recent legislation. Emphasizing the "safeguarding of our own industry and agriculture," the plat-

[2] Of the seven Senators not voting on the last issue, four were paired and two were announced as being in favor of the straight extension. This left Senator Moore of Oklahoma as the only one whose position was not known.
[3] "Protektionistische Tendenzen in Amerika," May 25, 1948.

form said, "we shall support the system of reciprocal trade and encourage international commerce." [4] At Bonham, Texas, in September, Truman stressed the importance of the Hull program for American foreign trade and accused the Republicans of planning to kill the program if they came to power. The next month, in Brooklyn, he repeated his accusation and said that the choice of Governor Dewey as his opponent had been "master-minded" by Joseph R. Grundy, the outstanding protectionist of the Republican party. Dewey said nothing about the trade agreements in any of his major speeches.

By January 1949, when the victorious President sent to Congress a State of the Union message calling for full restoration of the Trade Agreements Act, the matter had become more urgent because of the imminence of the new tariff negotiations under the Geneva agreement. The Congress that was now asked to restore the integrity of the Hull program was a very different body from the one which had passed the "crippling amendments" of which Marshall had complained. Not only were there sizable Democratic majorities in both houses, but 63 Republican Representatives and 6 Republican Senators who had voted against renewing the Act in 1948 had lost their seats to Democrats. Knutson and Gearhart were absent from the House for the first time in years; Brooks of Illinois and Robertson of Wyoming no longer sat in the Senate. Later, in a letter to Representative Doughton, who was once more in his familiar role as chairman of the House Ways and Means Committee, President Truman asked for speedy action on the bill to help out the impending tariff negotiations at Annecy. Some had expected him to request that the Trade Agreements Act be put on a permanent basis, but instead he asked for only a two-year extension.

The open House hearings resumed their familiar form, with a long parade of witnesses pro and con. Two Republicans joined the majority in reporting a bill that met the President's requests by eliminating the "peril-point" procedure. The House

[4] The drafting committee had gone a bit further, pledging support for "the reciprocal trade agreements."

passed it 319 to 69 on February 9. Six Democrats voted against the measure, but over 80 Republicans, including former Speaker Martin, supported it once their amendments were defeated. In the Senate the bill took its place on an overcrowded calendar where it would have to compete for legislative attention with such other pressing foreign policy matters as extension of ERP, ratification of the North Atlantic Treaty, and military aid to western Europe.

Meanwhile, of the 23 countries that signed the Geneva Agreement on Tariffs and Trade in the fall of 1947, 22 had put it into effect by the middle of July 1948.[5] Hence many U.S. imports were paying lower rates of duty. Delegates of the GATT countries met in Geneva for a month in the late summer of 1948. The issues they dealt with gave a preview of the sort of questions which would frequently come up under the agreement and later, if it were adopted, under the ITO Charter. Brazil, Cuba, Ceylon and Pakistan were given permission to re-negotiate some of the duties set in the original agreement because of unforeseen difficulties. The United States was permitted to grant tariff preferences to products coming from the Pacific islands it held as trust territories. Changes in the general provisions of GATT were made to bring the document more closely into line with the Havana Charter. A dispute between the United States and Cuba on the latter's licensing system for textile imports was resolved with a recommendation to Cuba to change its policy. The conference postponed final settlement of a politically delicate legal tangle arising from the refusal of India and Pakistan to apply GATT to South Africa because of that country's treatment of Indians. On the initiative of the United States a number of countries agreed to give reciprocal most-favored-nation treatment to western Germany, though not as part of GATT.

The Geneva meeting also settled on a procedure for negotiating with other countries which wished to join the group. A conference was set for April 1949 in Annecy, France. At that

[5] Chile was granted an extension of time and became the twenty-third signatory on February 4, 1949, its accession to take effect a month later.

time the original parties to GATT would negotiate tariff concessions with Colombia, Denmark, the Dominican Republic, Finland, Greece, Haiti, Italy, Liberia, Nicaragua, Sweden and Uruguay.[6] For the United States this meant that the regular trade agreements procedure had to be set in motion. The Committee on Reciprocity Information began hearings in December. Under the revised law adopted in 1948, the Tariff Commission also had to hold hearings as the basis for its report on "peril points."

The 11 new countries with which the United States would be negotiating at Annecy were much less important to world trade than the original 23 which had met at Geneva. Still, they were far from negligible, and had accounted for 8.8 percent of United States imports and 9.6 percent of the United States exports during 1948. Trade agreements were already in effect with six of them.[7] Reductions in United States duties on quite a long list of items were being considered. Some of them promised to give some trouble, such as Danish butter, cheese from Italy and Denmark, a number of manufactured products, especially from Sweden, and such perennial sore spots as leather goods, Italian textiles, hats, and hand-made lace. Other difficulties loomed as Czechoslovakia, only Cominform signatory of GATT, made known its intention to bring eastern Europe's fight against the U.S. export control policy[8] before the Annecy meeting. These controls, the Czechs alleged, violated the equal-treatment provisions of GATT by discriminating against Czechoslovakia on political grounds. The United States was expected to counter this charge by reference to the GATT provision authorizing exceptional trade measures where national or international security was involved.

Aside from tariff concessions negotiated in connection with the Geneva agreement, the United States unilaterally made a few adjustments in its tariff during 1948. Because of domestic

[6] Peru and El Salvador were originally in the list but dropped out.

[7] Colombia, Haiti, Finland, Nicaragua, Sweden and Uruguay. However, the tariff rates and some other provisions of the Nicaraguan agreement had been suspended since 1938.

[8] See above, p. 202.

shortages, the suspension of duties on imports of copper, scrap iron and steel, and lead was continued. The same treatment was given to standard newsprint and various minor items. Negotiations continued over the revision of duties on Mexican imports from the United States that followed Mexico's invocation in 1947 of the escape clause in the United States-Mexican reciprocal trade agreement.[9]

Though protectionist groups warned about the threat of heavy imports as the result of lower duty rates, there was little evidence of damage to domestic producers. The Tariff Commission dismissed pleas to invoke the escape clause of GATT on behalf of domestic producers of certain distilled liquors, candied marrons and marrons in syrup. The worries of the wool-growers about low prices resulting from heavy imports seemed to have vanished in a surprisingly rapid liquidation of world wool stocks, except in the lower grades, with which the Commodity Credit Corporation (CCC) was well supplied. The closing of the Waltham Watch Company early in 1949 led to agitation for higher duties on Swiss watches. Secretary of Labor Maurice J. Tobin, formerly Governor of Massachusetts, espoused the watchmakers' cause. Members of a delegation which called on the President said that he suggested an investigation by a special subcommittee of the House Ways and Means Committee. However, the weight of the evidence at the 1949 hearings on renewal of the Trade Agreements Act showed that internal factors, and not imports, were the cause of Waltham's troubles.

While the United States Government was moving ahead on GATT and the Trade Agreements Act, it marked time in handling the draft Charter for an International Trade Organization. Though the United States delegation had brought this document home from Havana at the end of March 1948, the Administration, facing a Republican Congress and an election, made no move during 1948 to send the document to the Hill. The Democratic platform endorsed the ITO, and when the re-elected President told Congress his program at the beginning

9 See *The United States in World Affairs, 1947-1948*, 129.

of 1949 he stressed the importance of adopting the Charter. At the end of April Truman sent the Charter to both houses of Congress, where adherence would be sought through joint resolution rather than through the treaty procedure.

Meanwhile opinion in the country was showing itself, but slowly. The American Tariff League and various protected interests came out against the Charter, as was to be expected. But other business groups which had been in favor of the general idea of an ITO had grown increasingly uneasy during the negotiations at the many concessions the United States had made to foreign demands for various kinds of protection. While still supporting the trade agreements program, a number of these groups showed doubt or outright opposition concerning the ITO Charter. A committee of the United States Chamber of Commerce condemned the Charter for not doing enough to further private enterprise. The annual National Foreign Trade Convention, sponsored by the National Foreign Trade Council, reflected the disagreement in business circles by ignoring the Charter in its "Final Declaration" in November. Two months later the Council announced its opposition to the ITO. One businessman, who was rated as an "internationalist," called it an "economic Munich." In March the National Association of Manufacturers denounced the Charter as "making the world safe for socialistic planning" and as legalizing "the economic jungle in which the world has lived since the early Nineteen Thirties."

On the other hand, the National Council of American Importers favored adherence, urging that the United States try to eliminate the Charter's imperfections from inside the organization, not by rejecting the agreement *in toto*. The Committee for Economic Development supported all but the investment provisions of the Charter. Other organizations, like the CIO and the League of Women Voters, endorsed the Charter. Republican Congressmen Javits of New York and Fulton of Pennsylvania, who had attended the Havana conference, issued a substantial report supporting acceptance of the Charter. The State Department and various private spokesmen set about explaining the complicated document to the general public and urged support of it as an essential part of American foreign policy and a necessary prop to the future of ERP.

The rest of the world showed only a modest interest in the ITO. "Empire-traders" in the British Commonwealth and official spokesmen for the U.S.S.R. attacked it, along with many people whose views fell in between. Most countries seemed to be waiting for action by the United States. For instance, Australia in the fall of 1948 adopted legislation enabling the government to become a member of the ITO, but made formal adherence conditional upon American and British ratification of the Charter. Britain, in turn, awaited action by the United States.

Meanwhile, the temporary organization set up at Havana began to function. The Executive Committee of the Interim Commission of the ITO met at Geneva in September 1948. Most of its work was concerned with preparatory arrangements for the administration of the ITO and with the latter's relations with other agencies, when it should come into being. Of greater significance were the fruitless negotiations with Switzerland about the terms on which that country might join the organization. Virtually the only European country not in balance-of-payments difficulties, Switzerland claimed that it would be at a disadvantage in dealing with its most important trade partners, since they could discriminate against its exports, especially of luxury goods, while Switzerland would be bound by the Charter not to retaliate. On this and some other issues the Swiss were looking for an interpretation or special provision that would provide them with an escape to equalize their bargaining power. While there was no final decision, the discussion made it quite clear that the prospects of finding a basis on which the Swiss could come in were very small.

The year ending in April 1949 reflected the cross currents that affected American foreign trade policy. A partial deviation from the course set in the Hull Trade Agreements Act and GATT was offset after the election by a return to the original path. But nothing happened during the year to show conclusively what the final American verdict would be on the largest trade question of all, the ITO.

2. International Agreement on Wheat

Shortage, scarcity, rationing, relief—these were the keynotes of the world's wheat and bread problems as the war ended. The wheat fields of much of western Europe and the Ukraine had been devastated; seeds, fertilizer and tools were scarce; the lack of rice in the Far East added to the world demand for wheat. The issues before the United States Government in 1945, 1946, and 1947 concerned the division of wheat supplies between home consumption and exports. Still, it required no clairvoyance to see that somewhere ahead lay not only the end of the shortage but perhaps surpluses and glutted markets as well. To many officials and growers, the way to avoid such a debacle seemed clear: an international agreement between the main producing and consuming countries to regulate world trade in wheat.

This approach appealed particularly to a group in the United States Department of Agriculture who believed that international commodity agreements would contribute to stability and prosperity, benefit producers and consumers alike, and help in avoiding the all-too-frequent pattern of former times in raw material markets: wide fluctuations of price, chronic depression, leading to restriction of production. They had a special interest in a wheat agreement. During the war years American farmers had been asked to increase their wheat acreage; by the end of the war they had record crops. A wheat agreement offered the chance of assuring American producers a foreign market in the years to come, thus avoiding a severe reduction in acreage or the accumulation of government-owned wheat bought at the support price under domestic legislation.

The idea was not new. An International Wheat Agreement born of the depression was signed in 1933 but broke down in less than a year, chiefly because Argentina, with good crops, exceeded its export quotas. The Wheat Advisory Committee set up in 1933 survived this breakdown and tried intermittently to lay the groundwork for a new agreement. The conflicting interests of consumers and producers and the rivalry for markets among the major grain-exporting countries frustrated this aim. Toward the end of the decade observers thought the chances for an agreement were improving, but the outbreak of war put an end to the effort. In 1942 the United States, Australia, Canada and Argentina, the principal wheat exporters, and the United Kingdom, the principal importer, drafted an interim wheat agreement. Only a few provisions came into immediate effect; the rest were to serve as a basis for later negotiation.

The 1942 agreement set up an International Wheat Council which in 1946 added eight countries to its membership and set about drafting a new agreement. Representatives of 41 countries attended the International Wheat Conference in London during March and April 1947. There was substantial agreement on a number of general provisions and on the main form the agreement should take, but negotiations broke down over the United Kingdom stand on the crucial issue of price. The year before the United Kingdom had signed a four-year bulk purchase contract with Canada. For the first two years the dominion was to sell the mother country 160 million bushels of wheat a year at $1.55 a bushel, about 30 percent less than the market price. The price for the 140 million bushels to be sold in each of the last two years of the contract was to be settled later but would not be less than $1.25 the third year and $1.00 the fourth.[10] This contract covered most of the United Kingdom's needs and the British, acutely conscious of their interest in relatively low raw material prices, saw no need to accept the maximum price of $1.80 for most of the five years of the international agreement that seemed agreeable to the other negotiating countries.[11] Without the participation of the United

[10] The price for the third and fourth years was ultimately fixed at $2.00. Continued high world prices and dissatisfaction among Canadian farmers at the "losses" they were incurring led to the pressure for this form of compensation.
[11] The price was to be $1.70 during the second year and $1.80 the rest of the time.

Kingdom, the world's biggest importer, there could be no effective general wheat agreement.

The next year the Wheat Council tried again and on March 6, 1948 announced that representatives of 36 countries meeting in Washington had signed a new agreement, subject to ratification. The pact was to cover the movement of 500 million bushels of wheat a year, about five-eighths of current world trade. Each year for five years, Canada, the United States and Australia agreed to sell 230, 185 and 85 million bushels, respectively, to the other 33 countries that signed the agreement. Each importing country agreed to buy a specified amount of wheat annually from the three exporters.[12] The maximum price was to be $2.00 a bushel, the minimum $1.50 the first year, falling by 10 cents a year to $1.10 in 1952–53.[13]

By the end of March, 1948, all the countries involved had signed the wheat agreement. A month later the President sent it to the Senate as a treaty and asked for speedy action since the agreement would have to be ratified by July 1 if it was to affect the next crop year. In mid-May a subcommittee of the Foreign Relations Committee, under Senator Lodge, held hearings for three days. Government officials and spokesmen for the major farm organizations urged acceptance of the agreement. Representatives of the millers and the grain trade objected to it for a variety of reasons, but mostly because they believed its operation would bring increased government intervention in wheat and flour exporting. The spokesman for the North American Export Grain Association called it "the greatest state trading deal ever presented to the Senate of the United States for ratification." [14] These groups saw little need for the

[12] That is, from the group as a whole. There were no allocations under the agreement for the specific amounts of wheat which each exporter was to sell to each importer.
[13] In Canadian currency for No. 1 Manitoba Northern wheat in store at Fort William or Port Arthur. Equivalents were set for other major types of wheat, and a procedure for determining still others.
[14] Testimony of William C. Schilthuis, *Hearings* before a subcommittee of the Senate Committee on Foreign Relations, 80th Congress, 2nd Session, on the ratification by the United States Government of the International Wheat Agreement (Washington, 1948), 132.

agreement as a means of ensuring export markets so long as ECA was in existence, and they doubted its efficacy afterward.

In mid-June, as the press of Congressional business grew before adjournment and political issues sharpened in anticipation of the electoral campaign, the subcommittee decided to let the issue lie until the next Congress met. Twelve countries, including the United Kingdom, Australia, and Canada, deposited their ratifications by the July 1 deadline; 16 others were prepared to do so shortly. At a meeting in Washington on July 6 and 7, delegates of the signatory countries agreed that there was no point in trying to make the agreement work without the United States. A new preparatory committee was appointed which would meet when the United States Government thought the "time propitious." The United Kingdom withdrew its ratification, followed by Australia. Secretary of Agriculture Brannan and Under-Secretary Norris E. Dodd predicted dire results. There would be a new scramble for bilateral bulk purchase agreements that would restrict the future market of the United States. For the first time since 1943 the Department of Agriculture asked farmers to cut their wheat acreage, by eight percent.

When Congress met in special session in July the only foreign policy action the President called for was consent to ratification of the wheat agreement. The lawyers had found ways to get around the July 1 deadline and the bargain could still be salvaged if the United States belatedly accepted it. On August 6 the Foreign Relations Committee unanimously reported the treaty to the Senate. The committee spoke of its "earnest belief that the principle of surplus marketing by international agreement is sound" but did not ask for Senate action before the next session. Delaying Senatorial action until the issues had been explored more fully, said Vandenberg, would "create a better domestic understanding of the issue and the widest possible degree of agreement upon the treaty."

Truman's reelection made the "time propitious" for a new wheat conference, which met in Washington on January 26, 1949. Using the 1948 agreement as an agenda, the 50 conferring countries on March 23 adopted substantially the same form for the new pact. But the balance of forces that affected bargaining on the key question of price had changed again. Good harvests all over the world, and the expectation of greater crops during the year to come, virtually ended the shortage of wheat. As a result, the maximum price set in the new agreement was $1.80, as it had been in 1947. The minimum price for the first year was to be $1.50, dropping by 10 cents a year to $1.20 in 1952–53. The new agreement was to last four years, instead of five as in the earlier case. France, which had been an importing country under the previous agreement, and Uruguay, which had not participated in it, both appeared as exporters under the new pact. There were to be 37 importers. The quantity of wheat guaranteed under the new agreement was less than before: 456,283,389 bushels, so the shares of the major exporters were also reduced, that of the United States dropping to 168,069,635 bushels.[15]

Argentina and the U.S.S.R. had both participated in the conference. Repeating their performance of the year before, the Argentine delegates withdrew from the negotiations in mid-February on the price issue. They reiterated their argument that Argentina could not accept such a ceiling on the price of its wheat exports until a ceiling was put on the cost of its imports of manufactured goods. The Russians stayed until almost the end of the conference but then dropped out on the issue of quantity. At first the Soviet delegation asked for a guaranteed export quota of 100 million bushels. They came down to 75 million in the course of negotiations but refused to go below that figure. Questioning the U.S.S.R.'s claim to so large a quota in view of the level of its past exports, and faced with a reduction in their own share, the other exporters would not offer more than a 50 million-bushel quota.[16] The Russians withdrew as participants but, like the Argentines, continued as observers.

[15] Canada—203 million, Australia—80 million, France—3.3 million, Uruguay—1.8 million.

[16] Secretary Brannan says, "The importers as a last resort offered a further compromise," presumably by buying more from the U.S.S.R. without cutting the shares of the other exporters, but it failed ("1949 International Wheat Agreement," *Foreign Agriculture*, XIII, May 1949, 99-102).

The new agreement, like the 1947 and 1948 drafts, differed from earlier proposals in that it did not try to regulate wheat production or limit exports by quotas. It was "essentially a multilateral bulk-purchase contract." [17] Buyers and sellers alike could deal with countries outside the agreement or trade with each other in excess of the guaranteed quantities at any prices they saw fit. The $1.80 maximum was less than the price at which most wheat was being sold. The theory of the agreement was that in return for this concession exporters got the assurance that for the next four years they would not lack markets for 456 million bushels of wheat at not less than the minimum prices. Both groups were taking a chance. If wheat prices stayed above the maximum, the sellers would feel they were losing by the agreement; if wheat prices fell below the minimum, the buyers would feel the burden of their obligation. Either development would put a strain on the agreement, particularly if the outsiders—Argentina, Russia, and the Danubian countries—should offer large quantities of wheat at low prices.

The 168 million bushels assigned to the United States under the agreements was a good bit less than it was currently exporting. Shipments to occupied Germany and Japan would add over 100 million bushels. For the first years of the agreement, at least, United States shipments to western Europe might also exceed the guaranteed quotas, but these sales would fall as European production expanded under the recovery program. Compared with prewar, however, 168 million bushels was more than the United States had exported since the late 1920's. In justification, the Department of Agriculture pointed to the record crops American farmers had produced to meet wartime demand—over a billion bushels a year for five years running. "Recognition of the enormous contribution made by the United States in the production and export of wheat during the war and postwar period is from the standpoint of United States producers the most important factor of the international wheat agreement," Acting Secretary of Agriculture Dodd told a sub-

[17] Edward G. Cale, "International Wheat Conference," Department of State, *Bulletin,* XVI, June 1, 1947, 1055.

committee of the Senate Foreign Relations Committee during hearings on the 1948 agreement.[18]

It would cost the United States Government money to live up to the wheat agreement. United States wheat was selling for over $2.00 a bushel, so exports would have to be subsidized to meet the lower maximum price set in the treaty. Even if the price of American wheat fell in later years, the domestic price-support program would almost certainly keep it higher than the level at which wheat would move under the agreement. Testifying on the 1948 agreement, Secretary Dodd held that subsidies would be cheaper than paying farmers not to produce wheat, as we had done in the late 1930's and early 1940's. Neither he nor the Senators who questioned him gave much attention to the issue whether billion-bushel wheat crops in the United States were likely to reflect the most efficient use of world resources after the current shortages were over.

The wheat agreement would not fix prices or establish a rigid pattern of trade. So long as each exporter could sell its share at not less than the minimum price, and each importer buy its quota at not more than the maximum, no special measures would be needed to make the agreement effective. If any country had trouble making sales or purchases on these terms it would appeal to the International Wheat Council, which would call on the exporters or importers to fulfill their obligations by supplying or buying their wheat quota at the agreed prices. Escape clauses provided means by which exporters could be relieved of their obligations when they had crop failures, and importers of theirs when they were short of foreign exchange.

Another article called on both exporting and importing countries to maintain stocks of wheat that would help guard against temporary shortages and make the agreement operate more smoothly. Under a rather vague provision the governments signing the agreement, "while reserving to themselves complete liberty of action" regarding internal agricultural policies, undertook "not to operate those policies in such a way as to impede the free movement of prices" between the limits set in the

18 *Hearings* . . . , *op. cit.*, 2

agreement, so far as transactions among the contracting parties were concerned. Bearing in mind the standards for an intergovernmental commodity agreement set out in the draft Charter for the ITO, the negotiators called for public reports on the working of the agreement and also provided for an "equal voice" for exporting and importing countries in administering it. This was done by giving 1,000 votes to all the importers together and an equal number to all the exporters together; within each group the votes were divided according to the wheat quotas. On some major issues, such as determining if the agreement had been violated, Council action required a majority of both groups, voting separately.

Once again the new agreement had to be ratified by July 1 if it was to take effect for the next crop year. This time the Americans felt more certain of Senate consent to ratification. Representatives of the six House and Senate committees concerned with the issues (agriculture, foreign affairs, finance) and of the major farm and grain trade organizations had been advisers to the U.S. delegation. The national budget called for an appropriation of $58 million to subsidize wheat exports under the new agreement. When the Senate ratified the agreement by voice vote on June 13 it looked as if after 16 years the world would once again have a wheat agreement.

Much more than wheat might be affected by this event. Secretary Brannan told the opening session of the 1949 conference: ". . . we will acquire valuable experience here, for the implications of this conference go far beyond the realm of wheat." What he meant was that the wheat agreement would be the first postwar intergovernmental commodity agreement and might set a pattern. The threat of future surpluses hung over a number of commodities; undoubtedly international agreements would be proposed as a way to avoid such troubles and secure stability in the raw material markets. The groundwork was being laid, but slowly. The ITO Charter provided standards for commodity agreements designed to prevent their becoming producer-controlled government cartels. The U.N. Economic and Social Council (ECOSOC) had created an Interim Coordinating Committee for International Commodity Arrangements to survey developments with the hope of keeping any new agreements in harmony with the ITO principles before the trade organization was set up.[19] The FAO was studying the problem. International groups met from time to time to survey the position of cotton, wool, tin, rubber and coffee.

Each commodity would have its peculiar problems, but all had some things in common on which the search for a formula had to concentrate. Past agreements had usually been unsatisfactory to consumers because they were run by producers; the producers were dissatisfied because the agreements tended to break down through the rivalry among exporting countries. Proponents of policies aimed at securing a prosperous and expanding world economy feared commodity agreements would become permanently restrictive. A committee of private Americans who had studied the problem put the issue this way:

> The justification for shelter under an intergovernmental commodity control agreement is that it gives time to change fundamental conditions, to move toward satisfying world demand from the most efficient sources, and to allow inefficient producers to shift into other lines. Otherwise, a commodity agreement becomes not an umbrella for emergencies, but a concrete shelter for permanent residence. The aim of commodity agreements should be to end the need for commodity agreements.[20]

3. Shipping Policy

The salient facts of the postwar shipping problem were already plain in the middle of the war. The United States was launching ships in unheard-of numbers. Production in the rest of the world was small. By agreement with the United States,

---

[19] This committee has issued two reports which summarize the economic position of major commodities, the status of international agreements concerning them, and activities of various organizations in this field: *Review of International Commodity Arrangements* (Geneva, 1947); *Review of International Commodity Problems 1948* (Lake Success, November 1948).

[20] "A Cartel Policy for the United States," Report of the Committee on Cartels and Monopoly appointed by the Trustees of the Twentieth Century Fund, appearing as Chapter 12 of George W. Stocking and Myron W. Watkins, *Cartels or Competition?* (New York, Twentieth Century Fund, 1948).

Britain was concentrating its efforts on naval vessels. Sinkings were heavy until near the end of the war; the principal merchant fleets outside of the United States would be reduced far below their prewar levels. Unlike most goods shipped abroad under lend-lease, title to ships was kept by the United States, so the wartime arrangements did not assure Britain, Norway, the Netherlands and our other Allies of any postwar tonnage. Yet these countries, and others, rated the restoration of their merchant shipping a major element of economic recovery. At the same time the preponderant position of the United States seemed likely to give an unequaled opportunity to the groups in this country who believed that the American merchant fleet should play a much larger role in world shipping than it had before the war.

In mid-1939 about 1,400 merchant vessels totaling 8.7 million gross tons, 14.4 percent of world shipping, flew the United States flag. By V-E Day this country had over 5,500 ships, totaling 40.3 million tons, nearly 60 percent of the world's merchant fleet.[21] Not even the most ardent big merchant navy advocates thought it would be possible to keep that much tonnage in use for very long. Moreover, many of the ships would prove uneconomical under peacetime sailing conditions: some were too old, some worn down by wartime service; many of the war-built vessels were not well adapted to the more selective markets of peace. Shippers remembered the bad days after the First World War when a large surplus of vessels hung over the market, and depressed it. While the bulk of the American ships belonged to the government, private and official plans envisaged a privately owned and operated merchant marine for the United

[21] Ocean-going ships of 1,000 gross tons or over. The 1945 figure includes 3.1 million tons of lend-lease shipping operated by foreign countries. Standard sources vary somewhat in the basis on which their statistics are computed and there are often discrepancies. Most of the data used in this section come from official sources and where comparisons are made the discrepancies have been checked to be sure they do not vitiate the general point even though there are differences in the detailed figures. Gross tonnage measures a ship's capacity and is usually between two-thirds and three-quarters of deadweight tonnage, which measures possible cargo weight. Both types of tonnage are mentioned in this section, depending on the source of the data. Figures usually refer to ships of 1,000 gross tons or over, but in some cases the basis is 100 or 1,600 gross tons.

States. Ship disposal was clearly the first practical task to be faced as the war ended.

It was a complicated matter, crossed with many conflicting interests. The first bill was introduced into the House on March 27, 1944. No law reached the books until two years later when the President signed the Merchant Ship Sales Act of 1946. He was not altogether satisfied with it but thought some legislation so badly needed that it was "better to sign the bill than to wait probably another year to get a better one." [22] The two years had been filled with pulling and hauling among the Congressmen, the Administration, and the shipping people on such issues as these: Ought nonsubsidized domestic operators to get better terms in buying ships than subsidized ones? How much of its original investment in the ships should the government try to recoup? How cheaply should the ships be sold, considering that the American operators would sooner or later have to compete against foreign shippers? How many ships should be sold abroad and on what terms? The last question epitomized the issues concerning the kind of postwar shipping policy the United States should follow, raising it as a practical matter before there was any agreement on general principles. And it split the Administration.

The State Department argued for liberal treatment of foreigners: They should be allowed to buy ships on equal terms with Americans, and should be able to charter them if they did not want to buy. It would be in the interests of the United States to help its allies resume merchant shipping as part of their economic reconstruction, and we had some obligations to do so. A policy that hindered this development and tried to maintain the United States' quasi-monopoly position would not only hold back recovery, but "would be distinctly out of harmony with the broad policy of promoting the flow of trade through the reduction of nationalistic restrictions and discriminations. If the Government of the United States were to attempt to take advantage of the war losses of other countries and of the wartime increase in its own merchant fleet to establish itself in a domi-

[22] *Congressional Record* (Daily edition), March 11, 1946, A1444.

nant shipping position, it would be acting contrary to its basic policy of promoting sound international economic relations and an increasing flow of commerce." "I do not agree with that," said Almon E. Roth, representative of the National Federation of American Shipping.[23] His group was willing to see some ships sold to foreigners, but not the faster and more efficient vessels, which they felt should be reserved for Americans. They were "unalterably opposed" to chartering, which would simply give the foreigners time to build new merchant ships without removing any vessels permanently from the surplus, and all at less cost than if they had to buy the ships.

The Maritime Commission agreed with the industry. Said Vice Admiral Emory S. Land, chairman of the Commission, ". . . if we charter a ship foreign, the bloom will be run off it in a year or two, and it will be turned back to us as an old crock, and all you have is something for scrap." [24] Similarly, the Commission opposed giving foreigners the privilege American operators had of trading in old ships when buying new ones. A "reasonable" foreign disposal policy was justified, said Admiral Land, not only as a reconstruction measure, but because it would minimize "the extent to which such nations might otherwise be forced into extraordinary shipbuilding programs, the effect of which in the long run would be inimical to our own interests." [25]

As finally passed, the Merchant Ship Sales Act of 1946 put foreigners and Americans on an equal footing so far as price and terms of sale were concerned. However, the Maritime Commission had to decide that the ships to be offered to foreigners were "not necessary to the promotion and maintenance of an American merchant marine," had to be satisfied as to the purchaser's financial responsibility and had to consult the

[23] *Hearings* before the House Committee on the Merchant Marine and Fisheries, 79th Congress, 1st Session, on H.R. 1425, A Bill to Provide for the Sale of Certain Government-Owned Merchant Vessels (Washington, 1945), Part 1, 483, 358.

[24] *Ibid.*, Part 2, 109-110.

[25] *Hearings* before a subcommittee of the Senate Committee on Commerce, 79th Congress, 1st Session, on S. 292, A Bill to Provide for the Sale of Certain Government-Owned Merchant Vessels (Washington, 1945), Part 1, 8-9.

Secretary of the Navy. Also, the foreigners only got a chance to buy vessels after they had been offered to citizens for at least 90 days (except for ten C-1's or C-2's which did not have to undergo the waiting period, so long as they were offered to domestic buyers first). Domestic purchasers had another advantage in that they could turn in old ships on rather favorable terms in part payment for their new purchases. After domestic applicants and Philippine citizens the order of preference among foreigners was to be determined by taking into consideration the extent to which war losses had been overcome by their respective countries.

The Act created a national defense reserve fleet into which the Maritime Commission would put whatever vessels it thought suitable after conferring with the Secretaries of War and Navy, and all the war-built vessels not disposed of by the end of 1947, unless they were not worth keeping. The Commission was authorized to convert its ships for commercial use, removing "war-service features" and installing "such special features" as would improve the ships for particular trades or general commercial utility. Except for specially authorized cases (like the Panama Railroad Company) the government was to get out of the shipping business as soon as it could transfer the vessels to private operators.

Sales began in June 1946. Applications from foreigners, including foreign governments, considerably exceeded those from American operators, as was to be expected. Since the Americans had first call they got the bulk of the faster and more efficient ships; the foreigners often had to be satisfied with Libertys that they could expect to use only for the time being, until more up-to-date ships were built for them. Originally supposed to expire in December 1947, the Ship Sales Act was extended until March 1949 but no sales were to be made to foreigners after March 1948. Under this authority the Maritime Commission sold foreigners 1,117 ships. Half were Libertys, the rest largely tankers, coastal cargo carriers and Victorys. Credits totaling $260 million were extended to 14 countries to finance these sales. The dispersal was wide, the largest buyer, the United

Kingdom, taking only 12 percent of the total. Panama, Italy, Greece, Norway, France and the Netherlands followed in that order.[26]

Some 850 ships were sold to domestic operators and over 1,600 put into the reserve fleet. As of September 1, 1948, 585 government-owned ships were on charter to private American operators. The active merchant fleet of the United States in mid-1948 had more than twice its 1938 tonnage. Over 70 percent of it was engaged in foreign trade, compared with less than 40 percent in the prewar year. Counting the reserve fleet, the United States still had the largest merchant navy in the world: 3,644 ships of 26.7 million gross tons, about 38 percent of the world total. But it was a sharp drop from the level of V-E Day.

The ship disposal program dealt with an immediate issue. However, it did not do much to establish long-run policy except in creating the defense reserve fleet. The policy declaration at the beginning of the Merchant Ship Sales Act of 1946 was for the most part taken from the Merchant Marine Act of a decade before. It said that American security and trade required "an efficient and adequate American-owned merchant marine":

1. that would carry "a substantial portion" of the foreign commerce of the United States, as well as all the coastwise trade and that with Alaska, Hawaii, Puerto Rico and the Virgin Islands, and "provide shipping service on all routes essential" for maintaining our foreign trade;
2. "capable of serving as a naval and military auxiliary in time of war or national emergency";
3. owned and operated by American citizens, and flying the United States flag;
4. composed of well-equipped, safe vessels built in the United States and manned by Americans;
5. "supplemented by efficient American-owned facilities for ship building and ship repair, marine insurance, and other auxiliary services."

[26] Most of the ships transferred to Panamanian registry were bought by people of other nationalities, primarily Americans. U.S. citizens buying ships for Panamanian registry were considered in a different category from alien purchasers under the Act.

Few challenged these general principles, but when it came to deciding on how some of them should be put into practice there was less agreement. The makers of United States shipping policy during the postwar years decided some of the many issues that faced them without serious controversy; others they postponed or settled by temporary expedients. Much of the controversy concerned three interrelated issues: (1) the size of the future merchant fleet; (2) the shipbuilding program; (3) the place of shipping in the European Recovery Program.[27]

Admiral Land, the energetic chairman of the Maritime Commission, had frequently urged as a postwar goal a merchant marine that would carry 50 percent of the country's foreign trade, a figure that had more magic than science in it. On National Maritime Day, May 22, 1945, he set 17 million deadweight tons as the size fleet that would accomplish this task. This represented a 50 percent increase over the prewar fleet and was endorsed as a desideratum by many people in shipping circles. A number of committees which studied various aspects of the subject proposed a smaller fleet. The Harvard Report of June 1945, prepared by the Harvard Graduate School of Business Administration on the request of the Maritime Commission and the Navy, estimated that the United States might reasonably maintain a fleet of from 8.9 to 13.35 million deadweight tons, depending on the level of world trade. A little less than half of this tonnage would be engaged in foreign trade. The Postwar Planning Committee of the Maritime Commission, which reported in 1946, contemplated a still smaller fleet: 10.5 million deadweight tons, of which 5 million would be engaged in foreign trade. This was less than the prewar tonnage but since the ships would be faster and more efficient was judged

[27] A fourth issue concerned the extent to which the United States would encourage and support the handling of shipping problems by an international organization. A convention creating an Intergovernmental Maritime Consultative Organization (IMCO) was signed March 6, 1948, after two years of preparatory work dating from the dissolution of the United Maritime Authority, which had controlled Allied shipping for six months after the end of the war. IMCO would be concerned primarily with technical matters, such as safety at sea, but would have powers of discussion and recommendation on private and governmental discriminatory practices. Hearings on ratification began in March 1949.

to represent a carrying capacity equal to about 14 million deadweight tons of the older ships. The next year another Maritime
Commission committee envisioned a fleet of 11.4 million deadweight tons. An Advisory Committee appointed by the President, headed by K. T. Keller of the Chrysler Corporation,
reviewed these and other estimates. While avoiding setting
another figure itself, the committee expressed "its belief that
. . . a reasonable minimum of an active sea-going merchant
fleet" would be between 11 and 12 million deadweight tons,
the mean of the estimates made by other groups.[28]

All these figures concerned the future. The United States
fleet was still well above that level. Demand for shipping was
particularly high because of a number of emergency needs, especially to carry coal from the United States to Europe. As conditions improved the demand slackened; the number of government-owned ships on charter to American operators decreased
from over 1,400 in mid-1947 to about 350 at the end of 1948.
As European fleets grew, the share of United States water-
borne foreign trade carried in American-flag vessels dropped,
from nearly 100 percent at V-E Day to 60 percent in 1946, 54
percent in 1947 and 48 percent in 1948. This was still well
above the prewar level of about 25 percent.

Freight rates were high and the financial position of most
American shipping companies had improved greatly during the
war. The Maritime Commission recaptured $17 million of sub-
sidies out of operators' profits.[29] Operating subsidies had been
suspended during the war but the Commission agreed to resume
payments to ten operators beginning January 1, 1947, and a
year later to the remaining two of the lines which had been
subsidized before the war. Under the provisions of the 1936
Act, the subsidies would be paid to American companies maintaining service on designated routes, in amounts equal to the
difference between their costs of operation and those of foreign
operators. In the summer of 1948 the Maritime Commission

[28] *Report of the President's Advisory Committee on the Merchant Marine* (Washington, 1947), 52.
[29] Half the profits in excess of 10 percent of the capital employed by a subsidized operator must be used to repay subsidies previously granted.

estimated that subsidies would be higher than before the war because American costs had doubled while foreign costs had not risen so fast. Also, more American ships would be plying the subsidized routes.

Meanwhile, high demand and the large American share of the world's shipping postponed the day when the United States would have to decide how to keep a large merchant fleet in operation. The reserve fleets gave flexibility to the supply and insurance of national defense needs. But with shipbuilding it was different. There current activity depended on future wants and the delay in deciding on a clear-cut national policy left the industry in an uncertain state.

From a peak of 12.8 million gross tons in 1943, United States ship production dropped to 501,000 tons in 1946 and then plummeted to 126,000 in 1948. The wartime mass-production shipyards closed down. European production, on the other hand, increased as each country raced to revive its merchant marine, or to increase its exports by selling ships abroad. This process was accelerated by delays in U.S. ship sales to foreigners, and by restrictions on the types of vessels offered. Over nine times as much tonnage was launched in Britain during 1948 as in the United States, well above the prewar ratio. American shipbuilders and the Maritime Commission were alarmed. They saw the virtual disappearance of the American industry, or at least its decay to the state it was in before the Maritime Commission began its long-term building program in 1937. Reporting in November 1947, the Keller Committee found that during the past few months the shipbuilding industry had been sustained at a "general satisfactory level of total employment" by virtue of repair and conversion work. But "the dearth of new construction work has resulted even now in a serious depletion of essential skilled and technical groups in the industry." The committee warned that by early 1948, "unless new contracts are forthcoming, shipbuilding in this country will be at a virtual standstill."

The reasons for the low level of building were fairly clear. The Maritime Commission's ten-year building program was virtually completed during the war. Though the speed, quality and age level of the American merchant fleet were greatly improved, the increase in tonnage had been mostly in dry-cargo carriers and tankers; there was a relative shortage of passenger ships, combination passenger-freighters, and various kinds of specialized vessels. Though the number of tankers had increased greatly, demand exceeded supply. American operators professed interest in contracting for the construction of ships of this sort, but high costs and an uncertain future made them hesitate. Private operators wanted a 50 percent subsidy on the construction of new vessels. The Maritime Commission would not offer more than a 38-41 percent subsidy, based on a study of foreign building costs. It pointed out that:

"With few exceptions American shipowners are in better financial condition to undertake a reasonable amount of new construction than at any time in the recent past. The aggregate net worth of the 12 operators now holding subsidy contracts with the Commission is more than 6 times what it was in 1937." [30]

The Keller Committee found, on the other hand, "that the uncertainty of industrial conditions . . . prevents a satisfactory determination of" the difference between foreign and domestic construction costs. Added costs for safety devices and crew conditions on American ships, plus "the pressing national security needs for ships and shipbuilding," led the committee to recommend 50 percent subsidies for the next three years at least.

In June 1947 the Maritime Commission recommended a new 25-year building program. For ten years, beginning in 1949, the United States should produce 250,000 deadweight tons a year to improve the balance of the merchant fleet, according to this plan. During the last 15 years of the program, annual production would be 640,000 tons, aimed largely at replacing war-built tonnage. The Keller Committee recommended "the building of a number of prototype high-speed dry-cargo and tanker vessels" but made specific proposals only for a passenger-carrying ship program. Forty-six ships in four years, including two 50,000-ton

[30] *Report to Congress for the Fiscal Year Ended June 30, 1948, 3.*

vessels for the New York-Channel Ports run, were called for in the committee's plan; the cost would be between $500 and $600 million in all. Then Washington fell silent on the subject. The President's budget message for fiscal 1949 asked for only $15 million for new construction to supplement the $84 million the Maritime Commission still had in hand, far less than the big building proposals would require.

The industry took its troubles to Congress. After long committee hearings the House in June 1948 passed two resolutions embodying most of the program drawn up by the Long Range Planning Committee of the National Federation of American Shipping. Fifty-percent construction subsidies, liberalized trade-in allowances, easier depreciation terms, lower interest rates, and a number of other financial benefits for private operators were the main features of the legislation. Caught with a rush of business at the end of the session, the Senate failed to act.

The Administration's policy had meanwhile taken a new turn. On March 15, 1948 the President appointed a Cabinet committee made up of the Secretaries of Defense, Commerce, Treasury and Labor to review all the reports and recommend a shipping policy. At the House hearings on April 8, Secretary of the Navy John L. Sullivan outlined the committee's building plan: 50 passenger ships with a troop-carrying capacity of 2,000-10,000 men each, 116 tankers and some dry-cargo vessels. A week later the President asked for more money to subsidize ship construction. "This action was taken as an integral part of the security program which recent events have compelled me to place before the Congress," he wrote to the Chairman of the Maritime Commission. Congress provided $94 million and gave the Commission 90 days of the new fiscal year in which to spend the $84 million already on hand. On the President's request a liaison committee of the Maritime Commission, the military establishment and the shipping industry was formed which by July reported "reasonably good prospects" for building 18 fast passenger and combination vessels under subsidy, and 20 fast tankers with the government paying only for their increased speed as a "national defense feature." But in the absence of legislation for a long-term shipbuilding program, the industry still held back, wanting larger subsidies. A compromise was reached and in August the Maritime Commission agreed to pay a 45 percent subsidy on two 20,000-ton passenger liners which could carry 5,000 troops apiece. Contracts followed for combination passenger and freight vessels and a number of new tankers. As of September 1 five times as much new tonnage was on order in American shipyards as a year previously. By the end of 1948, 407,000 gross tons of shipping was actually under construction in American yards, compared with 136,000 at the end of 1947. Most of the ships being built were tankers for private account, some of them ordered by foreigners because of U.S. quick delivery. The oil shortage of the previous winter, not government subsidy, was the motivating factor.

When the new Congress assembled in January 1949 the stage seemed set for action on a long-range shipping program involving a heavy expenditure of public money on grounds of national defense. The National Security Resources Board had set up a permanent Ship Facilities Committee. The Maritime Commission was working on shipbuilding proposals, and the industry was preparing another long-range program. However, although two bills were introduced in the House and proposals were made for investigation of the whole merchant marine picture, no legislative action appeared likely in 1949.

The new budget for fiscal 1950 called for $91 million for new construction; this, added to left-over allotments, would provide building subsidies for a considerable number of ships. In April the Maritime Commission authorized construction of the largest passenger liner ever built in American yards, the government paying 60 percent of the $70 million it would cost. Instead of the usual talk about "luxurious accommodations" and the prestige of American shipping, attention focused on the simple fact that the new ship would carry 12,000 soldiers.

Meanwhile, the United States' new predominance in world shipping was having an impact on other sectors of policy. Before the war the United States was a debtor in its international shipping account, paying more to foreigners for shipping services than it took in with its own merchant marine. The ships of many western European countries, on the other hand, earned foreign exchange which helped pay for the import of goods. Thus shipping was an important part of the national economy of countries like England, Norway and the Netherlands.[31] With European merchant fleets depleted and American ships carrying most of the world's trade, the position was reversed at the end of the war. The net foreign exchange earnings of the United States merchant fleet were $900 million in 1946, $1,008 million in 1947 and $439 million in 1948. The United States was helping Europe rebuild its economy and overcome the deficit in its balance of payments. That meant helping to rebuild the European merchant fleets and improve their earning capacity. Inevitably that meant more competition and a smaller share of world trade for American shipping. At the same time, the United States Government was subsidizing American operators and builders to counter lower European costs. The apparent conflict of these two policies appeared in the controversies over the disposal of surplus ships to foreigners, and showed up again in the Marshall plan.

The Paris Report of the Committee of European Economic Cooperation, issued in September 1947, showed that the participating countries planned to build 15.5 million deadweight tons of merchant and passenger shipping during the next four years. In addition, they wished to purchase about 3 million deadweight tons of United States ships at a cost of $300 million. These countries had lost almost two-thirds of their 1938 tonnage during the war. New building and the purchase of American surplus ships had restored them to about 80 percent of the prewar level by the summer of 1947. If the reconstruction programs submitted to the CEEC were completed, the tanker tonnage of the participating countries would reach the 1938 level by the end of 1947, the total tonnage by the end of 1949, and the dry-

---

[31] For instance, in 1937 Norway's net shipping receipts were more than one-third as large as exports of Norwegian goods, and over 11 percent of Norway's national income came from shipping. Comparable figures for Britain are 13.4 percent of exports and 1.3 percent of national income; for the United States, 1.9 percent of exports and .09 percent of national income.

cargo tonnage by the end of 1950.[32] They intended to replace many of the Libertys and Victorys they had bought from the United States with new ships better adapted to their needs. Through 1950 the CEEC countries expected that their demand for United States shipping services would exceed the "normal" supply. Over the four years planned for at Paris, the participants in the European Recovery Program expected to pay $1.7 billion in freight charges to countries that would require dollars.

The Harriman Committee disliked the CEEC shipping program. "The United States needs an active merchant marine for national defense and we must not create conditions in which that merchant marine cannot survive . . . It is pointless for Europe to be building up a world surplus of vessels at this juncture." There were plenty of vessels laid up in the United States. To the objection that the Europeans wanted modern ships of high quality, tailored to their special needs, the committee retorted that "in an emergency period like the present they perhaps could manage with some tonnage not ideally suited to their purposes in the interest of conserving resources for the production of items which, from a world point of view, are more desperately needed." Half the steel being requested from the United States was accounted for by the European shipbuilding program. A smaller shipbuilding program would free men and resources for more urgent needs. At the same time, the report conceded, "in fairness to the Paris planners it must be admitted that our ship sales policy has not encouraged the European nations to expect any further sales of our war-built vessels in appreciable quantities." [33]

The Harriman Committee proposed that the United States transfer to the CEEC countries more than the 3 million tons of surplus ships they suggested—provided the European shipbuilding program was curtailed. On the other hand, the committee thought western Europe would need more tankers than were

[32] Western Germany, forbidden to have a merchant fleet by the Potsdam agreement, is excluded from both prewar and postwar figures.
[33] *European Recovery and American Aid: A Report by the President's Committee on Foreign Aid* (Washington, 1947), 65, 210, 213.

called for by current plans and recommended increased building of these vessels in Europe (at the expense of dry-cargo tonnage) and also transfer of Liberty tankers from the United States, to be replaced by newer, faster vessels built here. Ship transfers and more realistic calculations would reduce the $1.7 billion which the CEEC countries planned to pay out in dollar freights to $1 billion, in the opinion of the committee.

In sending its proposals for the Marshall plan to Congress, the Administration adopted much of the Harriman Committee's line of reasoning. The State Department recommended the sale of 200 war-built ships (about 2 million deadweight tons) and also the bareboat chartering of another 300 to ERP countries. The latter step would save $350 million of the cost of the Marshall plan over four years, and the sale would save $300 million, which the European countries would otherwise have to pay out in dollar freight charges.[34] In return for these transfers the European countries would be expected to cut their dry-cargo building programs, but not those for tankers or passenger vessels.

The Herter Committee, in its turn, examined the shipping problem, pointing out that there were plenty of ships available, so that "the principal issues . . . revolve around the question of whose ships are to get the business." The strongest argument for greater use of foreign ships was the saving of dollars; on the other side lay the need to maintain a sizable American merchant fleet for national security. Transfer of vessels would undoubtedly throw American seamen out of work, but "this is largely a question of timing, since no one believes that our present level of maritime employment can be maintained for more than a few years under any policy . . ." An immediate shift might be preferable because the business boom would make it easier for the men to find other jobs. Balancing these factors, the Herter Committee recommended, among other things: sale and charter of vessels to European countries, reduction of Euro-

[34] Senate Foreign Relations Committee, 80th Congress, 1st Session, *Outline of European Recovery Program: Draft Legislation and Background Information Submitted by the Department of State* (Washington, 1948), 57.

pean building of dry-cargo carriers, increased tanker production at home and abroad, no arbitrary requirements for the shipment of recovery cargoes in American vessels. If these recommendations were not accepted and the ships were not transferred abroad, or carriage in American bottoms were required, the Herter Committee held that "the additional cost of such provisions should be made a part of the defense budget and not of the recovery program appropriation." [35]

The idea of selling or chartering more American ships to Europe brought an outcry from the shipping industry and the maritime unions. The money involved was only one or two percent of the cost of the recovery program, said the National Federation of American Shipping, but a quarter of our shipping reserve would be lost and 20,000 to 25,000 men thrown out of work. "The future of American shipping is to be sacrificed or placed in jeopardy, for a consideration of no relative value." [36] Then the Maritime Commission came out against any further sale or charter of American vessels to foreign countries. Instead, it held, American efforts should concentrate on building up our own fleet to meet the competition it would have to face as European replacement programs were carried out. [37] In answer to a question from Senator Vandenberg, Secretary of Defense Forrestal said that though the transfer of 500 vessels would have some effect on our military strength, "we stand to gain more by such charter or transfer, from an over-all national security standpoint, than we stand to lose." [38] The Maritime Commission challenged this view, arguing that Forrestal had overlooked the fact that by increasing competition the transfer of ships abroad would reduce the size of the American operating fleet, not of the laid-up reserve.

The European aid bill introduced into Congress provided for the sale of 200 vessels and the chartering of 300 more, as recommended by the State Department. While the bill was before

[35] *Final Report of the House Select Committee on Foreign Aid,* House Report No. 1845, 80th Congress, 2nd Session, May 1, 1948, 312-317.
[36] NFAS press release, December 30, 1947.
[37] *Congressional Record* (Daily edition), March 24, 1948, A1938.
[38] Department of State, *Bulletin,* XVIII, March 7, 1948, 313.

the Committee on Foreign Relations, the Senate unanimously passed the Tobey resolution extending the Ship Sales Act but forbidding sales or chartering to foreigners. The committee then struck out the sales provision of the aid bill, but retained the chartering arrangements. When the bill came to the floor, Brewster of Maine offered an amendment to strike out the chartering provision. In the debate Vandenberg said that this was the only section of the bill on which there had been sharp division in the committee. Speaking for himself he said that "since Congress itself within the past sixty days has passed a bill . . . prohibiting the charter or sale of any of our ships to foreign countries, this provision in this bill would be, to put it mildly, inappropriate." Barkley, Connally, Lodge and other leaders of the fight for the recovery program supported him and the amendment was accepted. The Senate also approved an amendment submitted by Knowland of California requiring that half of all ERP cargoes shipped from the United States be carried in American vessels.[39] The bill was passed by the House in the same form despite the adverse recommendation of the Committee on Foreign Affairs on the ground that "it would be an expensive paradox to divert funds from European recovery to the purpose of maintaining United States maritime operations at a level which all concede is inflated far above the predicted permanent postwar operations. The aim of the program is to restore Europe, not to save American interests from the impact of peace." [40]

To administer the 50 percent shipping provision, the ECA decided it would have to rely largely on the procurement agencies of recipient countries, subject to spot checking by ECA officials. Before long American shippers complained that the provision was being violated. Some cargoes that appeared to be commercial shipments when they left the United States were

[39] The ancestry of this provision included Public Resolution 17 of the 73rd Congress, which provided that all goods bought with government loans be shipped on American vessels, subject to certain qualifications. Never fully applied, this law was apparently used to bolster the United States merchant marine's position during 1946 and 1947. See *The United States in World Affairs, 1945–1947*, 373.

[40] House Report No. 1585, 80th Congress, 2nd Session, March 20, 1948, 35.

later transferred to ECA financing. Some European countries were alleged to be evading the rule deliberately to benefit their own merchant fleets. The ECA responded by announcing improved policing of the regulation through pre-shipment identification of cargoes. The OEEC countries were asked to prepare a joint plan for allocation of total ERP shipments between American and foreign shipping. When they did not produce one by October 1, 1948, Hoffman said in a letter to each government that "unless a satisfactory plan is submitted in the very near future, the requirements of the statute must be fulfilled by each country." [41] If that happened, each country, even those with large merchant fleets, would have to apply the 50 percent rule to its own ECA imports even if that were more burdensome than application of the rule to recipient countries as a group.

European opposition to the 50 percent rule was sharpened by the fact that American shippers were receiving substantially higher rates for carrying ECA bulk cargoes than were their European competitors. The Economic Cooperation Act said the 50 percent rule was to apply "to the extent such [United States] vessels are available at market rates." The ECA took the view that this did not mean that American shippers would have to meet the lower rates foreign shippers could offer. Instead, "the rate for American-flag ships should be a reasonable rate permitting a reasonable opportunity for profit to American operators and assuring the existence of an American fleet in the market." [42] As foreign freight rates fell, the rates paid American shippers continued at a high level based on the Maritime Commission's charter rates set the year before. Late in October ECA Deputy Administrator Howard Bruce wrote to the Maritime Commission asking that its charter rates for bulk cargoes to Europe be reduced. He pointed out that on coal shipments to France the rate on American ships was $4.50 a ton higher than on foreign vessels. He hinted that the ECA might be unable to enforce the fifty-fifty cargo rule if American rates

[41] *New York Times*, October 9, 1948.
[42] Statement of Col. Arthur G. Syran, ECA transportation director (*ibid.*, July 9, 1948).

did not come down. Grenville Mellen, a member of the Commission, charged that European shippers had deliberately depressed their rates to force ECA and Congress to change the 50 percent rule and would raise them as high as or higher than current American rates once they succeeded in diverting business from American vessels.[43]

On December 3, Hoffman wrote to Senator Bridges, chairman of the Congressional "watchdog committee," saying that he would stop applying the 50 percent rule after the first of the year unless American rates were lowered. At the outset of the program the differential in rates had been justified by the need to keep American ships in operation to move bulk cargoes; now conditions had changed and there was no longer need to follow this expensive course. (Twelve percent of ECA funds were being spent for shipping.) To apply the 50 percent rule in these circumstances "would result in a subsidy to American shipping out of dollar appropriations for European recovery and would correspondingly reduce the amount of dollars available for assistance to Europe. I do not believe this was intended by the act."[44]

Congress was not in session, but throughout the country a number of Senators and Representatives announced that Congress had intended just that. The Maritime Commission protested to the White House; one of its members said the proposed action amounted to "selling out our merchant marine" and would reduce the United States to "a second-rate maritime power." It would mean "mothballs for a sixth of the American merchant marine and 'berry picking' for 600 ships' captains and mates," said an official of the National Union of Masters, Mates and Pilots.[45] The AFL and CIO seamen's unions and the ship operators struck the same note; Harry Lundeberg of the Seafarers International Union (AFL) threatened to picket

[43] *Ibid.*, November 14, 1948.
[44] *Ibid.*, December 8, 1948. The ECA's legal argument was that the "market rates" clause did not require payment of higher rates to American shippers and that the other qualification to applying the 50 percent rule—"so far as it is practicable"—gave the Administration some discretion.
[45] *Ibid.*, December 11, 1948.

foreign ships carrying ECA cargoes. The blow would fall largely on the unsubsidized American vessels engaged in tramp operations, a field in which there was almost no American activity before the war because of lower foreign costs. Most liner rates were set by private international conferences, so there were fewer discrepancies between American and foreign charges.

Senator Flanders of Vermont suggested a possible way out. He approved the proposed change in ECA policy but suggested that any justified subsidy of American shipping should be paid out of other funds than those appropriated for European recovery. Under considerable pressure from Congress and the shipping interests, Hoffman delayed the application of his proposed ruling until Congress had a chance to make up its mind on the matter. He suggested that if the 50 percent rule were continued, the ECA appropriation should be increased to make up the added cost. In April 1949 the Senate passed the ECA renewal with the original shipping provision, expanded to make it clear that "market rates" applied to United States rates and not world rates. The House put in a proviso that would allow the Administration to suspend the rule if American rates were above world rates by more than a "reasonable differential," but accepted the Senate version in conference.[46]

A somewhat similar problem, involving a good deal less money, plagued the ECA in the matter of marine insurance. Because its operations were so large the ECA, like the Lend-Lease Administration before it, found it more economical to be a self-insurer—spreading any loss on its shipments over its total expenses—than to pay premiums to private firms. Foreign importers, however, often wanted to insure their interest in ECA cargoes. The ECA did not believe it should advance dollars for this purpose, since that would reduce the amount to be spent on recovery supplies. Foreign governments were anxious to conserve dollars and usually took the same view. The result was that a large part of the insurance business

[46] The renewal act also provided that the 50 percent rule should apply separately to dry bulk carriers, dry-cargo liners, and tankers. The Administration was directed to try to get "a fair and reasonable participation by United States flag vessels in cargoes by geographic area."

on these cargoes was placed in European markets. American marine insurers objected that this practice discriminated against them.[47] They wanted ECA to require that some of the insurance on the shipments it financed be placed in the American market, and got some Congressional support for their view. Mr. Hoffman rejected this contention but in February 1949 announced that if foreign importers wished to insure ECA cargoes in the American market, ECA would provide dollars for the premiums. This meant, he said, that the insurers would be put on the same basis as other American exporters (and on a competitive basis with foreign insurers) but not given a privileged position. When it renewed the Economic Cooperation Act for a year Congress instructed the Administration to provide dollars when marine insurance was placed "on a competitive basis" in accordance with prewar trade practices.[48]

Thus by special governmental measures of various sorts the American merchant marine was sustained at a higher level of activity than it could have achieved in a competitive world market. The ship operators and maritime labor were not altogether satisfied and were worried about many other issues, such as the possible revival of German and Japanese shipping, foreign discrimination directed against American shipping, and the growing practice of registering United States-owned vessels in Panama or elsewhere to escape United States regulations that raised costs. Somewhere ahead lay further readjustment as European merchant fleets grew and the proportion of world trade financed by ECA fell. How great that readjustment would be and how it would be met depended in part on the kind of long-range shipping policy the United States Government adopted. For the foreseeable future, national defense needs—modified by Congressional willingness to appropriate

[47] The same issue had come up before with regard to foreign purchases financed by Export-Import Bank loans. The Bank finally agreed that insurance proceeds would have to be payable in dollars. See *The United States in World Affairs, 1945–1947,* 343-344.
[48] The Senate version contained language intended to prevent foreign governments from limiting the placing of insurance in the American market, but this was dropped.

funds—would be the strongest force shaping that policy; but it remained to be seen just what those needs would dictate.

4. Paying for United States Exports [49]

The extent of American aid to the rest of the world may be measured in various ways. One of the most significant, though general, indicators is the amount by which the goods the United States sends abroad and the services it renders to for-

TABLE I

UNITED STATES FOREIGN TRADE AND SERVICES
1947 AND 1948
(in billions of dollars)

	1947		1948	
U.S. got dollars from:				
Exports	14.4		12.6	
Other transfers abroad	1.6		.8	
Income on investments	1.1		1.2	
Other services	2.6		2.2	
Total		19.7		16.8
Foreign countries got dollars from:				
Imports into the U.S.	5.7		7.1	
Other transfers	.3		.6	
Income on investments	.2		.3	
Other services	2.2		2.5	
Total		8.4		10.5
Leaving a balance which had to be financed some other way of		11.3		6.3

Source: "International Transactions During 1948," *Survey of Current Business*, XXIX, March 1949, 14-18.

eigners exceed the goods and services it receives from them. Table I shows this discrepancy for 1947 and 1948. In the former year United States exports hit their all-time peak and were supplemented by $1.6 billion worth of goods shipped to occupied territories, sold as surplus property or otherwise trans-

[49] Much of this section is a continuation of pages 344-383 of *The United States in World Affairs, 1945–1947.*

ferred to foreigners without being officially classified as "exports." Though the value of exports fell in 1948, they were still substantially higher than in any other year of peace, and about four times the 1937–39 average. Imports were at record levels both years.

The 1947 gap between exports and imports of goods and services was cut almost in half in 1948. Reduction of exports and other transfers abroad, coupled with a 25 percent increase in the value of imports, accounted for most of the contraction. A third factor was a shift in the service account (excluding income on investments) that made the United States a net debtor in this category for the first time since the war. This change was due primarily to a drop of half a billion dollars in foreign payments for United States shipping.[50] Larger expenditures by the U.S. Government abroad and some increase in foreign travel by Americans accounted for most of the rest of the change.

Even the reduced gap of $6.3 billion between exports and imports of goods and services in 1948 was sizable; it was more than 25 percent larger than the ECA's first annual appropriation for European recovery. The 1947 gap of $11.3 billion was of record size for peacetime. Table II shows how the gap was filled in each of these years.

Some striking contrasts between 1947 and 1948 in Table II epitomize the international financial relations of these two years. Foreign liquidation of gold and dollar balances and loans by the U.S. Government are the two biggest items in the 1947 column. The reduction of foreign reserves by nearly $5 billion reflected in part the Latin American countries' use of their accumulated dollar balances, but was primarily due to the heavy European demand for American goods during the first half of the year and the virtual drying up of dollar sources for many countries. The British loan accounted for three-quarters of the $3.9 billion which the U.S. Government lent abroad during 1947. England's bad winter and heavy import

[50] However, the United States was still a net creditor of $439 million on shipping account.

TABLE II
HOW THE EXCESS OF UNITED STATES EXPORTS WAS FINANCED IN 1947 AND 1948
(in billions of dollars)

	1947	1948
On balance foreigners owed the United States for goods and services	11.3	6.3
We gave them:		
Through ECA, interim aid, etc.	1.8	4.2
Through private gifts	.6	.6
We lent them:		
Through the government	3.9	.5
From private sources	.7	.9
	7.0	6.2
Leaving a balance due us of	4.3	.1
They sold us gold and used up their dollar balances to the amount of	4.5	.9
And got from the International Bank and Monetary Fund	.8	.4
	5.3	1.3
This leaves a balance in their favor that is not accounted for in the official statistics of	1.0	1.2

Source: Adapted from "International Transactions During 1948," *Survey of Current Business*, XXIX, March 1949, 14-18. The figures are net. Figures for loans refer to actual draft of funds, not the formal granting of credits.

needs contributed largely to the fact that more than half the $3.75 billion loan was drawn down by the middle of the year. Although there were hints of trouble in store, the British did not ask for any postponement of their obligations, under the loan agreement, to make sterling arising out of current transactions freely convertible into dollars on July 15. A tremendous drain on Britain's dollars quickly followed. By the time the British Government ended convertibility on August 20, $1.3 billion more of the loan was spent. The United States stopped drawings on the remaining $400 million of the loan while the British set up new controls. The funds were freed again in December and on March 1, 1948 the last $100 million was used. Nineteen and a half months had passed since Congress appropriated the funds which were expected to last Britain for four years.

Neither government lending nor liquidation of foreign reserves was anything like as important in 1948 as it had been the year before. Although foreign governments spent $920 million of their gold and dollar balances in the first half of the year, liquidations dropped to $156 million in the third quarter and during the last three months of the year foreigners actually increased their reserves (by $216 million), for the first time since the end of 1945. The main factor in bridging the gap in the U.S. balance of payments in 1948 was government gifts to foreign countries. About 40 percent of the $4.2 billion total came from ECA and another 27 percent in the form of supplies for Germany, Japan and other occupied countries. Most of the rest was made up of shipments under the Greek-Turkish and Interim Aid programs. Governmental foreign aid thus filled more than two-thirds of the gap between what we gave and what we got in goods and services.

Loans under the Marshall plan, though they were to total $1 billion of the first year's appropriation, were for the most part not made until the spring of 1949. Apart from the British loan, the principal source of U.S. Government credits during 1947 and 1948 was the Export-Import Bank. It disbursed $824.5 million in 1947 and $428.9 million the following year. Over 85 percent of the 1947 disbursements was for purposes of European reconstruction. During the next year, however, reconstruction payments fell well below trade financing. This shift reflected the Bank's decision, announced early in 1947, to leave reconstruction financing to other agencies.[51] Of the $614 million of new loans authorized in 1947, only $100 million to Italy and $30 million to Finland were classed by the Bank as being "reconstruction credits." None of the $138.3 million authorized during 1948 fell into this category. However, nearly one-fourth of the new "trade" credits advanced during these two years were to finance exports to ERP countries. The Export-

51 See *The United States in World Affairs, 1945–1947*, 379.

Import Bank acts as agent for the ECA in making loans to European countries under the Economic Cooperation Act. These transactions do not involve the Bank's own funds and are not included in these figures.

A $300 million credit to Canada in November 1947 to help that country keep up its purchases of U.S. goods in spite of its difficulties in getting dollars was the Bank's largest loan during 1947 and 1948. A $50 million credit to Belgium was the largest European advance, apart from the Italian reconstruction loan. The Bank financed the sale of United States cotton to Germany and Japan and loaned Austria some $14 million to buy American machinery and other equipment for industrial reconstruction. Finland was the only "iron curtain" country to get new credits, about $48 million being authorized during the two years for the purchase of American goods. A $7 million cotton credit for Hungary was authorized during the first part of 1947 but canceled in July of that year. During 1947 and 1948, Czechoslovakia drew $7.9 million and Poland $32.3 million from credits previously granted.

Latin Americans, once the Bank's principal clients, hoped that the shift away from reconstruction loans would mean that more funds would flow in their direction. Though they got only about $120 million in new credits during 1947 and 1948, their share of the Bank's new loans increased as the two years passed. At the Bogotá conference Secretary of State Marshall announced that the President would ask Congress to increase the Bank's lending authority by $500 million, principally for the benefit of Latin America. Truman did so in April. The Senate passed the bill, but it died in committee in the House. By the end of 1947 the Bank had only $497 million of uncommitted funds out of an original $3.5 billion. Repayments and the expiration or cancellation of unused credits (notably $100 million committed to the Netherlands East Indies in September 1945) were more than four times the new loans made during 1948, so that lendable funds had increased to $967 million by the end of the year. At the low rate of lending that prevailed during 1947 and 1948 the funds were sufficient for a while, but they would certainly have to be supplemented if the Bank was to have an important role in the "bold new program" of assistance to underdeveloped areas.

Two lesser sources of U.S. Government credit were ship sales arrangements and the disposal of surplus property. Foreign countries actually used $195 million of ship sales credits during 1947 and 1948. Surplus property credits were drawn on to the extent of $120 million in 1947 and $208 million in 1948. Termination of the Office of the Foreign Liquidation Commissioner (OFLC) as of June 30, 1949 was announced in March 1949. By then the OFLC had sold for about $2 billion a wide variety of goods and installations in all corners of the globe which had originally cost five times as much.

The massive wartime operation of lend-lease had also not entirely stopped. Repayments of lend-lease obligations by various foreign countries (a credit item in the U.S. balance of payments) came to $206 million in 1947 and $10 million in 1948. Negotiations for settlements continued in 1947 and 1948, but at a much slower pace than during 1946. Final agreements were signed with the Union of South Africa and the Netherlands in 1947, and with Norway, Brazil and Czechoslovakia in 1948. The Dutch agreed to pay $67.5 million, about half of which took the form of a credit to be repaid over 30 years beginning in 1951. The South Africans paid $100 million in two installments in 1947 to clear their accounts. The other settlements involved smaller sums and no extensive credits. Off and on during the two years there were negotiations with the Russians about the settlement of their accounts, but there was no final agreement. Some of the tangled minor issues of the complex wartime lend-lease relations were cleared up in a series of agreements, but accounts remained unsettled with half a dozen European and Asiatic countries (of which the principal one was China) and most of the Latin American republics.

Some of the dollars with which foreign countries paid for goods and services in the United States came from the International Monetary Fund. From the time of its first transaction in May 1947 to the end of February 1949 the fund advanced

$688.6 million in U.S. currency to its members.[52] The largest share went to Britain, which got $300 million, followed by France with $125 million, India with $92.5 million, and the Netherlands with $62.5 million. Eleven other countries acquired smaller sums. In addition the Fund advanced $11.4 million worth of Belgian francs to Norway and the Netherlands, and also $6 million worth of pounds sterling to the latter country. Most of the Fund's dollar sales took place in 1947, when Europe's dollar shortage was most intense. On April 20, 1948 the Fund announced that it would advance dollars to countries eligible for ECA aid "only in exceptional or unforeseen cases," and no such transactions took place after the middle of 1948. This decision had the approval of U.S. financial authorities and was in line with their view that the Fund should conserve its resources for the post-transitional period, after the termination of the European Recovery Program, when they could be used more directly and effectively "for the attainment of exchange stability and the elimination of discriminatory currency practices." [53]

The Fund met a crisis in January 1948 when the French Government announced its intention of setting up an exchange system under which the franc would be cheaper in terms of the dollar and the Portuguese escudo than in relation to other currencies. While recognizing the need to devalue the franc the Fund refused to approve this arrangement. It opposed multiple exchange practices and feared that the French action might become a precedent leading to competitive devaluation in other countries. The U.S. Government and the British—who feared the effect of the French proposal on the pound and their foreign trade—backed the Fund's decision. The French went ahead with their plan, thereby losing access to the Fund's supply of dollars and other currencies but retaining membership. In several less important cases the Fund sanctioned multiple exchange ar-

---

[52] $6.1 million represents a purchase of gold from Norway; the rest is covered by the Fund's purchase of each member's own currency.

[53] *First Special Report of the National Advisory Council on the Operations and Policies of the International Monetary Fund and the International Bank,* House Doc. No. 656, 80th Congress, 2nd Session (Washington, 1948), 21.

rangements with the understanding that they were temporary
and would be ended as soon as possible. While the United
States supported this action, the National Advisory Council
believed "that greater efforts must be made by the Fund and
by the member countries to eliminate multiple currency practices . . ." [54]

Gold also created trouble for the Fund. Concerned about the
effect on official currency values of gold sales at premium prices
and subsidies on its production, the Fund tried to discourage
these practices. As the world's largest gold buyer, the United
States professed great interest in this matter and supported the
Fund's actions. While some particular issues were settled for
the time being by compromises, the fundamental question
seemed likely to persist and rise in new forms as time passed.
More important, in the spring of 1949, was the question of de-
valuing European currencies. Statements by American officials,
hints from the OEEC, and occasional suggestions in the Fund's
documents all indicated that the time was approaching when
some kind of concrete attack would be made on this difficult
and complex problem. Whatever the approach and whatever
the program, it seemed certain that the Fund, as guardian of
the parities and devotee of "exchange stability" and "orderly
exchange arrangements," would have an important role. That
was plainly the intention of the United States, which casts
about 30 percent of the votes in the Fund.

The Fund's Bretton Woods sister, the International Bank for
Reconstruction and Development, also provided some of the
dollars with which foreigners met their American obligations.
After long delays caused by organizational trouble and differences of opinion on policy the Bank made its first loan on May
9, 1947: $250 million to France to cover a number of recon-
struction needs. Smaller loans to other western European countries brought the total loans to $509 million by the end of 1948,
all but $6 million of it advanced in U.S. dollars. In the first
quarter of 1949, Mexico borrowed $34.1 million to develop
electrical power and Belgium $16 million to import equipment

[54] *Ibid.,* 16.

for building two steel mills and a power plant in Liége. In addition loans of $16 million to Chile and $75 million to Brazil, mostly for hydroelectric developments, were authorized but had not yet been ratified by the borrowing governments by April 1949.

The Bank was pursuing a cautious policy, anxious to make a good showing with sound loans. The great demand was for dollars, and a major source of dollars for the Bank was the sale of its own bonds on the U.S. market. In view of their own balance-of-payments difficulties, most member governments were unwilling to let the Bank lend the part of its capital held in their own currencies. During 1948 the Bank received a number of applications for loans and sent missions to many countries. But developmental projects, requiring engineering surveys, take a long time to prepare. During the first year of the Marshall plan the Bank deliberately refrained from making reconstruction loans to European countries while waiting to see how it could best fit its operations into the recovery program. All were agreed that the Bank had an important role to play, but its exact nature was still unclear in the spring of 1949.

The same obvious reasons that made the International Bank a cautious lender put a damper on foreign ventures by private investors in the United States. American businessmen and government officials alike talked about the desirability of large private foreign investment and of the many "nonbusiness" risks it involved which people were unwilling to take: economic nationalism, blocked currencies, foreign bankruptcy, discrimination, socialization, war. There were many proposals for getting around the difficulties but few produced practical results. The provisions of the Bogotá agreement on this subject satisfied neither potential investors nor the U.S. Government. The investment articles added to the ITO Charter at a late stage offered little present comfort to American investors. U.N. discussions of an international investment code moved slowly, as did the negotiation of American commercial treaties. Plans were afoot to permit investment in occupied Germany and Japan, but delicate issues created difficulties and the danger of carpetbagging delayed action. The ECA's investment guarantees were of very limited use during its first year; more was hoped for from the revised law in the second year.[55] Other guarantee and insurance plans abounded, but few got very far toward the essential point—tapping the public purse—during 1947 and 1948.

Still, private investment was not negligible in these two years. During 1947 over $1.1 billion of American funds were put into direct investments abroad, mostly by the oil industry in the Caribbean and Middle East. Norway and the Netherlands floated loans for $30 million in the American market, Australia engaged in refinancing, loans to Canada continued; a good bit of short-term capital moved abroad. However, there was also some repatriation of funds and the net outflow of private capital for the year was $727 million.[56] In 1948 the figure rose to $876 million, the highest level in 20 years. Of course, the fall in the value of money reduced the material significance of this amount, but it was sufficient to fill 14 percent of the gap in the goods and services account for the year.

Large as they were, the private foreign investments of these years were small compared with the sums that would probably have moved under more favorable conditions. Would-be investors found a new source of hope in Truman's inaugural address. "Point Four" sounded very much like an announcement that the time had come for government and private business to pull together all the proposals, plans and pronunciamentos and make something practical out of them.

[55] The law was originally drafted so that the guarantees had to be subtracted from a country's dollar allocation, thus making recipient governments reluctant to approve investment arrangements.
[56] This does not include the purchase of bonds issued by the International Bank.

CHAPTER SEVEN

AMERICAN POLICIES IN THE FAR EAST (I)

To THE peoples of Asia the first years of nominal world peace brought further conflict, upheaval and revolution, hunger and suffering. Large areas remained in the throes of political unrest and open warfare. Guerrillas in China, Indonesia and Indochina were "scorching the earth" in resistance to the authority of governments which they no longer accepted. Everywhere insecurity discouraged production, and shortages fostered greater insecurity. The low level of exports made it impossible to count on regular imports of badly needed supplies. Exports from the southeast Asian rice bowl (Burma, Siam and Indochina), on which neighboring countries were dependent, were far below the prewar average. Even where food production levels were maintained or increased, as in India, they could not keep up with the rise in population. The shortage of goods underlay the disastrous inflation which struck everywhere in the Far East. It was bad in India, worse in Indonesia, and reached calamitous heights in China.

These economic conditions strengthened the pressures for political and social change, manifest in the form of nationalism and of movements for a new social order. Nationalism, in many ways a product of the influence of the west, had appeared chiefly as a movement directed against the west, against the "imperialist" powers which had long dominated large parts of Asia. The end of extraterritoriality in China, the winning of independence by India, Burma and Ceylon, the rebellion of Indonesians and Vietnamese against Dutch and French rule, and the violence of Arab feeling on Palestine bore witness to the growing strength of nationalism. The revolt against the west tended to bring Asian peoples together. But where would nationalism, a world religion but one which divides the world instead of uniting it, lead after that? Could these peoples develop a regional system as foreseen by the Asian Relations Conference of 1947 or were they entering a period of rivalry and conflict among themselves? Would they work out a basis for cooperation with western Europe and America or find themselves in ever closer alignment with the Soviet Union? These were questions to which there could be no ready answers.

In many areas the national revolution was becoming or had become a social revolution as well. In both independent and colonial countries there was increasing pressure for agrarian reform and for higher living standards. Many of the nationalist leaders were also socialists, although generally not doctrinaire Marxists and guided mainly by local conditions; some few were Communists whose first allegiance was to Moscow. U Kyaw Nyein, Burma's Minister of the Interior, was typical of many nationalists in his reply to a question put to him by Edgar Snow: "Our immediate aim is a semisocialist state, based first of all on radical agrarian reforms. In general our program is the same as Mao Tse-tung's program for the New Democracy in China—adapted to Burmese conditions. We are Marxists, but we are creative Marxists. We follow the line which is best for Burma, not what somebody who has never seen Burma decides is good for us." [1]

Into this situation the worldwide rivalry between the Soviet Union and the United States had projected itself. For all their gains along the road to independence, the peoples of Asia were destined to be drawn, as in the past, into the currents of world politics. On the other hand Asia could not easily be controlled from outside. In competing for stakes in Asia those powers which played the game of world politics inevitably had to take account of the forces at work within that continent, to concern themselves with the idiosyncrasies, the likes and dislikes, the needs and the aspirations of its peoples. The stakes were high, for Asia is the home of half the world's population; it possesses

[1] Edgar Snow, "The Rover Boys Rule Burma," *Saturday Evening Post*, CCXX, May 29, 1948, 114.

a wealth of human and material resources. Just as it behooved Asia's leaders, if they wished to serve their peoples, to understand the nature of the world struggle, it behooved the leaders of outside powers, if they wished to ride the storm in Asia, to understand the major forces behind the political manoeuvres, violence and rebellion that were its surface manifestations.

The strategic situation in the Far East at the close of the war, as between Soviet and American power, was roughly the following: the U.S.S.R. had acquired southern Sakhalin and the Kuriles, and with them a dominant position in the seas north of Japan, had occupied northern Korea, established preponderant influence in Manchuria, and maintained its position in Outer Mongolia; the United States, having established beyond dispute its predominance in the Pacific, had assumed control of Japan, occupied southern Korea, and continued its leading role in China through aid to and close relations with the Chiang Kai-shek government. In southern and southeast Asia, a vast area which historically had been a sphere of British influence, neither the U.S.A. (except in the Philippines) nor the U.S.S.R. was directly involved although both were following closely the conflict there between the European colonial powers and the strong nationalist movements.

During the three years which followed the war the positions of the two powers underwent little change, except in China where the increasing military successes of the Chinese Communists made it probable that the zone of Soviet influence and control would expand southward. U.S. policy was directed toward strengthening the Nanking government, in the hope that it might at least hold its own, pending a settlement which would unite China. That was a major motive behind the extension of economic aid for civilian relief, financial stabilization and the purchase of military supplies. But the year 1948 was one of new and greater military victories by which the Chinese Communists won absolute possession of all Manchuria, took most of north China, and appeared in force in the Yangtze Valley not far from the capital, Nanking.

For the United States these developments raised strategic

questions of the first magnitude. Was eastern China a crucial area like western Europe that must be kept free from Soviet control in the interest of American security? Or were our island positions in Japan, Okinawa and the Philippines adequate to safeguard American interests in Asia and the western Pacific? Could the United States afford to see the Chinese Communists in a position to organize the manpower and resources of all China for the benefit of the Soviet Union? If not, what measures could be taken to stop them?

The emergence and growth of "Red China" was a development deserving the most serious consideration of those responsible for American policy. They had to consider not only its military implications but also its moral and political effect in India, Malaya, Indonesia and elsewhere. They had to judge whether the policy of containment could be applied in the Far East, and by what methods. Above all, in order to see the problems clearly, they had to pay particular attention to the objectives, policies and tactics of the Soviet Union in its dealings with the peoples of the world's largest and most populous continent.

1. Nationalism, Communism, and Soviet Strategy

The rulers of the Soviet Union had their own estimate of the situation in Asia, derived from their Marxist interpretation of history and politics. On this estimate they had built their policies and determined their strategy. They believed Asia to be ripe for revolutionary changes, not necessarily for communism but for revolt against "exploiting" foreign interests and their local retainers, against native landlords, war lords and "reactionaries." In pursuing their aims they appeared to follow two policies. As prophets of a new revolutionary faith who had renounced the "imperialist" treaties concluded under the Tsarist regime, they inveighed against the imperialism of other powers. As leaders of a great state and heirs of the Tsars, however, they did not balk at annexing territory or establishing spheres of influence of their own. The first policy was most evident, in point of time, when the Soviet Union was comparatively weak, and, in point of space, in countries at some distance from the Soviet frontiers. The second was most apparent when the Soviet state was strong, and in regions adjoining the U.S.S.R. itself. To the Soviet mind there was no inconsistency in this pursuit of imperialism by the great "anti-imperialist" power. The growth of world communism was furthered by the expansion of the territory and influence of the world's only communist state, and vice versa. Tactics were often shifted to meet changing conditions, but the objectives remained the same: to assure the security of the Soviet Union and to extend its influence throughout Asia.

Certain regions were of obvious strategic importance: Korea, Manchuria, Mongolia, Sinkiang, Iran. They were potential bases for any power wishing to attack the U.S.S.R., or for the U.S.S.R. should it wish to strike at Japan, China, or the Middle East. These were regions which lay in the path of Russia's historic drive toward warm water or which opened gateways into the heart of China. The Soviet Union made persistent efforts, both by diplomacy and by more direct methods, to establish its power in them. At Yalta in 1945 it obtained recognition of its "preeminent interest" in Manchuria, specified in railway and port rights—an interest which was secured beyond question when the Chinese Communists won control of all Manchuria in 1948. By the arrangement for military occupation of northern Korea, the Soviet Union was able to establish there a "friendly" regime, backed by a Korean armed force, which was preparing to take over southern Korea as well when the opportune moment should come. In Outer Mongolia, Soviet influence had been uncontested since the 1920's. In Sinkiang, nominally under Chinese sovereignty, it waned during the years of the life and death struggle with Germany, but was again active in the post-war years; Soviet agents seem to have had a hand in the movement which set up a separate East Turkestan Republic in 1944. By delaying withdrawal of its troops from Iran after the war and by pressing for far-reaching oil concessions, the Soviet Union attempted to establish itself in that strategically located country, but here met less success, for strong Anglo-American opposition made itself felt both through the United Nations and through encouragement to the Iranian Government to assert its independence.

Whatever the temporary successes and setbacks, one could count on Soviet interest in and pressure on these peripheral regions as a constant factor in international relations. Further afield—in Japan, China, India, southeast Asia—where Soviet strategic interests and Soviet influence were less direct, the approach was necessarily different. The Japanese home islands had been kept beyond the reach of Soviet influence, first by the power of Japan itself and after the war by the dominant American role in the occupation. In China, Moscow had a double-edged and flexible policy. Without losing interest in the Chinese Communists, it had maintained relations with the Nanking government, supplied aid to Chiang Kai-shek in his struggle against Japan in order to lessen the Japanese threat to the U.S.S.R., and even concluded a comprehensive treaty of friendship and alliance with him in 1945. These commitments did not prevent the Soviet Government from giving support to the Communists as they enlarged the area under their control in Manchuria and north China. Soviet propaganda exploited the widespread desire for land reform, dissatisfaction with the Kuomintang regime, and anti-foreign feeling. This feeling was now directed chiefly against America as the power which had assumed a leading role in China and was the obvious target of blame for China's woes. The combined appeal to nationalism and to the desire for social change was a most effective weapon. In China main emphasis was on the latter, in colonial Asia on the former. Belief in dialectical materialism never blinded the Soviet leaders to the strength of nationalism in Asia. On the contrary, from the time of their coming to power they had had a carefully thought-out policy on nationalities and the colonial question.

Capitalism, as Lenin saw it, was marching toward its own destruction. Imperialism, however, had temporarily given it a new lease on life. Only with the profits derived from the exploitation of colonial peoples, he held, was the bourgeoisie able to maintain its position in the advanced capitalist countries. Seeing in Asia and Africa hundreds of millions of potential allies of the workers of Europe, Lenin set about planning a twofold attack on the citadels of capitalism through agitation for social revolution in the metropolitan countries and for national independence in their colonies. On coming to power the Bolsheviks announced themselves as champions of movements of national liberation. In the organization of their own state, they gave recognition to differences of nationality within the limits of the rigid discipline of a one-party system and a centrally directed economy. Nationalities in the Soviet Union were not permitted to look forward to political independence; nevertheless, the grant of full cultural autonomy, in contrast to the "Russification" policy of the Tsars, could not fail to impress non-Russian peoples both inside and outside the U.S.S.R. Since the Soviet regime also raised standards of literacy, medical care and the like in its non-Russian republics in Asia, these republics exercised an undeniable power of attraction over neighboring and sometimes ethnically related peoples in Mongolia, Central Asia, Iran and eastern Turkey.

In the more distant countries under direct colonial rule, the Soviet Union's immediate purpose was to weaken the imperial powers. Unceasingly its propaganda mill ground out testimonials of sympathy for the exploited colored peoples and exhortations to them to cast out the white imperialists. After the war it used United Nations bodies as a forum for attacks on the colonial system. Championship of the principle of racial equality was a powerful weapon of Soviet propaganda in Asia.

The Soviet Union did not support movements of national liberation merely as a matter of principle, but entered them actively and made constant efforts to turn them into channels advantageous to the U.S.S.R. and to Soviet Communism. In the pursuit of this general program Soviet agents and native Communist leaders attempted to build up party organizations in colonial countries, and to work with and infiltrate the groups whose main objective was national independence.

The unsettled period at the end of the second World War offered great opportunities. The Soviet Union, as a strong victor power, had great prestige, as did local Communists, who had distinguished themselves in the resistance movement against the Japanese. Moreover, the war and the attempts of some of the colonial powers to restore by force an approximation of the pre-war status created an atmosphere favorable to extremism. Communist parties grew in numbers and in influence. Not all of them were controlled by Moscow. Many who called themselves communists had no clear conception of Marxist-Leninist doctrine; their interest was in radical reform measures *per se* rather than as part of a world revolutionary strategy. This was true of some the communist factions in Burma. Ho Chi Minh, leader of the Vietnamese nationalist movement in Indochina, had spent a part of his career in the Soviet Union and had worked in the Comintern, but his allegiance to Soviet Communism in 1948 was not beyond question. Nor was there any public evidence that the radical Hukbalahap movement in the Philippines was linked with Moscow. Nevertheless, the activities of all these groups served the interests of Soviet policy in making trouble for the western powers and for the moderate, noncommunist nationalists. And the Soviet Union was the beneficiary of those policies of the colonial powers which drove the moderates into collaboration with the Communists.

In China, where communism scored its greatest successes, it was not altogether clear to what extent its leadership was consciously serving the Kremlin's rather than its own interests. That the acknowledged leader, Mao Tse-tung, followed all turns of the Moscow line, including the condemnation of the Tito regime in Yugoslavia, seemed to put the burden of proof on those who maintained that his was an independent Chinese movement not under Soviet direction. Yet it had real roots in China. This was no artificial, imported revolution.

Coordination of Communist leadership in various countries of Asia might be deduced from the frequency of visits made by individual leaders to the U.S.S.R. and to Yenan, the "capital" of Red China. The intensification of Communist activity throughout the Far East in the spring and summer of 1948 led to considerable speculation whether it was part of a campaign planned by the Soviet Union.[2] Often in the course of Russian history a lull in Russian expansion to the west has been accompanied by a concentration of effort on the Far East. In this case, the setback to Soviet policies represented by the launching of the European Recovery Program may have turned the Soviet leaders toward more aggressive moves in the east, where they could simultaneously seek political gains and attack ERP at a vulnerable point, its dependence on Asia's raw materials.

The Soviet strategy was to gain for tried and true Stalinists key positions in the movements for national liberation and social revolution, and to gain maximum mass support for those movements which had been or could be brought under their control. To this end the points of concentration were the industrial working class and the peasantry. As the labor movement was in its infancy, Communist efforts were directed both toward building up trade unions and toward turning them into revolutionary channels. Slogans demanding organization, increased wages and better working conditions were mixed with others calling for the overthrow of the imperialists and their native lackeys. New labor organizations such as the Korean General Confederation of Labor, the Pan-Malayan and All-Indonesian Federations of Trade Unions and the Arab Workers' Congress were organized under Communist guidance and affiliated with the World Federation of Trade Unions.

Communists knew that the labor movement could not provide a base, except possibly in Japan, strong enough to immobilize national economies or to take power. At the base of society in Asia stood the peasant, whose land hunger could be used in the struggle to overturn the existing order. The success of the Chinese Communists was due in large part to the appeal which

[2] A number of journalists have referred to reports of the adoption of a common plan in February 1948 at Calcutta, where Communist representatives from many countries, including the U.S.S.R., were present at a congress of the Indian Communist party. Burmese Premier Thakin Nu alleged that Communists in his country were obeying written instructions brought back from India ("Asia's Old Order Crumbles," *New Republic*, CXIX, December 13, 1948, 16).

they made to the peasants and to the agrarian reforms which they instituted in areas brought under their control. Often taking the lead in organizing peasant unions and other associations, native Communists put forward demands for lower rents, systematization of the tax structure, liquidation of "feudal bondage," confiscation of the large estates and distribution of land to the peasants. A great number of peasants had been given land in Communist China.[3] In northern Korea large holdings were confiscated and redistributed to landless peasants and owners of dwarf plots. Mao Tse-tung wrote that Communists had come to realize that the revolution in the East was a "peasant revolution." "Its basic characteristic is that the peasants, not the workers, form the principal mass that resists the oppression of foreign capital and the left-over medieval elements in the . . . countryside." [4]

Emphasis on the revolutionary possibilities of the peasantry, the writings of both Lenin and Stalin point out, should not obscure the main goal, the dictatorship of the proletariat. The peasants were needed to overthrow the old order, but satisfaction of their land hunger would inevitably make them conservative elements in society. The march to socialism had then to be headed by the Communist-led working class.

In addition to the workers and peasants, the Communists have given another group, the armed forces, a major place in their calculations. Oriental armies have generally had political importance only in relation to the ambitions and policies of their leaders. The Communist appeal was to the rank and file, to the ordinary soldier, who was held to be potential revolutionary material whether he had fought in wartime resistance movements

---

[3] Soviet sources give estimates as high as 43 million and 60 million as the number of peasants who had received land by the end of 1947 (G. V. Efimov, *Borba dlya Demokratsii protiv Reaktsii v Kitae* [Leningrad, 1948], 8; V. Maslennikov, "Borba kitaiskogo naroda za natsionalnuyu nezavisimost i svobodu," *Mirovoe Khozyaistvo i Mirovaya Politika*, December 1947, 19). The basic law for the redistribution of land, intended to complete earlier reforms, went into effect in the autumn of 1947 after the holding of a special agrarian conference in September.

[4] Anna Louise Strong, "The Thought of Mao Tse-tung," *Amerasia*, XI, June 1947, 163.

or served in regular armies. Infiltration and agitation was one facet of Communist technique in this field. The other was the organization, wherever possible, of "people's armies." To do this most effectively the Communists required actual control of territory. Thus the most extensive experience and greatest success were gained in Communist China, where over a period of 20 years a "Red Army" had been built up, trained to fight both guerrilla and positional warfare, especially the former, and educated in Marxism by political commissars. It served, *mutatis mutandis,* as model for the army created in northern Korea and for Communist forces operating in Burma and Indonesia.

The work of organization and propaganda, aimed at winning the support of workers, peasants and soldiers, proceeded steadily. Everywhere the Communists proclaimed themselves to be in the vanguard of the struggle against inequality, exploitation, feudalism and imperialism. Their slogans were directed both to self-interest and to sentiments of universal freedom and brotherhood. By the "popular front" technique they won the cooperation of many non-Communist intellectuals and middle-class liberals. By their campaign against "big bureaucratic capitalists" they made a strong appeal to the traders and small capitalists.

Mao Tse-tung, whose *New Democracy* has become a minor classic of Communist doctrine in undeveloped countries, envisaged a Communist-led "people's democracy" such as had come into existence with Soviet support in countries of eastern Europe. The people's democracy, he wrote, is based on the bloc of partners of the united front, having the broad support of the millions of industrial workers, artisans and peasants, who constitute the overwhelming majority of the population, and also of the "small, liberal bourgeoisie and other patriots." [5] The stage of socialism, according to Mao, would come later. If the analogy with eastern Europe may be carried further, the "united front" and the "people's democracy" might be expected to pave the way to full Communist control and a totalitarian system. Mao himself, in a speech delivered at the end of 1947, proclaimed

[5] Efimov, *op. cit.,* 6.

that the united front "should be under the firm control of the Chinese Communist party." [6]

Political democracy has something less of an attraction than national and social equality to those living at the subsistence level and subjected to colonial rule or local despotism. Wherever it could make effective use of the force of nationalism in Asia, the Soviet Union could assure itself of a potent weapon with which to combat and destroy western influence. Even without it, communism and Soviet influence had an unparalleled opportunity to grow and prosper in Asia if they could succeed in taking the leadership of the forces making for social change. That possibility, which proved itself to be very real in 1948 and 1949, posed a challenge to western nations, especially to the United States, and to those in Asia who feared and opposed the spread of Communist totalitarianism.

2. The Plight of Nationalist China

The vast and populous country called China seemed destined to be the main Asian battleground between Soviet Communism and the western world. At any rate, it was the scene of large-scale civil war between two factions, one of which professed to be guided by the principles of Marx and the example of the Soviet Union, while the other pictured itself as a bulwark against communism and was openly dependent on aid from the United States. Chiang Kai-shek, after the failure of General Marshall's attempt to bring a truce and a political settlement in 1946, had declared war to the bitter end on the Communists as rebels against constituted authority and agents of Soviet imperialism. Mao Tse-tung replied by denouncing Chiang and his associates as traitors to the Chinese people and "running dogs of American imperialism." There was no further talk of compromise.

Unfortunately for the Kuomintang regime, its armies were unable to carry out Chiang's promise to dispose of the Communist menace by military action. At the beginning of the year

[6] Quoted in *Pravda*, January 6, 1948.

1948, government troops held only a very small part of Manchuria, a narrow corridor connecting the cities of Changchun and Mukden with the coast. The Communists were making gains in Shantung, Shansi, and other provinces of north China. They held scattered areas even in the Yangtze Valley, the heart of Kuomintang China. Mao Tse-tung announced that the decisive turning point in the war had been successfully passed.

Chiang Kai-shek was receiving from the United States economic support and military advice in training programs. While the Chinese Communists had the benefit of Soviet military advice, were consistently supported by Soviet propaganda, and had picked up a large quantity of Japanese military equipment when Soviet troops evacuated Manchuria, probably they were not receiving material aid from Russia comparable to what the government obtained from the United States. How much came directly across the long Soviet-Chinese land frontier outsiders had no way of knowing. The Soviet Government would hardly publicize such assistance, since it would be in open violation of its treaty of August 1945 with the Chinese Government, and if known would probably lead to increased American aid to the other side and to a greater danger of international conflict. Besides, with the Chinese Communists winning, there was no need for open intervention on the part of the Soviet Union.

Why was Chiang losing the trial of arms? Reports from the battlefronts pointed to the inescapable conclusion that the morale of the Communist forces was higher than that of their opponents. This was no proof that the Chinese people welcomed communism. It is a safe assumption that the great mass of the Chinese people was heartily sick of war and almost entirely absorbed in the struggle for the necessities of life. Those enrolled in the Communist ranks, however, fought with greater enthusiasm and effectiveness than the soldiers of the national army. Even Chiang's best-equipped divisions had poor leadership and low morale. Many of the arms supplied by the United States wound up in Communist hands, by capture or by other means.

If the loyalty and effectiveness of the government armies was dubious, it was because the government itself had lost prestige and no longer inspired confidence in the country. Many foreign observers, including General Marshall and General Wedemeyer, had called the world's attention to the maladministration and corruption of the Kuomintang regime. Political power remained in the hands of Chiang himself and of a limited number of generals and politicians, who relied for support on their armies, on the party machinery, and on certain privileged economic groups. What had been a popular revolutionary party in the 1930's had become more and more an authoritarian, bureaucratic regime concerned with preserving its power. Its methods, such as the use of secret police and control of the universities, alienated the liberal elements which might have led such a movement for reform as American envoys had so often advised. It did not meet the popular demand for social reform. China was in a ferment of continuing social revolution, which the Kuomintang no longer had the capacity to lead, whereas the Communists, while equally authoritarian, advocated a program which carried them along on the revolutionary tide.

Discontent with the government, even in Kuomintang circles, was apparent when the first National Assembly under the new constitution, in force since December 1947, met at the end of March 1948. The Assembly was empowered by the constitution to exercise power on behalf of the whole body of citizens. Because of its unwieldy size (approximately 3,000 members) and infrequent meetings, its important functions were limited to the election of the president and vice-president of the republic and amendment of the constitution. The actual functions of government were assigned to the president and to five yuans (legislative, executive, judicial, examination, and control). In practice, real political power remained in the hands of the Kuomintang, which had not brought the period of one-party "tutelage" to an end nor established civil liberties despite the adoption of a democratic constitution. The presence within the government of two minor groups, the Democratic Socialist and Young China parties, gave the outward impression of a coalition regime, but their representatives were a symbol of the pledge to establish a representative regime rather than a proof of its existence.

In the elections for the National Assembly some 700 independent Kuomintang members and nonparty men won seats even though they were not official candidates put forward by the party. Most of these seats had actually been promised to the Young China and Democratic Socialist parties, which won but 140 of the 560 seats assigned to them.[7] The resulting wrangle developed into a minor revolt against the leadership of the party machine. The leader of the Democratic Socialists, although his party suffered from the failure of the election to go according to plan, drew the conclusion that it proved the existence of such a thing as public opinion in China, a public opinion which refused to be molded by organized interests and groups. He was "both surprised and encouraged by the emergence of this unknown quantity." [8]

Ostensibly the controversy centered on the issue of manipulation and irregularities affecting the legality of the election. Actually it reflected growing dissatisfaction and alarm within the Kuomintang itself over military reverses, stifled trade and high living costs. Chiang himself was losing prestige. General Li Tsung-jen became the spearhead of this opposition movement when, without official sanction, he announced his candidacy for the vice-presidency with a statement of the need of new leadership, reorganization of the army, an end of corruption, and a wider popular base for the government. He expressed himself in favor of democratic control over public finance and the redistribution of land. These were the major points on which the Communists were basing their propaganda against the Kuomintang regime. General Li, while loyal to the Kuomintang, took the line that it could not defeat the Communists by military force alone, that it must solve the problem of "the

[7] The same situation arose in connection with the election for the Legislative Yuan in January 1948. When it met in May, it was boycotted by the two minor parties.
[8] Letter of Carson Chang to the editor of the *New York Times*, March 10, 1948 (*New York Times*, March 21, 1948).

people's livelihood," one of the famous three principles of Sun Yat-sen, or resign itself to defeat.

Chiang Kai-shek, on April 4, announced his intention not to be a candidate to succeed himself as President of China, but when other Kuomintang leaders insisted that he continue and the Assembly elected him, he overcame his reluctance. At the same time the Assembly approved temporary constitutional provisions for granting the president emergency powers "during the period of national crisis." These results were to be expected, as this was in essence a Kuomintang assemblage and Chiang, standing above the various factions, was both the symbol and the active leader of the Kuomintang. However, loyalty to him as a national leader did not preclude widespread criticism of recent governmental policies and the conduct of the war.

In the balloting for the vice-presidency Li won an unexpected victory over the incumbent, Sun Fo, who had the backing of the party machine. His election, amid turbulent scenes in the assembly hall, was a demonstration of a general lack of confidence in the Nanking politicians. Constitutionally, Li as vice-president would have little power. Yet he had considerable prestige and potentialities. A leader of the southern province of Kwangsi, he had ties with powerful generals in other provinces whose attitudes would be of increasing importance if Chiang's armies should suffer further defeats in the civil war.

In his inaugural address as the first constitutional President of the Republic on May 20, Chiang pledged allegiance to the constitution, administrative reform, and practice of the principle of the people's livelihood, including land reforms. But the immediate and urgent task, he said, was the "eradication of anti-democratic forces," the Communists.[9] To help him in this task he could count on American aid in the amount of $400 million appropriated by the 80th Congress under the Foreign Assistance Act of 1948. The purpose behind the extension of the grant was clearly set forth in the report of the Senate Foreign Relations Committee stating that "at this critical moment . . . China is an important part of a common front against aggres-

[9] *China Information Bulletin* (New York), I, June 1, 1948.

sive Communism." "There exist in China," said the report somewhat optimistically, "the social and political elements and ideals which can combat the hard core of a disruptive, alien-orientated communism in open rebellion." [10] Of the total sum appropriated, $275 million was to be devoted to helping China stabilize economic conditions; $125 million was granted for such purposes as the Chinese Government should desire, with the expectation that it would be spent for American military supplies.

The debate in the United States over aid to China raised fundamental questions concerning American policy in the Far East. In the heat of the current controversy between those who wished to "stop communism" at all costs and those who opposed giving anything to support a "corrupt and reactionary dictatorship," the permanent elements of American policy in China were often forgotten. One was the principle of the open door, enunciated by John Hay in 1899. The other was the principle of the territorial integrity of China, which the United States and other nations had formally agreed to respect in signing the Nine-Power Treaty of 1922. It was true that the United States was not committed to go to war in defense of those principles and had not done so when Japan violated them in the 1930's. However, they still stood as principles which America supported and hoped that other nations would respect. With the defeat of Japan in 1945 a new vista of freedom from foreign domination had seemed to be opening for China. Counted on as a potential great power and stabilizing force in the Far East, China was accepted as one of the five permanent members of the U.N. Security Council and as a member of the Council of Foreign Ministers. American policy, in the new postwar setting, had the declared aim of helping the Chinese to build a peaceful, democratic and united nation, one which could maintain its independence and integrity, keep open the doors to world trade, and contribute to the maintenance of world peace and security.

[10] *Aid to China*, Senate Report No. 1026, 80th Congress, 2nd Session, March 25, 1948, 4-5.

What had happened to that policy between 1945 and 1948? A genuine effort, General Marshall's mission of 1946, had been made to bring about a settlement of differences between the Chinese Government and the Communists, in order that they might work together to rebuild China instead of fighting a civil war. That effort had failed. General Marshall's report on his mission stated that extremists on both sides, the Communists and the right wing of the Kuomintang, had made agreement impossible and that the liberal elements who favored a middle course lacked power and authority to make their influence felt. Thenceforth, with Marshall as Secretary of State, American policy was one of watchful waiting. The United States continued, however, to be involved in Chinese affairs by virtue of the fact that it continued to provide aid and advice to the Chinese Government. The Chinese Communists, seeing their opponents strengthened by American help, found added reason to take up the current Moscow propaganda line denouncing America's "imperialistic intervention" and "support of reaction" in China.

The result of this half-involvement in China's civil war was that the United States became identified with the cause of the central government without giving that government effective support against the Communists. In that China had not been made peaceful, united or democratic, American policy had failed. The question was: Could anything be done about it? An influential current of opinion felt that the United States must give the government greater and more effective assistance. This group, whose chief spokesmen in Congress were Representative Judd and Senator Bridges, also included leading military men with experience in China, Generals Wedemeyer and Chennault, and prominent private individuals such as William C. Bullitt. They had the support of the Luce publications and the Scripps-Howard press, and the general sympathy of a number of individual newspapers including the *New York Times*. Broadly, their argument ran as follows: The government of Chiang Kai-shek, whatever its defects, stood for China's independence and friendship with the United States; it was fighting

America's battle in the struggle against communism, which was not confined to Europe but was world-wide; substantial American assistance would enable Chiang to defeat the Chinese Communists or at least to check Communist, and Soviet, influence in China; if necessary, the United States should send a prominent general, in agreement with the Chinese Government, to assume over-all direction of the fight against communism in China; direct military intervention with American troops would be unnecessary if material aid were given promptly.

An opposing current of opinion held that such a policy would be fruitless and mistaken. According to this view, the Kuomintang regime had lost the sympathy and support of the Chinese people; further American intervention in its favor would involve the danger of outright participation in a civil war in which the mass of Chinese would be against us; communism in China, riding a wave of social change, could not be countered by purely military force, and Chiang's regime had shown its inability to compete with the Communists on the political and social plane; the United States, therefore, should stay out of the fight while continuing to express interest in the welfare of the Chinese people and to seek opportunities, as the situation developed, to work toward the achievement of the basic aims of our China policy.

Either course would represent an attempt, at great risk, to make the best of a very discouraging situation. The Administration seemed inclined to follow the second, although it did carry through a limited aid program authorized by Congress in 1948. Secretary Marshall made no public statement of American aims and policies in China. The State Department did not feel confident that American aid, even in much larger quantities than had been authorized, would suffice to retrieve the Chinese Government's military fortunes or rectify the disastrous economic situation in Kuomintang China. It desired to avoid commitments which might involve the United States deeply in the Chinese civil war to the detriment of our European policy.

On August 19, the Chinese Government came forward with

a bold plan of currency reform intended to check the spiraling inflation. The old notes were replaced by a new issue of gold yuan currency at the rate of three million to one. Promising additional financial reorganization and economic stability, Chiang called on the people to prove their patriotism by observing the regulations. Utilizing American advice and financial support, the government made a serious effort to carry the reform through successfully. Drastic punishment, even the death penalty, was inflicted on hoarders and speculators. Closely linked with the fight against inflation was a new scheme for rural rehabilitation, also undertaken with American help, which had possibilities of countering the political appeal of the agrarian reforms promised by the Communists. But the lateness of the hour, difficulties of local enforcement, and growing dissension and conflict within the ranks of the Kuomintang combined to reduce virtually to zero the chance that real economic and social reforms could be put into effect. The new currency could not withstand the pressure of shortages, panic buying, black market operations, and the devotion of most of the national budget to military expenditures. By autumn the economic outlook in the cities seemed hopeless. On November 1 the government, admitting failure, abolished price ceilings. The flow of food, cotton and other goods under the ECA program slowed but did not halt the economic decline. Only $81.6 million worth of goods had actually been shipped by that time. The rural areas, where peasants struggled for a bare existence, were not so deeply affected by financial chaos, but in Shanghai and other large cities it was virtually impossible to carry on any orderly business activities, and there were food riots as the price of rice shot up out of reach. On the military front, meanwhile, government forces were suffering a series of calamitous defeats.

3. Red Star in the Ascendant

For some months the government had held only isolated points in Manchuria: Changchun, Mukden, Chinchow, and a few others. In north China most of the government's gains made in Shantung in 1947 had to be given up in 1948 and were more than counterbalanced by the expansion of Communist-controlled "liberated areas" both north and south of the Yellow River. On September 1 the Communists announced the formation of a North China People's Government "on the basis of a patriotic democratic united front for the striking down of American imperialism and Kuomintang reactionary rule in China." [11]

In September Tsinan, capital of Shantung, fell to the Communists. In October they completed the conquest of Manchuria. This debacle, in which the government lost thousands of its best troops, enabled the Communists to regroup their armies and carry their offensive southward toward the Yangtze River and Nanking itself.

The national government faced the prospect of complete defeat. Chiang reaffirmed his determination to fight on to the end. The people had fought for 14 years, he said, to save China from the Japanese and to recover Manchuria. They would fight for 14 more years to save China and win back Manchuria from the Communists. Whether Chiang would be able to fight on depended on his ability to rally his armies and the people in support of his cause and to obtain additional American assistance to meet the emergency. He found that he could do neither.

The national armies were demoralized. Some units went over to the Communists. The military leaders in charge of various theaters of war became increasingly independent of Nanking. Foreseeing collapse, some of them prepared to make what arrangements they could with the Communists. Among the people no real enthusiasm for continuing the war was evident. Chiang himself admitted that the Communist "rumor offensive" was gaining momentum, "so much so that the general public has been taken in by the vicious propaganda and become panicky." [12] The Communists were using the slogans of "peace"

[11] New China News Agency broadcast, North Shensi, September 1, 1948.
[12] Speech of November 8, 1948 at Nanking (Chinese News Service, New York, Press Release No. SA 429, November 9, 1948).

and "people's livelihood" against the government with considerable success. Talk of peace, even among high Nanking officials, grew louder as the Communists massed for an assault on Suchow, key junction north of the capital.

Would the United States do anything to prevent a complete disaster for the Chinese Government? Chiang Kai-shek and his colleagues had some hope that a Republican victory in the American elections would bring about a more active policy in support of their cause in view of Dewey's campaign references to the need of standing by China and the Republican pressure in Congress for greater aid. Whatever Dewey may have intended to do or could have done for China if elected, the news of his defeat at the polls created an atmosphere of the deepest gloom at Nanking. It shattered the last real hope that new and massive support could be expected from America.

A report by ex-Senator D. Worth Clark, who went to China on behalf of the Senate Appropriations Committee, indicated the scale of any program "properly calculated to attempt the rescue of China from communism at this stage." It included immediate and extensive military aid in the form of guns, planes, and ammunition, authority to direct the military campaign, and sufficient financial aid to stabilize the Chinese currency and remove a major cost of the war from the Chinese budget, with strict American supervision of expenditures of money supplied by the United States.[13] Clark did not attempt to estimate the cost of such a program or the political consequences of its adoption. But the mere statement of what far-reaching measures would be necessary to save the Nanking government from defeat was instructive. For it was not likely that such direct and large-scale intervention, which might even involve the eventual use of American troops, would be acceptable to the Administration, the Congress, or the American public.

The Administration did not intend to be forced into a huge and expensive gamble in support of a cause that appeared beyond salvation. That was the reason for the cool reception given to Mme. Chiang when she flew to Washington in Decem-

13 *New York Times,* November 21, 1948.

ber to make a last-minute plea for help. Truman and Marshall did not wish even to make a public declaration of support for the Chinese Government. They thought it wiser to keep their hands free to deal with whatever new situation might develop. The United States had already lost much of its influence in China. A new declaration which would associate the U.S. Government formally with Chiang's cause and could not be backed would only tie American prestige even more closely to a losing cause. The United States, officials announced, would do what it could to speed up the existing aid program, but nothing more.

The Kuomintang regime broke under the pressure to which it was subjected. Chiang remained inflexible in his opposition to any peace overtures to the Communists, who left no doubt of their refusal to make any kind of deal with him. A growing group within the government, however, was unwilling to follow Chiang in resistance to the bitter end. To work toward peace, on the basis either of a division of China into two states or of a coalition regime for the whole country, they had to have some assurance that the Communists would negotiate and some assurance that Chiang would step aside. A new cabinet formed late in December with Sun Fo as premier contained some members who favored Chiang's resignation as a step toward a negotiated peace.

On what terms and with whom would the Communists negotiate? Their radio announced, on December 25, a list of "first-class war criminals who have committed such crimes that the people of the nation would agree upon death sentences for them." As might have been expected, Chiang Kai-shek, T. V. Soong, H. H. Kung and the Chen brothers were included in this category. These "four families" were the target of the most virulent Communist attacks as the high priests of bureaucratic capitalism and exploiters of the Chinese people. The "not yet complete" list also contained the names of Vice-President Li Tsung-jen, Premier Sun Fo, ex-Premier Chang Chun, ex-Foreign Minister Wang Shih-chieh, Wellington Koo (Ambassador to Washington), Mme. Chiang Kai-shek, and many others. Seven members of Sun Fo's cabinet were included.

Who, then, could negotiate on behalf of the Nanking government? This Communist pronouncement was a blow to the "peace party" at Nanking as well as a shock to world opinion. Killing off all the leading figures of a government which had fought with the Allies against the Axis and still was the recognized legal Government of China did not commend itself as a civilized procedure. In Washington, Under-Secretary Lovett called it "unthinkable" that these Chinese leaders should be regarded as war criminals.

Yet the military situation seemed to offer Nanking only two alternatives, to negotiate for peace or to suffer complete defeat. An attempt to bring the American, British and Soviet governments into the picture to help arrange a settlement met with complete failure. Moscow wished to let matters take their course. Washington and London wanted no further responsibility. Chiang finally brought himself to say, in his New Year's message, that peace could be negotiated "if the Communists were sincerely desirous of peace." But he was not the one to undertake such negotiations, certainly not on the conditions set by Mao Tse-tung and announced over the Communist radio. Mao listed eight points: "(1) punishment of war criminals; (2) repeal of the fictitious constitution; (3) abolition of the traditional legal institutions established by the Kuomintang; (4) reform of all the reactionary armies in accordance with democratic principles; (5) confiscation of bureaucratic capital; (6) reform of the agrarian system; (7) repeal of treacherous treaties; (8) convocation of a Political Consultative Council without the participation of reactionary elements, with the object of forming a democratic coalition government and of taking all authority away from the reactionary Nanking Kuomintang government and its local organs." [14] In other words, the Communists would insist on taking over the government of all China and on putting into effect, with political allies chosen by themselves, their own program.

On January 21, 1949, Chiang announced his "retirement,"

[14] North Shensi radio broadcast, January 14, 1949, reproduced in *Izvestia* (Moscow), January 19, 1949.

leaving Nanking for his home in Chekiang province. His fare-well statement expressed the hope that the Communists would order a cease-fire and agree to begin peace talks. After Chiang's departure, most of the higher officials in Nanking were talking about peace, but none of them could do much about it. The Communists denounced the "peace campaign" as an American plot to rob them of their victories and to give Chiang Kai-shek a breathing space to build up new armies in south China. They were not interested in a truce which would merely stop the fighting and open the way to peace talks. They would negotiate only on the basis of their eight points, which would amount to capitulation and the end of the Kuomintang as a factor in the government of China. The "coalition" regime which they had in mind was not a sharing of authority with the Kuomin-tang but a government dominated by the Communists, who would permit the participation of certain "safe" non-Communist groups such as the left-wing Democratic League and, possibly, the dissident Kuomintang group which, from exile in Hong Kong, had long been preaching the need of peace.

The fall of Tientsin and Peiping, giving the Communists complete military control of north China, gave added weight to their demands. Acting President Li Tsung-jen, on January 22, announced that he was ready to talk terms on the basis of the eight conditions laid down by Mao Tse-tung. He appealed to the dissident Kuomintang group in Hong Kong to cooperate with him. At the same time he took belated measures to reform and liberalize the Nanking regime. Meanwhile, however, Premier Sun Fo, the cabinet and many of the government officers were moving to Canton. Military units, funds and supplies were being transferred to the south and to Formosa, as if in preparation for continued resistance. Some of the generals remained personally loyal to Chiang, not to the Nanking government. Nationalist China seemed to be disintegrating into a number of zones in which actual authority was in the hands of local "war lords." Li might be unable to make a peace settlement for China as a whole, since his government's control over areas beyond the lower Yangtze Valley was shadowy.

Attempting to hold the government together in order to present the strongest possible front in peace talks, Li gathered the principal military leaders round him at Nanking, and persuaded Sun Fo to return from Canton; not long afterward Sun Fo resigned under pressure from the Legislative Yuan. Toward the end of February, a "preliminary" peace mission from Nanking and Shanghai, made up of men with whom the Communists were willing to talk, was received by Mao Tse-tung at his headquarters in north China. More formal negotiations opened in April, only to break down when the Nanking mission saw that there was no hope of compromise and when the Communists demanded unopposed crossing of the Yangtze. On April 21-22 they crossed the river in force, renewing large-scale military operations.

Communist victories represented a resounding defeat for the United States. American influence, which had stood at a high point at the end of the war, was reduced virtually to zero. In the last two years Chinese opinion on both sides, in so far as it found public expression, had turned increasingly against America, for a variety of reasons—because we had intervened, or because we had not intervened effectively, or because of our policies in Japan.[15] In any case, anti-Americanism colored all the thinking and all the propaganda of the victorious Chinese Communists.

The great danger to the United States was not that the new China emerging from the civil war should reject American influence but that it should be an appendage of the Soviet Union. For China to become a part of the Soviet system, as Poland and Rumania were parts of it, would represent a great shift in the world balance of power. Communist spokesmen asserted that the triumph of communism in China shifted the balance decisively in their favor. Many in the United States, especially those who had deplored our failure to send more aid to Chiang Kai-shek, agreed with them. The sentiment in Congress favor-

[15] Dorothy Borg, "America Loses Chinese Good Will," *Far Eastern Survey*, XVIII, February 23, 1949, 37-45; Thurston Griggs, *Americans in China: Some Chinese Views* (Washington, Foundation for Foreign Affairs, 1948).

ing more aid to anti-Communist forces in China had by no means disappeared. In mid-March a group of 50 Senators, a majority of the Senate, announced their support of a bill providing up to $1,500 million in credits for economic and military aid to the Nanking government in fighting the Communists. In return, China would accept American direction of its armed forces and pledge the tax revenues of its major ports as collateral for the loan. This was no partisan Republican manoeuvre, for half the signatories were Democrats. But the proposal found no more favor with the State Department than had those put forward by the Republicans alone. Secretary Acheson's views were stated bluntly in a letter to Senator Connally apparently not intended for publication. The extension of such a huge loan, Acheson said, "would embark this Government on an undertaking the eventual cost of which would almost surely be catastrophic." Even under stable conditions, China could not repay such loans, and the conditions proposed would be deeply resented. Finally, the Secretary concluded, in the absence of a Chinese government able to achieve stability and win popular support, U.S. aid would be dissipated as the more than $2 billion already extended since the war had been dissipated.

The most that the State Department favored in the way of aid to China was that the $54 million of unexpended funds remaining under the ECA appropriation expiring April 1 should be made available to areas of China still outside Communist control. This the Congress did by including a provision to that effect in the new Economic Cooperation Act of April 19, 1949. But many Congressmen were far from satisfied and talked of "investigating" the whole question of U.S. policy in the Far East and the State Department's responsibility for the current disastrous situation.

The situation contained many imponderables from which Americans might take some consolation. The Chinese Communist movement had its roots in China's soil. It had maintained itself as a political and military force for some 30 years. The Communists were winning control of China by their own efforts. Would they be mere puppets of Moscow? There was no doubt

of their Marxist-Leninist-Stalinist orthodoxy. Mao's pronouncements followed the party line without noticeable deviation.
American imperialism, he wrote in the Cominform journal,
was menacing the world. Against it the united anti-imperialist
front, headed by the Soviet Union, must be strengthened. The
Chinese Communist party, he wrote, was an integral part of
that front. Its struggles were not isolated, but were supported
by the Communist parties throughout the world.[16] On the other
hand, China was one of the world's oldest nations. Nationalism and anti-foreign feeling were deeply embedded in the
Chinese character. Even a Communist regime, in adapting itself
to Chinese conditions, might, as in Yugoslavia, be independent
rather than subservient to Moscow. That the Soviet Union itself
foresaw the possibility of such a development was a possible explanation of efforts to strengthen its own position in the immediate border areas such as Manchuria and Sinkiang.

Furthermore, China was a huge, unorganized country. The
Communists, in taking over the government, would fall heir
to the vast problems which had plagued the Kuomintang. Lacking sufficient cadres of trained officials, they would find governing the large cities a new and difficult experience. They might
find it impossible to control local war lords. They would have to
deal with the economic chaos which had engulfed the Kuomintang regime. They would have a huge problem in trying to
develop the country, probably without American capital and
technical assistance. China was exhausted by years of war; its
people were ground down by poverty and weakened by disease.
As an industrial nation China did not count. Even if China was
drawn into the Soviet empire, in material terms it was likely
for many years to be an element of weakness rather than of
strength. A great many things could happen before China's
resources and manpower could be mobilized for effective use as
an adjunct to Soviet military power. No such time lag would
exist in Europe, where the main American effort to contain Soviet power was being made.

American policy, so far as it could be judged by Washing-

16 *For a Lasting Peace, For a People's Democracy!*, November 1, 1948.

ton's reaction to events in China, was to withdraw from all involvement, to wait and see how matters developed, and to keep hands free for more positive action when the situation should become clearer. American naval units and marines were withdrawn from Tsingtao. The U.S. military mission was called home. Recognition of the Communist government was a question for the future. Whether the United States would attempt to keep any strategic points in south China, or Formosa, out of Communist hands was not apparent. With all of China lost, the American strategic position in the western Pacific would rest on island strong points in the Philippines, Okinawa, and Japan. The debacle in China seemed destined to make Japan, the recent foe, the fulcrum of American policy in the Far East.

CHAPTER EIGHT

AMERICAN POLICIES IN THE FAR EAST (II)

1. Changes in Occupied Japan

Three years after the surrender of Japan there was no peace treaty. In contrast to the situation with respect to Germany, the subject of lengthy sessions of the Council of Foreign Ministers during 1947, not even a beginning was made toward a peace settlement with Japan. The reason was not far to seek. The big powers could not agree even on procedure. The United States had proposed an 11-nation conference, with decisions to be made by two-thirds majority vote. The U.S.S.R. maintained that the Council of Foreign Ministers, where each of the four members would have a veto, was the proper body to draft the treaty. The Chinese Government, resentful over what had happened at Yalta in its absence and desiring legal safeguards to compensate for China's actual weakness, also supported the veto. China would accept the American proposal only if amended to provide that final decisions required the concurring votes of the Big Four.

As none of the powers gave way, there the matter stood. The United States, Britain, and other states which had indicated their readiness to begin discussions did not attempt to go ahead without Russia and China. There could be no genuine peace settlement in the Far East unless those two countries were parties to it. China could see no reason to join in framing a treaty which Russia was not obligated to observe, and both were specifically pledged, under their treaty of August 1945, not to conclude a separate peace with Japan. Furthermore, China's future was so much in doubt that the Chinese could not play their proper role in a Japanese peace settlement at that time.

The indefinite postponement of peace negotiations meant that the United States had to adapt its occupation policies to a situation under which the "armistice period" had acquired a more or less permanent status. Occupation policy, however, was undergoing considerable changes and would undergo more as relations between Japan and the Allied powers approached a normal peacetime basis, in fact if not in law. In other words, the United States had to take stock of the situation in Japan in the light of present conditions, rather than of policy statements made three years before, and to set the lines of a long-term policy on the assumption that there would be no formal peace settlement for some time to come.

The basic directives on "post-surrender policy," drafted in 1945,[1] had two guiding principles which could be described in general terms as punishment and reform. In the former category were all those measures intended to render Japan militarily impotent and to chastise the men and organizations responsible for Japan's career of aggression: demobilization, disarmament, destruction of war industries, reparation, punishment of war criminals, purge of militaristic elements, dissolution of ultra-nationalistic societies. In the category of reforms, the ultimate purpose of which was to make the Japanese a more democratic and therefore a more peaceful nation, were such measures as renunciation of the Emperor's alleged divinity, abolition of state Shinto, the new democratic constitution, general elections, reform of local government, decentralization of the police power, deconcentration of industry, land reform, encouragement of labor unions, emancipation of women, and reeducation.

Generally speaking, the measures of the first type were completed rapidly and successfully, with the notable exception of

---

[1] These were the Potsdam Declaration of July 26, 1945, the Presidential Policy Statement sent to General MacArthur on September 6, 1945 (amended and approved by the Far Eastern Commission on June 19, 1947), and the Basic Initial Post-Surrender Directive sent to General MacArthur on November 8, 1945. For texts, see Department of State, *Occupation of Japan, Policy and Progress* (Washington, 1946), 73-81; *Activities of the Far Eastern Commission* (Washington, 1947), 49-58; Department of State, *Documents and State Papers*, I, April 1948, 32-45.

the reparation program. Japan was deprived of its armed forces and rendered incapable of military action. The major war criminals were tried by an international court, and the chief offenders ultimately executed on December 23, 1948. The purge removed from public life the most notorious leaders of the old regime. The reform measures were less easy to apply and, by their very nature, less certain of success. Revolutionary changes in political and social institutions were imposed by the occupation authorities and accepted, at least superficially, by the Japanese. The weakness of many of the reforms lay in the general approach, which was to attempt to make Japan over somewhat in America's own image, and in the speed with which they were imposed. Whether they would take permanent root in Japanese society was an open question; at least they laid the foundation of a system of political democracy and individual freedom. The rest depended on the Japanese themselves. Once these major reforms had been instituted, the main emphasis of occupation policy shifted to another field, economic recovery.

This shift in emphasis was the result of no sudden decision but of a number of factors which had gradually assumed increasing importance. One was the cost of supporting the Japanese economy, by 1948 about $400 million per year, borne entirely by the United States as the power principally responsible for the occupation. Another was the continuing chaos elsewhere in the Far East, which made Japan appear as the only stable country and one whose economic revival was necessary in the interest of the entire region. A third element in the picture was the failure of the major Allies to develop a common policy in Japan and the Far East. Japan came to be looked upon as a part of the American strategic system which could not be allowed to fall into the Soviet orbit; accordingly, it was an American interest that Japan be made a going concern, that it not be allowed to remain in a state of grave economic weakness, either during or after the occupation.

American policy in Japan was determined by the State Department, by the Department of the Army, which had direct responsibility for the occupation and for obtaining funds from Congress to support it, and also by General MacArthur, who enjoyed a good deal of freedom in translating into concrete measures the general directives which came to him from Washington. MacArthur, who acted as Supreme Commander for the Allied Powers (SCAP), theoretically carried out Allied rather than strictly American policies, receiving directives from the 11-nation Far Eastern Commission. In practice, however, the Commission generally endorsed policies worked out by the United States, sometimes long after they were actually in effect. Occasionally, as on the question of reparation, when a decision was blocked through lack of agreement in the Commission—where each of the Big Four had a veto—the United States took action by exercising its right to issue an interim directive. Neither the Far Eastern Commission nor the advisory Allied Council in Tokyo represented an effective check on American policy in Japan.

In the spring of 1948 William H. Draper, Under-Secretary of the Army, and George Kennan, chief of the State Department's Policy Planning Staff, visited Tokyo. Although they made no official statement, Draper outlined to reporters his own views on the directions which American policy was taking.[2] The principal objective was Japanese economic recovery to the point where Japan would be self-sustaining, which should be reached by 1952 or 1953. To increase production and exports to the necessary levels probably would require an annual grant from the United States, some half-billion dollars the first year, probably less thereafter. It would require a "common-sense" attitude on reparation and on the deconcentration of industry, perhaps also an expansion of Japan's merchant marine. The United States did not propose permanent restrictions on peacetime industries. Draper did not talk in terms of specific measures, and all funds would of course have to be voted by Congress, but the emphasis on recovery, as opposed to the earlier emphasis on reform, was unmistakable. The United States was preparing to go ahead on the path indi-

[2] *New York Times*, March 27, 1948.

cated by Under-Secretary of State Dean Acheson about a year before when he said that we must push the reconstruction of those two great workshops, Germany and Japan, upon whose production Europe and Asia were dependent.[3]

A detailed analysis of the situation in Japan was being made by a committee of private citizens, headed by Percy H. Johnston, which at the invitation of the Department of the Army had accompanied Draper to Japan. The two main questions before the committee were how the United States could eventually be relieved of the burden of supporting Japan, and how Japan could contribute to the recovery of the Far East. Its report, submitted on April 26, contained a number of major conclusions: that the industrial recovery of Japan on a peaceful basis was necessary to bring about a self-supporting economy; that this program had properly become a primary objective of the occupation; that the U.S. Government in the national interest should support a "reasonable recovery program"; that revival of the economic life of a disarmed Japan should improve the chance of maintaining peace. "The accepted responsibility has been to maintain order, to stimulate reform, to prevent disease and unrest. Now we should concentrate upon the ways of revival and provide certain minimum essentials without which Japan cannot become self-supporting."[4]

The first economic needs of Japan were increased production and trade. The existing level of industrial production was no higher than 45 percent of that of 1930–1934. Exports were far below imports. Exchange of Japanese manufactures for the iron ore, petroleum, wool, rubber, rice and sugar of Japan's former overseas possessions and other Asian countries ceased with Japan's defeat and had not been revived. The Johnston committee mentioned the lack of essential raw materials, the bad condition of many factories, and the poor state of transport as the main physical obstacles to recovery. In addition it cited other deterrent influences which affected adversely the desire

[3] Speech at Cleveland, Miss., May 8, 1947 (Department of State, *Bulletin*, XVI, May 18, 1947, 991).
[4] *Report on the Economic Position and Prospects of Japan and Korea . . .* (Department of the Army press release, May 19, 1948).

to produce, work, plan and invest. Among these were the threat of removal for reparation hanging over much of Japan's industry, the uncertainty over changes being effected in control of industry, and the serious inflation. The committee recommended that a decision be reached promptly on what plants would be removed as reparation, that the deconcentration program be carried out with minimum disturbance to production, and that the Japanese Government and people be helped to take the drastic measures necessary to combat inflation. In order to carry out these plans, the committee believed that the United States must provide funds not merely under the "disease and unrest" formula, as heretofore, but to foster economic revival, chiefly through the purchase of raw materials. The idea was that of the Marshall plan, to spend more over a definite period for recovery in order to avoid spending indefinitely for relief. The report recommended passage of the proposal then before Congress for the appropriation of $144 million for recovery in addition to the $424 million requested for the expenses of government and relief in Japan in the fiscal year 1948–1949. For the immediate future there was little prospect that foreign private investors could provide needed capital, in view of the absence of a peace treaty and the many uncertainties of Japan's economic position.

Having recently voted many millions for assistance to China, Congress was reluctant to spend additional money on Japan. The appropriation for recovery was not voted, but Congress did recognize the recovery principle, as opposed to relief, and set up a revolving credit fund of $150 million to be used by all occupied areas for buying American agricultural commodities and raw materials. In addition, the Export-Import Bank joined with several commercial banks to give Japan a $60 million credit for the purchase of American raw cotton. Thus it was possible to make a start on a recovery program such as the Johnston committee had recommended.

The report of the Johnston committee was not officially adopted as American policy, although the United States was on record, in a statement to the Far Eastern Commission made in

January 1948, as favoring all possible and necessary steps consistent with the basic policies of the occupation to bring about the early revival of Japan on a peaceful, self-supporting basis. In principle the report's conclusions were accepted by the Department of the Army and by responsible officers of the State Department, although the two departments did not commit themselves to support its specific recommendations and were not always in full agreement with each other. American policy in the following months on the various subjects covered by the report followed lines roughly parallel to its recommendations.

The revival of production and trade proceeded slowly but steadily. The additional funds provided by the United States brought in more raw materials. A drive for increased coal production brought encouraging results. Textiles, the most important item in Japanese exports, had remained at a very low level of production since the war owing to the slow rehabilitation of productive capacity and shortages of labor and fuel. Output was increased during the first half of 1948, although it still did not reach 25 percent of the 1930–1934 level. The general index of industrial production in September, as the fourth year of the occupation began, showed a brighter picture. For the first time it reached and passed 50 percent, and by the end of the year stood at nearly 65 percent, of the level of 1930–1934.

The Japanese Government's Economic Stabilization Board worked out a plan to regain the 1930–1934 standard of living by 1953. This was an ambitious goal in view of the increase in population which had occurred since 1934, and would necessitate production above the level of that period—110 percent in the case of agricultural production and 145 percent in the mining industries.[5] A major difficulty was the inability or unwillingness of the government to enforce price and wage controls. Removal of economic controls was urged by some as a means of stimulating productive activity, but so long as real shortages remained it was doubtful whether it would be sound

5 SCAP, *Summation of Non-Military Activities in Japan*, No. 35, August 1948, 299-300.

politics or economics to try the experiment of free economy. The production effort called for by the plan would require responsible cooperation and self-discipline on the part of Japanese business and labor such as they had not shown in the past few years. This posed to SCAP the question of how much direction and control it would assume over the planning and execution of the necessary program.

In July 1948 MacArthur urged on the Japanese Government a comprehensive program covering tax rates and tax collection, wage stabilization, price control, foreign trade control, food collection, rationing, rationalization of enterprises, and balancing the budget. When the response proved inadequate, on instructions from Washington he took the step of issuing a directive to the government to carry out such a program. This return to the earlier practice of SCAP directives, replaced during the last couple of years by informal "suggestions" to the Japanese, was proof of the seriousness with which the United States regarded the inflation and the failure of the Japanese to take adequate measures against it. The State and Army departments announced in Washington that the Japanese performance in carrying out the directive would be weighed in connection with future requests for the appropriation of funds for Japan.[6] Since the program entailed drastic changes in established institutions and practices, the Japanese Government could be expected to be, at the very least, cautious and hesitant.

The interim directive on which the new program was based, sent to Tokyo on December 10, was submitted to the Far Eastern Commission for its information six days later. There it encountered vigorous Soviet opposition on two grounds, that issuance of such a directive on "fundamental changes in the regime of control" required the consent of the Commission, and that in substance it was inconsistent with earlier FEC decisions. But formal Soviet protests in Washington, which the United States rejected as unfounded, did not have any effect on the direction of affairs in Japan, where MacArthur went ahead on the basis of the new directive.

[6] Department of the Army, Joint State-Army press release, December 18, 1948.

The program would stand or fall on the effort to increase Japan's foreign trade beyond the prewar volume. Although the bulk of Japan's trade was still carried on through government-to-government arrangements, limited private trading had been permitted since August 1947. One year later, on August 15, 1948, SCAP granted permission for export contracts to be made directly between foreign buyers and Japanese producers. On November 18, the Far Eastern Commission confirmed U.S. policy by approving a directive providing that Japanese foreign trade should be so conducted as to foster its growth to a level consistent with Japan's peaceful needs. Exports were to be encouraged, in order to meet the cost of imports required to prevent disease and unrest and to reestablish a self-sustaining economy, and in order that Japan might provide goods needed in international trade.[7]

The basis for Japan's trade, previously confined to dollar transactions or to barter, was broadened by an arrangement with the sterling area, thus opening new markets and new sources of raw materials. Trade agreements were made with the Netherlands Indies, Pakistan and Siam. In November a one-year £55 million trade agreement with five countries of the British Commonwealth (Great Britain and its colonies, Australia, New Zealand, India, South Africa) was announced. More than half of Japan's exports under this agreement would consist of cotton textiles; imports would be largely raw materials.

The revival of Japanese trade with other countries of the Far East was a condition *sine qua non* of recovery to the self-sustaining level. Japan could count on some trade with the United States after the period of special grants was over, and the United States probably would have to take a considerable volume of Japanese exports in order to fill at least a part of Japan's need of foreign exchange. Yet the ninefold increase in exports required to enable Japan to pay for necessary imports

[7] Far Eastern Commission, *Second Report by the Secretary-General* (Department of State publication 3420, Washington, 1949), 9-10.

and sustain its population (to approximately $1,575 million at current prices, according to the Johnston committee) could hardly take place without a widening of its markets all over the world and without a flourishing trade with those countries which imperial Japan had once hoped to include in the "Greater East Asia Co-Prosperity Sphere." That prospect might create political problems as big as the economic problems it was intended to solve. Trade relations with Communist China would affect not only Japan's balance of payments, but possibly the future orientation of Japan itself.

Another aspect of the shift in emphasis from reform to recovery was its effect on the policy of breaking up excessive concentrations of economic wealth and power. This reform was aimed primarily at the so-called Zaibatsu, the great family trusts which had dominated economic life and collaborated with the militarists in Japan's career of aggression. The occupation authorities had set out to break up the Zaibatsu holdings, on the assumption that a more even distribution of these assets would make for a more peaceful and democratic Japan and would promote free enterprise in place of monopoly. Directives and "suggestions" from SCAP brought about the enactment of a number of laws by the Japanese Government for the execution of this policy, ending with the Law for the Elimination of Excessive Concentrations of Economic Power, passed by the Diet on December 9, 1947. Under these measures the Japanese Government took into custody the securities of the Zaibatsu families and of the holding companies that were listed for dissolution, and some of the larger combines were actually broken up.

All in all, the program for giving Japan a more democratic and competitive system was carried forward on a broad front, although to the accompaniment of criticism by those who felt that it did not go far enough and those who believed that it had already gone too far. Adherents of the latter view, who found some support in the Department of the Army and in Congress, contended that some phases of the program amounted to confiscation, that others represented a doctrinaire campaign against successful companies merely because of their size, and that in any case the disruption of business operations caused by the new laws was harmful to recovery.

The detailed directive on deconcentration submitted by the United States to the Far Eastern Commission, which attained a certain notoriety as FEC-230, was subjected to considerable criticism in Congress. Actually, much of that criticism was misdirected, since there was a wide gap between the general language of FEC-230, which was intended to provide the broad authority, and what was actually being done in Japan. What was important was not the text of directives and laws but the amount of pressure put on the Japanese to carry them out. SCAP had established the legal framework for drastic action against large companies but was proceeding quite cautiously, advised by a board of American businessmen. Of the 325 companies originally designated for reorganization, 194 were later exempted, and others were being treated with comparative leniency. Ultimately, the United States suspended consideration of FEC-230 in the Far Eastern Commission, and on December 9, 1948, withdrew its support of the draft directive on the ground that its "outmoded" terms might do the program more harm than good.

General Frank McCoy, in explaining American policy to the Commission, noted that under the new conditions it had been possible to reconsider the standards to be applied to the big banks and combines still existing, without affecting the broad purposes of the program. The major points of FEC-230, he said, had already been implemented; other points either had been adopted or had become unnecessary or inappropriate.

The ultimate success of the deconcentration program, of course, would depend on the Japanese themselves, and the conservative groups which were the strongest force in Japanese politics were not particularly enthusiastic about trust-busting or unfriendly to the Zaibatsu. Some companies still had to be reorganized. The problem of disposing of assets taken over by the Japanese Government remained. But these operations, in the view of the U.S. Government, did not call for any declaration of policy on the part of the Far Eastern Commission. American officials apparently felt that a detailed and rigid policy decision on the part of the Commission might interfere with efforts for rapid Japanese recovery, which had become a much more important aspect of American policy than the deconcentration program.

The same consideration affected American views on reparation. The original proposals which the United States placed before the Far Eastern Commission were based on the same formula that was applied to Germany at Potsdam: that reparation should take the form of deliveries of capital equipment over and above the level of industry necessary for the defeated nation to meet its peacetime requirements, including exports sufficient to pay for essential imports. Such a program of removals was intended to serve the objective of security against Japanese aggression and to provide Japan's victims with at least partial compensation for their war losses in the form of equipment needed to restore their economies and raise living standards. How much was to be taken and from what industries were not easy problems to solve in view of the difficulty of estimating what capacity would be necessary to meet the needs of a future population, what industries could be operated at peak efficiency, and what export markets would be open to Japan.

In 1947 the Far Eastern Commission defined the level of peacetime requirements (per capita) as that of the period 1930–1934. It also arrived at definitions of the armaments industries, which were to be removed or destroyed, and of a number of "war-supporting industries" (such as iron and steel, chemicals, light metals, shipbuilding, automobiles, electric power, oil refining, synthetic rubber), the excess capacity of which was to be made available for reparation deliveries. Two major items remained, the setting of actual capacity levels in specific industries and the division of the spoils among the claimants. An interim removals program designed to make available plants which were obviously surplus had been adopted in 1946 but nothing was moved owing to the disagreement over shares. In April 1947, to break the stalemate, the U.S. Government issued a unilateral interim directive authorizing MacArthur to allocate and ship 30 percent of this surplus to China, the Philippines, the Netherlands and Great Britain (for their Far Eastern possessions). Nothing was actually shipped until December of that year, and as there was still no Allied agreement in the FEC, the political value of the gesture was largely lost.

The economic value of transplanted factories and used equipment was also much less than the claimant countries had hoped. The Johnston committee concluded that even if the Allied claimants received all they asked for they would gain little because of the costs involved in moving the plants and their limited usefulness to their new owners. As final agreement in the Far Eastern Commission was held up more or less indefinitely, sentiment in the United States turned toward cutting down the removals program or ending it altogether except for war plant equipment. The Johnston report pointed out that the loss of plants and tools needed to make Japan self-sustaining would have to be made up by the United States, and that as long as uncertainty prevailed as to what would be taken it was impossible to plan intelligently for the rehabilitation of Japanese industry. The committee regarded "early definitive and authoritative action" as imperative. It then made specific recommendations as to what should be made available, chiefly from armaments industries plus minor shipbuilding and other facilities. The total available under this proposal would be a mere fraction of what the other Allied claimants wanted, and of what the original American recommendations of 1946 had envisaged. The reasoning behind it was that the American program for the economic recovery of Japan would be jeopardized by either a drastic program depriving Japan of equipment useful to the recovery effort or a delay in reaching final decision, whether drastic or not. Accordingly, the need was for a quick operation, very restricted in scope, to settle the matter once and for all.

The big difficulty was political. The other victims of Japanese aggression could not easily be persuaded to give up their hopes of getting some substantial reparation from Japan. Even when the governments knew that Japanese factories and equipment would be of very doubtful value, they felt obliged to press their claims because of strong public feeling on the subject. The Department of the Army might disagree with their views, but the State Department, charged with the conduct of relations with those nations, had to take account of them. Consequently, all through 1948, while the matter remained undecided by the Far Eastern Commission, the United States took no step to put through a unilateral solution. But the mere passage of time without action seemed to confirm the fears of the Chinese, Filipinos and others that they would never receive anything substantial in the way of reparation from Japan. Finally, on May 12, 1949, the U.S. representative on the Far Eastern Commission announced that the United States saw little or no prospect of agreement in the Commission, considered that further reparation removals could seriously jeopardize the economic objectives of the occupation, and was therefore discontinuing advance transfers under the interim directive and would take no further unilateral action to make possible additional reparation removals.

Friction over the reparation issue was indicative of the distrust and opposition which American policies in Japan had aroused elsewhere in the Far East, especially in China and the Philippines. There was a strong current of feeling in those countries that the United States, obsessed by the Russian danger, had been deceived by Japan's "conversion" to the ways of peace and democracy and was mistakenly building up Japan's economic, and therefore potential military, power while neglecting the legitimate needs of Allied nations which had suffered Japanese invasion in the past and would be exposed to it again. The argument that Japan had to be put on its feet in order to take the burden from the American taxpayer did not impress them. Nor did they see why the bad state of Soviet-American relations should require giving preference to Japan. Themselves militarily weak, they did not agree that Japan could not again be a menace to their security for many years.

In China, resentment over America's Japanese policies was the one point on which most nationalists and Communists agreed. It was the cause, or at least the pretext, of widespread anti-American student riots during the spring and summer of 1948. U.S. Ambassador Stuart, with the approval of the State Department, felt it necessary to take the unusual step of making a public statement explaining American motives in Japan. The editor of the influential *Ta Kung Pao* of Shanghai wrote a letter to an American periodical setting forth what he declared was "the general Chinese view of the Japanese question." That view was that America, "contradicting every moral code and in defiance of the Potsdam Declaration," was promoting the recovery of Japan by every possible means as a part of the cold war with the U.S.S.R. In so doing, he contended, America was reviving the reactionary forces of the past, encouraging war-minded extremists, abandoning necessary reforms, and providing the Japanese with the means to attack their neighbors.[8] Expressing the same view in more diplomatic terms, Carlos P. Romulo spoke of the "profound misgivings" of the Filipino people over the recent trend of American policy on such matters as reparation and economic reform.[9]

In India, Australia and New Zealand the feeling was less intense but still present. The Australian Government, for example, was in favor of permanent controls over the growth of Japanese industry and had serious reservations to the theory that Japan should be the workshop of the Far East. Considerations of security and fear of economic competition were both present in Australian thinking. Whether justified by the facts or not, these were the two factors which caused so many throughout the Far East to doubt and to criticize American motives and policies in Japan.

Preoccupation with the Russian danger had certainly become a major factor in determining those policies. The growing successes of the Communists in China made the United States all

[8] Wang Yun-sheng, "Japan—Storm-Center of Asia," *Pacific Affairs*, XXI, June 1948, 195-199.
[9] *New York Herald Tribune*, July 19, 1948.

the more inclined to see in Japan the one stable country in the Orient. Talk of Japan as a "bastion against communism," which had become so common among both critics and supporters of American policies, was somewhat misleading, since the Japanese had no armed forces and there was no intention of permitting them any, other than a police force to maintain internal order. The problem was not one of using Japan against Russia, as critics alleged, but of making sure that Russia would not use Japan against the United States. Japan was very close to the U.S.S.R. Should occupation forces be withdrawn, it would be open to Soviet penetration or attack.

To minimize these dangers, the men in charge of American policies felt that Japan must be helped to achieve sufficient economic stability to prevent communism from getting a foothold there. The external danger would be countered by the presence of American occupation forces. From this point of view it was fortunate that the drafting of a peace treaty had been indefinitely postponed. Whether and how Japan would be protected against possible attack after the withdrawal of American troops were questions still to be faced. From the standpoint of military planning, overpopulated Japan might be a liability in time of war, as Secretary of the Army Royall was reported to have intimated in an "off-the-record" press conference in Tokyo in February 1949; Okinawa, according to this reasoning, might be sufficient for American strategic purposes. But official denials of the supposed Royall statement left the impression that no such decision had yet been made. MacArthur announced that "we never intended to use Japan as an ally. All we want her to do is to remain neutral." But he added that the United States would defend Japan against a Russian attack, and described the American line of defense as running from the Philippines through Okinawa, Japan, and the Aleutians.[10]

The American program for Japan envisaged a stable, democratic political system as well as a self-sustaining economy. Whether such a system would take root would not be apparent until the occupation was over and the firm guiding hand of

[10] Interview with G. Ward Price (*New York Times*, March 2, 1949).

General MacArthur removed. The political reforms put into effect since 1945 established the institutional framework for representative government. On the whole the Japanese co-operated surprisingly well with the occupation authorities, although they did not neglect opportunities to block and sabotage measures which they did not like. Since SCAP was dependent on the Japanese Government for execution of its policies, such opportunities were manifold.

After the elections of April 1947 Japan was governed by an unstable coalition of center parties, the Democrats, Social Democrats and People's Cooperatives. Revelations of corruption, incessant political bickering and the absence of competent leadership brought the coalition into considerable disrepute, the cabinet of Hitoshi Ashida, Democratic leader, finally coming to an inglorious end in October 1948 in the midst of a public scandal. Shigeru Yoshida, leader of the right-wing Democratic Liberal party, which had been working to unseat Ashida's government, headed a stop-gap ministry until the elections of January 23, 1949, ordered by SCAP, gave Japan a new Diet and a new cabinet.

This third general election since the war resulted in a sweeping victory for the most conservative of Japan's political parties, the misnamed Democratic Liberals. They won approximately 44 percent of the popular vote and an absolute majority of seats, 264 out of 466, in the lower house. The Democrats and Social Democrats suffered big losses, while the Communists increased their seats from 4 to 35, with 9.6 percent of the popular vote. MacArthur, in an official statement, hailed "this enthusiastic and orderly Japanese election which at a critical moment in Asiatic history has given so clear and decisive a mandate for the conservative philosophy of government."

The trends shown by the election pointed up some of the problems with which the United States would have to deal in the future. The gains of the Communists, who held a strong position in the labor movement, particularly in the Congress of Industrial Organizations, indicated that their propaganda against occupation policies was having some success. Mac-

Arthur's denial of the right of government workers to strike or to bargain collectively, an issue which had aroused resentment in the unions, was another factor which may have increased the Communists' strength at the expense of the Social Democrats and bettered their chances of winning control of organized labor, which had had a mushroom growth during the occupation. Union membership had stood at about 400,000 before the war. Encouraged by SCAP under American and FEC directives, it rose to more than six and one-half million, without a corresponding growth in responsibility, discipline, or knowledge of the functions of unions in a democratic society.

The disintegration of the center parties redounded even more to the benefit of the extreme right. The Democratic Liberal party, which took over the government after the election, was closer than any other party to the groups which had held power in Japan before and during the war. It stood solidly with MacArthur in opposition to communism, but its loyalty to the political system and other reforms which he had introduced was not beyond question. Yoshida's party was, above all, nationalistic in outlook. Its electoral victory was likely to increase the distrust felt elsewhere in the Far East, where the "conservative philosophy of government" which it represented tended to be equated not with western democracy but with reaction and with Japanese imperialism.

In the economic field as well, the prospects for the achievement of the goals of U.S. policy were far from assured. The plans for recovery required, on the one hand, an American decision to put in enough money to give the necessary impetus to production and trade, and on the other, Japanese willingness to make effective use of American assistance and to carry out the comprehensive measures laid down in the SCAP directive of December 1948. Yoshida's reluctance to take unpopular measures of taxation and economic control was understandable, especially since his party had campaigned for election on a platform of laissez-faire. The Japanese Communists' attitude, the uncertainty over how persistently and effectively the United States would pursue its announced aims, and the chaotic con-

ditions in other Far Eastern areas on whose trade Japanese recovery would in large part depend, made it seem ever more
doubtful whether the hoped-for revival of industry and trade,
to which other aspects of occupation policy had been sacrificed,
could really be attained by the target date of 1952, or 1953, or
even later.

2. Two States in Korea

When the U.N. General Assembly, on the proposal of the
United States, considered the problem of Korea in November
1947, the resolution which emerged from its debates called for
free elections throughout the country, the creation of a nine-
member Temporary Commission to observe them, the formation of a Korean national government to which governing
power would be transferred by the United States and Soviet
military authorities, and the withdrawal of occupation forces
as soon as practicable. [11] But the Soviet Union, whose troops
occupied the northern half of Korea, had no intention of cooperating in carrying out the Assembly's resolution. The decision of the "Little Assembly," in February 1948, that the
commission should go ahead with its program "in such parts
of Korea as were accessible to it" took cognizance of what had
become an obvious fact. Korea, divided in 1945 into Soviet
and American zones of occupation, was not one but two states.
Two years of negotiations between the two occupying powers
had not brought the unity which all professed to desire, and
the resolution of the General Assembly made a Soviet-American
agreement on the subject even more unlikely than it had been.
The Soviet zone in Korea had become a part of the Soviet "empire." Southern Korea, with all its problems, remained under
American control, but with the United Nations, through its
Assembly resolutions and the activities of its Temporary Commission, taking an increasing share of responsibility.

The elections called for by the U.N. resolution of November
1947 were held on May 10, 1948, under the observation of the

[11] The United States in World Affairs, 1947–1948, 178.

Temporary Commission. Although confined to southern Korea, boycotted by the pro-Communist left and by some rightist and moderate parties, and marked by violence, they were termed by the commission "a valid expression of the free will of the electorate in those parts of Korea which were accessible to the Commission." [12] The new national assembly, largely of right-wing complexion, promptly adopted a liberal-democratic constitution, elected the veteran nationalist, Syngman Rhee, as president of the "Republic of Korea," and passed a resolution appealing to the people of northern Korea to send duly elected representatives to the assembly. On August 15 American Military Government came to an end.

While southern Korea was setting up a government whose authority, it was hoped, would later extend over the whole country, the Soviets and their Korean collaborators in the north were taking similar steps. In April 1948 they had convoked a conference at Pyongyang, capital of the Soviet-occupied zone, which was attended also by two prominent leaders from the south, Kim Koo and Kimm Kiu Sic, in addition to representatives of the Soviet-sponsored regime in the north. This conference laid down a program calling for withdrawal of all occupation troops, formation of a provisional central government, nationwide elections, and adoption of a national constitution for the "Democratic People's Republic of Korea." What kind of government and constitution the delegates envisaged was apparent from the character of the North Korea People's Committee and other governing institutions which had already been set up in the Soviet zone. This regime was, in all essentials, a dictatorship run by the Communists under the supervision of the Soviet authorities. It was not recognized in any way by the United States, and General Hodge, Commander of the U.S. Army forces in Korea, would have no dealings with it.

On August 25, 1948, Soviet-type elections were held in

[12] *Report of the United Nations Temporary Commission on Korea, Part One,* I (U.N. General Assembly, *Official Records: Third Session,* Supplement No. 9 [A/575]), 47; cf. George M. McCune, "The Korean Situation," *Far Eastern Survey,* XVII, September 8, 1948, 199.

northern Korea for a Supreme People's Assembly, which declared, on September 9, the establishment of a People's Republic of Korea, claiming authority over the entire country. This government the Soviet Union later recognized. Thus when the General Assembly met in Paris in mid-September, there were two rival governments in Korea, each committed to the extension of its authority over the entire country.

A major point in the Assembly's 1947 resolution had been the recommendation for the withdrawal of Allied troops as soon as practicable after the establishment of a national government. But this was a decision which would be made by the occupying powers themselves in the light of the strategic and political situation as they saw it. The United States, apparently, was anxious to rid itself of the responsibility of governing southern Korea and keeping troops there. The U.S.S.R., for its part, was preparing to withdraw its occupation forces when it had set up a functioning regime in north Korea and built up a native army of the desired strength.

In September 1948, before the U.N. General Assembly met, the U.S.S.R. announced that, pursuant to a request from the People's Republic of Korea, Soviet troops would be withdrawn by the end of the year. This announcement was a potent propaganda stroke which the United States found it hard to counter. The State Department said that the question of withdrawal of Allied forces was a part of the larger question of the unity and independence of Korea. The critical question was: Unity and independence on whose terms? Even if no vital American strategic interest required that southern Korea be held, the United States could hardly abandon the new republic, which it had fostered, to almost certain extinction at the hands of the Communists merely because the latter had trained a larger armed force. A Communist-led revolt in south Korea which was suppressed with some difficulty in October served notice that the Rhee government would be hard pressed to defend itself against an assault from the north unless American troops remained.

The report submitted to the Assembly by the Temporary Commission described conditions in south Korea (the only part it was permitted to visit) as generally satisfactory. But any hopeful signs on that score were overshadowed by "the grim reality of a divided Korea." The vital industrial resources of the north (coal, iron, chemicals, hydroelectric power) were absolutely necessary to the agricultural south, which otherwise could not exist without substantial foreign aid, the report pointed out. But the commission had no solution to offer except to urge that some procedure for peaceful negotiation be established "before military evacuation of the occupying forces abandons Korea to the arbitrary rule of rival political regimes whose military forces might find themselves driven to internecine warfare." [13]

In the course of a debate in which the arguments were reminiscent of those of the year before, the United States succeeded in obtaining virtually unanimous support for its position among states outside the Soviet bloc. On December 12 the Assembly, by a vote of 48 to 6, approved the report of the Temporary Commission, declared the government in southern Korea a lawful government, recommended that the two occupying powers withdraw their forces as early as practicable, and established a new Commission on Korea to replace the Temporary Commission. Composed of Australia, China, El Salvador, France, India, the Philippines, and Syria, this commission was directed to lend its good offices to bring about the unification of Korea and the integration of Korean security forces, to try to facilitate the removal of barriers to friendly intercourse between north and south, to be available for observation and consultation in connection with the development of representative government, and to observe the withdrawal of occupying forces.

The new commission was confronted with practically insurmountable obstacles in trying to carry out these assigned tasks. Without the cooperation of the Soviet Union and the regime in northern Korea, it could do nothing about unification or the

[13] *Report of the United Nations Temporary Commission on Korea, Part Two,* I (U.N. General Assembly, *Official Records: Third Session,* Supplement No. 9 [A/575/Add. 3]), 14.

easing of intercourse between north and south. Furthermore, it had to contend with the opposition of President Rhee and his government. They did not want the commission to approach the "illegal" regime in the north or to try to work out any scheme for conciliation; they did not even wish to have the commission talk to Rhee's political opponents, Kim Koo and Kimm Kiu Sic, who had boycotted the election of May 1948. The function of the commission, as Rhee saw it, "was that of helping to mobilize world opinion in favor of the Korean Government." If the U.S.S.R. could be induced not to intervene, he felt that his government could then unify the country "with the support of friendly forces in north Korea." [14] In north Korea, at the same time, the Soviet-sponsored regime was talking of unifying the country under its own aegis, with the help of friendly forces in south Korea.

After the Soviet Union withdrew its last occupation forces at the end of 1948, the only remaining foreign troops in the country were the Americans in the south. These the United States was preparing to withdraw as soon as the government in south Korea, whose lack of popular appeal was undeniable, had at least gained sufficient assurance of stability, armed forces adequate to maintain order and to balance those of northern Korea, and wide international acceptance as the lawful government of Korea. The General Assembly resolution of December 12, 1948, was a big step in that direction. Another was the agreement signed on December 10 by the United States with Rhee's government, under which it was contemplated that ECA, as of the beginning of the new year, would take over the administration of the Korean aid program authorized by Congress in June 1948. The agreement envisaged the provision of American financial, material and technical assistance to "avert economic crisis, promote national recovery, and insure domestic tranquility in the Republic of Korea." The State Department later proposed to Congress the appropriation of $150 million for the fiscal year 1949–50.

[14] U.N. Commission on Korea, *Second Information Report,* March 26, 1949 (U.N. Doc. A/830, April 11, 1949), 7-10.

The United States extended full diplomatic recognition to the Republic of Korea on January 1, 1949, and on April 8, in the Security Council, supported its application for membership in the United Nations, an application promptly vetoed by the U.S.S.R. The similar application of the regime in northern Korea, which was recognized by the U.S.S.R. and its satellites and concluded a series of formal economic and cultural agreements with the Soviet Government during March, was not even referred to the Security Council's membership committee since it was supported only by the Soviet and Ukrainian representatives.

On April 18, 1949, President Rhee announced that his government's defense forces were "rapidly approaching the point at which our security can be assured, provided the Republic of Korea is not called upon to face attack from foreign sources." Discussions were in progress with the United States, with the assistance of the U.N. Commission, regarding the withdrawal of the U.S. troops, which was already in progress. But this step, Rhee concluded, in no way signified a lessening of the American commitment and interest in the Republic of Korea. The United States would continue to provide assistance of various kinds, and to maintain a military mission there.

The self-congratulation in each half of Korea on the ending of foreign occupation and the attainment of independence could not obscure the fact that the main problem, unsolved since the end of the war, remained. This was the problem of the partition of the nation by an artificial line, 38° north latitude. The prospective withdrawal of all occupation troops added to the uncertainty, as the commitments of the U.S.S.R. and of the United States to their respective "wards" were not clear. Since one of the latter was dedicated to arch-conservatism and the other to the principles of "people's democracy," and since each was dedicated to the achievement of Korean unity through the destruction of the other, the situation contained elements of danger which the participation of the United Nations in the affair did not remove. Unity was what Koreans on both sides wanted. Yet it could hardly be expected that the

Koreans themselves could find the way to unity so long as the line which divided their country also divided the Soviet from the non-Soviet world.

3. The Indonesian Conflict

In southeast Asia the problems confronting American policy were not the same as in Japan, Korea and China. In this large and wealthy region the United States did not find itself in direct competition with Soviet power, although Communist victories in China seemed to bring closer the day when it would be. Communist elements in southeast Asia could not fail to profit from the expected surge of communism to the borders of Indochina, Burma and India. The presence of large Chinese minorities in the countries of southeast Asia made the situation even more hopeful from the Communists' viewpoint. This challenge of communism remained in the background while the western world occupied itself with the more immediate issue of reconciling Asian nationalism with the desire of European colonial powers to retain what they could of their rights and influence in these countries. The United States, which had at first stood aside, tended to be drawn more and more into these conflicts, both because of its increasingly intimate association with western Europe and because of its growing concern over the danger that all Asia might be swept into chaos to the profit of communism and of Soviet power.

Indonesia provided the foremost example of the issues at stake and of America's new, more active role. The agreement signed by the Netherlands and the Indonesian Republic aboard the *U.S.S. Renville* on January 17, 1948, was made possible largely through the efforts of the American member of the U.N. Good Offices Committee, Dr. Frank Graham. Besides providing for a military truce, the Renville agreement laid down the principles on which a political settlement was to be negotiated. Confirming the gains won by Dutch military action in the past year, it left the latter in control of large areas previously recognized as parts of the Republic; these included the rich agricultural regions of east and west Java and important plantations and mineral-producing areas in Sumatra (see map, page 314). However, the final disposition of these areas was to be determined by plebiscites after the conclusion of the detailed political agreement.

The goal set by the Renville agreement, as by the earlier Linggadjati agreement of 1947, was the creation of a sovereign United States of Indonesia linked with the Netherlands in a union under the crown. In the meanwhile the Netherlands was to be considered as retaining sovereignty over the whole of Indonesia, but it might transfer power to a provisional federal government as soon as possible. The major question was how the Republic, which had dealt on virtually equal terms with the Dutch over two years of negotiation, and which the U.N. Security Council (although avoiding judgment on the question of its juridical status) regarded as a party to the dispute, would fit into the provisional government and into the future U.S.I.

It was the job of the Good Offices Committee to help the two parties work out the political settlement agreed to in principle aboard the *Renville*. Batavia was the scene of these talks. Major disagreements soon appeared on the old issues which had plagued conciliation efforts in the past. The admission of Dutch sovereignty in the interim period, even over the areas controlled by the Republic, gravely damaged the latter's negotiating position. The Netherlands criticized the Republic for continuing to maintain relations with foreign states despite the promise to accept Dutch sovereignty. There was no agreement on how the proposed plebiscites would be carried out, on when and how the provisional federal government of the U.S.I. would be constituted, nor on what powers currently exercised by the Netherlands and the Republic in the areas they respectively controlled would be transferred to it.

The Good Offices Committee, in its report of June 21, 1948, remarked that lack of agreement on basic issues "has recently begun to have an unwholesome effect upon the atmosphere." [15] Contributing to the unwholesome atmosphere were the condi-

[15] U.N. Doc. S/848, June 21, 1948, 5.

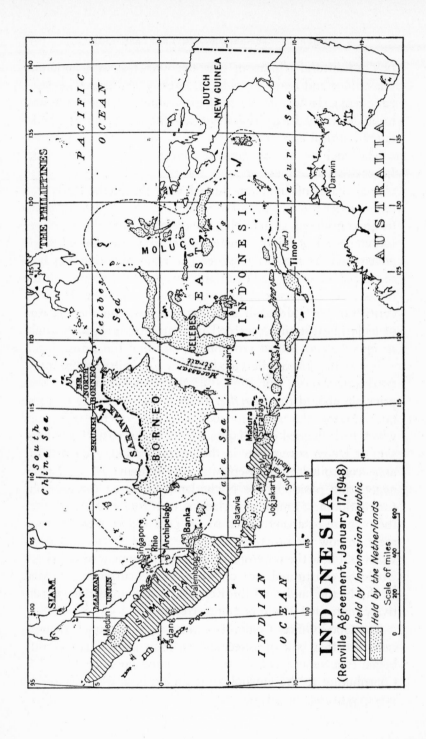

INDONESIA
(Renville Agreement, January 17, 1948)

▨ Held by Indonesian Republic

▦ Held by the Netherlands

Scale of miles
0   200   400   600

tions in Republic-held areas, where the large quantity of arms in private hands made it virtually impossible for the government to maintain order and security. Other factors were the virtual Dutch blockade of Republican areas, although the Renville terms called for trade and intercourse on as free a basis as possible, and the insistence of the Dutch on going ahead with plans to set up, in the territory they held, separate states intended to be members of the future U.S.I. Such measures would have the effect of counterbalancing the power which the Republic, because of its numbers and wealth, could be expected to exert in the U.S.I. In addition to the states which they had created in East Indonesia and Borneo, the Dutch proceeded early in 1948 to foster new states in regions of Sumatra and Java which they had taken from the Republic by military action. On March 9 the Netherlands Indies Government established a "Provisional Federal Government of Indonesia" without the Republic, and on May 27 it convened a conference at Bandoeng, Java, to work out the organization of the U.S.I. The Republic protested these steps as violations of the Renville agreement. The Dutch replied that they were of a provisional and purely consultative character.

By the end of May the political negotiations under the auspices of the Good Offices Committee had broken down. The Australian and American members, T. V. Critchley and Coert duBois, then drew up their own proposals for a settlement, presenting them informally early in June to Van Mook, the Dutch Lieutenant-Governor, and to Premier Hatta of the Republic. These proposals provided for elections to a constituent assembly for all Indonesia which would also act as a provisional parliament and name a provisional government of the U.S.I. The Dutch reaction was unfavorable. Using as a pretext the alleged "leak" of the terms to the press, the Dutch negotiators refused to discuss them. That marked the end of any serious attempt to reach an accommodation at Batavia on the basis of the Renville agreement.

Twice during the summer of 1948 the Indonesian question came again before the Security Council, which by its earlier cease-fire resolutions and its role in promoting the Renville agreement had assumed a certain responsibility for a pacific settlement. The Council took up the reports of the Good Offices Committee and listened to Dutch and Republican complaints against each other. The Soviet and Ukrainian members consistently denounced the Netherlands and the Good Offices Committee, calling the latter a guardian of Dutch colonial interests. India and the Philippines, nonmembers invited to be present because of their interest in the question, also took the side of the Republic, criticizing the Dutch blockade and the policy of fragmentizing Indonesia into a series of small "puppet" states. Romulo of the Philippines accused the Netherlands of being determined to subject the Republic to "the double squeeze of political disintegration and economic disaster." [16] There was no majority on the Security Council, however, in favor of taking definite action against Holland. The western European members and the United States preferred to keep up the effort for a negotiated settlement. On July 29 the Council approved, with the U.S.S.R. abstaining, a resolution calling on the two governments, with the assistance of the Good Offices Committee, to maintain strict observance of the political and economic articles of the Renville agreement.

This exhortation did not arrest the deterioration of the situation in Indonesia. The delay in achieving a settlement had serious consequences for the Republic, where critical shortages and political difficulties favored popular discontent. The Communists, seeking to turn the situation to their own advantage, launched a revolt in September which the Republic hastened to put down in order to forestall Dutch intervention.[17] But the tension remained. Experience in Palestine had shown that no military truce could be expected to last indefinitely when the parties remained in complete disagreement on the political issues that had brought them into conflict.

Dutch and Republican representatives met again for direct

[16] U.N. Security Council, *Official Records: Third Year*, No. 99, July 29, 1948, 20.
[17] See below, pp. 326-327.

talks in November 1948, without much hope on either side that an agreement would result. After a few meetings the Dutch told the Committee of Good Offices that the talks had made clear the Republic's inability to control its armed forces and its refusal to accept Dutch sovereignty in the interim period. In their view, therefore, they had no choice but to proceed with the establishment of an interim federal government, in which they planned to include the Republican areas. To this end another "police action" like that of July 1947 was being prepared. On December 17 the Republican negotiators in Batavia were given a list of terms which they were to accept within 18 hours. These terms called upon the Republic to accept incorporation in the proposed federal organization on the same footing as other federal areas.

Just before the expiration of the time limit, H. Merle Cochran, duBois' successor as U.S. representative on the Good Offices Committee, delivered a note to the Dutch deploring the setting of a time limit and describing the Dutch action as aimed not at resuming negotiations but at imposing "surrender to the position of your government on every material point." [18] That same evening, December 18, the Dutch announced that the truce had been disregarded by the Republic and was therefore terminated. Dutch troops moved swiftly to overrun the remaining Republican areas, capture the capital, Jogjakarta, and take into custody the Republic's leaders, among them President Soekarno and Premier Hatta. Cochran and the deputy Australian member of the Good Offices Committee, cut off from their colleagues by the fighting, sent a report to the Security Council sharply critical of the Netherlands. The United States and Australia immediately called for an emergency meeting of the Council to deal with the situation resulting from the renewal of hostilities.

The Security Council, meeting on December 22 after the Dutch forces had gained their major military objectives, was faced with the same problem as after the Dutch "police action" of July 1947. It could order the Dutch to return to the

[18] U.N. Doc. S/1129, December 19, 1948.

positions held before the truce was broken, as the Indonesian representative demanded, or it could order a cease-fire and then try to help in patching up a new agreement between the two parties. The first solution, as the Netherlands Government knew, was not likely to be tried, as the United Nations had no armed force at its disposal, and in any case there was no majority in favor of sanctions. The Council heard some strong talk from Australia, India, and the U.S.S.R., calling the Dutch action a deliberate act of aggression, but the resolution approved on December 24 merely ordered the cessation of hostilities and the release of political prisoners. Four days later, no results having been attained, the Council voted a new resolution calling on the Netherlands to free the political prisoners and report within 24 hours, neither of which demands was complied with.

Dutch officials had discovered that they were more successful in Indonesia when they took action first and then let the other United Nations discuss what might be done about it. That was a good formula for practical success, but Indonesia was by this time a matter of world concern. Although the Security Council did not act on Indonesian demands that the Dutch be ordered to withdraw their troops to the Renville truce line, most of its members, in no uncertain terms, let the Netherlands know their opinion that the "police action" was an unjustified violation of the truce.

Feeling in the United States was particularly strong in condemnation of the Dutch. Soon after Dutch troops moved against the Republic, ECA suspended the allocation of the grant made to the Netherlands for reconstruction in Indonesia; this affected some $11.2 million remaining from the $72.7 million already allotted for Indonesia in addition to the much larger sum allocated to the Netherlands itself.[19] Considerable sentiment developed in Congress in favor of barring Holland from ECA grants and from military aid programs so long as it did not comply with Security Council resolutions on Indo-

[19] Economic Cooperation Administration, *The Netherlands: Country Study (European Recovery Program)* (Washington, 1949), 23.

nesia.[20] Philip Jessup, in the Security Council, took a position more critical of the Netherlands than any taken by the United States hitherto. "The continuance of military action of the Netherlands authorities after the adoption of the Security Council resolution of 24 December," he said, "was clearly an act of defiance on the part of the Netherlands authorities . . . In the opinion of the Government of the United States, the representative of the Netherlands has failed to relieve his Government from the serious charge that it has violated the Charter of the United Nations . . . Further, my Government cannot but recall a history of non-cooperation on the part of the Netherlands in the work of the Committee of Good Offices . . . It appears that even prior to the resumption of military action . . . the Netherlands pursued a policy which had the effect of weakening the Republic, working unnecessary hardship on the population, isolating the Republican Government economically and politically, and presenting it with a prefabricated administration for Indonesia with which it was to associate itself but which it had no part in forming . . ." [21]

Meanwhile, on January 20 in New Delhi a conference of 19 "Asian" countries (including Australia, New Zealand, and Ethiopia) met in order to discuss Indonesia and to give the Republic some moral support. The advisability of Australia's participation in what might become an anti-western bloc was questioned both in Britain and in Australia itself, but Herbert Evatt, Minister for External Affairs, called the New Delhi meeting of crucial significance to his country. "Geographically," he said, "Australia is closely linked with Southeast Asia. Those who are devoted to Australia's welfare will desire to live in the closest harmony with these new neighbor nations, three of which, India, Pakistan and Ceylon, are new and very im-

[20] This issue held up Senate approval of the new Economic Cooperation Act for some days and was settled temporarily only by the adoption of an amendment suggested by Senator Vandenberg to the effect that the United States would terminate assistance to any state against which the United Nations was taking preventive or enforcement action.

[21] U.N. Security Council, *Official Records: Fourth Year,* No. 2, January 11, 1949, 5, 6.

portant members of the British Commonwealth of Nations."
No permanent Asian organization was established by the conference, although the participants agreed to consult and to
cooperate more closely in the future. On Indonesia, the specific
reason for the calling of the conference by Prime Minister
Nehru, a resolution was passed calling for the withdrawal of
Dutch troops from Republican areas, the return of Republican
political prisoners, the formation of an interim government,
and a transfer of sovereignty to the U.S.I. by January 1, 1950.

This resolution was forwarded to the Security Council, where
four states, China, Cuba, Norway and the United States, had
meanwhile submitted a joint resolution providing for immediate discontinuance of military operations, immediate release
and return to Jogjakarta of the Republican officials, the formation of an interim government by March 15, elections to a constituent assembly by October 1, and the transfer of sovereignty
to the U.S.I. no later than July 1, 1950. The Good Offices
Committee would be reconstituted as the U.N. Commission for
Indonesia, with enlarged powers permitting it, for the first
time, to make recommendations both to the parties and to the
Security Council. The Commission was to recommend the extent to which areas formerly under control of the Republic
under the Renville agreement should be progressively returned
to it. This resolution was passed by the Council on January 28,
1949, with France, the U.S.S.R. and the Ukraine abstaining on
most of its provisions.

The Netherlands Government took the position that its
main job was to go ahead with the formation of a provisional
government. Holland hoped, its representatives said, to complete the transfer of sovereignty earlier than July 1, 1950. That
the Dutch had no intention of allowing the Republican leaders
to set themselves up again as a government at Jogjakarta or to
exercise control over any part of former Republican territory
was clear. They proposed instead a conference at The Hague
to prepare the way for an interim federal government for Indonesia. They wanted the Republican leaders to attend as individuals, not as members of a government.

The United States and other members of the Security Council took a jaundiced view of this Dutch move, which seemed to ignore the Council's recent resolutions. However, they wished to explore every possibility of a negotiated settlement which did not contravene the resolution of January 28, and to persuade the Netherlands Government to be more conciliatory. Hence the decision of the Security Council on March 23 to authorize the U.N. Commission for Indonesia to assist the parties in reaching agreement on the terms and conditions for the proposed Hague conference as well as on the implementation of the January 28 resolution. Hence Secretary Acheson's attempt to impress on Netherlands Premier Stikker, when the latter came to Washington to sign the Atlantic pact, the seriousness with which the U.S. Government and American opinion regarded his country's apparent intention to get its way by force in Indonesia in violation of Security Council resolutions.

On April 14 Dutch and Indonesian leaders met once more in Batavia, with the assistance of the U.N. Commission for Indonesia, in what was perhaps the final attempt to reach a negotiated settlement between the Netherlands and the now nonexistent Republic. Increasing guerrilla activity against the Dutch forces pointed to the danger of further bloodshed for an indefinite period if no agreement should be reached. On May 7 delegates of the two sides arrived at a provisional understanding based on restoration of the Republican government to Jogjakarta, cooperation in restoring peace and maintaining law and order, and early convocation of the round-table conference at The Hague; but it remained to be seen whether this was the beginning of a permanent solution or merely the opening of another round of recriminations.

The persistence for so long a time of a dispute which was embittering relations between the United States and the Netherlands struck a sour note in all the talk of western solidarity on the occasion of the conclusion of the Atlantic pact. Although neither government allowed the issue to prevent the Netherlands' participation in the pact, it remained a factor which weakened the western bloc in Europe and which encouraged anti-western elements, Communist and extreme nationalist, in Asia.

4. *Ferment and Communism in Southeast Asia*

Elsewhere in southeast Asia the same elements of unrest and conflict present in Indonesia made their appearance in varying forms: civil war in Burma, colonial war in Indochina, attempted revolution in Malaya. Economic conditions were conducive to mass violence, and constituted governments had the greatest difficulty in making their authority felt. While nationalism remained a powerful factor in the equation, especially in Indochina, the influence of communism and of Communist leaders was increasingly evident.

Three conferences were held in Calcutta under Communist auspices in February and March 1948, those of the Indian Communist party, the New Democratic Youth League, and the students of southeast Asia. Representatives from all the countries of the Far East, including the U.S.S.R., were present at one or another of these conferences. The opportunity was taken, apparently, to lay down a new party line, that of direct Communist action instead of attempts to conciliate and work with popular movements having a wider than purely Communist basis. These were the same tactics being adopted by Communist parties all over the world at this time, a phenomenon which seemed to point to central direction from Moscow. In any event, Communists had a leading role in the violence which broke out in Burma, Malaya, and other countries of southeast Asia in 1948, whether the major motivation was the desire of Moscow to stir up trouble for the western powers or that of local Communists to take advantage of chaotic conditions.

Burma's experience was particularly tragic for a nation which had just won its independence. Under the leadership of Premier Thakin Nu, Burma became an independent state on January 4, 1948, after concluding a series of political, military and economic agreements with the former sovereign power, Great Britain, and apparently settling the problem of the non-

Burmese national minorities through a system of graded autonomy for the different national communities. The new government was pledged to a program of democratic socialism which seemed likely to be popular in a country whose upper and middle classes had been largely foreign (British, Indian and Chinese). However, the forces making for disunity and disorder soon proved too strong for the government to control. Nationalism no longer held conflicting groups together once the battle for independence was won. The governing coalition, which had led the movement for independence as the Anti-Fascist People's Freedom League (AFPFL) but had lost its best leaders when Premier Aung San and his colleagues were assassinated in 1947, began to split into factions. The Communists took advantage of the situation to launch a revolt.

There were two Communist parties in Burma, known as Red Flag and White Flag Communists. The former, who were Trotskyites, or at any rate non-Stalinists, had been outlawed and forced underground in 1946. The latter were Stalinists, who had broken with the AFPFL before Burma became independent. In March 1948 government troops swung into action to put down a rebellion of the Red Flag Communists. Shortly afterward they were confronted with an armed revolt of the White Flag group.

Attempting to make use of political methods as well as military force, the government of Thakin Nu announced in June a new and more left-wing program which called for broader measures of socialization, an end to exploitation by foreigners, and the establishment of closer ties with the U.S.S.R. A bill for the nationalization of a considerable amount of British property was hurriedly passed. The government did not intend to join the Soviet camp against the west, but rather to follow a middle course. Such a course, however, was not satisfactory to the Communists, nor even to powerful groups within the AFPFL which now went over to the Communist side. Personal ambitions and rivalries had a great deal to do with the split, the political and ideological differences being anything but clear.

The difficulties of the government in dealing with the Communists encouraged the Karens, the largest of the national minorities, to start a rebellion of their own in September. Dissatisfied with their position in the new republic, they demanded the autonomy of those parts of Burma where they lived, not an easy area to define since in many districts they were mixed with the Burmese. The three-cornered struggle among Karens, Communists and government brought the country dangerously close to chaos, as if to justify the gloomy predictions of Churchill and the British Conservatives who, in deploring Burma's departure from the Commonwealth, had argued that the Burmese were not yet capable of governing themselves. Government forces had to yield large pieces of territory to the Karens and to the Communists during the last part of 1948 and the early months of 1949. The Burmese economy, never restored to its prewar level, was thoroughly disorganized. Not only did Burmese oil and minerals cease to flow in the channels of international trade, but the rice crop, on which India and other countries depended, also fell off.

When the Burmese Government appealed to London for help in exporting its rice and reconstructing its finances, the British Government communicated with other interested members of the Commonwealth. Prime Minister Nehru of India, believing that the Commonwealth governments might do something constructive to help end the fighting in Burma, convened a conference of representatives of the United Kingdom, Australia, Malaya and Ceylon. Meeting in New Delhi on February 28, 1949, they agreed on and submitted to Premier Thakin Nu a list of suggestions on making peace in Burma, including an offer to mediate the conflict with the Karens. The Burmese Government, however, was not interested in outside mediation in its own civil war. Even in the country's desperate plight, in the midst of civil strife, deteriorating economic conditions, and unsolved political problems, Burmese nationalism was too strong to permit the government to accept outside mediation even from friendly nations.

In Malaya there was the same complex picture of nationality conflicts and Communist rebellion. But Malaya was still a

British colony and had a government able to take effective counteraction. The Communists, most of whom were Chinese, dominated some of the labor unions, which they attempted to use for their own ends. In May and June they set off a series of strikes and terrorist actions which spread rapidly, reaching a climax with the murder of three British planters. The government assumed emergency powers and mobilized its security forces. In July, British armed forces went into action to put down the rebels. These strong measures enabled the government to weather the immediate crisis by October, although terrorism and scattered guerrilla warfare continued.

Malcolm MacDonald, British Commissioner-General for Southeast Asia, with headquarters at Singapore, reported that the disorders in Malaya were the result of a deliberate plan of the Malayan Communists to take over the government. Bevin, speaking in the House of Commons, declared: "This problem has been in existence ever since the Marxist-Leninist theory was adopted. It has existed not only in Malaya but elsewhere. It is part and parcel of a clash between two philosophies and it will keep on breaking out everywhere it can, not merely in Malaya and Burma and India, but elsewhere." [22] Yet a substantial part of the explanation lay in conditions in Malaya: discontent among plantation workers, anti-European feeling, and above all the antagonism between Malays and Chinese. While the Malay people and the Malay labor unions, for the most part, rallied to the side of the British in opposing the Communists, the Chinese tended to be anti-government, anti-Malay, and submissive to intimidation, and were influenced by events in China, where the Communists were winning sweeping victories.

The Communist offensive in southeast Asia was aimed at disrupting the flow of critical materials, such as tin and rubber, to western Europe; thus, indirectly, it was an attack on the Marshall plan. It was directed also at weakening the position and prestige of the western powers and of those moderate

[22] *Parliamentary Debates, Weekly Hansard,* House of Commons, September 15, 1948, 91.

Asian leaders who sought to work out an understanding with the west. In Indonesia, as in Burma, the Communist revolt broke out in territory held not by a European power but by a nationalist government enjoying the first fruits of independence.

While the leaders of the Indonesian Republic were engaged in difficult negotiations with the Netherlands, they were faced with a growing left-wing movement ready to capitalize on the failure of the government to achieve either economic security or a settlement with the Dutch. Premier Hatta, in the summer of 1948, was attempting to reach an understanding with the leftists, but the arrival in Java of a certain Muso, a long-time militant Communist who had lived in Russia since the 1920's, turned the situation definitely toward open conflict. Muso took over the leadership of the Communist party. Soon afterward the Communists were joined by the Socialists, the Labor party, and the Socialist Youth Organization to form a new "Workers' Front." Former Premier Amir Sjarifoeddin gave added prestige to the new leftist alliance by announcing that he had been a secret member of the Communist party since before the war.

On September 18, the Communist leaders launched a revolt at Madioen, in Central Java, proclaiming an independent republican regime. For a while they controlled the surrounding area, including the city of Soerakarta, but the expected support of the masses did not develop. The government of the Indonesian Republic moved swiftly and effectively. Within a month its forces had taken Madioen and extinguished the Communist "republic." The specter of a Communist state in southeast Asia was laid for the time being.

However, the factors which had produced the leftist movement in Indonesia remained, and as the moderate nationalists continued to meet intransigence on the part of the Dutch and apparent indifference on the part of the western powers, the Communists had a new opportunity to regain their strength and to win new recruits from the ranks of those nationalists who were disillusioned by the failures of the policy of moderation or impressed by the Soviet Union's self-assumed role of champion of colonial peoples. The Dutch "police action" of December 1948 and the failure of the United Nations to act decisively probably made many new friends for the Communists in Indonesia.

In Indochina, where fighting between French troops and the Vietnamese (Annamese) had been more or less continuous since the end of 1946, the role of the Communists was not so clear. Ho Chi Minh, president of the "Democratic Republic of Vietnam," which claimed to represent the people of the three most populous provinces (Tonkin, Annam and Cochinchina),[23] had once been a leading Comintern agent in China and southeast Asia. His coalition regime included Socialists, Democrats and independents as well as Communists. Ho himself professed to be a nationalist rather than a Communist. The extent of Communist influence in the Vietnamese government was not known to the outside world. What was apparent was that the immediate objective was to win national independence from the French (possibly inside the French Union, but only on condition that Vietnam's autonomy should be complete), and that Ho's considerable popular support resulted from his leadership of resistance to French rule.

France, after abortive attempts to reach an understanding with Ho Chi Minh, in 1947 ruled out further dealings with him on the ground that he was a Communist and could not speak for the Vietnamese people. The French Government, after an unsuccessful experiment with a hand-picked regime for Cochinchina, turned to Bao Dai, former emperor of Annam and an exile in France, as the man to play off against Ho Chi Minh. On June 5, 1948, General Nguyen Van Xuan, French-designated president of Cochinchina, who had proclaimed a provisional government of Vietnam, signed an agreement in Bao Dai's presence bringing Vietnam into the French Union as an associated state. What this would involve was left to later negotiations with Bao Dai.

The difficulty was that Bao Dai, if he was to have any chance

[23] The other two provinces, Laos and Cambodia, had joined the French Union as associated states.

of success, had to hold out for virtually the same terms that Ho was demanding. Negotiations went on during 1948 and the first part of 1949. News of Communist triumphs in China and fear of what might happen when the Chinese Communists should reach the frontier of Indochina brought home to the French the urgency of the question, and the agreement with Bao Dai was finally signed on March 8, 1949. Though not immediately made public, it was understood to provide for the creation within the French Union of an autonomous Vietnam which would include Tonkin, Annam and Cochinchina and would enjoy some measure of independence in military, diplomatic and financial affairs.

Bao Dai returned to Indochina at the end of April 1949, after a special assembly in Cochinchina had voted to include that province in the proposed Vietnam state. The big question, for French policy, was what kind of reception Bao Dai would get on his return to Vietnam. The Bao Dai experiment had some measure of support from all French political parties except the Communists. It was far from certain, however, that it would have the support of the people of Vietnam. Should it fail, France might not be willing or able to keep on supporting a seemingly endless war which cost so much in men and money. Other powers with interests in Asia, having left affairs in Indochina almost entirely in the hands of the French, might have to take a more positive attitude themselves in working out in Indochina, as elsewhere, the major issue facing the western world in southeast Asia: how to deal with rising nationalism and at the same time combat the menace of communism and of Soviet power.

For the United States, relations with southeast Asia promised to take on added importance after the Communist successes in China. The American position in Asia, presumably, would rest on Japan, on southeast Asia including the Philippines, and on India and Pakistan. Thus far there was no coordinated U.S. policy, particularly economic policy, for the Far East as a whole. In many ways the region was not adapted to treatment as a whole. In the matter of loans and technical assistance for the industrialization and economic development on which the nations of Asia, like those of Latin America, seemed intent, the United States might find it wiser and more practical to deal with individual countries rather than act through a cumbersome regional body such as the U.N. Economic Commission for Asia and the Far East. Prospects for investment in India, for example, might be much better than in less advanced and less stable countries. Yet the United States had to look at the entire region in order to formulate a policy taking account of over-all American strategic and economic requirements.

The revival and growth of trade between Japan and the rest of Asia was already a definite American objective. With Manchuria and all of China likely to be cut off, the hoped-for recovery of Japan to a self-sustaining level probably would require a substantial increase in trade with southeast Asia, thus raising thorny political problems. Japan and Communist China would need desperately to trade with each other. Would that trade increase the Communist threat to Japan, or would it modify the course of Communist rule in China? In any case the United States faced the necessity of working out a coordinated and consistent approach to the Far East based on a careful estimate of what should or should not be done to prevent economic collapse in any one country or group of countries, to maintain such influence as the United States had in the region, and to counter the propaganda and the diplomatic activities of the Soviet Union and its agents.

CHAPTER NINE

RELATIONS WITH NEW WORLD NEIGHBORS

IN THEIR concern with the problems of relations with Russia, problems involving the issue of war or peace, many Americans have tended to overlook the importance of relations with Great Britain and the dominions. They have overlooked also the fact that the United States, the United Kingdom and some of the dominions have acted in informal partnership in dealing with the major issues of war and peace, that is, in dealing with the Soviet Union and the problems raised by Soviet expansion. In certain vital areas, such as Germany, the United States and Britain gradually worked out in the postwar years what amounted to joint policies. In strategic regions important to both powers they found it advantageous to work together. In the Middle East, for example, despite the disagreements over Palestine, there developed something very like a common Anglo-American system, to which the United States contributed chiefly material and financial support while Britain's contributions consisted largely in bases, some armed forces, political experience, and special treaty relations with Middle Eastern countries.

The United States remained vitally interested in the security and stability of Great Britain, one reason being its potentialities as an "unsinkable aircraft carrier" off the coast of Europe, another its importance in world trade. The $3.75 billion loan to Britain in 1946 and the European Recovery Program, under which the largest share of U.S. aid goes to Britain, emphasized the American stake in Britain's position. Reciprocally, under the Bevin regime British foreign policy was generally in alignment with that of the United States, not, as some of Bevin's critics charged, because he was the "puppet" of American interests, but because British and American objectives, for the present at least, were so nearly the same. Both were concerned with checking further Soviet expansion, with the revival of western Europe and the survival of western civilization.

As the United States was drawn into closer relations with Britain, so also did it develop its ties with the dominions. Together the United States and the British Commonwealth were attempting to maintain a world-wide strategic position and to provide leadership for non-Communist forces throughout the world.

This was a period of change within the Commonwealth. In some ways the trend which began with Lord Durham's report of 1839 was reaching in these years a century later its logical conclusion, as the dominions had become fully independent states constitutionally linked together only by common allegiance to the crown. The role of the dominions, especially Canada and Australia, in the war added to their importance, and to their sense of their own importance, in world affairs.[1] The real change in the postwar period, however, lay in the application of Lord Durham's principles to former parts of Britain's dependent empire inhabited by Asian peoples. India and Pakistan became dominions in 1947, Ceylon in 1948.

From the point of view of the United States, it was desirable that the transition from British rule to independence in these parts of Asia should be peaceful, and that the newly emancipated nations should remain within the British Commonwealth. Such a peaceful transition would set a good example to other parts of Asia, while the free association of Asian nations in the Commonwealth would give promise that these nations would cooperate with the west in matters affecting world security; in achieving stability and maintaining free institutions

---

[1] Although the dominions were fully independent after 1931, they still did not have a system of separate citizenship. Their growing nationalism, however, led to changes in this matter as well after Canada, in 1946, passed a law establishing separate Canadian citizenship, though ruling also that Canadian citizens would be British subjects. The new British Nationality Act of July 30, 1948, took account of the new situation by conferring the status of "British subject" upon "citizens" of the United Kingdom and the dominions (not including Eire). Any person having this status could be known either as a British subject, a citizen of a dominion, or both.

they would constitute a barrier to the advance of communism and of Soviet power in Asia. In the light of India's aspirations to leadership in Asia it was significant that India chose to remain within the Commonwealth if, as a republic, it would be permitted to do so. That a formula satisfactory to all was found at the meeting of Commonwealth prime ministers at London in April 1949 was a tribute to the flexibility of British institutions and to the statesmanship of those present, particularly of Attlee and Nehru. For the United States, seeking to work out a long-term policy in Asia, the relative stability shown by India and Pakistan (despite their conflict over Kashmir), in contrast to the turbulence and chaos in China, Burma, Indonesia and elsewhere, offered possibilities for more constructive political and economic policies than had yet been undertaken.

Of all the dominions, Canada has had the most intimate relations with the United States, for well-known geographical and historical reasons. The two countries were drawn together by the great volume of trade between them and by many common interests. Canada, however, remained very jealous of its sovereignty, and the disparity in strength sometimes made the conduct of relations a difficult and delicate task. Canada wished to remain a member of the British Commonwealth despite its close ties with the United States. Lacking bonds of interest and sentiment with Latin America, it remained cool to offers to join the inter-American system. By contrast, the Canadian Government and people welcomed the concept of a North Atlantic community, in which their close ties to Britain and to the United States could be reconciled, and gave full support to the project of an Atlantic pact.

Canada, in cleaving to the British Commonwealth, remained the missing link in the American "commonwealth of nations," the inter-American system built up gradually over more than a half-century, which finally acquired a formal constitutional structure at the Bogotá conference of 1948. For the United States the ties with Latin America, as with Canada, were of primary importance to its security. The recent war had shown what inter-American cooperation could mean in terms of nec-

essary bases, supplies of strategic materials, and joint action in
checking enemy efforts to gain a foothold in the western hemisphere. It would be important in any new world crisis. Peacetime, meanwhile brought difficulties which put new strains on
the bonds of inter-American solidarity. Political instability in
Latin America brought in its wake a series of revolutions and
in some states a setback in the laborious progress toward democracy. Economic troubles, particularly the dollar shortage and
the failure to obtain loans from the United States, combined to
build up in Latin America a feeling of neglect and resentment.
All these difficulties came to the fore as the delegates of 21
American republics came together at Bogotá in the spring of
1948.

1. Canada's Trade and Dollar Problem

It was inevitable that Canada, as a major exporting nation,
should be profoundly affected by the revolutionary changes in
world trade patterns that occurred during the war and early
postwar years. The industrial expansion which helped to supply
the requirements of the Allied fighting fronts increased Canada's economic importance in an absolute sense. At the same
time the war increased its dependence on foreign commerce,
while disrupting the system of trade relationships that had
enabled it to keep its international payments in equilibrium
before 1939.

The Canadian economy emerged from the war in a flourishing condition that seemed to promise a high level of prosperity
and to offer rich possibilities of further development, especially
in mining and industry. At a time when many countries were
suffering depletion of their mineral resources, much of Canada's
fabulous mineral wealth still invited exploitation. Aside from
gold, nickel, iron, lead, copper and zinc, Canada possessed
titanium, uranium and other metals which were expected to be
in heavy postwar demand. Oil was newly discovered in Alberta,
and plans were being laid to exploit for the first time the vast
iron ore deposits of the Quebec-Labrador region. A high level of

industrial output was relied upon to support a national income which had more than doubled during the war years and a standard of living which was already the second highest in the world.

To receive the full benefit of these advantages Canada would have to maintain a large volume of foreign trade, since the domestic market could not begin to absorb the output of Canadian farms, forests, mines and factories. Canadian trade, however, was a part of world trade, and was bound to feel the effect of the dislocations and impediments which were so conspicuous a feature of the postwar years. Until world trade revived, Canada would be caught in the same net of currency and payments difficulties that beset its war-ravaged Allies.

Historically the salient feature of Canadian foreign trade was a heavy surplus of imports from the United States and an excess of exports to Great Britain and the rest of Europe. These tendencies were accentuated during the war as Canada expanded the flow of manufactured goods across the Atlantic and further increased its dependence on the United States for many industrial materials and products and fuels. Canadian exports to the United States meanwhile remained limited in the main to a few important staples. Between 1939 and 1945 the share of the United States in total Canadian imports increased from 66.2 percent to 76.8 percent, while its share in Canadian exports actually declined from 41.6 percent to 37.2 percent.

In prewar years Canada's chronic deficit on current account with the United States had been compensated by its chronic surplus with the United Kingdom, whose sterling payments were freely convertible into the dollars Canada needed to balance accounts with the United States. This smoothly working triangle was destroyed by Britain's postwar dollar deficit. Emerging from the war with an unprecedented need to import from the United States and export to the United Kingdom, Canada found that its sterling exports would no longer serve to pay for its dollar imports.

In so far as these difficulties could be attributed to temporary dislocations induced by the war, Canadians had every incentive to work toward the reconstruction of world trade along the same liberal lines being pursued by the United States. Restoration of the trading position of former trade partners was a first requisite, and in the early postwar years Canada went even further than the United States (in relation to population and resources) in extending loans and credits to its war-impoverished Allies. Canada's heavy wartime financial assistance to the United Kingdom was supplemented by a new credit of $1,250 million extended to the mother country in May 1946; in the same year it signed a four-year agreement to supply most of the United Kingdom's wheat requirements.[2] To other countries export credits were granted to a total of $594 million. Beyond this, Canada vigorously joined in efforts to reduce the barriers to free multilateral world trade through the Geneva agreement on tariffs and trade and the proposed International Trade Organization.

But the expectation that measures such as these would enable Europe to recuperate fairly rapidly, once the initial postwar readjustments were accomplished, proved to be overoptimistic. In 1947 Canada found itself facing a crisis in its international payments of comparable severity to that of the countries of western Europe and Latin America. The worsening of its position was evidenced by a rapid depletion of gold and U.S. dollar resources, which at the end of 1945 had stood at the high figure of $1,508 million. During 1947 a combination of developments —heavy imports of U.S. capital goods and consumers' goods at increased prices, a cessation of the inflow of American capital, and the failure of expected hard-currency payments from Europe to materialize—dissipated these reserves at an alarming rate. From $1,245 million at the beginning of the year they declined to $700 million in April and to $480 million at the end of November.

The steps taken by the Canadian Government to meet this emergency were as drastic as the situation that prompted them. On November 17, 1947, the finance minister announced a comprehensive program to curtail dollar expenditures. This program featured an import ban on a wide variety of consum-

[2] See above, p. 221.

ers' goods; a 25 percent excise tax on many of the same goods manufactured in Canada; import quotas or individual import license requirements for still other groups of commodities, including all metals and metal products not affected by the import ban; and restriction of individual pleasure travel in the United States. Although applied on a theoretically nondiscriminatory basis, the import restrictions were avowedly designed to maximize the saving of dollars while minimizing interference with the export trade of non-dollar countries. Meanwhile Canadian manufacturers were encouraged to find ways of lessening their dependence on U.S. materials and components, and of buying less and selling more in the American market; and a loan of $300 million was secured from the Export-Import Bank to help tide Canada over the immediate emergency.

It was unofficially estimated that these measures might reduce the drain of U.S. dollars by as much as $300 million a year. Actually results were better than anticipated. During 1948 several other factors intervened to help improve the dollar position. The dollar yield of exports to the United States increased markedly, thanks to the higher prices paid for Canadian forest products, base metals and other exports; the removal of controls on Canadian exports of meat, cattle and coarse grains; increased U.S. demand for Canadian metals and other products for rearmament and stockpiling; and reductions in American tariffs under the Geneva agreement of 1947. Meanwhile Canadian imports were being substantially curtailed through the austerity program, with the result that the over-all commodity deficit with the United States for the year was reduced to $283.6 million, as compared with $918 million in 1947.

Even more important in improving Canada's dollar position during 1948 was the financing of Canadian exports to Europe by ECA as a part of the European Recovery Program. In the last nine months of 1948, ECA authorized offshore purchases from Canada and Newfoundland to a total of $593 million, payable in U.S. dollars. About one-half of this amount was allocated for purchases of wheat, mostly for shipment to the

United Kingdom; the remainder was used to acquire such typical Canadian products as timber, wood pulp and newsprint, zinc, lead, copper, aluminum, cheese and bacon. In effect, ECA was restoring something resembling the prewar trade pattern by paying for Canada's exports to western Europe in a currency valid for transactions with the United States. Canada too was doing its part to make ERP succeed by providing credits to recipient countries and selling its wheat below the world price; but thanks to ECA financing it was itself a major—if temporary—beneficiary of the program.

By the end of 1948 gold and dollar holdings were back around the $1,000 million mark, and many of the controls instituted a year before could be relaxed or dropped. What remained of the British loan of 1946 had been frozen at the height of the dollar crisis but was now unblocked. These favorable developments emphasized the vigorous over-all condition of the Canadian economy in the winter of 1948–49. During the year just closed, income and employment had stood at the highest levels in history; production and foreign trade had never been higher in peacetime. Expansion and development were confidently going forward on many fronts. Capital investment in new plant, equipment, housing and construction was absorbing 20 percent of the national income.

Yet the situation did not lack disquieting features. Persistent shortages of steel and textiles, the closing of the English market to Nova Scotia apples and British Columbia salmon, uncertainty and apprehension in the lumbering and other industries, emphasized the perils for Canada of the persistent instability of world trading relationships. Offsetting the growth of exports to the United States during 1948 was a decline in the value of export trade with Great Britain and the Marshall plan countries, Australia and New Zealand, the British West Indies and Latin America. To some observers Canada seemed to be gradually falling out of the British trading orbit, without acquiring the ability to hold its own in trade with the United States. ECA, which was helping to bridge the immediate difficulties, would not last forever; in fact, the prospect of a wheat

surplus in the United States made it unlikely that offshore purchases in Canada would be continued in 1949 on anything like
the same scale as in 1948.[3] Trade figures for the first three
months of 1949 indicated that Canadian exports were running
into fresh difficulties, while the debit balance with the United
States showed a disquieting increase. The gains registered in
1948 began to look rather ephemeral.

The hazards of the United States market combined with
political and sentimental factors to make Canadians anxious to
retain and solidify their relations with the United Kingdom
and the sterling area as a whole. Imports of British steel and
manufactured goods were desired as a dollar-saving substitute
for American products and as the only means of enabling Great
Britain to absorb its share of Canadian exports. But while
Canada's imports from Britain increased materially during 1948,
its exports to the United Kingdom declined in spite of the
fact that three-fifths of them were being financed by Canadian
credits and ECA offshore procurement. Early in 1949 Sir Stafford Cripps, Britain's Chancellor of the Exchequer, intimated
that still further cuts were in prospect. "It is quite unrealistic,"
he said in a published interview, "to imagine that we can in
the foreseeable future earn enough Canadian dollars with
which to buy supplies from Canada on a wartime scale. That
is why we have already had to make plans to bring our purchases from Canada more into line with our ability to pay for
them. It is on food that the reductions have mainly to come,
but we have also had to reduce our purchases of some other
products like timber."[4]

Canadians did not see the problem in quite the same light.

[3] ECA was prohibited by law from authorizing offshore purchases of agricultural
commodities which had been declared surplus in the United States. In April
1949, anticipating formal declaration of a wheat surplus, ECA advised the British
that no further authorizations for offshore purchases of Canadian wheat would
be granted as long as American wheat stocks were sufficient to cover Europe's
entire import requirements. Although Britain was still committed under the
1946 agreement to purchase 140 million bushels of Canadian wheat at the read-
justed price of $2 a bushel during the year 1949–50, the unavailability of
Marshall plan dollars for this purpose promised some embarrassment for both
Britain and Canada.
[4] Quoted from *Financial Post* (Toronto), March 19, 1949.

To them the British tendency to rely on bilateral barter-type agreements with non-dollar countries, often involving imports from other sources of products which Canada could supply at a lower cost, was unsound both economically and politically. It seemed to threaten the creation by Britain of a separate high-cost trading area from which the North American countries, with their better competitive position, might be permanently excluded by exchange restrictions and similar devices. Such a development, Canadians felt, would be to the long-run advantage of neither Canada, the United States, nor the sterling area itself.

If Canadian hopes for a restoration of multilateral world trade were to prove illusory, Canada would have to find other means of safeguarding its economic well-being. Self-sufficiency hardly seemed a practical alternative, and the attempt to achieve it would certainly spell a lowered standard of living and the death of free enterprise. A reversal of present trade policies in favor of bilateralism or Empire preference would require heavy sacrifices in exchange for dubious benefits. A third alternative, economic union with the United States, was one that most Canadians viewed with misgivings for political reasons. Nevertheless it was bound to receive serious attention in view of the real uncertainty whether Canada could continue to occupy its traditional intermediate position between the British and American economies. Merging of its own with the American economy might be a remedy for the present chronic imbalance.

Among those Canadians who were attracted by the idea of economic union with the United States were certain large industrialists with faith in the competitive potentialties of Canadian industry in an expanded continental market, and farmers interested both in new outlets for their produce and in improved sources of supply. The opposition, apart from industrial interests which depended on protection against U.S. competition, was mainly political in character. The old suspicion of American imperialism had not wholly died out, and an editorial in *Life* proposing a customs union occasioned such an uproar in the Canadian press that the London *Economist* was able to say: "Mr. Henry Luce has made Canada safe for the Commonwealth for some time to come." [5]

In the United States these problems had received scant attention until the dollar-saving measures invoked by Ottawa at the end of 1947 effectively dramatized the plight of this country's "biggest cash customer." Conversations between Canadian and American officials at that time appear to have produced agreement that ways of furthering increased economic cooperation between the two nations should be carefully explored. On the official plane no serious consideration was given to the idea of a full economic or customs union, but the possibility of following up the Geneva tariff reductions with further reciprocal concessions—possibly through the medium of a new reciprocal trade agreement—would undoubtedly demand further consideration. Whatever might be the course of Canada's future overseas trading relationships, few could doubt that Canadian products must enter the American market in greater volume if the postwar promise of Canada's richly endowed economy was to be realized.

2. The Defense of North America

In the course of the Second World War Canada achieved maturity as an independent nation. The rapid economic expansion of the war years was part of a larger process of growth whose results were equally apparent in the fields of politics, military affairs, and national psychology. A new sense of nationhood was developed which gave substance and meaning to the status of constitutional independence guaranteed by the Statute of Westminster. At the close of the war Canada was ready to take its place as one of the world's "middle powers" and to speak with the authority of an independent nation of 12 million North Americans.

This new adulthood did not necessarily imply a relaxation of Canada's ties of sentiment and tradition with the United King-

[5] "Customs Union With Canada," *Life*, XXIV, March 15, 1948, 40; *The Economist*, CLV, April 3, 1948, 547.

dom and the other nations of the Commonwealth, or of the "working relations" habitually maintained with them on defense and other matters. Few Canadians doubted that a third world war would find the senior dominion aligned with the mother country as promptly as in 1914 and 1939. Nevertheless the assumption of full responsibility for foreign policy, combined with drastic changes in world political alignments and in the balance of world military power, meant that the peculiarities of Canada's own position in the western hemisphere would affect its international relations more directly than ever before.

From every standpoint the decisive feature of Canada's world situation was its position on the North American continent and its contiguity with the United States. As the basic solidarity of interest between the United States and the rest of the English-speaking world became manifest in the years preceding the Second World War, this relationship had ceased to be a major cause of anxiety to Canadians. In matters of security the common interest and reciprocal dependence of the two nations had been recognized when President Roosevelt declared in 1938 that "the people of the United States will not stand idly by if domination of Canadian soil is threatened . . ." and Prime Minister Mackenzie King replied that one of Canada's obligations as a good neighbor was to see that, "should the occasion ever arise, enemy forces should not be able to pursue their way by land, sea or air to the United States across Canadian territory." [6]

Canada's concern with American affairs, moreover, did not and could not stop at the United States in view of the latter's active role in Latin America and the strength of the "hemisphere" concept in political and military thinking of the 1930's and 1940's. It was to a Canadian audience that Roosevelt delivered the famous address in the summer of 1938 in which he described all of the Americas as linked in a common destiny.[7] It was true that few Canadians showed great eagerness to act on the theory that their fate was bound up with that of a con-

[6] *The United States in World Affairs, 1938,* 218-221.
[7] *Ibid.,* 218.

geries of Latin American republics which seemed much more remote, geographically and in every other sense, than Europe itself. Yet the development of air communications was inexorably bringing Canada into closer relationship with more than one portion of the globe that had hitherto seemed inaccessible.

Although the United States did not follow Canada into the Second World War until more than two years after the German attack on Poland, close cooperation in military affairs was instituted by the two governments soon after the fall of France. At Ogdensburg, New York, on August 18, 1940, Roosevelt and Mackenzie King agreed on the establishment of a Permanent Joint Board on Defense to conduct "studies relating to sea, land, and air problems" and "consider in the broad sense the defense of the north half of the Western Hemisphere." At Hyde Park, on April 20, 1941, they established the principles for cooperative utilization of the productive facilities of North America in the interests of "local and hemisphere defense" and of assistance to Great Britain and the other democracies.[8] Cooperation under these and kindred agreements was steadily intensified even before Pearl Harbor. Among its ultimate results were the development of integrated procurement and supply programs, formulation of joint strategic plans, creation and cooperative use of military facilities and installations on Canadian territory, vast construction projects such as the Alaska Highway and the Northwest Staging Route, and Canadian participation in the development of the atomic bomb.

At the end of the war most of the American-built military installations in Canada were purchased by that country in accordance with wartime agreements. The new posture of world affairs that followed the defeat of the Axis, however, seemed to increase rather than diminish the need for Canadian-American military cooperation. The revolution in military technology signalized by the development of long-range aircraft, guided missiles, and the atomic weapon had greatly lessened the security both nations had formerly enjoyed by virtue of their

[8] S. Shepard Jones and Denys P. Myers, eds., Documents on American Foreign Relations, III (Boston, World Peace Foundation, 1941), 160-162.

geographic remoteness; and the polarization of world politics around the conflict between the United States and the Soviet Union raised the strong possibility that Canada would find itself in the middle of any future clash among the great powers. The shortest routes between Russia and the United States lay across the arctic regions and Canada.

In seeking a means of exit from this predicament, Canadians attached first-rate importance to strengthening the prospects of peace through the United Nations, and deprecated actions from any quarter that seemed to make war more likely. The role of the United States in opposing Soviet expansion was viewed with considerable misgivings by some sections of Canadian opinion which regarded any move to continue Canadian-American military cooperation as an outright provocation of the U.S.S.R. The old mistrust of Canada's powerful southern neighbor was fortified by a natural reaction against the close association of the two powers in wartime and by an intense desire to escape involvement in quarrels which many Canadians felt were no concern of theirs.[9]

In Canada as elsewhere, however, the behavior of the Soviet Union itself did much to lessen these misgivings as time went on. Revelation of Soviet espionage activities in Canada, irritation over Soviet press attacks on Canadian military policies in the Arctic, annoyance at Soviet diplomatic discourtesies, and increased familiarity with the ruthlessness of Soviet world policy all helped to produce the realization that Canada's interests were inseparably linked with those of the United States for reasons even more fundamental than the accident of geographical propinquity. The solidarity of Great Britain with the United States in resisting Soviet expansionism made it easier for Canadian opinion to move in the same direction.

It was implicit in Canada's whole situation that any future war in which the country might become involved would be a war of great powers on a global scale. If Canada were attacked, as Defense Minister Brooke Claxton told the House of Com-

[9] This state of mind is well exemplified in the work of a Canadian journalist, Leslie Roberts, *Home From the Cold Wars* (Boston, Beacon Press, 1948).

mons in June 1948, it would be "as an incident of a world war." Accordingly, he said, Canada's defense policy was based on the assumption that Canadian armed forces would be used only in association with those of friendly great powers; and its immediate defense aims were "(1) to provide the force estimated to be necessary to defend Canada against any sudden direct attack; (2) to provide the operational and administrative staffs, equipment, training personnel and reserve organization which would be capable of expansion as rapidly as necessary to meet any need; (3) to work out with other free nations plans for joint defense based on self-help and mutual aid as part of a combined effort to preserve peace and restrain aggression." Basic to this program was maximum cooperation with the armed forces of the United Kingdom and the United States, with which, added the minister, the Canadian armed forces worked more closely than did those of any other country.[10]

The general character of this collaboration with the American armed services had been known since February 12, 1947, when it was officially announced that following discussions in the Permanent Joint Board on Defense the two governments had decided that their national defense establishments should, "to the extent authorized by law, continue to collaborate for peacetime joint security purposes." Specific aspects of this intended collaboration, it was stated, were the interchange of selected individuals to increase mutual familiarity with each other's defense establishments; cooperation and exchange of observers in connection with exercises and tests of material; encouragement of common designs and standards in arms, equipment, organization, methods of training, and new developments; and mutual availability of military, naval and air facilities in each country, including transit privileges for military aircraft and public vessels. All such arrangements would be in keeping with the obligations assumed under the United Nations Charter and were to be "without impairment of the control of either country over all activities in its territory"; each

[10] Statement of June 24, 1948 (*Official Report of Debates, House of Commons,* 1948, VI, 5783-5784).

country would "determine the extent of its practical collaboration" and would remain free to discontinue collaborations in any field at any time.[11]

In commenting on these arrangements, Canadian statesmen endeavored to allay the suspicions of the Soviet Union by minimizing their scope and to reassure Canadian opinion by emphasizing that they did not in any way encroach on Canada's sovereignty or its Commonwealth relationship. Prime Minister King explained that the announced principles of cooperation closely paralleled the working arrangements which had long been operating among the Commonwealth nations without formal intergovernmental agreement. Deprecating as "unwarranted" and "fantastic" the talk of a program of large-scale defense works approximating a northern "Maginot Line," he conceded that the polar regions had assumed new importance as "the shortest routes between North America and the principal centers of population in the world." But Canada's northern program, he asserted, remained what it had been for many years—"primarily a civilian one to which contributions are made by the Armed Forces." The United States, which also recognized the need for greater familiarity with northern conditions, would participate in the work of the "small winter experimental establishment" at Churchill, on Hudson's Bay, whose tests of clothing, equipment, transport, etc. "will be of general benefit to all who live in the north." [12]

Infrequent announcements during the ensuing two years indicated that activities under the February agreement lay well within the officially defined limits. In March 1947 it was reported that the two governments had agreed to establish nine jointly operated weather stations in the arctic region. Further disclosures had to do mainly with meteorological research, navigation aids, and cold-weather tests of men and equipment. The military program was obviously playing a significant part —though not the only part—in the opening of the Canadian

[11] Department of State, *Bulletin*, XVI, February 23, 1947, 361.
[12] Statement in the Canadian House of Commons, February 12, 1947 (*Official Report of Debates, House of Commons*, 1947, I, 347).

northlands to scientific investigation and economic development.

That American military authorities would be willing to extend the scope of these joint activities was made clear in 1946 and again in 1947 in their testimony to Congressional committees on the proposed Inter-American Military Cooperation Act, which was designed to facilitate standardization in the organization, training and equipment of the armed forces of other American states.[13] Although this legislation was conceived primarily with reference to Latin America, both General Eisenhower, and General Vandenberg of the Army Air Force, testifying before the House Foreign Affairs Committee, emphasized the importance of including Canada in the proposed arrangements. General Guy V. Henry, as senior U.S. Army member of the Permanent Joint Board on Defense, stated that the act was necessary to provide the United States with legal authority for a general standardization of arms, matériel, tactical doctrine, organization and training such as would be essential if the Canadian and American armed forces were to react quickly and effectively against attack.[14] Since the measure did not reach the floor of Congress, the Canadian Government was not obliged to take a position on the proposal.

Canadian sensitivity on the issue of American military personnel in Canada was strikingly evidenced in June 1947 when a bill was introduced in the Canadian Parliament to facilitate the internal administration of U.S. troops in the country. During peacetime special legislation was required to allow the administration and discipline of American military personnel in Canada to remain under the jurisdiction of the United States Army. The Visiting Forces Act, authorizing American military authorities to try American soldiers accused of committing crimes or breaches of the peace in Canada, provoked a three-day debate on Canadian-American relations and was passed only after the government made a positive statement that the num-

---

[13] Cf. *The United States in World Affairs, 1947–1948,* 109-112.

[14] *Hearings* before the House Committee on Foreign Affairs, 79th Congress, 2nd Session, on Inter-American Military Cooperation Act (Washington, 1946), *passim;* same, 80th Congress, 1st Session (Washington, 1947), 39-40, 76-78, 80-81, 95-100.

ber and disposition of American troops in Canada would be regulated and controlled by Parliament. Still later, Foreign Minister Louis St. Laurent once again emphasized American acceptance of the principle that all joint defense undertakings on Canadian territory—which, he said, were "of a very limited character with very few United States personnel involved"—should be under Canadian control.[15]

A visit of Defense Secretary Forrestal to Ottawa in August 1948 unloosed a new spate of nervous rumors featuring such grandiose projects as the construction of a radar screen across northern Canada. The actual talks between Forrestal and Claxton, according to the public announcement, were exploratory in character and dealt mainly with the role of Canadian manufacturing plants and raw materials in any future emergency, the interchange of weapons and ammunition between Canada, the United States and the United Kingdom, and the standardization of American and Canadian arms and ammunition. The supreme importance of industrial factors in all defense planning was fully recognized by both governments, and their collaboration in this field was capable of results at least as significant as their picturesque ventures in the frozen north. The two nations were quietly pursuing their cooperation in the development of atomic energy, a field in which Canada's large uranium deposits at Great Bear Lake had special relevance. Problems of industrial mobilization and its relation to the broad picture of Canadian-American defense were also receiving increased attention, and on April 12, 1949 an agreement was announced on the establishment of a Joint Industrial Mobilization Committee "to exchange information and coordinate the views of the two Governments in connection with planning for industrial mobilization in the event of an emergency." [16]

One phase of Canadian-American cooperation that progressed less rapidly was the Great Lakes-St. Lawrence seaway and power project. This enterprise, under consideration since the

---

[15] Statement of April 29, 1948 (*Official Report of Debates, House of Commons, 1948*, IV, 3443).
[16] Department of State, *Bulletin,* XX, April 24, 1949, 537.

First World War, involved the construction of a channel around the International Rapids to enable ocean-going vessels to reach ports on the Great Lakes and also the erection of hydro-electric plants at suitable points along the St. Lawrence. The two governments had made repeated agreements to carry out the project, most recently in 1941. The enterprise was strongly opposed, chiefly on economic grounds, by some Canadian groups as well as by certain American transportation and power interests and by local sentiment in East Coast cities which feared a diversion of their traffic to lake ports. Legislation to implement the 1941 agreement produced abundant controversy in each new Congress, but no affirmative action. A resolution introduced by Senator Vandenberg in the Eightieth Congress was favorably reported by the Foreign Relations Committee but failed to gain Senate acceptance and was recommitted for further study in February 1948, a step which effectively buried the measure for the duration of that Congress.

During the summer of 1948 various agencies of the U.S. Government were directed to prepare analyses of specific aspects of the seaway project, mainly of a technical nature, for the guidance of the Foreign Relations Committee. The Secretary of Defense was asked for an evaluation in terms of national defense and resource mobilization. Reporting back in February 1949, Secretary Forrestal expressed the view that the undertaking would be clearly advantageous from the standpoint of national defense, since it would facilitate the use of Great Lakes shipbuilding and repair facilities for all types of cargo vessels, give ready access to the Quebec-Labrador iron ore deposits, provide an abundance of cheap, dependable electric power, and relieve the strain on existing transportation facilities in case of an emergency. Completion of the project, the Secretary held, would not involve excessive demands for materials and manpower needed for other purposes. The Permanent Joint Board on Defense, he recalled, had recently reaffirmed its opinion that completion of the project would be "of great value to the peacetime economy and to the defense potential" of both Canada and the United States and had recommended that every effort be made to overcome the obstacles that were delaying its completion.[17] Meanwhile a new Congress had met but took no action on the matter during the early months of the session, although as usual a number of bills on the subject were introduced.

Another complicating factor in defense arrangements between the two countries was introduced by the accession of Newfoundland, with its dependency of Labrador, to the Dominion of Canada on April 1, 1949. After many years as a separate dominion and repeated refusals to enter the Canadian union, Newfoundland in the early 1930's had been driven by bankruptcy to accept temporary government by a royal commission appointed by the Dominions Office in London. During the war both the United States and Canada acquired defense sites in the area on 99-year leases, adding to the importance which geography gave to Newfoundland in the whole strategy of the North Atlantic. At the close of the war arrangement was made for the island's 300,000 inhabitants to determine their future allegiance through a national convention and a popular referendum. This was ultimately held in the summer of 1948 and resulted in a small majority for confederation with Canada.[18]

Among the alternatives that had theoretically been open to Newfoundland was union with the United States, a solution advocated by a minority of Newfoundlanders who believed this country would be better able than Canada to assure their economic future. A plan to send an exploratory delegation to Washington was heavily defeated by the National Convention in April 1947, but some opponents of confederation with Canada resumed vigorous agitation for "economic union with the United States" in the weeks preceding the referendum. Some

[17] Senate Committee on Foreign Relations, 81st Congress, 1st Session, *The St. Lawrence Seaway and Power Project: Reports Prepared by Government Agencies . . .* (Washington, 1949), 72-75.
[18] The first ballot, on June 3, failed to produce a majority for any of the three solutions offered, confederation (64,066 votes), restoration of responsible government (69,400), or continuation of commission government for five years (22,311). Accordingly a second referendum was held on July 22 in which confederation received 78,408 votes to 71,464 for responsible government.

natural annoyance was caused in Canada when 50 American Senators, including Taft and Vandenberg, responded affirmatively to a telegraphic inquiry asking whether they would be willing to discuss the matter with a Newfoundland delegation; Senator Brooks of Illinois even declared that a delegation would be warmly received and that "satisfactory terms could be worked out." The Gloucester Fisheries Association, on the other hand, let it be known that New England fishing interests would go the limit in opposing any arrangement that would permit free entry of Newfoundland fish into the U.S. market.[19] Although the many islanders who voted for a return to self-government undoubtedly included some who regarded this as a first step toward closer association with the United States, there was no evidence that pro-American sentiment in Newfoundland was sufficiently intense to cause difficulty for the new Canadian administration.

From a military point of view the acquisition of Newfoundland and Labrador gave Canada for the first time the great advantages that went with direct control of its Atlantic bastions. On the other hand, the prior rights of the United States in the bases it had developed at Argentia, St. John's and Stephenville on lease from the United Kingdom ran counter to the principle, laid down in the agreement of February 12, 1947 and repeatedly reaffirmed, that "all cooperative arrangements [between Canada and the United States] would be without impairment of the control of either country over all activities in its territory." The union agreement signed by Newfoundland representatives in Ottawa on December 11, 1948 made no mention of these American bases, but it was generally understood that the matter was considered one for future negotiations between Canada and the United States. These two governments and that of the United Kingdom had already gained so much experience in the cooperative solution of defense problems that there was reason to hope a satisfactory adjustment could be achieved without serious difficulty.

[19] *Christian Science Monitor*, May 22, 1948; *New York Times*, June 1, 1948; *New York Herald Tribune*, July 22, 1948.

3. Pan America or Atlantic Community?

Those Canadians who reluctantly acknowledged that their security was indissolubly bound up with that of the United States found it much more difficult to conceive that they could have any interest in association with the American nations as a group. Although a "twenty-second chair" had stood ready for Canada at Pan American Union headquarters in Washington since 1910, no formal invitation to occupy it had ever been extended. It had long been assumed that the United States would view with reluctance the participation of a member of the British Commonwealth at meetings of the American states; and Canadian governments were well content that this potentially embarrassing issue should not be raised.

Although the war stimulated some Canadian interest in closer ties with Latin America, especially among French Canadians, there was little enthusiasm for any association more intimate than that involved in occasional participation in technical conferences of the American states. When the Inter-American Conference at Chapultepec in 1945 adopted a resolution expressing the desire "that Canada's collaboration with the Pan American system may daily become closer and closer," Prime Minister King confined himself to a friendly but noncommittal acknowledgment in which he welcomed "the increased collaboration in all matters of mutual interest and concern with our neighbors of the Americas." [20]

Eventually it appeared likely that Canada would be forced to take a more positive stand. The spring of 1947 was marked by two American pronouncements which, though unofficial, suggested a possible change in the American attitude toward Canadian membership in the Pan American Union. Senator Vandenberg declared on April 14 in the course of a Pan American Day address:

"I express the wish that the time may soon come when our continental fellowship will be geographically and spiritually

[20] F. H. Soward and A. M. Macaulay, *Canada and the Pan American System* (Toronto, Canadian Institute of International Affairs, 1948), 31-32.

complete through the association with us, on some appropriate basis, of the great and splendid Dominion of Canada . . . By every rule of reason we should wish her here. I would welcome the final and total New World unity which will be nobly dramatized when the twenty-second chair is filled and our continental brotherhood is complete from the Arctic Circle to Cape Horn." [21]

A week later Sumner Welles, former Under-Secretary of State, endorsed the Vandenberg proposal in a radio address. Past reasons for the exclusion of Canada had disappeared, he said, and the great bulk of American opinion "would warmly share in the hope expressed by Senator Vandenberg." [22]

Further impetus to discussion was provided by the action of the Rio Conference in September 1947 in including both Canada and Greenland within the security zone defined by the Inter-American Treaty of Reciprocal Assistance.[23] Any armed attack within this area was to be considered an attack against all the American states, requiring them to take specific measures as prescribed by the treaty. The language of the treaty left open the possibility that Canada might become a party to it, and Senator Vandenberg on his return from Rio underlined this feature by a reference to the fact that Canada and Greenland were not "presently" among the signatories but might be included later.[24]

It was widely expected that the issue of Canadian participation in the inter-American system would be raised again, perhaps in more direct and for Canada more embarrassing terms, at the Ninth Inter-American Conference at Bogotá in the spring of 1948. The general desire of the American republics to include Canada in their fellowship played some role in the Bogotá deliberations and had an influence on the final form of the Charter of the Organization of American States, the main achievement of the conference.[25] The term "American

21 *New York Times,* April 15, 1947.
22 Quoted by Soward and Macaulay, *op. cit.,* 32.
23 *The United States in World Affairs, 1947–1948,* 116-118.
24 Department of State, *Bulletin,* XVII, September 14, 1947, 504.
25 See below, pp. 363-367.

States" was deliberately used in preference to "American Republics" in order to leave the way clear for accession by Canada or any new American state; membership was declared open to "all American states that ratify the present Charter"; and the Charter was left open for signature indefinitely.[26]

This intermittent courtship gave rise to considerable debate in Canada and disclosed some real sentiment in favor of hemispheric ties. Advocates of Pan Americanism held that Canadian participation would lead to expanded trade with Latin America, an enhancement of regional security, and increased Canadian influence in the affairs of a hemisphere in whose problems Canada was inextricably involved by geography. Opponents argued that trade was determined by other factors, that Canada's security needs were adequately safeguarded by existing arrangements with the United States, that a hemisphere orientation would be inconsistent with Canada's world outlook and affiliation with the British Commonwealth, and that membership in an organization of American republics would mean loss of independence in foreign policy, subservience to the United States, and an obligation to take sides in local quarrels which were no Canadian concern.

The air of artificiality that pervaded the debate on western hemisphere association was noticeably absent from the discussions that preceded Canada's adherence to the North Atlantic security pact in April 1949. For Canadians the concept of a North Atlantic region embracing Canada, the United States, the United Kingdom and western Europe corresponded to a concrete and familiar reality. As Lester Pearson, the new Secretary of State for External Affairs, wrote early in 1949:

"The North Atlantic Community effectively meets the needs of Canadian foreign policy. In contrast with the Pan American Union . . . it reflects political, economic and cultural interests which in the history of Canada have been of importance in the growth of its freedom and security. These interests also are

[26] Department of State, *Ninth International Conference of American States: Report of the Delegation of the United States of America* (Washington, 1948), 14-16.

more generally shared by other members of the Commonwealth of Nations, in which Canada is determined to maintain her membership. The North Atlantic grouping, moreover, is the association which most directly corresponds to the need which Canada has for increased security, because Canadians, perhaps more than any other people in the Americas, consider that the safety of their country is bound up with that of Western Europe." [27]

Although participation in an Atlantic pact involved commitments which were as radical a departure for Canada as for the United States, in a deeper sense it was thoroughly consistent with the whole postwar trend of Canadian foreign policy. Canadian statesmen had been most active in admonishing the U.N. Security Council to live up to its responsibility for maintaining international confidence and security, and, when these pleas proved unavailing, in promoting the concept of more limited associations to accomplish the same end within the United Nations framework. Prime Minister King had warmly endorsed the Brussels treaty of March 17, 1948 and declared that "Canada will play her full part in every movement to give substance to the conception of an effective system of collective security by the development of regional pacts under the Charter of the United Nations." [28] Canadian and American observers were present at the subsequent military discussions of the five Western Union nations in London, and Canada was a full participant in the diplomatic conversations at Washington which began in July 1948 and resulted in the signature of the North Atlantic pact nine months later.[29]

Canadian association with the United Kingdom and the

[27] Lester B. Pearson, "Canada and the North Atlantic Alliance," *Foreign Affairs,* XXVII, April 1949, 374-375. Cf. the similar views of Vincent Massey, leading opponent of Canadian membership in the Pan American Union, in *Foreign Affairs,* XXVI, July 1948, 694.

[28] Speech in the Canadian House of Commons, March 17, 1948, quoted, with other related pronouncements, in the *Report of the Department of External Affairs, 1948* (Ottawa, 1949), 15-19.

[29] See below, pp. 529 ff. Canada was also the first nation to ratify the North Atlantic Treaty, by unanimous action of the House of Commons on April 29, 1949.

United States in a single instrument for integrated regional defense was a logical consummation of the long series of events which, during the preceding decade, had brought the new Canada into full defense cooperation with the neighboring power while leaving its ties with the mother country undisturbed. The Atlantic pact was not, Canadian statesmen realized, a wholly satisfactory answer to the problem of world security. Louis St. Laurent, Mackenzie King's successor as Prime Minister, exposed the heart of Canada's and the world's postwar problem when he said in an address in September 1948:
"Any political association on other than a universal basis in this shrinking world cannot be an end in itself, but only a means to an end. The end is that set out in the Charter we have all signed, the erection of a structure of international cooperation and understanding, in which all men of every creed and race and color may exist together in peace and prosperity." [30]

4. The Bogotá Conference

In the midst of the crisis in Europe a large United States delegation, headed by General Marshall and including two other cabinet members, left Washington for Bogotá, Colombia. There the Ninth Conference of American States opened on March 30, 1948. Special inter-American conferences and meetings of the foreign ministers had been held in the past decade, but this was the first formal conference in the regular series since the meeting at Lima in 1938. No matter how urgent the demands of the European situation might be, the United States could not afford to slight this conference, already postponed several times, or to neglect relations with the other American republics.

The agenda consisted of a number of general topics: reorganization, consolidation and strengthening of the inter-American system; economic cooperation; recognition of *de facto* governments; defense and preservation of democracy; European colonies in America; development and improvement of

[30] Quoted in *Foreign Affairs*, XXVII, April 1949, 376.

inter-American social services. These were, for the most part, matters of long-term organization rather than of immediate political urgency. Yet some were more urgent than appeared on the surface. Under the heading "economic cooperation" the Latin American nations were preparing to put forward demands for help from the United States, probably for more help than the United States would be willing to provide. Under the heading "defense of democracy" the conference would discuss what to do about the menace of communism, the topic of the moment both in the United States and in Latin America. The subject of European colonies covered long-standing territorial disputes between certain American republics and Great Britain which had recently boiled up again in a series of incidents, claims and counterclaims, and acrimonious official statements.

In its first week the conference no more than began its discussion of these and other items on the agenda. Then, striking like a tornado, violence and rioting swept Colombia's capital. Law and order broke down. There could not have been a more unexpected and dramatic proof of the existence of revolutionary forces seething just beneath the surface in this as in many other Latin American countries. On April 9 the leader of the left wing of the Liberal party, Jorge Eliécer Gaitán, was assassinated. Immediately, as if at a given signal, rioters were racing through the streets of Bogotá, killing, looting, and destroying property. One of the first buildings to be pillaged was the Capitolio, the seat of the conference. For a few days no one knew whether the conference could or would continue. The delegations were entirely taken up with assuring their own safety. A number of governments sent planes to evacuate their representatives. Secretary Marshall, however, threw his great influence on the side of those who believed that the conference should carry on even under the almost insuperably difficult conditions. After a week of rioting which devastated the center of Bogotá, a reorganized Colombian government brought the situation under control. The conference was able to resume its sessions in a suburban school building.

General Marshall made the flat statement that the violence

in Bogotá was no isolated phenomenon but was related to the strikes in Italy and in France, that all were part of an international pattern of Communist action directed from Moscow. He did not reveal the information on which his conclusion was based, nor did the Colombian Government produce evidence to support it. After arresting the leading Communists on the charge of instigating rebellion, it let them go later for lack of sufficient evidence to prosecute. Nevertheless, it was clear that the Communists took advantage of the outbreak if they did not actually start it. They did their best to disrupt and discredit the conference, which was certainly in Moscow's interest. It was only natural that the disturbances and the Communist share in them should have the effect of giving prominence to the anti-Communist resolution which was before the conference. After what had happened, there was little doubt that the resolution would be strongly worded and that it would have unanimous support. Many Latin American governments were genuinely concerned over the threat of communism to the existing order. Practically all of them saw that they could lose nothing and might gain something by declaring their solidarity with the United States against communism.

On the agenda was an item on "defense and preservation of democracy in America," a Guatemalan proposal for nonrecognition of "antidemocratic regimes" on the ground that they were a danger to the solidarity and the peace of the continent. The Guatemalan Government had in mind the right-wing dictatorships in a number of American states. Other governments were more concerned over communism. For some months Chile, which had broken relations with the Soviet Union and dealt harshly with its own Communists, had been the vanguard of the anti-Communist crusade. Brazil and Peru were not far behind. Together with these three states, the United States submitted a draft resolution on the subject. The essence of it was the declaration that the American republics were convinced that international communism was an "instrument of aggression" constituting a threat to free democratic and republican institutions in the western hemisphere.

Other delegations had some changes to suggest. The Argentines wished to make absolutely sure that the right of each government to deal with its local Communists in its own way was recognized. They also wanted to include some reference to the ideas of social justice and "planned democracy" which they said inspired the Perón regime. On the other hand Rómulo Betancourt, ex-president and head of the delegation of Venezuela, took occasion to denounce dictatorial regimes existing in the Americas, including, by implication, Argentina. He wanted the resolution to condemn the suppression of human rights and civic freedoms. No delegation, however, took exception to the heart of the resolution, the denunciation of communism and the pledge to take measures to combat it. The text finally adopted declared that "the political activity of international communism or any other totalitarian doctrine" was incompatible with the concept of American freedom. It reiterated the faith of the peoples of America in the ideal and the reality of democracy, "under the protection of which they shall achieve social justice." The American republics resolved to condemn interference in their public life "by any foreign power or by any political organization serving the interests of a foreign power," to condemn the methods of every system tending to suppress civil rights and liberties, and to adopt measures necessary to prevent activities instigated or assisted by foreign governments aimed at fomenting disorder or at the violent overthrow of their institutions.

As an indication of inter-American solidarity in opposition to communism, the resolution gave welcome support to the United States in its propaganda battle with the Soviet Union. What it would mean in a practical way was uncertain. A consultative organ for "political defense" already existed in the form of an Emergency Advisory Committee, set up in 1942, which had done good work in combating Nazi and Fascist infiltration during the recent war. So far as it was really a matter of Soviet penetration, all American governments could find profit in cooperation to combat it. But the strength of communism was in many instances a direct reflection of widespread poverty and ignorance. Police measures alone could not deal with it. Moreover, the issue was clouded by the tendency of some American governments to pin the Communist label on all political opposition. There was a certain amount of hypocrisy in the support of a resolution condemning the methods of "every system tending to suppress political and civil rights and liberties" by such regimes as the governments of Paraguay, Nicaragua and the Dominican Republic, and Argentina. But hypocrisy was nothing new in inter-American declarations.[31]

On another of the items before the conference, the status of European colonies in the American hemisphere, no general wording could be found to cloak the differences of opinion between the United States and other republics. Argentina and Chile had claims to territory in the Antarctic which conflicted with those of Great Britain. Argentina also claimed the Falkland Islands, long held by the British, and Guatemala regarded British Honduras as illegally occupied Guatemalan territory. These claims were hardy perennials. They had never been taken very seriously by Great Britain. Within the past year, however, the Latin American countries had become bolder in twisting the lion's tail. President González Videla of Chile visited "Chilean territory" in the Antarctic in February 1948. Guatemalan mobs stoned the British Legation in Guatemala City. Britain reacted by sending warships into Antarctic waters and landing troops in British Honduras. Argentina, Chile and Guatemala thought the moment propitious to reinforce their claims by an appeal to the spirit of American solidarity, which other American states would find it difficult to oppose. Guate-

---

[31] Some experienced observers felt that the concentration of attention on the menace of international communism tended to obscure other and more important factors making for unrest and revolution in Latin America and for strained relations with the United States. Sumner Welles, one of the architects of the good neighbor policy, took the extreme view that obsession with the "hemisphere Red scare" obscured the fact that the inter-American system was in real danger of collapse (*New York Herald Tribune*, April 20, 1948). Samuel Guy Inman, a consultant to the U.S. delegations at former inter-American conferences, felt that at Bogotá democracy suffered a crushing defeat because the tactic of blaming everything on the extreme left strengthened the hand of dictators of the extreme right ("What Went Wrong at Bogotá?," *The Nation*, CLXVI, June 5, 1948, 625-627).

mala took the initiative by placing before the Bogotá conference a draft resolution declaring it to be the just aspiration of the American republics that the status of colonies in the Americas be terminated.

The Guatemalan, Argentine and Chilean delegates introduced a great quantity of historical and geographical data in support of their claims, which met with considerable sympathy. The United States was placed in the embarrassing position of wishing neither to disturb its good relations with Britain nor to appear to oppose the "just aspirations" of other American republics. Its decision was to abstain from voting on the resolution, explaining that the settlement of these territorial disputes involving non-American states was outside the jurisdiction of a purely inter-American conference. Marshall reaffirmed the devotion of the United States to two cardinal principles: that the peoples of dependent territories should be helped to attain a constantly increasing measure of self-government, and that disputes should be settled by peaceful means available to all parties and consistent with the U.N. Charter. By the Monroe Doctrine the United States had long ago declared its opposition to the extension of European colonies in the western hemisphere, but the British, French and Dutch colonies in existence did not fall within the scope of the doctrine. In regard to the current disputes, the United States did not wish to take sides or to support any resolution "which would appear to prejudge the conflicting claims of friendly nations." [32]

When the matter came up for discussion, Argentina submitted some strongly worded amendments to the original Guatemalan draft. They stated, among other things, that the existence of colonies or of "*de facto* occupations" (the latter phrase inserted to cover the Falklands, considered not as a colony but as illegally occupied Argentine territory) was in-

[32] Department of State, *Ninth International Conference of American States,* 85-86. On the subject of Antarctica, the United States later (August 28) announced that it regarded "some form of internationalization" as the most effective solution of the territorial problem but recognized that no early agreement could be expected in view of the multiplicity of conflicting interests, claims and legal arguments.

compatible with American ideals, contrary to principles proclaimed at inter-American conferences, and a menace to the peace and security of the continent. To the declaration that the end of colonial dependencies was the just aspiration of the American republics, Argentina proposed a second point recognizing the "rights, responsibilities and titles" of the American republics as against outside nations occupying American territory. The resolution ultimately approved by the conference was a good deal milder than the Argentine proposal. Condemning in general terms the existence of colonial regimes and recalling the American ideals of emancipation and independence, it provided that the controversies between American and European states over certain territories and the whole problem of dependent and occupied territories should be studied by a new American Committee on Dependent Territories in Havana.[33]

Brazil and the Dominican Republic joined the United States in abstaining. The Brazilian delegation, in a formal and well-reasoned declaration, reminded the conference that it was not a proper forum for passing on questions affecting the interests of non-American states; that the destinies of those European possessions which were in dispute should be resolved by direct negotiation or by other recognized pacific means for the settlement of disputes; and that with reference to other possessions it was appropriate to call attention to Article 73 of the U.N. Charter, under which the states responsible for their administration assumed the "sacred trust" of preparing them for self-government.

Another question of current political interest was the recognition of *de facto* governments, one to which the frequency of governmental changes by nonconstitutional methods in Latin America gave special importance. For years there had been controversy over the use of recognition or nonrecognition as a political instrument to show approval or disapproval of a revolutionary government. At Bogotá opinion was divided between states favoring the doctrine of automatic recognition of any

[33] The committee met for the first time on March 15, 1949, after 14 states had appointed representatives to it.

government in actual control of a given country and those which held that recognition or the maintenance of diplomatic relations should be contingent upon the observation of certain principles. States such as Ecuador, where revolutions were frequent, supported the former doctrine, as did Mexico and Argentina, the latter having recently been the subject of an experiment in nonrecognition on the part of other republics, including the United States. Venezuela and several others, distinctly a minority, felt that nonrecognition should be used as a deterrent to revolutions directed against democratic governments. Uruguay urged that in the event of the extensive violation of human rights by an American government, the other governments should consult on whether recognition should be withheld or diplomatic relations broken. This proposal reflected the same general outlook as the Rodríguez Larreta doctrine of collective intervention proposed by Uruguay in 1945 but not accepted by other Latin American states.

The United States, which in 1945 had given public support to the Rodríguez Larreta doctrine, leaned more toward the strict nonintervention approach at Bogotá. The U.S. delegation introduced a resolution stating that continuity of diplomatic relations among the American republics was desirable and that the establishment or maintenance of relations with a given government did not involve any judgment as to the domestic policies of that government. These two points were included in a resolution finally adopted, together with a third proposed by Mexico to the effect that the right of maintaining, suspending or renewing diplomatic relations with another government should not be exercised as a means of obtaining unjustified advantages. A Colombian proposal for inter-American consultation prior to recognition of a new government was not accepted. More detailed consideration of the subject of recognition of *de facto* governments was put off until the next conference, to which the Inter-American Juridical Committee was to submit a project and report.

The resolution on recognition was criticized in some quarters as an encouragement to revolution, since under its terms any group of rebels could feel sure of international recognition as soon as they succeeded in seizing power. It was, however, in line with the principle of nonintervention, and the argument could be made that recognition or nonrecognition was not only an improper but also an ineffective means of chastising or expressing disapproval of another government. That seemed to be the lesson of recent experience in dealing with revolutionary regimes in Argentina, Bolivia and Nicaragua. Not long after the conference, however, revolutionary *coups d'état* brought military juntas to power in Peru in October 1948 and in Venezuela in November, replacing regimes which had been trying since 1945—without great success, it is true—to move toward constitutional democracy and social reform. Following the principles of the Bogotá resolution the United States decided, after a short delay in which it consulted the other American republics, to maintain normal relations with the new government in Peru. In the case of Venezuela it waited longer, finally recognizing the new regime on January 21, 1949, but taking the occasion to call attention to the principle that the solidarity of the American states required that their political organization be based on "the effective exercise of representative democracy," words which appeared in the new Charter of the Organization of American States. Washington was disturbed, however, by this reappearance of military dictatorships in Latin America. Even before recognizing the new Venezuelan regime the State Department had sent a circular note to the other American republics expressing "growing concern with respect to the overthrow of popularly elected governments by military forces in certain of the countries of this hemisphere" and asking for their comments on what action the inter-American organization might appropriately take to strengthen democracy.

The discussions on recognition, European colonies, and communism took up a good deal of the time of the Bogotá conference. Its major task, however, and major accomplishment, was the establishment of a permanent constitutional status for the inter-American system, henceforth to be known as the Organization of American States. The growth of the system had been a gradual process since the first conference of American states in 1889. It was based on a number of treaties, resolutions and declarations, the work of a whole series of conferences. It functioned through various and sundry organs set up at different stages in the development of the system. Vagueness of definition, inefficiency, and lack of coordination pointed to the need for reorganization, which was recognized by a resolution of the Mexico City conference in 1945. That resolution laid down the lines which the reorganization was to take, leaving the adoption of the new constitutional document to the next regular conference of American states in Bogotá.

By and large the work of drawing up the new Charter of the Organization of American States, on the basis of a draft prepared by the Pan American Union, proceeded without major controversies. The Argentines were concerned about certain articles which, they felt, leaned toward making the organization a superstate, and succeeded in obtaining some modifications, but they did not appear in an obstructionist role to the same degree as they had at many earlier inter-American conferences. The charter, as it finally emerged from the debates, represented the constructive labors of the American republics, all of which wanted to strengthen and consolidate their regional organization. The inter-American system remained what it was before, a loose organization of sovereign states, but for the first time it had a formal constitution.

The charter began with a statement of purposes and principles, most of them taken from earlier declarations. One new element was the reference to the United Nations. The Organization of American States was declared to be a regional agency within the United Nations, among the purposes of which was the fulfillment of its regional obligations under the U.N. Charter. One chapter of the new American charter listed the fundamental rights and duties of states. Another, dealing with the pacific settlement of disputes, provided that all disputes arising between American states should be submitted to peaceful procedures set forth in the charter before being referred to the U.N. Security Council. A special treaty, called the Pact of

Bogotá, set forth those procedures in detail. The charter repeated the accepted principle that every act of aggression against an American state should be considered an act of aggression against the other American states. In the event of such aggression, they would apply the measures and procedures laid down in special treaties, the most important of which was the Rio treaty of September 1947.

These agreements were speedily put to the test. On December 3, 1948, the Rio treaty came into force. Eight days later Costa Rica invoked it, alleging the invasion of armed forces from Nicaragua. The new Council of the Organization of American states acted quickly, sending a committee to investigate on the spot. By Christmas Eve the committee, after a flying trip, reported its conclusions to the Council: that Costa Rican political exiles had organized on Nicaraguan territory an armed revolt against the Costa Rican Government; that the Government of Nicaragua did not take adequate measures to prevent it; that no proof was found of participation in the revolt by Nicaraguan armed forces. It reported also that the Caribbean Legion, whose purpose was the overthrow of certain existing governments, including that of Nicaragua, had been given moral and material support by Costa Rica. The Council, on the basis of this report, requested the two governments to take measures to remedy this dangerous situation and to observe strictly the principle of nonintervention. They did take such measures and, with the prompting and assistance of the Council, finally signed a pact of amity in Washington on February 21, 1949. This was a notable victory for the new inter-American peace machinery.

The organs of the new Organization of American States were the Inter-American Conference, the meetings of Foreign Ministers, the Council, the Pan American Union, the specialized conferences, and the specialized organizations. The Inter-American Conference, meeting once every five years, was the supreme authority of the organization. When necessary the Foreign Ministers would meet as an organ of consultation to consider "problems of an urgent nature" such as an armed attack against an American state, which would bring the Rio mutual assistance treaty into effect. Such meetings had already been held in the past: at Panamá in 1939 to deal with the outbreak of war in Europe, at Havana in 1940 to consider the threat to the hemisphere caused by Germany's victories and the situation of European colonies in America, and at Rio de Janeiro in 1942 to adopt common measures against the Axis states. To advise the Foreign Ministers on military matters an Advisory Defense Committee was established. Originally conceived by the United States and other republics as a permanent body and organ of the newly established Council, it was given a more restricted status after the Argentine and other delegations at Bogotá objected that creation of a continuously functioning military body would not be in keeping with the pacific traditions of the inter-American system. Argentina had wanted to set it up by a special protocol to the Rio treaty, making it independent of the Council. The compromise devised to meet these divergent viewpoints was not entirely satisfactory to the United States, but in order to meet the need for a continuously functioning body the existing Inter-American Defense Board, although not mentioned in the Charter itself, was by a separate resolution continued until such time as a two-thirds majority of the American states should decide to abolish it.

At the center of the Organization of the American States was the Council, the successor to the Governing Board of the Pan American Union. The Pan American Union itself became the Secretariat of the Organization.[34] Composed of one representative of each state, the Council was the executive body of the Organization, with definite political and administrative functions. Argentina led a bloc of states which believed that to give it political powers would create a superstate and open the door to intervention. The final decision of the conference was a compromise. The Council was to exercise the functions of a provisional consultative organ given to the old Governing Board under the Rio treaty. It would also take cognizance of

[34] The Director General of the Pan American Union, Alberto Lleras Camargo, became Secretary-General of the Organization of American States.

any matter referred to it by the Inter-American Conference. It was empowered to exercise general supervision over the existing Inter-American Economic and Social Council and two new bodies, the Cultural Council and the Council of Jurists. The Council was certainly no superstate. On the other hand, it had some political functions and might be given more.

The Charter of the Organization of American States was a notable achievement, the culmination of many years of effort in building an American commonwealth of nations. To the credit of the delegates gathered at Bogotá, they carried through this task despite the unnerving events of the week of April 9 which nearly broke up the conference. It was an accomplishment likely to endure long after those events had been forgotten.

5. Economic Aid and Good Neighbor Policy

The delegates at Bogotá heard much speechmaking and praise of the unshakable solidarity of the American republics. Yet the persistent differences over economic issues made some of the speeches sound somewhat hollow. Latin America's most pressing need was for U.S. goods and for the dollars with which to buy them. Aid from the United States, in Latin American eyes, was required both for readjustment to a normal peacetime economy and for the fulfillment of ambitious national development plans. That Latin America, after its cooperation in the war effort, received so little while Europe was granted billions was a source of some resentment. This resentment was already evident at the Rio conference of 1947, but was mollified to some extent when General Marshall made a special plea for the postponement of economic problems to the meeting at Bogotá.

In his opening address at Bogotá, Marshall told the conference of the "tremendous problems" the United States was facing, of the "staggering and inescapable responsibilities" assumed by the American people. He expressed understanding of the desires of the other American republics to achieve balanced economies through development of industries, mechanization of agriculture, and modernization of transportation. The U.S. Government, he said, was prepared to increase its economic assistance to Latin America. But it could finance "no more than a small portion of the vast development needed." Progress could best be achieved, as the experience of the United States had shown, "through individual effort and the use of private resources." The implication was that private U.S. capital would be available if Latin American governments would set specific and realistic goals in their development programs and make the investment climate sufficiently attractive. Marshall's speech was a frank and logical exposition of two fundamental points: U.S. resources were not unlimited and the decision had been taken to give priority to the European Recovery Program.

The assembled Latin American delegates were not encouraged by Marshall's statement. What they wanted was an assurance of direct government-to-government loans from the United States. Alternatively, they might have favored an inter-American development corporation financed largely by the United States. Having largely assumed direction and control of national development programs, the Latin American governments did not wish to be dependent for needed capital on conditions set by private foreign investors. To meet those conditions, such as allowing the transfer of profits abroad, they would have to retreat from the extreme nationalism which was their stock in politics. What they preferred was a series of loans such as they had received from the Export-Import Bank in the 1930's, not what they feared would be a revival of the unfortunate era of private loans of the 1920's, which had left a legacy of ill feeling and resentment on both sides.

The Export-Import Bank, however, did not have unlimited resources. Most of its authorized funds had been committed to Europe and the Far East. As a great concession Marshall announced during the conference that Truman had just requested an increase in the Bank's lending authority by $500 million. His statement, according to news reports, was received in cold silence. The Latin Americans were thinking in terms of billions.

The atmosphere was hardly propitious for discussion of the agreement which was to lay down the broad principles of economic cooperation among the American states. As it finally emerged, the Economic Agreement of Bogotá contained a number of points dear to the Latin Americans such as the need for reducing the disparity in prices between raw materials and manufactured goods, the need for general development and sound industrialization, and the elimination of any element of coercion in the economic relations of the American states. At the instance of the U.S. delegation the agreement also contained a detailed statement on the treatment of private foreign investment capital. There were to be no unjustified restrictions on the transfer of capital and earnings, no discriminatory action against foreign enterprises, and no expropriation without prompt, adequate and effective compensation. On the other hand, foreign investment was to be made with a view not only to profit but to the sound development and social welfare of the receiving state.

The Economic Agreement of Bogotá left unresolved the basic conflict of philosophies and policies. The United States entered a number of reservations, while many Latin American nations made reservations on the provisions relating to private investment. More would be heard, at the forthcoming inter-American technical economic conference scheduled for Buenos Aires if not before, of Latin American proposals for government loans, for an inter-American development corporation, and for an inter-American bank.

The great financial effort which the United States was making to save western Europe left little for direct loans or grants to Latin America. International Bank loan agreements for Latin American countries at the end of 1948 totaled only $16 million, although the Bank subsequently allotted an additional $75 million for Brazil and $34.1 million for Mexico. The Bank's president, John J. McCloy, told the Bogotá conference that "it is in the Latin American countries that, for the immediate future, I regard the Bank as having its greatest opportunity to render constructive assistance in the development field"; but he emphasized that loans from the Bank would have to meet rigorous tests of their "soundness" and that the ultimate objective was to blaze the trail for private international investment.[35] Nor was the Export-Import Bank interested in "political" loans. The proposed $500 million increase in its lending authority failed to secure Congressional approval, and such funds as it had available it was willing to use only on carefully scrutinized projects. Its loans to Latin American countries during 1948 totaled $53.9 million.[36]

Another source of dollars, which proved quite disappointing to most Latin American states, was the Marshall plan. They had the chance to glean something from the system of offshore purchases of Latin American goods for Europe. The State Department, in presenting its original ERP proposals to Congress, estimated that dollar purchases in Latin America would total $2,615 million on the first 15 months of the program.[37] Hopes raised by this estimate proved vain, for as ERP was put into operation there was no such flow of dollars into Latin American coffers. In the first six-month period only some $116 million was authorized for the purchase of Latin American commodities. For the 12 months ending March 31, 1949 the total came to $442 million.[38] The chief factor was the improvement in world food prospects; Europe's own harvest was good, while the United States and Canada had bumper wheat crops. Under the Economic Cooperation Act, products of which the United States had a surplus could not be bought by ECA outside the country. This list included a number of items usually exported by Latin America.

ECA offshore purchases included Chilean nitrates, Cuban

---

[35] International Bank for Reconstruction and Development, *Address by John J. McCloy before the Economic Commission of the Ninth International Conference of American States,* April 5, 1948.

[36] Export-Import Bank of Washington, *Sixth Semiannual Report to Congress for the Period January-June 1948* (Washington, 1948), 4; *Seventh Semiannual Report . . . July-December 1948* (Washington, [1949]), 5.

[37] Senate Foreign Relations Committee, 80th Congress, 1st Session, *Outline of European Recovery Program: Draft Legislation and Background Information Submitted by the Department of State* (Washington, 1948), 107.

[38] Economic Cooperation Administration, *Eleventh Report for the Public Advisory Board* (Washington, 1949), 50.

sugar, Venezuelan oil, and copper and other nonferrous metals from Chile, Peru, and Mexico. Argentina, called by the Herter Committee "the focal point of the problem of bringing Latin America's productive capacity to bear on European recovery," was near the bottom of the list, with only $286 million in paid shipments (mostly hides, skins and leather and dairy products) through February 1949.[39] Bumper crops elsewhere partially accounted for Argentina's meager contribution. Another factor was the Argentine Government's own price and trade policies and its refusal to meet conditions set by the United States. There was no disposition on the part of ECA to pay inflated prices for Argentine grain, meat, and hides. While attempts were made to reach an agreement in the summer of 1948, U.S.-Argentine relations took on the aspects of small-scale economic warfare.

Argentina held firm on its price demands and clamped restrictions on foreign exchange, a severe blow to American business interests in Argentina. Perón presented the controversy to his public as a struggle which capitalist nations, in league with his domestic opponents, were waging against the Argentine people. He reiterated his intention to push ahead with his program of economic nationalism, embodied in a grandiose five-year plan. The main difficulty was that he needed the capitalist nations' trade and financial cooperation, which he professed to scorn. U.S. Ambassador Bruce pushed the idea of expanded private trade as the only way out of the present difficulties for both countries. But there was no fundamental change in the policies of either government.

Argentina, thanks to several years of a sellers' market in foodstuffs, had been able to liquidate its foreign debt, buy out foreign owners of its railways and other public utilities, and even extend credits to a number of Latin American and European countries. The Perón government stated on many occasions that it did not desire any foreign loans. Other Latin

[39] *Final Report of the House Select Committee on Foreign Aid,* House Report No. 1845, 80th Congress, 2nd Session, May 1, 1948, 459; Economic Cooperation Administration, Division of Statistics and Reports, *Paid Shipments* (Washington, February 28, 1949), 6.

American governments were not so proud. They admitted frankly that they needed loans. They knew that these could come only from the United States and openly intimated that refusal by the United States would be regarded as a betrayal of inter-American solidarity and of the good neighbor policy.

In the United States a certain sector of opinion concerned with inter-American relations, led by former Under-Secretary of State Sumner Welles, defended the view that the other American republics were entitled to large-scale economic support and that their demands could not be ignored without incurring their lasting ill will and jeopardizing our leadership in the hemisphere. Assistant Secretary of State Norman Armour conceded publicly that the Latin Americans "keenly feel that in our plans to help meet the needs of other parts of the world we have given too little thought to theirs. It has been said that their dissatisfaction over the degree of United States assistance to them has led to a deterioration in relations with the United States." [40]

It was true, as an American official admitted in a published article, that Latin American affairs were "in temporary eclipse" in Washington.[41] What Latin Americans deplored as indifference, however, was the almost inevitable consequence of the United States' concentration first on Europe and second on the Far East. The resources available for shoring up the economic structure of large parts of the world were not unlimited. Despite continued official adherence to the good neighbor policy, neither Congress nor the Administration was willing to pour loans into Latin America. This attitude was reinforced by the fact that the Latin American governments had not done their part by putting their own financial house in order or modifying nationalistic practices, and also by the conviction of leaders of the business community in the United States who felt that the only sound long-run solution was through private investment and private trade.

[40] N.B.C. radio broadcast, March 20, 1948 (Department of State Press Release No. 224, March 20, 1948).
[41] Americus, "Making Good Neighbor Policy Work," New York Herald Tribune, January 26, 1949.

The situation called for some form of practical implementation of the good neighbor policy which would convince the Latin Americans of the interest of the United States in their welfare, give them a measure of constructive economic support, and at the same time remain within the bounds of the possible. Point Four of President Truman's inaugural address in January 1949 proposed a "bold new program" of aid to underdeveloped areas. This program would avoid vast outlays of public funds and stress the "export" of special knowledge and techniques. It would be carried out through close cooperation and association between governments and private interests, the latter having the major role in providing capital for development. Such a program for Latin America would have some solid foundations on which to build. Through the projects of the Institute of Inter-American Affairs in such fields as public health the technical knowledge of the United States was being made available to Latin America on a basis involving the gradual decrease of the commitment of U.S. public funds. The work of the International Basic Economy Corporation, whose leading spirit was Nelson Rockefeller, former wartime Coordinator of Inter-American Affairs and Assistant Secretary of State, illustrated how private U.S. capital and technical skill could be made available for sound agricultural and industrial development in two countries, Brazil and Venezuela. As a preliminary to reappraising the whole question of future economic development in Brazil, a Joint Brazil-United States Technical Commission was set up in 1948. Its terms of reference included estimating Brazil's capacity for economic expansion through the maximum use of domestic resources, considering measures designed to encourage the flow of private capital to Brazil, and analyzing that country's position in the world economy. The commission's report, submitted to the two governments in March 1949, laid the basis for consideration of the question of U.S. technical and financial assistance on the political level when President Dutra visited Washington in May.

The initial Latin American reaction to Point Four, however, was not one of unbridled enthusiasm. Discussion in the Economic and Social Council in February found Latin American delegates chiefly concerned with the methods of financing economic development operations and pessimistic about the availability of sufficient foreign capital in view of the competing demands of the Marshall plan. How to work out a compromise between ambitious development plans and a "common sense" program of mainly technical aid, between economic nationalism and insistence on a proper climate for private foreign investment, was a challenging problem. But if the good neighbor policy had any reality, if each side could see that cooperation with the other was necessary to its own security and welfare, it would not have to be an insoluble problem. Point Four promised long-term results. The question was whether Latin America was prepared to wait out the long term.

CHAPTER TEN

WAR AND PEACE IN PALESTINE

PALESTINE, a problem for which no amount of study, negotiation, or discussion in the United Nations seemed to provide a solution, continued throughout 1948 to be a subject of heated debate. Only in the first months of 1949, with the conclusion of armistice agreements between the new state of Israel and its Arab neighbors, could the outlines of the future settlement be clearly seen.

Ever since the British Government had decided to give up its mandate over Palestine, the situation in that small but bitterly contested land had been explosive in its possibilities, although it did not carry the same threat of world war as those disputes which brought the western powers into direct conflict with the U.S.S.R. The immediate struggle for Palestine was between two intense nationalisms, Zionist and Arab, which would admit of no workable compromise. In the background—often not very far in the background—were the great powers. With each pursuing its own interests, together they proved incapable of the concerted action needed to control or to settle the Arab-Jewish conflict.

The U.S.S.R. was hopeful of exploiting that conflict in order to loosen the Anglo-American grip on the Near East, but faced the handicap of having to act indirectly, by propaganda, by activity in the United Nations, and by Communist agents in the Near East. Great Britain and the United States, on the other hand, probably could have brought about a settlement regardless of Soviet desires if they could have agreed on one course and taken the necessary decisions to put it into effect, for Palestine lay well within the sphere of Anglo-American strategic power. But they did not agree even on the principles of a settlement until the latter part of 1948, and at no time were they willing to impose a solution by force. British commitments to the Arab states and American sympathies with the Zionist cause pulled the two powers in opposite directions at the expense of their common interest in the stability of the Near East and the maintenance of their strategic position there.

In the absence of decisive action on the part of the great powers, the Palestine issue became the subject of a long series of indecisive actions on the part of the United Nations. The General Assembly dealt with the problem of a permanent political settlement, the Security Council with that of keeping the peace. But the Assembly's partition plan and the Council's cease-fire resolutions did not prevent civil strife and the invasion of Palestine by armies of the Arab states, nor did they prevent the subsequent military offensives of Israel. Meanwhile, the problem of Palestine seemed to be approaching a solution through the interplay of forces in Palestine itself, and the strongest force there was the new Israeli army. In this process of settlement the United Nations played its most effective role, that of mediation between Arabs and Jews. It was the hard work, patience and sincerity of U.N. Mediator Count Bernadotte, and even more of his successor, Ralph Bunche, that made possible the long period of truce and the later formal armistice agreements which terminated hostilities between Israel on the one hand and Egypt, Lebanon and Transjordan on the other. These agreements, stabilizing the military situation, foreshadowed a political and territorial settlement under which the Jews would have won by far the greater part of Palestine.

Whatever the immediate fate of Palestine, Zionism and Arab nationalism would continue to confront one another in the Near East. Their relations, whether of conflict or of accommodation, would affect the entire Arab world and the interests of the great powers in that strategic region. Both the U.S.S.R. and the western powers had to determine whether to base their policies primarily on Israel or on the Arab states. The Soviet Union, with a Moslem population of its own, could be counted on to attempt to expand its influence and its power in the

Moslem Middle East. On the other hand, in the United Nations it consistently supported Israel. Whether Communists would have any influence in the new state was very doubtful, and there was no indication that Israel would follow the Soviet lead in international affairs. It was not impossible, however, that Israel's very success in establishing itself would cause turmoil and unrest in the Arab countries of a kind that the Kremlin would be able to turn to its own advantage.

Britain and the United States, in working out long-range policies in the Middle East—toward the movement for Arab unity, toward the economic development of the region, toward political and social trends in the Arab countries and in Israel— had to take account of a Soviet expansionism which combined the historic push toward warm water with Communist theory and advocacy of social change. And this was not only a long-range question. Soviet pressure on the Middle East in 1948 and 1949, especially on Iran, was an existing fact. If the Russians could not control the region, they wished at least to deny it to the west. The position of Great Britain, traditionally the most influential power in the area, had grown weaker in recent years. Egypt's attack on the Anglo-Egyptian treaty of 1936, Iraq's refusal to enter into a new alliance with Britain in January 1948, and the decision of Britain to give up Palestine were symptoms of the changing situation. Britain still had, however, the benefit of the friendship of King Abdullah of Transjordan, and improved its position when the pro-British Nuri Pasha returned to power in Iraq in January 1949.

The western position was strengthened, of course, by the increasing interest in the region shown by the United States, especially in Turkey, Iran and Saudi Arabia. Under special aid programs beginning in 1947, Turkey was the recipient of U.S. military advice and equipment intended to modernize the Turkish armed forces and to reduce the great burden on the Turkish budget of a large semimobilized army. In Iran also the United States had a military mission to advise the Iranian army. In Saudi Arabia the large air base at Dhahran and the expanding activities of the Arabian-American Oil Company, largest American enterprise in the Middle East, testified to the growing American influence.[1]

Iran was the most exposed point of this western defense triangle, and here Soviet pressure was strongest. The Iranian parliament was so bold, in November 1947, as to reject the oil concession in northern Iran which the government had agreed to grant to the U.S.S.R. in 1946. The Soviet radio repeatedly denounced the Iranian Government as made up of lackeys of the Anglo-American trusts and monopolies. They were accused of allowing the Americans to fortify the country and to establish bases intended for aggression against the U.S.S.R. The Soviet Ambassador delivered protests in Teheran. The Iranian Government talked back and even took the step, in February 1949, of dissolving the pro-Soviet Tudeh party. Naturally the Iranians, nervous over Soviet intentions, looked to the United States for an ironclad guarantee of their frontiers. This was what many nations wanted, but what none, not even the parties to the Atlantic pact, could get. On several occasions, as a substitute, the United States issued statements assuring the world of the American interest in Turkey and Iran. Actually, not only those two countries but the entire Middle East, owing to its geographic position and its vast oil resources, had become an area of continuing and permanent interest to the United States.

1. Partition Plan Abandoned

The U.N. General Assembly, by its resolution of November 29, 1947, proposed the only solution of the Palestine problem that appeared to have any chance of being effective, the partition of the country into a Jewish and an Arab state. One point on which most of the various commissions and experts who had studied the problem agreed was that the two peoples could not live peaceably together in the same state. On the other hand, Palestine was a small enough country as it was; to divide it into

---

[1] The air base at Dhahran, completed early in 1946, was under direct U.S. operation for a period of three years under the terms of an Army contract with King Ibn Saud.

two antagonistic and competitive states might make it impossible for either to live. The answer of the U.N. Special Committee on Palestine was to combine political division with economic union. This solution the Assembly accepted.

The proposed solution was fraught with hazards, inasmuch as the factors which made political union impossible would also operate against the success of the experiment of economic union. It required a very large degree of cooperation from both sides and, should that not be forthcoming, a willingness on the part of the great powers to enforce the Assembly's recommendation regardless of Jewish or Arab opposition. Unfortunately, while the Jews welcomed the partition plan as giving them an independent state, small though it would be, the Arabs openly opposed it and refused all cooperation. Their active opposition, which took the form of local warfare in Palestine aided and abetted by surrounding Arab states, posed the question of what the United Nations, and in particular the Security Council, would do to enforce the Assembly's decision.

That decision, of course, was merely a recommendation, which was as far as the Assembly could go. Yet it was widely considered as having validity as a binding decision because Great Britain, in bringing the matter before the Assembly for consideration, had announced its intention to give up the Palestine mandate. The solution proposed by the Assembly, therefore, was the only alternative to Palestine's becoming, on the departure of the British, a juridical vacuum, a prey to open war between Arabs and Jews. Partition had been supported in the Assembly by both the United States and the Soviet Union, a circumstance which appeared to assure its success.

The Assembly, however, had underestimated Arab resistance to partition, British unwillingness to cooperate, and the obstacles to Soviet-American collaboration in putting the agreed solution into practice. The six states of the Arab League which were members of the United Nations (Syria, Lebanon, Iraq, Egypt, Saudi Arabia, Yemen), and Transjordan which was not, immediately set about wrecking the partition plan. Arab "volunteers" streamed into Palestine to join the Palestine Arabs in

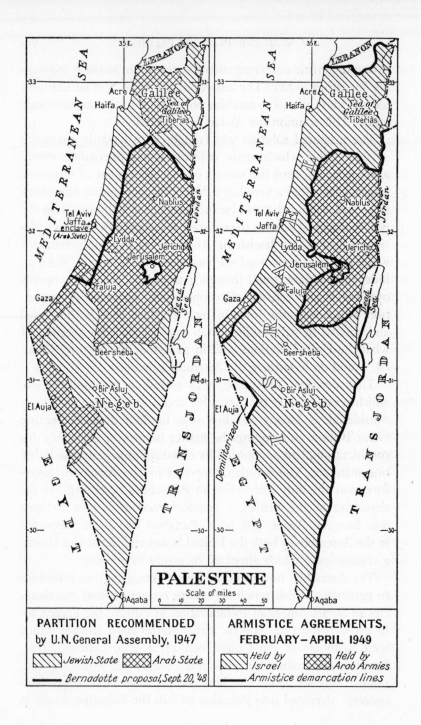

PALESTINE

Scale of miles
0 10 20 30 40 50

PARTITION RECOMMENDED
by U.N. General Assembly, 1947

⧄ Jewish State ⧄ Arab State
— Bernadotte proposal, Sept. 20, '48

ARMISTICE AGREEMENTS,
FEBRUARY—APRIL 1949

⧄ Held by Israel ⧄ Held by Arab Armies
— Armistice demarcation lines

open resistance. Great Britain, which had stated many times its refusal to join in the enforcement of any settlement not acceptable to both Jews and Arabs, was unwilling to use force against the Arabs or to facilitate the task of the five-member Palestine Commission,[2] set up by the Assembly to prepare the way for the transfer of power to the two new states. The British announced that they would terminate the mandate on May 15, 1948. Determined not to jeopardize their position in the Arab world, they would not share control prior to that date with any U.N. body. The situation, as the Palestine Commission reported to the Security Council, promised only more violence and chaos after May 15 unless the Council should provide the necessary force to make partition stick.

Britain could not or would not provide such force, or even cooperate with other powers in enforcing partition. The United States, which had watched with dismay the rising tide of violence, did not wish to supply American troops, wished even less to see Soviet troops in Palestine, and could not persuade smaller countries to undertake the job. As the partition plan began to seem unworkable, officials of the State and Defense departments who had never been enthusiastic for partition, largely a White House policy, felt confirmed in their fears that to insist on it would antagonize the Arab world and endanger American strategic interests, especially in petroleum, in the Middle East. These American misgivings, which had been present though not expressed even when the United States supported the partition plan, came to the fore as soon as it became apparent that partition as voted could not actually be effected unless forced on the Arabs. It was then decided to abandon partition as an American policy, or at least abandon it as the necessary immediate solution to the problem of Palestine. On February 24, 1948, U.S. representative Warren R. Austin first announced to the Security Council that the United States did not believe that force could be used to support a recommendation of the General Assembly. A few weeks later, on March 19, he stated that, since partition could not be effected peaceably at

Composed of Bolivia, Czechoslovakia, Denmark, Panama, and the Philippines.

the present time, the United States favored a temporary U.N. trusteeship over Palestine.

The effect of this announcement, in Palestine, was to encourage the Arabs, believing that the United States had recognized the partition plan as a blunder, to continue their display of force. The effect on the other members of the Security Council was one of bewilderment. They waited to see what proposals the United States would present. Keeping the trusteeship proposal in the background, it presented two resolutions, one calling for an immediate end to violence in Palestine, the other requesting a special session of the General Assembly. One year before, the British Government had asked for a special session "to consider the question of the future government of Palestine." Now the United States asked that such a session be called "to consider further the question of the future government of Palestine."

The Council accepted both American proposals. On April 17 it ordered a general truce and six days later it set up a truce commission to observe it.[3] But there was no improvement in the situation in Palestine. The commission could hardly supervise the truce when both Jews and Arabs ignored it completely. As the end of the mandate and the withdrawal of British troops approached, confusion and chaos increased. The Security Council had neither enforced the partition scheme nor stopped the fighting. The problem was squarely put to the Assembly to reaffirm its partition resolution of November 1947 or to find some alternative solution.

When the Assembly opened on April 16, under the presidency of José Arce of Argentina, there was little optimism among the delegates. Austin explained the trusteeship plan, assuring them that it was not a substitute for partition but an emergency measure to ensure public order and the public services. The immediate necessity, in the American view, was to adopt a temporary solution, such as a trusteeship administered by the United Nations, which would stop the fighting, maintain

[3] The commission was composed of the three non-Arab members of the Security Council having consulates at Jerusalem (Belgium, France, and the United States).

order, and make it possible to negotiate a final political settlement. Only when the Arabs and the Jews agreed on a plan of government would the trusteeship come to an end. In the meantime the United States would be willing to send troops to uphold the trusteeship plan if other states did the same. As an inducement to Arabs and Jews to accept it, Austin alluded to possible U.N. aid to help both in developing the economic potentialities of the country.

This proposal, which made no mention of the General Assembly's partition resolution, could only be interpreted as the abandonment of American support for that resolution. The Jews were bitterly opposed to the new proposal. The Arab leaders, though pleased by the prospect that partition would not be forced upon them, said that they would accept trusteeship only if assured that it would be followed, after a limited period, by establishment of Palestine as an independent Arab state.

At the Assembly itself the lack of enthusiasm for the American plan was apparent to all. The U.S.S.R. and its client states still stood firm for partition, as did Australia, New Zealand and others. The British still held the position that they would get out of Palestine according to the schedule they had set, and would help to enforce no solution not agreeable to both Jews and Arabs, a condition that could not be met. The U.S. delegation at Lake Success continued its efforts to gain support for the trusteeship plan and to persuade other states to join in the policing job required in Palestine, without much success in either, and the time was growing short.

2. The New State of Israel

While the Assembly discussion dragged on without results, British power in Palestine was contracting. As the end of the mandate approached, the British authorities were principally concerned with protecting their own forces and officials as they prepared to withdraw. They did not attempt to enforce law and order throughout Palestine. Arab and Jewish organizations, therefore, were already fighting for position and assuming functions of government. The United Nations might talk about trusteeship, Rabbi Silver of the Jewish Agency told a committee of the General Assembly, but partition had already "become a political and economic reality."[4] In matters of defense the Jews were already on their own in some parts of the country. Their authorities carried on health and social services and other governmental functions. A central Jewish authority began to collect taxes. All preparations were made to set up an independent government the moment the mandate ended on May 15.

The fighting between Jews and Arabs in Palestine became increasingly serious as the Assembly talked. After the French delegate urged that an effort be made at least to safeguard Jerusalem and its Holy Places, the Assembly asked the Trusteeship Council to look into the matter. The Council had already drawn up a draft statute for an international city of Jerusalem in accordance with the partition resolution of November 1947. It was at this point, when it appeared that all or part of Palestine might be placed under the supervision of the Trusteeship Council, that a Soviet representative took his seat in the Council for the first time, ending a year's boycott.

The Trusteeship Council succeeded in getting the Arabs and the Jews to accept a cease-fire in the old walled city of Jerusalem. It failed to accept an American proposal for a U.N. trusteeship over Jerusalem alone, then suggested the appointment by the British of a neutral commissioner to carry on the minimum necessary administrative services in Jerusalem after the expiration of the mandate. But such measures were not solving the problem of Palestine, and of what to do after May 15. The Assembly spent its last days in a futile endeavor to find an alternative to the partition plan. On May 3 British Colonial Secretary Creech Jones told the Assembly that there was not time to set up a trusteeship, and not much point in trying to do so since both Arabs and Jews opposed it. He proposed setting up a "neutral authority" to control essential services and to seek a settlement by mediation. A subcommittee was set up to work

4 U.N. General Assembly, *Official Records of the Second Special Session* (Lake Success, 1948), II, 46.

out such a plan, and an American, Harold Evans, was ultimately appointed to exercise strictly limited administrative functions in the Holy City. But by this time the end of the mandate was at hand. The British Palestine administration was dissolving, the last troops were departing, and the country was left to be fought over by those who claimed it.

In Washington President Truman watched the trend of events with a critical eye. The role which the U.S. delegation had been instructed to play at Lake Success seemed to be accomplishing nothing and to be winning no friends for the United States. The pro-Zionist influences and sentiments which had brought about President Truman's previous interventions in the Palestine question, notably his support of the partition plan in 1947, led him at this point to a new and dramatic stroke. Eliahu Epstein, the representative of the Jewish Agency in Washington, wrote to the President on May 14, stating that a Jewish state called Israel, within the frontiers approved by the General Assembly's resolution of November 29, 1947, would become an independent republic at one minute after 6 P.M. (Washington time) on that same day. Truman acted immediately. A few minutes after 6 P.M. he announced American recognition of the provisional Jewish government in Tel Aviv as the *de facto* government of the new state of Israel.

News of the President's action reached Lake Success during the debate on Palestine. The American delegation, surprised and disconcerted, officially announced the recognition as soon as confirmation arrived. There could be no further talk of a temporary trusteeship for Palestine on the part of the American delegation. The United States was back where it had been before, supporting partition. If the existence of the state of Israel within the frontiers set by the Assembly resolution was a recognized fact, then the partition of Palestine was also a recognized fact. Three days later the U.S.S.R. also recognized Israel.

May 14, the birthday of Israel, was the last day of the Assembly session. Before it adjourned it called upon the Security Council to appoint a U.N. Mediator to use his good offices with the local and communal authorities in Palestine to arrange for the operation of essential services, assure the protection of the Holy Places, and work toward a peaceful settlement. The Mediator was to cooperate with the truce commission set up by the Security Council. On May 20 Count Folke Bernadotte, the head of the Swedish Red Cross, was appointed to the post.

The new turn of events did not deter the surrounding Arab states from their plan to invade Palestine at the end of the mandate. They were welcomed by the Arab Higher Committee in the name of the Arabs of Palestine, who were already fighting the Jews without any great success. The governments of Egypt and Transjordan and the Secretary-General of the Arab League all announced the military campaign as aimed at freeing Palestine from Zionist terror and restoring law and order.

The coming military struggle was a supreme test for Israel and also for the Arab League. This group of seven Arab states was held together largely by the Palestine issue. On it they could act together despite the dynastic and other rivalries which set Egypt against Saudi Arabia and both against Transjordan and Iraq. King Abdullah of Transjordan's plan for a "Greater Syria" under his leadership also kept him at odds with Syria and Lebanon. The expectation was widespread that the Arab armies, unless outside powers intervened, could deal heavy and perhaps mortal blows to the young Jewish state. However, the myth of Arab military strength was soon to be exploded in Palestine, and with it went the myth of Arab political unity.

In view of the undisguised state of war in Palestine, the Security Council met in urgent session on May 15. Within a few days it had passed two American-sponsored resolutions. The first called for sending questionnaires to the Arab states, the Arab Higher Committee, and the provisional government of Israel in order to get their versions of the facts. The second called for a cease-fire. Unfortunately for the prestige of the United Nations, these resolutions brought no improvement; the fighting in Palestine went on. On May 29, the Council tried once more to bring its influence to bear to stop the fighting, and this time was more successful. It called for a four-week truce during which no war material or fighting personnel were to enter Palestine or the Arab states. After conferring with Bernadotte, both Jewish and Arab leaders accepted the truce, and on June 11 it went into effect.

By this time the strength of the Jewish military formations had been proved. The Arab armies advanced into Palestine, but principally into the Arab-inhabited areas not assigned to the Jews by the General Assembly's resolution of November 1947. The Jews were generally successful in defending their main coastal area and even their outlying settlements. Furthermore, they took control of the new city in Jerusalem—Transjordan's Arab legion captured the old city—but despite severe fighting were unable to open the road from Tel Aviv to Jerusalem.

3. Truce and Mediation Efforts

Bernadotte was confronted by problems which were both formidable and complex. His major tasks were two: (1) to supervise the operation of the truce in cooperation with the three-power truce commission previously established by the Security Council, and (2) to promote a peaceful settlement of the Arab-Jewish dispute over Palestine, a problem that had defied solution for some 30 years.

To assist him in carrying out his assignment Bernadotte had only a handful of military officers, guards and technical personnel, and obviously insufficient equipment. He found it impossible to maintain permanent observers in the various Arab states and in all the places where they were needed in Palestine. His observers, moreover, were powerless to enforce the truce and to punish violators.

Throughout the four weeks of the truce Bernadotte's organization had to deal with many charges and countercharges of violations, generally without being able to tell which side was at fault. Yet on the whole the truce was observed, thanks largely to the good work done by Bernadotte and the respect which he won. He had to report only three violations, which were isolated incidents. During the four-week period not one case of large-scale military action occurred in Palestine.

With his political mediation the Mediator had less success. The indecisiveness of the fighting that preceded the truce left neither side in a mood to compromise. To give them something to discuss, Bernadotte presented some ideas of his own to the provisional government of Israel and to the Arab states. Starting from the premise that the solution recommended by the General Assembly in November 1947 had been left behind by events, he proposed new territorial and economic arrangements. The Negeb, the southern desert region of Palestine, he proposed should go to the Arabs, and western Galilee in the north to the Jews. In each case his proposal was a reversal of the U.N. partition plan. Jerusalem, which the partition plan would have placed under a special international regime, he thought might go to the Arabs. He proposed that there be a free port at Haifa and a free airport at Lydda, both in Jewish territory. He retained the idea of an economic union of Jewish and Arab Palestine. On the touchy subject of immigration he proposed that either of the two states, after a period of two years, would have the right to ask the central council of Palestine to rule on the policy of the other, and in the last resort could take an appeal to the U.N. Economic and Social Council.

This "reasonable framework of reference," as Bernadotte described it, struck both Jews and Arabs as neither reasonable nor worthy of discussion. Israel criticized his departure from the U.N. partition plan. The Israeli leaders hoped that they might improve the territorial provisions of that plan, but firmly rejected any suggestion that they accept less. Israel was "deeply wounded," they said, by the Mediator's "disastrous" and "startling" suggestion for Jerusalem. It would accept no infringement of its independence in respect of immigration policy. The Mediator, said the Israeli Government, should reconsider his whole approach to the problem. On the other side of the fence, the states of the Arab League were no more willing to compromise. For years they had been asking for a unitary state including all Palestine, in which the Jews would have special rights as a minority, and they had not changed their minds. They told Bernadotte that his suggestions were aimed at "the realization of all Zionist ambitions" and tended to grant them more than they would get under the U.N. partition plan.[5]

Unsuccessful in making progress toward a political settlement, Bernadotte had also to report failure in his efforts to prolong the truce by agreement. Although Israel was willing, the Arab states refused his plea, and fighting began again on July 9. The Mediator flew to Lake Success to plead for firm action. On July 15 the Security Council, on the proposal of the United States, ordered the cessation of fighting. Acting under Chapter VII of the Charter, the Council served notice that any breach of the truce would be met with punitive action of some kind. The order was effective, and Bernadotte went back to Palestine to supervise the new truce, this one having no time limit. This time he was given more observers and more equipment. U.N. observers patrolled the land, sea and air approaches to Palestine to keep out war materials and to control the immigration of men of military age. Of the two parties Israel was the more directly affected by this control, for Bernadotte's organization had to concentrate its attention on Palestine and could not patrol all the Arab states. Nevertheless, Israel's strength continued to grow; the army improved in organization and received a certain amount of smuggled equipment and munitions, including shipments by air from Czechoslovakia. While building up their forces, the Israelis continued to supply and to maintain the outlying Jewish settlements in the Negeb. Israel regarded the Negeb as Jewish national territory, assigned to it by the United Nations, even though Arabs still controlled most of it.

Clashes which took place during the second truce period were more serious than in the first. Bernadotte reported a number of truce violations, but they were about evenly divided between the two sets of disputants. In Jerusalem, where the truce was handled by the three-power truce commission, the Jews stayed in the new city, while the Arabs held the old. Sniping

[5] *Progress Report of the United Nations Mediator on Palestine* (U.N. General Assembly, *Official Records: Third Session*, Supplement No. 11 [A/648]), 21, 25.

and rifle-fire were almost continuous. The Jews, remembering Bernadotte's earlier suggestion that Jerusalem go to the Arabs, would not risk losing their foothold. Bernadotte reported a disquieting tendency on the part of local commanders to disregard the authority of the United Nations. Any of these clashes might have developed into full-scale hostilities.

Attempting to renew his mediation during the second truce, Bernadotte found that the Israeli attitude had stiffened. In the brief period between the two truces the Jews had gained new territory and new confidence. They had extended the *de facto* boundaries at several points beyond the limits set by the U.N. partition plan. Henceforward the government of Israel tended to count less on the United Nations and to be more critical of its interventions. Israeli leaders warned the Arab states that if they continued to violate the truce, it would mean war. At the same time they indicated that they were prepared to negotiate peace directly with the Arab states. The latter, however, were not prepared to negotiate with Israel or even to recognize its existence in any way.

As the truce dragged on, punctuated by sporadic local fighting, especially in Jerusalem, Bernadotte prepared a progress report for submission to the coming session of the General Assembly. The truce, he warned, could not be maintained indefinitely. Furthermore, his attempt to mediate could not be successful "so long as either party believes that it can, with relative impunity, resort to armed force and thereby achieve for itself a more favorable settlement." [6] Believing that he saw indications of moderation and sober counsel "in at least some important quarters," he considered the time ripe for a settlement.

Four points, said Bernadotte's report to the Assembly, were fundamental in considering the problem of Palestine. The first was that the Assembly's resolution of November 29, 1947, which had taken for granted a cooperation between Arab and Jew which did not exist, "has already been outrun and irrevocably revised by the actual facts of recent Palestine history."

[6] *Ibid.*, 3.

One of those incontrovertible facts, and Bernadotte's second fundamental point, was the establishment of the Jewish state, "the most significant development in the Palestine scene since last November." It was "a living, solidly entrenched and vigorous reality," thanks to a "combination of Jewish strength and international intervention." The Arab dilemma was that only by force could the Jewish state be eliminated, whereas the Arab military forces had proved too weak to apply such force and now could not continue their attempt to do so without violating the orders of the Security Council. Bernadotte's third point concerned Jewish immigration. In contrast to his earlier view, he now conceded that if the Jews were to have a sovereign state, they could determine their own immigration policy.

On all three of these points Bernadotte intimated that Arab attitudes, which had remained unchanged, had become quite unrealistic. The fourth factor which he cited was both a political and a humanitarian question, the existence of several hundred thousand Arab refugees who had fled from their homes in territory taken over by the Israeli authorities. Jaffa, an Arab city which the U.N. partition plan had assigned as an enclave in the proposed Jewish state, was virtually cleared of its population by a mass flight of Arab refugees. If these people wished to return to their homes, Bernadotte believed that their right to do so should be safeguarded; if not, they should be helped to settle elsewhere. In the meantime they had to have emergency aid. Despite help given by the Arab states they were in desperate need of shelter, food, clothing, and medicines. This was a displaced persons problem rapidly surpassing the proportions of that of the displaced Jews of Europe.

The major specific recommendations of Bernadotte's report to the General Assembly were the following: (1) replacement of the truce by a formal peace or at least an armistice involving withdrawal and demobilization of the armed forces or the creation of demilitarized zones between them; (2) revision of the frontiers laid down by the original Assembly resolution, so as to give western Galilee to the Jews and the Negeb to the Arabs; (3) merger of Arab Palestine with Transjordan, with possible frontier rectifications in favor of other Arab states; (4) Haifa to be a free port and Lydda a free airport; (5) an international regime for Jerusalem, with the right of unimpeded access to it; (6) assistance to Arab refugees and recognition of their right to return to their homes and to be compensated for their loss of property; (7) creation of a U.N. conciliation commission to supervise the working out of any arrangements decided by the United Nations and to aid in the search for peaceful adjustment of the situation. Bernadotte also expressed the view that it was useless to wait for Arabs and Jews to agree on a solution. Given the permanent injunction of the Security Council against military action, he wrote, he was reasonably confident that both sides would "acquiesce, however reluctantly, in any reasonable settlement on which is placed the stamp of approval of the United Nations." [7]

There was another part of Bernadotte's report worthy of mention, his comments on the casualties among unarmed U.N. observers doing their best to make the truce effective. Four had been killed (three French officers and a Norwegian guard) and seven wounded. U.S. Consul General Thomas C. Wasson, the American representative on the Security Council's truce commission, was also killed in performing his duties, on May 23, 1948. When the Mediator's report finally reached the Assembly, another name had been added to the list. Bernadotte himself was assassinated, apparently by Jewish extremists of the Stern Gang, on September 17. The shocking news stunned the delegates gathering in Paris. In the course of the solemn service held in memory of the late Mediator, French Foreign Minister Schuman referred to the final report as "his last will, sealed in blood, which shows us the way to lasting peace."

4. Solution by Fait Accompli

Count Bernadotte's proposals seemed to offer a solution on which for the first time the United States and Great Britain might be able to agree, thus removing what had been for the

[7] *Ibid.*, 4.

past few years the greatest obstacle to a settlement. Secretary Marshall, in Paris, endorsed the plan as "a generally fair basis for settlement" and "the best possible basis for bringing peace to a distracted land." The British Government, after some discussion, also accepted the Bernadotte plan in principle. This decision represented real concessions for the sake of finding a common policy with the United States; up to this point Britain had pointedly refused to recognize the existence of Israel as a state and had consistently maintained that it would support no solution not acceptable to both Arabs and Jews.

The apparent Anglo-American agreement on Palestine might have opened the way for a settlement on those lines had it been acted on with dispatch. There was, however, little disposition at Paris to discuss Palestine early in the session. There was an American election in the offing, and hardly anyone outside the U.S. delegation maintained that American domestic politics had no bearing on the Palestine problem, and vice versa. When President Truman, goaded by Zionist and Republican demands for a clarification of the U.S. Government's position, made his own statement on October 24, other delegations found it reasonable to wonder whether Marshall, in accepting the Bernadotte proposals, was not giving the views of the State Department alone rather than those of the President. Truman said in his statement that he stood squarely on the provisions of the Democratic platform, which had approved the boundaries laid down in the U.N. resolution and expressed the view that no changes should be made in them which were not fully acceptable to Israel. The result was complete confusion in Paris concerning where the United States stood in the matter and a growing desire to put the whole thing off until after the American election. By that time the newly found Anglo-American harmony on Palestine was evaporating, and developments in Palestine itself were becoming harder for the United Nations to influence or to control.

Ralph Bunche, Bernadotte's American deputy, who succeeded him as Acting U.N. Mediator, appeared before both the Security Council and the General Assembly in Paris. In the

Council he discussed the difficulties of keeping the peace in Palestine. To the Assembly's Political Committee he said that the Assembly should make a decision once and for all on a political and territorial settlement. He barely had time to warn that the truce was breaking down before fighting broke out in the Negeb between Israeli and Egyptian forces. At issue was the failure of both sides to accept arrangements worked out under the truce for the supplying of Jewish settlements in the Negeb. Both had used obstructive tactics to hinder the work of the truce organization; as Bunche said, "each side has its soiled hands in the grim business of trying to win a war through the instrumentality of an enforced truce." [8]

It was impossible to maintain the truce in a political vacuum. The Bernadotte report had suggested fundamental territorial adjustments, which the Jews were determined to prevent. Bernadotte had proposed that the Negeb go to the Arabs instead of to the Jews. Secretary Marshall had expressed his approval of the Bernadotte report. Britain, which was known to favor Arab control of the barren but strategic Negeb, had also endorsed it. But the leaders of Israel made it clear that they would not give up this area which had been promised to the Jewish state in the Assembly resolution of 1947. To make that refusal stand, they saw the advantage of first getting possession of the territory itself. The Egyptians, however, who had moved in virtually unopposed when the British mandate ended, were not in a mood to withdraw.

In mid-October the Israeli army on the Negeb front took the offensive. Despite new Security Council resolutions calling for a cease-fire, the fighting continued. Egypt then formally appealed to the Council, but before any decision was taken the Israelis had routed the Egyptian army in a series of smashing victories. Bunche tried to enforce the principle that neither side should be permitted to gain any advantage as the result of fighting. Yet Israel would not give up what it had gained, despite assurances from Bunche that withdrawal would not prejudice

[8] U.N. Security Council, *Official Records: Third Year*, No. 118, October 19, 1948, 3-4.

the final settlement. As political realists the Israeli leaders knew that the Council did not have force available to make them withdraw, and that their military victories very likely would influence the final political settlement.

The Security Council decided to take a rather strong position. On November 4 it passed a resolution, which had the full support of the United States, calling upon the two parties to withdraw to the positions they had held on October 14, behind provisional demarcation lines determined by the Acting Mediator. If either party failed to do so, the Council would consider whether appropriate measures could be taken under Chapter VII of the Charter, dealing with threats to the peace, breaches of the peace, and acts of aggression. The U.S.S.R. abstained from voting on the proposal. Only the Ukraine voted against it. Despite the near-universal support, however, the Jewish leaders were not impressed. By the time Bunche was ready to draw the provisional demarcation lines, Israel had defeated another Arab army in the north, in Galilee.

In Palestine as in Indonesia the United Nations could not act as policeman. When a truce was broken, it was next to impossible to restore the *status quo ante*. About all the United Nations could do was to try to patch up the situation and prevent further outbreaks. The Security Council, on November 16, acted on Bunche's suggestion that conclusion of a formal armistice was the least that should be done. The new resolution, without prejudice to the action of the Mediator in implementation of the resolution of November 4, directed the parties to seek agreement by negotiations conducted either directly or through the Mediator, with a view to the immediate conclusion of an armistice, delineation of permanent armistice lines, and such withdrawal and reduction of armed forces as would make possible the transition to a lasting peace.[9] The Jews did not like the reference to the resolution of November 4, but the Israeli representative, Aubrey Eban, stated Israel's willingness to enter into negotiations. The Arab states, having refused to recognize Israel's existence, officially clung to their

[9] U.N. Doc. S/1080, November 17, 1948.

insistence that they could not negotiate with it, although privately they were not nearly so aloof to Israel's peace feelers as they stated in public.

By this time, with the American election over, the General Assembly was well into its discussion of a British draft resolution endorsing the Bernadotte report and calling for the establishment of a conciliation commission to implement it. Jessup, for the United States, expressed general agreement with the report's conclusions but added the proviso that modifications in the frontiers laid down in the Assembly's resolution of November 1947 should be made only if fully acceptable to Israel, and that if there were changes in Israel's favor there should be equivalent changes in favor of the Arabs. The Soviet delegate, Tsarapkin, stood firmly on the 1947 partition plan as the only proper solution. British and American attempts to substitute the Bernadotte plan for it, he charged, were aimed at strengthening their own influence in the Middle East and imposing their will on the United Nations in the interest of the militarists and the oil monopolies.

From support of partition in 1947 the United States had swung to the idea of trusteeship early in 1948, only to recognize the existence of the Jewish state as soon as it was proclaimed. It then went back to the 1947 partition plan as the basis for the territorial settlement, adding the principle that any changes should be equalized so as not to give one side an advantage. But whether strong American action would be taken to enforce that principle against the Jews was questionable, in view of the support which the new Jewish state enjoyed in a broad segment of American public opinion and in the White House itself. The considerations which had prompted the momentary abandonment of the partition plan—chiefly the fear of alienating the entire Arab world and jeopardizing the American position in the Middle East—did not disappear, but the actual situation made it no longer practical to base American policy on the idea of a trusteeship for all Palestine. It was hoped that the Arab states would somehow adjust to the fact that the Jewish state could not be disposed of or ignored, and that Arab resentment over American support of Israel could be kept within bounds.

Besides showing that the United States and the U.S.S.R. no longer were on common ground on the Palestine question, and that the United States had not yet found common ground with Great Britain, the discussion in the Assembly had a certain air of unreality because of what was happening in Palestine itself. The Jews had no idea of accepting the loss of the Negeb, nor of giving up western Galilee, which they had conquered. The Negeb, they felt, was the sole area suitable for large-scale settlement and development by the thousands of immigrants they expected. Nor would they accept being cut off from the Dead Sea, which had been developed by Jewish initiative and capital and was the main source of mineral wealth in Palestine. Thirdly, the Jews wished by holding the Negeb to maintain a foothold on the Gulf of Aqaba, their gateway to the eastern seas. What the United Nations had granted to them in 1947 they did not intend to let the United Nations take away in 1948. Jewish arms, they felt, would decide the future of the Negeb, and of all Palestine, while the Assembly debated.

The generally unexpected successes of the Israeli armies were matched by the unexpected political and military weaknesses of the Arab League. Although the full measure of Arab defeats was kept from the people of the Arab states, bad news from the war fronts combined with economic distress at home produced unrest, and even disorder and rioting, in Egypt, Syria and Iraq. The rivalry among the various Arab states was brought out into the open.

Abdullah of Transjordan had the only effective Arab army left in the field. He alone, as logical heir to those parts of central Palestine which Israel had not taken, stood to gain by avoiding an all-out fight and waiting until a settlement could be negotiated with Israel. Other Arab states, however, stuck to the old idea, now hardly practical, of an Arab Palestine state. Egypt, Syria, Lebanon, Iraq and Saudi Arabia had granted recognition to the phantom government set up at Gaza in September by the Arab Higher Committee, but they were unable to give it a respectable piece of territory in Palestine on which to function. Saudi Arabia, which had not taken an active part in the Palestine fighting, avoided further involvement. Lebanon, with its mixed Christian-Moslem population, was less fanatic on the subject of Palestine than the other Arab states; the Lebanese, knowing that they would have to live as neighbors of Israel, were not anxious to continue a losing fight indefinitely.

Adversity had brought most of the Arab states to the realization that they could not wipe Israel off the map, and had reduced them to quarreling among themselves. In December a conference of Palestine Arabs at Jericho proclaimed Abdullah "King of All Palestine." Although the Arab League, Islamic authorities and several Arab rulers denounced the move, Transjordan's parliament on December 13 unanimously authorized Abdullah to add Arab Palestine to his kingdom, a step he appeared quite ready to take as soon as conditions were propitious.

The discussion on Palestine in the United Nations at Paris gave the Arab states no reason to hope that they could get a settlement as favorable to them as the recommendations of the Bernadotte report or even the U.N. plan of November 1947, both of which they had rejected as unjust to their cause. Even their staunchest defender among the great powers, Great Britain, had become reconciled to the existence of Israel and was preparing to grant recognition. The British were trying above all to reach agreement with the United States, in the realization that continuing Anglo-American agreement was a firmer foundation for the British position in the Middle East than a series of shaky alliances with Arab governments whose weaknesses had just been glaringly exposed. The American position was now clearly in favor of Israel's getting at least what was assigned to it under the original U.N. partition plan, while Russia had consistently supported the Jewish cause.

The outcome of the Assembly discussion was a resolution, adopted on December 11, creating a three-member conciliation commission which was directed to assist in achieving a final settlement in Palestine. In addition, the commission was to present to the next session of the Assembly recommendations on the protection of the Holy Places in Jerusalem and on an international regime for the city, and also to facilitate the solution of the problem of Arab refugees through repatriation and resettlement. What the final political and territorial settlement would be the Assembly did not attempt to say. There was not the confidence of a year before in the Assembly's ability to decide it, nor was there the same measure of agreement. The Assembly, in effect, now proposed that a settlement be reached by conciliation and negotiation between the parties. The major factors in such a settlement would be, it was realized, the balance of forces in Palestine itself and the degree to which the great powers would intervene to change or to maintain that balance.

The Jews, meanwhile, were doing what they could to tip the balance even more in their favor, and the Arabs were doing what they could to prevent it. On December 22, 1948, fighting broke out again in the Negeb, as Israeli troops swept down toward Gaza and the Egyptian frontier. Egypt brought the situation before the Security Council, alleging a flagrant violation of the Council's cease-fire order by the Jews. Whoever was to blame for the outbreak of hostilities, which grew out of disagreements over withdrawal of troops to previous positions and release of Egyptian forces trapped in a pocket at Faluja, the Acting Mediator was prevented from supervising the truce effectively and the Security Council was unable to do anything to stop the fighting.

Again the Israeli armies swept forward almost without opposition, pushing the Egyptian forces into the narrow coastal strip between Gaza and the Egyptian frontier and even penetrating into Egyptian territory. This decisive offensive action, more than any United Nations resolution, paved the way for serious negotiations for a settlement, for it convinced Egypt and the other Arab states that they would have to deal with Israel. The conciliation commission established by the Assembly was not yet functioning. A new resolution of the Security

Council, of December 22, calling for implementation of earlier cease-fire resolutions and complete supervision of the truce by U.N. observers, had no appreciable effect on the actual situation in Palestine. For some time it had been obvious that the Arab states would have to come to terms with Israel. They had to recognize its existence at least to the extent of negotiating an armistice with the Israeli Government. On January 6, 1949, Bunche informed the Security Council that both Israel and Egypt had unconditionally accepted a cease-fire proposal and would proceed immediately to direct negotiations for an armistice, with his mediation, on the island of Rhodes.

5. United Nations Mediation

When Egyptian and Israeli delegates presented themselves at Bunche's headquarters in the Hotel des Roses at Rhodes on January 12, 1949, Israel in effect had already won the Palestine war in the teeth of the combined Arab armies, the unconcealed hostility of the United Kingdom, and the repeated admonitions of the United Nations. The commencement of negotiations found Israel in possession not only of most of the territory allotted to the proposed Jewish state under the original U.N. partition resolution, but also of large areas in Galilee, central Palestine and the northern Negeb which that resolution had assigned to the Arab state. The eastern sector of the proposed international city of Jerusalem was also under Israeli occupation, together with small areas of Lebanon and Syria. During the armistice negotiations the Israeli forces, once again disregarding the truce agreement of July 18, 1948,[10] took steps to make their occupation of the southern Negeb effective right down to the Red Sea and the Transjordan border opposite Aqaba, thus severing land communications between Egypt and Transjordan.

Israel's political and diplomatic position meanwhile was being rapidly consolidated in a way that would help it to draw

[10] Conclusion of the U.N. Acting Mediator (U.N. Doc. S/1295, March 23, 1949).

the maximum advantages from its favorable military situation; and the commencement of armistice negotiations, in turn, created favorable auspices for the emergence of the new Jewish state. National elections were held on January 25, a constituent assembly of nationalist complexion met in Jerusalem three weeks later to adopt a liberal democratic constitution, and on February 17 Chaim Weizmann was ceremoniously installed as president of the republic. A series of diplomatic recognitions promised early and full acceptance into the international community: even Great Britain accorded *de facto* recognition on January 29, while the United States on January 31 granted *de jure* recognition to both Israel and the Kingdom of Transjordan, which was on the point of joining in the armistice negotiations. Israel's application for membership in the United Nations, rejected by the Security Council on December 17, although the United States and the U.S.S.R. both supported it, was reexamined by that body at the beginning of March and recommended for favorable consideration by the General Assembly.

Israel could thus enter the negotiations with the confidence born of military and political success. Conditions in the opposing camp were altogether different. Here the shock of defeat by a despised and underrated foe was threatening the stability of the existing governments and the Arab coalition was dissolving amid bitter recriminations. The traditional antagonism between Egypt and Transjordan had been heightened by King Abdullah's independent course during the war and his seeming ambition to annex what remained of the Arab parts of Palestine. The "government" of Arab Palestine set up at Gaza was evaporating into nothingness, having virtually no territory to govern; central Palestine remained under the control of Abdullah's Arab legion. Egypt, in turn, while complaining of desertion by its Arab allies, laid itself open to their bitter censure when it decided to face the consequences of an untenable military situation and began negotiations with an antagonist whom all of them had confidently expected to extirpate. Once Egypt had taken the plunge, however, and the pressure on Israel's southern front had been relieved, it could be only a matter of time before the other Arab states would be forced to follow the Egyptian example. The most they could hope for was a stabilization based substantially on existing military positions. There was no longer any real possibility of forcing Israel back within the lines of the U.N. partition resolution, still less of eradicating the Jewish "intruder" as the Arab peoples had been encouraged to expect.

Under such circumstances the scope for United Nations mediation was decidedly limited. Nominally the terms of reference for the Acting Mediator's efforts were the Security Council resolutions of November 4 and November 16, 1948. Actually there was never much prospect of securing compliance with the first of these resolutions, which would have required the Israelis to withdraw to the lines of October 14 and thus relinquish the fruits of both the Negeb and Galilee offensives. The most the U.N. officials could do was to make available their facilities and their diplomatic skill in an effort to save the faces of all concerned and secure general acceptance of the situation created by force of Israeli arms.

The assumption by the United Nations of formal responsibility for promoting a return to peaceful conditions did not prevent the United States and Great Britain from exerting a substantial influence on the course of negotiations. For the United States humanitarian sentiment and sympathy for victorious Israel both counseled an early settlement, and Washington made strong and repeated representations in this sense in Cairo and Tel Aviv. The position of Great Britain was more complicated. Reinforcing the British Government's general pro-Arab proclivities were specific treaty relationships with Egypt and Transjordan which entitled the United Kingdom to maintain military forces on their soil and obligated it to come to their aid in case of attack. But the presence of British forces in the neighborhood of the fighting fronts was bound to appear to Israel as a form of pressure and was not calculated to moderate the temper of the Egyptian and Transjordan governments.

Incidents involving these British forces actually provided more drama than the armistice negotiations themselves and at one stage strained Israeli-British relations almost to the breaking point. On January 7 British military aircraft on reconnaissance flights just within the Egyptian frontier were attacked by Israeli fighters who inflicted a loss of five planes. The British lodged strong protests with the U.N. and with Israeli representatives, who gave the situation a touch of comedy by refusing to accept British communications addressed to the "Jewish authorities at Tel Aviv" rather than to the unrecognized provisional government. Simultaneously the Foreign office announced that London's concern over the situation created in Palestine by Israeli action had prompted it to dispatch a British force to Aqaba under the terms of the Anglo-Transjordan treaty.

Although both British and Israelis vented their irritation with considerable force, no irreparable crisis developed. The United States sought to exert a moderating influence. After a series of conferences between Acting Secretary Lovett and the British Ambassador, Sir Oliver Franks, in which the former developed the general theme that Israel was there to stay and nothing could be gained by British resistance to that fact, signs of mitigation in the British attitude toward Israel appeared. *De facto* recognition was announced on January 29, after Bevin had explained to a skeptical House of Commons that the delay had been occasioned by the necessity for consultation with the dominions and the Brussels powers.[11] Tension revived again in March in connection with Israel's objection to the reinforcement of British troops in Aqaba, its own action in sending an armored force into the adjacent southern Negeb, and Transjordan's unheeded request for British aid in manning its frontiers. So far as the course of the military armistice negotiations was concerned, however, the British appeared reconciled to letting the Arab belligerents make what terms they could.

[11] *Parliamentary Debates, Weekly Hansard,* House of Commons, January 26, 1949, 946-947.

Only four of the Arab states—Egypt, Transjordan, Lebanon and Syria—were directly contiguous to Israel and immediately concerned with the details of the armistice settlement. Saudi Arabia and Iraq, responding to an invitation to join the Rhodes negotiations, advised the Acting Mediator that they would in effect accept any decisions agreeable to the other four.[12] The Egyptian negotiations, as the first in the series, proved to be the most difficult and time-consuming, but established a pattern which was easier to apply in later instances.[13]

Questions of prestige inevitably occupied the foreground throughout the negotiations and presented a constant challenge to the tact and ingenuity of the Acting Mediator and his staff. After confirming the cease-fire order which had enabled negotiations to begin, Egyptians and Israelis proceeded to take up irreconcilable positions on virtually all of the concrete points in dispute. During the entire six weeks of negotiations the danger of a breakdown was never absent. Only the indefatigable energy and resourcefulness of Dr. Bunche and his assistants in bridging differences, sparing susceptibilities, devising compromises, and judiciously invoking the moral authority of the world organization enabled the negotiators to surmount one after another of the intricate problems confronting them and agree on a draft which both governments could accept.

The document finally signed on February 24,[14] although recognized by the parties as "an indispensable step toward the liquidation of armed conflict and the restoration of peace in Palestine," was explicitly declared to be a military armistice agreement which in no way prejudiced "the rights, claims and positions of either party . . . in the ultimate peaceful settlement of the Palestine question." Both parties pledged themselves to scrupulous respect "henceforth" for the Security Council's injunction against resort to military force in settlement of the

[12] U.N. Docs. S/1241, February 23, S/1265, February 24, 1949.
[13] Informal conferences of Israeli military representatives with their Transjordan and Lebanese opposites had been taking place intermittently for some time, but no formal talks were initiated until after the Egyptian armistice was signed on February 24.
[14] U.N. Doc. S/1264, February 23, 1949.

Palestine question; promised that no aggressive action would be undertaken, planned or threatened by either's armed forces against the other; and recognized each other's right to "security and freedom from fear of attack" by the other's armed forces. Provision was made for the exchange of all prisoners of war under U.N. supervision, and for the establishment of a mixed commission under U.N. chairmanship to supervise the execution of the terms.

With regard to the military positions of the two parties, the agreement provided that (1) the Egyptian military forces which had been trapped in the Faluja area since the previous October would be withdrawn under U.N. supervision; (2) Egypt would be permitted to retain defensive forces in the southern part of the Gaza coastal strip; (3) the disputed El Auja area near the Egyptian frontier would be demilitarized and serve as the seat of the mixed armistice commission; and (4) positions on the central front would be left in suspense pending an armistice agreement with Transjordan. In effect, therefore, the agreement of February 24, far from securing a return to positions of the previous autumn as demanded by the Security Council, drew an inviolable line around Israel's conquests in the Negeb.

The agreements with Lebanon and Transjordan likewise had the effect of ratifying Israeli conquests beyond the territorial limits originally contemplated by the U.N. resolution of November 1947. The Lebanese-Israeli agreement,[15] signed on March 23 at the frontier village of Ras en Naqura after 23 days of negotiations, reaffirmed the basic principles of the Egyptian armistice and laid down an armistice demarcation line along the international boundary, thus securing Israel's evacuation of certain occupied Lebanese villages but leaving it in control of the whole of Galilee.

The armistice with Transjordan,[16] which culminated negotiations carried on at Rhodes from March 1 to April 4, also left Israel in possession of substantially the areas it had oc-

[15] U.N. Doc. S/1296, March 23, 1949.
[16] U.N. Doc. S/1302, April 4, 1949.

cupied by force of arms during the preceding months, including the western portions of the projected international city of Jerusalem. Special features of the Transjordan agreement were the provisions for replacement of Iraqi by Transjordan forces in the sector held by the former; for deviations from the existing military lines in Israel's favor, mostly in the interest of improved communications, in central Palestine; and for compensatory modifications in favor of Transjordan from the Dead Sea southward to Aqaba.

Syria agreed late in March to take its turn in negotiating under U.N. auspices, but negotiations were delayed by a *coup d'état* at Damascus which replaced the existing parliamentary regime with a military dictatorship under Colonel Husni Zayim at the end of the month. Preliminary indications, as delegates met with U.N. representatives in tents on the frontier near Mishmar Hayarden, were that local positions held by the two armies would constitute the main issue and that, as in the case of Lebanon, the most logical demarcation line would coincide with the international frontier.

Despite the universal insistence that these were armistice agreements and in no way prejudged the eventual settlement in Palestine, there could be little doubt that they established the broad lines of the future territorial settlement. Intricate questions of all kinds—the delimitation of the actual frontiers, the disposition of what remained of Arab Palestine, the future of the Jerusalem area, the repatriation or resettlement of Arab refugees (now numbering over 700,000)—would undoubtedly delay a return to genuinely peaceful conditions for many months to come. Some of these problems had been examined in a preliminary way by the conciliation commission established by the General Assembly,[17] which planned to hold an exploratory conference with Israeli and Arab representatives in Lausanne late in April.

---

[17] This three-nation commission (France, Turkey and the United States) was expected eventually to take over the functions assigned to the U.N. Truce Commission and the Acting Mediator, but had declined to intervene in the armistice negotiations. See the commission's first progress report, U.N. Doc. A/819, March 15, 1949.

It was to be assumed that the settlement of these questions would be involved at every turn with the larger politics of the Middle East and the interests of the great powers. Abdullah's British connections, his ambitions to annex Arab Palestine, and his continued espousal of the Greater Syria scheme would remain a focus of Middle Eastern intrigue. Moreover, the popular forces unchained by the Palestine war would be a source of instability throughout the Middle East and a possible field for Soviet manipulations as long as economic and social conditions in the Arab world remained unimproved. Britain's reluctant acceptance of the accomplished fact of Israel, and the Kremlin's apparent disillusionment with the results of its pro-Israel policy, promised no cessation in either power's pursuit of its own aims at this crossroads of imperial interests. The United States, deeply involved in the area by virtue of its petroleum interests, its championship of Israel, its concern for the well-being of underdeveloped areas, and its general stake in world security, would face a continued challenge to its best statesmanship. Meanwhile, amid these many sources of uncertainty one fact stood out, clear and unchallengeable: The Jewish state had been born. Israel was a reality.

CHAPTER ELEVEN

ISSUES BEFORE THE UNITED NATIONS

SUPPORT of the United Nations, according to many official American statements during 1948 and 1949, had been and would continue to be the cornerstone of U.S. foreign policy. That did not mean, however, reliance on the United Nations for objectives that it could not achieve or tasks that it could not fulfill. The two major American efforts in the foreign field, the Marshall plan and the Atlantic pact, were carried through outside the United Nations. The recovery and consolidation of western Europe was a prime objective of American policy, as a means of checking Soviet expansion and restoring the world balance. There was no indication that this objective could have been achieved by acting through the United Nations. Indeed, as the United States and the nations of western Europe saw the problem, it was the very inadequacy of the United Nations as a means of checking Soviet expansion and assuring the recovery of western Europe that made the Marshall plan and the Atlantic pact necessary.

The United Nations organization was limited, of course, both by its Charter and by the reluctance of individual states to accept its authority. The General Assembly and the Economic and Social Council had the power only to make recommendations, with which member states were not bound to comply. The Security Council, entrusted with "primary responsibility" for the maintenance of international peace and security, did have the power to make binding decisions, but it was hamstrung by the right of veto which the Charter granted to the five permanent members. Although only one of the five, the Soviet Union, made extensive use of this right, the succession of Soviet vetoes which continued during 1948 provided ample illustration of the weakness of the United Nations. The Security Council was incapable of taking any effective action to maintain or restore peace in critical situations brought on by the expansionist policies of the Soviet Union, and those were precisely the situations which kept many nations in fear of a new world war.

The United Nations could function as an organization to keep the peace only if the great powers were united in their basic objectives, as the peoples of the world had hoped that they would be, or if there were general acceptance of a world authority superior to national governments. In the present state of international relations neither of these conditions could be met. That was why the State Department regarded as unrealistic such proposals as were voiced from time to time in the U.S. Congress and elsewhere for the immediate transformation of the United Nations into a veto-less world policing authority or a rudimentary world government. As a world organization dedicated to the maintenance of peace the United Nations had potential rather than actual significance. It was important, however, as General Marshall pointed out in a statement to the House Committtee on Foreign Affairs, to keep it in being as an all-embracing framework for building the structure of peace, as an alternative to the division of the world into hostile military blocs.[1]

In the fourth year of its life, despite disillusionment caused by the conflicts among the great powers and the ever-present threat of war, the United Nations continued to flourish as a going concern. It had its value as a forum for negotiation and for the exchange of views, even when the views were irreconcilable. The General Assembly, wholly aside from what its resolutions did or did not accomplish, served its purpose as the "town meeting of the world," as Senator Vandenberg had predicted at San Francisco. Other U.N. organs which attracted less public attention—the Economic and Social Council and its subsidiary commissions, the Trusteeship Council, the spe-

[1] Statement before the House Committee on Foreign Affairs, May 5, 1948 (Department of State, *Bulletin*, XVIII, May 16, 1948, 623-625).

cialized agencies which had been brought into formal association with the United Nations, and a host of specialized international conferences—were building, without fanfare, a substructure of understanding and practical cooperation on which a future effective world organization could rest. The Economic Commission for Europe, for example, although not unaffected by the east-west split, did yeoman service for the economic recovery of Europe as a whole by the practical work of its technical committees and its secretariat.

How far such constructive efforts could be carried in the face of unchecked great-power conflicts and the paralysis of the Security Council was open to question. The United Nations had to be given the chance to survive and to carry on its slow progress toward a functioning world order without being pulled apart by the east-west conflict and saddled with burdens which it could not bear. The challenge to world statesmanship was to create conditions in which the United Nations could grow and develop into a true world community as envisaged in the Charter, and not to permit the failures of national leaders and parochialism of national governments to discredit the concept of world organization for peace or to destroy the fledgling institution in which 59 nations were participating.

1. Continued Failure on Disarmament

Two years of study and discussion brought the U.N. Atomic Energy Commission, in the spring of 1948, to the conclusion that "no useful purpose can be served by carrying on negotiations at the Commission level." This situation resulted from the apparently unbridgeable gap between the proposals of the U.S.S.R. and those of the majority of the Commission for the control of atomic energy. The majority accordingly recommended that work be suspended until the major powers should find that some basis for agreement existed.[2] At about the same

[2] *Third Report of the United Nations Atomic Energy Commission to the Security Council, May 17, 1948* (Atomic Energy Commission *Official Records: Third Year*, Special Supplement), 5.

time the Commission for Conventional Armaments, after a year of desultory existence, was still waiting for "an atmosphere of international confidence and security" without which a system of regulation and reduction of armaments could not be put into effect.[3]

The impasse at which both commissions had arrived confirmed the feeling that the approach to world security through control of armaments, without fundamental political agreement among the big powers, was virtually hopeless. An armaments race was actually in progress because of the prevailing political tension and fear of a new war. In a world-wide struggle for power, in which the position of each side depended in large measure on its armed strength, any proposal for the control, reduction or abolition of particular weapons was certain to be looked at in the light of its effect on the comparative strength of the contending powers. In the field of atomic energy control the Soviet leaders did not want any scheme which would place the U.S.S.R. at a disadvantage, and they believed, rightly or wrongly, that such would be the result of adoption of the plan supported by the United States and a majority of the commission. Similarly, in the field of general disarmament in "conventional" weapons, the western powers were naturally skeptical toward Soviet suggestions such as the proposed reduction of all armaments by one-third, put before the U.N. General Assembly at Paris in September 1948.

The Atomic Energy Commission, after detailed study of the proposals submitted by the Soviet Union in 1947, adopted in April 1948 a report which found that they ignored the existing technical knowledge and did not provide an adequate basis for effective international control. The differences which separated the Soviet from the majority plan were the same which had been evident throughout the lengthy discussions of 1946 and 1947 in the Atomic Energy Commission, Security Council, and General Assembly.[4] The principal differences concerned

[3] United Nations, Commission for Conventional Armaments, Resolution of August 12, 1948 (U.N. Doc. S/C.3/31, August 15, 1948).
[4] See *The United States in World Affairs, 1945–1947*, 391-417; *The United States in World Affairs, 1947–1948*, 345-351.

the nature and scope of the control machinery, the timing of the institution of controls and disposition of existing stocks of atomic weapons, and safeguards against violations and evasions.

The majority plan, which grew out of the original U.S. proposals of 1946 known as the Baruch plan, envisaged an international authority with real power to detect and prevent diversion of fissionable materials to "dangerous" uses at all stages from the mine through the plant. The Soviet plan, on the other hand, provided for an international control commission with powers strictly limited so as not to infringe the sovereignty of individual states. Moreover, the first and most urgent step, in the Soviet view, was the conclusion of a convention prohibiting the possession or manufacture of atomic weapons, without regard to the stages by which effective international control would be instituted. As to enforcement action in case of violation, the Soviets regarded the Security Council as the only appropriate body, that is, they insisted on the veto. In the view of the United States and the other nations which made up the majority of the commission, the Soviets had proposed a plan fundamentally inadequate for the control of atomic energy and then added the stipulation that even this feeble plan could not be established until all atomic weapons had been outlawed. They felt that they could not possibly accept it.

These deep differences of view made it unlikely that any amount of negotiating could produce agreement. In its First Report to the Security Council, drafted at the end of 1946, the Atomic Energy Commission had set forth general principles for a system of international control. Its Second Report, completed in 1947, contained specific proposals for the functions of the proposed control agency. Both were accepted by all members of the commission except the U.S.S.R. and the two states of the Soviet bloc that were successively represented on it, Poland and the Ukrainian S.S.R. Soviet objections, of course, had the result of holding up the progress on a system of international control, since to be effective it would have to be world-wide or at least include all powers having the potential capacity to develop atomic energy. The commission had a plan of control, but it did not see how it could go on to the preparation of a draft treaty "incorporating its ultimate proposals," as it had been directed to do by the Security Council. Its Third Report, adopted on May 17, 1948, confessed failure by recommending that further negotiations in that body be suspended.

When the Security Council considered the matter in June, the United States introduced a resolution approving the plan embodied in the Atomic Energy Commission's earlier reports and accepting the recommendation that its work be suspended. Supported by nine members of the Council, the resolution was killed by a Soviet veto. The Council then voted to transmit to the General Assembly the reports of the Atomic Energy Commission, together with the record of the Council's own discussions on the subject.

The parallel efforts of the Commission for Conventional Armaments were meeting with no greater success. Proceeding under a "plan of work" approved by the Security Council in 1947, the commission endeavored to establish a set of principles to govern the regulation and reduction of armaments and armed forces. Here again the gulf between the Soviet Union and the United States, the former supported only by the Soviet Ukraine and the latter by the remaining members of the commission, was too wide to leave any hope that it might be bridged by negotiation. In the absence of concrete American proposals, the Soviet Union took the lead in pressing for immediate "practical" measures to reduce armaments, limit the strength of existing armies, navies and air forces, and restrict production of war material. The western powers regarded such proposals as propaganda measures rather than as serious propositions, especially in view of the secrecy surrounding the size, strength, and equipment of the Soviet armed forces. Besides objecting to the Soviet proposals as providing no adequate system of control and no safeguards against violations and evasions, the other members of the commission took exception to the Soviet attempts to bring atomic energy control into the picture and to include the outlawing of atomic weapons in its proposals on disarmament. The United States considered atomic energy a special problem urgently requiring agreement on a system of international control, while the reduction of armaments was a more general problem on which agreement could only come at some later date when much greater confidence existed.

Since the thesis that an atmosphere of greater security must precede any serious consideration of disarmament was firmly held by the western powers, there was no likelihood that the Commission for Conventional Armaments would make any early concrete recommendations for the reduction of armaments. A resolution adopted on August 12, 1948, over the opposition of the U.S.S.R., mentioned certain conditions essential to confidence and security, which in turn were essential before nations could be asked to disarm. These included (1) conclusion of agreements under which the great powers would make armed forces available to the Security Council in accordance with Article 43 of the Charter, a subject which the U.N. Military Staff Committee had been discussing for over two years without result; (2) the international control of atomic energy; and (3) the conclusion of peace settlements with Germany and Japan. The mere listing of these conditions, major outstanding issues between east and west on which there was no prospect whatever of early agreement, indicated without need of further illustration the western powers' views on the possibilities for disarmament. The remaining provisions of the resolution of August 12 merely emphasized the divergence of views on the nature of a hypothetical international system for the regulation of armaments. Following the western powers' approach to atomic energy control, they stated that the system should include adequate safeguards to detect violations and ensure observance of the agreed restrictions, and should provide for effective enforcement action in the event of violation.

The Soviet Union and the Ukraine were the only members of the commission which voted against this resolution. As in the Atomic Energy Commission, the U.S.S.R. stood alone in opposition to the proposals of the majority. It could not prevent the majority from adopting resolutions. It could, however, block all progress toward an effective treaty either on atomic energy control or on the general regulation of armaments. Meanwhile, the Soviet Government extracted full propaganda advantage from its sponsorship of general proposals, which it knew had no chance of acceptance, for the prohibition of atomic weapons and for the reduction of armaments and armed forces.

Among the peoples of the world there was, undoubtedly, a feeling of anxiety and apprehension over the failure of the United Nations to achieve progress in this field. That feeling was present among the delegations of the 58 countries gathered in Paris in September 1948 for the third regular session of the General Assembly. The Soviet leaders apparently believed the situation ripe for a spectacular stroke. In his opening speech to the Assembly, Vyshinsky proposed that the five permanent members of the Security Council (U.S.A., U.K., U.S.S.R., France and China), as a first step toward disarmament, reduce their land, sea and air forces by one-third. His draft resolution also contained the familiar proposal for the prohibition of atomic weapons. Vyshinsky supported his proposal with a ringing denunciation of the United States for provoking a new armaments race and of the imperialists and reactionaries who were fomenting a new world war.[5]

Foreign Secretary Bevin voiced the suspicion with which most of the delegations at Paris viewed the Soviet initiative when he called it a scheme "to induce the rest of us to disarm while the Union of Soviet Socialist Republics maintains absolute secrecy about their own military strength and activities." [6] General Marshall, in his principal speech, reiterated the American view that the most urgent and necessary step was the early adoption of an international system for the control of atomic energy, which could then be followed by "a progressive reduction in armaments as rapid as the restoration of political confidence permits." Having reached an impasse in the Atomic Energy Commission, the United States wished to obtain the

[5] U.N. Doc. A/PV.143, September 25, 1948, 36-47.
[6] U.N. Doc. A/PV.144, September 27, 1948, 37.

approval of the Assembly for the majority plan of control. Although such approval might be helpful in marshaling world opinion, there was no illusion that it would bring agreement with the Russians any closer. Vyshinsky maintained that only those "cherishing plans for attacks on other countries" favored the American plan for atomic energy control. The majority proposal that the international authority should itself own atomic energy raw materials, in order to ensure their use for peaceful purposes, he regarded as an American plot to seize the sources of raw materials in other countries "with the aid of the so-called international control body where the United States expects to be backed by its own majority."

Atomic energy control was the first item on the agenda of the Assembly's Political and Security Committee. There the Soviet delegation submitted a new proposal recommending that the Atomic Energy Commission prepare two conventions, one on the prohibition of atomic weapons and another on the establishment of international control over atomic energy, which would be signed and brought into operation simultaneously. This proposal received a good deal of publicity as a major Soviet retreat from the position that atomic weapons should be outlawed before the convention on control was negotiated, but other delegations were not impressed. Frederick H. Osborn of the United States explained that the Soviet proposal did not meet the fundamental point that control should be introduced, and weapons given up, by stages. Whether two treaties were concluded at the same time, General McNaughton of Canada pointed out, was not particularly important. The question at issue was whether the two conventions proposed by the U.S.S.R. would be based on the three reports of the Atomic Energy Commission and on the majority views on control embodied in them.

Canada introduced a resolution, which had the support of the United States, similar to the one which the Soviet Union had vetoed in the Security Council the previous June. It called for endorsement of the three reports of the Atomic Energy Commission, and thus of the majority plan, and asked the five permanent members of the Security Council and Canada, as sponsors of the original Assembly resolution of 1946, to consult together to determine whether a basis for international control existed. A number of smaller nations took exception to the paragraph of the Canadian resolution calling for suspension of work in the Atomic Energy Commission, feeling that it must be kept going despite the hopeless outlook. When the United States gave in to this view against its own better judgment, the way was cleared for the overwhelming endorsement of the majority plan.

On November 4 the Assembly rejected the Soviet resolution, 40 to 6, and adopted the amended Canadian resolution by the same vote.[7] The Assembly approved the majority plan "as constituting the necessary basis for establishing an effective system of international control of atomic energy." It expressed concern over the impasse in the Atomic Energy Commission, requested the six original sponsoring powers to consult together, and called on the Atomic Energy Commission to resume its sessions. By this vote, as President Truman's annual report on U.N. activities points out, the plan of the majority in the commission became the United Nations plan.[8] But it still could not be put into effect without Soviet cooperation, which was not forthcoming. Vyshinsky, in opposing the Canadian resolution, sharply rejected the proposed consultations as "unnecessary." The Soviet Government, however, wished to carry on in the Atomic Energy Commission, even though it was almost certain to remain in the minority there, supported only by its own Ukrainian S.S.R. In any case, so long as the major powers continued formal discussions on control, they did not openly concede the hopelessness of trying to reach some agreement before an atomic armaments race threw the world once more into war.

When the Political and Security Committee turned next to the question of disarmament, the Soviet proposal for a general one-third reduction was subjected to a broadside of objections

---

[7] There were five abstentions on the first resolution, and four on the second.
[8] *United States Participation in the United Nations, Report by the President . . . for the Year 1948 . . .* (Washington, 1949), 33.

on the part of the western powers. Since the Soviet ground forces were at the time far superior in numerical strength to theirs, a one-third cut across the board would leave them at an even greater disadvantage, while such a reduction in naval and air armaments would destroy the balance, and thus the effectiveness, of their forces. The British delegate called the Soviet plan a "rough and unjust system of quantitative disarmament" which took no account of the postwar reductions made by Britain and the United States or of the lack of security afforded France by its existing level of armaments. Osborn of the United States said that the Soviet proposal "would perpetuate the present Soviet superiority in aggressive forces," apparently on the theory that Soviet ground troops were "aggressive forces" while American bomber fleets and atomic bombs were not. The most substantial objection to the Soviet scheme was its complete lack of provision for inspection and verification. Soviet insistence on "sovereignty" would make it impossible for an international body to check on Soviet compliance. The western powers were convinced that the Soviet leaders were aware of these factors, and that, like the prewar proposals for complete disarmament made by Litvinov at Geneva, their new scheme was put forward not with any serious hope of acceptance but primarily for propaganda purposes.

The western counter-resolution, an amended French proposal to which the United States gave its support, recognized that a reduction of armaments could only be brought about "in an atmosphere of real and lasting improvement in international relations." It then recommended that the Security Council, through the Commission for Conventional Armaments, pursue its study of the regulation and reduction of armaments and armed forces, and suggested that it devote first attention to formulating proposals for receiving and checking relevant information to be supplied by member states. This resolution the Assembly passed by a vote of 43 to 6 with one abstention, only the Soviet bloc voting against it. And only the Soviet bloc voted for the proposal for a general one-third reduction, which was rejected by 39 to 6, with 6 abstentions. This final outcome of the Assembly's deliberations was hardly a bold step toward the goal of disarmament. In the existing state of their relations with the U.S.S.R., however, it was the most that the western powers felt they could do.

Later discussion of atomic energy and disarmament problems in the Security Council, Atomic Energy Commission, and Commission for Conventional Armaments added nothing to what had been said before. The Security Council, after rejecting various resurrected Soviet proposals on atomic weapons and the reduction of armaments, transmitted the Assembly's disarmament resolution to the Commission for Conventional Armaments "for action according to its terms." On February 15, 1949, the commission met for the first time since the previous August. Three days later the Atomic Energy Commission resumed its sessions. In neither body was there any sign of a change in the fixed positions of east and west, or any reason to expect progress in the near future. The fact that they continued to meet, however, showed that the United Nations, officially at least, had not yet given up hope.

2. The Balkans Again

The troubles between Greece and its three northern neighbors had been a hardy perennial of United Nations deliberations ever since the world organization began to function. First came the many discussions in the Security Council in 1946 and 1947. They reached a dead end when the Soviet Union by a series of vetoes prevented the taking of any steps to condemn or curb the governments of Yugoslavia, Bulgaria and Albania, which a commission of investigation (with Russia and Poland dissenting) had found guilty of giving aid to the Communist-led guerrillas in their rebellion against the authority of the Greek Government. Then it was the turn of the General Assembly, which on October 21, 1947, voted to establish a special committee to observe the frontiers and help the four Balkan governments to reestablish normal relations.[9]

[9] See *The United States in World Affairs, 1945–1947*, 91-93, 146-149, 474-475; *The United States in World Affairs, 1947–1948*, 386-394, 398-400.

Greece being one of the most touchy and explosive issues between east and west, the failure to reach a solution through U.N. agencies was scarcely surprising. As the Soviet Union and its allies, from mid-1947, refused to cooperate in the attempts at investigation and conciliation made by such agencies, the latter's activities were necessarily restricted and one-sided. They became, for all practical purposes, a means of exposing and condemning Communist penetration into Greece from across the northern borders. In a sense they supplemented the "Truman doctrine" and the program of American aid to Greece. While Greek resistance to communism and Soviet pressure were stiffened by direct American material aid and advice, the United States also took the initiative, in the United Nations, in support of efforts to deal with certain aspects of the problem internationally instead of unilaterally. In finding and publicizing the facts on the violation of Greece's frontiers, the United Nations performed a notable service to American and British policy in the Balkans.

If one looked at the Greek civil war simply as an aspect of the east-west conflict, it was plain that American "intervention" was far greater than that of the Soviet Union and its satellites. Since the Soviet leaders chose to consider the Greek Government as an unrepresentative "monarcho-fascist clique," it was natural that they should regard American support of that government as unwarranted intervention against the rights and interests of the Greek people. It so happened, however, that the Greek monarchy had been confirmed by a plebiscite in 1946, and that the Greek Government was based on an election which a British-French-American mission of observers declared to be free and fair. Accordingly, American aid to the legitimate and recognized Government of Greece, with its consent, and Albanian or Yugoslav aid to the guerrillas attempting to overthrow that government were in quite different legal categories. The latter was a violation of international law and of the U.N. Charter. The Greek Government's strong legal position, plus the general sympathy with Greece's attempt to maintain itself as an outpost of the western world, had the effect of leaving the Soviet bloc in an isolated minority when "threats to the political independence and territorial integrity of Greece" were discussed and voted upon by the United Nations.

By its resolution of October 21, 1947 the General Assembly called upon Albania, Bulgaria and Yugoslavia "to do nothing which could furnish aid and assistance to the [Greek] guerrillas." At the same time it urged those three nations and Greece to cooperate in the settlement of their disputes by peaceful means, recommending that they establish normal and good neighborly relations, conclude frontier conventions to control the frontiers and settle incidents, solve refugee problems, and study the practicability of the voluntary transfer of minorities. To observe compliance and assist the four governments in implementing these recommendations, the Assembly established the United Nations Special Committee on the Balkans (UNSCOB) with its principal headquarters at Salonika. Two of the eleven designated members, the U.S.S.R. and Poland, ignored the committee completely and never took their seats.[10]

The committee could not expect to accomplish much in the way of promoting cooperation and peaceful settlements between the right-wing government in Athens and the Communist governments in Belgrade, Sofia and Tirana. The attitude of the latter, ever since the Security Council's Balkan Investigating Commission in the spring of 1947 had found them guilty of supporting the Greek rebels, was one of noncooperation with all attempts at investigation and conciliation under U.N. auspices. Following the cue of the Soviet Union, they denounced UNSCOB as an illegal body which the Assembly had no right to establish. Although they made many charges of frontier violation by the Greeks, they would not permit the committee to do any observing on their territory and even refused to answer its communications.[11] The Government of Greece, on the other hand, was only too willing to cooperate, since any

---

[10] The others were the United States, United Kingdom, France, China, Australia, Brazil, Mexico, the Netherlands, and Pakistan.

[11] The only exception was on one occasion when Bulgaria allowed some members of the committee to visit an island (claimed by Greece) in the Maritza River where a frontier incident had taken place.

evidence which the committee might turn up in the frontier districts was likely to help the Greek case.

The U.N. Special Committee, after holding over 90 meetings in Paris, Athens, Salonika and Geneva, signed its principal report to the General Assembly on June 30, 1948. Returning to Greece in the summer, it drew up a supplementary report covering events up to September 10, a few days before the Assembly opened its session in Paris. Since the Soviet bloc representatives who had done much to render difficult the work of the Security Council's Balkan Commission in 1947 took no part in the work of the Special Committee, the latter was able to do its assigned job, so far as circumstances would permit, and to reach some unanimous conclusions. Yet its proceedings were by no means a staged affair under American direction as the Soviet Union and its satellites alleged. There were some real differences in viewpoint, especially between the Australian and American delegations, which made drafting the reports no easy task. In general, the Australians tended to stress the conciliatory over the investigative functions of UNSCOB. They felt that there could not be any real pacification in Greece or lessening of the international tension over the Greek situation until the Balkan nations themselves could be brought together and encouraged to work out a settlement. They did not want the committee to become merely a body engaged in collecting incriminating evidence against Greece's northern neighbors. The U.S. delegation, while agreeing that every reasonable step should be taken to normalize relations among the Balkan states, saw little possibility of accomplishing anything on that line unless the Soviet Union and its satellites should decide to call off their intervention in Greece. Since they showed by their attitude toward UNSCOB that they had no intention of doing so, the United States wanted the committee to do what it could to investigate and publicize the extent of that intervention.

The Special Committee was in fact unable to do anything about improving relations between Greece and its neighbors or promoting agreements on frontier control, repatriation of refugees, and transfer of minorities. In carrying out the other part of its mandate, observing compliance with the General Assembly's resolution, it established a number of observation groups which visited various parts of the frontier area. The evidence collected by these groups convinced the committee that the Greek guerrillas had received and were still receiving considerable support from outside Greece. Government-sponsored committees for aid to "democratic Greece," set up in most of the states of the Soviet bloc, had given moral and financial support to them. War material was supplied to them from Albania, Yugoslavia and Bulgaria. The guerrillas had used the territory of those nations in their operations, crossing and recrossing the frontiers in accordance with the needs of the military situation. UNSCOB observers saw groups of fighting men entering Greece from all three countries. They saw artillery and machine guns firing into Greece from across the border. The assistance was on such a scale, the committee concluded, that it had been given with the knowledge of the three governments.[12]

In its recommendations to the General Assembly the Special Committee recorded its conviction that the functions of exercising vigilance and of attempting to bring about a peaceful settlement should remain entrusted to a United Nations body so long as the present disturbed conditions along the northern borders of Greece continued. The outside support being given to the guerrillas, the report concluded, constituted a threat to the independence of Greece and to international peace and security in the Balkans and was inconsistent with the principles of the U.N. Charter.[13] The attitude which the United States would adopt when the subject came up for debate in the Assembly was apparent when the State Department, on the eve of the meeting, released a statement calling attention to the

[12] While accepting this conclusion and the facts on which it was based, the Australian delegation made a general reservation, contending that UNSCOB was not empowered to investigate aid to the Greek guerrillas. See U.N. General Assembly, *Official Records: Third Session*, Supplement No. 8 (A/574), 35-36.
[13] The Australian delegation abstained from voting on the conclusions and recommendations of the report on the ground that it was up to the Assembly, not the committee, to pass judgments and make decisions.

supplementary UNSCOB report and to its conclusions which flatly contradicted the protestations of innocence of Albania, Bulgaria and Yugoslavia.

The discussion in the Assembly added little, except some colorful epithets, to what had already been said. Vyshinsky, taking the lead for the Soviet bloc, dismissed the UNSCOB report as "a pile of garbage." According to him, the blame for the Balkan crisis fell on the Greek Government, with its senseless expansionist ambitions, and on the United States, which, in following a plan for world domination in league with reactionary forces in many countries, was using Greece as a military base for its own strategic purposes. John Foster Dulles, for the United States, used the Balkan question as a jumping-off place for an attack on Moscow's efforts to extend the power of Soviet communism throughout the world. He was especially vehement in his denunciation of Communist methods: coercion, fear, violence, terrorism, revolution. The pattern was the same, he said, in Berlin, Korea, wherever one looked, whether in Europe, Africa, Asia or the Americas. Such strong words as these on both sides had the effect of showing all other nations how hopelessly wide the gulf between the two strongest powers had become and how unlikely was any settlement in Greece at this stage.

There had been some curiosity over what position Yugoslavia would take in view of the widening breach between Belgrade and Moscow. The final UNSCOB report had noted that "in recent months there has been less evidence of receipt of supplies from Yugoslavia by the guerrillas." [14] Aleš Bebler, in a series of marathon speeches, left no doubt where Yugoslavia stood. He was as abusive as ever in his denunciations of the Greek Government and of what he called American imperialism. He praised the "democratic army" of General Markos and his "Provisional Democratic Government of Free Greece." So far as public pronouncements went, Yugoslavia was still 100 percent with the Soviet bloc, and presumably would continue to

[14] General Assembly, *Official Records: Third Session*, Supplement No. 8A (A/644), 9.

aid General Markos, the guerrilla leader, no matter how serious
the doctrinal quarrel with the Cominform and no matter what
condemnatory resolutions might be passed by the United
Nations.

The United States, Britain, France and China submitted a
draft resolution stating that the continued aid given by Albania,
Bulgaria and Yugoslavia to the Greek guerrillas endangered
peace in the Balkans and was inconsistent with the principles
of the Charter. It called on them to cease such aid forthwith
and to cooperate with Greece in settling their disputes by peaceful means. The resolution also proposed extending the life of
the Special Committee. The Soviet delegation came forward
with its own draft resolution providing for the abolition of
UNSCOB and the withdrawal of all foreign (meaning American and British) forces stationed in Greece. Other points in
the Soviet resolution proposed that the Balkan governments
establish normal relations and take steps to settle refugee problems, and that Greece cease discrimination against minorities.
The result of the voting on major issues presented by these
various resolutions was never in doubt. The four-power resolution, fought every inch of the way by the six states of the Soviet
bloc, was passed on November 27 by a vote of 47 to 6. The
various paragraphs of the Soviet resolution were voted on
separately. Those calling for the termination of UNSCOB and
the withdrawal of foreign troops were decisively rejected. In
contrast, the three paragraphs dealing with normalizing relations between Greece and its three northern neighbors were
passed unanimously.

The President of the Assembly, Herbert Evatt of Australia,
regarded this latter vote as an endorsement of the position the
Australian delegation had taken in the Special Committee and
of the recent efforts which he and Trygve Lie, in pursuance of
an Australian resolution passed by the Political Committee,
had been making to bring Greece and the other Balkan states
together. These talks were continued. Evatt apparently believed
that informal negotiations between the small nations directly
concerned, with the big powers absent, might produce a solu-

tion or at least some improvement in the situation.[15] However, Greece was not likely to agree to compromise its independence, nor were the other states likely to call off their intervention unless told by Moscow to do so. The talks broke down early in December when the Bulgarians issued a blast against the Greek attitude and the Greeks, although in general conciliatory, refused to renounce definitively their claim to Northern Epirus (Southern Albania), technically still before the Council of Foreign Ministers. Evatt planned to continue his mediation when the Assembly met again at Lake Success in April 1949.

The United Nations, as all realized, could not deal decisively with the Balkan question. However, the Special Committee, now given a new lease on life, could keep the world informed on what was taking place on the Greek side of the frontier. Its mere presence there possibly had the effect of holding the intervention from the north at a level below what it might have been if allowed to pass unobserved. But the Greeks and the western powers were not relying on the agencies of the United Nations or the power of world opinion to stop Russia and its allies from taking over Greece. They were relying primarily on America's Greek aid program, which had been a permanent feature of U.S. foreign policy since the passage of the Greek-Turkish aid bill in May 1947.

On the credit side of that program the United States could point to the fact that Greece remained outside the Soviet orbit. On the other side, the civil war continued to sap the strength of the Greek nation despite the efforts of the Greek national army, advised by American officers and supplied with American equipment. The army mounted a series of well-prepared offensives in the summer of 1948 in the Grammos mountains along the Albanian border and the Vitsi area near the junction of the Greek, Yugoslav and Albanian frontiers. But these territories could not be permanently cleared of guerrillas. The

[15] Evatt had long been a proponent of the theory that the middle powers (notably Australia) could play an active part in world affairs by mediation and conciliation. See his speech to the Carnegie Endowment for International Peace, Paris, November 3, 1948 (*International Conciliation*, No. 445, November 1948, 667-680).

official progress report to Congress on the Greek aid program covering the quarterly period to September 30, 1948, conceded that there were still some 22,000 active guerrillas despite reported losses, since the first of the year, of approximately that number. The total guerrilla strength in the field showed no appreciable change from the period before American matériel began to flow into Greece. Terrorizing whole districts with their hit-and-run tactics, they would swoop down on cities and villages, killing some, carrying off others, then retreating to the hills while exacting a heavy toll in casualties among the regular troops. Thousands of Greek children were taken by the guerrillas and sent to camps in Yugoslavia, Bulgaria, Rumania, and Czechoslovakia.[16] So long as the frontiers were not sealed, the Greek army and air force of some 154,000 men found it impossible to defeat the much smaller but elusive "democratic army" of General Markos. The guerrillas, moreover, were active not only in the northern border districts but also in central Greece and the Peloponnesus. The prospect of the indefinite continuation of this warfare was discouraging both to the people of Greece, who had to endure the suffering and privation, and to the people of the United States, who had to pay the money to keep the Greek Government's military effort going.

Politically, Greece remained unstable. Themistocles Sophoulis, the venerable Liberal politician who took over the premiership in September 1947, remained at the helm of a coalition regime through recurrent cabinet crises. The U.S. Department of State and the American Mission [17] on several occasions made known their preference for a broadly representative coalition, and would not have welcomed a return to a purely right-wing regime under the Populist party led by Vice Premier Tsaldaris,

---

[16] The Greek Government maintained that these children were abducted by force; the other Balkan governments held that they were refugees who had fled from Greek terror. The UNSCOB report stated that the majority was forcibly taken. The General Assembly on November 27, 1948, passed a resolution calling for the return to their homes of all children who wished to go back, or whose parents or close relations wanted them back.

[17] After the resignation of Dwight Griswold as chief of the American Mission for Aid to Greece, in September 1948, the office was held by the U.S. Ambassador to Greece, Henry F. Grady.

although it had the largest representation in the parliament. Greece, being dependent on ERP funds to sustain its recovery as well as U.S. military support to combat the guerrillas, naturally paid some heed to American preferences, although the decisions were made by the Greeks themselves. The big difficulty was how to get a government with sufficient authority, efficiency and popular support to conduct the necessary military campaigns and make effective use of American economic aid. Whether the Sophoulis government, under public attack from several directions, reflected the popular will may have been open to question, but it was hardly possible to hold a national election under existing conditions, and there was no alternative government which could command the support of party leaders and public.

While the Greek question was under debate at the U.N. General Assembly in Paris in November 1948, a new crisis caused Sophoulis to submit his resignation. He himself admitted that his government had not been able to prosecute the war successfully nor to take necessary measures against the "economic and political oligarchy." Subsequent wrangling among the politicians and delay in the forming of a new government led King Paul at one point to consider naming a nonpartisan government of strong, competent men without reference to party representation in the parliament. Such a regime in Athens might have handled public affairs more honestly and expeditiously, but its mere existence, reminiscent of the prewar dictatorial regime of Metaxas, would give substance to the Communist charge of "monarcho-fascism" and would certainly not help the Greek case, and the case for American aid to Greece, before the bar of world opinion.

Ultimately, the ministerial crisis ended when the leaders of all parties in the parliament agreed to support a new coalition headed by Sophoulis. He resumed office on January 20, 1949, backed by a decisive vote of confidence. At about the same time, General Alexander Papagos, hero of the campaign of 1940–41 against the Italians, was placed in charge of the military operations against the guerrillas. These developments held out the promise of more coherent and effective action on the part of the Greek Government. Reporting to Congress on the operation of the Greek-Turkish aid program in the last quarter of 1948, President Truman conceded that guerrilla strength had increased by 1,000 but professed to see signs that the tide was turning against them "as a result of the training, regrouping, and tenacious holding operations of the Greek armed forces." [18]

The guerrillas, meanwhile, seemed to be having internal troubles of their own. Early in February their radio announced that Markos had been "relieved of his responsibilities." Presumably his removal was considered a necessary preliminary to a shift in the guerrillas' political strategy which appeared directed against Tito's Yugoslavia no less than against the Greek Government. The guerrilla movement had always counted among its supporters a substantial number of Macedonians whose separatist political outlook tended to diverge from that of the Greek Communists. The idea of an autonomous Macedonian state within the framework of a Balkan federation had never been completely submerged and was now permitted to come to the surface again in Communist resolutions calling for Macedonian self-determination and, by implication, the dismemberment of both Greece and Yugoslavia. The personnel of the guerrilla "government" was reshuffled in line with this concept, and as spring advanced, the Cominform war of nerves against Tito was stepped up concurrently with the guerrilla military offensive against the Greek national army.

Although the guerrilla leaders now had less basis than ever for posing as champions of Greek national interests, there was no immediate indication that the Greek people could hope for early surcease from their travail. They were caught in a vicious circle. There could be no political stability when the country was torn by the civil war. Conversely, military force alone did not seem adequate to end the guerrilla menace; a political solution was also necessary. It was obvious, moreover, that neither the internal conflicts of Greece nor the disputes with other

[18] *Sixth Report to Congress on Assistance to Greece and Turkey, for the Period ended December 31, 1948* (Washington, 1949), i, 8.

Balkan nations would find any solution, military or political, until the great powers whose policies clashed in Greece could themselves establish the basis for a settlement or *modus vivendi* in that region.

3. Accomplishments of the General Assembly

The General Assembly met in its third regular session at the Palais de Chaillot, in Paris, on September 21, 1948, in an atmosphere of uncertainty, concern and fear for the peace of the world. This was nothing new. The Assembly had met in 1946 and again in 1947 in just that atmosphere. But this time the tension was greater and the danger of war more real because of the crisis over Berlin. In the opening round of speeches General Marshall recalled his statement of a year before that "a supreme effort is required from all of us if we are to succeed in breaking through the vicious circles of deepening political and economic crises." Despite the efforts of most nations to rebuild peace, he continued, tension had increased and "the leaders of the other nations are creating a deep rift between their countries and the rest of the world community." [19]

The "other nations," of course, were the Soviet Union and its satellites. There was some fear, especially among the smaller nations, that the Soviet Union might decide that it was no longer worth while to stay in the United Nations, and that a Soviet withdrawal would be a prelude to war. Such fears proved unfounded. Although it might be regularly outvoted and subjected to considerable abuse at U.N. meetings, the Soviet Union still found it more useful than not to continue its participation. The meetings of the General Assembly afforded the Soviets their best opportunity to place their views before the world. They sent to Paris their most colorful and effective spokesman, Andrei Vyshinsky, to take advantage of that opportunity.

The theme of Vyshinsky's speeches was that the western nations, led by the United States, were following a war policy

[19] U.N. Doc. A/PV 139, September 23, 1948, 23-25.

directed at the Soviet Union. The United States, he maintained, was aiming at world domination in open alliance with reactionary and fascist groups all over the world. It was suppressing democratic forces, organizing military blocs, building air and naval bases, indulging in a wild armaments race, and conducting a "cold war" against the U.S.S.R. and the "people's democracies." Having heard a similar set of speeches by Vyshinsky the year before, the Assembly was not overly impressed. Bevin voiced the thoughts of many when he pointed out that "there has been a war of nerves, but it has not been instituted by us." Spaak made the most effective reply for the west. With devastating directness he reminded the Assembly that Vyshinsky's accusations, if sincere, revealed "such a lack of comprehension of our spirit . . . such an ignorance of our wishes, of our thoughts . . . that it is imperative to redress these mistakes and to allow the Union of Soviet Socialist Republics to base its policies on an accurate understanding of what is happening, and of what is being thought." Not the so-called warmongering of the United States and Britain, he said, but the audacious and ambitious foreign policy of the U.S.S.R. itself had driven the smaller nations of western Europe to organize themselves for their collective self-defense. The basis of their policy was fear— "the fear of you, the fear of your Government, the fear of your policy." [20]

The general concern over the Berlin dispute and the danger of war found expression in a resolution, based on a Mexican proposal, appealing to the great powers to compose their differences and establish a durable peace. Recalling the declarations of cooperation made at Yalta in February 1945 and the Moscow agreements in December of that year, the resolution recommended that the great powers "redouble their efforts, in a spirit of solidarity and mutual understanding, to secure in the briefest possible time the final settlement of the war and the conclusion of all the peace settlements." This resolution, passed unanimously on November 3, had no noticeable effect on the great-power deadlock over the peace settlements with Germany,

[20] U.N. Doc. A/PV 147, September 28, 1948, 51-80.

Austria and Japan, or on the later work of the Assembly itself
—which was, in the words of President Truman's report on
the year's activities, "conditioned largely by the continuing
differences between the Soviet Union and the other Members." [21]

Interest in the Paris session of the Assembly, when it was not
diverted to the Berlin question then under discussion in the
Security Council, centered in the major political issues on which
the United States was attempting to obtain resolutions record-
ing the Assembly's approval of the American position or something very close to it. In general, the U.S. delegation was successful in getting what it wanted on Greece, Korea, atomic
energy, disarmament, and the Little Assembly.[22] In each case
the resolution which had American support had close to the
maximum number of votes that could be expected; except for
the six negative votes of the Soviet bloc and a few abstentions,
all the votes cast were affirmative.

This is not to say that support of the U.S. position on the
part of the middle and smaller powers was automatic. On the
contrary, these nations voted according to their independent
judgment. The United States won their support partly by modifying its own position to meet their points of view. On the
atomic energy question, for example, the United States gave
in to the widely held desire that the Assembly should urge the
Atomic Energy Commission to continue its sessions. Perhaps
an even more decisive factor was the conduct of the Soviet and
other eastern European delegates, whose offensive talk and
failure to show any spirit of compromise alienated the other
nations and contributed to the establishment of a solid bloc
against them when it came to voting. All the members of the
Assembly had had an additional year of experience with Soviet
tactics. Many of them, for that reason, showed a greater appreciation of the position of the United States and of Great Britain
than at former sessions. This evidence of solidarity tended to
substantiate the argument that on these major issues the lineup

[21] *United States Participation in the United Nations . . . 1948*, 5.
[22] The General Assembly's debates and resolutions on Greece, Korea, Palestine,
atomic energy and disarmament are discussed elsewhere in the present volume.

was not the U.S.S.R. against the United States but the U.S.S.R. against the rest of the world.

This opposition came out clearly in the discussions on the Interim Committee, or Little Assembly. This body, composed of all members of the United Nations, had been established for one year at the 1947 session with the purpose of facilitating the work of the Assembly itself and providing a convenient means of taking up matters arising between the regular annual Assembly sessions. Its establishment also reflected the disillusionment of the United States and other nations over the failure of the Security Council to live up to their expectations and the consequent tendency to place more emphasis on the General Assembly in the field of pacific settlement of disputes and maintenance of international security. The Soviet bloc had opposed the creation of the Interim Committee, had boycotted its sessions, and now fought against its renewal. According to Soviet spokesmen it was an illegal body, not authorized under the Charter, attempting to exercise functions rightly belonging to the Security Council.

Other nations, including the United States, were not altogether satisfied with what the Interim Committee had done but felt that the experiment should be continued. It had considered the general problem of the promotion of international cooperation in the political field and that of the peaceful adjustment of disputes. It had made an extensive study and report on voting in the Security Council.[23] It had taken an important decision on Korea, instructing the Assembly's Temporary Commission on Korea to observe elections in that part of the country which was accessible to it even though its original mandate covered all Korea. The member states had failed to use the committee for what was meant to be one of its most important functions, the preliminary consideration of situations and disputes prior to their coming before the Assembly itself. It had acquired only limited experience, and the search for the most effective methods of organizing the work of the General Assembly was still going on.

[23] See below, p. 447.

For these reasons it was the general feeling that the committee should be continued at least for another year. The proposed resolution gave it approximately the same functions that it had had before. It was again empowered to advise the Secretary-General when any matter before it seemed to require a special session of the General Assembly. It was authorized to conduct investigations and appoint commissions of inquiry (by a two-thirds vote), and to request advisory opinions of the International Court of Justice; moreover, the Assembly's resolutions on Korea and on Greece authorized the Commission on Korea and the Special Committee on the Balkans to consult with the Interim Committee in regard to the performance of their functions. All this was anathema to the Soviet Union, which regarded as undesirable and illegal not only the Interim Committee but also the Assembly's committees on Korea and the Balkans. When the resolution came to a vote, however, only the six votes of the Soviet bloc were cast against it, while 40 were cast in its favor. The Little Assembly was thus given another year's lease on life, with the assurance that the boycott of the U.S.S.R. and the other Slav states would continue.

The Assembly passed a number of resolutions concerned with dependent territories and the trusteeship system, two matters that usually found the Soviet bloc and the Middle Eastern and Asian states lined up against the European colonial powers while the United States endeavored to play a moderating role. A committee set up in 1947 with power to receive voluntary reports from administering governments and make general recommendations on economic, social and educational problems in dependent territories was continued for another year. The Assembly expressed regret that the Union of South Africa had not brought its former mandated territory of South West Africa under the trusteeship system, and asked the Union Government to continue submitting reports on the area pending an agreement on its future. Four resolutions dealing with the work of the Trusteeship Council were passed in a form unlikely to cause serious embarrassment to the government responsible for administering trust territories.

One of the most publicized, and possibly the most portentous, accomplishments of the General Assembly lay outside the field of immediate political controversy. This was its adoption of a Universal Declaration of Human Rights. "Historians will, I think, refer to this session as the Human Rights Assembly," declared John Foster Dulles, Acting Chairman of the U.S. delegation, at the final meeting. "We have met in a country where the Declaration of the Rights of Man was inspired. We have met on a continent which has seen mankind's greatest struggle against tyranny. And we have met at a time when the paramount issue is the preservation of human freedom." [24]

The declaration was a product of some two and one-half years of work in the Economic and Social Council and its Commission on Human Rights, presided over by Mrs. Franklin D. Roosevelt. Described in its preamble as "a common standard of achievement for all peoples and all nations," it included such traditional Anglo-Saxon civil rights as freedom of speech, religion, and assembly, and in addition a number of others such as the right to work, the right to an adequate standard of living, and the right to participate freely in the cultural life of the community. This was, of course, a declaration, not a treaty binding its signatories to secure such rights to their citizens. Yet it had considerable significance as showing what world opinion, speaking through the General Assembly, regarded as the fundamental rights of human beings. Forty-eight nations voted for the declaration. None voted against it. The six states of the Soviet bloc, Saudi Arabia, and the Union of South Africa abstained.

If the paramount issue of our time, as Mr. Dulles said, is the preservation of human freedom, then the difference between the Soviet and western conceptions on the subject of human rights and the relation of the individual to the state was a fundamental one, more difficult to bridge than disputes over the balance of power in the Balkans or the unity of Germany. Vyshinsky's speeches in the final debate on the declaration were illuminating in this regard. The Soviet delegation, he

[24] *United States Participation in the United Nations . . . 1948*, 3.

emphasized, did not object to the aims of the declaration, but only to its omissions and to the abstract and theoretical formulation of rights which it had vainly sought to endow with a specific ideological content. Answering western critics who maintained that the Soviet concept of human rights subordinated the individual personality to the state, he denied that any antagonism between state and individual could exist in a society like that of the Soviet Union, where class conflict had been eliminated and the interests of the individual and the government were "fully harmonized." Passing over the actual denials of widely recognized human rights in the U.S.S.R. and its satellites, he denounced the framers of the declaration for their timid avoidance of any principle whose acceptance could threaten the existing order.[25]

Among the Assembly's other accomplishments was a resolution on genocide, passed unanimously. On December 9 it approved a convention which declared the destruction, in whole or part, of a national, ethnical, racial or religious group to be a crime under international law. The convention was signed two days later by the representatives of 20 nations including the United States. It would come into force 90 days after ratification by 20 signatory states.

The Assembly, at its Paris session, also carried out its routine procedural and housekeeping tasks. It elected Cuba, Norway and Egypt to succeed Colombia, Belgium and Syria on the Security Council, thus preserving the geographic distribution of seats. Belgium, Chile, China, France, India and Peru were elected to the Economic and Social Council. With the concurrence of the Security Council, the five retiring judges of the International Court of Justice were reelected for full nine-year terms. The Assembly voted the adoption of Spanish as a third working language (in addition to English and French), despite the adverse recommendation of the Fifth Committee, which was worried about the expense; the solid bloc of Latin American votes assured passage of the measure.

[25] U.N. Docs. A/PV 180, December 9, 1948, 16-40; A/PV 183, December 10, 1948, 71-101.

Finally, the Assembly adjourned on December 12, 1948, after being in session for nearly three months without completing its agenda. To the "second part" of the session, to be held in New York in April, it left the disposition of the former Italian colonies, an issue inherited from the Big Four Council of Foreign Ministers as a result of the latter's failure to agree on any plan for the disposal of Libya, Eritrea and Italian Somaliland within a year after the Italian peace treaty went into effect on September 15, 1947. Although the Foreign Ministers' deputies had worked on the problem from February to August 1948 and a commission of inquiry had been sent to ascertain the views of the local populations, the council was unable to reach agreement at a hastily convoked session on the eve of the Assembly's Paris meeting. Also left for consideration in April were three draft conventions worked out at a conference on freedom of information held at Geneva in the spring of 1948, and a number of perennial standbys such as the Franco regime in Spain, the treatment of Indians in South Africa, and the veto.

At the close of the Paris session the international atmosphere was less ominous and less tense than when it opened in September. A similar easing of tension had taken place during the autumn sessions of 1946 and 1947. In each case, the mutual recrimination, the bitter debate, and the decisive defeats suffered by the U.S.S.R. in the voting did not noticeably worsen relations between the powers or increase the prospects for war. The Soviet delegation stayed in the Assembly and fought its battles with sharp words and long speeches. The Assembly was, of course, a talking and not an acting body. Possibly its greatest service was that it allowed the Russians and their allies to talk as much as they liked, and at the same time allowed the force of world opinion, in the form of the speeches and votes of other nations, to make itself felt.

4. The Record of the Security Council

In the public mind the success or failure of the United Nations was measured by its ability to keep the peace, and that was the task for which primary responsibility, under the Charter, rested with the Security Council. In attempting to fulfill this task, the Council had severe handicaps. It had no armed forces at its disposal, and it was continuously hamstrung by the veto power so freely used by the Soviet representative. In its first years the Security Council had had some successes, notably its part in influencing the U.S.S.R. to withdraw its troops from Iran in 1946. The total record, however, counted more frustration and failure than success. These failures were cumulative, since the inevitable loss of prestige in each case encouraged disrespect for the Security Council's authority in the future.

It was taken for granted by those who framed the Charter that the Security Council would not be able to coerce one of the great powers. To bring great-power conflicts before the Council, therefore, was to do it a disservice. Yet such considerations did not prevent member states from submitting such cases to the Council, often for purposes of propaganda rather than with any genuine expectation of corrective action. Thus there was never any real possibility that the Council would take positive action on such matters as Greece, Berlin, and Czechoslovakia. The resolutions put up by the U.S.S.R. uniformly met defeat at the hands of the majority, while the resolutions supported by the western powers were blocked by the exercise of the veto. The Balkan case, which came before the Council in 1947, provided a good example of the Council's limitations. Clearly the acts of Albania, Yugoslavia and Bulgaria against Greece constituted a threat to the peace and a breach of the peace, as the Council's investigating commission reported. But the U.S.S.R. proceeded to veto all resolutions which condemned its satellites or proposed action distasteful to them.

The two issues which took up most of the Security Council's time and attention in 1948 and 1949 were Palestine and Indonesia. In one form or another they were continuously on the Council's agenda. The prestige of the United Nations was committed in each case to preventing the use of force and violence and to promoting a negotiated settlement. Lying outside the danger zone of direct east-west conflict, these two controversies gave the great powers the opportunity to act together in search of solutions which could be pressed on the disputant parties with all the weight of the world organization behind them. However, national strategies and propaganda were stronger factors than consideration for the prestige and effectiveness of the United Nations. Even the small powers found that by bold action they could ignore the United Nations and get away it. That, essentially, was what happened in Palestine and Indonesia.

In both cases the Soviets were not so directly involved that they found it necessary to use the veto power. They followed a definite line, supporting the Jewish position in Palestine and the cause of the Indonesian Republic, but did not block resolutions which fell short of their demands. The Council was able to pass cease-fire resolutions and to recommend methods of settlement. Unfortunately, neither the Arabs nor the Jews in Palestine, when they thought that they had a military advantage, were prepared to deny themselves the fruits of that advantage in order to comply with such resolutions. The Dutch found it possible to engage in "limited police actions" in Indonesia, after which the Security Council would help to restore peace and stabilize the situation on terms more advantageous to the Dutch than before. The "police action" of December 1948 actually put an end to the Indonesian Republic as a *de facto* government, beyond the power of the Security Council to restore it.[26]

The dispute between India and Pakistan over Kashmir was another question in which the great powers did not have a vital and direct interest, and another example of how states other than the big powers did not hesitate to put their conception of national interest first and support of the United Nations second. It was, however, not without its encouraging aspects from the point of view of the United Nations. After months of trying to help the two dominions to work out a compromise by direct negotiation, the Security Council had passed a resolution on April 21, 1948, providing for a five-member U.N. Commission for India and Pakistan, which was to aid in the

[26] See above, p. 317.

restoration of order and in the holding of a plebiscite to determine the future status of Kashmir.[27] Both parties objected to this resolution, for different reasons, but the commission decided to go ahead with its task. Arriving on the scene, it found itself confronted with an undeclared war in Kashmir. India had sent in troops in 1947, on the invitation of the ruling Hindu Maharajah of this predominantly Moslem state, in order to help put down a rebellion aided by Moslem tribesmen coming into Kashmir from Pakistan's Northwest Frontier Province. In May 1948, as the Foreign Minister of Pakistan informed the commission to its surprise, Pakistan troops were sent in to help check the Indian army's spring offensive against the forces of the Moslem tribesmen and the "free" government set up in the Moslem-held areas.

After some weeks of unsuccessful effort to arrange for a cease-fire agreement and to find some basis for a settlement, the commission on August 13 put forward a three-point proposal: (1) a cease-fire; (2) a truce agreement providing for the withdrawal from Kashmir of Pakistan troops and of the bulk of the Indian forces there; (3) a reaffirmation by both states of their willingness to have Kashmir's future status be determined in accordance with the will of its people. Both countries accepted, but with interpretations and conditions which nullified the nominal agreement. Unable to find a middle ground between India's insistence on the immediate withdrawal from Kashmir of the Pakistan troops and invading Moslem tribesmen and Pakistan's insistence that the military settlement be subordinated to the acceptance of conditions for a plebiscite, the commission reported to the Security Council in November that it had temporarily exhausted the possibilities of negotiations for restoring order in Kashmir. Nevertheless, at this moment of failure, further negotiations were in progress at Paris between the delegations of India and Pakistan. A new set of arrangements for a plebiscite, including provision for a plebiscite administrator with ample authority, was worked out with

[27] See *The United States in World Affairs, 1947–1948*, 209-214. Argentina, Belgium, Colombia, Czechoslovakia and the United States composed the commission.

the help of the U.N. commission. Together with the commission's August proposals on cease-fire and truce arrangements, the new suggestions were accepted by Nehru for India on December 23 and by Sir Mohammed Zafrullah Khan for Pakistan two days later. Hostilities in Kashmir were ordered stopped by both sides on January 1, 1949.

Receiving the report of this success, members of the Security Council indulged in expressions of satisfaction. The chairman, General McNaughton of Canada, called the settlement "a most important and encouraging event in the history of the United Nations . . . its effects will extend to peoples far beyond those territories [India and Pakistan], who will be inspired by the good example which has been set and encouraged by the fact that this very difficult and grave controversy has yielded to patience and persistent effort by the parties through the medium of an agency created by the United Nations." [28]

The real settlement, however, had still to be worked out in Kashmir itself, under pressures from both sides. The complexities of the problem were overwhelming. Admiral Chester Nimitz, named as Plebiscite Administrator by Secretary-General Lie on March 21, 1949, had no perfunctory job ahead of him. Territorial disputes are notoriously hard to solve by peaceful means when each party considers its national interest involved. Moreover, a plebiscite in such a remote and comparatively primitive region as Kashmir would be something new in plebiscites and a real challenge to those responsible for obtaining a true reflection of the will of the people.

Several other problems of the Indian subcontinent came before the Security Council in 1948 without being dealt with in any decisive fashion. Most of them were matters of direct controversy between India and Pakistan, such as the Pakistan charge of "genocide" against India's treatment of Moslems and the dispute over the state of Junagadh. In a slightly different category was the question of Hyderabad, a large princely state entirely surrounded by Indian territory. The Nizam of

[28] United Nations Security Council, *Official Records: Fourth Year,* No. 3, January 13, 1949, 4.

Hyderabad, Moslem ruler of a preponderantly Hindu population, would not meet the Indian Government's terms on the legal relationship which his state was to have with the Dominion of India. Under a "standstill" agreement concluded on November 29, 1947, India was to conduct Hyderabad's foreign relations for one year, during which the definitive relationship was to be worked out. When there seemed no prospect of working it out by agreement, however, the Indian Government decided to resort to force.

Early in September 1948, Indian troops invaded the princely state from all sides. The Nizam sent an appeal to the Security Council, which took it up on September 16. While the Council discussed whether Hyderabad was a state competent to bring a dispute before the United Nations, Indian forces broke the opposition of the Nizam's troops and occupied his capital. The Indian representative was then able to tell the Council that the Nizam had instructed him to head the Hyderabad delegation and to withdraw the complaint. India considered the case closed. This novel situation left the Security Council in no position to challenge the accomplished facts, unless it could be proved that the Nizam had acted under duress. In the end, the Council merely dropped the subject without any decision. The episode scarcely added luster to the record of the Security Council. It was true that the only logical consequence of Hyderabad's position, after the withdrawal of British power from India, lay in accession to the new dominion. But this further illustration of the effectiveness of using force first and talking afterward did no service to the prestige and authority of the United Nations.

On subjects where there was a direct conflict of interest between eastern and western blocs—such as Czechoslovakia, Trieste and Berlin—the Security Council generally ended by doing nothing, since the Soviet Union could veto any decision it did not like but could not garner sufficient votes to pass the resolutions that it did like. After the *coup* which brought the Communists to power in Czechoslovakia in February 1948, Chile brought a complaint before the Security Council alleging that the Soviet Union, by the threat of force, had violated Czechoslovakia's independence and created a situation dangerous to international peace and security. Citing statements made by Jan Papanek, Czechoslovakia's permanent representative to the United Nations until the *coup,* the Chilean delegate contended that a *prima facie* case against the U.S.S.R. had been made out, justifying further investigation. The American and British statements before the Council dwelt on the general pattern of Communist seizure of power with Soviet support throughout eastern Europe. It was common knowledge that the Communist leaders in those countries were Soviet agents. Evidence of actual Soviet participation in the change of regime in Prague, however, was not easy to find. Chile, supported by the United States and a majority on the Council, put forward the proposal that a subcommittee should be set up to hear witnesses and seek further information. The U.S.S.R., which had already shown on the Greek question that it wanted no U.N. bodies investigating and reviewing what went on in the countries of the Soviet bloc, promptly vetoed a resolution which called the proposal a procedural question, then vetoed the Chilean resolution itself.

In the case of the complaint on Berlin brought before the Security Council by the western powers in September 1948, the U.S.S.R. again exercised the veto to defeat a settlement supported by a majority of members.[29] In the case of Trieste there were no vetoes, for here the complaints were brought by the eastern bloc and were defeated by failure to win enough votes. For more than one year following the signature of the Italian peace treaty, the four big powers had vainly sought agreement on the choice of a governor for the Free Territory of Trieste. In effect, they vetoed each other's choices, although these talks were all informal four-power meetings without voting. No one candidate of the many proposed was acceptable to all four powers. Consequently, though the Free Territory of Trieste came into being, it had no governor. For all practical purposes it remained split by the old Morgan line of 1945.

[29] See below, p. 458.

Anglo-American forces remained in the city itself, while the southern area under Yugoslav occupation was being absorbed into Yugoslavia. Then on March 20, 1948, the three western members proclaimed their willingness to see the Free Territory restored to Italy. Thereafter they saw no point in continuing to discuss choosing a governor. Those provisions of the peace treaty, they held, had proved unworkable. Meanwhile, both parts of the territory remained under military government, while recriminations continued on each side concerning conditions in the other's zone of occupation.

Yugoslavia finally brought the situation before the Security Council at the end of July, 1948, on the ground that the United States and Great Britain had violated the Italian peace treaty. The Yugoslav complaint cited the financial agreements tying the Anglo-American zone of Trieste to Italy as proof that the western powers were seeking to annex the Free Territory to Italy. The United States and Britain replied that these were temporary agreements permitted by the treaty and that the Yugoslavs were in no position to raise the issue, having virtually incorporated their own zone of occupation into Yugoslavia and made the peace treaty provisions unworkable. After two weeks of inconclusive debate the Council engaged in some inconclusive voting. A Yugoslav proposal, sponsored by the Ukraine, to invalidate the Anglo-American economic agreements with Italy on Trieste got two votes (U.S.S.R. and Ukraine) with nine abstentions. A second Ukrainian resolution urging the speedy choice of a governor for the Free Territory received four votes, with six abstentions.[30] Yugoslavia submitted a new complaint in October 1948, protesting the inclusion of Trieste in ERP, but the Council did not take it under consideration. The results could hardly have been different from those of the previous August.

On one further subject, the admission of new members to the United Nations, the Security Council maintained its record of deadlock and inaction. The U.S.S.R. continued to keep out

[30] Great Britain did not participate at all, claiming that the proposal was not properly presented.

Austria, Italy, Eire, Portugal and Transjordan by the simple expedient of the veto or the threat of its use. The western powers continued to oppose Albania, Bulgaria, Hungary, Rumania, and the Mongolian People's Republic, on the ground that they had not shown themselves able and willing to carry out the obligations of the Charter. Finland's application was favorably regarded by both sides, but the U.S.S.R. would not accept Finland unless Bulgaria, Hungary and Rumania were also admitted. Burma was the only candidate which won the Security Council's approval and was duly admitted by the General Assembly on April 19, 1948. Until Israel was admitted on May 11, 1949, no other new members came in.

The General Assembly in its session of 1947 had expressed its concern over this situation, which was freezing the United Nations in its present membership, by recommending that the Security Council reconsider the applications of Austria, Italy, Eire, Portugal, Transjordan and Finland. It had also urged consultations among the five permanent members of the Security Council and asked the International Court to render an advisory opinion on two points: (1) whether a member is entitled to make its consent to the admission of a state dependent on conditions not expressly provided by Article 4 of the Charter (which says that membership is "open to all peace-loving states which accept the obligations contained in the present Charter and, in the judgment of the Organization, are able and willing to carry out these obligations"); and (2) whether a member can make its affirmative vote on the application of one state conditional on the admission of other states.

Neither the Assembly resolution, however, nor the opinion of the Court, which answered both questions in the negative, changed the situation. On April 10, 1948, the U.S.S.R. again vetoed Italy's application, and when it was made clear that no member of the Security Council had changed its position on the others, no further votes were taken. Ceylon's application, submitted in May, was vetoed by the U.S.S.R. in August and again in December. Many member nations, concerned over the deadlock, sought ways of breaking it, either by changing the procedure for admission or by acting on the "principle of universality." At the Paris session of the Assembly in 1948, Argentina proposed that if an applicant received seven votes in the Security Council, whether or not a permanent member cast a negative vote, it should be deemed a recommendation for admission. The United States, in discussing voting procedures in the Security Council, stated the view that the permanent members should voluntarily agree to waive the veto power in passing on membership applications. Sweden took another line, presenting a resolution emphasizing the ultimate goal of universal membership. The Argentine resolution was withdrawn before a vote, but the Swedish resolution was passed in amended form by a vote of 33 to 0, with 10 abstentions. Noting the advisory opinion of the International Court of Justice and "the general sentiment in favor of the universality of the United Nations," the resolution asked the Security Council to reconsider individually the applications of the 12 states whose membership it had thus far failed to approve. A second resolution, introduced by Australia and adopted by a vote of 32 to 10, called on the members of both the Security Council and the Assembly to be guided by the opinion of the Court in voting on the admission of new members.

The Assembly also passed separate resolutions affirming that it considered Italy, Austria, Finland, Eire, Portugal, Transjordan and Ceylon qualified for membership and requesting the Security Council to reconsider their applications. No Assembly resolution, however, was sufficient to enable the applicant states to run the Security Council gauntlet. The western powers, which were charging the Soviet satellites with violation of the peace treaties, were not prepared to support their admission to the United Nations as peace-loving nations able and willing to fulfill the obligations of the Charter. Nor was the Soviet Union prepared to relax its opposition to those states which the Assembly and the rest of the Council supported; it was prepared to keep on casting vetoes to keep them out.

The greatest obstacle to the effective operation of the Security Council remained, as before, the veto. Between the 1947 and 1948 regular sessions of the Assembly the Soviet Union cast vetoes on four important occasions—to block an investigation on Czechoslovakia, to reject the report of the Atomic Energy Commission, and to deny admission to Italy and Ceylon. In October was added a veto of a compromise resolution on the settlement of the Berlin dispute. Whether used or not, the continued threat of the veto affected all the work of the Security Council. As in previous years, many of the smaller nations at Paris in 1948 urged that something be done about it; Argentina came forward with its old proposal for a conference to revise the Charter by eliminating the veto. The United States and the other permanent members of the Council, except the U.S.S.R., favored less drastic remedies, while the U.S.S.R. itself defended the "principle of unanimity" as absolutely essential and fundamental to the existence of the United Nations.

The 1947 Assembly had given the problem to the Interim Committee for study. That body, which the U.S.S.R. and its satellites boycotted as illegal, came up with a series of recommendations based on suggestions put forward by the United States. It proposed one list of 36 questions which could be considered as procedural, and thus not subject to the veto, and another of 21 questions, including the pacific settlement of disputes and the admission of new members, on which the five permanent members might agree among themselves that the veto would not apply. These proposals, brought before the Assembly in the autumn of 1948, were adopted without important change by the Ad Hoc Political Committee. The vote was 33 to 6, with 4 abstentions, the negative votes being those of the Soviet bloc, which bitterly opposed the recommendations as contrary to the Charter.

The Assembly did not have time at its Paris session to vote on this resolution. It finally did so at New York in April 1949, passing it by a vote of 43 to 6, with 2 abstentions. But Soviet spokesmen left no doubt that the resolution would have no practical effect on voting in the Security Council. The veto, in the view of the Soviet Government, was a necessary protection against majority decisions contrary to vital Soviet interests. It was an essential condition of Soviet participation in the United Nations.

The veto was widely denounced in the United States and elsewhere as the great obstacle to an effective United Nations organization. Actually it was a symptom rather than a cause, a reflection of the fact that the organization did not have the means or the authority to coerce the great powers. No matter what the voting procedures in the Security Council might be, a dispute involving the great powers that could not be resolved by agreement would involve the possibility of a major war.

Abolition of the veto was impossible under the Charter without Russia's concurrence. Should it be done without Russia, the effect would be to break up the United Nations as it then existed. None of the great powers wished that to happen. The western powers knew that the existence of the United Nations would not be a bar to Soviet aggression. To guard themselves against that eventuality they turned to military alliances and regional pacts. The U.S.S.R., in its eastern European sphere, was doing virtually the same thing. These pacts paid lip service to the United Nations and were concluded within the framework of the Charter. Article 51, which recognizes the right of collective self-defense, and Articles 52 and 53, sanctioning regional arrangements, were cited in support of this thesis. The Vandenberg Resolution,[31] which laid the groundwork for U.S. participation in a security pact with the nations of western Europe, tied together the two concepts of strengthening the United Nations and protecting the security of particular regions through the conclusion of special regional pacts. Senator Vandenberg himself, a leading figure in the conclusion of the Rio pact of 1947 and of the Atlantic pact, was one of the architects of the Charter and a firm supporter of the United Nations. He believed that effective regional pacts, giving real protection and security to participating states, were a means of giving life to the Charter, of overcoming the obstacle of the veto without attacking it head on and destroying the United Nations in the process. Nevertheless, some concern was voiced outside

31 See above, pp. 11-13.

official circles over the possibility that such pacts, especially the proposed Atlantic pact, would transfer attention away from the United Nations and toward rival blocs, foster a bi-polar division of the world, and thus harm rather than help the successful development of the United Nations.[32]

Both supporters and critics of the conclusion of regional pacts and alliances were in agreement that the United Nations must be maintained and strengthened. Whatever its shortcomings, it did carry the hope that it might be developed into an effective world authority in the future. The State Department supported, as contributions furthering this development, the policy of limited regional arrangements to circumvent the veto and the proposed modifications of the veto power contained in the Assembly resolution. Against the Atlantic pact the Soviet Union could do little except protest. To the proposed modifications of the veto it had an effective reply: it could veto any change. Nevertheless, while there seemed to be no hope that the Assembly's resolution would be put into practice, it did point to means by which, if and when the tension should relax, the Security Council, and the United Nations, might gain effectiveness and authority in the task of preserving peace and security. For this it was important not only that the veto be modified but also that the peoples of the world continue to take the United Nations seriously and lend authority to its decisions by complying with them.

[32] Cf. Grayson Kirk, "The Atlantic Pact and International Security," *International Organization*, III, May 1949, 239-251.

CHAPTER TWELVE

THE WEST AGREES ON GERMANY

THE so-called German problem has been intimately involved
in the origins of nearly every major international conflict since
the year 1864. In the summer of 1948, at a time when the
world was still struggling to overcome the disastrous consequences of Nazi aggression, Germany's ruined capital again
became the point at which the immediate chances of peace or
war would be decided. It was the crisis over Berlin that finally
dispelled any lingering illusions concerning the state of postwar international affairs and forced hundreds of millions
throughout the world to reckon with the possiblity of a third
world war.

Unlike similar crises in the past, that of 1948 was neither of
German making nor one on whose outcome Germans could
exert great influence. Conquered Germany was simply the arena
in which the world-wide political struggle between the Soviet
Union and the western democracies reached a degree of tension beyond which a continuation of peaceful intercourse
seemed impossible. That this ultimate test of strength and will
should occur in Germany was, indeed, no accident. With its
commanding European position, its disciplined population and
its largely unimpaired industrial potential, Germany had been
predestined to become the focal point of the east-west struggle. No accommodation between east and west was possible
while the fate of Germany remained in suspense; and meanwhile the competitive efforts of the two sides to bend German
developments to their advantage had steadily deepened the gulf
between them. The crisis over Berlin was incidental to a larger
competition whose stakes were the shattered but still weighty
fragments of Hitler's Reich.

The Berlin crisis overshadowed but did not suspend other activities in Germany which were of equal importance to the future of the world. In the western zones major emphasis was laid on expeditious construction of the new federal republic decided upon at London and its early integration into the developing community of western Europe, a process that necessarily involved a relaxation of the remaining occupation controls and a mitigation—though not the abandonment—of the punitive and security measures originally envisaged. This reorientation of policy in western Germany was not accomplished without prolonged negotiation among the United States, France and Great Britain, who differed materially in their evaluation of the various perils among which they were endeavoring to pick their way. France in particular, always primarily concerned with security against German aggression, mistrustful of any too-facile German democratic regeneration, and loath to push matters to a crisis with the one strong military power on the European continent, fought a long-continued delaying action against the new trend.

In the final resort, however, the common interest of the western powers in face of Soviet intransigence outweighed their separate preoccupations in regard to the German question as such. In 1948, the reality of the Berlin blockade impelled them to take up a common position in Moscow and in the Security Council. In 1949, the decision of the Soviet Union to lift the blockade and transfer the struggle back to the diplomatic level occurred just as they were successful in sinking their remaining differences. In April they reached definitive accord on such fundamental matters as the final form of the new west German state and the nature of the occupation controls to be retained, and formalized their agreements on reparation, demilitarization and control of the Ruhr.

In the background of these manoeuvres the German people, denied a direct voice in the settlement of their destinies, seemed to be recovering from the prostration of the early postwar years and preparing to play a more decisive role when circumstances should permit. While lending themselves without undue hesitation to the broad objectives of the Allies in the west, and unable to oppose effectively the will of the occupant in the east, they seemed more preoccupied with the fate of Germany as a nation than with what political forms might be immediately acceptable to one or other of the victorious powers.

1. Berlin Before the Security Council

The United States took the lead in bringing the question of Berlin before the United Nations. Great Britain and especially France were less convinced of the desirability of the move, but both agreed to join in presenting the case, thus maintaining the three-power solidarity already established in the Moscow and Berlin negotiations. Obviously the United Nations could not be expected to settle the struggle over Berlin, as long as both sides maintained their respective positions. The Soviet Union could veto any action proposed in the Security Council and refuse to carry out any recommendation made by the General Assembly. The purpose of the western powers was to present their case before world opinion, to rally the smaller nations to their side, to improve their bargaining position and thus to make matters more difficult for the Russians.

The first question to decide was whether to appeal to the Assembly or the Security Council. In the former an impressive majority vote in favor of the western powers might be obtained. At the Assembly session of 1947 the United States had been able to overwhelm the Russians with votes on such major issues as Korea, the Balkans, and the Little Assembly. The Assembly, with its large membership and its rules of voting, which excluded the veto, was the logical place to appeal to world opinion and to seek a demonstration of support. There was a danger, however, on the question of Berlin, that support for the western position might fall short of expectations. The American and British delegations could not be sure that Evatt, the President of the Assembly, or other representatives of the middle and smaller powers might not take the initiative out of their hands.

To take the case to the Security Council involved certain risks. It was not practical to proceed under Chapter VI of the Charter, dealing with pacific settlement; since the parties to a dispute, in this case four of the permanent members, were barred from voting, it would be almost impossible to get any decision at all. To proceed under Chapter VII, dealing with threats to the peace, breaches of the peace and acts of aggression, raised the question of sanctions and possible military action. It would call for skillful and cautious handling to get the maximum propaganda value out of discussions in the Security Council, to obtain a resolution condemning the Soviet Union, and at the same time to avoid setting in motion the machinery for sanctions which might, whether vetoed or not, lead the world into war.

The decision was taken to appeal to the Security Council under Chapter VII. The official notification of the American, British and French governments to the Secretary-General, delivered on September 29, 1948, drew attention to the "serious situation" caused by the Soviet blockade of Berlin, which was described as contrary to the principles of the United Nations (Article 2 of the Charter) and as constituting a threat to international peace and security. "The issue is that the Soviet Government has clearly shown by its actions that it is attempting by illegal and coercive measures, in disregard of its obligations, to secure political objectives to which it is not entitled and which it could not achieve by peaceful means." The conduct of the Soviets, said the note, revealed their purpose to reduce the other occupying powers in Berlin to a position of complete subordination, to obtain absolute authority over the political and economic life of the people of Berlin, and to incorporate the city into the Soviet zone of Germany.

Once this step was taken, all attention at Paris was turned to the Security Council. Tension had been building up over the Berlin situation all through the past summer. Now, for the first time in the brief history of the United Nations, three of the great powers, permanent members of the Security Council, were directly accusing a fourth of threatening international peace and security. There was real fear that this step might lead to the breakup of the United Nations and to war. A proposal for sanctions, or a decision by the Soviet Government to withdraw from the United Nations, whatever its reasons might be, would mean the end of the world organization as conceived and established at San Francisco. As the debate opened, the western powers brushed aside a last-minute Soviet proposal that the Council of Foreign Ministers be convened to take up the entire German question. They insisted on going ahead with the Berlin case before the Security Council. Vyshinsky, maintaining that this action was itself in violation of the Charter and of other agreements, announced that the Soviet Union would not be a party to such violations. Whether this declaration meant that the Soviet delegation would walk out of the Security Council, and perhaps out of the United Nations, remained a subject for speculation on the part of all other delegations.

The western representatives went ahead with their arguments why the Council should consider the Berlin question. To Vyshinsky's contention that it was beyond the competence of the Council, they replied that the blockade was clearly a threat to the peace within the meaning of the Charter and that the Security Council was the only existing machinery for dealing with such threats. To his argument that Article 107 prohibited the Council from taking action in relation to the former enemy states,[1] they answered that this was not a matter of dealing with Germany but a dispute between the Allied powers themselves, one of which was threatening international peace. With his statement that no blockade of Berlin existed, they emphatically recorded their disagreement. To his contention that the four interested powers should settle the dispute among themselves, they replied that the negotiations of the past months had shown that they were unable to settle it.

[1] Article 107 of the Charter reads as follows: "Nothing in the present Charter shall invalidate or preclude action, in relation to any state which during the Second World War has been an enemy of any signatory to the present Charter, taken or authorized as a result of that war by the Governments having responsibility for such action."

On October 5 the Security Council voted, 9 to 2, to put the Berlin question on the agenda. Vyshinsky and Manuilsky, who cast the two negative votes, immediately served notice that the Soviet and Ukrainian delegations "would not participate" in its consideration. It became apparent the next day that the announced boycott applied only to the discussion, not to the meetings of the Council. Vyshinsky, according to one reporter, "sat brooding at the Council table" while the representatives of the western powers presented their case.

Philip C. Jessup, of the United States, carried the main burden of argument for the western powers. In a lengthy speech he reviewed the entire Berlin controversy in order to justify the contention that the Soviet blockade was a threat to the peace. The United States, he said, was not unwilling to negotiate with the Soviet Union on Germany or on any other outstanding problem, but it could not be expected to negotiate under duress. The three western spokesmen described how their governments had used every reasonable means to persuade the Soviet Government to lift the blockade, and had failed. They had therefore appealed to the Security Council. But they did not make any specific proposal for action by the Council. Although the appeal was made under Chapter VII, they avoided talk of sanctions and apparently did not contemplate pushing matters that far. Jessup pointed out that the Council was not precluded from using the provisions for pacific settlement found elsewhere in the Charter. He asked merely that the Council assist in removing the threat to the peace. The moment that the blockade was lifted, he concluded, the United States was ready to have an immediate meeting of the Council of Foreign Ministers to discuss any and all questions relating to Germany.

What the three western powers wanted from the Council was a resolution calling upon the Russians to lift the blockade. Their plan was to have such a resolution presented by one or more of the smaller powers. The latter, however, proved somewhat hesitant. Canada, Belgium and China shared the views of the three western powers but were reluctant to put themselves in the front line. Argentina, Colombia and Syria did not wish to take sides in a dispute which threatened to wreck the United Nations, but desired to find some formula which both east and west could accept without loss of face. Under the leadership of Bramuglia of Argentina, who was serving at this time as president of the Security Council,[2] all six undertook to work together informally with a view to finding a compromise solution.

Despite all the fire and fury of the speeches before the Council, the Russians and the western powers were not so far apart that a compromise seemed impossible. Judging from the earlier negotiations, the Russians would lift the blockade if a settlement of the Berlin currency question could be reached. An agreement in principle, the Moscow directive of August 30,[3] was still on the record. Unless the western powers should insist on having the Security Council vote on a resolution calling for an end to the blockade, which the Soviet Union would certainly veto, the opportunity to work for a solution was there. The delegates of the smaller powers, genuinely frightened at the prospect of a showdown on Germany, resolved to seize it.

Their object was to find a solution acceptable to the west which would avoid a Soviet veto. Bramuglia shuttled back and forth between the Soviet and western delegations in search of a gentleman's agreement under which the German question could be taken up by the Council of Foreign Ministers simultaneously with the raising of the blockade and an agreement on the currency. He had to try to persuade the "nonparticipating" Soviet delegation to countenance the adoption of a resolution by the Security Council, and to persuade the western representatives not to insist on a resolution censuring Soviet conduct in Berlin.

The six smaller powers finally produced a compromise resolution of their own on October 22. It called upon the four parties to the dispute to put into effect the following measures: (1) the immediate lifting of the blockade of Berlin and

[2] He served during October in place of Warren Austin, who did not take his regular turn, the United States being a party to the Berlin dispute.
[3] See above, pp. 143-144.

of the western counter-restrictions on transport and commerce with the Soviet zone; (2) an immediate meeting of the four military governors to arrange for the acceptance of the Soviet mark as the currency for all Berlin in accordance with the terms and conditions laid down in the Moscow directive of August 30, that is, under a system of quadripartite control, this measure to be completed by November 20, 1948; (3) within ten days of that date, or on any other date agreed by the four powers, the Council of Foreign Ministers would meet to negotiate on all outstanding problems concerning Germany as a whole.

Before they submitted this resolution, the "neutral six" had received assurances that the three western powers would accept it. Having won support for their main point, that the blockade should be raised at once, those powers did not insist on a resolution naming the Soviet Union as responsible for the Berlin situation. Vyshinsky gave no such prior clearance to the resolution, although he had proved unusually cooperative and cordial in his contacts with Bramuglia. From the Soviet viewpoint, the resolution contained a catch in that the blockade was to be lifted immediately, simultaneously with the beginning of negotiations on the Berlin currency question, not with the successful conclusion of these negotiations. As the supposed agreement embodied in the directive of August 30, referred to in the resolution, had already been shown by the September talks in Berlin to be no agreement at all, the prospect of completing the currency arrangements by November 20 or any other fixed date was dubious. In his conversations with Bramuglia, Vyshinsky proposed a gradual lifting of the blockade as the currency negotiations proceeded, with both operations to be completed at the same time—a plan which did not meet with the approval of the western powers nor even of all the "neutral six," although Bramuglia himself apparently looked on it favorably.

On October 25 the three western delegates announced in the Council that they would accept the six-power resolution, although it did not fully meet their original complaint. They said that they would vote for it in a spirit of compromise and hoped that the Soviet delegate, now participating in the discussion in preparation for "utilizing" his right to vote, would do likewise. Vyshinsky's instructions, however, gave him no choice. Citing the differences in dates—the blockade to be raised at once, the Soviet mark to be introduced at some future date assuming agreement could be reached—he called the draft resolution a departure from the directive of August 30. He would therefore be compelled to vote against it.

Before the vote, Jessup made a final and forceful exposition of the U.S. position in the light of the promised veto. Brushing aside the Soviet arguments, he asked what the Soviet Government really wanted. Did it want a four-power conference on Germany? An arrangement for the introduction of the Soviet mark into Berlin under four-power control? Assurances that the west would not use currency arrangements to interfere with the economy of the Soviet zone? If it would only lift the blockade, it could have any and all of those things. But the western powers would not negotiate under duress. If, on the other hand, the Soviet purpose was to drive them out of Berlin, Jessup assured Vyshinsky that it could not be achieved by maintaining the blockade. Although the six-power draft resolution had purposely avoided such a judgment, he reminded the Council that Soviet action had created a threat to peace.

The vote on the resolution was 9 to 2. Vyshinsky and Manuilsky were alone in the minority, but the former's vote, under the terms of the Charter, killed the resolution. No other conclusion of the Council's consideration of the Berlin dispute had been at all likely, although the patient efforts of Bramuglia and his colleagues to achieve a compromise seemed to fall just short of success. From the standpoint of justifying their position before world opinion, the western powers had done fairly well. They had presented their case exhaustively and convincingly. By accepting the compromise resolution put forward by the six smaller nations they had shown themselves to be conciliatory. The final voting found them together with all other states represented in the Council, placing on the Soviets the onus of blocking a settlement by the exercise of the veto. The latter, in contrast, gave the impression of not having handled their case well. Their assertions that no blockade existed and that the United Nations had no jurisdiction over the dispute were not very convincing. Their nonparticipation in the discussion left the initiative in the hands of the other side. Vyshinsky's speech in defense of his veto was brief and remarkably ineffective. Finally, the veto itself branded the Soviet Union as the one power unwilling to accept a laboriously worked out compromise which took some account of the Soviet viewpoint.

As if to counter the relative success of the western powers in the propaganda war, Stalin chose this moment to issue a blast against them in the form of answers to the questions of a correspondent of *Pravda,* published on October 28. He bluntly accused the United States and Great Britain of going back on two agreements on the Berlin question and of seeking to unleash a new world war. The two "agreements" were the directive of August 30, which the western powers said not they, but the Soviet Union itself, had discarded and which had therefore never been implemented, and a last-minute proposal of Bramuglia's in Paris which apparently had received Soviet but not western approval.[4] Although Stalin pointedly omitted France from his accusations, Schuman hastened to declare France's solidarity with Britain and the United States and to deny that France had accepted any such agreement as Stalin had mentioned.

[4] Stalin stated that Bramuglia had in his hands an agreed draft decision which the U.S. and U.K. representatives declared to be null and void. Tass, the Soviet news agency, made public on October 30 the text of a draft resolution allegedly agreed upon by Vyshinsky and Bramuglia, "who represented the other powers," on October 24. The draft coincided with the resolution actually voted upon the next day except in one particular: it provided that the lifting of the transport restrictions and the arrangements for introducing the Soviet mark as sole currency in Berlin were to be completed by November 20. Thus the blockade would not be lifted at once but would be conditional upon the simultaneous implementation of the currency arrangements. Bramuglia gave the Security Council no report on these informal negotiations. Whatever agreements he may have made with Vyshinsky, he was not authorized to accept the terms mentioned above in the name of the western powers.

Stalin's statement, underlining the Soviet veto, dashed all reasonable expectations that a settlement of the dispute was possible at that time. The western powers decided not to bring it before the General Assembly, whose agenda was already overloaded. They had already demonstrated that the Soviet Union was responsible for blocking a settlement, and a vote in the Assembly could do no more than that. The lengthy consideration of the Berlin situation by the Security Council, moreover, had taken some of the edge off the dispute and given the tension existing in September a chance to diminish. By November, the blockade and the airlift, both well established, were coming to be regarded as normal rather than alarming aspects of the international scene.

The optimistic Bramuglia, remaining as president of the Security Council during November, continued his efforts to bring the parties together. He noted in a press interview that only "subtle" differences separated their respective positions.[5] The so-called Vyshinsky-Bramuglia compromise proposal of October 24 was, in content, not very different from the Moscow directive of August 30, in that the raising of the blockade and the currency arrangements were to be worked out simultaneously. The western powers, however, after their experience with Marshal Sokolovsky in Berlin in September, had brought the dispute to the United Nations for the very reason that the Moscow agreement, in their view, had broken down because of Soviet bad faith. They were not anxious to make the same bargain again.

Jessup, paying a short visit to Berlin at the end of October, reiterated publicly the conviction of the U.S. Government that the deadlock was due not to technical difficulties over currency but to "the fundamental desire of the Russians to get us out of Berlin." [6] Since there was no evidence that they had abandoned that desire, the Americans and British could not accept the view that only slight differences stood in the way of a settlement. This was the principal reason why the appeal made

[5] *New York Times,* October 30, 1948.
[6] *Ibid.,* October 31, 1948.

by Herbert Evatt, President of the General Assembly, and Secretary-General Trygve Lie for immediate conversations to settle the dispute had a very cool reception in Washington and London.

On November 13 Evatt and Lie sent a letter to the four great powers invoking a resolution recently passed by the General Assembly urging renewed efforts to compose their differences and conclude the postwar peace settlements. The first step, the letter suggested, should be the Berlin question, as the deadlock was endangering peace and undermining the work of the United Nations in every field. It then urged the four powers to begin conversations at once and to give full support to the mediation efforts of Bramuglia. Undoubtedly this appeal reflected the general feeling of many of the nations represented at Paris. A direct attempt by the big powers to settle the dispute seemed the only hope of relieving the international tension. But from the point of view of the Americans and British, the Evatt-Lie appeal, which asked them to negotiate under the duress of the blockade and made no mention of the Security Council resolution vetoed by the U.S.S.R., was anything but helpful. It struck a blow for the Soviets in the propaganda war in that it proposed essentially what Vyshinsky himself had proposed. The Soviet reply referred to the earlier Soviet proposal for a session of the Council of Foreign Ministers to consider Berlin and other German questions, implying that Evatt and Lie were to be congratulated for agreeing with it. The replies from the three western powers politely pointed out that they already had tried direct discussions with the Soviet Union, in July and August, and that these had failed because of the refusal to lift the blockade. They mentioned that the Security Council had proposed a fair solution, which the Soviet Government had chosen to veto. The three western governments were willing to cooperate with Bramuglia in his efforts to bring about a settlement, but they would not, they reiterated, negotiate under duress.

The failure of the Evatt-Lie proposal did not put an end to mediation efforts. Bramuglia and Lie, working with representatives of the six smaller powers on the Security Council and their experts, tried to work out a technical plan, based on the four-power directive of August 30, to solve the Berlin currency question. Nothing in the attitudes of the four powers gave much hope that this approach would succeed. Bramuglia, however, when he retired as president of the Security Council at the end of November, announced that he was inviting the six smaller nations on the Council to appoint experts to a committee to evolve such a plan. Bramuglia's proposal met no objections, but the western powers reserved their position on any recommendations the new committee might submit to the Council, pointing out that measures being taken by the Soviets in Berlin itself at that very moment were widening the split in the city administration and making it more difficult to apply any scheme for four-power control of the currency.

Developments in Berlin were, indeed, marching rapidly toward the creation of two separate and mutually hostile administrations in the Soviet and western sectors. The elected assembly and the city council, minus their pro-Soviet members, were now meeting in the British sector, being unable to function in the Soviet sector. On November 30 the SED and other Communist organizations, with the blessing of the Soviet authorities, brought into being in the Soviet sector a body which claimed to be the provisional government of all Berlin. Friedrich Ebert, son of the first president of the Weimar republic, was ceremoniously installed as "Mayor of Berlin." This was the climax of a long series of actions taken by the Soviets in splitting the city administration.

Elections, scheduled for 1948 under the temporary constitution approved by all four powers, could not be held throughout the city. When the Berlin administration, with the support of the western powers, rejected certain conditions stipulated by the Soviet authorities, the latter forbade the holding of the elections in the Soviet sector and refused to recognize their validity in the other sectors. Held on December 5 in the western sectors alone and boycotted by the SED, the elections served as an informal plebiscite against the Communists and against Soviet policies. The heavy vote (86 percent of the electorate) and the smashing victory of the Social Democrats, who gained 65 percent of the total vote, seemed to leave no room for compromise or for a return to a united city government under four-power direction. The three western powers took account of this fact some weeks later by recreating the Allied Kommandatura in western Berlin on a three-power basis.

The committee of experts appointed under Bramuglia's proposal, working assiduously to produce an acceptable plan for Berlin's currency, came up early in January with a detailed scheme providing for two separate banking systems. Agreement on it by the four powers was not forthcoming, however. The United States, in particular, was skeptical of the possibility of finding any way out of the Berlin impasse by this means. In view of what had happened in the past three months, the Moscow directive of August 30, on which the committee of experts based its proposals, seemed no longer to offer a solution which would safeguard the rights and interests of the western powers in Berlin. Stalin, in his open letter to Kingsbury Smith of International News Service on January 30, 1949, did not mention the currency question as the obstacle to agreement on Berlin. He did mention the decision to establish a west German state, postponement of which would make it possible to raise the blockade. This was a condition which the United States, as Secretary of State Acheson pointed out on February 2, had no intention of meeting.[7]

Through the whole course of the discussions on Berlin after the matter was brought before the Security Council, neither the United States nor the U.S.S.R. was sufficiently anxious for an agreement to make major concessions. In view of the success of the airlift and the prospect that it could be continued through the winter months, the United States was inclined to

[7] See below, pp. 493, 537. The committee of neutral experts notified the Security Council on February 11 that it saw no early prospect of reconciling the widely divergent viewpoints of the four occupying powers' experts (Department of State, *Documents and State Papers,* I, May 1949, 749-783), and on March 20 the western military governors finally declared the western mark to be the sole legal tender in the western sectors of Berlin.

let the dispute remain unsolved, meanwhile putting the onus on the Russians for maintaining the blockade, using force in an attempt to starve the city into submission, and threatening international peace. From the propaganda standpoint, especially within Germany, the American position was showing favorable results.

Behind the problem of Berlin was the problem of Germany. Should a compromise be reached on Berlin, the next step would be a meeting of the Council of Foreign Ministers to discuss Germany as a whole. The United States was in no hurry to hold such a meeting, where the Russians might well seize the initiative with proposals for the establishment of a central German government and the withdrawal of occupation forces. It would be difficult to counter such proposals, which would have an undeniable appeal to the Germans, until the plans for western Germany were carried further and until the work of recovery and consolidation in western Europe should reach the point where it could handle a united Germany freed of Allied forces of occupation. Another Council of Foreign Ministers talking-match would be of no particular help to the western powers. The U.S.S.R. would certainly insist on abandonment of the program for western Germany, to which the western powers could not agree. The immediate need, as they saw it, was to strengthen their position by reaching agreement among themselves on western Germany, while maintaining their position in Berlin. Strengthening their bargaining power in this way, they would be better able at some future date to deal with the Soviets on a settlement for Germany as a whole with a good chance of attaining their own political and security objectives.

2. Agreement on the Ruhr

The United States and Britain had not worked out a policy for all Germany to meet the new conditions. They did have a policy for western Germany, which seemed to be meeting with success. Soviet attempts to get them to give up this policy and the unending stream of abuse showered on it by Soviet-controlled propaganda organs indicated that Moscow was very much concerned over the recovery and consolidation of the larger part of Germany under western leadership while difficulties were piling up in the Soviet zone. Whatever advantages the Soviet Union might be winning in the struggle for Berlin, the western powers appeared to be gaining ground in the struggle for Germany.

Anglo-American policy in western Germany was frankly aimed at German revival, economic and political though not military. It was a far cry from the approach of the early postwar period, when the emphasis had been on holding Germany down, on a fixed low level of industry, and on satisfying the needs of Allied nations at Germany's expense. The Soviet Union and its satellites scored the Anglo-American policy of reviving German industry, especially in the Ruhr, as an attempt to build up German war potential for aggressive purposes. France and the smaller western nations also had serious reservations concerning policies which, they felt, neglected essential long-term security considerations. There were groups in England and America also which expressed opposition to what seemed to them the abandonment of necessary vigilance against Germany's recovery of military power in the haste to produce quick results, to lighten the burden of American taxpayers, and to win German support in the political struggle with Russia.

Generals Clay and Robertson, and their superiors in Washington and London, were not oblivious of the danger to world peace of a strong and united Germany. They saw no reason why it was not possible to guard against that danger while promoting a maximum expansion of German peacetime industry. There was no intention of allowing Germany to maintain armed forces or to produce armaments. To prevent it, the United States and Britain counted on close observation and forceful preventive action. While the occupation lasted, this was a simple matter. After the occupation, an effective system of inspection and a determination to intervene at once in case of violation would be required. The French were not inclined to leave so much to chance and to the will of the English-speaking powers to enforce disarmament on Germany for the indefinite future. They had more confidence in such positive measures as the removal of German plants, restrictions on German industrial capacity, and Allied control of the Ruhr, with the purpose of making Germany permanently inferior to France in industrial strength. The effort to devise an agreed tripartite policy toward western Germany revolved round these issues. The English-speaking powers, especially the United States, attempted to whittle down the French demands when they tended to interfere with the economic recovery of western Germany. The French, in a much weaker position, did what they could to win Anglo-American support for what they regarded as legitimate and necessary safeguards for the security of France.

British and American policy in regard to control of the Ruhr, for some years after the war, consisted largely in denying Soviet and French demands for the creation of a special international regime. The British took the position that there would be no special regimes in their zone alone. The Americans had accepted the principle of some kind of international control of the Ruhr. "The resources and industrial potential of the Ruhr . . . should not be left under the exclusive control of any future German government but should be used for the benefit of the European community as a whole," Secretary Marshall said at Chicago on November 18, 1947.[8] But they were in no hurry about establishing such a control. No special arrangements were necessary as a security measure while Allied armies still occupied Germany; as for long-term control, that was a matter for the peace treaty. Meanwhile, with the economic merger of the U.S. and U.K. zones, the Ruhr came under the joint responsibility of both powers. Together they worked out arrangements intended to maximize current production of coal, steel and other products essential to recovery. Plans to socialize the Ruhr mines and industries, once favored by Britain, were put aside. Decisions on the whole question of future ownership

[8] Department of State, *Bulletin*, XVII, November 30, 1947, 1028.

and management, which seriously concerned the French, were put off to the indefinite future.

Actual management of the Ruhr industries was in the hands of Germans under Anglo-American supervision. But if this situation was satisfactory to British and American military government officials in Germany, who did not conceal their lack of sympathy with French demands, the State Department and the Foreign Office felt obliged to be more conciliatory. The three western powers were standing together in the European Recovery Program and in the Berlin crisis. All three had every interest in reaching a common policy on western Germany, including the Ruhr, in order not to jeopardize the success of the great effort to save western Europe, in which western Germany was expected to play such an important role.

By the agreement on western Germany reached in London on June 1, 1948, the principle of an international regime for the Ruhr was accepted by the three western powers and the Benelux nations. The functions of the new International Authority for the Ruhr, as outlined in the agreement, were limited to (1) allocation of coal, coke and steel between export and German consumption, and (2) cooperation with Allied agencies charged with the enforcement of disarmament in the Ruhr.[9] Nothing was decided as to the ownership and management of Ruhr industries. The United States and Britain, mindful of the German reaction and of the possible effects on production, did not intend that anything should be decided, as they wished them to remain in German hands. The French Assembly, however, in reluctantly accepting the London agreements, added a reservation in the form of an instruction to the Foreign Minister to insist, in his negotiations with the Americans and British, on placing those industries under international management. Thus the main issue dividing France from the other two powers remained unsolved.

Representatives of the six powers met again in London on November 11, to work out the detailed statute of the new Ruhr authority. The day before the conference opened, Gen-

[9] See above, pp. 75-76.

eral Clay and General Robertson announced a new law, Law No. 75,[10] by which ownership of the Ruhr industries was to be vested temporarily in "trustees," who would hold them until their final disposition was decided. According to the preamble of the law, that decision would be made by a freely chosen German government. These trustees would be Germans, named by the military authorities "after consultation with appropriate German bodies." [11]

From the standpoint of what the Anglo-American authorities were trying to do in Germany, this law was a logical step. The ideas behind it were to end the uncertainty which kept both managers and workers from putting forth their best efforts, to permit necessary improvements, to increase efficiency, and to rationalize and decentralize control by breaking up some of the big cartels. From the standpoint of relations with France, however, it was ill-advised, or at least singularly ill-timed. The French reaction, though perhaps not its vehemence, was foreseen in Washington and London. Those who opposed the step, or who favored holding back at least until the London talks had made some progress, did not have sufficient opportunity or influence to get their counsel accepted. On the American side, the moving spirit was General Clay, not the State Department.

At the London conference the French had intended to plead their case once more for an international authority with power to control production and investment in the Ruhr. The rapid advance shown by German industry since June seemed to strengthen their deeply rooted fear of German industrial power. Then, on the eve of Armistice Day, without regard to French views and sensibilities, came the announcement of Law

---

[10] Law 75 applied to the U.S. zone. A similar law was promulgated simultaneously in the U.K. zone.

[11] The list of 12 trustees for the steel industry proposed by the Bizonal Economic Council in February 1949, containing the names of some men closely associated with the old ownership and management and no representatives of the trade unions, seemed to justify the fears of those who felt that Law 75 opened the way to restoration of the prewar situation. The 12 men ultimately selected by the Anglo-American military governors, however, included only three who had not previously been declared acceptable by the trade unions.

75. The French Government immediately protested that the decision regarding ownership of the Ruhr mines and industries could not be made by Britain and the United States alone, but only by all interested powers. Léon Blum, who had long courted unpopularity in France by deprecating ultra-nationalism on the German question and urging understanding of the Anglo-American policy, said that "London and Washington have struck a severe, perhaps irreparable, blow at the French system of security." [12] President Auriol, in an unprecedented and vehement speech, denounced it as an unforgivable mistake and a violation of justice, exposing Germany's victims to the danger of a new aggression. The entire French press joined in condemning an act which seemed to prejudice the future and to cut the ground from under the French position just as the London negotiations were about to begin.

The disregard shown for French desires reflected the growing impatience felt by many American and British officials toward what they considered French delaying and blocking tactics which interfered with the recovery effort. They regarded the scope of the international Ruhr authority as already settled by the London decisions of the previous June, which said nothing about international ownership and management. The French Foreign Office, however, had no choice but to protest, especially since the French Assembly had expressed itself in favor of pressing the case for international ownership. The French Government had a very difficult row to hoe. It was not strong enough to defy a public opinion genuinely concerned over a Ruhr industrial colossus controlled by Germans, whether publicly owned or returned to the industrialists, "Hitler's accomplices." De Gaulle was making the most of French resentment against the Anglo-Saxon policy of "remaking the German Empire." It was true that France had little bargaining power on the Ruhr issue. In the end it probably would have to give up its more far-reaching demands. But the British and American governments, though not wishing this rift to threaten western solidarity on the Berlin question or on ERP, seemed

[12] *Le Populaire*, November 19, 1948.

bent on making it difficult rather than easy for the French to retreat.

Hervé Alphand, chief of the French delegation at London, recalling the stand taken by the French Assembly, protested against the Anglo-American decision to leave the question of ownership to a future German government. The other delegates gave him a respectful hearing, but left the subject to be dealt with further through diplomatic channels. France pressed its case in formal notes and in a long talk which Schuman had with Marshall and McNeil in Paris.[13] The United States and Britain then assured France that the final decision would not be taken until the peace settlement. Thus neither the military governors nor a provisional west German government could make that decision. Marshall told a press conference that "the final determination of the security problem of Europe in relation to the future of the Ruhr must await the terms of the peace treaty which will be conclusive in the matter." [14] This was a definite assurance to France. There was, however, no intention on the part of either the United States or Great Britain to withdraw Law 75.

Alphand's second major point, the necessity of international supervision and control over the management of the Ruhr industries, was taken up in connection with the agreed task before the London conference, elaboration of the functions of the international authority already agreed upon in June. An authority with power only to allocate the products of three major industries, as outlined in the June agreement, did not seem adequate to the French. What was necessary, in their view, was the power to exercise supervision over production and investment. To meet this view, at least partially, the United States and Britain agreed to admit France to a share in the control over the coal and steel industries during the occu-

13 The French Assembly, by a vote of 377-181 on December 2, 1948, upheld the government's protest and rejected "the policy expressed in the preamble of Law 75." The negative votes were cast by the Communists, not because they approved General Clay's policies but for internal political reasons.
14 Statement to the press, November 24, 1948 (Department of State, *Bulletin,* XIX, December 5, 1948, 715).

pation period. What concerned the French much more was what would happen when the occupation was over, especially if the industries were then turned over to German ownership. They urged the establishment of an ironclad system of control over management and planning which would prevent the excessive development of steel production while encouraging full production of coal and coke. This proposal was not accepted, but in the interests of avoiding a deadlock the representatives of the three powers agreed to postpone final decision on it.

The draft agreement on a Ruhr statute, announced on December 28, 1948, provided for the establishment of an International Authority for the Ruhr, on which the six signatory powers and Germany would be represented. Most decisions of the Authority were to be taken by majority vote. Until the establishment of a German government and its accession to the agreement, the three votes allotted to Germany would be cast as a unit by a representative of "the occupation authorities concerned," that is, of the United States, Britain and France. Each of these powers would have in addition three votes, while Holland, Belgium and Luxembourg would have one apiece. The jurisdiction of the proposed Authority covered a precisely defined area including the Ruhr Valley itself and additional territory on the left bank of the Rhine extending to the Dutch border.[15]

The functions of the Authority were to include fixing minimum amounts of coal, coke and steel to be made available for export. It was given the right to look into transport, trade and price policies affecting these three products to see whether they prejudiced the accomplishment of the purposes of the agreement; if so, the Authority could insist on necessary changes, having due regard for the requirements of international security, for Germany's obligations under the European Recovery Program, and for Germany's need for legitimate protection in its international trade. All these points had already been

[15] See map on p. 68. For text of the draft agreement and accompanying communiqué see Department of State, *Bulletin*, XX, January 9, 1949, 43-52.

agreed upon in June. In practice they would presumably be worked out in harmony with the plans of the OEEC in Paris, tying Ruhr production into the general recovery effort.

At the end of the occupation or "control period" or at an agreed earlier date, such of the existing powers of the occupation authorities over the management of the coal, coke and steel industries as were necessary to ensure that policies and programs relating to production, development and investment were in conformity with the purposes of the agreement would be transferred to the Authority, to the Military Security Board or its successor,[16] or to some other body created by international agreement. Which of these powers should be continued and what agency should exercise them the signatory governments would not decide for a year at least and perhaps not until just before the occupation ended. Thus the major point raised by France was put off for future decision in the light of the Authority's experience and such new conditions as might develop.

The part which the Authority would play in enforcing the disarmament of Germany was left to be settled by the peace treaty or by some other international agreement. It was stated to be Allied policy not to permit the development of any "excessive concentration of economic power" in the Ruhr coal, coke or steel industries and to exclude men who had furthered Nazi aims from positions of ownership and control. Before the end of the control period the signatory governments would decide which powers were to be continued and whether they would be transferred to the Authority, the Military Security Board, or some other body.

Thus a great deal was left for future decision. A Ruhr Authority would come into being after approval by the six governments [17] and would have important functions in respect of the allocation of the Ruhr's chief products, but the scope of its activities after the control period remained in doubt. The

---

[16] See below, p. 481.
[17] An agreement establishing the Ruhr Authority was signed in London on April 28, 1949.

French could continue to hope that it would become an effective instrument in making sure, as the first sentence of the draft agreement's preamble put it, "that the resources of the Ruhr shall not in the future be used for the purpose of aggression but shall be used in the interests of peace."

Whether the Ruhr agreement represented a victory for the French thesis, as the press in many countries described it, was open to question. The December decisions were based on those of June, without any great change. Security considerations were given more attention, but the main function assigned to the Authority was still the allocation of Ruhr production in the interest of Germany and Europe. The crucial decisions on who should own and who should control or manage the Ruhr industries were still to be made. The mere existence of a Ruhr Authority did not guarantee its effectiveness, particularly if basic disagreement among the powers represented on it should continue to exist. Be that as it may, it was important, in December 1948, that France appeared satisfied with the agreement, the French delegate at the London conference calling it an unprecedented achievement in postwar understanding.[18] It made possible a greater unity among the three powers in other phases of the German problem, more particularly in opposing Soviet policies in Germany.

Possibly the most notable feature of the Ruhr agreement was the fact that the Soviet Union was not a participant. The Ruhr, the greatest center of heavy industry in Europe, would work for the recovery of western Europe. Communist propaganda attacked the agreement from two directions. The Soviet organs, which since the war had urged the establishment of a special regime of four-power control over the Ruhr, continued their familiar theme that American monopolists were taking charge of the Ruhr combination with the German "coal and

[18] Certain sectors of American opinion, such as that represented by the Society for the Prevention of World War III, were much more critical than the French Government in their reaction. They regarded the proposed Ruhr Authority as ineffective and the agreement as mere sugar-coating for the reality that the Ruhr would be left in German hands (see Society for the Prevention of World War III, News Release No. 33, January 13, 1949).

steel barons," who were willing to serve Wall Street as they served Hitler. They planned to use the Ruhr, said Moscow, to buttress the iniquitous Marshall plan for the enthrallment of Europe and aggression against the U.S.S.R. The German Communists, appealing to German nationalism, denounced the agreement as "the rape of the Ruhr" and a threat to Germany's survival. Max Reimann, Communist leader in the western zones, told a public meeting that German politicans who were prepared to accept the Ruhr statute would be regarded as quislings and would face reprisals, a remark which led to his arrest, trial, and sentencing to three months' imprisonment by a British military court.[19]

There were objections from all sectors of German opinion, not merely from the Communists. All the points which tended to make the agreement acceptable to the French made it undesirable from the point of view of the Germans. Political leaders in western Germany, becoming more vocal and less hesitant in speaking the language of nationalism, registered outraged protests at this "servitude" imposed on Germany for an indefinite period. German Socialists opposed the concept of international control on the ground that it ruled out socialization and made it impossible for a German government to run the Ruhr industries for the welfare of the German people. German opinion in general, judging from press reports, regarded the Ruhr Authority as an instrument with which other nations, especially France, would try to hold down German production for the benefit of their own. Nevertheless, aside from the Communists, the German political leaders did not talk of sabotage and actual resistance to the Allied decision. They intended rather to work for its modification by negotiation. Former owners and managers, who were now coming back to positions of influence in the Ruhr industries, could be counted on to do what they could to prevent its working out in practice to their disadvantage.

German criticism often raised the point that it was wrong

---

[19] Reimann's sentence was suspended temporarily and he was released February 12 to permit his attendance at the Bonn assembly. He was later sent back to jail.

to single out the Ruhr for international control unless the same thing were done in other heavy industrial areas such as Belgium and northeastern France. The same idea had gained adherents elsewhere, even in France,[20] and had been discussed informally at the time of the London meeting on the Ruhr. It was supported both as a means of making the Ruhr statute acceptable to the Germans and as a desirable step toward a closely knit European economy. This was something for the future, however, which might possibly be worked out through the OEEC. There was no intention on the part of the western powers to hold up action on the Ruhr, Germany's "arsenal for aggression," in order to work out a European scheme which few Allied nations would be likely to accept at this time. The Germans might complain that the Ruhr scheme was a *Diktat* which would make European economic cooperation impossible. The western powers were willing to take that chance. They were not willing to set aside an agreement reached among themselves with such travail merely because of German protests. They proposed to go ahead and put it into effect in the hope that cooler counsels would prevail in Germany and that the Germans, by cooperating, would seize the opportunity which it offered for their return to the European community.

3. *Reparation and Security*

Encouragement of all-out production in the Ruhr raised questions concerning the level of industry and the reparation

[20] Cf. the speech of André Philip in the French Assembly on November 30, 1948 (*Journal Officiel, Débats de l'Assemblée Nationale, Séances,* November 30, 1948, 7314, 7315). Stephen Raushenbush, *The Ruhr: A Better American Policy* (Public Affairs Institute, Occasional Paper 2, Washington, 1948) endorses the same solution from the American point of view, as does *The Economist* (December 11, 1948, 957; January 15, 1949, 92) from the British. *Feet on the Ground* (London, 1948), a Labor party pamphlet, recommends (p. 19) international control of all European basic industries. A British official in Germany, the chairman of the Anglo-American coal control group, stated on January 15, 1949, that success of the Ruhr experiment might lead to application of the idea over other areas; but before this could take place, the Germans would have to create in other nations a feeling of confidence that they were determined to serve the cause of peace and contribute to European recovery (*Manchester Guardian,* January 17, 1949).

program. Here again the Anglo-American emphasis on recovery clashed with the French insistence on security. What was to remain of the Potsdam program under the new conditions in which the American policy no longer showed any trace of the "Morgenthau plan" approach? In 1947 the United States and Great Britain had already abandoned the four-power level-of-industry agreement of 1946, setting a new level for Bizonia (that of 1936) which left the Germans a greater "peacetime" industry and cut down correspondingly the amount of plant and equipment available for reparation deliveries to Allied nations. The salient item was the limit of 10.7 million tons on the annual production of crude steel, compared to the 5.8 million-ton level set for all Germany in the four-power agreement of 1946.[21] Under this new program, which France did not like but had to accept, 767 plants in the three western zones were designated as surplus capacity to be removed as reparation.

By this time, virtually nothing was being delivered to the Soviet Union, which under the Potsdam agreement was entitled to 25 percent of the surplus plant and equipment in the western zones, to cover its own share and that of Poland.[22] As a result of the Soviet refusal to treat Germany as an economic unit, in violation of the Potsdam agreement, the western powers had delivered very little to the east, some $25 million worth of factories and machinery by the end of 1947. In the same period the other 18 Allied nations which were entitled to reparation had received only about $125 million, shared out among them by the Inter-Allied Reparation Agency (IARA) in Brussels according to percentages agreed upon at the Paris conference of 1945. France and the smaller European allies were especially anxious to speed the dismantling, allocation and delivery of the 767 plants declared available for reparation under the new 1947 level of industry. The same considerations, however, which had led to the curtailment of the reparation pro-

[21] *The United States in World Affairs, 1947–1948*, 82-84.
[22] Ten percent without payment, 15 percent in return for goods to be delivered by the U.S.S.R.

gram in 1947 were still present and threatened to cut it down further. As in Japan, the longer the problem dragged on without a rapid and decisive solution, the smaller were the chances that the erstwhile enemies would ever have to pay a heavy reparation bill.

In the U.S. Congress there was strong criticism of the continuation of dismantling. German factories, said the critics, would make a greater contribution to recovery if left in Germany than if moved elsewhere; since the United States was proposing to spend billions for European recovery, it was merely increasing the cost to itself by going on with the reparation program. From the economic standpoint this was a reasonable argument. A Ruhr steel plant could not be torn down, shipped to France, and reassembled there without a loss to European production as a whole. But the French, Belgians, and others entitled to reparation did not look at the problem quite that way. They had their own plans for increased national production, counting on equipment from Germany. Furthermore, they felt that Germany owed them something for the frightful damage caused by Hitler's war. Even if reparation payments amounted to little compared to the volume of American aid, and second-hand machinery was less useful than new machinery bought with ERP dollars, they did not wish to see the Germans get off scot-free. In Czechoslovakia and other nations not receiving American aid, the scaling-down of the reparation program was regarded not only as a violation of inter-Allied agreements but also as another proof of American determination to rebuild German industry and war potential with callous disregard for the interests of Germany's neighbors.

The British and French governments were proceeding on the basis that the list of 767 factories to be dismantled was final. The U.S. State Department, early in 1948, took the same view. As an answer to Congressional criticism, Secretary Marshall wrote to Senator Vandenberg in February 1948 that the United States had undertaken an obligation to other Allied nations and could not unilaterally hold up the reparation program. He also gave assurance that the removals did not interfere with

European recovery since the factories being dismantled were either war plants or surplus capacity well above the level of production Germany was likely to reach for some time. A report put out by IARA, reflecting the views of the smaller nations, emphasized the importance to their economic recovery of the German plant and equipment that they had received or hoped to receive.[23] The power of decision, however, lay not with the smaller claimant nations but with those powers in control of western Germany, and especially with the United States.

A number of factors were pushing the U.S. Government toward a reconsideration of the entire question in the light of new circumstances. One of these was the attitude of the Germans, both industrialists and workers. The Germans had been making complaints about dismantling for a long time, but more heed was paid to their views now than in 1945. A major purpose of the attempt to deal with reparation claims through a plant-removals program was to get the whole thing out of the way in one fairly rapid operation. This had not been done. Allowed to drag on, it had become a constantly disturbing factor, since the Allied nations felt that they had been cheated and the Germans felt that their means of livelihood were being taken away. Once ERP became the touchstone of policy in western Europe, and western Germany was included in it, pressure to review the reparation program in the light of the over-all objective of western European recovery followed as a logical consequence. The U.S. Congress included in the Economic Cooperation Act a specific instruction to the Administrator to "request the Secretary of State to obtain the agreement of those countries concerned that such capital equipment as is scheduled for removal as reparations from the three western zones of Germany be retained in Germany if such retention would most effectively serve the purposes of the European recovery program." [24]

[23] IARA, *Allied Economic Recovery: The Contribution of Industrial Capital Equipment delivered by Germany as Reparation* (Brussels, March 1, 1948).
[24] Public Law 472, 80th Congress, 2nd Session, approved April 3, 1948, 19.

In the first six months of 1948 dismantling was continued, with plants scheduled for allocation by IARA and delivery to claimant states. Then in August, at the request of ECA Administrator Hoffman, Marshall proposed that dismantling be temporarily stopped until a committee of American businessmen could examine the factories on the spot and make recommendations as to which ones would best serve European recovery if left in Germany and which ones could be removed. The British and French governments were not enthusiastic. To them the question was political and psychological as well as economic. They did not want to ask their own peoples, or those of other Allied nations, to accept a higher level of German industry and a cut in reparation deliveries. Coming at a time when German industrial production, under the stimulus of the currency reform, was beginning to bound upward, the American proposal seemed to confirm the complaints of those who charged America with a policy of deliberately favoring Germany at the expense of the victims of German aggression and exploitation; it seemed to put an end to hopes that Germany would ever have to pay anything substantial as reparation for wartime losses. Ultimately, however, London and Paris agreed to hold up all dismantling until the American committee, headed by George M. Humphrey, could visit the factories and make its report.

In January 1949 the Humphrey committee recommended that 167 of the 381 plants it had been asked to examine be left in Germany, where they could make a contribution to European recovery. There were immediate objections from Britain and France, followed by long negotiations in London, where the Humphrey report was discussed in conjunction with a report from the military governors of the western zones on a revised list of prohibitions and restrictions which should be applied to German industry on security grounds. The negotiations were difficult, as the French wished to save what they could of the reparation program and maintain a maximum of restrictions on key German industries, while the British, without questioning the American emphasis on recovery, leaned toward the French rather than the American side.

The agreements finally reached at London and approved by the three foreign ministers in Washington in the first week of April, 1949, revised the Humphrey proposals on plant removals only by adding eight plants to the list of those to be dismantled and delivered as reparation. These eight plants, however, included some of the largest in Germany, such as the *August Thyssen Hütte* at Duisburg and the *I. G. Farben* buna and caustic soda plants at Ludwigshafen.

The agreement on prohibited and restricted industries was announced at the same time. The production of war materials, radioactive materials, certain machine tools, synthetic rubber, synthetic oil products (with a few exceptions), primary magnesium, and beryllium was to remain absolutely prohibited. The steel, shipbuilding, aluminum, synthetic ammonia, ball bearings, and certain other industries were limited to specific levels of capacity or production. The level of 10.7 million tons per year for steel production in Bizonia, set in 1947, was retained with the addition of 400,000 more tons to be produced in the French zone. Shipbuilding was limited both as to total capacity and as to the size and speed of vessels which could be built. All the prohibitions laid down in the agreement were to remain in force until the peace settlement, and the limitations would remain until January 1, 1953 or until the peace settlement, whichever was the earlier, and thereafter as might be agreed.[25]

As security was the main consideration behind the reluctance of France to accept the American approach to the Ruhr and reparation problems, it was up to the United States to demonstrate that, in its zeal for Germany's industrial recovery, it was not overlooking the legitimate fears of France and other Allied nations. It was fundamental to the American approach that economic restrictions on German industry did not hold the key to security against renewed German aggression; if enforceable, they might keep Germany weak, but economic stagnation was considered too high a price to pay; an impoverished and frustrated Germany might prove more dangerous to peace than

[25] Department of State, *Bulletin*, XX, April 24, 1949, 524-531.

a productive, prosperous Germany. The key to the security question, as the United States saw it, lay in vigilant control to ensure Germany's disarmament. The decisions taken to set up such control were not mere paper concessions to gain French acceptance of Anglo-American views on the Ruhr or on reparation. They represented a serious attempt to set up effective control machinery. After all, France was not the only nation concerned about the possible revival of Germany as an aggressive military power.

When Secretary Byrnes's draft four-power treaty to ensure Germany's disarmament, proposed in 1946, was turned down by the Soviet Union and had to be abandoned, the three western powers set out to find a substitute by which they could maintain the demilitarization and disarmament of those parts of Germany in which they could take action. In the London agreements of June 1, 1948, they laid the foundation for a permanent system of control by proposing the establishment of a tripartite Military Security Board, with controls over prohibited and restricted industries, to enforce disarmament in the three western zones. Formation of this board was finally announced in January 1949.

The Military Security Board's responsibilities, according to its terms of reference, would "cover the whole field of disarmament and demilitarization, taking into consideration the laws and directives which have been agreed already on a quadripartite basis." [26] It would carry out necessary inspections and recommend to the military governors measures necessary to prevent the revival of military organizations, to ensure that there would be no manufacture or import of war material, and to prevent the use of scientific research for warlike ends.

In the Military Security Board the three western powers had at their disposal the machinery to look into and control all activities which might contribute to the revival of German militarism and Germany's war potential. So long as Allied armies remained in occupation of Germany, a German threat to security through rearmament was not likely to arise. That

[26] *Ibid.*, XX, February 13, 1949, 195.

was the very period during which the Military Security Board was to be in operation. If it proved its usefulness, however, the three western powers would be likely to propose its continuance, or its replacement by some comparable body, in the terms of the peace treaty for Germany.

The three-power agreements on German economic and security matters settled, or at least appeared to settle, some of the most vexatious questions that had kept the western nations at odds on German policy ever since the war. At about the same time, agreement was finally reached on the outstanding political differences. Completed on the eve of a new meeting of the Council of Foreign Ministers, the series of agreements marked a new high point in western solidarity. This evidence of solidarity and the nature of the agreements themselves, which were meant for the western zones but were potentially applicable to the Soviet zone as well, would be important factors strengthening the hands of the western delegates in the forthcoming four-power negotiations.

4. The West German Constitution

Western Germany, through the operation of the European Recovery Program, was being drawn into close economic association with the nations of western Europe. That process was not without political implications. As the war faded into the past, as the Germans recovered from the shock of defeat and the chaos of the early postwar years, the problem of Germany's political future had to be faced. First, what political institutions would Germany be permitted or encouraged to establish? Second, in what ways would Germany, or parts of Germany, be associated with other nations of Europe?

Because these questions went to the heart of the German problem and bore directly on the world balance of power, they proved incapable of settlement through four-power negotiation in the Council of Foreign Ministers. The only extended formal discussion on the nature of a provisional government for Germany took place at the Moscow conference in the spring of

1947. It revealed wide disagreement on methods and practice despite nominal agreement on generalities such as the desirability of a peaceful and democratic Germany. After Moscow there was no real effort by either side to reach an accord. Each occupying power sought to influence the future political organization of Germany by propaganda and by concrete measures in those parts of Germany under its control. While the Soviets were implanting in their zone a political system embodying their conception of the type of regime Germany should have, the three western powers, much more hesitantly, set out to reconcile their own differences and prepare the way for the establishment of a government in the west. The Americans and British felt that military government could not be continued indefinitely; if Soviet moves in the political field were to be countered and impetus given to the economic recovery of western Germany, the Germans would have to be given greater responsibility for governing themselves and gradually associated with the western European community. At the six-nation London meeting in 1948 France and the Benelux nations accepted this approach on the understanding that there must be adequate guarantees of their security against the revival of German military power.

The London decisions set the framework for the new political structure of western Germany. Communicated by the three military governors to the minister-presidents of the *Länder* of the western zones, and modified somewhat in order to meet the latters' objections,[27] they were the starting point for the drafts submitted to the constituent assembly which met at Bonn on September 1, 1948. One hundred years before, at Frankfort-on-the-Main, representatives of German liberalism had met to draft a federal, democratic constitution for Germany. Some 30 years before, delegates meeting at Weimar had drawn up a constitution for the new German republic. Both constitutions had succumbed to the powerful authoritarian and antidemocratic forces that had been a feature of German political life since the rise of Prussia. The delegates at Bonn had to take account not only of those forces but also of two very important

[27] See above, pp. 97-98.

considerations which overshadowed everything they did. First, they were drafting a constitution while their country was under foreign occupation. Second, they spoke only for a part of Germany. No representatives from the Soviet zone were present. Berlin was represented by a delegation of five men who took part in the discussions but did not have the right to vote.[28]

The delegates at Bonn were very sensitive to the accusation, made time and again by the Russians and the German Communists, that they were engaged in a manoeuvre to split Germany. Although the London decisions provided for the drafting of a "constitution," the German political leaders insisted that their meeting be a "parliamentary council," not a constitutent assembly, and that the document be not a constitution (*Verfassung*) but a "basic law" (*Grundgesetz*). This document, hammered out at Bonn in the last months of 1948, was being prepared not for all Germany but for a "state-fragment," western Germany, although the preamble on which the delegates agreed stated that they "acted also on behalf of those Germans to whom participation was denied." The preamble stated the resolve of the German people "to preserve its national and political unity . . . ," and the final article declared: "This Basic Law shall become invalid on the day when a constitution adopted in a free decision by the German people comes into force."

Another phrase which appeared in an early draft of the preamble reflected the feeling of the German representatives that they were not free agents: ". . . with the realization that the occupation of Germany by foreign powers subjected the exercise of a right of free national self-determination to severe restrictions . . ."[29] They were, in a sense, excusing themselves for taking full responsibility for the document they were drafting, for their assembly was being held as a consequence of a decision taken by the occupying powers and the document would have to

[28] Among the five were Ernst Reuter, who became mayor of the western sectors of Berlin after the election of December 5, and Jakob Kaiser, former leader of the CDU in the Soviet zone who had fled to the west after being ousted by the Soviet authorities.

[29] This passage did not appear in the final text of the basic law.

be approved by the military governors. Nevertheless, having made these reservations, the delegates at Bonn went ahead with their work of drafting a workable, democratic basic law for a German government. The document which resulted from their labors gave the appearance of being a serious attempt to establish the framework for a political system which, with necessary changes, would outlast the occupation and eventually serve as a constitutional law for all Germany. Thus, while they disclaimed any intention of writing a constitution for Germany, their basic law could stand as a model of the kind of constitution which a democratic Germany, associated with the western powers, might expect to have. It might serve as a potent instrument in the competition between east and west, between totalitarianism and constitutional democracy, for the sympathy and allegiance of the German people.

The Bonn assembly consisted of 65 delegates named by the *Land* parliaments according to the strength of the political parties represented in them. Since those parliaments had been elected some time before, the delegates could not claim to be directly representative of German opinion in 1948 or to have any popular mandate to draft a constitution. Such considerations made them all the more sensitive to public criticism and anxious to avoid offense to German national feeling. No great volume of criticism was evident; on the other hand, they failed to rouse any noticeable popular enthusiasm for their work. The people of Germany appeared to have little genuine interest in the constitution being framed for them.

The Christian Democratic and the Social Democratic parties had 27 delegates each; the remaining eleven were scattered, nine belonging to conservative parties and two to the Communists. The latter took part in the discussions and voting despite their contention that the assembly had no authority to draft a constitution. Although the two big parties tended to dominate the proceedings, the others could not be ignored since they held the balance in case of disagreement. The job of constitution-making consisted principally in the search for compromises between the CDU and the SPD, which were at odds on many issues. Of these the most important concerned the division of powers between the central government and the *Länder*.

According to the draft evolved at Bonn, the *Bundesrepublik Deutschland*, a "democratic and social federal state," would be a true federal state in that powers not expressly granted to the central government were reserved to the *Länder*. In the absence of specific provision to the contrary, federal laws were to be executed by the *Länder*. Moreover, the latter had an important role in the field of federal legislation through the upper house, or *Bundesrat*, whose members were appointed by the *Land* governments. In most matters the *Bundesrat* could be overridden by the lower house, the *Bundestag*, but in certain important matters of finance and administration its concurrence was required.

These were concessions to the CDU viewpoint. They made the new governmental system less centralized than that of Weimar. On the other hand, the powers granted to the central government by the preliminary drafts at Bonn were so extensive as to go far beyond the "letters of advice" in which the three Allied governments had given their views on the application of the London formula of "a federal form of government which adequately protects the rights of the respective states and which at the same time provides for adequate central authority . . ." The central government was given exclusive legislative power in the fields of foreign affairs, citizenship, customs, foreign trade, federal railroads, posts and telecommunications, and federal criminal police. It had priority of legislation over a long list of subjects such as civil and criminal law, public health and welfare, social security, and economics (including mining, industry, trade, and banking). Moreover, on the crucial question of taxation the Bonn draft hardly gave adequate safeguards to the *Länder*. Its provisions tended to place them in a position of financial dependence on the central government which could not but affect the autonomous status granted them by other articles of the constitution.

In general, the Bonn draft provided for a balanced, democratic constitutional system. It contained a detailed bill of rights. It affirmed specifically the doctrine that sovereignty emanates from the people and that the government is responsible to the people. It provided for the separation of powers. As compared to the Weimar constitution, the powers of the president were reduced. The provisions for the exercise of emergency power by the executive were limited and strictly defined, in order to guard against a repetition of the procedure by which the democratic process was subverted under the Weimar constitution.

One novel article in the draft constitution provided that Germany might, by law, transfer sovereign power to international authorities. In order to preserve the peace it might "join a system of collective security; in so doing it will consent to those limitations of its sovereign powers which will bring about and secure a peaceful and lasting order in Europe and among the nations of the world." In this way the German politicians expressed good intentions in the matter of organization for peace, and also their desire to have Germany again playing an active part, as an equal, in international politics.

Overshadowing all the discussions at Bonn was the fact that western Germany was still under foreign occupation. Whatever the delegates wrote into their "basic law" would have to be approved by the three occupying powers. Furthermore, the constitution would go into effect only in conjunction with an occupation statute, which would lay down the limits within which it would operate. The occupation statute, to be agreed upon by the three powers and promulgated by them, would serve as a sort of preliminary peace treaty. Yet the west German government would by no means be a free agent under the statute, by which the three powers would reserve to themselves supreme authority and certain specific powers such as the conduct of foreign relations. Thus certain provisions of the Bonn basic law, drafted as it was in the form of a constitution of an independent state, obviously would be inapplicable during the period in which the statute remained in force. For the Germans, the statute would represent a great advance over the existing situation, in which there was no limitation on the powers of the occupation authorities, but it would not bring the "control period" to an end. The Germans, according to a resolution passed by the Bonn assembly, wanted the occupying powers to reduce their own role to maintaining the security of their occupation forces and protecting western Germany. But the Allies were not prepared to make any such surrender of authority at this stage.

At the same time that the German constitution-makers were meeting at Bonn, the military governors were negotiating the terms of the occupation statute. Until they knew its terms, the Germans could not put their constitution in final form. They had been told in general terms, in July, the powers which would be reserved to the military governors: foreign relations; some control over foreign trade and internal matters affecting foreign trade; controls over the Ruhr, the level of industry, reparation, decartelization and demilitarization; protection of occupation forces and satisfaction of their requirements; measures necessary to ensure observance of the new constitution.[30]

Because of differences among the three occupying powers, it proved no simple matter to draw up the statute. At issue were questions concerning the merger of the three occupation zones, the nature of the combined tripartite authority, and the degree of supervision to be exercised over the new German government. The French, following their consistent policy of maximum Allied control, favored circumscribing quite narrowly the governmental powers granted to the Germans in matters where the Americans and British were willing to grant them greater leeway to run their own affairs. As usual, the three powers had to fight the battle of Germany all over again on each important question. By November, however, negotiations of the military governors had reduced the differences to a few points, and these were submitted to the three governments for settlement on that level.

The military governors, meanwhile, were keeping an eye on the deliberations at Bonn. Without exercising continuing guid-

[30] Office of Military Government for Germany (U.S.), Frankfort, press release, July 1, 1948.

ance, they did on several occasions make known their views when the assembly appeared to be departing from them. Thus at the end of November, reminding the Germans that the Allied objective was "a democratic, decentralized, federal government," they laid down a number of principles to be followed. They dealt, *inter alia*, with the division of powers between the federal and *Land* governments, limitations on the executive power, and the power of an independent judiciary to review federal laws and adjudicate between federal and *Land* authorities. On some points the Bonn draft, in the opinion of the military governors, had already disregarded these principles in going too far in the direction of centralization.

The much-discussed issue of federalism may well have received an undue amount of attention. All three occupying powers and the great majority of Germans agreed that Germany should be a federal state (*Bundesstaat*). Only the Communists were true centralists, and only the Bavarian separatists were true representatives of the concept of loose federation (*Staatenbund*). The interplay of SPD and CDU viewpoints and of British, American and French viewpoints presumably would produce a solution somewhere in the middle ground between the two extremes. Even when solved, it was not certain how long any particular constitutional formula would last if there should develop strong pressure in Germany for its evasion or revision. It would not be easy for outside powers to enforce indefinitely a degree of decentralization that did not correspond to public sentiments, economic conditions and political forces within Germany.

Progress toward the creation of a west German government was falling behind the original time schedule, owing to long party wrangles in the Bonn assembly and persistent differences between Paris, Washington and London on the controls to be retained by the western Allies after the basic law went into effect. The inter-Allied log jam was not broken until early April 1949, when Bevin, Schuman and Acheson, gathered in Washington for the signature of the North Atlantic Treaty, unexpectedly announced that they had also reached agreement on "the whole range of issues now pending in connection with Germany." In addition to approving the London agreements already referred to on plant dismantling, prohibited and restricted industries, and the establishment of an International Ruhr Authority, the three foreign ministers at last found themselves in accord on the text of an occupation statute and of an "agreement on tripartite controls" to regulate the exercise of Allied authority after the fusion of the three western zones and the establishment of the provisional German government.[31]

The occupation statute followed the expected lines in stipulating that "supreme authority" remained with the three governments, whose representatives would continue to exercise direct supervision in such fields as disarmament and demilitarization, industrial and economic controls, foreign affairs, foreign trade and exchange, and respect for the basic law and the *Land* constitutions. The general tone of the document, however, was decidedly liberal. It declared that the three governments desired and intended the German people to "enjoy self-government to the maximum possible degree" consistent with the occupation, and that within the prescribed limits the federal state and the participating *Länder* should have "full legislative, executive and judicial powers in accordance with the Basic Law and with their respective constitutions." Provision was made for a review of the statute, which was much simpler in form than the earlier unagreed drafts, within 12 to 18 months, "in the light of experience with its operation and with a view to extending the jurisdiction of the German authorities." [32]

The trizonal fusion agreement, which was to become effective simultaneously with the inauguration of the provisional German government, provided for the establishment of a three-man Allied high commission, to serve as the "supreme Allied agency of control" in all matters except the strictly military

[31] Agreements were also reached on certain recommendations concerning the German basic law; on postponing action with regard to proposed modifications of the Württemberg-Baden *Land* boundaries; and on the protection of French interests in the Rhenish port of Kehl. Department of State, *Bulletin*, XX, May 1, 1949, 551; May 8, 1949, 589-590.
[32] *Ibid.*, XX, April 17, 1949, 500-501.

functions of the occupation authorities. As a result of concessions by the French, decisions in the high commission would be reached by majority vote, unanimity being required only in regard to modifications of the federal constitution; appeals might, however, be carried to the governmental level in matters concerned with demilitarization, security, reparation and other fields reserved under the occupation statute. Special provisions relating to foreign trade and exchange matters protected the interests of the United States in the event that increased appropriations of American funds should become necessary. Staff personnel of the Allied establishments was to be kept to a minimum "in order to permit the German federal republic to exercise increased responsibilities over domestic affairs and to reduce the burden of occupation costs." An explanatory statement referred to the expectation of the western governments that the exercise of direct controls, except in security matters, would be of a "temporary and self-liquidating nature." [33]

In announcing these decisions the three governments emphasized their desire to apply them in a liberal and conciliatory spirit, to hasten western Germany's democratic progress, and to "encourage and facilitate the closest integration, on a mutually beneficial basis, of the German people under a democratic federal state within the framework of a European association." The German federal republic, they made clear, would be expected to participate in the OEEC as a full and responsible partner in the European Recovery Program, adhering to the Convention for European Economic Cooperation and concluding a bilateral ERP agreement with the United States. Responsibility for supervising the use of American relief and recovery funds made available to the German economy would be entrusted to ECA.[34]

Statements such as these, however welcome in themselves, did not suffice to win for the Washington agreements an enthusiastic reception in Germany, where attention naturally focused on the substantial restrictions which were still to be

[33] *Ibid.*, XX, May 8, 1949, 589-590.
[34] *Ibid.*, XX, April 17, 1949, 499; May 8, 1949, 590.

maintained. In conjunction with other announcements on dismantling, economic controls, and rectifications of the western German frontier,[35] it would have been too much to expect that the projected arrangements would be accepted without protest by German opinion, now increasingly outspoken in its nationalism. A grudging acknowledgment of the occupation statute by the 11 western minister-presidents, calling attention to the "weighty German wishes" which were left "still unfulfilled," cautiously remarked that "the value of the document will . . . be decided through its practical execution."[36]

Paradoxically, nationalist resistance to Allied plans for western Germany had come to center mainly in the Social Democratic party, which was continuing to hold out against any solution of the constitutional issue that would seriously impair the authority of the future central government. During the fortnight that followed announcement of the Washington agreements, prospects for a settlement of the constitutional difficulty seemed to grow daily more remote. The Social Democrats apparently were prepared to give up the whole Bonn experiment if the occupying powers insisted on forcing their views on the assembly. Time was pressing, however, and the western governments were not prepared to wait indefinitely. On April 25 the three military governors met with envoys of the Bonn assembly at Frankfort and gave them to understand that further delay was definitely inadmissible. After six hours of intensive debate, General Clay emerged to announce that all differences between the occupation powers and the Germans and among the Germans themselves had been resolved. The Social Democrats gave way on some of the powers of the proposed central government. The final compromise embodying the changes required by the occupying powers, especially on police and financial matters,

---

[35] A communiqué issued on March 26 announced that a six-power agreement had been reached to effect 31 "minor rectifications" in the German frontier with the Netherlands, Belgium, Luxembourg, the Saar and France. These adjustments, affecting a total area of some 52 square miles and a population of about 13,500 persons, would be subject to confirmation or modification by the terms of the final peace settlement. Department of State, Bulletin, XX, April 3, 1949, 427.

[36] New York Times, April 13, 1949.

represented an attempt to assure the independence of both central and *Land* governments, and seemed to achieve that objective so far as the language of a constitutional law could do so. On May 8, the fourth anniversary of V-E Day, the Bonn assembly adopted the new constitution.

The sense of urgency which enabled the three western governments thus rapidly to bridge both their own and the Germans' long-standing differences owed much to their knowledge of an impending shift in the political strategy of the Soviet Union. Since the Moscow conversations of the preceding summer it had been apparent that the Soviet leaders were deeply worried by the prospective west German government, whose formation they regarded as intimately if not formally linked with the issue of the Berlin blockade. At the end of January Stalin, in answering four questions posed by Kingsbury Smith of the International News Service, had intimated that if the western governments agreed to postpone the creation of a separate west German government pending a meeting of the Council of Foreign Ministers to consider the German problem as a whole, the Soviet Government would see no objection to lifting the Berlin blockade—provided the other powers lifted their own restrictions on transport and trade at the same time.[37]

If four-power discussions were to be renewed in this way, the Soviets unquestionably would spare no effort to secure abandonment of the Allied plans for western Germany; and they might be expected to put forth demagogic proposals for German unification and withdrawal of occupation troops under conditions which would restore to the U.S.S.R. the advantages it had forfeited in Germany during the last two years. The western powers had been in no hurry to place themselves in such a position, in which most of the propaganda advantages would lie with the other side; and the success of the Berlin airlift had enabled them to proceed at leisure with their own arrangements for safeguarding their collective interests in western Germany. Nevertheless they too remained committed to the principle of German unity, and they had made it clear that

[37] *USSR Information Bulletin,* IX, February 11, 1949, 65-66.

they would be ready to discuss any and all aspects of the German problem with the Soviets once the blockade had been lifted. And it now seemed increasingly probable that the Soviet Government, recognizing the failure of the blockade,[38] oppressed by economic difficulties in its own zone of Germany, and faced with a steady consolidation of the entire western world in opposition to its policies, was prepared to do exactly that.

The United States, which was carrying the major burden of the airlift operation, apparently took the initiative in following up Stalin's January statement to the press. In a conversation in February between Dr. Philip C. Jessup and Jacob A. Malik, American and Soviet representatives at the United Nations, the former inquired whether there was any significance in Stalin's failure to mention the much-discussed currency issue in his statement of the conditions under which the blockade might be lifted. A month later Mr. Malik replied that this omission on Stalin's part was "not accidental"; the currency question, though important, was one that could be discussed at a meeting of the Council of Foreign Ministers together with other aspects of the German problem. In response to further inquiries, Malik then stated on March 21 that a reciprocal lifting of trade and transport restrictions (blockade and counterblockade) could take place in advance of a meeting of the Council of Foreign Ministers, provided the date for such a meeting was first agreed upon. This in effect would meet the western conditions as laid down at Paris the previous autumn. Subsequent exchanges, concerning which the British and French were fully informed, served to confirm the Soviet position, which was made public by Tass almost simultaneously with General Clay's announcement at Frankfort that agreement had been reached on the German constitutional issue. The State Department, in turn, declared on April 26 that, although various matters still required clarification, if the Tass statement was correct "the way appears clear

---

[38] On April 15-16, 1949, U.S. and British fliers shattered all records by flying 12,941 tons of supplies into Berlin in 1,398 flights during a single 24-hour period.

for a lifting of the blockade and a meeting of the Council of
Foreign Ministers." [39] The long-delayed treaty for Austria,
under discussion for over two years and most recently by the
Foreign Ministers' deputies in London, was also likely to be
taken up once more by the Council.

The knowledge that four-power conversations on Germany
might be resumed in the near future had given the western
governments ample incentive to hasten their arrangements in
western Germany in preparation for a new trial of diplomatic
skill. The Russians held strong cards and could be expected
to make a powerful appeal to German national sentiment. On
March 19 the People's Council which they sponsored in their
zone approved their previously prepared constitution intended
for all Germany,[40] and followed it with appeals for a meeting
of eastern and western German leaders to discuss unity. Raising of the blockade would itself be a popular measure whose
effect they would seek to reinforce by well-chosen variations on
the theme of German unity. It was true that the western powers
were avowedly working toward the same goal. The west German state, to quote the London agreement of June 1, 1948, was
intended to pave the way to "eventual reestablishment of German unity, at present disrupted." But the western powers could
not simply agree to German unity on any terms, and did not
care to see the kind of reunified Germany that might tread
either the path of Hitler's Reich or that of postwar Hungary,
Rumania and Bulgaria. The further advanced was their own
political creation in western Germany, the better would be their
chances of extending a similar pattern to all Germany.

The political leaders in western Germany for the time being
had unequivocally accepted the course of cooperation with the
western powers. In dealing with them they had done their best
to protect German interests as they saw them, but, regarding
Russia as the greatest threat to their nation, they had felt that

[39] *New York Times,* April 26, 27, 1949. A four-power communiqué issued on
May 5 announced that the blockade and counterblockade would be lifted on
May 12 and that the Council of Foreign Ministers would convene in Paris on
May 23.
[40] See above, p. 82.

permanent German interests demanded a western orientation. In this they were following, consciously or not, the advice given by Admiral Dönitz in a speech made at the time of surrender: "Land that was German for a thousand years has now fallen into Russian hands. Therefore our political line is plain. We must go along with the western powers and work with them in the occupied territories in the west, for only by working with them can we have hopes of later retrieving our land from the Russians . . . Most important, we must keep a zealous watch over the greatest boon given to us by National Socialism— our unity." [41]

Recovery of German unity and independence of action were, indeed, fixed objectives for which practically all German leaders could be counted upon to strive, whether the talk was of democracy, of federation, of European union, or of Christian civilization. The partition of the country, brought about by the victorious Allies, was still the major aspect of the German problem. In its anxiety to end this condition, there was danger that German opinion would prove receptive to Soviet proposals which might lay insufficient stress on the necessity for democratic safeguards. But unless partition could be terminated, and terminated in a manner consistent with the legitimate security interests of all of the wartime Allies, it was difficult to see how any stable settlement could be found for Germany and for Europe.

[41] Quoted in *The Times,* of London, August 17, 1948.

CHAPTER THIRTEEN

DEFENSE OF THE WEST

THE Marshall plan had been America's way of recognizing that Europe could not find its way back to economic health unassisted and that it was in the interest of the United States to encourage, guide, and, within reasonable limits, support Europe's recovery effort. The North Atlantic Treaty signed on April 4, 1949 constituted the American answer to a parallel problem in the field of military security, where the uneven development of old-world power relationships had left the western European nations, America's bulwark of defense in two world wars, too weak to withstand an attack by the one strong military power remaining on the continent of Europe. Both problems were interrelated because it was the practice of that one power, the Soviet Union, to use the class struggle and the Communist parties of other countries as instrumentalities of what Dean Acheson once called its "aggressive and expanding" foreign policy. Economic stagnation and hardship weakened the fabric of European life and aided these parties in their work of social and political disruption. At the same time, the fear of Soviet aggression and Communist revolution held back the spirit of optimism and drive essential to economic recovery.

That the United States could not afford to disinterest itself in these conditions was fully recognized by the leaders of American foreign policy and, in the abstract at least, by the American public. The massive new commitments they entailed for the United States were, in the last analysis, no more than commensurate with the growth of America's position and influence in the international community. The urgent and self-evident necessities of the postwar era were inexorably outmoding the American tradition of aloofness toward foreign affairs and invigorating the parallel tradition which, ever since the early days of the Republic, had seen the most effectual safeguard for American freedom in resistance to hostile encroachments beyond our frontiers.

But American support of western Europe, though its necessity was widely understood, was never conceived as a unilateral American responsibility. The aim of the United States in both the economic and military fields was to help the peoples of western Europe to help themselves, encouraging them to find cooperative solutions of their own problems and providing only such aid as was essential to make their own efforts effective. This concept reflected not only a keen understanding of American public psychology but also an awareness that American resources were not unlimited and a conviction that American cooperation with western Europe was, in the fullest sense, a matter of mutual interest.

Not unnaturally, Americans sometimes tended to lay more stress on the virtues of European cooperation as such than on the magnitude of the American aid it presupposed. Part of the American enthusiasm for European political and economic "integration" sprang from the desire to find a magic formula that would somehow reduce the burdens to be assumed by the United States. It was easy to overlook the fact that even the most efficient and public-spirited use of western Europe's resources over the next several years would leave a large gap that only the United States could fill.

Anxiety to limit the scale of American efforts in relation to western Europe was particularly evident in Congress, whose zeal in whittling down the details of important foreign policy legislation occasionally threatened to compromise the policy itself. Isolationism, if discredited as a distinct political philosophy, continued to assert itself vigorously as a restraining influence on the acts of the Administration. Europeans were forced again and again to ask themselves how much reliance could be placed on a government whose convictions appeared, at best, to be imperfectly reflected in Congress and the country. Inevitably their misgivings were multiplied during the latter half of 1948 by the imminence of a presidential election and the likelihood that the next Administration would be more responsive to isolationist sentiment than its predecessor.

1. The Presidential Election

As the United States has become more deeply involved in world affairs, its international relations have been increasingly affected by the vagaries and uncertainties attendant on each new presidential election. At home, every political move is weighed in relation to its effect on the voters, creating an inevitable tendency on the part of both the Administration and the opposition candidate to shun unpopular courses and encourage hopes which may be inconsistent with the long-term national interest. Partisan attacks on the conduct of foreign relations weaken the American hand in current international negotiations. Abroad, there is fevered speculation on the chances and intentions of the rival candidates, and uncertainty whether the American policies of today may not be repudiated tomorrow.

These features were present in 1948 as in former election years. As in the recent wartime elections, however, they were tempered by the existence of a measure of fundamental agreement between the two major parties, expressed in the so-called bipartisan foreign policy, which limited the scope of debate and the potential fluctuations of national policy. Events since V-J Day, with the emergence of Soviet expansionism as the chief threat to American interests, had if anything widened the area of genuine agreement between the two parties. The Republicans were already on record as supporting the major Administration policies regarding Europe and the Soviet Union. It was far from certain, however, what a Republican Administration would mean concretely in terms of ERP, military aid to western Europe, international trade, and the relative emphasis given to Europe and the Far East.

The bipartisan principle in foreign policy was not, and in the nature of American politics could not be, expressed in any formal commitment binding on either side. In certain important areas of foreign relations, moreover, the bipartisan approach found little or no application. American policy in occupied areas, although dependent on Congress for funds, had remained largely a military responsibility. In general, Republican leaders were not consulted on the problem of Palestine or on China; in regard to Latin America, Republican spokesmen complained that although their party had first suggested the Rio pact they were not even allowed a voice in hemisphere economic policy. Despite these exceptions, however, Senator Vandenberg declared in the course of the 1948 campaign that bipartisanship in foreign affairs did "apply to most contemporary principles"; and with respect to other issues Republican campaign criticism was confined largely to the plane of generalities.[1]

It was characteristic of this lack of any vital disagreement on foreign affairs that the bipartisan concept itself furnished one of the main debating points of the campaign, with each party claiming the credit for its development and accusing the other of grossly violating its spirit.[2] Much campaign oratory was devoted to attempts to define the bipartisan "neutral" area in a manner advantageous to one side or the other. Early in the summer Governor Dewey indicated that in attacking the Administration he would accord special treatment to those issues on which Republican leaders had been consulted. Insisting on his right to discuss foreign policy problems in broad terms, he rejected Truman's contention that international problems subject to multilateral negotiation should not be made the subject of unilateral proposals. The President himself repeatedly accused his opponent of disappointing his hope that foreign policy would not become a campaign issue, of tearing off the bipartisan mask to reveal the "ugly partisan passion beneath,"

[1] Blair Bolles, "Bipartisanship in American Foreign Policy," *Foreign Policy Reports*, XXIV, January 1, 1949, 192.
[2] The Democratic platform made no reference to the bipartisan foreign policy. The Republican platform declared: "We are proud of the part the Republicans have taken in those limited areas of foreign policy in which they have been permitted to participate. We shall invite the minority party to join us under the next Republican Administration in stopping partisan politics at the water's edge." *New York Times*, June 23, 1948.

and indiscriminately "dragging American foreign policy into party politics." [3]

In reality, Republican criticism on foreign issues was highly selective. Soviet-U.S. relations, the Italian colonies and China were almost the only specific foreign policy problems on which Governor Dewey took a clear-cut and independent stand. Without disputing the Administration's basic objectives, Republican spokesmen denounced what they chose to call the long course of appeasement of the U.S.S.R. "In a series of easy victories," said Dewey in his Salt Lake City speech, "the Soviet achieved domination of the Baltic countries, the Balkans, Poland, Czechoslovakia. Now she's moved on to similar conquests in the Far East. It serves no purpose to review the concessions made by our Government to the Soviet in Manchuria and in Northern China at the expense of the Chinese people and without even consulting them. These things are done. The tragedies have occurred. Month after month, the area of human freedom has been pressed back and back, as communism marched on and on. The question is: What lies ahead?" [4]

In August Governor Dewey told a group of Italian-Americans that he favored the restoration of Italy's former colonies under a United Nations trusteeship. This statement, closer to the Soviet stand than to the American position then being maintained in discussions by the deputies of the Big Four Foreign Ministers, incurred a sharp presidential reproof. On China, Dewey repeatedly and unequivocally attacked the Administration policy toward the Nationalist government as "niggardly and faltering and inconsistent and blundering to the point of tragedy." [5] Here he was following a clear-cut Republican line developed in the debates on the foreign aid program. The fact that the later stages of the electoral campaign coincided with the crumbling of the Chinese Nationalist position in Manchuria did not, however, prompt the Administration either to defend

[3] Speech at St. Paul (October 13), statement (October 24), and speech at Brooklyn (October 29), *New York Times,* October 14, 25, 30, 1948.
[4] *New York Times,* October 1, 1948.
[5] *New York Times,* June 27, 1948.

or to modify its previous China policy. For the Democrats China apparently had no significance as a campaign issue.

It was the Administration's actual conduct of foreign relations, as distinguished from its choice of objectives, that gave the Republicans their major ground for criticism. On May 5, weeks before his nomination, Dewey declared in a speech at Eugene, Oregon: "The real trouble with our national Administration, the real reason it has failed in its leadership for peace—is not that it has so many bad policies. It has just had no policy at all. In this period of grave crisis, we need, more than anything else, a real, a firm and intelligent leadership in foreign affairs in order to start rebuilding a tottering and shaky peace." It was on this issue also that Senator Vandenberg mainly dwelt when he was persuaded to make a campaign broadcast on October 4. The chief Republican architect of the bipartisan foreign policy lamented "past lapses" on the part of the Administration— "such lapses as the failure to make our peace aims just as much matters of contract at the time as we did our war aims; such lapses, now bitterly apparent, as the fateful concessions to Stalin at Yalta and Potsdam . . ."

An unexpected opportunity for Republican criticism in this vein was presented in the last weeks of the campaign by the President's abortive plan to send Chief Justice Fred M. Vinson to Moscow as a personal envoy. According to press reports which appeared on October 8, the Chief Executive had personally planned this dramatic move in the hope of persuading the Soviets to lift the blockade of Berlin, but had postponed action when it was pointed out to him that the mission would undercut the negotiations then being conducted jointly by the three western powers in the Security Council. Following Secretary Marshall's return to Washington the next day, the President issued a statement indicating that his idea—prompted by concern not over Berlin but over the Soviet attitude on the atomic energy problem—had been dropped after the Secretary had convinced him in a transatlantic telephone conversation of "the possibilities of misunderstanding to which any unilateral action, however desirable otherwise, could lead at present." The Secretary likewise made public a statement in which he deplored reports that the incident betokened a "split" between the President and himself.

To Republican strategists the Vinson project, on which no Republican had been consulted, appeared as made-to-order confirmation of all they had been saying about the Administration's irresolution and ineptitude. Governor Dewey and his advisers, however, decided—not unostentatiously—to treat the incident on a high plane of national responsibility. This attitude was calculated to reassure the world of America's fundamental unity and determination to fulfill its commitments, and also to place the Republican candidate in a posture of dignified and responsible statesmanship which would make his opponent look all the more vacillating and incompetent. Dewey immediately issued a statement on behalf of "the people of America" stressing their united support of their U.N. delegation and their "friends of the free world." At no time did he refer directly to the Vinson affair in his campaign utterances. His personal and highly uncomplimentary opinions on the subject, however, were made abundantly available to the newspapermen covering his campaign.

President Truman undertook to justify his action by insisting that the supreme responsibilities of the President, extending to "the ultimate realities—the final consequences of war and peace," could not be confined within the formal and fallible channels of conventional diplomacy.[6] It may be that his vigorous speeches on this theme played a part in repairing the damage of an incident which many believed had shattered even the remotest possibility of his election. It may be that the electorate at large was less disturbed by the contretemps than were persons immediately concerned with foreign affairs. Conceivably the President's manifest good will and desire for peace even helped to turn the tide in his favor.

In Paris, where both General Assembly and Security Council were in session, the Vinson affair was a blow to the prestige and authority of the U.S. delegation, then endeavoring to

[6] Miami speech, October 18. Brooklyn speech, October 29, 1948.

attract all possible support for firm policies toward the Soviet Union. In the last weeks before the election the delegation's position became even more difficult because of the general expectation of a change in administration, and on many problems the Assembly merely marked time awaiting the outcome. The President's stand on Palestine once again caused deep discomfiture to his foreign policy aides when, a week before the election, he undertook to reaffirm his support of the General Assembly's partition resolution after the Secretary of State had publicly endorsed the Bernadotte partition plan, which was less favorable to Israel.[7] Finally, Truman provided further embarrassment for the ranking Republican member of the delegation, John Foster Dulles, when in his Chicago speech of October 25 he attacked the backers of the Republican party as "reactionary" and, by implication, fascist, the very epithets with which Vyshinsky and his colleagues were denouncing Dulles at the Assembly.

The unwillingness of the Republicans to challenge the essentials of American foreign policy as developed by the Democratic Administration meant that really fundamental criticism could come only from minority political groups. It was indicative of the degree to which relations with the Soviet Union had come to dominate American thinking that the situation admitted of only one well-defined minority viewpoint, which was indistinguishable from that of the U.S.S.R. and the world Communist movement.[8] The function of representing the Soviet view on world affairs devolved upon the small Communist party of the United States and upon a heterogeneous assemblage of dissident Democrats, idealists, pacifists, radicals and malcontents united in the new Progressive party of Henry A. Wallace. Although this group had an independent domestic program, its analysis of the international situation did not differ markedly from that of the Communists, and its candidate was un-

---

[7] See above, p. 393.
[8] The Socialist party leader, Norman Thomas, though critical of the Administration's handling of foreign policy, did not dispute its identification of the Soviet Union as the main threat to peace and democracy.

equivocally endorsed by the Communist party, which refrained from entering a candidate of its own. The platform adopted by the Progressive party contained what amounted to a blanket condemnation of the existing, foreign policy of the United States. Among other drastic reversals it called for repudiation of the Truman doctrine and the Marshall plan, abandonment of the "inter-American military program," early peace treaties with Germany and Japan, Big Four control of the Ruhr, destruction of existing stocks of atomic bombs, abandonment of "military bases designed to encircle and intimidate other nations," and the opening of direct negotiations with the U.S.S.R. in the spirit of the Wallace-Stalin letters of the preceding spring.[9]

During the campaign there were many indications that their close association with the Communists was proving an embarrassment to the Progressive leaders and to many of the rank and file, whose enthusiasm seemed to flag as November 2 approached. Nevertheless the small final vote rolled up by the Wallace party was not the least of the surprises of the election. In contrast to its original declared hope of polling up to 10 million votes, the final tabulation showed a Wallace vote of only 1,157,000, nearly half of which was polled in New York State. While this overwhelming rejection did not in itself signify a national endorsement of the bipartisan foreign policy, it showed clearly that the American people found no merit in the program urged by that policy's chief domestic and foreign critics.

For different reasons, the Republicans also fell short of realizing their pre-November expectations. Unable or unwilling to attempt a frontal assault on foreign policy and unable to sell the electorate on their domestic program, they failed to capture the Presidency and lost their control of both the Senate and the House. Harry S. Truman, handicapped by the manifold shortcomings of his own record and by the competition of the Progressives on the left and of bolting Southern Democrats on the right, upset every calculation except his own by capturing 28

[9] See above, p. 27. Text of platform draft and amendments in *New York Times,* July 25, 26, 1948.

States and 24,104,836 votes to Dewey's 16 States and 21,969,-
500 votes. In Congress the Democrats gained control of 54
Senate seats to 42 for the Republicans, and in the House they
secured a majority of better than three to two.

Amazement at Truman's victory was world-wide. In western
Europe, and in Israel, relief and encouragement were the prevailing reaction. European Socialists were heartened by the decisive role of American labor in the election, liberals by the
prospect of increased continuity and stability in Washington's
policies. There was relief that there would be no "interregnum"
and no shift in leadership. Everywhere except on the extreme
left there was unmistakable satisfaction at the disappearance of
the supposed danger of an American retreat from Europe.
One striking feature of the European comment was the post-
humous attention bestowed on the Vinson project, especially
in France, where several organs of the left and center expressed
interest in seeing it revived. By contrast with western Europe,
the reaction in the Arab states and in Kuomintang China, where
officials had hoped for better things at the hands of the Republicans, was one of scarcely concealed dismay.

More problematical was the response of the Soviet Union.
During the campaign Soviet propaganda, while clearly anticipating a Dewey victory, had minimized the differences between Republicans and Democrats—both equally tarred with
the imperialist brush—to concentrate its favors on the Progressive party as the one refuge of peace-loving and democratic
American voters. The defeat of Dewey and the overwhelming
repudiation of Wallace confronted the Kremlin with a major
problem in rationalization and readjustment. Foreign Minister
Molotov produced the answer on November 6 in his address
marking the thirty-first anniversary of the Bolshevik Revolution: "The defeat of the Republican party and of Dewey, who
came to the elections with an openly reactionary and most
aggressive program, has shown that the majority of the American people reject that program." In other words, the will to
peace which the Soviets had hitherto imputed exclusively to the
Wallace faction had miraculously transferred itself to the mil-

lions of voters whose choice had fallen on the author of the Truman doctrine and of American rearmament. Here, in germ, was the concept which was to guide Soviet political warfare during the winter of 1948–49 and to inspire the various "peace offensives" with which the Soviet Union sought to disrupt and check the growing consolidation of the western world.

For Americans and foreigners alike, November 2 brought a much-needed clarification of the U.S. position. While reasons of domestic policy probably were responsible for the Democratic victory, it could not but be taken as an endorsement of the Truman foreign policy as well, and would not be without its effect in the foreign field. Many of the die-hard isolationists had been defeated. The popular mandate seemed to assure the continuance of active American participation in world affairs, full support of ERP, and early conclusion of the negotiations for a North Atlantic treaty. The advent of a Democratic Congress meant the probable revival of the Trade Agreements program in its original form and a better chance for U.S. acceptance of the International Trade Organization. For all practical purposes the election seemed to eliminate the possibility that further aid would be extended to Nationalist China. Likewise excluded—if, indeed, it had ever been a practical possibility— was any radically new approach to the central problem of American-Soviet relations. Dean Acheson, designated to succeed General Marshall at the outset of the new Administration, had little difficulty in convincing the Senate that there would be no "appeasement" of the U.S.S.R. while he was Secretary of State.

Doubts on this score were even more difficult to entertain after the President's solemn rededication to the ideals of social justice and advancement of all peoples in his inaugural address of January 20, 1949. Following a strong condemnation of the "false philosophy" of Communism as the major challenge to world order, the President charted four major courses of American action for the pursuit of peace and freedom in the coming years: (1) unfaltering support of the United Nations, (2) continuation of the program for world economic recovery, (3) strengthening of freedom-loving nations against the dangers of aggression, and (4) "a bold new program for making the benefits of our scientific advances and industrial progress available for the improvement and growth of under-developed areas." Three of these points represented the continuance of policies already well established; the significance of the fourth, which immediately gave rise to much speculation, could become apparent only after due analysis and discussion of its possibilities and implications.

As was appropriate on an occasion of national solemnity, the President made no reference to party politics or to the future role envisaged for the Republican party in foreign affairs. There were indications that the Administration might feel itself under less obligation than in the past to seek Republican counsel and assistance. The election of Democratic majorities in both houses of Congress appeared to lessen the Administration's dependence on Republican legislative backing. The reduction from six to five of the minority representation on the Senate Foreign Relations Committee early in January was characterized by Republican leaders as a body blow to the concept of bipartisanship.

On the other hand, there were weighty reasons for continuing a practice which had proved its value time and again in earlier Congresses irrespective of party control. Apart from the evident need for maintaining a high degree of national unity on major foreign issues, the absence of party discipline in Congress set a high value on the cooperation of at least a portion of the Republican legislators. A further reason for maintaining the existing bipartisan relationship lay in the practical wisdom and accumulated experience of such men as Dulles and Vandenberg. The President's appointment of the former to head the American delegation to the General Assembly in the absence of Secretary Marshall indicated that these assets would not be lightly discarded. On the whole it appeared likely that bipartisanship would continue, not as a formalized institutional arrangement but as the practical expression of a real community of views on the fundamental issues of American foreign relations.

2. ERP Enters the Second Year

"We can now say with assurance that Europe is through the first phase of its economic recovery. In the months ahead, Europe must tackle the more difficult problem of making major readjustments which break away from its traditional, and now inadequate, ways of paying its way in the world." With these words, Paul Hoffman summarized his justification of ECA's first year of operations and its request for funds for another year.[10] As indications of recovery he pointed to the fact that industrial production in the participating countries in 1948 was 14 percent higher than in 1947 and agricultural production 20 percent higher. However, 1947 had been a bad crop year and the level of agricultural production was still below prewar, whereas the output of manufactured goods had reached the prewar level for the ERP area as a whole and was higher than that if western Germany was excluded from the comparison. Electric power production, railway traffic, exports and other forms of economic activity also showed considerable increases.

American aid was, of course, not the main driving force in the western European economy. The funds supplied by ECA probably equaled about 5 percent of the national income of the participating countries as a group. This was, however, aid of a strategic kind the value of which greatly exceeded the arithmetical measure: it supplied dollars, which the Europeans might otherwise not have been able to get at all, and at best only with a cut in their living standards; and with the dollars they were able to get commodities without which there would have been serious gaps and breaks in the productive process so that not 5 percent, but some multiple of it, would have been lost. Emphasizing the uncertainty of any forecasts, Hoffman

---

[10] *Hearings* before the Senate Committee on Foreign Relations, 81st Congress, 1st Session, on S. 833 (Extension of European Recovery) (Washington, 1949), 11. Subsequent quotations are taken from Hoffman's initial statement at these hearings.

pointed out to the Congressmen that ECA had made it a practice to cut European estimates of the dollar aid they would need in any given period. Accordingly, he emphasized, he was asking for less money in the fiscal year 1950 than ECA had spent the year before.

Looking at Europe's position in the world, Hoffman pointed to a satisfying improvement in the foreign trade of the participating countries. Britain's 1948 exports were 25 percent higher than in 1947, those of the Benelux countries about 30 percent higher, and Italy's foreign sales had increased by half. These were better than average performances; the group as a whole, excluding western Germany, had exported about 20 percent more in 1948 than in the previous year. "In this current fiscal year, the earnings of the ERP countries on exports and 'invisibles' such as income from the tourist trade, will probably pay for a little more than half of the imports they need from the outside world. In the calendar year 1947, these earnings paid for only 40 percent of imports from the outside. As European production and exports have gone up, Europe's degree of dependence on us for assistance has diminished."

Hoffman warned against misinterpretation of the pessimistic conclusions of the OEEC's *Interim Report*.[11] It was, he said, "the most helpful appraisal of the obstacles that face Europe . . ." The $3 billion balance-of-payments deficit mentioned for 1952 "was not a forecast of future defeat, but a diagnosis of present weaknesses for which the remedy is to be found in cooperative readjustments." Its purpose was to find ways to avoid running that deficit. The conclusion he drew from the report was that "this is the time to hit hard for European recovery—time for the Europeans to take the drastic and sometimes painful steps necessary for real recovery, time for the United States to back their efforts to the full." The American purpose in doing this was not just to fill a gap in Europe's balance of payments; that was only a means to a broader end: "that the free nations of Europe should, through their own efforts, with substantial help from us, attain a standard of living

[11] See above, p. 178.

that is not just barely enough to sustain life but high enough to give people an incentive to work, live, and progress as free men."

While stressing the fact that ECA was an economic agency, Hoffman did not ignore the political effects of American aid to Europe. At the beginning of his statement to Congress he referred to the Mindszenty case and said that without the Marshall Plan "similar events might now be taking place in several other countries of Europe. Politically, it is beyond doubt that the ERP already has greatly strengthened the forces of freedom in Europe."

Political considerations of this sort played a great part in the Congressional debate on renewing the Marshall plan, from Connally's opening speech on. Though the Senate debated for over two weeks there was no really strong opposition to extending the ECA for another year, at least in principle. Those who might be suspected of opposing the whole idea of aid to Europe tended to attack particular features of the first year's activity, often at considerable length. Financing British socialism, building up foreign competition for American business, British trade with eastern Europe, impending "national bankruptcy" for the United States, skepticism whether ERP would end in 1952 were some of the themes of these critics. The most serious threat to the Administration's program, however, came from the attempt to reduce the authorization of funds for the year's activities. Taft proposed a 10 percent cut in the authorization for fiscal 1950, from $4.28 to $3.852 billion.[12] He challenged the idea that a specific amount of money was needed to do the job and argued the need for general cuts to avoid a deficit in the national budget. His amendment was defeated, 54 to 23, in a vote which later proved to have been only a temporary setback for the economy advocates.

Fulbright again tried, unsuccessfully as he had the year before, to strengthen the bill's language with regard to European unification. Many other changes were proposed, mostly with a view to attaching more conditions to aid. Most were rejected,

[12] And of the three-month interim appropriation from $1.15 to $1.035 billion.

but a number of changes were made in the Act. On April 8 the bill passed the Senate 70 to 7,[13] with 19 not voting. Under a rule limiting debate the House spent only three days on the bill, passing it 354 to 49 on April 12. In capsule form the debate and proposed amendments largely repeated those of the Senate. A one-day conference session was needed to eliminate the differences in the House and Senate versions. Both houses accepted the conference report by voice votes on April 14 and the President signed the bill on the 19th. The new law ensured another 15 months of Marshall aid, changed some of the rules, and put additional responsibilities on the Administrator.[14] But another hurdle lay ahead—the appropriation—which threatened to offer as much difficulty in 1949 as it had the year before.

3. Development of the Brussels Union

The cooperation of 16 European governments and two occupied areas in the OEEC was but one expression of the overall trend toward closer association in western Europe during 1948 and 1949. Stimulated on the one hand by unmistakable signs of American interest and on the other by recurrent manifestations of Soviet and Communist aggressiveness, the parliamentary democracies of western Europe were displaying on various fronts an unprecedented determination to seek in unity the strength which they could no longer hope to possess individually. Britain, France and the Benelux nations pushed forward with the implementation of the "western union" established by the Brussels treaty of March 17, 1948. Responding to the initiative of the various groups that had organized the Hague Congress,[15] they also developed plans for a wider political association of European states to be known as the "Council of Europe." In the military field the same governments worked out plans and institutions for common defense and joined with the United States and Canada to lay the groundwork for a

---

[13] Butler, Capehart, Ellender, Jenner, Kem, Langer and Wherry. Johnston (S. C.), Malone, Taylor, Williams and Byrd were announced as being against it.
[14] Some of these changes are mentioned on pp. 164 and 246-248 above.
[15] See above, pp. 56-58.

security system, within the framework of the U.N. Charter, embracing the entire North Atlantic area.

The Brussels treaty had expressed the intention of the five Western Union governments to coordinate their efforts not only in the sphere of collective military defense but also in a wide variety of economic, social and cultural fields. To this end it provided for the establishment of various councils and other machinery which the signatory countries immediately set to work to develop. The initial meeting of Western Union foreign ministers in Paris on April 17, 1948, decided on the establishment of the main coordinating organs: a secretariat and Permanent Committee of diplomatic representatives in London, and a Consultative Council, consisting of the five ministers for foreign affairs, which would meet successively in each of the western European capitals at least once a quarter. Provision was also made for meetings of the five defense ministers at London, where a Chiefs of Staff Committee, a permanent Military Committee and other organs were established, and for periodic gatherings of economic, social and cultural ministers or experts and the establishment of appropriate committees in these fields.

While the five ministers for foreign affairs used the meetings of the Consultative Council both for organizational business and for discussions of such wide-reaching issues as the Berlin situation, the question of a European parliament or council, and the proposed North Atlantic treaty, the various subsidiary bodies concentrated on the detailed work of converting Western Union from abstract principle into reality. The financial and economic relations among the five governments were too intimately involved with their participation in the OEEC to be susceptible of completely independent planning, but a series of measures looking toward intensified commercial exchanges and tourist trade among the Brussels nations were worked out for approval by the Consultative Council at its meeting in July 1948. In October a special committee of experts was set up to study the economic and financial questions connected with the organization of western Europe's defense. In the social and cultural field the Consultative Council decided not to set up special machinery but to promote intensified relations among existing cultural and educational organizations, recommend the conclusion of bilateral social security conventions as a preliminary to eventual multilateral agreements, and establish expert committees on public health, manpower, and labor conditions.

On the crucial task of creating a unified military organization enough progress had been accomplished to permit a public announcement in the early autumn. The policy on which the five defense ministers had then agreed, in the presence of American and Canadian observers, was aimed, to quote the official communiqué, at assuring the security of the five powers *as a group* within the framework of the Brussels Treaty and the U.N. Charter. A permanent organization, comprising elements of a unified ground, air, and naval command under a permanent military president, was being set up to implement this policy, deal with procurement and supply matters, and study the technical and tactical problems involved in the defense of western Europe.

Field Marshal Montgomery of Alamein was designated military president; General Jean de Lattre de Tassigny was appointed as ground commander-in-chief, Air Marshal James Robb as air commander-in-chief, and Vice Admiral Robert Jaujard as flag officer, western Europe. Dutch, Belgian and Luxembourg staff officers were integrated into the general staff structure. It was officially emphasized that an integrated procurement program would be worked out, taking account of the special economic capabilities of each of the participating countries.[16] During the following months the appearance at Fontainebleau of a western European staff headquarters, responsible through Montgomery to the Western Union Chiefs of Staff Committee in London, and the invention of the name "Uniforce" bore witness to the concrete progress being accom-

[16] Press interview of Raoul de Fraiteur, Belgian Minister of National Defense, October 4, 1948 (*Chronique de Politique Étrangère*, I, November 1948, 15, 17).

plished in this new experiment in combined military planning.
It was recognized from the outset that no plan for the collective defense of western Europe in the next few years could
succeed without the strong backing of the United States, both
as a source of large quantities of up-to-date military equipment
and, in the final resort, as a military ally. Strategic planning on
behalf of the Western Union was bound to be somewhat
academic as long as the American position remained unclari-
fied; yet it was essential to make a start if only to convince
American opinion that western Europe was seriously bent on
applying principles of "self-help and mutual aid" in the military field. For the time being the United States made no commitment but displayed its sympathetic interest by assignment
of high-ranking military "observers" who participated actively
in the discussions of the Western Union military organs. Meanwhile, as an augury of more concrete American assistance to
come, informal conversations on a North Atlantic defense
treaty were opened in Washington in July 1948, attended by
representatives of the Brussels powers and Canada.

For obvious reasons no details of the military staff planning
at London and Fontainebleau were made public. The elements
of the problem, however, were clear. The only conceivable objective of any joint military action by the Brussels powers under
existing circumstances would be the attempt to prevent the
Soviet Union from overrunning western Europe in case of
hostilities. Planning to this end involved, fundamentally, ascer-
taining the extent of western Europe's presently or potentially
available resources in manpower and matériel and devising the
most effective methods for their use, bearing in mind the influence of geography and terrain and the presumed intentions of
the Soviet Union and the United States.

Immediately available force in western Europe was clearly
inadequate for effective defense. A program for training and
equipping larger forces over the next few years would not
only present serious financial problems but also necessitate
a difficult choice between considerations of military security and
the need for continued full production in the interests of the

common recovery effort. The possibility of drawing on the reserves of manpower and industrial capacity in western Germany was one that for political reasons could not be seriously considered at this stage.

The inadequacy of available force, in turn, would largely determine the strategic plan for using what little could be brought to bear. From a political point of view the concept of a defense of the entire territorial area of western Europe, based on or beyond the Rhine, seemed the only one from which the war-weary peoples of western Europe, uncertain but fearful of the destructive potentialities of modern warfare, could derive any of the feeling of confidence so essential to general recovery. From a military point of view, however, there seemed to be no prospect that the Rhine could be held at present, even with the assistance of the small American forces stationed in Germany.

Uncertainty and apprehension on this point were apparent during the latter half of 1948, when fear of war in Europe was at its height. Partly because of the prominent role assigned to British officers in the new military organization, it was widely believed that the Western Union strategy was of British or American origin and envisaged a defense based not on the Rhine but on the Channel and perhaps the Pyrenees—in other words, that France and probably the Low Countries would be thrown open to a new enemy occupation and the defense of Europe conducted from London. General de Gaulle sharply criticized the new military arrangements on this ground in a press conference on October 1.[17]

Although no American commitment could yet be expected, signs of American interest were sufficiently numerous during the winter of 1948–49 to restore a measure of plausibility to the concept of a defense on the Rhine or even an eventual advance beyond the Rhine. In November Marshal Montgomery outlined his preliminary defense plans to the British, American and French commanders in Germany, and American Secretary of Defense Forrestal held "casual" discussions of western Eu-

[17] New York Times, October 2-4, 1948; cf. Chronique de Politique Étrangère, I, November 1948, 18-20.

ropean defense problems with the highest British military authorities. In December United States observers were attached to the various sections of Montgomery's new headquarters at Fontainebleau, and conversations between American and western European military men were intensified on various levels. In his first report as Secretary of Defense, issued December 29, Forrestal spoke of "the military self-reliance of Western Europe" as a question that "will have to be dealt with in decisive fashion by the United States in the coming months," and in such a way as to show "that we intend to follow through the actions involved in the European Recovery Act." [18]

The negotiations looking toward a North Atlantic security pact had meanwhile regained sufficient momentum to justify the hope that western Europe's frail defensive structure would never have to stand alone against the full impact of a Soviet onslaught. The efficacy of the North Atlantic pact, however, would depend less on the precise wording of its provisions than upon the response of the American people to the situation that was bringing it into being. Unless Americans were convinced that the collective defense of western Europe was both necessary to their own security and realistically possible, they would be loath to assume the risks and burdens attendant on their participation in it. In making up their minds Americans would be influenced by numerous factors outside the military realm. Not least important would be their judgment of western Europe's moral and spiritual vitality as it revealed itself in efforts toward cooperative solution of common problems, and particularly in the development of broader forms of political and economic association.

4. The Council of Europe

The various steps toward closer association among the nations of western Europe during 1948 were taken to the accompaniment of unceasing encouragement and exhortation from across the Atlantic. Desire for western European "integration"

[18] *First Report of the Secretary of Defense* (Washington, 1948), 13-14.

was nowhere keener, or less troubled by a realization of its practical difficulties, than in the United States. The prospective refashioning of even a portion of the European "crazy-quilt" into a broadly consolidated, geographically extensive and politically homogeneous union was well suited to capture the imagination of American legislators, diplomatic officials, and wide sections of the public. Some Americans laid primary stress on the prospect that European integration would eliminate the nationalistic rivalries which had so often been a cause of war in the past; others were more attracted by the concept of an extensive free-trade area or of a third great power center emerging in western Europe to discourage Soviet aggression and supersede the present direct confrontation of the U.S. and the U.S.S.R. Not a few looked upon a western European union as one link in an eventual globe-girdling chain of security systems and hoped that it would exert a magnetic attraction on countries behind the iron curtain. Almost all saw in unity a powerful guarantee of peace. The few who questioned the timeliness, feasibility, or long-run expediency of European union were but scattered voices without noticeable influence.

The assumption that Europe was a well-defined and homogeneous entity whose common cultural, economic and political interests called for fuller institutional expression was implicit in Secretary Marshall's Harvard speech of June 1947 and in virtually all major American policy pronouncements thereafter. "We welcome and encourage the sturdy progress toward unity in western Europe," said the Republican party's 1948 campaign platform. "We pledge continued support of . . . the developing Western European Union," echoed the Democratic platform. The State Department announced on August 27, 1948: "As stated in the preamble of the Economic Cooperation Act, this Government strongly favors the progressively closer integration of the free nations of western Europe. We believe that the world of today requires the taking of steps, which before the war would have seemed beyond the range of practical politics." Governor Dewey declared on September 30 that "the program of European aid . . . must not be just relief. We shall use it as a means for pushing, and if I may say so, prodding and encouraging the nations of western Europe toward the goal of European union . . ." [19] And in November John Foster Dulles, in an address before the American Club of Paris which was cleared with the State Department, emphasized the desire of the American people to see a Europe so united that it "will no longer be dependent but strong and free for itself and a contributor of strength and inspiration to all the world." [20]

So keen was Congressional interest in European unity that it occasionally threatened to force the hand of the western European governments and of the State Department, as well as to give substance to the Soviet charges of American interference in Europe's affairs. Secretary Acheson, in reporting to House and Senate committees in February 1949 on the progress of European recovery, found it necessary to point out that "the form and nature of these developments along economic and political lines must, if they are to be strong and lasting, come from the people of Europe themselves." The United States, he warned, would not apply coercion to bring about a type of political integration which would be impossible until existing economic disparities had been lessened. The achievement of political unity was "very decidedly . . . the duty and the concern and the business of the European countries." Our role was "to encourage and urge and help at every point in bringing that about." [21]

This official caveat reflected an awareness that within western Europe itself the response to the idea of unity had been less uniformly enthusiastic than in the United States. Europeans had to ask themselves not only whether union was a good thing in principle but also what degree or kind of union was both attainable and suited to the requirements of the situation. They also had to take some account of American views even if unconvinced of their validity.

[19] Salt Lake City speech (*New York Times*, October 1, 1948).
[20] Speech of November 18, 1948 (State Department Press Release No. 915, November 17, 1948).
[21] *Hearings* before the Senate Committee on Foreign Relations, 81st Congress, 1st Session, on S. 833 (Washington, 1949), 19, 193.

For many the issue was complicated by the convergence of two distinct types of pressure which did not necessarily call for an identical response: the decades-old trend of opinion in favor of the development of common European policies and institutions, and the immediate problems created by Soviet expansionism in Europe and by American sponsorship of European recovery efforts. Although both of the latter influences had given rise to different forms of *ad hoc* association, neither seemed to require the full panoply of a European parliament or government. An attempt to go the whole way to a United States of Europe—necessarily confined for the present to the area west of the iron curtain—might even create new difficulties which could prejudice the attainment of immediate and essential ends. Even among the ardent proponents of union there were various schools of thought concerning both the geographic scope and the substantive character of any European association.

The group of European countries lying to the west of the Lübeck-Trieste line was both extensive and diverse. In addition to Britain, France and the Benelux nations it included no fewer than 11 states which were participating in the European Recovery Program (together with Trieste and the western zones of Germany) and one other country—Spain—whose key relationship to the strategy of western defense was as impossible to overlook as was the unpalatability of its domestic regime. These states in turn fell into a number of distinct groupings based on geographic, historical and political factors. Italy, as the largest and most important western state outside the original Western Union, seemed a sure candidate for inclusion in any new or expanded grouping. Its developing rapprochement with France, notably in the steps toward a customs and economic union, already had set it far forward on the path of western association. The Scandinavian countries, on the other hand, despite their participation in the OEEC, were set apart by traditions of neutrality and (except for Iceland) by their proximity to the Soviet Union. Switzerland's neutral and isolationist traditions placed it in a somewhat similar position.

Portugal and Spain had in common their Atlantic position and an official aversion to Communism and the U.S.S.R., but remained outside the political currents prevailing elsewhere in western Europe. Western Germany and Austria, inevitably destined to be in the forefront of any east-west clash, were still under Allied military occupation and lacking in many of the essential attributes of sovereignty. Finally, Greece and Turkey presented unique problems and while threatened by Soviet expansion were remote from the organizing centers of the west.

Most of the projects for European union put forward during 1948 took for their point of departure one or the other of the two going concerns already in the field, the OEEC and the Brussels union. Use of the OEEC framework was strongly urged by the Italian Government, both on principle and presumably because it seemed to promise a larger role for Italy than the alternative procedure.[22] Because of its authority to make decisions binding on the participating governments, it was not illogical to regard the OEEC as a potential framework for European cooperation extending beyond the economic sphere. On the other hand, its very inclusiveness was a serious obstacle. Some of the "neutral" countries participating in ERP would almost certainly refuse to countenance such a redefinition of the OEEC functions; practically all of them would find it difficult to accept any further surrender of "sovereignty" to so heterogeneous a group. Commencement with the narrower grouping represented by the Brussels union therefore seemed from the beginning to enjoy a better prospect of success.[23]

Ideas on the form and functions of a European union ranged all the way from the limited goal of a multilateral military alliance to outright political federation. Full federal union, with

[22] See especially the statement of Count Carlo Sforza, Italian Foreign Minister, to the Chamber of Deputies, September 28, printed in *Relazioni Internazionali*, XII, October 9, 1948, 672-675, and the Italian notes to France (August 24) and to the OEEC governments (October 27), reprinted *ibid.*, November 6, December 4, 1948, 744-745, 800-801.
[23] The Brussels treaty expressly provided for the association or outright inclusion of other like-minded states with the five original signatories.

a European government based on universal suffrage, could
hardly be considered a practical possibility at this stage but
remained the avowed goal of most of the doctrinaire federalists, who continued to advance their ideas with undiminished
ardor throughout the year 1948. A larger and more influential group which held that Europe was not yet ripe for
federation urged that a start be made by establishing a European deliberative assembly that could explore concrete issues,
make recommendations to governments, and serve as a symbol
and rallying point of the "European idea." A third view, prom-
inently represented in the British Labor government, saw danger in even this modest proposal and desired merely to encourage practical cooperation among European governments
on immediate issues which required action.

The practical limits of the discussion as it developed during the latter part of 1948 were set by the cautious empiricism
of the British on the one hand and, on the other, by the unexpectedly radical and internationalist approach of the French,
who vigorously championed the project of a European assembly as the symbolic embodiment of Europe's moral unity. On
August 18 the French Government formally espoused a proposal in this sense by the International Committee of the Movements for European Unity, which had organized the Hague
Congress and assumed responsibility for carrying out its recommendations.

Drawn up by a commission under former French Premier
Ramadier and addressed to all of the OEEC countries, this
memorandum called on the five Brussels governments to take
the lead in convoking a European assembly with representatives from all of the ERP countries. Though the proposed assembly would have no legislative or executive power, its advocates held that it could play an important deliberative and
advisory role, give expression to the desire of the European
peoples for unity and peace, study the constitutional, economic
and social problems involved in European integration, promote
ideological and cultural evolution in this direction, adopt a
Charter of Human Rights and a plan for a European Court of

Justice, and make appropriate recommendations to governments and intergovernmental bodies.[24]

The promptness with which the French Government endorsed this proposal was attributable to a variety of factors. The various unofficial movements for European unity had always had a large and influential following in France. Many Frenchmen, impressed with the collapse of France's old position and the manifold threats to its future security—conditions which were in a measure common to most countries of western Europe—had come to accept the idea that greater unity was actually essential to Europe's survival. Some transfer of the focus of government away from the national level might enable France to regain an influence in European affairs that was denied it under existing conditions. To statesmen conditioned to think in terms of the German menace, union commended itself not only as a salutary restraining influence on a revived Germany, but also as a means of encouraging the moral regeneration of Germany itself. In forwarding this enterprise the government thus could count on the active support of Socialist, MRP and many independent and rightist leaders, tolerance from the de Gaullist element, and stubborn opposition only from the Communist left.

British opinion was less unalterably opposed to European parliaments and federations than might have been inferred from the attitude of the Labor government during most of 1948. An opinion poll conducted in September by the unsympathetic *Daily Express* indicated that Britons as a whole were 68 percent for military, 65 percent for economic, and 58 percent for full political integration of western Europe. Percentages among Conservatives and Liberals were, however, noticeably higher than among Laborites.[25] British hesitations seem, in fact, to have owed much to the self-consciously socialistic outlook of the Labor party and government, mistrustful of a project which was being so vigorously promoted by the Con-

[24] *Assemblée européenne: Memorandum présenté aux gouvernements par le Comité International des Mouvements pour l'Unité Européenne* (Paris, 1948).
[25] *New York Times*, September 14, 1948.

servative opposition, although whether the Conservatives would have been so strong for European union if in power as they were in opposition was another question. Moreover, the Conservatives' proposals seemed to envisage the political and economic unification of Europe on a basis of liberal capitalism. At its June congress the Labor party had affirmed that only socialist methods could lead to real western union—an assumption that continued to color the British attitude more strongly than it did that of the continental Socialists.

Aside from partisan and doctrinaire consideration and the traditional British distaste for constitutional experiments, the government was influenced by persistent uncertainty as to how Britain's participation in any European superstate could be related to its responsibilities as the key member of the British Commonwealth. The Commonwealth Prime Ministers, at their London meeting in the autumn of 1948, approved Great Britain's existing association with other western European nations under the Brussels treaty, but their final communiqué made no reference to any wider association. Under all the circumstances British preferences definitely inclined toward the "functional" method of *ad hoc* collaboration to meet practical situations, rather than to any formal or legalistic method which, it was asserted, might raise insuperable constitutional obstacles to real cooperation where it was needed. Answering charges of lukewarmness in the House of Commons on September 15, Bevin once again deprecated reliance on simple and spectacular measures and urged a continuation of the patient, empirical approach by way of treaties, agreements and collective action on real problems.

That British and French views would clash on the governmental level was made certain by the action of France and Belgium in bringing the proposal for a European assembly before the Consultative Council of the Brussels union. At its October meeting the Council decided to set up a special committee to study and make recommendations on projects of this order. When the committee convened in Paris on November 26 it had before it both the Franco-Belgian proposal and a cautious British counterproposal suggesting not an assembly but a European Council of Ministers, limited initially to the five Brussels nations, made up of government appointees, meeting at stated intervals, and free to discuss "all matters of common concern"—with the noteworthy exception of defense problems and of economic matters falling within the domain of the OEEC.

In the course of long weeks of discussion by the committee, under the chairmanship of Edouard Herriot, the issue of representative assembly versus ministerial council was eventually resolved by a decision to establish both bodies. Protracted argument then took place concerning the nature of the assembly. The British insisted that Communists be excluded outright, a principle which the French, with their large Communist electorate, were hesitant to accept. The French and Benelux delegates were thinking in terms of an assembly of prominent personalities who would enjoy wide latitude in pressing their individual views; the British thought in terms of disciplined national delegations which would support only the official views. When the deadlocked committee adjourned on January 20, 1949 it could point to no more positive achievement than a tentative choice of Strasbourg as the headquarters of any European union that might eventually be set up.

Despite this failure, the Consultative Council at the conclusion of its London meeting a week later announced that it had reached agreement in principle on the establishment of a "Council of Europe" comprising both a ministerial committee and a consultative body. Further details were disclosed by the Permanent Commission of the Brussels union on February 5.[26] These decisions, which were to be presented for consideration by a later conference at which other European countries would be represented, went a long way to meet British views. The Consultative Assembly, which by universal consent would be restricted to deliberative and advisory functions, would meet only once a year and its agenda would be carefully circumscribed. Each participating government could choose its own

[26] *Relazioni Internazionali,* February 12, 1949, 100.

method of selecting delegates. Nothing was announced about how national representation would be weighted in terms of population.

The agreement provided that other European countries would be invited to take part in negotiations preliminary to setting up the Council of Europe. World attention by this time had focused on the projected North Atlantic security pact to a degree that made a purely political organism seem innocuous by contrast. Italy, Norway and Denmark were already veering toward inclusion in the Atlantic treaty and would hardly refuse an invitation to become founding members of the Council. Even Sweden, which had refused to have anything to do with the Atlantic treaty, announced its readiness to participate in the preliminary conference. Ireland likewise found that the special political obstacles that were holding it aloof from the Atlantic pact did not apply in this instance. Of the western continental nations originally considered for membership only Portugal, with its corporative and authoritarian government and its distrust of parliamentary processes, remained aloof despite its willingness to join in an Atlantic security system.

Representatives of Norway, Denmark, Sweden, Italy and Ireland met with delegates of the Brussels powers in London at the end of March to examine a draft constitution for the new European Council and prepare the ground for a full-dress conference of foreign ministers to be held the following month. Before autumn, it was hoped, the Ministerial Committee and European Assembly would actually be meeting in Strasbourg.[27]

What these new organs would be able to accomplish no one could say. It was certainly much easier to create imposing new European institutions than to begin a real clearance of the legal, financial and psychological underbrush that had flourished on the European soil during centuries of separate national life. Weighty problems remained unsolved—the future role of Germany, the relations of the Council of Europe to the United Nations and to the British Commonwealth, the capacity for com-

---

[27] The statute of the Council of Europe was signed by representatives of the ten governments in London on May 5, 1949.

mon action of countries with such heterogeneous social, political and economic structures. In the best of cases it was uncertain how far their united efforts could suffice to lessen Europe's long-term dependence on outside aid. The competing demands of European military defense, capital investment, direct consumption and social expenditure would place a heavy strain on the available resources for the indefinite future. Clearly, union would be no panacea. But the rapid emergence of the Council of Europe bore witness to a new and urgent sense of community among the western European peoples which augured well for their determination to grapple successfully with the difficult problems of the future.

5. North Atlantic Pact

The idea of a North Atlantic security pact did not originate with any single individual or government. It grew spontaneously out of the situation in which the countries bordering on the North Atlantic found themselves during the years 1948 and 1949. The decisive factors in this situation were the failure of the United Nations to provide adequate guarantees of world peace and security, a general loss of confidence in the peaceful intentions of the U.S.S.R., and the inability of Great Britain, France and the lesser nations of western Europe to develop an effective counterpoise to the Soviet military power. In these circumstances the security of both western Europe and North America seemed to require an active association of the like-minded nations on both continents in the pursuit of their common peaceful objectives. Specifically, as the Senate Foreign Relations Committee pointed out in its report on the Vandenberg Resolution, it was clear that "the great power and influence of the United States must be thrown into the scales on the side of peace." [28]

[28] Quoted in U.S. Senate, *North Atlantic Treaty: Documents Relating to the North Atlantic Treaty,* printed for the Senate Foreign Relations Committee, 81st Congress, 1st Session (Washington, 1949), 80. Except as otherwise indicated, all statements and documents referred to in this section are included in this publication or in "North Atlantic Treaty," *National Peace Council Papers* (London), No. 6, May 1949.

In an informal way such an association between the United States, Canada and the western European democracies was already in existence. With or without a formal commitment, there was every likelihood that Soviet aggression in western Europe would be answered by American armed force, especially while American occupation troops were stationed on the continent. The purpose of a North Atlantic treaty would be to strengthen and give durability and legal status to this *de facto* association and to determine the manner in which it would operate in certain definite eventualities. This in itself, it was assumed, would be a powerful deterrent to potential aggressors, and incidentally would provide the nations of western Europe with the long-desired guarantee of American assistance against German as well as Soviet aggression.

A regional security pact for the North Atlantic area was not the only possible response to great-power disunity and western European weakness. Many observers feared that a military alliance might aggravate rather than diminish the dangers of the existing situation. Such a treaty, its opponents argued, seemed to ignore the fact that some western nations were more threatened by internal subversion than by external aggression. It would further weaken the United Nations, widen the chasm between Russia and the west, impede European economic recovery, expose the small nations on Russia's borders to reprisals, and commit the United States to a course of action that might be wholly inappropriate to the circumstances obtaining at some future date. Even those Americans who accepted the necessity for urgent action by the United States differed widely in their recommendations. Some advocated the development of a general rather than a regional security system within the United Nations framework; some argued for limiting the geographic scope of the proposed alliance, others for extending it; some felt that Europe should be given military assistance without a formal treaty; others professed to favor a treaty but to be reluctant to back it up with tangible military assistance.

For the western European governments the form of their relationship with the United States was less important than a clear assurance of American aid in rebuilding their defenses and, should it prove necessary, in forestalling aggression from the east. An effective defense could not be based on the assumption that the United States would come to their aid after the damage was done; it required full American participation in preparations to meet the danger before it materialized. If the United States Government favored basing this participation on a formal treaty of defensive alliance, Europeans had little incentive to question this preference. Many of them had vainly desired such an alliance for the past 30 years.

The diplomatic conversations which laid the groundwork for the Atlantic pact began in Washington on July 6, 1948, when the representatives of Canada and the five Brussels nations met with Under-Secretary Lovett for a first "informal and exploratory exchange of views." In the course of the summer agreement was reached both on the necessity for a defensive North Atlantic treaty and on its general nature. Recessed in September, the conversations resumed on December 10, by which time a draft treaty prepared by the permanent commission of the Western Union in London was available for discussion.

The principles and aims of the proposed treaty were expounded at length in a State Department release of January 14, 1949 [29] and, more briefly, by President Truman in his inaugural address on January 20. As the third of the four major courses of action to be emphasized in American foreign policy during the coming years, the President said, "we will strengthen freedom-loving nations against the dangers of aggression" through the conclusion of "a joint agreement designed to strengthen the security of the North Atlantic area" and the provision of "military advice and equipment to free nations which will cooperate with us in the maintenance of peace and security." The primary purpose of the proposed North Atlantic treaty, like that of the Rio treaty of 1947, declared the President, was "to provide unmistakable proof of the joint deter-

[29] "Collective Security in the North Atlantic Area," *Foreign Affairs Outlines: Building the Peace*, No. 19, Spring 1949.

mination of the free countries to resist armed attack from any quarter . . . If we can make it sufficiently clear, in advance, that any armed attack affecting our national security would be met with overwhelming force, the armed attack might never occur."

In putting its name to a treaty, the United States had nevertheless to face the possibility that its provisions might some day be invoked and positive action called for. The search for a formula to cover this eventuality, in terms that would be sufficiently clear-cut to impress allies and potential aggressors and yet sufficiently elastic to gain acceptance by the Senate, consumed two more months of intensive negotiation, rendered more difficult by the fact that the congressional foreign policy leaders had not as yet been fully acquainted with the intentions of the Administration. Dean Acheson, the new Secretary of State, was required to negotiate simultaneously with six foreign ambassadors and with the members of the Senate Foreign Relations Committee, two groups whose views often seemed virtually irreconcilable. The problems which caused most difficulty in the final drafting of the pact concerned its relationship to the Charter of the United Nations and especially to the constitutional practice of the United States.

To bring the pact within the terms of the United Nations Charter required some flexibility of interpretation. Article 24 of the Charter unequivocally assigns the primary responsibility for maintaining international peace and security to the Security Council, acting on behalf of all members of the United Nations. Except for action against former enemy states, the Charter does not provide for any limitation on the Security Council's authority in this field. Article 51 recognizes "the inherent right of individual or collective self-defense," but only until the Security Council has "taken the measures necessary to maintain international peace and security." Articles 52-54, which authorize "regional arrangements or agencies for dealing with such matters relating to the maintenance of international peace and security as are appropriate for regional action," again explicitly reserve the rights of the Security Council as the supreme authority. The Charter makes no reference to "other" (i.e., non-regional) collective arrangements such as the Vandenberg Resolution endorsed.

The North Atlantic Treaty, in the form in which it was made public on March 18, 1949, did not purport to be a "regional arrangement" under the Charter. It did invoke Article 51 as authority for the specific measures of mutual assistance contemplated in the event of an armed attack on any of the parties. In conformity with that article it provided for immediate report to the Security Council of all action taken, and for terminating such measures when the Security Council had itself taken the measures necessary to restore and maintain international peace and security. In addition, it explicitly affirmed that the rights and obligations of the parties under the Charter, and the primary responsibility of the Security Council for the maintenance of international peace and security, remained unimpaired.

In a purely formal sense, therefore, there was no marked inconsistency between the provisions of the Atlantic pact and those of the Charter. In a wider sense, however, the Charter rested on the assumption that the Security Council would, as a matter of course, take whatever measures were necessary to maintain international peace and security, whereas the whole meaning of the Atlantic pact derived from the tacit assumption that the Security Council would do no such thing. The Charter had presupposed a degree of unanimity among the great powers that would itself afford a reasonable guarantee of world security. Events since 1945 had shown that no such unanimity existed; on the contrary, one of those great powers had revealed itself as the major threat to world security. It was this realization that impelled the members of the "North Atlantic community" to devise measures which, though claiming the authority of the Charter, were in effect designed to take the place of those sections of the Charter in which experience forbade them to repose confidence.

The effort to keep the treaty consistent with American constitutional principles without sacrificing its political impact in

Europe also required ingenuity. What the European representatives desired was a guarantee that the United States would, among other things, go to war in case any one of them were a victim of aggression. This, however, was an undertaking no American government was prepared to give in view of the exclusive power of Congress to declare war. The problem therefore was to devise language which came as close as possible to the commitment desired by the Europeans without transgressing the bounds of constitutional propriety as interpreted by Connally, Vandenberg, and other leaders of the Eighty-first Congress. The result—an undertaking by each of the parties to "assist the Party or Parties so attacked by taking forthwith, individually and in concert with the other Parties, such action as it deems necessary, including the use of armed force, to restore and maintain the security of the North Atlantic area"—was a formula whose precise effect would depend on later interpretation. It certainly fell far short of the clear-cut commitment of the Brussels treaty signatories to afford the victim of aggression "all military and other aid and assistance in their power"; on the other hand, it was a long step forward for a country that had eschewed military alliances throughout its history.

There were other features of the draft treaty for which there were obvious political reasons but no easy logical explanation, especially in conjunction with the geographic location and political complexion of the five governments—Denmark, Iceland, Norway, Italy and Portugal—which were invited to adhere to the pact as original signatories. The concept of a "North Atlantic area" which excluded Spain and Eire but included Italy, the Algerian departments of France, and the entire North American territory of the United States and Canada was, to say the least, a novel one. The inclusion of Italy and Portugal among the signatories of a treaty whose text made repeated professions of devotion to the United Nations slurred over the fact that those states had not yet been admitted to membership. Also, the presence of quasi-fascist Portugal in an association ostensibly founded on a common heritage of democratic principles and individual liberty was not without its incongruous aspect. The heart of the treaty was the signatories' pledge to "maintain and develop their individual and collective capacity to resist armed attack"; to consult together in case of a threat to the "territorial integrity, political independence or security" of any of them; to regard an armed attack against one or more of them in Europe or North America as an attack against them all; and to provide assistance in case of an armed attack on their European (or Algerian) or North American territories, their occupation forces in Europe, their North Atlantic islands, or their vessels or aircraft in the area. To implement these undertakings the treaty provided for a council representing all of the signatories and a defense committee to recommend appropriate measures in the military field. The pact was to remain in force indefinitely, with provision for review at the end of 10 years and optional withdrawal after 20 years. Other European states in a position to further the principles of the treaty and "contribute to the security of the North Atlantic area" might be invited to accede by unanimous agreement of the parties.

The final list of signatories was not fixed until the middle of March. There were many states throughout the world that felt themselves threatened with aggression and would have welcomed guarantees of support. The governments sponsoring the Atlantic pact had to balance the advantages of inclusiveness against the danger of assuming commitments too far-flung to be carried out. Greece and Turkey were excluded because of their remoteness, although Acheson and Bevin subsequently made statements emphasizing that this implied no lessening of determination to support their integrity and independence, as well as that of Iran.[30] Western Germany was ruled out if only because none of the participating states was in a mood to countenance German rearmament.

Italy was in the peculiar position of a non-Atlantic state and an ex-enemy country whose military forces were limited by the

[30] Acheson broadcast, March 18, 1949 (Department of State, *Bulletin*, XX, March 27, 1949, 386); Bevin in *Parliamentary Debates, Weekly Hansard*, House of Commons, March 18, 1949, 2547.

peace treaty and could contribute little to the coalition's armed strength. The Italian Government wished to accede to the pact in order to seal its solidarity with the west and also to promote a favorable settlement on the disposition of its former colonies. France supported Italy's inclusion; Great Britain tended to oppose it, primarily on military grounds, but was persuaded to drop its opposition, largely by the United States, usually sympathetic to Italian aspirations. Spain and Portugal had stronger historical, geographic and strategic claims to membership in the Atlantic community. Portugal, however dubious its attachment to democratic principles, was early slated for inclusion. Spain, however, was ruled out because its internal regime was not acceptable to other nations of western Europe, notwithstanding the favorable opinions of such prominent Americans as James A. Farley and Chan Gurney, chairman of the Senate Armed Services Committee in the Eightieth Congress, whose interviews with Franco in the fall of 1948 had impressed them with Spain's potentialities as a partner in an anti-Communist bloc. Eire, equally anti-communist and equally important in the strategy of the North Atlantic, expressed sympathy with the aims of the pact but counted itself out because of its territorial quarrel with the United Kingdom. "As long as Ireland is partitioned," said Minister for External Affairs MacBride, "the first essential of Irish participation is denied."

The most intricate membership problems concerned the Scandinavian countries, among which only Iceland was clearly in a position to enroll itself in the North Atlantic column. For Norway, Denmark and Sweden the issue was tragically complicated by their proximity to the U.S.S.R. and the danger that they would immediately be engulfed by any forcible Soviet reaction to the pact. The strength of the Scandinavian neutrality tradition varied in the three countries, being most persistent in Sweden and least so in Norway. All three, however, were seriously embarrassed by the Atlantic pact negotiations, which confronted them with an unwelcome choice between lining up with the west and incurring the threat of Soviet reprisals or remaining aloof and forfeiting the possibility of bolstering their defenses with American equipment.

As an escape from this dilemma Sweden, as early as May 1948, had taken the initiative in urging the formation of a Swedish-Norwegian-Danish defensive bloc which would be strong enough to assure the armed neutrality of the three countries in the event of war. Although the Soviet press warned that Moscow would view this combination with no less disfavor than outright Scandinavian accession to an Atlantic pact, the project was discussed at numerous conferences of Scandinavian ministers during the latter part of 1948 and the beginning of 1949. It failed of adoption primarily because of Norway's conviction that its security lay in association with the Atlantic powers and that outside military aid was required if Scandinavian defenses were to be built up to an adequate level. Doubtful about the capacity of Swedish industry to carry the rearmament load, the Norwegian Government turned its eyes increasingly toward Washington, especially after the State Department made known in mid-January that military supplies were unlikely to be available for countries to which the United States had no previous commitments and which remained outside the proposed treaty.

A Soviet note to Norway at the end of January brought the issue to a head. Did Norway mean to defer to the aggressive aims of the western powers by joining the Atlantic alliance, asked the U.S.S.R., and was it undertaking any commitments regarding the establishment of air or naval bases on its territory? The Norwegian Government immediately replied with a frank statement of its position. Forced by the disappointing performance of the United Nations to seek increased security through regional cooperation, it had looked into the possibilities of a northern defense union without positive result and now intended to investigate more closely the matter of participation in a regional security system comprising countries on the Atlantic. But it would never lend itself or its territory to a policy of aggression, nor would it grant bases for foreign armed forces as long as Norway was not attacked or threatened. The U.S.S.R. then dispatched a second note reiterating its belief in the aggressive aims of the Atlantic pact, affirming its own "good neighborly intentions" toward Norway, and ominously offering to confirm them by means of a non-aggression pact.

By the time this note was received, on February 5, the Norwegian Government had already decided to send Foreign Minister Halvard M. Lange to Washington to seek urgent clarification of the United States position. In conversations with Secretary Acheson and other high officials Lange was told in substance that an unattached Scandinavian defense union could not expect political or military support from the west; that Norwegian participation in the Atlantic pact would not involve requests to establish U.S. or joint bases on Norwegian soil; and that the United States was unable to give any assurances regarding the quantities of military equipment that might be made available to Norway after that country signed the pact or during the critical period before the pact came into operation. Returning with these clear-cut if not very inspiriting replies, Lange on March 3 obtained authorization from the Storting to join the Washington talks, in which the Norwegian Ambassador participated from March 4 onward. The Soviet Union was advised of this decision and of the Norwegian Government's opinion that there was no need to duplicate the pledges of non-aggression both nations had given in subscribing to the United Nations Charter.

The Norwegian action determined the attitude of Denmark, which now could choose only isolation, an impractical alliance with Sweden, or the Atlantic pact. Foreign Minister Rasmussen made the pilgrimage to Washington in mid-March, and parliamentary authorization to sign the treaty was obtained before the end of the month. Iceland likewise accepted the invitation of the sponsoring powers after its foreign minister had received the customary assurance that it would not be required to make military bases available in peacetime. Sweden, amid expressions of uneasiness in high military quarters, prepared to make the best of its precarious neutrality.

The hostility with which the U.S.S.R. regarded the Washington negotiations was only partially concerned with their Scandinavian aspect. Its disapproval of the whole project was expressed with a bitterness surpassing even that of previous anti-warmongering campaigns. The old fear of anti-Soviet coalitions and capitalist encirclement may have helped some of the Soviet leaders to persuade themselves that the proposed treaty really was, as they insisted, an aggressive instrument directed at Anglo-American world domination. Yet they could hardly fail to perceive that it was their own policy, in the United Nations and elsewhere, that had precipitated this unwelcome development.

The Soviet campaign against the North Atlantic Treaty was not confined exclusively to propaganda blasts, Communist agitation, and hectoring of neighboring states like Finland and Norway. It also embraced sundry conciliatory gestures which appeared designed to relieve tension and strengthen opposition to the treaty within the western countries. On January 30, for instance, simultaneously with the first Soviet note to Norway and a lengthy statement by the Soviet Foreign Office intemperately recapitulating Moscow's objections to the Western Union and the Atlantic treaty, the Soviet radio broadcast a superficially very conciliatory declaration by Stalin on Soviet-American relations.

Stalin's statement, which was to inaugurate the process that led to the raising of the Berlin blockade and the reassembly of the Council of Foreign Ministers,[31] took the form of answers to four questions posed by Kingsbury Smith of International News Service. Aside from his remarks on the Berlin issue, the Soviet leader in effect declared himself willing to consider publishing a joint Soviet-U.S. declaration that neither government intended to make war against the other, to cooperate with the United States in measures leading toward a peace pact and gradual disarmament, and to meet President Truman at a mutually suitable place for discussions to this end. This specious overture was scarcely calculated to yield more positive

---

[31] See above, pp. 493-495.

results than the earlier projects for direct American-Soviet discussions that had arisen in connection with the Smith-Molotov exchange of the previous May and the abortive Vinson mission in October.[32] Neither Stalin nor Truman, it soon appeared, was able to leave his own bailiwick to meet the other; and an ironic exposure by Secretary Acheson of the logical inconsistencies and diplomatic pitfalls lurking in the Stalin statement assured the plan an early burial.[33]

Whether or not as a result of this rebuff, the following weeks saw a hardening of the intransigent Communist opposition to the pact. The fury of Communist propaganda and parliamentary obstruction steadily mounted. Thorez, Togliatti and their confreres made gratuitous statements about assisting the Soviet forces in the event of war and Soviet military occupation of their countries. In the Italian Parliament the Communists and left-wing Socialists filibustered against the Atlantic pact with a parade of speakers that held the Chamber in continuous session for 56 hours before a vote could be taken. Meanwhile another phase of the "peace offensive" gained momentum with a monster "Cultural and Scientific Congress for World Peace" in New York and preparation for a similar gathering in Paris. And on March 30, five days before the scheduled signature of the treaty, the Soviet Government in a formal protest to the seven sponsoring governments reiterated its assertions with regard to the pact's aggressive aims, anti-Soviet orientation, and incompatibility with United Nations obligations.

The foreign ministers assembled in Washington for the signature contented themselves with a brief statement that there was nothing new in the Soviet protest and affirming that "the text of the treaty itself is the best answer to such misrepresentations and allegations." For the United States, Secretary Acheson had already given a far more forceful reply in a broadcast on March 18:

"Anyone with the most elementary knowledge of the processes of democratic government knows that democracies do

[32] See above, pp. 24-28, 502-503.
[33] Department of State, *Bulletin*, XX, February 13, 1949, 192-194.

not and cannot plan aggressive wars. But for those from whom such knowledge may have been withheld I must make the following categoric and unequivocal statement, for which I stand with the full measure of my responsibility in the office I hold: This country is not planning to make war against anyone. It is not seeking war. It abhors war. It does not hold war to be inevitable. Its policies are devised with the specific aim of bridging by peaceful means the tremendous differences which beset international society at the present time. Allegations that aggressive designs lie behind this country's signature of the Atlantic pact can rest only on a malicious misrepresentation or a fantastic misunderstanding of the nature and aims of American society." [34]

The Soviet Union did not, as some observers feared, resort to forceful action when the North Atlantic Treaty was signed on April 4, 1949. Instead, it went ahead with the conversations that preceded the agreement for raising the Berlin blockade and the first real slackening of international tension in many months. Whether this line of action resulted from a radical change of Soviet policy, presaging a retreat to isolation or a shift of attention to the Far East, it was too early to say. A belated realization of the unity and determination of the west, signs of declining Communist strength in western Europe, local conditions in Germany and the Soviet orbit—all were factors which may have influenced the Soviet decision.

Whatever lay behind the Kremlin's new tactic, it seemed to fit in with Moscow's continuing effort to obstruct the consolidation of the western world. "The real test of our Atlantic Alliance," Canada's Foreign Minister, Lester Pearson, had written, "will come if and when the threat to peace seems to recede and we are allowed to see that silver lining which the iron curtain is said to possess." [35] If, as seemed possible, Soviet policy was now entering a conciliatory phase—a phase which could be terminated whenever it might suit the Politburo—there was

[34] *Ibid.*, XX, March 27, 1949, 387.
[35] Lester B. Pearson, "Canada and the North Atlantic Alliance," *Foreign Affairs*, XXVII, April 1949, 377-378.

danger that the momentum behind the Atlantic pact might be lost at a time when the security of the west had still to be established.

For the signature of the North Atlantic pact was at most no more than a step toward the lofty goals enumerated in its preamble. The possibility of realizing those aims would depend on the spirit in which the peoples of western Europe and North America carried out its provisions. In the United States it was uncertain whether the mass of the people fully realized as yet the magnitude and gravity of the commitment undertaken in their behalf. There was no magic about the treaty that would deter an aggressor by sheer force of rhetoric. If the pact was to be effective it would first have to be faced and accepted in all its implications.

The most immediate of these, aside from the question of Senate ratification, was Europe's need for tangible American support in the form of military equipment with which to begin redressing the military balance on the old continent. A program of military assistance to foreign countries, based on the "self-help and mutual aid" principle which was written into the pact, had been worked out by the National Military Establishment, the State Department and ECA. In May it was announced that Congress would be asked to make a single appropriation for military aid for the fiscal year 1950 amounting to approximately $1,450 million, of which some $1,130 million would be for the North Atlantic pact countries and some $320 million for Greece, Turkey and "certain other nations whose security is important to the United States." This program, the State Department pointed out, was "part of the price we must pay for peace and security in present world conditions." [36]

There was no assurance that Congress, once again at grips with ERP and faced with a substantial budgetary deficit, would

---

[36] "The U.S. Military Assistance Program," *Foreign Affairs Outlines: Building the Peace*, No. 22, Spring 1949, 7. An exchange of notes in which the Western Union countries, Denmark, Italy and Norway called attention to their need for military aid and the State Department outlined its intention of going to Congress was released a few days after the pact was signed. See Department of State, *Bulletin*, XX, April 17, 1949, 493-498.

see the matter in that light. The Atlantic pact, however, seemed fairly sure of ratification. By accepting its obligations, elastic though they might be, the United States would formally join a military alliance in peacetime, a new departure in American policy. For the long term it was a continuing commitment to defend the security of the nations of western Europe against aggression from Germany, Russia, or any other quarter. In the immediate situation it was a logical step in the already established policy of containing Soviet expansion and restoring the balance of power in Europe. Many vital decisions in world affairs remained for the future, decisions which would test the wisdom and the realism of the American government and people. But with the Atlantic pact they had come a long way, in a few short years, in the exercise of America's potentialities and responsibilities as a world power.

SELECTED BIBLIOGRAPHY

The following titles represent but a fraction of the literature on the subjects touched upon in this book. It is hoped that the process of selection has contributed to the usefulness of the list. In view of the sparing use of footnotes, an attempt is made to include the principal documentary and secondary sources on which the narrative is based. This bibliography is intended also to provide a guide to further study of the subjects covered. Articles are included as well as books since they contain much recent material not available elsewhere. Explanatory or critical comment is added when it appears necessary or helpful. Most of the books listed were published in 1948 or 1949. A few important books of earlier date which were omitted from the bibliography of the preceding volume of this survey are also included. A few others, listed there, are again mentioned here because of their relation to material in the text. In order that the bibliography may be of maximum use to the general reader, it is confined to works in the western languages, with a heavy emphasis on material in English. All official United States documents listed are published by the Government Printing Office, and all British documents by H.M. Stationery Office, unless otherwise indicated.

GENERAL

BLACKETT, P. M. S. Fear, War and the Bomb. New York, Whittlesey House, 1949, 244 p.
  An analysis of the military and political consequences of atomic energy, supporting Soviet views on control. First published in London in 1948.
EBON, MARTIN. World Communism Today. New York, Whittlesey House, 1948, 536 p.
GROSS, FELIKS (ed.). European Ideologies: A Survey of Twentieth Century Political Ideas. New York, Philosophical Library, 1948, 1075 p.
KEETON, GEORGE W., and GEORG SCHWARZENBERGER (eds.). The Year Book of World Affairs, 1948. London, Stevens, 1948, 376 p.
  A series of articles on various international topics.
U.S. CONGRESS (80TH, 1ST SESSION). House Doc. 619 (The Strategy and Tactics of World Communism). Report from Subcommittee No. 5 of House Committee on Foreign Affairs. Washington, 1948–1949, 4 pts. (incl. supp. I-III).
WRIGHT, QUINCY (ed.). The World Community. Chicago, University of Chicago Press, 1948, 332 p.
  A discussion of the practicability of proposals for a world government.

U.S. POLICY

I. DOCUMENTS

U.S. Foreign Policy

DENNETT, RAYMOND, and ROBERT K. TURNER. Documents on American Foreign Relations, Vol. VIII (1945–1946). Princeton, Princeton University Press, 1948, 962 p.
  The latest volume of an important series.

U.S. COMMISSION ON ORGANIZATION OF THE EXECUTIVE BRANCH OF THE GOVERNMENT. Foreign Affairs. Report of the Commission to the Congress. Washington, 1949.

U.S. CONGRESS (80TH, 2ND SESSION). S. Report 855 (The United States Information Service in Europe). Report of the Senate Committee on Foreign Relations pursuant to S. Res. 161. Washington, 1948.
Report of the Congressional group which investigated USIS activities in Europe in the fall of 1947.

————. S. Res. 239 (Reaffirming the Policy of the United States to Achieve International Peace and Security through the United Nations and Indicating Certain Objectives to be Pursued), June 11, 1948. S. Report 1361, May 19, 1948. Washington, 1948.
The Vandenberg Resolution.

U.S. CONGRESS (81ST, 1ST SESSION). Inaugural Address of Harry S. Truman, January 20, 1948 (S. Doc. 5). Washington, 1949.

U.S. DEPARTMENT OF STATE. Report to Congress on Assistance to Greece and Turkey. Washington, quarterly, 1948–1949.

U.S. Military Policy

U.S. CONGRESS (80TH, 2ND SESSION). Public Law 547 (H.R. 6226), approved May 21, 1948 (Supplemental National Defense Appropriation Act, 1948). Subcommittee of House Appropriations Committee, Hearings, April 8-9, 1948; H. Report 1729, April 14, 1948; S. Report 1223, April 30, 1948; H. Report 1905, May 5, 1948. Washington, 1948.

————. Public Law 753 (H.R. 6772), approved June 24, 1948 (Department of the Navy—1949 Appropriations). Subcommittee of House Appropriations Committee, Hearings, May 19-21, 1948; Supplemental Hearings, May 19-22, 1948; H. Report 2136, June 2, 1948; Subcommittee of Senate Appropriations Committee, Hearings, June 11-12, 1948; S. Report 1621, June 14, 1948; H. Report 2385, June 16, 1948. Washington, 1948.

————. Public Law 759 (S. 2655), approved June 24, 1948 (Selective Service Act of 1948). S. Report 1268, May 12, 1948; H. Report 2438, June 19, 1948.

————. Public Law 766 (H.R. 6771), approved June 24, 1948 (Military Appropriation Act, 1949). Subcommittee of House Appropriations Committee, Hearings, March 29-May 22, 1948; H. Report 2135, June 2, 1948; Subcommittee of Senate Appropriations Committee, Hearings, June 14-17, 1948; S. Report 1763, June 17, 1948. Washington, 1948.

U.S. DEPARTMENT OF NATIONAL DEFENSE. First Report of the Secretary of Defense. Washington, 1948.

U.S. Economic Policy

U.S. CONGRESS (80TH, 2ND SESSION). Public Law 792 (H.R. 6556), approved June 26, 1948 (Extension of Reciprocal Trade Agreements Act). Subcommittee on Tariffs and Foreign Trade of the House Committee on Ways and Means, Hearings, May 3-8, 1948; H. Report 2009, May 24, 1948; S. Report 1558, June 8, 1948. Washington, 1948.

U.S. CONGRESS (81ST, 1ST SESSION). H.R. 1211 (Extension of the Reciprocal Trade Agreements Act). House Committee on Ways and Means, Hearings, January 24-February 1, 1949; H. Report 19, February 4, 1949; S. Report 107, March 11, 1949. Washington, 1949.

U.S. CONGRESS (80TH, 2ND SESSION). Executive F (International Wheat Agreement). Message from the President, April 30, 1948; Subcommittee of Senate Committee on Foreign Relations, Hearings, May 14-17, 1948; Executive Report 12, August 6, 1948. Washington, 1948.

U.S. CONGRESS (81ST, 1ST SESSION). Executive M (International Wheat Agreement of 1949). April 19, 1949. Washington, 1949.

————. Public Law 11 (S. 548), approved February 26, 1949 (Continuation of Export Controls). House Committee on Banking and Currency, Hearings on H.R. 1661, January 31–February 2, 1949; H. Report 18, February 7, 1949; Subcommittee of the Senate Committee on Banking and Currency, January 28–February 3, 1949; S. Report 31, February 4, 1949. Washington, 1949.

U.S. EXPORT-IMPORT BANK. Sixth Semiannual Report . . . January–June 1948; Seventh Semiannual Report, July–December 1948. Washington, 1948–1949.

U.S. DEPARTMENT OF STATE. Aspects of United States Participation in International Civil Aviation. International Organization and Conference Series IV, 2. Washington, 1948, 118 p.

II. SECONDARY MATERIAL

U.S. Foreign Policy

ADAM, THOMAS R. Education for International Understanding. New York, Institute of Adult Education, 1948, 181 p.

A critical analysis of the groups trying to direct American opinion toward world cooperation.

ARMSTRONG, HAMILTON FISH. Coalition for World Peace. (Foreign Affairs, XXVII, October 1948, 1-16.)

————. Regional Pacts: Strong Points or Storm Cellars? (Ibid., XXVII, April 1949, 351-368.)

DAHL, ROBERT A. Congress and Foreign Policy. New Haven, Yale Institute of International Studies, Memorandum No. 30, 1949, 42 p.

GRAHAM, MALBONE W. American Diplomacy in the International Community. Baltimore, Johns Hopkins Press, 1948, 279 p.

LANGER, WILLIAM L. The Mechanism of American Foreign Policy. (International Affairs, XXIV, July 1948, 319-328.)

MARKEL, LESTER, and others. Public Opinion and Foreign Policy. New York, Harper for the Council on Foreign Relations, 1949, 227 p.

MOSELY, PHILIP E. Face to Face with Russia. New York, Foreign Policy Association, Headline Series, 1948, 63 p.

MOWRER, EDGAR A. The Nightmare of American Foreign Policy. New York, Knopf, 1948, 313 p.

The author criticizes the failure to use the power of the U.S. to prevent recurring world wars.

RESTON, JAMES. Prospects for Stability in our Foreign Policy. (Foreign Affairs, XXVII, October 1948, 34-43.)

THOMSON, CHARLES A. H. Overseas Information Service of the United States Government. Washington, Brookings Institution, 1949, 397 p.

WARBURG, JAMES P. Put Yourself in Marshall's Place. New York, Simon and Schuster, 1948, 93 p.

A review of the problems faced by Secretary Marshall during his first year in office, with documentary appendix.

U.S. Military Policy

BALDWIN, HANSON W. The Price of Power. New York, Harper for the Council on Foreign Relations, 1948, 261 p.

BOLLES, B. Arctic Diplomacy. (*Foreign Policy Reports,* XXIV, June 1, 1948, 58-67.)
KENT, SHERMAN. Strategic Intelligence for American World Policy. Princeton, Princeton University Press, 1949, 220 p.
NEWMAN, JAMES R., and BYRON S. MILLER. The Control of Atomic Energy: A Study of Its Social, Economic, and Political Implications. New York, McGraw-Hill, 1948, 434 p.

U.S. Economic Policy

BIDWELL, PERCY W., and WILLIAM DIEBOLD, JR. The United States and the International Trade Organization. (*International Conciliation,* No. 449, March 1949, 185-239.)
BLINKEN, DONALD M. Wool Tariffs and American Policy. Washington, Public Affairs Press, 1948, 168 p.
HARRIS, SEYMOUR E. (ed.). Foreign Economic Policy for the United States. Cambridge, Harvard University Press, 1948, 503 p.
A symposium.
LEWIS, CLEONA. The United States and Foreign Investment Problems. Washington, Brookings Institution, 1948, 377 p.
METZGER, LAURE. American Loans in the Postwar Period. Washington, Foundation for Foreign Affairs, 1948, 60 p.

ECONOMIC AFFAIRS

I. DOCUMENTS

General

U.N. DEPARTMENT OF ECONOMIC AFFAIRS. Major Economic Changes in 1948. Lake Success, 1949.
Third of a series of reports dealing with world economic conditions.
U.N. ECONOMIC COMMISSION FOR EUROPE. Economic Survey of Europe in 1948. New York, Columbia University Press, 1949, 300 p.
U.S. DEPARTMENT OF AGRICULTURE. World Food Situation, 1949. Washington, Office of Foreign Agricultural Relations, 1949.
U.S. DEPARTMENT OF STATE. General Agreement on Tariffs and Trade, Geneva, October 30, 1947. Treaties and Other International Acts Series 1700. Washington, 1949, 2044 p.
U.N. INTERIM COMMISSION FOR THE INTERNATIONAL TRADE ORGANIZATION. United Nations Conference on Trade and Employment, Havana, Cuba, November 21, 1947, to March 24, 1948. Reports of Committees and Principal Subcommittees. Geneva, 1948 (ICITO 1/8).
——————. Final Act [of the U.N. Conference on Trade and Employment, Havana, Cuba] and Related Documents. Lake Success, 1948.
U.S. DEPARTMENT OF STATE. Havana Charter for an International Trade Organization, March 24, 1948, including a guide to the study of the Charter. Commercial Policy Series 114. Washington, 1948.

European Recovery Program

ORGANIZATION FOR EUROPEAN ECONOMIC COOPERATION. History and Structure. Paris, OEEC, 1948.
——————. Agreement for Intra-European Payments and Compensations, October 16, 1948. Paris, OEEC, 1948.

————. Report on the Work of OEEC Since Its Inception. Paris, OEEC, 1948.

————. Interim Report on the European Recovery Program. Paris, OEEC, 1948, 2 vols.

————. Report to the Economic Cooperation Administration on the 1949–1950 Program. [Paris] OEEC [1949].

————. Report to the Economic Cooperation Administration on the Second Annual Program, July 1, 1949–June 30, 1950. [Paris] OEEC, 1949.

U.S. CONGRESS (80TH, 2ND SESSION). Public Law 472 (S. 2202), approved April 3, 1948 (Economic Cooperation Act of 1948). S. Report 935, February 26, 1948; H. Report 1585, March 20, 1948. Washington, 1948.

————. Public Law 793 (H.R. 6801), approved June 28, 1948 (Foreign Aid Appropriations). H. Report 2173, June 3, 1948; Senate Committee on Appropriations, Hearings, May 13–June 11, 1948; S. Report 1626, June 14, 1948. Washington, 1948.

U.S. CONGRESS (81ST, 1ST SESSION). Public Law 47 (S. 1209), approved April 19, 1949 (Economic Cooperation Act—Extension). Senate Committee on Foreign Relations, Hearings [on S. 833], February 8-23, 1949; S. Report 100, March 8, 1949; H. Report 440, April 14, 1949. Washington, 1949.

————. S. Report 13 (Progress of the Economic Cooperation Administration), January 10, 1949. Report of the Joint Committee on Foreign Economic Cooperation. Washington, 1949.

U.S. ECONOMIC COOPERATION ADMINISTRATION. Reports for the Public Advisory Board of the Economic Cooperation Administration. Washington, Economic Cooperation Administration, 1948–1949.

————. Reports to Congress of the Economic Cooperation Administration: First Report for the Period April 3 to June 30, 1948 and Supp.; Second Report for the Quarter Ended September 30, 1948; Third Report for the Quarter Ended December 31, 1948. Washington, 1948–1949.

————. A Report on Recovery Progress and United States Aid. Washington, ECA, 1949.

II. SECONDARY MATERIAL

General

CHAMBER OF COMMERCE OF THE UNITED STATES. America and the International Trade Organization. Washington, 1948, 101 p.

HUTCHESON, HAROLD H. Problems of the Underdeveloped Countries. (*Foreign Policy Reports,* XXIV, September 15, October 1, 1948, 98-106, 110-119.)

ISAACS, ASHER. International Trade: Tariff and Commercial Policies. Chicago, Irwin, 1948, 838 p.

WILCOX, CLAIR. A Charter for World Trade. New York, Macmillan, 1949, 333 p.
The ITO Charter, by a former U.S. official who had a large part in its creation.

European Recovery Program

APCHIÉ, M., and others. Le Continent américain et le déséquilibre mondial. Paris, Marcel Rivière, 1948, 227 p.
A collection of articles on the problems of European recovery, issued by the Centre d'Etudes de Politique Etrangère.

CROWTHER, GEOFFREY. The Economic Reconstruction of Europe. Claremont, Cal., Claremont College, 1948, 88 p.
Three essays by the editor of *The Economist.*

DIEBOLD, WILLIAM, JR. East-West Trade and the Marshall Plan. (*Foreign Affairs*, XXVI, July 1948, 709-722.)

GORDON, LINCOLN. ERP in Operation. (*Harvard Business Review*, XXVII, March 1949, 129-150.)

HABERLER, GOTTFRIED. Some Economic Problems of the European Recovery Program. (*American Economic Review*, XXXVIII, September 1948, 495-525.)

HARRIS, SEYMOUR E. The European Recovery Program. Cambridge, Harvard University Press, 1948, 309 p.

————. ERP: Progress and Prospects. (*Foreign Policy Reports*, XXV, April 15, 1949, 30-39.)

WILLIAMS, JOHN H. Europe After 1952: The Long-Term Recovery Problem. (*Foreign Affairs*, XXVII, April 1949, 426-448.)

EUROPEAN UNION AND THE ATLANTIC PACT

I. DOCUMENTS

UNITED KINGDOM. Treaty of Economic, Social and Cultural Collaboration and Collective Self-Defence between Great Britain and Northern Ireland, Belgium, France, Luxembourg, and the Netherlands, Brussels, March 17, 1948. London, Cmd. 7367, 1948.

INTERNATIONAL COMMITTEE OF THE MOVEMENTS FOR EUROPEAN UNITY. Congress of Europe, The Hague, May 1948, Resolutions. London, 1948.

U.S. CONGRESS (81ST, 1ST SESSION). Executive L (The North Atlantic Treaty). Message from the President of the United States transmitting a Copy of the North Atlantic Treaty Signed at Washington on April 4, 1949. Washington, 1949.

————. Documents Relating to the North Atlantic Treaty, printed for the Senate Foreign Relations Committee. Washington, 1949.

UNITED STATES. Report of the Secretary of State to the President on the North Atlantic Treaty, April 7, 1949. (*Department of State Bulletin*, XX, April 24, 1949, 532-536.)

II. SECONDARY MATERIAL

BOYD, ANDREW and FRANCES. Western Union. London, Hutchinson, 1948, 175 p.
  A discussion with documentary appendixes.

The British Commonwealth and European Union. (*Round Table*, March 1948, 520-544; June 1948, 633-642; September 1948, 742-761.)
  A series of articles expressing various points of view.

COURTIN, RENÉ. French Views on European Union. (*International Affairs*, XXV, January 1949, 8-22.)

————. Le problème de l'union économique européenne. (*Revue d'économie politique*, LVIII, May–June 1948, 366-393.)

DEAN, VERA MICHELES, and BLAIR BOLLES. North Atlantic Pact—Background and Pros and Cons. (*Foreign Policy Reports*, XXIV, February 15, 1949, 226-232.)

KIRK, GRAYSON. The Atlantic Pact and International Security. (*International Organization*, III, May 1949, 239-251.)

KNORR, KLAUS. What Manner of Union? (*World Politics*, I, January 1949, 233-242.)
  An analysis of the economic and constitutional problems of European union.

MACKAY, R. W. G. You Can't Turn the Clock Back. Chicago, Ziff-Davis, 1948, 367 p.

An M.P., leader of the British delegation to the Hague Congress of May 1948, argues for federal union of Europe.

MANSERGH, NICHOLAS. Britain, the Commonwealth, and Western Union. (*International Affairs*, XXIV, October 1948, 491-504.)

WARD, BARBARA. The West at Bay. New York, Norton; London, Allen & Unwin, 1948, 288 p.

By the foreign editor of *The Economist*.

UNITED NATIONS

I. DOCUMENTS

General

GOODRICH, LELAND M., and EDVARD HAMBRO. Charter of the United Nations: Commentary and Documents. Second and revised edition. Boston, World Peace Foundation, 1949, 710 p.

U.N. GENERAL ASSEMBLY (3RD SESSION). Annual Report of the Secretary-General on the Work of the Organization, 1 July 1947–30 June 1948. U.N. Doc. A/565, July 30, 1948 (printed as Supplement 1, General Assembly *Official Records*, Third Session).

U.S. DEPARTMENT OF STATE. The 80th Congress and the United Nations. International Organization and Conference Series III, 17. Washington, 1948.

——————. United States Participation in the United Nations: Report by the President to Congress for the Year 1948 on the Activities of the United Nations and the Participation of the United States Therein. International Organization and Conference Series III, 29. Washington, 1949.

General Assembly

U.N. GENERAL ASSEMBLY. Official Records of the Second Special Session. Lake Success, 1948. 2 vols., annex and 2 supp.

——————. Official Records of the Third Session, Part I. Paris, Lake Success, Geneva, 1948. 9 vols., 3 annexes and 12 supp.

——————. Universal Declaration of Human Rights approved by the General Assembly . . . on 6 December 1948. U.N. Doc. A/811, December 16, 1948.

Security Council

U.N. GENERAL ASSEMBLY (3RD SESSION). Report of the Security Council to the General Assembly Covering the Period from 16 July 1947 to 15 July 1948. U.N. Doc. A/620, September. 1948 (printed as Supplement 2, General Assembly *Official Records*, Third Session).

U.N. SECURITY COUNCIL. Official Records, Third Year. Lake Success, Paris, 1948.

——————. Official Records, Fourth Year. Lake Success, 1949.

Atomic Energy Commission

U.N. ATOMIC ENERGY COMMISSION. Third Report to the Security Council, 17 May 1948. U.N. Doc. AEC/31/Rev. 1, June 27, 1948 (printed as Special Supplement, Atomic Energy Commission *Official Records*, Third Year). Published also by the Department of State as International Organization and Conference Series III, 7, Washington, 1948.

U.S. DEPARTMENT OF STATE. Atomic Impasse, 1948: A Collection of Speeches by Frederick Osborn. International Organization and Conference Series III, 14. Washington, 1948.

By the deputy U.S. representative on the U.N. Atomic Energy Commission.

Economic and Social Council

U.N. GENERAL ASSEMBLY. Report of the Economic and Social Council Covering the Period from 18 August 1947 to 29 August 1948. U.N. Doc. A/625, September 1948 (printed as Supplement 3, General Assembly *Official Records,* Third Session).

U.N. ECONOMIC AND SOCIAL COUNCIL. Conference on Freedom of Information. Final Act. U.N. Doc. E/CONF.6/79, April 22, 1948.

————————. Economic Commission for Asia and the Far East. Interim Report to the Economic and Social Council. U.N. Doc. E/1088–E/CN.11/180/Rev. 1, December 12, 1948.

————————. Economic Commission for Europe. Annual Report, 15 July 1947– 8 May 1948. U.N. Doc. E/791, May 18, 1948.

————————. Economic Commission for Europe. Interim Report for the Period 8 March 1948–11 November 1948. U.N. Doc. E/1074–E/ECE/85, January 10, 1949.

————————. Economic Commission for Latin America. Interim Report for the Period 10 July 1948–10 January 1949. U.N. Doc. E/1099, January 10, 1949.

Trusteeship Council

U.N. GENERAL ASSEMBLY. Report of the Trusteeship Council Covering Its Second and Third Sessions, 29 April 1947–5 August 1948. U.N. Doc. A/603, August 20, 1948 (printed as Supplement No. 4, General Assembly *Official Records,* Third Session).

Specialized Agencies

FOOD AND AGRICULTURE ORGANIZATION. CONFERENCE (4TH SESSION). Work of FAO, 1947/48: Report of the Director General. Washington, 1948.

INTERNATIONAL LABOR ORGANIZATION. Second Report to the United Nations. Geneva, 1948.

INTERNATIONAL BANK FOR RECONSTRUCTION AND DEVELOPMENT. Third Annual Report, 1947–1948. Washington, 1948.

INTERNATIONAL MONETARY FUND. Annual Report of the Executive Directors for the Fiscal Year Ended April 30, 1948. Washington, 1948.

U.S. NATIONAL ADVISORY COUNCIL ON INTERNATIONAL MONETARY AND FINANCIAL PROBLEMS. First Special Report on the Operations and Policies of the International Monetary Fund and the International Bank for Reconstruction and Development, covering the first two years of operations of these institutions. 80th Cong., 2nd Sess., House Document No. 656, May 18, 1948. Washington, 1948.

INTERNATIONAL REFUGEE ORGANIZATION. Report to the General Council by the Executive Secretary of the Preparatory Commission, 1 July 1947 to 30 June 1948. Geneva, 1948.

U.N. ECONOMIC AND SOCIAL COUNCIL. Report of the International Civil Aviation Organization. U.N. Doc. E/808/Add. 2, August 16, 1948.

U.N. EDUCATIONAL, SCIENTIFIC AND CULTURAL ORGANIZATION. Report of the Director General on the Activities of the Organization in 1948. Paris, 1948.

II. SECONDARY MATERIAL

General

EVATT, HERBERT V. The United Nations. London, Oxford, 1948, 148 p.
By the Australian Minister of External Affairs and president of the Assembly's third regular session.

Security Matters

PADELFORD, NORMAN J. The Use of the Veto. (*International Organization,* II, June 1948, 227-246.)

Dependent Areas

GREEN, JAMES FREDERICK. The Trusteeship Council: Third Session. (*Documents and State Papers,* I, February 1949, 629-640.)
HALL, H. DUNCAN. Mandates, Dependencies and Trusteeships. Washington, Carnegie Endowment for International Peace, 1948, 429 p.
LIU, CHIEH. International Trusteeship System. (*International Conciliation,* No. 448, February 1949, 99-184.)

Specialized Agencies

HANSON, SIMON G. Case Study in Futility: United Nations Economic Commission for Latin America. (Inter-American Economic Affairs, II, Autumn 1948, 81-99.)
KOTSCHNIG, WALTER M. ECOSOC 1948: a Review and Forecast. (*Department of State Bulletin,* XX, January 2, 1949, 3-17.)
    By the Chief of the State Department's Division of U.N. Economic and Social Affairs.
MCKEON, RICHARD. The Pursuit of Peace through Understanding. (*Yale Review,* XXXVIII, Winter 1949, 253-269.)
    A discussion of UNESCO.
SHARP, W. R. The Specialized Agencies and the United Nations—Progress Report II. (*International Organization,* II, June 1948, 247-267.)
    Part I appeared in August 1947.

BRITISH COMMONWEALTH

I. DOCUMENTS

General

CANADA. DEPARTMENT OF EXTERNAL AFFAIRS. Official Communiqué at the Close of the London Meeting of Commonwealth Prime Ministers, October 22, 1948. (*External Affairs,* I, November 1948, 13-14.)
UNITED KINGDOM. The Colonial Empire, 1947–1948. London, Cmd. 7433, 1948.

United Kingdom

UNITED KINGDOM. Statement on Defence, 1949, presented by the Minister of Defence to Parliament by command of His Majesty, February 1949. London, Cmd. 7631, 1949.
    Includes a section on "Co-operation Within the Commonwealth and With Other Countries."

Canada and Newfoundland

CANADA. DEPARTMENT OF EXTERNAL AFFAIRS. Canada and the United Nations. Ottawa, 1949.
————. Report and Documents Relating to the Negotiations for the Union of Newfoundland with Canada. Conference Series No. 2. Ottawa, 1948.
————. Information Division. Reference Papers. No. 24. Newfoundland;

No. 26. Background of the Great Lakes-St. Lawrence Seaway and Power Project; No. 30. Canada's Foreign Trade; No. 33. Statements Made by the Canadian Government on the Proposed North Atlantic Treaty, January 20, 1948–October 25, 1948. Ottawa, 1948.

India and Pakistan

U.N. SECURITY COUNCIL. Commission for India and Pakistan. Interim Report. U.N. Doc. S/1100, November 22, 1948.

II. SECONDARY MATERIAL

General

HODSON, H. V. Twentieth Century Empire. London, Faber & Faber, 1948, 186 p.
  Brilliant expository essay on the Commonwealth's position in the world.
MANSERGH, NICHOLAS. The Commonwealth and the Nations: Studies in British Commonwealth Relations. London, Royal Institute of International Affairs, 1949, 236 p.
————. Postwar Strains on the British Commonwealth. (*Foreign Affairs*, XXVII, October 1948, 129-142.)
McGUIRE, PAUL. Experiment in World Order. New York, William Morrow, 1948, 412 p.
  The British Commonwealth.
MEYER, F. V. Britain's Colonies in World Trade. London, New York, Toronto, Oxford University Press, 1948, 281 p.
  Issued under the auspices of the Royal Institute of International Affairs.

United Kingdom

ADAMS, MILDRED, and WILLIAM W. WADE. Britain's Road to Recovery. New York, Foreign Policy Association, Headline Series, 1949, 62 p.
BALOGH, T. Britain's Foreign Trade Problem. (*Economic Journal*, LVIII, March 1948, 74-85.)
BRINTON, CRANE. The United States and Britain. Revised Edition. Cambridge, Harvard University Press, 1949, 326 p.

Canada and Newfoundland

BREBNER, J. BARTLET. A Changing North Atlantic Triangle. (*International Journal*, III, Autumn 1948, 309-319.)
  Discusses Canada's relations with the U.S. and the U.K.
GIBSON, J. D. (ed.). Canada's Economy in a Changing World. Toronto and London, Macmillan for the Canadian Institute of International Affairs, 1948, 380 p.
PEARSON, LESTER B. Canada and the North Atlantic Alliance. (*Foreign Affairs*, XXVII, April 1949, 369-378.)
  By the Canadian Secretary for External Affairs.
SOWARD, F. H. Canada in a Two-Power World. (Toronto, Canadian Association for Adult Education and Canadian Institute of International Affairs, *Behind the Headlines*, VIII, April 1948, 1-28.)
SOWARD, F. H., and A. M. MACAULAY. Canada and the Pan American System. Toronto, Ryerson Press for the Canadian Institute of International Affairs, 1948, 47 p.

India and Pakistan

BARTON, W. A Year of Independence in India and Pakistan. (*Quarterly Review,* CCLXXXVI, October 1948, 469-484.)
CHATTERJEE, ATUL. The New India. London, Allen & Unwin, 1948, 201 p.
Brief and lucid picture of India at the time of the transfer of power.
GRIFFITHS, PERCIVAL. India and Pakistan: The Second Year. (*Asiatic Review,* XLV, April 1949, 547-565.)
Kashmir. (*Indian Information,* XXII, April 1, 1948, 345-409.)
RAJPUT, R. B. Muslim League Yesterday and Today. Lahore, Shaikh Muhammad Ashraf, 1948, 288 p.
Interesting account by a Pakistani of the rise of Pakistan.
TALBOT, PHILLIPS. The Rise of Pakistan. (*Middle East Journal,* II, October 1948, 381-398.)
THORNER, ALICE. The Kashmir Conflict. (*Ibid.,* III, January 1949, 17-30; April 1949, 164-180.)

Ceylon

JENNINGS, W. IVOR. The Dominion of Ceylon. (*Pacific Affairs,* XXII, March 1949, 21-33.)

Malaya

DOBBY, E. H. Malaya and the Malayans. London, University of London Press, 1948, 186 p.
REES-WILLIAMS, DAVID R., and others. Three Reports on the Malayan Problem. New York, Institute of Pacific Relations, 1949, 46 p.

West Indies

WHITSON, A., and L. HORSFALL. Britain and the West Indies. London, Longmans Green, 1948, 87 p.

WESTERN EUROPE

I. DOCUMENTS

ITALY. Statement on foreign policy by Count Carlo Sforza in the Italian Chamber of Deputies, September 28, 1948. (*Relazioni Internazionali,* XII, October 9, 1948, 672-675.)
FRANCE-ITALY. Report of the Mixed Commission on the Franco-Italian Customs Union (*Ibid.,* XII, March 12, 1949, 172-174.)

II. SECONDARY MATERIAL

General

ALMOND, GABRIEL A. The Christian Parties of Western Europe. (*World Politics,* I, October 1948, 30-58.)
—————. Western European Politics and American Policy. New Haven, Yale Institute of International Studies, Memorandum No. 26, 1948, 43 p.
HEATON, HERBERT, and ALVIN JOHNSON. Socialism in Western Europe. New York, Foreign Policy Association, Headline Series, 1948, 62 p.

Low Countries

SILZ, EDOUARD. La Hollande et la crise du relèvement européen. (*Politique Etrangère,* XIII, August 1948, 351-368.)

VAN RAALTE, E. Van Nederlands-Belgische toenadering tot samenwerking, 1848–1948. (*Etudes Internationales*, I, April 1948, 203-219.)

France

COWAN, L. GRAY. The Techniques of the Communist Party in France. (*International Journal*, IV, Winter 1948–1949, 33-46.)
DIETERLEN, PIERRE, and CHARLES RIST. The Monetary Problem of France. New York, Columbia University Press for the Carnegie Endowment for International Peace, 1948, 98 p.
EHRMANN, HENRY W. Political Forces in Present-Day France. (*Social Research*, XV, June 1948, 146-169.)
JOLLY, P. Aspects of the French Economy. (*Harvard Business Review*, XXVI, May 1948, 257-266.)
Le Plan Marshall et l'Avenir de la France. (*Esprit*, XVI, April 1948, 513-631.) A series of articles.
ROUABLE, M. La Vie économique de l'Union Française. Paris, Dunod, 1948, 303 p.

Italy

KAPLAN, JACOB J. Economic Stagnation in Italy? New Haven, Yale Institute of International Studies, Memorandum No. 32, 1949, 34 p.
PERNOT, M. Le Vatican, la guerre et la paix. (*Politique Etrangère*, XIII, April 21, 1948, 147-166.)

Spain

Espagne: problème des relations internationales. Brussels, Institut des Relations Internationales, 1948, 122 p.

Scandinavia and Iceland

Iceland, Its Importance in the Air Age. (*World Today*, IV, July 1948, 297-307.)
Norway and the Atlantic Pact. (*Ibid.*, V, April 1949, 154-160.)
SEIDENFADEN, E. Scandinavia Charts a Course. (*Foreign Affairs*, XXVI, July 1948, 653-664.)

CENTRAL EUROPE

I. DOCUMENTS

Germany

CONTROL COMMISSION FOR GERMANY (BRITISH ELEMENT). Monthly Reports. Berlin, 1947– .
OFFICE OF MILITARY GOVERNMENT FOR GERMANY (U.S.). Reports of the Military Governor, U.S. Zone. Berlin, monthly.
INTER-ALLIED REPARATION AGENCY. Allied Economic Recovery: The Contribution of Industrial Capital Equipment Delivered by Germany as Reparation. Brussels, 1948.
——————. Report of the Secretary-General for the Year 1948. Brussels, 1949.
U.S. ECONOMIC COOPERATION ADMINISTRATION. Report on Plants Scheduled for Removal as Reparations from the Three Western Zones of Germany. Washington, 1949.
GREAT BRITAIN. Germany: An Account of the Events Leading up to a Reference of the Berlin Question to the United Nations. London, Cmd. 7534, 1948.

U.S. DEPARTMENT OF STATE. The Berlin Crisis: A Report on the Moscow Discussions. European and Commonwealth Series 1. Washington, 1948.
Documents, with supplementary comment.

U.S.S.R. MINISTRY OF FOREIGN AFFAIRS. The Soviet Union and the Berlin Question (Documents). Moscow, 1948.

U.S.S.R. Documents and Materials on the German Question. (Supplement to *New Times*, No. 27, June 30, 1948.)
Contains the declaration of the Warsaw conference of June 24, 1948, and the Soviet currency reform.

UNITED STATES. Communiqué, June 7, 1948, on London Conference Recommendations on Germany. (*Department of State Bulletin*, XVIII, June 20, 1948, 807-810.)

—————. Draft Agreement on the Ruhr, December 28, 1948. (*Ibid.*, XX, January 9, 1949, 43-52.)

—————. Tripartite Agreements on Germany, April 8, 1949. (*Ibid.*, XX, April 17, 1949, 499-501; April 24, 1949, 524-531; May 8, 1949, 589-592.)

U.S. DEPARTMENT OF STATE. The Bonn Constitution: Basic Law for the Federal Republic of Germany. European and British Commonwealth Series 8. Washington, 1949.

II. SECONDARY MATERIAL

Germany

BAUER, WILHELM. Das Deutsche Bevölkerungsproblem in Europäischer Sicht. (*Europa-Archiv*, III, June–July 1948, 1395-1410.)

CAREY, J. P. C. Germany Today: Security vs. Recovery. (*Foreign Policy Reports*, XXIV, March 1, 1949, 234-247.)

—————. German Politics and the East-West Deadlock. (*Ibid.*, CCV, April 1, 1949, 14-27.)

CORNIDES, WILHELM, and HERMANN VOLLE. Die Londoner Aussenministerkonferenz der vier Grossmächte. (*Europa-Archiv*, III, January 1948, 1067-1086.)
The most detailed published account of the London conference.

DEUTSCHES INSTITUT FÜR WIRTSCHAFTSFORSCHUNG. Wirtschaftsprobleme der Besatzungszonen. Berlin, Duncker & Humblot, 1948, 288 p.
A series of studies by German economists.

DIEBOLD, WILLIAM, JR. The Choice in the Ruhr. (*Foreign Affairs*, XXVII, October 1948, 117-128.)

HOOVER, CALVIN B. Germany and European Economic Recovery. (*Yale Review*, XXXVII, Spring 1948, 385-399.)

Die Industriestruktur in der Sowjetischen Besatsungszone Deutschlands. (*Europa-Archiv*, III, June–July 1948, 1421-1436.)

LEWIS, HAROLD O. New Constitution in Occupied Germany. Washington, Foundation for Foreign Affairs, 1948, 145 p.

NEUMANN, R. G. New Constitutions in Germany. (*American Political Science Review*, XLII, June 1948, 448-468.)

RODNICK, DAVID. Postwar Germans. New Haven, Yale University Press, 1948, 233 p.
A sociological study based on observations in two towns of the U.S. Zone.

SCHÖNKE, ADOLF (ed.). Postwar Reconstruction in Western Germany. (*Annals of the American Academy of Political and Social Science*, CCLX, November 1948, 250 p.)
A series of articles by German authors.

Situation politique de la zone française. (*France en Allemagne*, No. 8, March 1948, 81 p.)

Austria

BRAUNTHAL, JULIUS. The Tragedy of Austria. London, Gollancz, 1948, 216 p.
HADSEL, WINIFRED N. Austria Under Allied Occupation. (*Foreign Policy Reports*, XXIV, November 1, 1948, 134-144.)

EASTERN EUROPE

I. DOCUMENTS

General

HOWARD, HARRY N. The Soviet Alliance System, 1942–1948. (*Documents and State Papers*, I, July 1948, 219-249.)
————. New Links in the Soviet Alliance System, 1948–1949. (*Ibid.*, I, March and April, 1949, 681-684, 727.)
ROYAL INSTITUTE OF INTERNATIONAL AFFAIRS. The Soviet-Yugoslav Dispute. London, New York, 1948.
Texts of the letters between the Soviet and Yugoslav Communist parties, the Cominform resolution, and the Yugoslav reply.

Satellite Countries and Greece

U.N. GENERAL ASSEMBLY. Special Committee on the Balkans. Report . . . U.N. Doc. A/574, June 1948 (printed as Supplement 8, General Assembly *Official Records*, Third Session); and Supplementary Report for the Period 17 June to 10 September 1948. U.N. Doc. A/644, September 16, 1948 (printed as Supplement 8A, General Assembly *Official Records*, Third Session).
UNITED STATES. U.S.-Yugoslav Claims Settlement Agreements, July 19, 1948. (*Department of State Bulletin*, XIX, August 1, 1948, 137-140.)
————. U.S. Notes to Bulgaria, Hungary and Rumania, April 2, 1949, charging violations of human rights provisions in the peace treaties. (*Ibid.*, XX, April 10, 1949, 450-453.)
YUGOSLAVIA. COMMUNIST PARTY. Fifth Congress. Reports. Belgrade, 1948.

II. SECONDARY MATERIAL

General

CAMPBELL, JOHN C. Diplomacy on the Danube. (*Foreign Affairs*, XXVII, January 1949, 315-327.)
CORNIDES, WILHELM, and others. Die Osteuropäische Wirtschaftsrevolution. (*Wirtschafts-Archiv*, III, October 1948, 1603–1618.)
KOHN, HANS. Eastern Europe, 1948. (*Current History*, XVI, February 1949, 72-78; April 1949, 193-198.)
MCKITTERICK, T. E. M. Russian Economic Policy in Eastern Europe. London, Fabian Publications, 1948, 41 p.
SHARP, SAMUEL L. Federation in Eastern Europe. (*American Perspective*, I, March 1948, 612-627.)
SZALAI, A. La Coopération des économies planifiées du bassin danubien. (*Politique Étrangère*, XIII, June 1948, 223-234.)
WARRINER, DOREEN. Economic Changes in Eastern Europe Since the War. (*International Affairs*, XXV, April 1949, 157-167.)

U.S.S.R.

ARMSTRONG, W. C. The Soviet Approach to International Trade. (*Political Science Quarterly*, LXIII, September 1948, 368-382.)

DOBB, MAURICE. Soviet Economic Development Since 1917. London, Routledge & Kegan Paul, 1948, 474 p.

HISTORICUS. Stalin on Revolution. (*Foreign Affairs*, XXVII, January 1949, 175-214.)

KELSEN, HANS. The Political Theory of Bolshevism: A Critical Analysis. Berkeley, Cal., University of California Press, 1948, 60 p.

MAGIDOFF, ROBERT. In Anger and Pity: A Report on Russia. Garden City, N.Y., Doubleday, 1949, 278 p.
An account of life in Soviet Russia by a correspondent expelled after 12 years in Moscow.

MIKHAILOV, NICHOLAS. Soviet Russia: The Land and its People. New York, Sheridan House, 1948, 374 p.

NEWLAND, BERNARD. Baltic Background. London, Hale, 1948, 280 p.

TOWSTER, JULIAN. Political Power in the U.S.S.R., 1917–1947. New York, Oxford University Press, 1948, 443 p.

VOZNESENSKY, NIKOLAI A. The Economy of the U.S.S.R. During World War II. Washington, Public Affairs Press, 1948, 103 p.
An important Soviet work whose author is now in eclipse.

WINTERTON, PAUL. Inquest on an Ally. London, Cresset Press, 1948, 288 p.
Indictment of recent Soviet policy by a British correspondent formerly stationed in Moscow.

Finland, Poland, Czechoslovakia

La Crise Tchécoslovaque. (*Chronique de Politique Etrangère*, I, May 1948, 67-82.)

DUCHACEK, IVO. The Strategy of Communist Infiltration: The Case of Czechoslovakia. New Haven, Yale Institute of International Studies, 1949, 47 p.

ENCKELL, ARVID. Democratic Finland. London, H. Joseph, 1948, 151 p.

FRANCE. MINISTERE DES AFFAIRES ETRANGERES. Le relèvement économique et le plan triennal polonais. (*Notes Documentaires et Etudes*, No. 924, June 9, 1948, 1-23.)

JACKSON, J. HAMPDEN. Finland Since the Armistice. (*International Affairs*, XXIV, October 1948, 505-514.)

MIKOLAJCZYK, STANISLAW. The Rape of Poland. New York, Whittlesey House, 1948, 309 p.
By Poland's leading political exile.

ROSE, WILLIAM J. Poland Old and New. London, Bell, 1948, 354 p.

Hungary, Rumania

MARKHAM, REUBEN H. Rumania Under the Soviet Yoke. Boston, Meador, 1949, 601 p.

NAGY, FERENC. The Struggle Behind the Iron Curtain. New York, Macmillan, 1948, 471 p.
By the former Prime Minister of Hungary who was ousted in 1947.

Yugoslavia, Bulgaria, Albania

FOTITCH, CONSTANTIN. The War We Lost: Yugoslavia's Tragedy and the Failure of the West. New York, Viking, 1948, 334 p.
By the former Yugoslav Ambassador in Washington.

KERNER, ROBERT J. (ed.). Yugoslavia. Berkeley, Cal., University of California Press, 1949, 558 p.

Economic, psychological and political studies by various authorities. A volume in the United Nations Series.

PADEV, MICHAEL. Dimitrov Wastes No Bullets: Nikola Petkov, The Test Case. London, Eyre and Spottiswoode, 1948, 160 p.

SKENDI, S. Albania Within the Slav Orbit: Advent to Power of the Communist Party. (*Political Science Quarterly*, LXIII, June 1948, 257-274.)

Greece

BLACK, CYRIL E. Greece and the United Nations. (*Political Science Quarterly*, LXIII, December 1948, 551-586.)

HOWARD, HARRY N. The Problem of Greece in the Third Session of the General Assembly. (*Documents and State Papers*, I, January 1949, 545-614.)

SMOTHERS, FRANK, and others. Report on the Greeks. New York, Twentieth Century Fund, 1948, 226 p.
Report of an on-the-spot inquiry in 1947.

MIDDLE EAST AND AFRICA

I. DOCUMENTS

UNITED KINGDOM. Palestine: Termination of the Mandate, 15 May 1948: Statement Prepared for Public Information by the Colonial Office and Foreign Office. London, 1948.

U.N. GENERAL ASSEMBLY. PALESTINE COMMISSION. Report. U.N. Doc. A/532, April 10, 1948 (printed as Supplement 1, General Assembly *Official Records*, Second Special Session).

U.N. GENERAL ASSEMBLY. Progress Report of the United Nations Mediator on Palestine. U.N. Doc. A/648, etc., September 18, 1948 (printed as Supplement 2, U.N. General Assembly *Official Records*, Third Session).
The Bernadotte report.

————. Progress Report of the United Nations Acting Mediator on Palestine: Assistance to Refugees. U.N. Doc. A/689, etc., October 18, 19, 1948 (printed as Supplement 11A, General Assembly *Official Records*, Third Session).

FRANCE. MINISTERE DES AFFAIRES ETRANGERES. Situation économique et politique des anciennes colonies italiennes d'après le rapport de la Commission d'enquête des quatre puissances. (*Notes Documentaires et Etudes*, Nos. 1025, 1026, November 27, 29, 1948.)

II. SECONDARY MATERIAL

General

BONNE, ALFRED. State and Economics in the Middle East: A Society in Transition. London, K. Paul, Trench, Trubner, 1948, 427 p.
Survey from the turn of the century to the present.

ELIOT, GEORGE FIELDING. Hate, Hope and High Explosives: A Report on the Middle East. Indianapolis, Bobbs-Merrill, 1948, 284 p.

HALL, HARVEY P. American Interests in the Middle East. New York, Foreign Policy Association, Headline Series, 1948, 61 p.

HINDUS, MAURICE G. In Search of a Future: Persia, Egypt, Iraq and Palestine. Garden City, N.Y., Doubleday, 1949, 270 p.

KIRK, GEORGE E. A Short History of the Middle East. London, Methuen, 1948, 301 p.

ROOSEVELT, KERMIT. Arabs, Oil and History: The Story of the Middle East. New York, Harper, 1949, 271 p.
WARRINER, DOREEN. Land and Poverty in the Middle East. London, Royal Institute of International Affairs, 1948, 148 p.

Turkey

LINGEMAN, ERIC R. Turkey: Economic and Commercial Conditions. London, H.M. Stationery Office, 1948, 228 p.
SARC, OMER CELAL. Economic Policy of the New Turkey. (*Middle East Journal*, II, October 1948, 430-446.)

Palestine

CUNNINGHAM, ALAN. Palestine: The Last Days of the Mandate. (*International Affairs*, XXIV, October 1948, 481-490.)
    By the British High Commissioner in Palestine.
EBON, MARTIN. Communist Tactics in Palestine. (*Middle East Journal*, II, July 1948, 255-269.)
GARCÍA GRANADOS, JORGE. The Birth of Israel: The Drama as I Saw It. New York, Knopf, 1948, 291 p.
    By the Guatemalan representative on the U.N. Special Committee on Palestine.
HOBMAN, J. B. (ed.). Palestine's Economic Future: A Review of Progress and Prospects. London, Lund Humphries, 1948, 310 p.
    Twenty-three contributions by various authors, with an introduction by Chaim Weizmann.
JOSEPH, BERNARD. British Rule in Palestine. Washington, Public Affairs Press, 1948, 286 p.
    A critical account.
WEIZMANN, CHAIM. Trial and Error. New York, Harper, 1949, 482 p.
    The autobiography of Israel's first president.

The Arab World

COLOMBE, M. La Grande Bretagne et le nationalisme arabe. (*Cahiers du Monde Nouveau*, IV, April 1948, 47-58.)
KIRK, GEORGE. Independent Syria and Lebanon. (*Journal of the Royal Central Asian Society*, XXXV, July–October 1948, 259-272.)
MIKESELL, RAYMOND F., and HOLLIS B. CHENERY. Arabian Oil: America's Stake in the Middle East. Chapel Hill, N.C., University of North Carolina Press, 1949, 201 p.
SETON-WILLIAMS, M. V. Britain and the Arab States. London, Luzac, 1948, 330 p.
    A brief survey of Anglo-Arab relations since 1920.

Iran

ELWELL-SUTTON, L. P. Political Parties in Iran. (*Middle East Journal*, III, January 1949, 45-62.)
WILBUR, DONALD N. Iran: Past and Present. Princeton, Princeton University Press, 1948, 234 p.

Africa

BATTEN, THOMAS R. Problems of African Development. Part I, Land and Labour, 186 p. Part II, Government and People, 190 p. London, Oxford University Press, 1947, 1948.

The Fate of Italy's Colonies: A Report to the Fabian Colonial Bureau. London, Fabian Publications and Gollancz, 1948, 96 p.

KRAFT, LOUIS. Pan-Africanism: Political, Economic, Strategic, or Scientific? (*International Affairs*, XXIV, April 1948, 218-228.)

LAVERGNE, B. Une Révolution dans la politique coloniale de la France: Le problème de l'Afrique du Nord. Paris, Librairie Mercure, 1948, 227 p.

PEKHAM, MARGERY. The Government of Ethiopia. London, Faber and Faber, 1948, 481 p.

RIVLIN, BENJAMIN. Unity and Nationalism in Libya. (*Middle East Journal*, III, January 1949, 31-44.)

THE FAR EAST

I. DOCUMENTS

General

INSTITUTE OF PACIFIC RELATIONS. Asian Relations: Report of First Asian Relations Conference, New Delhi, March–April, 1947. New York, 1949.

U.N. ECONOMIC COMMISSION FOR ASIA AND THE FAR EAST. Economic Survey of Asia and the Far East, 1947. Shanghai, 1948.

China

U.S. CONGRESS (81ST, 1ST SESSION). H. Report 329 (Amending the China Aid Act of 1948), March 28, 1949. Report from the House Committee on Foreign Affairs to accompany H.R. 3830. Washington, 1949.

U.S. ECONOMIC COOPERATION ADMINISTRATION. Economic Aid to China under the China Aid Act of 1948. Washington, 1949.

Japan

FAR EASTERN COMMISSION. Second Report by the Secretary-General, July 10, 1947–December 23, 1948. U.S. Department of State, Far Eastern Series 29. Washington, 1949.

SUPREME COMMANDER FOR THE ALLIED POWERS. Education in the New Japan. Tokyo, 1948.

Korea

U.N. GENERAL ASSEMBLY (3D SESSION). Report of the United Nations Temporary Commission on Korea . . . U.N. Doc. A/575, August–November 1948. 5 parts. (Printed as Supplement 9, General Assembly *Official Records,* Third Session).

U.S. DEPARTMENT OF STATE. Korea, 1945 to 1948: A Report on Political Developments and Economic Resources with Selected Documents. Far Eastern Series 28. Washington, 1948.

Southeast Asia

U.N. SECURITY COUNCIL. COMMITTEE OF GOOD OFFICES ON THE INDONESIAN QUESTION. First Interim Report . . . (U.N. Doc. S/649, February 10, 1948); Second Interim Report (S/787, May 26, 1948); Third Interim Report (S/848 and S/848/Add. 1, June 21, July 6, 1948); Fourth Interim Report (S/1085, November 15, 1948); Special Report to the Security Council, with Appendixes (S/1117 and S/1117/Add. 1, December 13, 15, 1948).

II. SECONDARY MATERIAL

General

CLYDE, PAUL HIBBERT. The Far East: A History of the Impact of the West on Eastern Asia. New York, Prentice-Hall, 1948, 862 p.

DALLIN, DAVID J. Soviet Russia and the Far East. New Haven, Yale University Press, 1948, 398 p.

GUILLON, J. Les Peuples d'Asie en lutte pour leur indépendance nationale: Chine et sud-est asiatique. (*Cahiers du Communisme,* XXV, November 1948, 1273-1286.)
A Communist interpretation.

LATTIMORE, OWEN. The Situation in Asia. Boston, Atlantic-Little Brown, 1949, 244 p.

LEVY, ROGER. Extrême-Orient et Pacifique. Paris, Armand Colin, 1948, 200 p.
A political and economic survey, a complete revision of the earlier edition.

SCHECHTMAN, JOSEPH B. Population Transfers in Asia. New York, Hallsby Press, 1949, 149 p.

China

BAND, CLAIRE, and WILLIAM BAND. Two Years with the Chinese Communists. New Haven, Yale University Press, 1948, 347 p.

COPLAND, D. B. United States Policy in China. (*Pacific Affairs,* XXI, December 1948, 339-347.)

FAIRBANK, JOHN KING. The United States and China. Cambridge, Harvard University Press, 1948, 384 p.

GRIGGS, DAVID THURSTON. Americans in China: Some Chinese Views. Washington, Foundation for Foreign Affairs, 1948, 59 p.
Chinese opinion on U.S. policy.

McLEAN, N. L. D. Sinkiang Today. (*International Affairs,* XXIV, July 1948, 377-386.)

MARKER, A. E. A Survey of Economic Problems in China. (*Ibid.,* XXV, January 1949, 23-36.)

PEFFER, NATHANIEL. What Is Our Stake in China? (*Virginia Quarterly Review,* XXIV, Summer 1948, 354-367.)

WINFIELD, GERALD F. China: The Land and the People. New York, William Sloane Associates in cooperation with the American Institute of Pacific Relations, 1948, 437 p.

Japan

BALL, WILLIAM MACMAHON. Japan, Enemy or Ally? London, Cassel, 1948, 239 p.
Review of the occupation by the former British Commonwealth representative on the Allied Council.

BISSON, T. A. Prospects for Democracy in Japan. New York, Macmillan, 1948, 143 p.
A critical study of SCAP's record by a former official. Published under the auspices of the Institute of Pacific Relations.

BRINES, RUSSELL. MacArthur's Japan. Philadelphia, Lippincott, 1948, 247 p.

COHEN, JEROME B. Japan's Economy on the Road Back. (*Pacific Affairs,* XXI, 264-279.)

GAYN, MARK. Japan Diary. New York, William Sloane Associates, 1948, 517 p.
A journalist's critical account of occupation policies.

LADEJINSKY, W. I. Trial Balance in Japan. (*Foreign Affairs*, XXVII, October 1948, 104-116.)
Evaluation of occupation results by a former SCAP consultant.
MARTIN, EDWIN M. Allied Occupation of Japan. New York, American Institute of Pacific Relations, 1948, 130 p.
A factual account by a State Department official.
OKUBO, GENJI. The Problem of the Emperor System in Postwar Japan. Tokyo, Japan Institute of Pacific Studies, 1948, 87 p.
QUIGLEY, HAROLD S. (ed.). Postwar Politics in Japan: A Symposium. (*American Political Science Review*, XVII, October 1948, 927-969; December 1948, 1149-1180.)
STRATTON, SAMUEL S. The Far Eastern Commission (*International Organization*, II, February 1948, 1-18.)

Korea

MCCUNE, GEORGE M. The Korean Situation. (*Far Eastern Survey*, XVII, September 8, 1948, 197-202.)
WEEMS, BENJAMIN. Behind the Korean Election. (*Ibid.*, XVII, June 23, 1948, 142-146.)

Southeast Asia

Communism in South East Asia. (*British Survey*, IX, November 1948, 1-16.)
DUBOIS, CORA A. Social Forces in Southeast Asia. Minneapolis, University of Minnesota Press, 1949, 78 p.
FURNIVAL, JOHN S. Colonial Policy and Practice: A Comparative Study of Burma and Netherlands India. Cambridge (England) University Press, 1949, 568 p.
JACOBY, ERICH H. Agrarian Unrest in Southeast Asia. New York, Columbia University Press, 1949, 287 p.
LANDON, KENNETH P. Southeast Asia: Crossroads of Religion. Chicago, University of Chicago Press, 1948, 236 p.

Burma

APPLETON, G. The Burmese Viewpoint. (*Asiatic Review*, XLIV, July 1948, 233-251.)
FURNIVAL, JOHN S. Twilight in Burma: Reconquest and Crisis. (*Pacific Affairs*, XXII, March 1949, 3-20.)
MACDOUGAL, SIR RAIBEART M. Burma Stands Alone. (*Foreign Affairs*, XXVI, April 1948, 542-553.)

Indochina

HAMMER, ELLEN J. Blueprinting a New Indochina. (*Pacific Affairs*, XXI, September 1948, 252-263.)

Indonesia

EMERSON, RUPERT. Reflections on the Indonesian Case. (*World Politics*, I, October 1948, 59-81.)
OVERDIJKINK, G. W. Het Indonesische Probleem: Nieuwe Feiten. Amsterdam, Keizerskroon, 1948, 268 p.
SJAHRIR, SOETAN. Out of Exile. Translated and with Introduction by Charles Wolf, Jr. New York, John Day Co., 1949, 261 p.
By the former Premier and Foreign Minister of the Republic of Indonesia.

Philippines

ROSINGER, LAWRENCE K. The Philippines: Problems of Independence. (*Foreign Policy Reports,* XXIV, September 1, 1948, 81-96.)

LATIN AMERICA

I. DOCUMENTS

General

ORGANIZATION OF AMERICAN STATES. Report on the Ninth International Conference by the Secretary General. (*Annals of the Organization of American States,* I, [Spring, 1949] 1-75.)
————. Charter of the Organization of American States. (*Ibid.,* 76-86.)
————. American Treaty on Pacific Settlement ("Pact of Bogotá"). (*Ibid.,* 91-98.)
————. Economic Agreement of Bogotá. (*Ibid.,* 99-108.)
U.S. DEPARTMENT OF STATE. Ninth International Conference of American States, Bogotá, Colombia, March 30–May 2, 1948: Report of the Delegation of the United States of America, with Related Documents. International Organization and Conference Series II, 3. Washington, 1948.

II. SECONDARY MATERIAL

General

An Appraisal of the Inter-American System: A Symposium. (*Inter-American Economic Affairs,* II, Spring 1949, 45-95.)
DORFMAN, A. Latin-American Economic Problems and International Cooperation. (*International Labour Review,* LVIII, November 1948, 601-624.)
DOZER, DONALD MARQUAND. Roots of Revolution in Latin America. (*Foreign Affairs,* XXVII, January 1949, 274-288.)
FENWICK, CHARLES G. The Inter-American Regional System. New York, Declan H. McMullen Co., 1949, 96 p.
JOSEPHS, RAY. Latin America: Continent in Crisis. New York, Random House, 1948, 503 p.
HALLE, LOUIS J. Significance of the Institute of Inter-American Affairs in the Conduct of U.S. Foreign Policy. Department of State, Inter-American Series 36. Washington, 1948.
KUNZ, JOSEF L. The Bogotá Charter of the Organization of American States. (*American Journal of International Law,* XLII, July 1948, 568-589.)
LOCKWOOD, J. E. The Economic Agreement of Bogotá. (*Ibid.,* XLII, July 1948, 611-620.)
MONSMA, GEORGE N. Organization of American States. (*Department of State Bulletin,* XIX, November 14, 1948, 591-597.)
PRICE, WILLARD. Roving South, Rio Grande to Patagonia. New York, John Day Company, 1948, 373 p.
  A correspondent's notes on Latin America.
SANDERS, WILLIAM. The Organization of American States. (*International Conciliation,* No. 442, June 1948, 383-433.)
  A summary of the Bogotá conference by a member of the U.S. delegation, with the text of the charter.
STUNTZ, ALBERT EDWARD. To Make the People Strong. New York, Macmillan, 1948, 298 p.

An account of projects undertaken in Latin America by the Institute of Inter-American Affairs.

WILLNER, ANN R. Case Study in Frustration: Latin America and Economic Issues at Postwar Inter-American Conferences. (*Inter-American Economic Affairs*, II, Spring 1949, 29-44.)

South American Countries

Constitutional Evolution in Brazil. (*World Today*, IV, August 1948, 354-362.)

HENNESSEY, J. F. Argentine-British Trade Pact. (*Bulletin of the Pan American Union*, LXXXII, May 1948, 272-278.)

————. National Economy of Brazil. (*Commercial Pan America*, No. 181, July 1948, 1-73; No. 183, November 1948, 1-34.)

KERSHAW, J. Q. Postwar Brazilian Economic Problems. (*American Economic Review*, XXXVIII, June 1948, 328-340.)

MORENO QUINTANA, LUCIO M. Politica Internacional de la Republica Argentina. Buenos Aires, Instituto de Derecho Internacional, 1948, 74 p.

SALZMAN, O. H. National Economy of Venezuela. (*Commercial Pan America*, No. 180, July 1948, 1-77.)

SPIEGEL, HENRY WILLIAM. The Brazilian Economy: Chronic Inflation and Sporadic Industrialization. Philadelphia, Blakiston, 1949, 246 p.

WHITAKER, ARTHUR P. The United States and South America: The Northern Republics. Cambridge, Harvard University Press, 1948, 280 p.

Mexico, Central America and the Caribbean

CARLSON, REYNOLD E. Economic Development in Central America. (*Inter-American Economic Affairs*, II, Autumn 1948, 5-29.)

HUMPHREYS, R. A. The Anglo-Guatemalan Dispute. (*International Affairs*, XXIV, July 1948, 387-404.)

TANNENBAUM, FRANK. The Anvil of American Foreign Policy. (*Political Science Quarterly*, LXIII, December 1948, 501-527.)
U.S. relations with Mexico.

CHRONOLOGY OF WORLD EVENTS

JANUARY 1–DECEMBER 31, 1948

In any such general chronology as this the selection of items must be somewhat arbitrary. An attempt has been made to include the most significant international agreements, statements of policy, changes in government, and general elections. The division is into broad geographical headings, plus one on the United Nations which covers the specialized agencies and other international organizations and conferences as well as the United Nations organization itself. Items under the heading "United States" are confined to events directly affecting foreign relations, chiefly acts and statements of the executive and Congress. The reader who desires a more complete and detailed chronology is referred to the *Chronology of International Events and Documents,* published fortnightly by the Royal Institute of International Affairs in London.

UNITED NATIONS

January 1948

1. India calls the Security Council's attention to the situation in Jammu and Kashmir resulting from invasion of armed raiders from Pakistan.

5. The Interim Committee holds its first meeting at Lake Success.

15. Pakistan replies to India's complaints and lodges a countercomplaint.

20. The Security Council establishes a commission to deal with the situation in Jammu and Kashmir.

23. The Soviet Government informs the U.N. that the Temporary Commission on Korea will not be permitted to visit northern Korea.

February 1948

2–March 11. Sixth session of the Economic and Social Council, at Lake Success.

10–March 10. The Trusteeship Council holds the second part of its second session at Lake Success.

19–March 6. A U.N. Maritime Conference meets in Geneva and draws up a convention establishing an Intergovernmental Maritime Consultative Organization.

25. The Economic and Social Council establishes an Economic Commission for Latin America with headquarters at Santiago, Chile.

26. The Interim Committee directs the Temporary Commission on Korea to observe the elections in those parts of Korea to which it has access.

March 1948

17. The Security Council decides to consider a Chilean request of March 12 for investigation into the part played by the U.S.S.R. in recent events in Czechoslovakia.

23. The Secretary General signs an agreement with the U.S. for an interest-free loan of $65 million to finance construction of permanent U.N. headquarters.

23–April 21. The U.N. Conference on Freedom of Information meets in

Geneva. The final act includes draft conventions on (1) gathering and international transmission of news; (2) international right of correction; (3) freedom of information.

24. The U.N. Conference on Trade and Employment, which convened in Havana on November 21, 1947, adjourns. Fifty-three states sign the final act establishing the International Trade Organization. Argentina and Poland refuse to sign.

April 1948

7. The World Health Organization comes into being, its constitution having been ratified by 26 U.N. members.

10. The Security Council recommends to the General Assembly that Burma be admitted to membership. Italy's application is again rejected because of a Soviet veto.

16–May 14. Second special session of the General Assembly meets at Flushing Meadow, New York to consider the Palestine question.

17. The Security Council approves by 9 votes to 2 (U.S.S.R. and Ukraine) a resolution calling for a truce in Palestine.

19. Burma is admitted to membership in the U.N.

21. The Security Council adopts a resolution creating a five-nation Commission for India and Pakistan.

21–May 4. The Trusteeship Council holds the third part of its second session.

23. The Security Council establishes a Palestine Truce Commission.

26–May 8. The Economic Commission for Europe holds its third session in Geneva.

May 1948

4–12. The Preparatory Commission of the International Refugee Organization meets in Geneva and asks that negotiations be carried on with governments for acceptance of their fair share of refugees and DP's.

17. The Atomic Energy Commission decides by 9 votes to 2 (U.S.S.R. and Ukraine) to suspend its work until such time as basic agreement between the great powers on fundamental problems is reached.

20. Count Folke Bernadotte, President of the Swedish Red Cross, is unanimously appointed Mediator in Palestine by the permanent members of the Security Council.

24. The U.S.S.R. twice exercises the veto in Security Council discussion of its alleged interference in the internal affairs of Czechoslovakia.

28. The International Court of Justice renders an advisory opinion requested by the General Assembly on the conditions of admission to U.N. membership.

29. The Security Council calls for a truce in Palestine for a four-week period and instructs the U.N. Mediator in concert with the Truce Commission to supervise its observance.

June 1948

1–12. The Economic Commission for Asia and the Far East holds its third session at Ootacamund, India.

1–21. The assembly of the International Civil Aviation Organization holds its second session in Geneva.

7–25. The first session of the Economic Commission for Latin America is held at Santiago, Chile. The Commission is instructed to prepare an economic survey of Latin America.

16–Aug. 5. The third session of the Trusteeship Council is held in New York.

17–July 10. The International Labor Organization holds its 31st general conference in San Francisco.

24–July 24. The first assembly of the World Health Organization is held in Geneva.

30. The Special Committee on the Balkans adopts a report to the General Assembly making recommendations with regard to relations between Albania, Bulgaria, Yugoslavia and Greece.

July 1948

15. The Security Council orders a truce in Palestine, to remain in force until a peaceful settlement is reached.

19–Aug. 29. The Economic and Social Council holds its seventh session in Geneva. It transmits to the General Assembly the draft International Declaration of Human Rights and draft conventions on Genocide and Freedom of Information.

28. Yugoslavia charges before the Security Council that financial agreements between the Anglo-American military government in Trieste and the Italian Government violate the Italian peace treaty.

29. The Security Council calls upon the Netherlands and the Republic of Indonesia to maintain strict observance of the Renville truce agreement.

August 1948

12. The Commission for Conventional Armaments decides that regulation and reduction of armaments is impossible under existing conditions.

13. The United Nations Commission for India and Pakistan presents a proposal for a cease-fire and plebiscite in Kashmir.

18. The U.S.S.R. vetoes Ceylon's application for membership.

19. The Security Council decides to take no action on the Yugoslav complaint concerning Trieste.

20. The International Refugee Organization (IRO) officially comes into being.

21. Hyderabad refers its dispute with India to the Security Council.

September 1948

6. The Commission for India and Pakistan reports that conditions imposed by both countries make it impossible to carry out a cease-fire resolution.

13–25. The General Council of the International Refugee Organization meets in Geneva and approves an agreement to bring IRO into relationship with the United Nations.

17. Count Folke Bernadotte, Mediator for Palestine, and Colonel André P. Serot, a U.N. observer, are assassinated in Jerusalem.

20. A report by Count Bernadotte containing new suggestions for a settlement in Palestine is published.

21–December 12. The first part of the third regular session of the General Assembly is held at the Palais de Chaillot in Paris. Dr. Herbert V. Evatt of Australia is elected President.

27–28. The Security Council holds inconclusive discussions of the Hyderabad case.

29. France, the United Kingdom and the United States request the Security Council to consider the Berlin situation at the earliest opportunity, charging that Soviet actions constitute a threat to peace.

October 1948

5. The Security Council by a vote of 9 to 2 decides to take up the Berlin question. The delegates of the Ukrainian S.S.R. and the U.S.S.R. announce that they will not participate in the discussion.

8. The General Assembly elects Cuba, Egypt and Norway for two-year terms as nonpermanent members of the Security Council, replacing Belgium, Colombia and Syria as of January 1, 1949.

19. The Security Council orders a new cease-fire in Palestine following the outbreak of renewed fighting in the Negeb.

24. Yugoslavia complains to the Security Council of fresh violations of the Italian peace treaty by the Anglo-American military administration in Trieste.

25. The U.S.S.R. vetoes in the Security Council the resolution for settling the Berlin dispute proposed by the six nonpermanent members.

November 1948

3. The General Assembly unanimously adopts a resolution appealing to the great powers to redouble their efforts to conclude peace settlements and establish a lasting peace.

4. The General Assembly adopts a resolution on atomic energy, requesting the six permanent members of the Atomic Energy Commission to seek a basis for agreement and urging the Commission to continue its work.

The Security Council calls upon the parties in the Palestine dispute to withdraw their forces to the lines held on October 14.

7. The International Court of Justice begins hearings on the Corfu Channel case.

15–30. The fourth annual conference of the Food and Agriculture Organization is held in Washington, D.C.

16. The Security Council calls on the parties in the Palestine conflict to negotiate for the immediate establishment of an armistice.

17–December 1. UNESCO holds its third annual conference in Beirut, Lebanon. The conference elects a new Director-General, Jaime Torres-Bodet of Mexico, to replace Dr. Julian Huxley.

19. The General Assembly recommends that the Security Council pursue the study of the regulation and reduction of conventional armaments and armed forces through the agency of the Commission for Conventional Armaments. The Assembly also approves a relief program for Palestine refugees.

25. The Security Council endorses the appeal of the Commission for India and Pakistan to the two governments to refrain from any action which might aggravate the military and political situation.

26. The General Assembly maintains its recommendation of December 14, 1946 that South West Africa be placed under the trusteeship system.

27. The Assembly calls on Albania, Bulgaria and Yugoslavia to cease rendering support to the Greek guerrilla forces, and decides to continue the Special Committee on the Balkans.

December 1948

1. The parties to the Berlin dispute agree to refer the currency question to a commission of experts.

3. The General Assembly reestablishes the Interim Committee with slightly broadened functions.

8. The Assembly asks the Security Council to reconsider individually the membership applications of Albania, Austria, Bulgaria, Ceylon, Finland, Hun-

gary, Ireland, Italy, the Mongolian People's Republic, Portugal, Rumania and Transjordan.

9. The General Assembly unanimously approves the Convention on the Prevention and Punishment of the Crime of Genocide.

10. The General Assembly adopts the Universal Declaration of Human Rights as "a common standard of achievement for all peoples and all nations."

11. The General Assembly establishes a three-nation Conciliation Commission on Palestine (France, Turkey, U.S.A.).

12. Before ending the first part of its third session the General Assembly endorses the government of the Republic of Korea; recommends that the occupying powers withdraw their forces from Korea as soon as possible; and establishes a new Commission on Korea.

15. In the Security Council the Soviet Union for the second time vetoes Ceylon's application for U.N. membership.

17. The Security Council fails to recommend Israel for membership in the U.N., the vote being 5 in favor, 1 against, and 5 abstentions.

23-25. India and Pakistan accept the arrangements for a plebiscite worked out in Paris with the U.N. Commission.

24. The Security Council calls on the parties in the Indonesian dispute to cease hostilities and release political prisoners arrested since December 18.

29. Following the outbreak of hostilities in Palestine, the Security Council calls on the parties to order an immediate cease-fire and to implement the resolution of November 4.

UNITED STATES *

March 1948

1. The Department of Commerce institutes export controls on all important shipments to Europe.

6. A new International Wheat Agreement is signed in Washington.

14. The Senate passes ERP by 65 to 17 votes.

17. President Truman calls on Congress to revive the draft temporarily, condemns Soviet aggressive policies, and endorses the Brussels treaty concluded the same day (see "Europe").

31. The House of Representatives passes ERP by 329 to 74.

April 1948

3. President Truman signs the Foreign Assistance Act of 1948, authorizing $5.3 billion for European recovery.

6. Truman nominates Paul G. Hoffman as Economic Cooperation Administrator.

May 1948

4. U.S. Ambassador W. B. Smith addresses a formal statement to Soviet Foreign Minister Molotov in which the U.S. declares its peaceful intentions, lays the onus for the current international situation on the U.S.S.R., but leaves the door "always open for full discussion and the composing of our differences."

5. Secretary Marshall makes a statement of U.S. foreign policy before the House Committee on Foreign Affairs.

9. In a reply to the aide-mémoire of May 4 the U.S.S.R. blames the U.S.

* For relations of the U.S. with individual countries see the appropriate geographical headings.

for "the present unsatisfactory state" of U.S.-Soviet relations and says it accepts the U.S. "proposal" to begin discussion and settlement of differences.

18. The State Department issues a formal statement on American-Soviet relations in connection with the Smith-Molotov exchange.

June 1948

4. The House passes an omnibus foreign aid appropriation bill reducing funds for ERP.

11. The Senate approves the so-called Vandenberg Resolution supporting the principle of U.S. association with certain types of regional collective security arrangements.

16. The Senate restores most of the cuts made by the House of Representatives in the ERP appropriation bill.

25. President Truman signs with strong criticism a Displaced Persons Act to admit 205,000 displaced persons from Europe outside the quota over two years.

28. President Truman signs the Foreign Aid Appropriations Act.

July 1948

6. Informal talks are begun with representatives of Canada, the U.K., France and the Benelux governments on the security of the North Atlantic region.

August 1948

6. The Senate Foreign Relations Committee approves the International Wheat Agreement but consideration by the Senate is deferred until January.

19. A note is handed to the Soviet Ambassador stating that the actions of the Soviet Consul General in New York in regard to Russian nationals in that area constitute abuse of his position and that his departure from the U.S. is requested.

24. The Soviet Government in reply to the U.S. note of August 19 rejects the criticism of its Consul General in New York, states that Soviet consular offices in the U.S. are being closed, and requests the closing of U.S. consular offices in the U.S.S.R.

27. The State Department declares that the U.S. strongly favors "the progressively closer integration of the free nations of western Europe."

November 1948

2. Harry S. Truman is elected President of the United States.

December 1948

10. Conversations with Canadian and western European representatives on the proposed North Atlantic treaty are resumed in Washington.

BRITISH COMMONWEALTH *

January 1948

1. *India* refers its dispute with Pakistan over Kashmir to the Security Council (for further references, see "United Nations").

4. *Burma* becomes an independent state.

21. *Malaya*—The nine rulers of the Malay States sign a treaty to establish the Federation of Malaya and also new treaties with the U.K.

* For relations of the U.K. with individual countries see the appropriate geographical headings.

22. *U.K.*—Foreign Secretary Bevin reviews foreign affairs in the House of Commons and proposes "a consolidation of western Europe."

30. *India*—Mahatma Gandhi is shot and killed by a Hindu while on his way to evening prayer at Delhi.

February 1948

4. *Ceylon* becomes a self-governing dominion in the British Commonwealth.

6. *Eire*—In a general election for the Dail, Premier Eamon de Valera's Fianna Fail party loses its majority.

18. *Eire*—The new Dail meets. James A. Costello is elected Prime Minister in place of de Valera.

March 1948

17. *U.K.*—Brussels treaty signed (see "Europe").

April 1948

6. *East Africa*—The new Central Legislative Assembly of East Africa meets for the first time in Nairobi.

May 1948

3. *India*—Sir Chakravarty Rajagopalachari is appointed Governor General to succeed Lord Mountbatten, who is to relinquish office on June 21.

17. *British West Indies*—The Colonial Office announces that a standing committee has been set up to make recommendations for closer association among the colonies in accordance with the resolution of the Montego Bay Conference in September 1947.

June 1948

3. *Newfoundland*—In a referendum to decide on the future position of Newfoundland no choice receives the required 51 percent of the vote.

South Africa—Dr. Daniel F. Malan, Nationalist leader, forms a new government with himself as Prime Minister and Minister for External Affairs. In a broadcast on June 4 he emphasizes South Africa's independent stand in Commonwealth and U.N. relations.

14. *Australia-New Zealand*—Prime Minister Chifley and New Zealand Finance Minister Nash issue a joint statement on economic cooperation.

30. *U.K.*—The Council for Colonial Economic Development publishes a report outlining five schemes involving a total expenditure of £28 million over the next ten years in Uganda, Nyassaland, Barbados, St. Vincent and Aden.

July 1948

22. *Newfoundland*—In a national referendum to decide between future self-government and confederation with Canada, the voters choose confederation by a vote of 78,408 against 71,464.

25. *India*—Prime Minister Nehru of India threatens war unless Hyderabad joins the Dominion.

30. *U.K.*—The British Nationality Act receives royal assent.

August 1948

19. *India*—The Prime Minister of Hyderabad states in a letter to Pandit Nehru that the government is referring their dispute to the United Nations,

India having broken the "standstill" agreement signed in November 1947 (see "United Nations," August 21).

31. *South Africa*—Prime Minister Malan tells the Assembly that the government believes South Africa has a right to incorporate South West Africa into the Union and that treatment of Indians in South Africa is a domestic matter in which neither the U.N. nor any other nation has a right to interfere.

September 1948

11. *Pakistan*—Mohammed Ali Jinnah, the first Governor-General, dies. Sir Khwaja Nazimuddin is appointed Governor-General on September 13.

13. *India*—Indian army forces enter Hyderabad from all points; aircraft attack military objectives.

18. *India*—The Indian commander receives the formal surrender of Hyderabad and places the state under military administration.

29. *U.K.*—A conference of unofficial members of the African Legislative Councils opens in London. The Lord President of the Council states that Britain wants to bring about the growth of responsible government in partnership with the colonial peoples.

October 1948

11–22. A *Commonwealth Conference* in London endorses U.K. participation in the Brussels pact.

18. *Eire*—Sean MacBride, Ireland's Minister for Foreign Affairs, informs the Commonwealth Conference that his government is determined to withdraw from the British Empire even if it means loss of trade and citizenship preferences.

November 1948

15. *Canada*—Louis St. Laurent succeeds Mackenzie King as Prime Minister.

23. *U.K.*—It is announced that on medical advice the King has canceled his visit to Australia and New Zealand.

December 1948

11. *Canada-Newfoundland*—The terms of the agreement for bringing Newfoundland into the Canadian Confederation, effective March 31, 1949, are signed at Ottawa preparatory to submission to the Parliaments of Canada and the U.K.

15. *India-Pakistan*—An agreement signed in Delhi provides for the establishment of a tribunal to settle the boundary disputes between east and west Bengal and between east Bengal and Assam.

18. *India*—The National Congress unanimously approves a resolution welcoming India's "free association" with the Commonwealth and expressing adherence to the U.N. Charter.

21. *Eire*—The Republic of Ireland Bill, providing for Ireland's complete independence effective April 18, 1949, is signed by President Sean O'Kelly.

EUROPE

January 1948

13. *Germany*—Soviet military authorities issue a decree conferring extensive new powers on a broadened and centralized German economic administration for the Soviet zone.

16. *Bulgaria-Rumania*—A pact of mutual assistance and friendship is signed in Bucharest.

24. *Hungary-Rumania*—A treaty of friendship and mutual assistance is signed at Budapest.

26. *U.S.S.R.-Poland*—A five-year trade treaty is concluded providing for an exchange of commodities to a value of $1 billion from 1948 to 1952.

27. *Germany*—The French Government sends a memorandum to Great Britain and the U.S. on the Anglo-American proposals for strengthening the economic machinery in the combined zones in Germany.

February 1948

2. *Italy-U.S.*—A ten-year treaty of friendship, commerce and navigation is signed in Rome.

4. *U.S.S.R.-Rumania*—A treaty of friendship and mutual assistance is signed in Moscow.

9. *Germany*—A German Bizonal Economic Administration is established at Frankfort.

10–Aug. 31. *Italy*—Deputies of the Council of Foreign Ministers meet in London to discuss the disposition of the former Italian colonies.

13. *Germany*—Soviet notes to the U.S., France and Great Britain protest their intention of holding three-power talks on Germany in London.

17–18. *Germany*—The Foreign Ministers of Czechoslovakia, Poland and Yugoslavia meet in Prague and declare that German issues should be handled on a quadripartite basis with consultation of other interested states.

18. *U.S.S.R.-Hungary*—A treaty of mutual assistance and friendship is signed in Moscow.

20–May 24. *Austria*—Deputies of the Big Four Foreign Ministers meet in London to discuss the Austrian treaty.

23–March 5. *Germany*—The three western powers hold talks in London in which Benelux representatives also participate.

25. *Czechoslovakia*—A Communist-fomented political crisis is resolved by the appointment of a new government under Communist leader Klement Gottwald.

26. *Czechoslovakia*—The U.S., France and Great Britain declare in a joint statement that the events in Czechoslovakia "jeopardize the very existence of the principles of liberty to which all democratic countries are attached."

27. *Finland*—In a letter to President Paasikivi, Stalin proposes the conclusion of a mutual assistance pact between Finland and the U.S.S.R.

March 1948

5. *Germany.*—The London conference adjourns with agreement in principle on international control of the Ruhr, German representation in ERP, closer economic integration of the western zones, a federal government for Germany, and association of the Benelux countries in German policy.

10. *Czechoslovakia*—Foreign Minister Jan Masaryk is killed by a fall from the window of his apartment at the Foreign Office. His death is officially termed suicide. At Lake Success Jan Papanek, Czechoslovak delegate to the U.N., demands an investigation of alleged Soviet influence in the February coup.

17. *Western Union*—The Foreign Ministers of Great Britain, France, Belgium, the Netherlands and Luxembourg sign a 50-year treaty of economic, social and cultural collaboration and collective self-defense in Brussels.

18. *U.S.S.R.-Bulgaria*—A 20-year treaty of friendship, cooperation and mutual aid is signed in Moscow.

20. *Germany*—Marshal Sokolovsky and the Soviet delegation walk out of the Allied Control Council's meeting after alleging that the western powers are

undermining quadripartite government in Germany and that the Council no longer exists as an organ of government.

Trieste—French Foreign Minister Bidault on a visit to Italy announces that the French, British and U.S. governments are proposing to the governments of the U.S.S.R. and Italy that a protocol be added to the Italian peace treaty returning the Free Territory of Trieste to Italian sovereignty.

France-Italy—Bidault and Count Sforza sign a protocol relating to the projected Franco-Italian customs union.

28. *Rumania*—In general elections the People's Democratic Front receives 90.8 percent of the votes and obtains 405 of 414 seats in the National Assembly.

30. *Germany*—The Soviet Deputy Military Governor advises the U.K., U.S. and French authorities that as of April 1 new regulations for the control of traffic between Berlin and the west will come into force.

April 1948

5. *Germany*—A British aircraft on its regular service to Berlin collides with a Soviet air-fighter and crashes in the Soviet zone.

Greece-Turkey—The Turkish Foreign Minister and the Greek Prime Minister in a joint statement in Athens reaffirm Greek-Turkish friendship as established by existing pacts.

6. *U.S.S.R.-Finland*—A treaty of friendship and mutual assistance is signed in Moscow.

13. *Rumania*—The National Assembly adopts a new constitution and elects a Presidium headed by Professor Constantin Parhon.

16. The Convention for European Economic Cooperation is signed in Paris by representatives of the 16 participating countries and the military government authorities in western Germany.

18. *Italy*—In hotly contested national elections the Christian Democrats win an absolute majority in the Chamber of Deputies and the Communist-Socialist bloc receives only 30 percent of the popular vote.

20–June 1. *Germany*—Six-power talks on Germany are held in London.

23. *Bulgaria-Czechoslovakia*—A treaty of friendship and mutual assistance is signed in Prague.

May 1948

7. *Congress of Europe*—With representatives of 22 countries in attendance, Winston Churchill, the honorary president, opens the first Congress of Europe in The Hague to discuss plans for European union.

9. *Czechoslovakia*—The constituent assembly unanimously adopts a new constitution.

11. *Italy*—Senator Luigi Einaudi is elected President.

Sweden—Foreign Minister Unden tells the Social Democratic party conference that the three Scandinavian countries can create an independent group of nations holding aloof from other international movements.

23. *Finland*—President Paasikivi dismisses Communist Minister of the Interior Yrjo Leino, who had refused to resign in spite of a parliamentary vote of no confidence.

Italy—The government resigns and a new government is formed with Alcide de Gasperi as Prime Minister and Count Carlo Sforza as Foreign Minister.

24. *Austria*—The Foreign Ministers' deputies conclude their treaty discussions without agreement.

30. *Czechoslovakia*—In national elections the Communist-dominated National Front receives 6,431,963 valid votes out of a total of 7,204,256.

June 1948

1. *Germany*—The six-power London conference concludes after reaching general agreement on coordination of economic policies, establishment of a west German government, and creation of an international authority for the Ruhr.

3. *U.S.S.R.-Finland*—The Soviet Government reduces its remaining war indemnity claim on Finland by one-half, or $75 million.

7. *Czechoslovakia*—President Eduard Beneš resigns on grounds of ill health.

7–8. *Benelux*—A conference attended by the Dutch, Belgian and Luxembourg Prime Ministers and Foreign Ministers ends with an agreement on measures to effect an economic union between the three countries on January 1, 1950.

8. *U.S.S.R.-Hungary-Rumania*—The U.S.S.R. announces that following a request from their governments it has decided to halve Rumania's and Hungary's remaining reparation obligations.

14. *Czechoslovakia*—The Assembly elects Communist leader Klement Gottwald as President to succeed Beneš.

15. *Czechoslovakia*—Communist Antonin Zápotocký succeeds Gottwald as Prime Minister.

16. *Germany*—Soviet representatives snap the last link in the four-power government in Berlin by walking out of the Allied Kommandatura.

17. *France*—The Assembly passes by 300 to 286 votes a resolution accepting with reservations the London agreement on Germany.

18. *Germany*—The British, U.S. and French authorities announce a currency reform in the western zones beginning June 20. Marshal Sokolovsky bans the use of the new Deutsche Mark in the Soviet zone and also in Berlin.

Hungary-Poland—A treaty of friendship and mutual assistance is concluded.

23. *Germany*—The Soviet Military Administration decrees a currency reform in the Soviet zone of occupation and in all four sectors of Berlin. The British, U.S. and French Military Governors announce their decision to introduce the Deutsche Mark into the western sectors of Berlin.

23–25. *Germany*—A conference of eastern European Foreign Ministers at Warsaw proposes a return to four-power control in Germany, conclusion of a peace treaty, and withdrawal of occupation forces one year thereafter.

24. *Germany*—Soviet authorities bar all rail traffic between the western zones and Berlin. The western powers launch a large-scale airlift.

28. *Yugoslavia*—A decision to expel the Yugoslav Communist party for doctrinal and other errors of its leadership is announced by the Cominform after a meeting in Rumania.

July 1948

1. *Finland*—The Communists lose 11 seats in Parliamentary elections. The distribution of seats is Agrarians 56, Social Democrats 55, Communists 38, Conservatives 32, Swedish party 14, and Liberals 5.

2. *Albania* breaks off economic relations with Yugoslavia and expels Yugoslav experts.

6. *Germany*—The U.S., Great Britain and France in notes to the U.S.S.R. protest the interruption of communications between their zones and Berlin.

14. *Germany*—Charging that the western powers had violated quadripartite agreements on Berlin, the Soviet Union rejects U.S., British and French protests against the Russian blockade.

Italy—Communist leader Palmiro Togliatti is shot and seriously wounded by a student.

19. *France*—The Schuman government is defeated on a vote of confidence and resigns.

Yugoslavia—Agreements are signed with the U.S. for release of $47 million in gold and other Yugoslav assets frozen since the war, in exchange for the payment by Yugoslavia to the U.S. of $17 million in compensation for nationalized U.S. property and for two U.S. transport aircraft shot down by Yugoslav fighters in 1946.

21. *Czechoslovakia-Rumania*—A treaty of friendship and mutual assistance is signed in Bucharest.

Yugoslavia—Opening the fifth congress of the Yugoslav Communist party at Belgrade, Marshal Tito replies to the charges made by the Cominform in its resolution of June 28.

24. *France*—André Marie is accepted as Prime Minister by the National Assembly.

26. *Germany*—British and U.S. authorities announce that they have stopped the movement of railway traffic across the Bizone between the Soviet zone and countries outside Germany until further notice.

Germany—At a meeting with the military governors, the west German minister-presidents agree to proceed immediately with the organization of western Germany on the basis of the London agreement.

28. *France*—The Foreign Affairs Committee of the National Assembly adopts a resolution calling for the creation of a European "constituent assembly."

29. *Finland*—The President approves a new Social Democratic cabinet headed by K. A. Fagerholm.

30–August 18. *Danube Conference*—The 10-nation conference on the future regime of the Danube meets in Belgrade.

30. *Hungary*—President Zoltán Tildy announces his resignation following the arrest of his son-in-law on charges of high treason and espionage.

August 1948

2. *Germany*—Representatives of the three western powers discuss the Berlin blockade and currency issues with Stalin and Molotov.

3. *Hungary*—Arpád Szakasits, chairman of the United Workers' party, is elected President by Parliament and assumes office immediately.

18. *Danube Conference* closes in Belgrade. The U.S., U.K. and France refuse to sign the convention drawn up by the Soviet-controlled majority.

23. *Germany*—Marshal Stalin with Foreign Minister Molotov again receives the British, French and U.S. envoys for discussion of the Berlin problem.

28. *France*—André Marie's cabinet falls when the Socialists refuse to support Finance Minister Paul Reynaud's economic program.

30. *Germany*—The western envoys reach agreement with Molotov on a directive to the military governors for solution of the Berlin blockade and currency problems.

31. *France*—The National Assembly gives Robert Schuman a vote of confidence authorizing him to form a cabinet.

September 1948

1. *Germany*—Representatives of the 11 western German states meet as a "Parliamentary Council" or constituent assembly at Bonn.

5. *Poland*—Wladyslaw Gomulka is relieved of his duties as Secretary-General of the Polish Workers' (Communist) party and expresses regret at his ideological errors.

6. *Germany*—In an attack on Berlin's City Hall in the Soviet sector, German Communists oust the legally elected Municipal Assembly and seize possession

of the building. The Assembly later meets in the British sector and calls for new elections.

Netherlands—Queen Juliana takes the oath of office in Amsterdam, Queen Wilhelmina having abdicated on September 4.

7. *France*—The Schuman cabinet falls after three days in office.

8. *Germany*—The military governors report their failure to agree on a solution of the Berlin currency issue.

10. *France*—The National Assembly endorses Henri Queuille as Premier. Robert Schuman becomes Foreign Minister.

13–15. *Italian Colonies*—The Council of Foreign Ministers meets in Paris but fails to reach agreement and refers the question to the U.N. General Assembly.

19. *Sweden.*—The Socialists remain the strongest party in elections for the lower house while the Communists lose 6 of their 15 seats. The distribution of seats is Social Democrats 109, Liberals 57, Agrarians 30, Conservatives 22, Communists 9.

21. *Portugal-Spain*—The Hispano-Portuguese friendship and nonaggression pact is extended for 10 years.

22. *Germany*—The U.S., Great Britain and France, in identical notes, demand that the Soviet Government state definitely whether it is ready to recognize their rights in Berlin, and that it clarify its attitude on the Berlin currency question.

26. *Germany*—The western powers inform the U.S.S.R. that they will refer the Berlin issue to the U.N. Security Council (for further references see "United Nations").

28. *Western Union*—Following a two-day meeting in Paris, the Defense Ministers of Great Britain, France, Belgium, the Netherlands and Luxembourg announce formation of a common military organization for the defense of western Europe.

October 1948

25–26. *Western Union*—The Foreign Ministers of the five countries, meeting in Paris, announce their complete agreement on the principles of a defense pact for the North Atlantic region and establish a committee to consider proposals for closer European union.

28. *U.S.S.R.*—Premier Stalin charges in an interview with a *Pravda* correspondent that the western powers have repudiated two agreements on the Berlin question and that the "policy of the present leaders of the U.S.A. and Great Britain is a policy of aggression."

November 1948

5. *Italy-Greece*—A treaty of friendship, commerce and navigation is signed at San Remo.

7. *France*—Gen. Charles de Gaulle's Reunion of the French People claims 107 (out of 320) seats in the Council of the Republic, while the Communists are reduced from 88 to 16 seats. Official figures for 262 seats representing metropolitan France give the RPF (without other affiliation) 55 seats; Radicals, 64; Socialists, 48; Radicals and Republican Independents, 41; Communists, 16; MRP, 15; Republican Liberal Party, 13; others, 10.

10. *Germany*—The U.S. and British Military Governments promulgate legislation providing that the Ruhr industries will be turned over to a group of German "trustees" pending decision as to their ownership by a future German government.

11–December 28. *Germany*—Representatives of Great Britain, the U.S.,

France, and the Benelux countries meet in London to discuss the establishment of an international authority for the Ruhr and related questions.

18. *Greece*—Themistocles Sophoulis forms a new coalition government, the previous government having resigned on November 12.

19. *Germany*—The French Government appeals to the U.S. and Great Britain to review their decision to vest management of the Ruhr industries in German trustees.

26. *Belgium*—Paul-Henri Spaak forms a new coalition government, the previous government having fallen on November 19.

26–December 17. *Western Union*—The committee on European union set up by the Consultative Council of the Brussels powers meets in Paris.

30. *Germany*—German Communists, with the support of the Soviet Military Government, establish a separate administration for the Soviet sector of Berlin.

December 1948

5. *Germany*—In elections held in the western sectors of Berlin, the Social Democrats receive 64.6 percent of the votes; Christian Democrats, 19.4; and Liberal Democrats, 16.1.

12. *Czechoslovakia-U.S.S.R.*—An important trade agreement is announced at the conclusion of a visit to Moscow by Premier Zápotocký and other high Czech officials.

13. *Italy-U.S.S.R.*—A number of trade and reparation agreements are signed in Moscow.

27. *Hungary*—The government announces the arrest of Jozsef Cardinal Mindszenty and other prominent Catholics on charges of plotting against the government, spying, treason, and black market money dealings.

U.S.S.R.-Yugoslavia—A new trade protocol provides for a seven-eighths reduction in commercial exchanges in 1949.

28. *Germany*—The U.S., Great Britain, France, Belgium, the Netherlands and Luxembourg announce a tentative agreement to establish an international authority to supervise the Ruhr industries for an indefinite period.

MIDDLE EAST AND AFRICA

January 1948

15. *Iraq*—A 20-year treaty of alliance and friendship with Great Britain is signed at Portsmouth.

21. *Iraq*—Following student riots in Baghdad, Regent Abdul Illah states that the treaty with Great Britain is unacceptable and will not be ratified.

29. *Iraq*—A new cabinet is formed under Mohammed el-Sadr, an opponent of the British treaty.

31. *Iran*—A Soviet note to Iran protests the terms of the U.S.-Iranian agreement of October 6, 1947.

February 1948

3. *Libya*—The U.S. Government rejects a Soviet protest against the reopening, with British consent, of the Mellaha airfield near Tripoli.

5. *Iran*—In a reply to the Soviet note of January 31 the government refutes the Soviet allegations and accuses the U.S.S.R. of having protected traitors.

19. *Yemen*—The Imam Yahya and three of his sons are assassinated.

March 1948

13. *Palestine*—The Arab League proclaims a state of war between the seven

Arab states and Palestine Jewry and announces that the Arab states will invade the Holy Land as soon as the U.K. gives up the mandate.

15. *Transjordan*—A new Anglo-Transjordan treaty is signed in Amman. An accompanying exchange of letters provides for British help in economic and social development and in financial matters.

21. *Yemen*—Sayif-ul-Islam Ahmad is recognized as Imam.

22. *Iraq*—The British military mission withdraws.

27. *Iran*—A note from the Soviet Government rejects the allegations contained in Iran's note of February 5.

April 1948

1. *Iran*—Replying to the Soviet note of March 27, the government insists that the Soviet assertions constitute interference in Iran's internal affairs.

30. *Palestine*—The mandatory government warns the Jewish Agency that severe military measures will be taken unless Jewish attacks on Arab positions cease.

May 1948

14. *Palestine*—High Commissioner Sir Alan Cunningham leaves Palestine. The British mandate ends at midnight. After a meeting in Tel Aviv the Jewish National Council (Vaad Leumi) proclaims the establishment of a Jewish state in Palestine. The U.S. Government recognizes the provisional government as *de facto* authority of the new state of Israel. Fighting between Arab and Jewish forces continues on an increased scale.

17. *Palestine*—Rabbi Chaim Weizmann accepts the Presidency of Israel; the new state is recognized by the U.S.S.R.

20. *Palestine*—Count Folke Bernadotte is appointed U.N. Mediator for Palestine.

22. *Palestine*—U.S. Consul General Thomas Wasson is fatally shot by a sniper and dies May 23.

23. *Turkey*—Foreign Minister Necmeddin Sadak states that Turkey sides always with those countries which respect other people's freedom and independence; alliance with Britain and collaboration and friendship with the United States are keynotes of Turkish policy.

June 1948

4. *Egypt*—The government Foreign Affairs Commission rejects a draft Anglo-Egyptian agreement on the Sudan negotiated by the British Ambassador and the Foreign Minister.

11. *Palestine*—A truce ordered by the Security Council goes into effect.

July 1948

7. *Egypt*—The Egyptian Government in a note to Britain protests the recent ordinance effecting constitutional reforms in the Sudan.

9. *Palestine*—The truce ends, followed by general resumption of hostilities.

18. *Palestine*—A new truce goes into effect.

29. *Palestine*—The Israeli Foreign Minister states that the provisional government rejects the Mediator's scheme for demilitarization of Jerusalem. He regards the U.N. resolution of November 29 as no longer binding in view of Arab aggression.

August 1948

12. *Transjordan* and *Saudi Arabia* agree to exchange diplomatic representatives.

September 1948

18. *Palestine*—Jerusalem is sealed and a curfew is imposed to aid in the search for the slayers of Count Bernadotte. Both the Stern gang and the Irgun deny any responsibility.

21. *Palestine*—The Irgun Zvai Leumi disbands after 11 years of underground activity. In Paris Secretary Marshall endorses the Bernadotte report (see "United Nations").

22. *Palestine*—The Arab Higher Committee announces the formation of a "Palestine Government" at Gaza.

October 1948

15. *Palestine*—Heavy fighting breaks out in the Negeb region.

22. *Palestine*—A new cease-fire becomes effective.

23. *Palestine*—Serious fighting breaks out on the northern front.

24. *Palestine*—A statement by President Truman indicates continued support of the U.N. partition resolution.

31. *Palestine*—A cease-fire goes into effect in northern Palestine as Israel claims control of the entire Galilee area.

November 1948

6. *Iran*—The government resigns, the Majlis having passed none of its bills and refused to adopt the budget. Mohammed Saed is elected Prime Minister by the Majlis on November 8.

16. *Palestine*—A meeting of the Arab League in Cairo resolves that the Arabs will never agree to partition.

18. *Egypt*—A speech from the throne at the opening of Parliament affirms the nation's resolve to see the evacuation of all foreign troops and the unity of Egypt and the Sudan.

30. *Palestine*—An agreement for a complete cease-fire in Jerusalem is signed by the Jerusalem commanders of the Israeli forces and the Arab Legion.

December 1948

1. *Palestine*—A meeting in Jericho of Arabs from all parts of the country proclaims Abdullah of Transjordan King of all Palestine.

28. *Egypt*—Prime Minister Nokrashy Pasha is assassinated in Cairo by a member of the dissolved Moslem Brotherhood. Ibrahim Abdul Hadi Pasha is named to succeed him.

THE FAR EAST

January 1948

4. *Burma* becomes an independent republic as British rule terminates.

13. *Indonesia*—The Dutch establish an "Interim Government" of the East Indies to prepare a constitution for the "preliminary Federative Government of Indonesia."

15. *Korea*—The U.N. Temporary Commission votes to invite the Soviet commander to cooperate in holding elections in Korea.

17. *Indonesia*—The Netherlands and the Republic of Indonesia sign a truce

agreement on board the *U.S.S. Renville,* including a statement of 12 principles to serve as a basis for political discussions.

21–23. *China*—Three-day national elections are held to designate 768 members of the Legislative Yuan.

29. *Siam*—In a general election the Democratic party of Premier Khuang Aphaiwong wins 36 out of 67 seats in parliament.

31. *Indonesia*—A new cabinet under Dr. Mohammed Hatta is announced.

February 1948

7. *Japan*—The Katayama government decides to resign *en bloc* as a consequence of dissension within the Social Democratic party.

12. *Japan*—The Far Eastern Commission adopts a comprehensive policy for disarming Japan and preventing the revival of its military strength.

21. *Siam*—The Supreme State Council designates Khuang Aphaiwong as Prime Minister.

March 1948

6. *Siam*—China, France, Great Britain, the Netherlands and the U.S. recognize the government.

9. *Indonesia*—The Dutch-established interim government which is to function until January 1, 1949, is installed under the chairmanship of Dr. Hubertus J. van Mook.

Japan—Hitoshi Ashida, head of the Democratic party, forms a cabinet of eight Socialists, six Democrats and two People's Cooperative representatives.

15. *Japan*—More than 200 Diet members meet to form a large opposition party, the Democratic Liberals, dedicated to restoration of a free economy. Former Premier Shigeru Yoshida is named party president.

16. *Indonesia*—The Republican government in a letter to the U.N. Good Offices Committee strongly protests the formation of the provisional federal government for Indonesia.

22. *Korea*—An extensive land reform program is announced by the U.S. Military Governor.

Japan—William H. Draper, U.S. Under-Secretary of the Army, arrives in Tokyo to study plans for Japanese economic rehabilitation.

29. *China*—The National Assembly is formally convoked by President Chiang Kai-shek with 1,639 delegates out of 3,045 attending.

Japan—SCAP prohibits a general strike for pay increases by several hundred thousand government employees.

April 1948

5. *China*—The Kuomintang Central Standing Committee decides to draft General Chiang Kai-shek as presidential candidate in spite of his announcement that he will not seek reelection.

9. *Siam*—Luang Pibul Songgram, who engineered the coup d'état of November 9, succeeds Khuang Aphaiwong as Premier.

19. *China*—General Chiang Kai-shek is reelected President by an overwhelming majority.

29. *China*—General Li Tsung-jen is elected Vice-President, receiving 1,438 votes to Dr. Sun Fo's 1,295.

May 1948

1. *Korea*—The North Korea radio announces the adoption by a "North and

South Korean Conference" at Pyongyang of a constitution for the "People's Democratic Republic of Korea" with jurisdiction over all Korea.

8. *Burma*—Former Premier U Saw and five others are hanged for the murder of seven Burmese officials July 19, 1947.

10. *Korea*—Elections are held in southern Korea under the observation of the U.N. Temporary Commission.

27. *Indonesia*—Dutch-Indonesian negotiations are resumed at Bandoeng, Java.

June 1948

5. *China*—Thousands of heavily armed police and troops throw cordons around all major universities at Shanghai to prevent demonstrations against the American policy of economic revival of Japan.

Indochina—By agreement signed on board a French cruiser at Haiphong, Vietnam becomes an associated state within the French Union.

10. *Japan*—The Far Eastern Commission authorizes General MacArthur to permit Japanese representatives to attend nonpolitical international meetings as observers.

16. *Malaya*—A state of emergency is declared following the murder of three European planters.

July 1948

7. *Malaya*—Commissioner Malcolm MacDonald attributes the disturbances in Malaya to a deliberate Communist plan to overthrow the government.

17. *Indonesia*—At the end of an eight-day conference at Bandoeng the leaders of the states outside the Republic and of the autonomous areas unanimously adopt a resolution urging the formation of an interim government.

23. *Indonesia*—The Republic breaks off the political discussions with the Netherlands under the auspices of the Good Offices Committee.

August 1948

15. *Korea*—The Republic of Korea is proclaimed at Seoul, South Korea, with Dr. Syngman Rhee as President.

20. *Burma*—Martial law is proclaimed throughout the country.

September 1948

1. *China*—A Communist radio report states that a "North China People's Government" was formed on August 19. Its aim is said to be the "striking down of United States imperialistic and Kuomintang rule in China."

6. *Burma*—The government announces that an understanding has been reached with Karen tribesmen who occupied Moulmein on September 1.

9. *Korea*—A "People's Republic" claiming authority over the entire country is established in northern Korea.

14. *Burma*—Parliament reelects Thakin Nu as Premier, to form an interim government to serve until after the general election of April 1949.

18. *Indonesia*—A "soviet government" is proclaimed at Madioen, Java, under the leadership of one Muso, who recently returned from Moscow.

Burma—U Tin Tut, former Foreign Minister who had resigned to serve in the army, is assassinated in Rangoon.

19. *Korea*—The Soviet Government states it is ready to withdraw Soviet troops from northern Korea and hopes the U.S. Government will agree to withdraw its troops from southern Korea.

October 1948

7. *Japan*—The Ashida government resigns, the Prime Minister accepting

"moral responsibility" for a situation in which a member of the cabinet was arrested for misappropriation of funds.

10. *Burma*—A commission of 30 members is appointed to deal with the autonomist claims of the Karens, Shans and other minorities.

11. *China*—Chiang Kai-shek in a speech in Peiping ascribes the deteriorating military situation to the "adverse psychological effect" of Communist propaganda.

14. *Japan*—The Diet elects Shigeru Yoshida (Democratic Liberal) as Prime Minister. A new government is formed on October 19.

20. *Korea*—Fighting is reported in various parts of southern Korea.

25. *Indonesia*—Republican President Soekarno announces that the Communist insurrection has been quelled.

29. *Indonesia*—The Queen signs a bill to set up the interim government. Dr. Louis J. M. Beel is appointed representative of the Crown.

30. *China*—Communist forces occupy Mukden, gaining control of all Manchuria.

November 1948

12. *Japan*—The International Military Tribunal sentences to death ex-Foreign Minister Koki Hirota, General Hideki Tojo, and five other generals found guilty of major war crimes.

21. *China*—The Communists broadcast a warning to the U.S. that they will regard any further military support of the Kuomintang regime as a hostile act.

26. *China*—Dr. Sun Fo is elected Prime Minister by the Legislative Yuan.

December 1948

10. *Japan*—General MacArthur is instructed to issue a directive to the Japanese Government to carry out an effective economic stabilization program.

Korea—An agreement is signed in Seoul providing for a program of American economic assistance to be carried out by the Army Department and the ECA.

12. *Indonesia*—The Netherlands Government announces that negotiations with the Indonesian Republic have broken down and that an interim federal government without the Republicans will be set up immediately.

18. *Indonesia*—The Netherlands Government issues a decree for the "government of Indonesia during the transitional period" and opens military action to "purge" Republican territory of "terrorists."

20. *China*—Prime Minister Sun Fo announces the formation of a new coalition cabinet.

22. *Indonesia*—The Committee of Good Offices reports that in launching military operations the Dutch Government has violated the Renville truce agreement. ECA Administrator Hoffman announces the suspension of Marshall Plan aid for Indonesia.

23. *Japan*—Ex-Foreign Minister Koki Hirota, General Tojo and five other leaders condemned to death by the International Military Tribunal are hanged.

Japan—Prime Minister Yoshida dissolves Parliament after a formal no-confidence vote and calls for a general election.

25. *Korea*—The Tass agency announces that the evacuation of northern Korea by Soviet troops has been completed.

China—The Communists publish a list of 40 Chinese, including 7 members of Dr. Sun Fo's cabinet, whom they consider as major war criminals.

31. *China*—In a New Year message General Chiang Kai-shek states that he is willing to conclude a negotiated peace on condition that national independence and sovereignty are respected.

LATIN AMERICA

January 1948

27. *Bolivia*—A state of siege is declared following the discovery of a plot to overthrow the government.

28. *Chile*—The British Government protests the establishment of a Chilean military base on Graham Land in the Antarctic. On January 31 Chile rejects the British protest and declares that the base is on Chilean national territory.

February 1948

5. *Venezuela*—Congress proclaims Rómulo Gallegos President of the Republic; he takes office officially on February 15.

8. *Costa Rica*—Elections for President and 31 members of Congress take place. The contest for the Presidency is between Otilio Ulate of the Democratic Union and former President Angel Calderón Guardia.

12. *Argentina*—An Anglo-Argentine trade treaty (Andes Agreement) is signed, including provision for the purchase of the British-owned railways in Argentina.

15. *Panama* is formally notified by the United States that American troops have been withdrawn from all the defense sites provided during the war.

Paraguay—J. Natalicio González, the only candidate on the ballot, is elected President for a five-year term, to take office on August 15.

19. *Argentina*—A squadron of the Argentine fleet leaves for the Antarctic.

24. *Chile*—In an address at Punta Arenas the President announces that Chile has formally annexed its sector of the Antarctic.

25. *Argentina*—Foreign Secretary Bramuglia tells the press that Argentina will not negotiate with Great Britain about the Falklands, which are unquestionably Argentine, although the Antarctic is another matter. Bevin tells the British House of Commons that rival claims in the Falkland Islands and dependencies should be referred to the International Court of Justice.

28. *Costa Rica*—A majority of the election jury announces that Otilio Ulate has been elected President by 10,000 votes (cf. February 8). On March 1 the Congress voids Ulate's election on charges of fraud.

Guatemala—A British warship arrives at Belize, British Honduras and marines are deployed at strategic points in the colony, claimed by Guatemala. Guatemala's President Juan José Arévalo calls on the U.S. to defend the interests of the Latin American countries in their territorial disputes with Great Britain.

March 1948

4. *Argentina-Chile*—An agreement for the joint defense of Chilean and Argentinean rights in the Antarctic is signed at Santiago. The Argentine Foreign Minister states that Argentina will raise the question at Bogotá.

5. *Guatemala* closes its British Honduras frontier.

12. *Costa Rica*—A revolt by followers of Otilio Ulate led by Col. José Figueres begins in southern Costa Rica.

23. *Argentina*—The Argentine delegate at the Havana Conference states that Argentina will not sign the ITO Charter and will never ask any international organization for prior approval of its economic policies.

30–May 2. *Bogotá Conference*—The Ninth International Conference of American States meets at Bogotá, Colombia.

April 1948

9. *Colombia*—Liberal party leader Jorge Gaitán is assassinated in Bogotá;

mobs storm the presidential palace and government buildings. Sessions of the Inter-American Conference are suspended.

12. *Colombia*—A government broadcast attributes the revolt to "foreign agents under the direction of Moscow" and reports that two foreign agents have been detained. The government announces that the Inter-American Conference will continue.

13. *Bogotá Conference*—Secretary of State Marshall declares that the disturbances in Colombia are part of "the same definite pattern as occurrences which provoked strikes in France and Italy."

14. *Costa Rica*—Members of the diplomatic corps arrange a truce between the government and the rebel forces, but fighting is resumed on expiration of the truce on April 17.

19. *Nicaragua-Costa Rica*—The U.S. protests against the crossing of the Costa Rican border by Nicaraguan troops to intervene in the Costa Rican conflict.

20. *Costa Rica*—President Picado surrenders the government forces and resigns. Santos León Herrera becomes acting president to hold office until May 8.

30. *Colombia*—The Secretary of the Communist party and 11 other Communists who had been under arrest are unconditionally released after a court hearing.

May 1948

2. *Bogotá Conference*—The Inter-American Conference adjourns after drawing up a Charter for the Organization of American States and other agreements.

4. *Colombia* breaks diplomatic relations with the U.S.S.R.

8. *Costa Rica*—A military junta headed by Col. José Figueres takes office.

9. *Panama*—The first presidential election since 1940 is held. Preliminary returns issued May 28 give former President Arnulfo Arias a slight lead over the government candidate, Domingo Díaz Arosemena, who charges fraud. (The final tabulation announced July 30 is Díaz, 72,210; Arias, 71,043.)

June 1948

3. *Paraguay*—President Morínigo is compelled to resign by a rebellious movement of the "Guión Rojo," a dissident group of the pro-government Colorado party.

July 1948

4. *Panama*—Ex-President Arnulfo Arias, who claims to be President-elect, flees to the Canal Zone.

5. *Peru*—Two army garrisons in southern Peru revolt as a result of the announcement by President Bustamente on June 28 that he will rule the country by decree. Constitutional guarantees are suspended but reinstated on August 4.

August 1948

6. *Argentina*—All Radical (Opposition) deputies resign their seats in protest against a decision by the Perónista majority to expel one of their number for criticizing newspaper articles by President Perón.

7. *Panama*—The national election jury proclaims Domingo Díaz Arosemena President-elect, his four-year term to begin October 1.

13. *Argentina*—The Chamber of Deputies approves a law giving the President unlimited powers when he deems a national emergency to exist.

14. *Argentina*—The Chamber of Deputies votes to reform the Argentine Constitution.

15. *Paraguay*—Juan Natalicio González is inaugurated President for a five-year term.

28. *Antarctic*—The U.S. Government announces its preference for "some form of internationalization" in the Antarctic.

September 1948

2. *Chile*—President Gabriel González Videla signs a bill outlawing the Communist party.

24. *Argentina*—Discovery of a plot to kill President Perón and his wife is announced.

October 1948

1. *Panama*—Domingo Díaz Arosemena is sworn in as President at a session of the National Assembly.

3–5. *Peru*—Revolts attributed to the Aprista party are suppressed.

10. *Cuba*—Dr. Carlos Prío Socarrás (Autentico party) is inaugurated as President to succeed Dr. Grau San Martín, who retires after a four-year term. (Dr. Prío was elected without incident on June 1.)

29. *Peru*—President José Luís Bustamente is deposed as the result of an army uprising. General Manuel Odría is named provisional President.

November 1948

3. *Peru*—General Manuel Odría outlaws the Aprista party.

9. *Guatemala* rejects the British proposal to refer their territorial dispute to the International Court.

23–24. *Venezuela*—The government is overthrown by a military *coup*. A military junta under Col. Carlos Delgado Chalbaud takes power.

December 1948

5. *Argentina*—The Perónista party wins a large majority in elections for a constitutional convention. It will hold 109 seats to 49 for the Radicals.

Venezuela—Exiled President Rómulo Gallegos states that the U.S. oil companies and local revolutionary groups were responsible for the recent army *coup*.

8. *Costa Rica*—President-elect Otilio Ulate's National Unity party wins an overwhelming majority in elections to a constituent assembly.

10. *Costa Rica* states that it has been invaded from Nicaragua by "armed forces of various nationalities" led by exiled former President Calderón Guardia.

14. *Costa Rica-Nicaragua*—The Council of the Organization of American States, meeting in Washington, invokes the Treaty of Rio de Janeiro and decides to send a commission of inquiry to the Costa Rican-Nicaraguan border.

El Salvador—President Salvador Castaneda resigns after fighting breaks out in the capital. The young army officers who seize control promise "faithfully to uphold the constitution."

27. *Costa Rica-Nicaragua*—The commission of inquiry having found that the invasion of Costa Rica was led by Costa Rican political exiles independent of the Nicaraguan Government, the Council of the Organization of American States calls on Costa Rica and Nicaragua to abstain from any hostile acts.

APPENDIX

TEXT OF THE NORTH ATLANTIC TREATY

The Parties to this Treaty reaffirm their faith in the purposes and principles of the Charter of the United Nations and their desire to live in peace with all peoples and all governments.

They are determined to safeguard the freedom, common heritage and civilization of their peoples, founded on the principles of democracy, individual liberty and the rule of law.

They seek to promote stability and well-being in the North Atlantic area.

They are resolved to unite their efforts for collective defense and for the preservation of peace and security.

They therefore agree to this North Atlantic Treaty:

ARTICLE 1

The Parties undertake, as set forth in the Charter of the United Nations, to settle any international disputes in which they may be involved by peaceful means in such a manner that international peace and security, and justice, are not endangered, and to refrain in their international relations from the threat or use of force in any manner inconsistent with the purposes of the United Nations.

ARTICLE 2

The Parties will contribute toward the further development of peaceful and friendly international relations by strengthening their free institutions, by bringing about a better understanding of the principles upon which these institutions are founded, and by promoting conditions of stability and well-being. They will seek to eliminate conflict in their international economic policies and will encourage economic collaboration between any or all of them.

ARTICLE 3

In order more effectively to achieve the objectives of this Treaty, the Parties, separately and jointly, by means of continuous and effective self-help and mutual aid, will maintain and develop their individual and collective capacity to resist armed attack.

ARTICLE 4

The Parties will consult together whenever, in the opinion of any of them, the territorial integrity, political independence or security of any of the Parties is threatened.

ARTICLE 5

The Parties agree that an armed attack against one or more of them in Europe or North America shall be considered an attack against them all; and consequently they agree that, if such an armed attack occurs, each of them, in exercise of the right of individual or collective self-defense recognized by Article 51 of the Charter of the United Nations, will assist the Party or Parties so attacked by taking forthwith, individually and in concert with the other Parties, such action as it deems necessary, including the use of armed force, to restore and maintain the security of the North Atlantic area.

Any such armed attack and all measures taken as a result thereof shall immediately be reported to the Security Council. Such measures shall be terminated when the Security Council has taken the measures necessary to restore and maintain international peace and security.

ARTICLE 6

For the purpose of Article 5 an armed attack on one or more of the Parties is deemed to include an armed attack on the territory of any of the Parties in Europe or North America, on the Algerian departments of France, on the occupation forces of any Party in Europe, on the islands under the jurisdiction of any Party in the North Atlantic area north of the Tropic of Cancer or on the vessels or aircraft in this area of any of the Parties.

ARTICLE 7

This Treaty does not affect, and shall not be interpreted as affecting, in any way the rights and obligations under the Charter of the Parties which are members of the United Nations, or the primary responsibility of the Security Council for the maintenance of international peace and security.

ARTICLE 8

Each Party declares that none of the international engagements now in force between it and any other of the Parties or any third state is in conflict with the provisions of this Treaty, and undertakes not to enter into any international engagement in conflict with this Treaty.

ARTICLE 9

The Parties hereby establish a council, on which each of them shall be represented, to consider matters concerning the implementation of this Treaty. The council shall be so organized as to be able to meet promptly at any time. The council shall set up such subsidiary bodies as may be necessary; in particular it shall establish immediately a defense committee which shall recommend measures for the implementation of Articles 3 and 5.

ARTICLE 10

The Parties may, by unanimous agreement, invite any other European state in a position to further the principles of this Treaty and to contribute to the security of the North Atlantic area to accede to this Treaty. Any state so invited may become a party to the Treaty by depositing its instrument of accession with the Government of the United States of America. The Government of the United States of America will inform each of the Parties of the deposit of each such instrument of accession.

ARTICLE 11

This Treaty shall be ratified and its provisions carried out by the Parties in accordance with their respective constitutional processes. The instruments of ratification shall be deposited as soon as possible with the Government of the United States of America, which will notify all the other signatories of each deposit. The Treaty shall enter into force between the states which have ratified it as soon as the ratifications of the majority of the signatories, including the ratifications of Belgium, Canada, France, Luxembourg, the Netherlands, the United Kingdom and the United States, have been deposited and shall come into effect with respect to other states on the date of the deposit of their ratifications.

ARTICLE 12

After the Treaty has been in force for ten years, or at any time thereafter, the Parties shall, if any of them so requests, consult together for the purpose of reviewing the Treaty, having regard for the factors then affecting peace and security in the North Atlantic area, including the development of universal as well as regional arrangements under the Charter of the United Nations for the maintenance of international peace and security.

ARTICLE 13

After the Treaty has been in force for twenty years, any Party may cease to be a party one year after its notice of denunciation has been given to the Government of the United States of America, which will inform the Governments of the other Parties of the deposit of each notice of denunciation.

ARTICLE 14

This Treaty, of which the English and French texts are equally authentic, shall be deposited in the archives of the Government of the United States of America. Duly certified copies thereof will be transmitted by that Government to the Governments of the other signatories.

In witness whereof, the undersigned plenipotentiaries have signed this Treaty.

Done at Washington, the fourth day of April, 1949.

For the Kingdom of Belgium:
P. H. SPAAK
SILVERCRUYS

For Canada:
LESTER B. PEARSON
H. H. WRONG

For the Kingdom of Denmark:
GUSTAV RASMUSSEN
HENRIK KAUFFMANN

For France:
SCHUMAN
H. BONNET

For Iceland:
BJARNI BENEDIKTSSON
THOR THORS

For Italy:
SFORZA
ALBERTO TARCHIANI

For the Grand Duchy of Luxembourg:
JOS BECH
HUGUES LE GALLAIS

For the Kingdom of the Netherlands:
STIKKER
E. N. VAN KLEFFENS

For the Kingdom of Norway:
HALVARD M. LANGE
WILHELM MUNTHE MORGENSTIERNE

For Portugal:
JOSÉ CAEIRO DA MATTA
PEDRO THEOTÓNIO PEREIRA

For the United Kingdom of Great Britain and Northern Ireland:
ERNEST BEVIN
OLIVER FRANKS

For the United States of America:
DEAN ACHESON

I CERTIFY THAT the foregoing is a true copy of the North Atlantic Treaty signed at Washington on April 4, 1949 in the English and French languages, the signed original of which is deposited in the archives of the Government of the United States of America.

IN TESTIMONY WHEREOF, I, DEAN ACHESON, Secretary of State of the United States of America, have hereunto caused the seal of the Department of State to be affixed and my name subscribed by the Authentication Officer of the said Department, at the city of Washington, in the District of Columbia, this fourth day of April, 1949.

DEAN ACHESON
Secretary of State

[SEAL]

By M. P. CHAUVIN
Authentication Officer
Department of State

INDEX

Abdullah, King of Transjordan, 377, 386, 397-398, 401, 407
Acheson, Dean, 285, 292, 321, 463, 489, 507, 530, 533, 536, 538; on Soviet policy, 36-37, 497; on Cardinal Mindszenty, 109; on aid to China, 285; on European unity, 519; on peaceful aims of U.S., 538-539
Agriculture, Department of (U.S.), 220, 223, 225
Alaska, 233, 342
Albania, internal affairs, 103, 111; foreign relations, 90, 115, 123-124, 419, 421, 423, 438, 445
Algeria, 532-533
Allied Control Council (Germany), 67, 72, 91, 134, 186
Allied Council for Japan, 291
All-Union Congress of Trade Unions (Soviet), 189
Alphand, Hervé, 470-471
American Federation of Labor, 47, 190 ff., 246
American Republics, American States, see Latin America
American Tariff League, 218
Annecy negotiations, 214-216
Antarctic, 359
Aqaba, 397, 400, 403, 406
Arab Higher Committee, 386, 397
Arab League, 379, 386, 397-398
Arab world, Arab states, 259, 375, 506; see also Palestine
Arabian-American Oil Company, 377
Arce, José, 382
Arctic regions, 342-343, 345, 352
Argentina, 191, 320, 358-359, 371; and international wheat agreements, 220, 224-225; territorial claims, 359-361; and nonrecognition, 361-362; and Organization of American States, 364, 366; foreign trade and price policies, 371-372; in U.N., 446-447, 456 ff.

Armour, Norman, 372
Army, Department of (U.S.), 290-292, 294-295, 297, 301
Ashida, Hitoshi, 304
Asia, upheavals in, 259-260; Soviet and Communist policy toward, 262-270; conference of "Asian" countries, 319; and U.S., 328-329
Asia, southeast, 20, 264, 312 ff., 322-329; U.S. policy toward, 328-329
Asian Relations Conference of 1947, 260
Atlantic pact, see North Atlantic Treaty
Atomic energy, 6, 8, 342, 347, 410-415
Attlee, Clement R., 332
Aung San, 323
Auriol, Vincent, 469
Austin, Warren R., 381-382, 456
Australia, 258, 309, 331, 337, 446; and ITO, 219-220; and international wheat agreements, 220, 222, 223-224; and Japan, 296, 302; and Indonesia, 318-319; and Burma, 324
Austria, 193, 521; and Danube conference, 128, 131-132; treaty negotiations, 128-129, 132, 432, 495; in ERP, 153, 154, 156, 160; U.S. loan to, 253; and U.N., 445-446

Balkans, 102, 103, 128, 452, 501; Soviet policy in, 36; proposed federation, 119, 123-124; Greek civil war, 419-429
Baltic countries, 501
Bank for International Settlements, 172
Baruch plan, atomic energy control, 412
Bao Dai, 327-328
Barkley, Alben W., 213, 244
Bebler, Aleš, 129, 131, 424
Belgium, 42, 180; and Germany, 71, 75, 88, 471, 475, 477, 492; and ERP, 156, 160, 164, 173; loans to, 253, 256; and U.N., 382, 436, 455; and

Western Union, 524-525; see also Benelux countries
Benelux countries, 75, 172, 180, 510, 520; and Western Union, 58-59, 512, 525
Beneš, Eduard, 112
Berlin, conflict over, 66-67, 79, 133-139, 147-149, 450-451, 463-464; Moscow negotiations, 130, 139-144; failure to carry out Moscow directives, 146-147; local aspects of, 76, 86, 97, 144-147, 462-463; consideration by the Security Council, 442-443, 452-464; attitude of U.S.S.R., 66-67, 79, 145, 463-464; agreement to lift blockade, 142, 493-495, 502; see also Germany, currency question
Berman, Jakob, 111
Bernadotte, Folke, 376, 387-389, 392-394; appointed mediator, 386; progress report of, 390-393; death of, 392
Betancourt, Rómulo, 358
Bevin, Ernest, 63-64, 330, 489, 533; and Western Union, 53, 55, 63, 524; and Germany, 92, 139; on communism in Far East, 325; and Palestine, 403; and Soviet policy, 415, 431
Bidault, Georges, 46, 63, 73-74, 76-78, 180
Bierut, Boleslaw, 111
Bled agreements, 124
Blum, Léon, 52, 469
Bogotá conference, 253, 257, 333, 352, 355-369; economic agreement, 369
Bolivia, 381
Bonnet, Henri, 167
Bradley, Gen. Omar N., 6
Bramuglia, Juan A., 456-461, 463
Brannan, Charles F., 223, 224, 227
Brazil, 373; and GATT, 215; lend-lease settlement, 254; loans to, 257, 369; and anti-communism, 357; on western hemisphere colonies, 361
Brewster, Owen D., 244
Bridges, Styles, 246, 276
British Commonwealth, 20, 32, 219, 320, 330-332; role of Canada in, 340-341, 345, 351, 353-354; and trade with Japan, 296; and Burma, 324; and Western Union, 524, 526-527; meeting of Prime Ministers (1948), 524; (1949), 332
British West Indies, 337

Brooks, C. Wayland, 214, 350
Bruce, David, 162
Bruce, Howard, 245
Bruce, James, 371
Brussels, Treaty of, see Western Union
Bukharin, N.I., 121
Bulgaria, 495; internal affairs, 103, 105-106, 107-108, 113, 114, 125; foreign relations, 89, 124-125, 204, 419, 421, 423, 427, 438, 445, 495
Bullitt, William C., 276, 280
Bunche, Ralph, 376, 393-394, 399, 400, 402, 404
Burma, 259-260, 266, 269, 312, 325, 332, 445; risings in, 322-324
Byrnes, James F., 2, 4, 10, 481

Calcutta, Communist meetings at, 267, 321
Canada, 258, 332, 455; and Western Union, 13, 354, 512, 515; and international wheat agreements, 221-224; U.S. loan to, 253, 336; and British Commonwealth, 331-332, 340-341, 345, 351, 353-354; trade and dollar problems of, 333-340; and ERP, 158, 336-338; proposed economic union with U.S., 339-340; and the defense of North America, 340-350; and Latin America, 332, 337, 351-353; and the Atlantic pact, 354-355, 528, 529, 532; and atomic energy control, 416-417
Cannon, Cavendish W., 133
Carey, James, 192 ff.
Caribbean Legion, 365
Ceylon, 215, 259, 319, 324, 331, 445-447
Chang Chun, 281
Chapin, Selden, 109
Chapultepec conference, 351
Chen brothers, 281
Chennault, Gen. Claire L., 276
Chiang Kai-shek, 14, 20, 261, 270-274, 276, 279-280, 281-284
Chiang Kai-shek, Mme., 280-281
Chile, 215, 436; and International Bank, 257; relations with U.S.S.R., 357; Antarctic claims, 359; and ERP, 370; on Czechoslovak issue, 443
China, 259, 261-264, 312, 325, 327, 329, 332, 501; U.S. relations with,

14, 15, 18, 19-20, 254, 261-262, 274, 277, 280, 284-286, 287, 501, 506, 507; Communists in, 209, 266-270, 281, 284, 285-286; Nationalist government, 261, 264, 270, 274-283, 286, 288, 506; future prospects, 284-287; and Japan, 288, 300-302; in U.N., 309, 320, 436, 455
Churchill, Winston, 28, 30, 56 ff., 135, 324
Clark, D. Worth, 280
Claxton, Brooke, 343, 347
Clay, Gen. Lucius D., 73, 465, 468, 494; and Berlin blockade, 137, 139; and ERP allocations, 183, 184-185
Clayton, William L., 212
Cochran, H. Merle, 317
Colombia, 356-357, 362, 436, 456
Cominform, 39, 102, 216, 286; and ERP, 33, 191, 194; and Yugoslavia, 92, 111, 118, 121, 127, 205-206, 425
Comintern, 37, 39, 327
Commerce, Department of (U.S.), 201, 238
Committee for Economic Development, 153
Committee of European Economic Co-operation, 165, 167, 240
Commodity Credit Corporation (U.S.), 217
Communism, international aspect, 6-7, 14-15, 21, 23, 265 ff., 286, 356-357, 424; doctrine, 34, 36-37, 39-40, 42, 100, 110, 118, 120-122, 123, 125, 264-266, 268, 286, 325, 507; in Europe, 19, 36-38, 39-40, 42-43, 78, 106-108, 110-116, 138, 145-146, 150, 202, 443, 497; nationalist deviations, 37-38, 102, 110, 116-127, 206; and labor movement, 189-197, 304; in Asia, 20, 260, 262-270, 285-286, 304, 312, 316, 322-329, 375-376; in Latin America, 356-359; in the U.S., 504-505
Congress, (U.S.), 167, 217; and military policy, 7-8; and the Vandenberg Resolution, 11-13; and military aid programs, 14, 215, 540-541; and first-year ERP appropriation, 17, 46, 150-151, 154-155, 183; and foreign information program, 22-24; and ERP administration, 153, 155, 159, 160, 163, 164, 165, 167, 175, 179;

and ERP extension, 151, 161, 164, 214-215, 511-512, 540; and European integration, 166, 511, 519; and ITO Charter, 210, 211-212, 217-218; and trade agreements program, 210-213, 214-215, 217; and international wheat agreements, 222-223, 226, 227-228; and shipping policy, 230, 231, 233, 238-239, 242-244, 246-247, 248; and loans to Latin America, 253, 372; and aid to China, 14-15, 274-275, 280, 284-285; and appropriations for Japan, 291, 293, 297-298; for Korea, 301; and Indonesia, 319; and inter-American military cooperation, 346; and Great Lakes-St. Lawrence seaway project, 347-349; and the U.N., 409; and German disarmament, 477-478; and 1948 election, 505-506, 508; and North Atlantic Treaty, 215, 527, 530, 532, 540-541
Congress of Europe, The Hague, 56, 58, 63, 512, 522
Congress of Industrial Organizations, 189-190, 191 ff., 195 ff., 218, 246
Connally, Tom, 166, 244, 285, 511, 532
Convention for European Economic Cooperation, 168
Costa Rica, 365
Cot, Pierre, 78
Council for Mutual Economic Assistance, 203-205
Council of Europe, 55, 512, 525-527
Council of Foreign Ministers, 4, 27, 88, 128, 141, 275, 426, 537; London meeting (1947), 5, 65, 80, 89, 91, 133; and Germany, 80, 88, 89, 91, 454-457, 464, 482, 493-495; and Austria, 128, 495; and Japan, 288; and ex-Italian colonies, 437; deputies, 88, 437, 495
Creech Jones, Arthur, 384
Cripps, Sir Stafford, 338
Critchley, T. V., 315
Cuba, 215, 320, 370, 436
Cultural and Scientific Congress for World Peace, 538
Cyrankiewicz, Józef, 106
Czechoslovakia, 118, 254, 381; and ERP, 38; Communist coup in, 55, 99, 104-105, 134, 442, 447; and Germany, 88-92, 99, 477; Soviet in-

fluence in, 103, 207; domestic politics, 106-107, 110, 112; church and state in, 109; nationalization and collectivization in, 113, 115; and Yugoslavia, 124, 205; at Danube conference, 128; and east-west trade, 199, 202, 216; economic agreement with U.S.S.R., 203; in Council for Mutual Economic Assistance, 204; U.S. loan to, 253; and Palestine, 389; and Greece, 427

Danube conference, 102, 127-133
Danubian countries, 130-132, 225
Deakin, Arthur, 191, 194, 196
Defense, Secretary of (U.S.), 238, 243
Defense Department (U.S.), 381
De Gasperi, Alcide, 41, 44, 47 ff.
De Gaulle, Gen. Charles, 50, 76, 469, 516
De Lattre de Tassigny, Gen. Jean, 514
Denmark, 61, 381; and Germany, 88; and ERP, 155-156; commercial relations, 216; and European union, 526; and North Atlantic Treaty, 532, 534, 536
Dhahran air base, 377-378
Dewey, Thomas E., 154, 214, 258, 280, 500-503, 506, 518-519
Dimitrov, Georgi, 108, 113
Disarmament, 410-419
Di Vittorio, Giuseppe, 196
Djilas, Milovan, 120, 123
Dodd, Norris E., 223, 225-226
Dominican Republic, 216, 359, 361
Dönitz, Admiral Karl, 496
Doughton, Robert L., 211, 214
Douglas, William O., 195
Draper, William H., 291-292
DuBois, Coert, 315
Dulles, John Foster, 424, 435, 504, 508, 519
Dunkirk, Treaty of, 59
Dunn, James Clement, 45
Dutra, Gen. Eurico, 373

East Turkestan Republic, 263
East-west trade and the Marshall plan, 31, 197-207; see also Intra-European trade
Eaton, Charles, 211
Eban, Aubrey, 395

Ebert, Friedrich, 462
Economic Cooperation Act of 1948 (U.S.), 154, 155, 158-159, 161-164, 202, 243, 245, 253, 478, 518
Economic Cooperation Act of 1949 (U.S.), 161, 164-165, 215, 247-248, 285, 319, 511-512
Economic Cooperation Administration (U.S.), 152-153, 170, 175, 179, 197, 223, 248, 250, 252-253; organization and operations, 153-157, 159-161, 180, 202, 258, 509-511; procurement authorizations, 157-159, 199; offshore purchasing, 158, 172, 175, 336-338, 370-371; and shipping policies, 244-248; counterpart funds, 161-162, 163-164; and strategic minerals, 162-165; and western Germany, 182-185, 479, 491; China program, 278, 280, 285; and Korea, 310; and Indonesia, 318
Ecuador, 362
Egypt and Palestine conflict, 376-405; Anglo-Egyptian treaty (1936), 377; in U.N. Security Council, 436
Eire, 60, 156, 160, 193, 445-446, 526, 532, 534
Eisenhower, Gen. Dwight D., 346
El Salvador, 216, 309
Epirus, Northern, 426
Eritrea, 437
Ethiopia, 319
Europe, 30-33, 77, 79, 335, 372; Soviet aims, 34-41, 127; see also European Recovery Program, European union, etc.
Europe, eastern, 31, 40, 123-124, 130; U.S. views on, 3-4, 25; Soviet policy in, 35-36, 91-92, 102 ff., 129, 133; and the German question, 81-82, 86-92; church and state in, 108-109; collectivism in, 113-115; economic conditions, 197-199, 202-207
Europe, western, 49, 74, 127, 141, 148, 150, 197, 198, 260, 331, 353, 512; U.S. policy toward, 5, 6, 9-14, 33, 497-499, 515-519; postwar weakness of, 30-33; economic cooperation in, 165-182; wheat position, 220, 225; shipping position, 240; currency devaluation, 255-256; see also Western Union, east-west trade, etc.
European Advisory Commission, 134

European Recovery Program, 1, 2, 20, 46, 59, 71-72, 79, 127, 148, 208, 219, 267, 293, 330, 336, 408, 469, 507, 520, 540; principles and objectives, 9, 15-18, 131, 150-152, 165-167, 497-499; accomplishments and prospects, 176-179, 509-512; administration and operation of, 152-182; western Germany in, 182-189, 471, 478, 482, 491; and world labor, 189-197; opposition to, 6, 18, 25, 38-39, 189 ff., 198, 325, 474, 505; and east-west trade, 197-207; bilateral aid agreements, 155-157, 161; labor and, 189-197; and U.S. shipping policy, 239-248; see also Economic Cooperation Administration, Organization for European Economic Cooperation, and geographic headings

European union, 53-64, 165-166, 197, 517 ff.; see also Council of Europe, Western Union

Evans, Harold, 385

Evatt, Herbert, 319, 425-426, 452, 461

Export-Import Bank (U.S.), 19-20, 209, 252-254, 293, 336, 368, 370

Fagerholm, Karl August, 107

Falkland Islands, 359 ff.

Far East, 20, 220, 259-262, 264, 292, 301-302, 372, 501; U.S. policies, 259-329; nationalism and communism in, 260-270, 319-328

Far Eastern Commission, 291, 293-294, 295, 298-301, 305

Farley, James A., 534

Federal Supply, Bureau of (U.S.), 165

Fierlinger, Zdenek, 106

Finland, relations with U.S.S.R., 103, 105, 115, 197, 537; internal politics, 115; foreign trade, 199, 216; reparations, 203; loans to, 252; and U.N., 445-446

Flanders, Ralph E., 247

Food and Agriculture Organization, 228

Foreign Assistance Act of 1948 (U.S.), 152, 274

Foreign Liquidation Commissioner, Office of the (U.S.), 254

Formosa, 283, 287

Forrestal, James, 8, 243, 347, 348, 516-517

France, 31, 32, 104, 357, 506, 520; domestic politics, 37, 41, 42, 49-53; labor movement in, 39, 51, 192-194, 196; and Germany, 70-79, 97, 139-149, 459, 465-473, 475, 476-483, 488-489, 492, 494; and ERP, 153-156, 162-163, 167, 169, 172-174, 177, 184-185; colonial questions, 162, 259, 327-328, 360, see also Indochina; and European union, 58-59, 64, 512-516, 522-523, 524-525; customs union with Italy, 58, 180-181, 520; shipping position, 223; and international wheat agreements, 224; and International Monetary Fund, 255-256; and International Bank, 256; and North Atlantic Treaty, 532, 534

Franco, Francisco, 437, 534

Franks, Sir Oliver, 403

Fulbright, James W., 166, 511

Fulton, James G., 218

Gaitán, Jorge Eliécer, 356

Gaza, 399, 405; Arab Palestine government, 397, 401

Gearhart, Bertram, 211, 214

General Agreement on Tariffs and Trade, 210, 215, 216-218, 219, 335, 336; 1948 negotiations under, 215-216; 1949 negotiations under, 213, 214, 215-216

Genocide, convention on, 436

Germany, 200, 342, 414, 431, 528, 541; conflicts of policy in, 65, 134, 148-149; Anglo-American policy, 65-67, 330, 465-470; U.S. policy, 4-6, 41, 292; French policy, 70-79, 451, 465-471; Soviet policy, 39-41, 65, 69, 79-88, 92, 493-494; eastern European views on, 88-92; four-power agreements on, 72, 83, 134-135; reparation and disarmament, 10, 83-84, 91, 475-482; territorial questions, 81, 92, 492; shipping, 131; currency question, 140-148, 463, 494, see also Berlin dispute; resumption of four-power negotiations, 493-495

Germany, eastern, 92, 97, 100, 102, 103, 135; People's Congress, 66, 80, 82; People's Council, 495; Soviet rule in, 79-80; political parties in, 80-82, 100

Germany, western, 510; administration and constitutional development, 67-69, 95-100, 184, 482-493; six-power meeting, London, 71, 90-91; London agreement, June 1948, 74-76, 92, 96, 97, 98, 140, 142-143, 149, 481, 483, 495; German politics in, 93-101, 483-486, 489-490, 492-493; currency reform in, 138, 185-187, 479; German criticism of Allied policies, 474-475, 491-492; Allied controls in, 183, 490-491; and ERP, 156, 160, 168, 172, 177, 182-185, 193; economic conditions, 182-183, 187-189, 215, 225, 241, 248, 252, 253, 257; agreement on the Ruhr, 464-475; reparation and security questions, 475-482; and European union, 98-99, 451, 516, 521, 523; and North Atlantic Treaty, 533
Gloucester Fisheries Association, 350
Gomulka, Wladyslaw, 111
Gottwald, Klement, 111
Graham, Frank, 312
Graziano, Rocky, 47
Great Britain, see United Kingdom
Great Lakes-St. Lawrence seaway and power project, 347-349
Greece, 38, 41, 119, 191, 209; American aid to, 14-15, 18-19, 540; civil war, 19, 125, 419-430; and ERP, 19, 153, 156, 160, 171, 216, 233; and European union, 521; and North Atlantic Treaty, 533
Greenland, 352
Gregg, John P., 212
Grundy, Joseph R., 214
Guatemala, 357, 359-360
Gurney, Chan, 534

Hague Congress, see Congress of Europe
Haiti, 216
Hall Patch, Sir Edmund, 169
Harriman, W. Averell, 153, 156, 170-171, 185
Harriman Committee, 241-242
Harvard Report on shipping policy, 234
Hatta, Mohamed, 315, 317, 326
Havana Charter, see International Trade Organization
Hawaii, 233

Hay, John, 275
Hebrang, Andrija, 121
Herriot, Edouard, 525
Herter Committee, 242-243, 371
Hitler, Adolf, 35, 40, 93, 450
Ho Chi Minh, 266, 327-328
Hoffman, Paul G., 153-155, 159, 175, 183, 184, 245-248, 479, 509-511
Hukbalahap movement, 266
Hull, Cordell, 2, 210
Human Rights, Universal Declaration of, 435
Humphrey, George M., 479
Humphrey committee, 479-480
Hungary, 495; internal affairs, 103-114; foreign relations, 38, 89, 109, 117, 128, 203-204, 253, 445
Hyde Park, declaration of, 342
Hyderabad, 441-442

Ibn Saud, 378
Iceland, 60, 156, 160, 520, 532, 534, 536
Impelliteri, Vincent, 47
India, 119, 215, 259, 262, 309, 322, 325, 328, 436; economic affairs, 255, 259, 329; and Far Eastern affairs, 296, 302, 312, 316, 318, 319-320, 324, 331-332; and British Commonwealth, 319-320, 324, 331-332; and Pakistan, 439-441; and Hyderabad, 441-442
Indochina, 259, 312, 322; conflict in, 327-328
Indonesia, 253, 259, 262, 269, 296, 332; conflict in, 312-322; Linggadjati agreement on, 313; Renville agreement on, 312-313, 315-316, 318; Asian conference on, 319-320; and the U.N., 315-321; Communist revolt in, 326-327
Inman, Samuel Guy, 359
Institute of Inter-American Affairs (U.S.), 373
Inter-Allied Reparation Agency, 476, 478-479
Inter-American Military Cooperation Act (U.S.), 346
Inter-American system, 332, 352, 364; see also Organization of American States
Inter-American Treaty of Reciprocal

Assistance, 12, 352, 365, 448, 500, 529
Intergovernmental Maritime Consultative Organization, 234
International Bank for Reconstruction and Development, 18, 199, 202, 209, 251, 256-257, 369-370
International Basic Economy Corporation, 373
International Children's Emergency Fund, 152
International Committee of the Movements for European Unity, 522
International Court of Justice, 434, 436, 445-446
International Federation of Trade Unions, 190
International Labor Organization, 181
International Monetary Fund, 18, 251, 254-256
International Trade Organization, 18, 208, 219-220, 335, 507; Charter of, 210, 215, 227, 257; American opinion on, 218-219; governmental action on, 217-218, 219; Interim Commission, 219
International wheat agreements, 208, 220-228
Intra-European trade, 171-172, 178, 200, 202; see also East-west trade
Iran, 263, 265, 377-378, 438, 533
Iraq, 377, 379, 386, 397, 404
Ireland, see Eire
Israel, 506; new state of, 383-387, 400-401; U.S. recognition, 385; admission to U.N., 445; see also Palestine
Italian Somaliland, 437
Italy, 32, 206, 357; domestic politics, 37, 41-44, 48-49, 538; elections, April 1948, 39, 41-49, 137, 150; labor movement, 39, 181, 189-190, 192, 196; and ERP, 150, 153-154, 156, 162, 172, 184-185, 189; former colonies of, 45, 437, 501, 534; and customs union with France, 58, 180-181, 520; and Trieste, 46, 444; commercial relations, 206, 216, 510; shipping position, 233; U.S. loans to, 252-253; and the U.N., 444-447; and European union, 520-521, 526; and North Atlantic Treaty, 532-534, 538

Japan, 275, 279, 312, 414, 432; in U.S. strategic thinking, 5, 14, 261-264, 287, 290, 302-303, 328; economic aid to, 154-155, 225, 252-253; economic situation and prospects, 248, 257, 292, 296-297, 305-306, 329; basic directives, 289; reform measures, 290; U.S. rehabilitation policy, 290 ff.; Johnston Committee, 292-294; stabilization program, 295-296; deconcentration in, 297-299; reparation, 299-301, 477; Far Eastern opposition to U.S. policies, 284, 300-302; domestic politics, 304-305
Jaujard, Admiral Robert, 514
Jerusalem, 384, 392, 399, 400, 406
Jessup, Philip C., 319, 396, 455, 458, 460, 494
Jewish Agency for Palestine, 384, 385
Johnston, Percy H., 292
Johnston Committee, 292-294, 300
Joint Export-Import Agency, 69
Joint Industrial Mobilization Committee (Canada-U.S.), 347
Jouhaux, Léon, 192
Jovanović, Dragoljub, 105
Judd, Walter H., 276

Kaiser, Jacob, 82, 484
Kardelj, Edvard, 120, 122
Kashmir, 332, 439-441
Keller, Karl T., 235
Keller Committee, 235-237
Kennan, George, 291
Kim Koo, 307, 310
Kimm Kiu Sic, 307, 310
King, W. L. Mackenzie, 341, 342, 345, 351, 354, 355
Knowland, William F., 244
Knutson, Harold, 210, 214
Koo, Wellington, 281
Korea, 154-155, 261, 263, 267-269, 306-312, 432, 434
Külz, Wilhelm, 82
Kung, H. H., 281
Kupers, Evert, 196
Kuznetsov, V. V., 192

Labor, Secretary of (U.S.), 217, 238
Labor and the Marshall plan, 152, 189-197
Labrador, 333, 348, 349-350
Land, Admiral Emory S., 231, 234

Lange, Halvard M., 536
Latin America, 335; U.S. economic relations with, 20-21, 250, 253-254, 329, 333, 367-374; and ERP, 158, 178, 370-371; labor in, 190; and Canada, 332, 337, 341-342, 351-353; U.S. political relations with, 333; and hemisphere defense, 346; communism and unrest in, 356-359; recognition of *de facto* governments in, 361-363; economic problems of, 367-374; *see also* Bogotá conference, Organization of American States
League of Women Voters, 218
Lebanon, 376, 379, 386, 397, 400, 404, 405
Lend-Lease Administration (U.S.), 247; lend-lease settlements, 254
Lenin, Leninism, *see* Communism
Li Tsung-jen, 273-274, 281, 283-284
Liberia, 216
Libya, 437
Lie, Trygve, 425, 460-461
Lima, Inter-American Conference, 355
Linggadjati agreement, *see* Indonesia
Lleras Camargo, Alberto, 366
Lodge, Henry Cabot, 166, 222, 244
Lombardo, Ivan Matteo, 43
London conferences, *see* British Commonwealth, Germany
Lovett, Robert A., 282, 403, 529
Luce, Henry, 276, 340
Lundeberg, Harry, 246
Luxembourg, 71, 156, 471, 492, 514; *see also* Benelux countries

MacArthur, Gen. Douglas, 291, 295, 300, 303-305
MacBride, Seán, 534
McCloy, John J., 369
McCoy, Gen. Frank, 298
MacDonald, Malcolm, 325
McNaughton, Gen. Andrew G. L., 416, 441
McNeil, Hector, 470
Macedonia, 124-125, 429
Malaya, 262, 322, 324; disturbances in, 324-325
Malik, Jacob A., 494
Manchuria, 261, 263, 271, 278-279, 286, 329, 501
Maniu, Iuliu, 105
Manuilsky, Dmitri Z., 455, 458

Mao Tse-tung, 260, 266, 268-270, 282-284
Marie, André, 52
Maritime Commission (U.S.), 231-232, 234-239, 243, 245-246
Marjolin, Robert, 169, 185
Markos (Gen. Markos Vafiades), 424-425, 427, 429
Marshall, Gen. George C., 3, 155, 355, 430, 502, 507, 508; on U.S. policy, 5, 15-16, 409; Harvard address, 16, 17, 38, 150, 181, 518; on Trade Agreements program, 211, 214; at Bogotá conference, 253, 356-357, 367-368; and China, 270, 272, 276, 281; and Palestine, 393-394, 504; on atomic energy control, 415; and Germany, 470, 477-478, 479
Marshall plan, *see* European Recovery Program
Martin, Joseph W., 211, 215
Marx, Marxism, *see* Communism
Mediterranean, 20, 37, 116
Merchant Ship, Sales Act of 1946 (U.S.), 230, 231-232, 233, 244
Metaxas dictatorship, 428
Mexico, 217, 256, 362, 363, 369, 371, 431
Middle East, 20, 258, 263, 330, 407; international politics in, 375-378
Mihailović, Gen. Drazha, 116
Mikolajczyk, Stanislaw, 104
Millikin, Eugene D., 211
Minc, Hilary, 114
Mindszenty, Cardinal Jozsef, 109 ff., 511
Molotov, V. M., 25, 83, 91, 127, 128, 141-144, 506, 538
Mongolian People's Republic, 445
Monroe Doctrine, 360
Montgomery of Alamein, Field Marshal, 514, 516
Moore, Edward H., 213
Moscow negotiations, *see* Berlin dispute
Murray, Philip, 194, 195
Muso, 326
Myrdal, Gunnar, 200

Nagy, Ferenc, 105
National Advisory Council (U.S.), 256
National Association of Manufacturers, 218

National Council of American Importers, 218
National Federation of American Shipping, 231, 238, 243
National Foreign Trade Council, 218
National Military Establishment (U.S.), 238, 540
National Security Resources Board (U.S.), 239
National Union of Masters, Mates and Pilots, 246
Navy, Secretary of (U.S.), 232, 238
Near East, 15, 38, 119; see also Middle East
Negeb, see Palestine
Nehru, Jawaharlal, 320, 324, 332, 441
Netherlands, 156; domestic politics, 42; in Western Union, 59, 514, 516; and Germany, 71, 75, 88, 471, 492; and ERP, 153, 163, 185; labor in, 196; shipping position, 229, 233, 240; financial relations, 254, 255, 258; and Indonesia, 259, 312-322, 439; and Japan, 300; colonies in western hemisphere, 360; in North Atlantic Treaty, 321; see also Benelux countries
Netherlands East Indies, see Indonesia
New Delhi, Asian conference at, 319-320; conference on Burma, 324
New Democratic Youth League, 322
Newfoundland, 336, 349-350
New Zealand, 296, 302, 319, 337
Nicaragua, 216, 359, 365
North American Grain Export Association, 222
North Atlantic community, 332, 353, 531
North Atlantic strategy, 14, 349
North Atlantic Treaty, 1, 215, 321, 408, 489, 497, 507, 513, 526; negotiation of, 515, 517, 529-530; Canada in, 332, 353-355; and the U.S., 531-532, 540-541; and the U.N., 408, 448-449, 530-531; provisions, 533; membership, 534-536; and the U.S.S.R., 535-539
Norway, 36, 61, 88, 156, 320, 436; shipping position, 229, 233, 240; financial relations, 254, 255, 258; and European union, 526; and North Atlantic Treaty, 532, 534-536, 537
Office of War Information (U.S.), 22

Ogdensburg agreement, 342
Okinawa, 262, 287, 303
Organization for European Economic Cooperation, 155-157, 197, 472, 475, 512, 513, 520, 521, 525; organization and operations, 59, 153, 168-175, 181-182, 183; western Germany and, 99, 183-185, 472, 475, 491; programs and allocations, 175-176, 179-180, 182; interim report, 176-179, 209, 510; and shipping policy, 245
Organization of American States, 352, 363-367
Osborn, Frederick H., 416, 418
Outer Mongolia, 261, 263

Pakistan, 215, 296, 319, 328, 331-332, 439-441
Palestine, 259, 330, 375-407, 438-439; termination of mandate, 381, 385; trusteeship proposal, 381-383; and U.S. election, 393, 396, 504; see also Israel
Pan American Union, 351, 364-366
Panama, 232-233, 248, 381
Pravda, 119, 122; Stalin's replies to, 459
Papagos, Gen. Alexander, 428
Papanek, Jan, 443
Paraguay, 359
Pastore, Giulio, 196
Patrascanu, Lucretiu, 110
Pauker, Ana, 124, 131
Paul I, King of Greece, 428
Pearson, Lester B., 353, 539
Permanent Joint Board on Defense (Canada-U.S.), 342, 344, 346, 348
Perón, Juan D., 358, 371
Peru, 216, 357, 363, 371, 436
Petkov, Nikola, 105
Philip, André, 475
Philippines, 232, 262, 266, 287, 303, 309, 316, 328, 381; and Japan, 300, 301-302
Pieck, Wilhelm, 81
Point Four, 165, 208-210, 258, 508; Latin American reaction, 373-374
Poland, 124, 198, 203-204, 205, 207, 342, 501; communism in, 38-39, 85, 103-104, 106, 109, 111, 113, 114, 118, 126, 203, 207; and Germany,

81, 83, 85, 89-90, 92, 99, 476; in
U.N., 202, 412; and east-west trade,
38-39, 199, 203, 254
Portugal, 60, 156, 157, 164, 445-446,
521, 526, 532, 534
Potsdam agreement, 40-41, 66, 79, 83,
90-91, 93, 147, 186, 241, 299, 302,
476, 502
Puerto Rico, 233

Queuille, Henri, 53, 162

Rákosi, Mátyás, 108, 111, 114, 124
Ramadier, Paul, 41, 53, 56, 522
Ranković, Aleksandar, 120, 122
Rasmussen, Gustav, 536
Reciprocal Trade Agreements Act
(U.S.), 219, 507; renewal (1948),
210-213; (1949), 213-214, 217
Reconstruction Finance Corporation
(U.S.), 154
Reimann, Max, 474
Renville agreement, see Indonesia
Reuter, Ernst, 97, 484
Reynaud, Paul, 56
Rhee, Syngmann, 307, 310-311
Rio conference (1942), 366; (1947),
352
Rio pact, see Inter-American Treaty of
Reciprocal Assistance
Robb, Air Marshal James, 514
Robertson, Gen. Sir Brian, 73, 139, 183,
465, 468
Robertson, Edward V., 214
Rockefeller, Nelson, 373
Rodríguez Larreta doctrine, 362
Romulo, Carlos P., 302, 316
Roosevelt, Eleanor, 47, 435
Roosevelt, Franklin D., and U.S.-Cana-
dian relations, 341-342
Roth, Almon E., 231
Royall, Kenneth C., 303
Ruhr, the, 95, 96, 451, 490; London
agreement, June 1948, 75-76, 467;
policies of western powers, 70-78,
464-467, 475; Soviet attitude on, 91,
141, 148, 473-474; London confer-
ence on, November-December 1948,
467-473; German reaction, 473-475
Rumania, 122, 495; internal affairs, 103,
105-108, 110, 113, 114; foreign relations, 89, 118, 121, 124, 203-204, 427,
445
Ryder, Oscar, 212

Saar, 70, 492
Saillant, Louis, 191, 193
St. Laurent, Louis S., 347, 355
St. Lawrence, 348
Sakhalin, 261
Saragat, Giuseppe, 43
Saudi Arabia, 435; and Palestine, 377,
379, 386, 397-398, 404
Scandinavia, 33, 60, 107, 193, 196, 520;
cooperative efforts, 181, 535; and
Western Union, 60-62, 526; and
North Atlantic Treaty, 535-537
Schilthuis, William C., 222
Schuman, Robert, 51-52, 73, 392, 459,
470, 489
Seafarers International Union, 246
Second Decontrol Act (U.S.), 201
Sforza, Carlo, 180, 521
Shipping policy (U.S.), 228-249
Siam, 296
Silver, Rabbi Abba H., 384
Sinkiang, 263, 286
Sjarifoeddin, Amir, 326
Smith, Kingsbury, 463, 493, 537
Smith-Molotov exchange, 24-28, 127,
538
Smith-Mundt Act (U.S.), 23
Smith, Walter Bedell, 24-25, 27, 127,
141, 538
Snow, Edgar, 260
Society for the Prevention of World
War III, 473
Soekarno, Achmed, 317
Sokolovsky, Marshal Vassili D., 72, 139,
146, 460
Soong, T. V., 281
Sophoulis, Themistocles, 427-428
South West Africa, 434
Spaak, Paul-Henri, 62, 169, 431
Spain, 33, 437, 520, 532, 534
Stalin Joseph V., 34-36, 123, 268, 502;
on Soviet-U.S. relations, 27; and Ger-
many, 83, 135, 141-143, 147; state-
ment to Pravda, 459; statement to K.
Smith, 463, 493-494, 537-538
Stalinism, see Communism
Stassen, Harold, 35, 154
State, Department of (U.S.), 22, 26, 46,
80, 294, 295, 301, 302, 308, 409, 427,
449, 494, 502, 535, 540; and Western
Union, 63, 518-519; and ERP, 153,
164, 167, 183; and trade agreements,
210, 212; and ITO, 218-219; and

shipping policy, 230-231, 242; denunciation of, 280, 285; and aid to China, 285; and Palestine, 381, 393
Stern gang, 392
Stikker, Derek U., 321
Stimson, Henry L., 47
Stuart, John Leighton, 302
Sullivan, John L., 238
Sun Fo, 274, 281, 283
Sun Yat-sen, 274
Switzerland, 60, 188, 193, 520; in ERP, 156; commercial relations, 202, 217, 219
Syria, 309, 436, 456; and Palestine, 379, 386, 397, 400, 404, 406
Szakasits, Arpád, 106
Sweden, 60, 61, 446; in ERP, 155, 156, 160; commercial relations, 216; and European union, 526; and North Atlantic Treaty, 534-535, 536

Taber, John, 154-155
Taft, Robert A., 211, 350, 511
Tariff Commission (U.S.), 211-212, 216-217
Tass, 494
Thakin Nu, 267, 322-324
Thomas, Norman, 504
Thorez, Maurice, 538
Tito, Josip Broz, 102, 111, 112, 115, 116-127, 204-206, 266, 429
Tobey, Charles W., 244
Tobin, Maurice J., 217
Togliatti, Palmiro, 44, 538
Transjordan, and Palestine conflict, 376-406; and U.N. membership, 445-446
Treasury, Secretary of (U.S.), 238
Trieste, 46, 119, 154, 156, 160, 442-444, 520
Trotsky, Leon, 121; followers of, 323
Truman, Harry S., 23, 27, 135, 152, 155, 168, 223, 253, 281, 368, 417, 508, 537-538; special message to Congress, 7, 77; and Trade Agreements program, 210, 213-214; and wheat agreements, 222-223; and shipping policy, 230, 235, 238; and Palestine, 381, 385, 393, 504; and proposed Vinson mission, 502-504; election campaign, 385, 393, 500-501, 504; inaugural address, 165, 208-209, 217-218, 258, 373, 507-508, 529-530

Truman doctrine, 2, 5, 15, 38, 41, 505, 506
Tsaldaris, Constantin, 427
Tsarapkin, Semyon K., 396
Turkey, 265, 521; U.S. aid to, 14, 38, 41, 377, 540; and ERP, 156, 160, 164, 171; and North Atlantic Treaty, 533

U Kyaw Nyein, 260
Ukrainian S.S.R., 128, 220, 316, 320, 412, 413-414, 455
Ulbricht, Walter, 81
Uniforce, 514
Union of South Africa, 254, 296, 434, 435, 437
U.S.S.R., 21, 520; and U.S., 1-7, 24-28, 254, 506-507, 518, 519; aims in Europe, 32-33, 34-42, 48; and Germany, 67, 69-71, 79-88, 91-92, 99, 133-149, 150, 152, 451-460, 463-464, 473-474, 476, 482, 483, 493-495; expansionist policy of, 16, 330-331, 377, 408-409, 497, 501, 541; and eastern Europe, 102-103, 107, 111-113, 115-116, 197-198, 203-204, 206-207; and Yugoslavia, 116-123, 124-127, 204-205; at Danube conference, 128-133; trade unions of, 189-192; and east-west trade, 201-203; at International Wheat Conference, 224-225; and the Far East, 259-270, 322, 329, 332, 539; and China, 270-271, 285-286; and Japan, 288, 295, 302-303; and Korea, 306-311; and Indonesia, 316, 318, 320; and Canada, 342-343, 345; and Latin America, 357-359; and the Middle East, 375-377, 379, 385, 397, 407; and disarmament problems, 410-419; and the Greek question, 18-19, 419 ff.; and Czechoslovakia, 442-443; in U.N. General Assembly, 430-431, 433-434, 435-436; in U.N. Security Council, 408-409, 438-439, 442-449, 455-459; and U.N. membership, 444-446; and Western Union, 61, 515; and North Atlantic Treaty, 527-528, 535-539
United Kingdom, 32; and European union, 53-54, 56, 63-64, 522-526; and ERP, 156, 161-163, 167, 173-174, 176, 178-179, 184, 510, 511; labor movement in, 189-191, 195-196; trade agreements with Yugoslavia and Poland, 199; and ITO, 219; and inter-

national wheat agreements, 221, 223; shipping position, 229, 232-233, 236, 240; U.S. loan to, 250, 252; and International Monetary Fund, 254-255; and Asia, 261; and Japan, 288, 296, 300; and Burma, 322, 324; and Malaya, 324, 325; and the U.S., 330-331, *see also* Germany, Middle East, etc.; and Canada, 334-335, 338-339, 340-341, 342, 347, 353; western hemisphere colonies, 356, 359 ff.; Palestine policy, 375-376, 381-382, 383, 392-393, 397, 398, 401, 402-403; and Middle East, 377, 407; and Germany, 139, 465-470, 479, 483, 489, 494, *see also* Germany, Anglo-American policy; and North Atlantic Treaty, 534

United Maritime Authority, 234

United Nations, 131, 202, 257, 343, 354, 360, 537; U.S. attitude toward, 1, 10, 15, 28-29, 408-410; and Korea, 306-311, 434; and Indonesia, 312-318, 320-321, 327, 438-439; relation of Organization of American States to, 364; and Palestine, 376, 378-406, 438-439; and disarmament, 410-419, 447; and the Balkan question, 419-426, 428, 434; and human rights, 435-436; and Kashmir, 439-441; and Hyderabad, 441-442; and Czechoslovakia, 442-443; and the Berlin dispute, 443, 452-463; and Trieste, 443-444; and admission of new members, 311, 401, 444-446; veto in, 4, 46, 311, 408-409, 412, 437, 443-449, 452, 456, 458-461; relation of Western Union to, 526; and North Atlantic Treaty, 513, 528, 530-531; Economic and Social Council, 209, 227, 373-374, 388, 408, 409, 435, 436; Economic Commission for Asia and the Far East, 329; Economic Commission for Europe, 58, 154, 181, 199-200, 410; General Assembly, 409, 452, 460, 503, accomplishments of, 430-437; Interim Committee, 306, 433-434, 447, 452; Security Council, 275, 311, 313, 318, 354, 364, 410, 436, 451, 453, 530-531, record of, 437-449; Trusteeship Council, 384, 409, 434

UNRRA, 27, 31, 276

United States (for relations with particular countries and areas *see* geographic headings; for references to Congress and to executive departments and agencies *see* organizational names), foreign policy, 1-29, 35-36, 43, 48, 381, 393, 497-499, 503-505, 507-508; military policy, 7-9; military aid programs, 9-10, 215, 377-378, 540; foreign assistance programs, 15-21, 157, 252, 274-275, 285, 310, *see also* European Recovery Program; foreign information program, 21-24, 161; exchange of notes with U.S.S.R., 24-27, 127, 538; and Western Union, 62-63, 516-517; strategic materials policy, 161-165; labor organizations of, 190 ff.; export control policy, 201-202, 206, 216; foreign economic policy, 18, 208-258, 336; and assistance to underdeveloped areas, 165, 208-210, 258, 373-374, 508; shipping policy, 228-249; exports, financing of, 249-258; foreign lending policy, 154, 250-255, 369-370; foreign investment, 161, 257-258, 293, 328-329, 335, 368-369, 372; and the U.N., 1, 10, 15, 28-29, 385, 408-409, 430, 432 ff., 447-449, 452-453; party politics and foreign policy, 280, 285, 393, 498-500, 508-509, 518-519; presidential election, 213-214, 217, 393, 396, 499-507; and ERP renewal, 509-512; and North Atlantic Treaty, 497, 528-530, 540-542

United States Chamber of Commerce, 218

Upper Silesia, 83

Uruguay, 216, 224, 362

Vandenberg, Gen. Hoyt S., 346

Vandenberg, Arthur, 153, 350, 477, 502, 508, 532; and foreign aid programs, 17, 154, 166; and trade agreements program, 211, 213; and shipping policy, 243-244; Pan American Day address, 351-352; on U.N., 409; on bipartisanship, 500

Vandenberg Resolution, 9-15, 448, 527

Van Mook, Hubertus J., 315

Van Zeeland, Paul, 56

Vatican, 44, 47

Venezuela, 358, 362, 371, 373

Vietnam, 259, 327-328

Vinson, Fred M., 502-503, 506, 538
Virgin Islands, 233
Vyshinsky, Andrei Y., at Danube conference, 129-130; and Berlin negotiations, 133-134, 454-455, 457-461; at U.N. Assembly, 415-417, 424, 430-431, 435-436, 504

Wallace, Henry A., 26-27, 504-505, 506
Waltham Watch Company, 217
Wang Shih-chieh, 281
War, Secretary of (U.S.), 232
Warsaw conference on Germany, 90 ff.
Wasson, Thomas C., 392
Wedemeyer, Gen. Albert C., 272, 276
Weizmann, Chaim, 401
Welles, Sumner, 352, 359, 372
Western hemisphere, 341-342, 353, 357; European colonies in, 355-356, 359-361
Western Union, 431, 537; establishment of, by Treaty of Brussels, 9-10, 13, 53-64, 79; operation of, 512-517, 529; military organization, 354, 514-516; and European union, 521, 522-526
Wheat, international agreement on, 220-228

Wilson, Woodrow, 30
Woll, Matthew, 194
World Federation of Trade Unions, establishment of, 189-191; and the Marshall plan, 191-194; split in, 194-197; Far Eastern affiliates, 267

Yalta agreements, 83, 90, 104, 147, 263, 288, 431, 502
Yemen, 379
Yoshida, Shigeru, 304-305
Yugoslavia, 89, 92, 102-103, 110-111, 266, 286; dispute with Cominform, 37-38, 116-127, 133; claims agreement with U.S., 126-127; at Danube conference, 127-129; trade agreement with U.K., 199; economic relations, 204-206; and Greece, 419, 421, 423-424, 426, 438; and Trieste, 443-444

Zafrullah Khan, Sir C. M., 441
Zápotocký, Antonín, 115, 203
Zayim, Col. Husni, 406
Zhdanov, Andrei, 33, 39
Zhukov, Marshal G. K., 135
Zujović, Sreten, 121